T0211425

THE DESCRIPTION LOGIC HANDBOOK

Description Logics are embodied in several knowledge-based systems and are used to develop various real-life applications. *The Description Logic Handbook* provides a thorough account of the subject, covering all aspects of research in this field; namely, theory, implementation, and applications. Its appeal will be broad, ranging from more theoretically oriented readers to those with more practically oriented interests who need a sound and modern understanding of knowledge representation systems based on Description Logics. As well as general revision throughout the book, this new edition presents a new chapter on ontology languages for the Semantic Web, an area of great importance for the future development of the web. In sum, the book will serve as a unique reference for the subject, and can also be used for self-study or in conjunction with Knowledge Representation and Artificial Intelligence courses.

THE DESCRIPTION LOGIC HANDBOOK

Theory, implementation, and applications

Edited by

FRANZ BAADER
DIEGO CALVANESE
DEBORAH L. McGUINNESS
DANIELE NARDI
PETER F. PATEL-SCHNEIDER

CAMBRIDGE
UNIVERSITY PRESS

CAMBRIDGE
UNIVERSITY PRESS

University Printing House, Cambridge CB2 8BS, United Kingdom

One Liberty Plaza, 20th Floor, New York, NY 10006, USA

477 Williamstown Road, Port Melbourne, VIC 3207, Australia

314-321, 3rd Floor, Plot 3, Splendor Forum, Jasola District Centre, New Delhi - 110025, India

103 Penang Road, #05-06/07, Visioncrest Commercial, Singapore 238467

Cambridge University Press is part of the University of Cambridge.

It furthers the University's mission by disseminating knowledge in the pursuit of education, learning and research at the highest international levels of excellence.

www.cambridge.org
Information on this title: www.cambridge.org/9780521150118

© Cambridge University Press 2003, 2007

First published 2003
Second edition published 2007
Reprinted 2008
Paperback edition 2010

A catalogue record for this publication is available from the British Library

ISBN 978-0-521-87625-4 Hardback
ISBN 978-0-521-15011-8 Paperback

Contents

Contributors

Franz Baader
Institut für Theoretische Informatik
Fakultät Informatik
TU Dresden
01062 Dresden, Germany
http://wwwtcs.inf.tu-dresden.de/~baader/

Alex Borgida
Department of Computer Science
Rutgers University
Piscataway, NJ 08855, U.S.A.
http://www.cs.rutgers.edu/~borgida/

Ronald J. Brachman
Yahoo!
http://www.brachman.org/

Diego Calvanese
Faculty of Computer Science
Free University of Bozen-Bolzano
Piazza Domenicani 3, 39100 Bolzano, Italy
http://www.inf.unibz.it/~calvanese/

Giuseppe De Giacomo
Dipartimento di Informatica e Sistemistica
Università di Roma "La Sapienza"
Via Salaria 113, 00198 Roma, Italy
http://www.dis.uniroma1.it/~degiacomo/

Francesco M. Donini
Political Science Department, Information Systems Research Group
University of Tuscia
Via San Carlo 32, 01100 Viterbo, Italy
http://dee.poliba.it/dee-web/doniniweb/donini.html

Enrico Franconi
Faculty of Computer Science
Free University of Bozen-Bolzano
Piazza Domenicani 3, 39100 Bolzano, Italy
`http://www.inf.unibz.it/~franconi/`

Volker Haarslev
Computer Science Department
Concordia University
1455 de Maisonneuve Blvd. W., Montreal, Quebec H3G IM8, Canada
`http://www.cs.concordia.ca/~faculty/haarslev/`

Ian Horrocks
School of Computer Science
University of Manchester
Manchester M13 9PL, U.K.
`http://www.cs.man.ac.uk/~horrocks/`

Ralf Küsters
Institut für Informatik und Praktische Mathematik
Christian-Albrechts-Universität zu Kiel
Olshausenstraße 40, 24098 Kiel, Germany
`http://www.ti.informatik.uni-kiel.de/~kuesters/`

Maurizio Lenzerini
Dipartimento di Informatica e Sistemistica
Università di Roma "La Sapienza"
Via Salaria 113, 00198 Roma, Italy
`http://www.dis.uniroma1.it/~lenzerini/`

Deborah L. McGuinness
Knowledge Systems Laboratory
Gates Building 2A, Stanford University
Stanford, CA 94305-9020, U.S.A.
`http://ksl.stanford.edu/people/dlm/`

Ralf Molitor
Swiss Life
IT Research and Development Group
General Guisan Quai 40, CH-8002 Zürich, Switzerland
`http://research.swisslife.ch/~molitor/`

Ralf Möller
Computer Science Department
University of Hamburg
Vogt-Kölln-Straße 30, 22527 Hamburg, Germany
`http://kogs-www.informatik.uni-hamburg.de/~moeller/`

Daniele Nardi
Dipartimento di Informatica e Sistemistica
Università di Roma "La Sapienza"
Via Salaria 113, 00198 Roma, Italy
`http://www.dis.uniroma1.it/~nardi/`

Werner Nutt
Faculty of Computer Science
Free University of Bozen-Bolzano
Piazza Domenicani 3, 39100 Bolzano, Italy
http://www.inf.unibz.it/~nutt/

Peter F. Patel-Schneider
Bell Labs Research
600 Mountain Avenue
Murray Hill, NJ 07974, U.S.A.
http://www.bell-labs.com/user/pfps/

Alan Rector
Medical Informatics Group
Department of Computer Science
University of Manchester
Manchester M13 9PL, U.K.
http://www.cs.man.ac.uk/mig/

Riccardo Rosati
Dipartimento di Informatica e Sistemistica
Università di Roma "La Sapienza"
Via Salaria 113, 00198 Roma, Italy
http://www.dis.uniroma1.it/~rosati/

Ulrike Sattler
School of Computer Science
University of Manchester
Manchester M13 9PL, U.K.
http://www.cs.man.ac.uk/~sattler/

Christopher A. Welty
Knowledge Structures Group
IBM Watson Research Center
19 Skyline Dr., Hawthorne, NY 10532, U.S.A.

Frank Wolter
Department of Computer Science
University of Liverpool
Ashton Building, Ashton Street
Liverpool L69 3BX, U.K.
http://www.csc.liv.ac.uk/~frank/

Preface to the second edition

Since the publication of the first edition of *The Description Logic Handbook* in 2003, the interest in Description Logics (DL) has steadily increased. This applies both to the number of active DL researchers working on DL theory and implementations of reasoning services, and to the number of applications based on DL technology. One effect of this growing interest was that the first edition of the *Handbook* has gone through quite a number of reprints. Another effect is, of course, that in the last three years there have been interesting new developments in the three areas (theory, implementation, and applications) that the *Handbook* covers. Despite that, we feel that most chapters of the *Handbook* still provide a good introduction to the field and lay a solid foundation that enables the reader to understand and put into context the research articles describing results since 2003. For this reason, we have decided to leave most of the chapters unchanged.

The principal exception is Chapter 14, which in the first edition was entitled "Digital Libraries and Web-Based Information Systems." This chapter provided a selected history of the use of Description Logics in web-based information systems, and the developments related to emerging web ontology languages such as OIL and DAML+OIL. Since the writing of this chapter, the new language OWL has been developed and recommended by the World Wide Web consortium as the standard web ontology language for the Semantic Web. In the second edition, Chapter 14, now co-authored by Peter Patel-Schneider, concentrates on OWL, which is reflected by its new title: "OWL: a Description-Logic-Based Ontology Language for the Semantic Web." The chapter still briefly reviews some early efforts that combine Description Logics and the Web, including predecessors of OWL such as OIL and DAML+OIL. But then it goes on to describe OWL in some detail, including the various influences on its design, its relationship with RDFS, its syntax and semantics, and a range of tools and applications.

A minor change was made in Chapter 2. In fact, Proposition 2.9 in the first edition, which tried to give a syntactic criterion for the existence of fixpoint models of cyclic terminologies, turned out to be wrong.[1] In the second edition, it has been replaced by a correct criterion, now given in Proposition 2.10. The new material starts with (the new) Proposition 2.8 and ends with Proposition 2.10.

We are indebted to David Tranah, our editor at Cambridge University Press, for his patience during the preparation of this second edition, but also for the gentle pressure he exerted, without which this second edition would probably not have been completed.

---

[1] This problem was independently detected by several Ph.D. students, including Yuming Shen, Hongkai Liu, and Boontawee Suntisrivaraporn. Thank you for your careful reading!

Preface

Knowledge Representation is the field of Artificial Intelligence that focuses on the design of formalisms that are both epistemologically and computationally adequate for expressing knowledge about a particular domain. One of the main lines of investigation has been concerned with the principle that knowledge should be represented by characterizing classes of objects and the relationships between them The organization of the classes used to describe a domain of interest is based on a hierarchical structure, which not only provides an effective and compact representation of information, but also allows the relevant reasoning tasks to be performed in a computationally effective way.

The above principle drove the development of the first frame-based systems and semantic networks in the 1970s. However, these systems were in general not formally defined and the associated reasoning tools were strongly dependent on the implementation strategies. A fundamental step towards a logic-based characterization of required formalisms was accomplished through the work on the KL-ONE system, which collected many of the ideas stemming from earlier semantic networks and frame-based systems, and provided a logical basis for interpreting objects, classes (or concepts), and relationships (or links, roles) between them. The first goal of such a logical reconstruction was the precise characterization of the set of constructs used to build class and link expressions. The second goal was to provide reasoning procedures that are sound and complete with respect to the semantics. The article "The tractability of subsumption in Frame-Based Description Languages" by Ron Brachman and Hector Levesque, presented at AAAI 1984, addressing the tradeoff between the expressiveness of KL-ONE–like languages and the computational complexity of reasoning, is usually regarded as the origin of research on *Description Logics*.

Subsequent research came under the label *terminological systems* to emphasize the fact that classes and relationships were used to establish the basic terminology adopted in the modeled domain. Still later, the emphasis was on the set of concept forming constructs admitted in the language, giving rise to the name *concept languages*. Recently, attention has moved closer to the properties of the underlying logical systems, and the term *Description Logics* has become popular.

Research on Description Logics has covered theoretical aspects, implementation of knowledge representation systems (modern frame-based systems) and the use of such systems to realize applications in several areas. This pattern of development is an example of one of the standard research methodologies, as is recognized by the Artificial Intelligence community. The key element has been the very close interaction between theory and practice. On the one hand, there are various implemented systems based on Description Logics, offering a palette of description formalisms with differing expressive power, and which are employed in various application domains (such as natural language processing, configuration of technical systems, databases). On the other hand, the formal and computational properties (like decidability, complexity) of various description formalisms have been studied in detail. These investigations are usually motivated by the use of certain constructors in systems or the need for these constructors in specific applications, and the results of such investigations have strongly influenced the design of new systems.

The Description Logics research community currently consists of at least 100 active researchers. In addition, other communities are now becoming interested in Description Logics, most notably the Databases community and, more recently, the Semantic Web one. After more than a decade of research on Description Logics there is a substantial body of work and well-established technical literature. However, there is no comprehensive presentation of the major achievements in the field, although survey papers have been published and workshop proceedings are available.

Now, since 1989 a workshop dedicated to Description Logics has been held, initially every two years but annually from 1994. At the 1997 workshop a Working Group was formed to develop a proposal for a book that would provide a systematic introduction to Description Logics, covering all aspects of the research in the field, namely: theory, implementation, and applications. Following the spirit that fostered this research, *The Description Logic Handbook* would provide a thorough introduction to Description Logics both for the more theoretically oriented reader interested in the formal study of Description Logics and for the more practically oriented reader aiming at a principled usage of knowledge representation systems based on Description Logics. Although some refinements have been made to the initial proposal to embody recent developments in the field, the final structure of the *Handbook* reflects the original intentions.

The *Handbook* is organized into three parts plus an initial chapter providing a general introduction to the field.

Part I addresses the theoretical work in Description Logics and includes five chapters. Chapter 2 introduces Description Logics as a formal language for representing knowledge and reasoning about it. Chapter 3 addresses the computational complexity of reasoning in several Description Logics. Chapter 4 explores the relationship with other representation formalisms, within and outside the field of Knowledge Representation. Chapter 5 covers extensions of the basic Description Logics introduced in Chapter 2 by very expressive constructs that require advanced reasoning techniques.

Chapter 6 considers extensions of Description Logics by representation features and non-standard inference problems not available in the basic framework.

Part II is concerned with the implementation of knowledge representation systems based on Description Logics. Chapter 7 describes the features that need to be provided, in addition to the inference engine for a particular Description Logic, to build a knowledge representation system. Chapter 8 reviews implemented knowledge representation systems based on Description Logics that have played or play an important role in the field. Chapter 9 describes the implementation of the reasoning services which form the core of Description Logic knowledge representation systems.

Part III addresses the deployment of Description Logics in the design and implementation of fielded applications. Chapter 10 discusses the issues involved in the development of an ontology for some universe of discourse, which is to become a conceptual model or knowledge base represented and reasoned with using Description Logics. Chapter 11 presents applications of Description Logics in the area of software engineering. Chapter 12 introduces the problem of configuration and the largest and longest lived family of Description Logic-based configurators. Chapter 13 is concerned with the use of Description Logics in various kinds of applications in medical informatics – terminology, intelligent user interfaces, decision support and semantic indexing, language technology, and systems integration. Chapter 14 reviews the applications of Description Logics in web-based information systems, and the more recent developments related to languages for the Semantic Web.

Chapter 15 analyzes the uses of Description Logics for natural language processing to encode syntactic, semantic, and pragmatic elements needed to drive semantic interpretation and natural language generation processes. Chapter 16 surveys the major classes of application of Description Logics and their reasoning facilities to the issues of data management, including the expression of the conceptual domain model/ontology of the data source, the integration of multiple data sources, and the formulation and evaluation of queries.

The syntax and semantics for Description Logics is summarized in an Appendix, which has been used as a reference to unify the notation throughout the book. Finally, an extended, integrated bibliography is provided and, within each chapter, comprehensive guides through the relevant literature are given.

The chapters are written by some of the most prominent researchers in the field, introducing the basic technical material before taking the reader to the current state of the subject. The chapters have been reviewed in a two step process, which involved two or three reviewers for each chapter. We have relied on the work of several external reviewers, selected both within the Description Logic community, and outside the field, to increase the readability for non experts. In addition, each chapter has been read also by authors of other chapters, to improve the overall coherence.

As such, the book is conceived as a unique reference for the subject. Although not intended as a textbook, the *Handbook* can be used as a basis for specialized courses on Description Logics. In addition, some of the chapters can be used as teaching material in Knowledge Representation courses. The *Handbook* is also a comprehensive reference to the subject in more introductory courses in the field of Artificial Intelligence.

We want to acknowledge the contribution and help of several people. First of all, the authors, who have successfully accomplished the hardest task of writing the chapters, carefully addressing the reviewers' comments as well as the issues raised by the effort in making the presentation and notation uniform. Second, we thank the reviewers for their precious work, which led to significant improvements in the final outcome. The external reviewers were:

Premkumar T. Devanbu,
Peter L. Elkin,
Jerome Euzenat,
Erich Grädel,
Michael Gruninger,

Frank van Harmelen,
Jana Koehler,
Diane Litman,
Robert M. MacGregor,
Amedeo Napoli,
Hans-Jürgen Ohlbach,
Marie-Christine Rousset,
Nestor Rychtyckyj,
Renate Schmidt,
James G. Schmolze,
Roberto Sebastiani,
Michael Uschold,
Moshe Y. Vardi,
Grant Weddell,
Robert A. Weida.

A special thank you goes also to Christopher A. Welty who, besides serving
as a reviewer, also coordinated the reviewing process for some of the chapters. Third, we express our gratitude to the Description Logics community as
a whole (see also the Description Logics homepage at `http://dl.kr.org/`)
for the outstanding research achievements and for applying the pressure that
enabled us to complete the *Handbook*. Finally, we are indebted to Cambridge
University Press, and, in particular, to David Tranah, for giving us the opportunity to put the *Handbook* together and for the excellent support in the
editing process.

1

An Introduction to Description Logics

Daniele Nardi
Ronald J. Brachman

Abstract

This introduction presents the main motivations for the development of Description Logics (DLs) as a formalism for representing knowledge, as well as
some important basic notions underlying all systems that have been created
in the DL tradition. In addition, we provide the reader with an overview of
the entire book and some guidelines for reading it.

We first address the relationship between Description Logics and earlier
semantic network and frame systems, which represent the original heritage
of the field. We delve into some of the key problems encountered with the
older efforts. Subsequently, we introduce the basic features of DL languages
and related reasoning techniques.

DL languages are then viewed as the core of knowledge representation
systems, considering both the structure of a DL knowledge base and its associated reasoning services. The development of some implemented knowledge
representation systems based on Description Logics and the first applications
built with such systems are then reviewed.

Finally, we address the relationship of Description Logics to other fields of
Computer Science. We also discuss some extensions of the basic representation language machinery; these include features proposed for incorporation
in the formalism that originally arose in implemented systems, and features
proposed to cope with the needs of certain application domains.

1.1 Introduction

Research in the field of knowledge representation and reasoning is usually
focused on methods for providing high-level descriptions of the world that
can be effectively used to build intelligent applications. In this context,

"intelligent" refers to the ability of a system to find implicit consequences of its explicitly represented knowledge. Such systems are therefore characterized as knowledge-based systems.

Approaches to knowledge representation developed in the 1970s – when the field enjoyed great popularity – are sometimes divided roughly into two categories: logic-based formalisms, which evolved out of the intuition that predicate calculus could be used unambiguously to capture facts about the world; and other, non-logic-based representations. The latter were often developed by building on more cognitive notions – for example, network structures and rule-based representations derived from experiments on recall from human memory and human execution of tasks like mathematical puzzle solving. Even though such approaches were often developed for specific representational chores, the resulting formalisms were usually expected to serve in general use. In other words, the non-logical systems created from very specific lines of thinking (e.g., early production systems) evolved to be treated as general-purpose tools, expected to be applicable in different domains and to different types of problems.

On the other hand, since first-order logic provides very powerful and general machinery, logic-based approaches were more general-purpose from the very start. In a logic-based approach, the representation language is usually a variant of first-order predicate calculus, and reasoning amounts to verifying logical consequence. In the non-logical approaches, often based on the use of graphical interfaces, knowledge is represented by means of some ad hoc data structures, and reasoning is accomplished by similarly ad hoc procedures that manipulate the structures. Among these specialized representations we find *semantic networks* and *frames*. Semantic networks were developed after the work of Quillian [1967], with the goal of characterizing by means of network-shaped cognitive structures the knowledge and the reasoning of the system. Similar goals were shared by later frame systems [Minsky, 1981], which rely on the notion of a "frame" as a prototype and on the capability of expressing relationships between frames. Although there are significant differences between semantic networks and frames, both in their motivating cognitive intuitions and in their features, they have a strong common basis. In fact, they can both be regarded as network structures, where the structure of the network aims at representing sets of individuals and their relationships. Consequently, we use the term *network-based structures* to refer to the representation networks underlying semantic networks and frames (see [Lehmann, 1992] for a collection of papers concerning various families of network-based structures).

Owing to their more human-centered origins, the network-based systems were often considered more appealing and more effective from a practical viewpoint than the logical systems. Unfortunately, they were not fully satisfactory, because of their usual lack of precise semantic characterization. The end result of this was that every system behaved differently from the others, in many cases despite virtually identical-looking components and even identical relationship names. The question then arose as to how to provide semantics to representation structures, in particular to semantic networks and frames, which carried the intuition that, by exploiting the notion of hierarchical structure, one could gain both in terms of ease of representation and in terms of the efficiency of reasoning.

One important step in this direction was the recognition that frames (at least their core features) could be given a semantics by relying on first-order logic [Hayes, 1979]. The basic elements of the representation are characterized as unary predicates, denoting sets of individuals, and binary predicates, denoting relationships between individuals. However, such a characterization does not capture the constraints of semantic networks and frames with respect to logic. Indeed, although logic is the natural basis for specifying a meaning for these structures, it turns out that frames and semantic networks (for the most part) did not require all the machinery of first-order logic, but could be regarded as fragments of it [Brachman and Levesque, 1985]. In addition, different features of the representation language would lead to different fragments of first-order logic. The most important consequence of this fact is the recognition that the typical forms of reasoning used in structure-based representations could be accomplished by specialized reasoning techniques, without necessarily requiring first-order logic theorem provers. Moreover, reasoning in different fragments of first-order logic leads to computational problems of differing complexity.

Subsequent to this realization, research in the area of Description Logics began under the label *terminological systems*, to emphasize that the representation language was used to establish the basic terminology adopted in the modeled domain. Later, the emphasis was on the set of concept-forming constructs admitted in the language, giving rise to the name *concept languages*. In more recent years, after attention was further moved towards the properties of the underlying logical systems, the term *Description Logics* became popular.

In this book we mainly use the term "Description Logics" for the representation systems, but often use the word "concept" to refer to the expressions of a DL language, denoting sets of individuals, and the word "terminology"

to denote a (hierarchical) structure built to provide an intensional representation of the domain of interest.

Research on Description Logics has covered theoretical underpinnings as
well as implementation of knowledge representation systems and the development of applications in several areas. This kind of development has
been quite successful. The key element has been the methodology of research, based on a very close interaction between theory and practice. On
the one hand, there are various implemented systems based on Description Logics, which offer a palette of description formalisms with differing
expressive power, and which are employed in various application domains
(such as natural language processing, configuration of technical products,
or databases). On the other hand, the formal and computational properties of reasoning (like decidability and complexity) of various description
formalisms have been investigated in detail. The investigations are usually
motivated by the use of certain constructors in implemented systems or by
the need for these constructors in specific applications – and the results have
influenced the design of new systems.

This book is meant to provide a thorough introduction to Description
Logics, covering all the above-mentioned aspects of DL research – namely
theory, implementation, and applications. Consequently, the book is divided
into three parts:

- Part I introduces the theoretical foundations of Description Logics, addressing
  some of the most recent developments in theoretical research in the area;
- Part II focuses on the implementation of knowledge representation systems based
  on Description Logics, describing the basic functionality of a DL system, surveying the most influential knowledge representation systems based on Description
  Logics, and addressing specialized implementation techniques;
- Part III addresses the use of Description Logics and of DL-based systems in the
  design of several applications of practical interest.

In the remainder of this introductory chapter, we review the main steps
in the development of Description Logics, and introduce the main issues
that are dealt with later in the book, providing pointers for its reading. In
particular, in the next section we address the origins of Description Logics
and then we review knowledge representation systems based on Description
Logics, the main applications developed with Description Logics, the main
extensions to the basic DL framework, and relationships with other fields of
Computer Science.

1.2 From networks to Description Logics

In this section we begin by recalling approaches to representing knowledge that were developed before research on Description Logics began (i.e., semantic networks and frames). We then provide a very brief introduction to the basic elements of these approaches, based on Tarski-style semantics. Finally, we discuss the importance of computational analyses of the reasoning methods developed for Description Logics, a major ingredient of research in this field.

1.2.1 Network-based representation structures

In order to provide some intuition about the ideas behind representations of knowledge in network form, we here speak in terms of a generic network, avoiding references to any particular system. The elements of a network are *nodes* and *links*. Typically, nodes are used to characterize concepts, i.e., sets or classes of individual objects, and links are used to characterize relationships among them. In some cases, more complex relationships are themselves represented as nodes; these are carefully distinguished from nodes representing concepts. In addition, concepts can have simple properties, often called attributes, which are typically attached to the corresponding nodes. Finally, in many of the early networks both individual objects and concepts were represented by nodes. Here, however, we restrict our attention to knowledge about concepts and their relationships, deferring for now treatment of knowledge about specific individuals.

Let us consider a simple example, whose pictorial representation is given in Figure 1.1, which represents knowledge concerning persons, parents, children, etc. The structure in the figure is also referred to as a *terminology*, and it is indeed meant to represent the generality or specificity of the concepts involved. For example the link between Mother and Parent says that "mothers are parents"; this is sometimes called an "IS-A" relationship.

The IS-A relationship defines a hierarchy over the concepts and provides the basis for the "inheritance of properties": when a concept is more specific than some other concept, it inherits the properties of the more general one. For example, if a person has an age, then a woman has an age, too. This is the typical setting of the so-called (monotonic) *inheritance networks* (see [Brachman, 1979]).

A characteristic feature of Description Logics is their ability to represent other kinds of relationships that can hold between concepts, beyond IS-A relationships. For example, in Figure 1.1, which follows the notation of

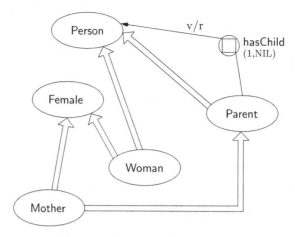

Fig. 1.1. An example network.

[Brachman and Schmolze, 1985], the concept of **Parent** has a property that is usually called a "role", expressed by a link from the concept to a node for the role labeled **hasChild**. The role has what is called a "value restriction", denoted by the label v/r, which expresses a limitation on the range of types of objects that can fill that role. In addition, the node has a number restriction expressed as (1,NIL), where the first number is a lower bound on the number of children and the second element is the upper bound, and NIL denotes infinity. Overall, the representation of the concept of **Parent** here can be read as "A parent is a person having at least one child, and all of his/her children are persons."

Relationships of this kind are inherited from concepts to their subconcepts. For example, the concept **Mother**, i.e., a female parent, is a more specific descendant of both the concepts **Female** and **Parent**, and as a result inherits from **Parent** the link to **Person** through the role **hasChild**; in other words, **Mother** inherits the restriction on its **hasChild** role from **Parent**.

Observe that there may be implicit relationships between concepts. For example, if we define **Woman** as the concept of a female person, it is the case that every **Mother** is a **Woman**. It is the task of the knowledge representation system to find implicit relationships such as these (many are more complex than this one). Typically, such inferences have been characterized in terms of properties of the network. In this case one might observe that both **Mother** and **Woman** are connected to both **Female** and **Person**, but the path from **Mother** to **Person** includes a node **Parent**, which is more specific then **Person**, thus enabling us to conclude that **Mother** is more specific than **Person**.

However, the more complex the relationships established among concepts, the more difficult it becomes to give a precise characterization of what kind of relationships can be computed, and how this can be done without failing to recognize some of the relationships or without providing wrong answers.

1.2.2 A logical account of network-based representation structures

Building on the above ideas, a number of systems were implemented and used in many kinds of applications. As a result, the need emerged for a precise characterization of the meaning of the structures used in the representations and of the set of inferences that could be drawn from those structures.

A precise characterization of the meaning of a network can be given by defining a language for the elements of the structure and by providing an interpretation for the strings of that language. While the syntax may have different flavors in different settings, the semantics is typically given as a Tarski-style semantics.

For the syntax we introduce a kind of abstract language, which resembles other logical formalisms. The basic step of the construction is provided by two disjoint alphabets of symbols that are used to denote *atomic concepts*, designated by unary predicate symbols, and *atomic roles*, designated by binary predicate symbols; the latter are used to express relationships between concepts.

Terms are then built from the basic symbols using several kinds of constructors. For example, *intersection of concepts*, which is denoted $C \sqcap D$, is used to restrict the set of individuals under consideration to those that belong to both C and D. Notice that, in the syntax of Description Logics, concept expressions are variable-free. In fact, a concept expression denotes the set of all individuals satisfying the properties specified in the expression. Therefore, $C \sqcap D$ can be regarded as the first-order logic sentence, $C(x) \wedge D(x)$, where the variable ranges over all individuals in the interpretation domain and $C(x)$ is true for those individuals that belong to the concept C.

In this book, we will present other syntactic notations that are more closely related to the concrete syntax adopted by implemented DL systems, and which are more suitable for the development of applications. One example of concrete syntax proposed in [Patel-Schneider and Swartout, 1993] is based on a LISP-like notation, where the concept of female persons, for example, is denoted by (and Person Female).

The key characteristic features of Description Logics reside in the constructs for establishing relationships between concepts. The basic ones are *value restrictions.* For example, a value restriction, written $\forall R.C$, requires that all the individuals that are in the relationship R with the concept being described belong to the concept C (technically, it is all individuals that are in the relationship R with an individual described by the concept in question that are themselves describable as C's).

As for the semantics, concepts are given a set-theoretic interpretation: a concept is interpreted as a set of individuals, and roles are interpreted as sets of pairs of individuals. The domain of interpretation can be chosen arbitrarily, and it can be infinite. The non-finiteness of the domain and the *open-world assumption* are distinguishing features of Description Logics with respect to the modeling languages developed in the study of databases (see Chapters 4 and 16).

Atomic concepts are thus interpreted as subsets of the intepretation domain, while the semantics of the other constructs is then specified by defining the set of individuals denoted by each construct. For example, the concept $C \sqcap D$ is the set of individuals obtained by intersecting the sets of individuals denoted by C and D, respectively. Similarly, the interpretation of $\forall R.C$ is the set of individuals that are in the relationship R with individuals belonging to the set denoted by the concept C.

As an example, let us suppose that Female, Person, and Woman are atomic concepts and that hasChild and hasFemaleRelative are atomic roles. Using the operators *intersection, union* and *complement* of concepts, interpreted as set operations, we can describe the concept of "persons that are not female" and the concept of "individuals that are female or male" by the expressions

$$\text{Person} \sqcap \neg \text{Female} \quad \text{and} \quad \text{Female} \sqcup \text{Male}.$$

It is worth mentioning that intersection, union, and complement of concepts have been also referred to as *concept conjunction, concept disjunction* and *concept negation*, respectively, to emphasize the relationship to logic.

Let us now turn our attention to role restrictions by looking first at quantified role restrictions and, subsequently, at what we call "number restrictions". Most languages provide *(full) existential quantification* and *value restriction* that allow one to describe, for example, the concept of "individuals having a female child" as $\exists$hasChild.Female, and to describe the concept of "individuals all of whose children are female" by the concept expression $\forall$hasChild.Female. In order to distinguish the function of each concept in the relationship, the individual object that corresponds to the second argument of the role viewed as a binary predicate is called a *role filler*. In the above expressions, which describe the properties of parents having female children, individual objects belonging to the concept Female are the fillers of the role hasChild.

Existential quantification and value restrictions are thus meant to characterize relationships between concepts. In fact, the role link between Parent and Person in Figure 1.1 can be expressed by the concept expression

$$\exists\mathsf{hasChild}.\mathsf{Person} \sqcap \forall\mathsf{hasChild}.\mathsf{Person}.$$

Such an expression therefore characterizes the concept of Parent as the set of individuals having at least one filler of the role hasChild belonging to the concept Person; moreover, every filler of the role hasChild must be a person.

Finally, notice that in quantified role restrictions the variable being quantified is not explicitly mentioned. The corresponding sentence in first-order logic is $\forall y.R(x, y) \supset C(y)$, where x is again a free variable ranging over the interpretation domain.

Another important kind of role restriction is given by *number restrictions*, which restrict the cardinality of the sets of role fillers. For instance, the concept

$$(\geqslant 3\ \mathsf{hasChild}) \sqcap (\leqslant 2\ \mathsf{hasFemaleRelative})$$

represents the concept of "individuals having at least three children and at most two female relatives". Number restrictions are sometimes viewed as a distinguishing feature of Description Logics, although one can find some similar constructs in some database modeling languages (notably Entity–Relationship models).

Beyond the constructs to form concept expressions, Description Logics provide constructs for roles, which can, for example, establish role hierarchies. However, the use of role expressions is generally limited to expressing relationships between concepts.

Intersection of roles is an example of a role-forming construct. Intuitively, hasChild ⊓ hasFemaleRelative yields the role "has-daughter", so that the concept expression

$$\mathsf{Woman} \sqcap {\leqslant}\, 2\, (\mathsf{hasChild} \sqcap \mathsf{hasFemaleRelative})$$

denotes the concept of "a woman having at most 2 daughters".

A more comprehensive view of the basic definitions of DL languages will be given in Chapter 2.

1.2.3 Reasoning

The basic inference on concept expressions in Description Logics is *subsumption*, typically written as $C \sqsubseteq D$. Determining subsumption is the problem of checking whether the concept denoted by D (the *subsumer*) is considered more general than the one denoted by C (the *subsumee*). In other words, subsumption checks whether the first concept always denotes a subset of the set denoted by the second one.

For example, one might be interested in knowing whether Woman ⊑ Mother. In order to verify this kind of relationship one has in general to take into account the relationships defined in the terminology. As we explain in the next section, under appropriate restrictions, one can embody such knowledge directly in concept expressions, thus making subsumption over concept expressions the basic reasoning task. Another typical inference on concept expressions is concept *satisfiability*, which is the problem of checking whether a concept expression does not necessarily denote the empty concept. In fact, concept satisfiability is a special case of subsumption, with the subsumer being the empty concept, meaning that a concept is not satisfiable.

Although the meaning of concepts had already been specified with a logical semantics, the design of inference procedures in Description Logics was influenced for a long time by the tradition of semantic networks, where concepts were viewed as nodes and roles as links in a network. Subsumption between concept expressions was recognized as the key inference and the basic idea of the earliest subsumption algorithms was to transform two input concepts into labeled graphs and test whether one could be embedded into the other; the embedded graph would correspond to the more general concept (the subsumer) [Lipkis, 1982]. This method is called *structural comparison*, and the relation between concepts being computed is called *structural subsumption*. However, a careful analysis of the algorithms for structural subsumption shows that they are *sound*, but not always *complete* in terms of the logical semantics: whenever they return "yes" the answer is correct, but when they report "no" the answer may be incorrect. In other words, structural subsumption is in general weaker than logical subsumption.

The need for complete subsumption algorithms is motivated by the fact that in the usage of knowledge representation systems it is often necessary to have a guarantee that the system has not failed in verifying subsumption. Consequently, new algorithms for computing subsumption have been devised that are no longer based on a network representation, and these can be proven to be complete. Such algorithms have been developed by specializing classical settings for deductive reasoning to the DL subsets of first-order logics, as done for tableau calculi by Schmidt-Schauß and Smolka [1991], and also by more specialized methods.

In the paper "The tractability of subsumption in frame-based description languages", Brachman and Levesque [1984] argued that there is a tradeoff between the expressiveness of a representation language and the difficulty of reasoning over the representations built using that language. In other words, the more expressive the language, the harder the reasoning. They also provided a first example of this tradeoff by analyzing the language $\mathcal{FL}^-$ (Frame Language), which included intersection of concepts, value restrictions and a simple form of existential quantification. They showed that for such a language the subsumption problem could be solved in polynomial time, while adding a construct called role restriction to the language makes subsumption a coNP-hard problem (the extended language was called $\mathcal{FL}$).

The paper by Brachman and Levesque introduced at least two new ideas:

1. "efficiency of reasoning" over knowledge structures can be studied using the tools of computational complexity theory;
2. different combinations of constructs can give rise to languages with different computational properties.

An immediate consequence of the above observations is that one can study formally and methodically the tradeoff between the computational complexity of reasoning and the expressiveness of the language, which itself is defined in terms of the constructs that are admitted in the language. After the initial paper, a number of results on this tradeoff for concept languages were obtained (see Chapters 2 and 3), and these results allow us to draw a fairly complete picture of the complexity of reasoning for a wide class of concept languages. Moreover, the problem of finding the optimal tradeoff, namely the most expressive extensions of $\mathcal{FL}^-$ with respect to a given set of constructs that still keep subsumption polynomial, has been studied extensively [Donini *et al.*, 1991b; 1999].

One of the assumptions underlying this line of research is to use worst-case complexity as a measure of the efficiency of reasoning in Description Logics (and more generally in knowledge representation formalisms). Such an assumption has sometimes been criticized (see for example [Doyle and Patil, 1991]) as not adequately characterizing system performance or accounting for more average-case behavior. While this observation suggests that computational complexity alone may not be sufficient for addressing performance issues, research on the computational complexity of reasoning in Description Logics has most definitely led to a much deeper understanding of the problems arising in implementing reasoning tools. Let us briefly address some of the contributions of this body of work.

First of all, the study of the computational complexity of reasoning in Description Logics has led to a clear understanding of the properties of the language constructs and their interaction. This is not only valuable from a theoretical viewpoint, but gives insight to the designer of deduction procedures, with clear indications of the language constructs and their combinations that are difficult to deal with, as well as general methods to cope with them.

Secondly, the complexity results have been obtained by exploiting a general technique for satisfiability checking in concept languages, which relies on a form of tableau calculus [Schmidt-Schauß and Smolka, 1991]. Such a technique has proved extremely useful for studying both the correctness and the complexity of the algorithms. More specifically, it provides an algorithmic framework that is parametric with respect to the language constructs. The algorithms for concept satisfiability and subsumption obtained in this way have also led directly to practical implementations by application of clever control strategies and optimization techniques. The most recent knowledge representation systems based on Description Logics adopt tableau calculi [Horrocks, 1998b].

Thirdly, the analysis of pathological cases in this formal framework has led to the discovery of incompleteness in the algorithms developed for implemented systems. This has also consequently proven useful in the definition of suitable test sets for verifying implementations. For example, the comparison of implemented systems (see for example [Baader *et al.*, 1992b; Heinsohn *et al.*, 1992]) has greatly benefitted from the results of the complexity analysis.

The basic reasoning techniques for Description Logics are presented in Chapter 2, while a detailed analysis of the complexity of reasoning problems in several languages is developed in Chapter 3.

After the tradeoff between expressiveness and tractability of reasoning was thoroughly analyzed and the range of applicability of the corresponding inference techniques had been experimented with, there was a shift of focus in the theoretical research on reasoning in Description Logics. Interest grew in relating Description Logics to the modeling languages used in database management. In addition, the discovery of strict relationships with expressive modal logics stimulated the study of so-called *very expressive* Description Logics. These languages, besides admitting very general mechanisms for defining concepts (for example cyclic definitions, addressed in the next section), provide a richer set of concept-forming constructs and constructs for forming complex role expressions. For these languages, the expressiveness is great enough that the new challenge became enriching the language while retaining the decidability of reasoning. It is worth pointing out that this new direction of theoretical research was accompanied by a corresponding shift in the implementation of knowledge representation systems based on very expressive DL languages. The study of reasoning methods for very expressive Description Logics is addressed in Chapter 5.

1.3 Knowledge representation in Description Logics

In the previous section a basic representation language for Description Logics was introduced along with some key associated reasoning techniques. Our goal now is to illustrate how Description Logics can be useful in the design of knowledge-based applications, that is to say, how a DL language is used in a knowledge representation system that provides a language for defining a knowledge base and tools to carry out inferences over it. The realization of knowledge systems involves two primary aspects. The first consists in providing a precise characterization of a knowledge base; this involves precisely characterizing the type of knowledge to be specified to the system as well as clearly defining the reasoning services the system needs to provide – the kind of questions that the system should be able to answer. The second aspect consists in providing a rich development environment where users can benefit from different services that can make their interaction with the system more effective. In this section we address the logical structure of the knowledge base, while the design of systems and tools for the development of applications is addressed in the next section.

One of the products of some important historical efforts to provide precise characterizations of the behavior of semantic networks and frames was a *functional approach* to knowledge representation [Levesque, 1984]. The idea was to give a precise specification of the functionality to be provided by a knowledge base and, specifically, of the inferences performed by the knowledge base – independent of any implementation. In practice, the functional description of a reasoning system is productively specified through a so-called "Tell&Ask" interface. Such an interface specifies operations that enable knowledge base construction (Tell operations) and operations that allow one to get information out of the knowledge base (Ask operations). In the following we shall adopt this view for characterizing both the definition of a DL knowledge base and the deductive services it provides.

Within a knowledge base one can see a clear distinction between *intensional knowledge,* or general knowledge about the problem domain, and *extensional knowledge,* which is specific to a particular problem. A typical DL knowledge base analogously comprises two components – a *TBox* and an *ABox*. The TBox contains intensional knowledge in the form of a terminology (hence the term "TBox", but "taxonomy" could be used as well) and is built through declarations that describe general properties of concepts. Because of the nature of the subsumption relationships among the concepts that constitute the terminology, TBoxes are usually thought of as having a lattice-like structure; this mathematical structure is entailed by the subsumption relationship – it has nothing to do with any implementation. The ABox contains extensional knowledge – also called assertional knowledge (hence the term "ABox") – knowledge that is specific to the individuals of the domain of discourse. Intensional knowledge is usually thought not to change – to be "timeless", in a way – and extensional knowledge is usually thought to be contingent, or dependent on a single set of circumstances, and therefore subject to occasional or even constant change.

In the rest of the section we present a basic Tell&Ask interface by analyzing the TBox and the ABox of a DL knowledge base.

1.3.1 The TBox

One key element of a DL knowledge base is given by the operations used to build the terminology. Such operations are directly related to the forms and the meaning of the declarations allowed in the TBox.

The basic form of declaration in a TBox is a concept *definition*, that is, the definition of a new concept in terms of other previously defined concepts. For example, a woman can be defined as a female person by writing this declaration:

$$\text{Woman} \equiv \text{Person} \sqcap \text{Female}.$$

Such a declaration is usually interpreted as a logical equivalence, which amounts to providing both sufficient and necessary conditions for classifying an individual as a woman. This form of definition is much stronger than the ones used in other kinds of representations of knowledge, which typically impose only necessary conditions; the strength of this kind of declaration is usually considered a characteristic feature of DL knowledge bases. In DL knowledge bases, therefore, a terminology is constituted by a set of concept definitions of the above form.

However, there are some important common assumptions usually made about DL terminologies:

- Only one definition for a concept name is allowed.
- Definitions are *acyclic* in the sense that concepts are neither defined in terms of themselves nor in terms of other concepts that indirectly refer to them.

This kind of restriction is common to many DL knowledge bases and implies that every defined concept can be expanded in a unique way into a complex expression containing only atomic concepts by replacing every defined concept with the right-hand side of its definition.

Nebel [1990b] showed that even simple expansion of definitions like this gives rise to an unavoidable source of complexity; in practice, however, definitions that inordinately increase the complexity of reasoning do not seem to occur. Under these assumptions the computational complexity of inferences can be studied by abstracting from the terminology and by considering all given concepts as fully expanded expressions. Therefore, much of the study of reasoning methods in Description Logics has been focused on concept expressions and, more specifically, as discussed in the previous section, on subsumption, which can be considered the basic reasoning service for the TBox.

In particular, the basic task in constructing a terminology is *classification*, which amounts to placing a new concept expression in the proper place in a taxonomic hierarchy of concepts. Classification can be accomplished by verifying the subsumption relation between each defined concept in the hierarchy and the new concept expression. The placement of the concept will be in between the most specific concepts that subsume the new concept and the most general concepts that the new concept subsumes.

More general settings for concept definitions have recently received some attention, deriving from attempts to establish formal relationships between Description Logics and other formalisms and from attempts to satisfy a need for increased expressive power. In particular, the admission of cyclic definitions has led to different semantic interpretations of the declarations, known as greatest/least fixpoint, and descriptive semantics. Although it has been argued that different semantics may be adopted depending on the target application, the more commonly adopted one is descriptive semantics, which simply requires that all the declarations be satisfied in the interpretation. Moreover, by dropping the requirement that on the left-hand side of a definition there can only be an atomic concept name, one can consider so-called *(general) inclusion axioms* of the form

$$C \sqsubseteq D$$

where C and D are arbitrary concept expressions. Notice that a concept definition can be expressed by two general inclusions. As a result of several theoretical studies concerning both the decidability of and implementation techniques for cyclic TBoxes, the most recent DL systems admit rather powerful constructs for defining concepts.

The basic deduction service for such TBoxes can be viewed as *logical implication* and it amounts to verifying whether a generic relationship (for example a subsumption relationship between two concept expressions) is a logical consequence of the declarations in the TBox. The issues arising in the semantic characterization of cyclic TBoxes are dealt with in Chapter 2, while techniques for reasoning in cyclic TBoxes are addressed in Chapter 2 and in Chapter 5, where very expressive Description Logics are presented.

1.3.2 The ABox

The ABox contains extensional knowledge about the domain of interest, that is, assertions about individuals, usually called *membership assertions*. For example,

$$\text{Female} \sqcap \text{Person}(\text{ANNA})$$

states that the individual ANNA is a female person. Given the above definition of woman, one can derive from this assertion that ANNA is an instance of the concept Woman. Similarly,

$$\text{hasChild}(\text{ANNA}, \text{JACOPO})$$

specifies that ANNA has JACOPO as a child. Assertions of the first kind are also called *concept assertions*, while assertions of the second kind are also called *role assertions*.

As illustrated by these examples, in the ABox one can typically specify knowledge in the form of concept assertions and role assertions. In concept assertions general concept expressions are typically allowed, while role assertions, where the role is not a primitive role but a role expression, are typically not allowed, being treated in the case of very expressive languages only.

The basic reasoning task in an ABox is *instance checking*, which verifies whether a given individual is an instance of (belongs to) a specified concept. Although other reasoning services are usually considered and employed, they can be defined in terms of instance checking. Among them we find *knowledge base consistency*, which amounts to verifying whether every concept in the knowledge base admits at least one individual; *realization*, which finds the most specific concept an individual object is an instance of; and *retrieval*, which finds the individuals in the knowledge base that are instances of a given concept. These can all be accomplished by means of instance checking.

The presence of individuals in a knowledge base makes reasoning more complex from a computational viewpoint [Donini *et al.*, 1994b], and may require significant extensions of some TBox reasoning techniques. Reasoning in the ABox is addressed in Chapter 3.

It is worth emphasizing that, although we have separated out for convenience the services for the ABox, when the TBox cannot be dealt with by means of the simple substitution mechanism used for acyclic TBoxes, the reasoning services may have to take into account all of the knowledge base including both the TBox and the ABox, and the corresponding reasoning problems become more complex. A full setting including general TBox and ABox is addressed in Chapter 5, where very expressive Description Logics are discussed.

More general languages for defining ABoxes have also been considered. Knowledge representation systems providing a powerful logical language for the ABox and a DL language for the TBox are often considered *hybrid* reasoning systems, since completely different knowledge representation languages may be used to specify the knowledge in the different components. Hybrid reasoning systems were popular in the 1980s (see for example [Brachman *et al.*, 1985]); lately, the topic has regained attention [Levy and Rousset, 1997; Donini *et al.*, 1998b], focusing on knowledge bases with a DL component for concept definitions and a logic-programming component for assertions about individuals. Sound and complete inference methods for hybrid knowledge bases become difficult to devise whenever there is a strict interaction between the knowledge components.

1.4 From theory to practice: Description Logic systems

A direct practical result of research on knowledge representation has been the development of tools for the construction of knowledge-based applications. As already noted, research on Description Logics has been characterized by a tight connection between theoretical results and implementation of systems. This has been achieved by maintaining a very close relationship between theoreticians, system implementors and users of knowledge representation systems based on Description Logics (DL-KRSs). The results of work on reasoning algorithms and their complexity have influenced the design of systems, and research on reasoning algorithms has itself been focused by a careful analysis of the capabilities and the limitations of implemented systems. In this section we first sketch the functionality of some knowledge representation systems and, subsequently, discuss the evolution of DL-KRSs. The reader can find a deeper treatment of the first topic in Chapter 7, while a survey of knowledge representation systems based on Description Logics is provided in Chapter 8. Chapter 9 is devoted to more specialized implementation and optimization techniques.

1.4.1 The design of knowledge representation systems based on Description Logics

In order to appreciate the difficulties of implementing and maintaining a knowledge representation system, it is necessary to consider that in the usage of a knowledge representation system, the reasoning service is really only one aspect of a complex system, one which may even be hidden from the final user. The user, before getting to "push the reasoning button", has to model the domain of interest, and input knowledge into the system. Further, in many cases, a simple yes/no answer is of little use, so a simplistic implementation of the Tell&Ask paradigm may be inadequate. As a consequence, the path one follows to get from the identification of a suitable knowledge representation system to the design of applications based on it is a complex and demanding one (see for example [Brachman, 1992]). In the case of Description Logics, this is especially true if the goal is to devise a system to be used by users who are not DL experts and who need to obtain a working system as quickly as possible. In the 1980s, when frame-based systems (such as, for example, KEE [Fikes and Kehler, 1985]; see [Karp, 1992] for an overview) had reached the strength of commercial products, the burden on a user of moving to the more modern DL-KRSs had to be kept small. Consequently, a stream of research addressed important aspects of the pragmatic usability of DL systems. This issue was especially relevant for those systems aiming at limiting the expressiveness of the language, but providing the user with sound, complete and efficient reasoning services. The issue of embedding a DL language within an environment suitable for application development is further addressed in Chapter 7.

In recent years, we might add, useful DL systems have often come as internal components of larger environments whose interfaces could completely hide the DL language and its core reasoning services. Systems like IMACS [Brachman *et al.*, 1993] and PROSE [Wright *et al.*, 1993] were quite successful in classifying data and configuring products, respectively, without the need for any user to understand the details of the DL representation language (CLASSIC) they were built upon.

Nowadays, applications for gathering information from the World Wide Web, where the interface can be specifically designed to support the retrieval of such information, also hide the knowledge representation and reasoning component. In addition, some data modeling tools, where the system provides a more conventional interface, can provide additional facilities based on the capability of reasoning about models with a DL inference engine. The possible settings for taking advantage of Description Logics as components of larger systems are discussed in Part III; more specifically, Chapter 14 presents Web applications and Chapter 15 natural language applications, while the reasoning capabilities of Description Logics in database applications are addressed in Chapter 16.

1.4.2 Knowledge representation systems based on Description Logics

The history of knowledge representation is covered in the literature in numerous ways (see for example [Woods and Schmolze, 1992; Rich, 1991; Baader *et al.*, 1992b]). Here we identify three generations of systems, highlighting their historical evolution rather than their specific functionality. We shall characterize them as *Pre-DL systems*, *DL systems* and *Current Generation DL systems*. Detailed references to implemented systems are given in Chapter 8.

1.4.2.1 Pre-Description Logic systems

The ancestor of DL systems is KL-ONE [Brachman and Schmolze, 1985], which signaled the transition from semantic networks to more well-founded terminological (description) logics. The influence of KL-ONE was profound and it is considered the root of the entire family of languages [Woods and Schmolze, 1990].

Semantic networks were introduced around 1966 as a representation for the concepts underlying English words, and became a popular type of framework for representing a wide variety of concepts in AI applications. Important and commonsensical ideas evolved in this work, from named nodes and links for representing concepts and relationships, to hierarchical networks with inheritance of properties, to the notion of "instantiation" of a concept by an individual object. But semantic network systems were fraught with problems, including vagueness and inconsistency in the meaning of various constructs, and the lack of a level of structure on which to base application-independent inference procedures. In his PhD thesis [Brachman, 1977a] and subsequent work (e.g., see [Brachman, 1979]), Brachman addressed representation at what he called an "epistemological", or knowledge-structuring level. This led to a set of primitives for structuring knowledge that was less application- and world-knowledge-dependent than "semantic" representations (like those for processing natural language case structures), yet richer than the impoverished set of primitives available in strictly logical languages. The main result of this work was a new knowledge representation framework whose primitive elements allowed cleaner, more application-independent representations than prior network formalisms. In the late 1970s, Brachman and his colleagues explored the utility and implications of this kind of framework in the KL-ONE system.

KL-ONE introduced most of the key notions explored in the extensive work on Description Logics that followed. These included, for example, the notions of concepts and roles and how they were to be interrelated; the important ideas of "value restriction" and "number restriction", which modified the use of roles in the definitions of concepts; and the crucial inferences of subsumption and classification. It also sowed the seeds for the later distinction between the TBox and ABox and a host of other significant notions that greatly influenced subsequent work. KL-ONE also was the initial example of the substantial interplay between theory and practice that characterizes the history of Description Logics. It was influenced by work in logic and philosophy (and in turn itself influenced work in philosophy and psychology), and significant care was taken in its design to allow it to be consistent and semantically sound. But it was also used in multiple applications, covering intelligent information presentation and natural language understanding, among other things.

Most of the focus of the original work on KL-ONE was on the representation of and reasoning with concepts, with only a small amount of attention paid to reasoning with individual objects. The first descendants of KL-ONE were focused on architectures providing a clear distinction between a powerful logic-based (or rule-based) component and a specialized terminological component. These systems came to be referred to as *hybrid systems*. A major research issue was the integration of the two components to provide unified reasoning services over the whole knowledge base.

1.4.2.2 Description Logic systems

The earliest "pre-DL" systems derived directly from KL-ONE, which, while itself a direct result of formal analysis of the shortcomings of semantic networks, was mainly about the implementation of a viable classification algorithm and the data structures to adequately represent concepts. DL systems, *per se*, which followed as the next generation, were more derived from a wave of theoretical research on terminological logics that resulted from examination of KL-ONE and some other early systems. This work was initiated in roughly 1984, inspired by a paper by Brachman and Levesque [Brachman and Levesque, 1984] on the formal complexity of reasoning in Description Logics. Subsequent results on the tradeoff between the expressiveness of a DL language and the complexity of reasoning with it, and more generally, the identification of the sources of complexity in DL systems, showed that a careful selection of language constructs was needed and that the reasoning services provided by the system are deeply influenced by the set of constructs provided to the user. We can thus characterize three different approaches to the implementation of reasoning services. The first can be referred to as *limited+complete*, and includes systems that are designed by restricting the set of constructs in such a way that subsumption would be computed efficiently, possibly in polynomial time. The CLASSIC system [Brachman *et al.*, 1991] is the most significant example of this kind. The second approach can be denoted as *expressive+incomplete*, since the idea is to provide both an expressive language and efficient reasoning. The drawback is, however, that reasoning algorithms turn out to be incomplete in these systems. Notable examples of this kind of system are LOOM [MacGregor and Bates, 1987], and BACK [Nebel and von Luck, 1988]. After some of the sources of incompleteness were discovered, often by identifying the constructs – or, more precisely, combinations of constructs – that would require an exponential algorithm to preserve the completeness of reasoning, systems with complete reasoning algorithms were designed. Systems of this sort (see for example KRIS [Baader and Hollunder, 1991a]) are therefore characterized as *expressive+complete*; they were not as efficient as those following the other approaches, but they provided a testbed for the implementation of reasoning techniques developed in the theoretical investigations, and they played an important role in stimulating comparison and benchmarking with other systems [Heinsohn *et al.*, 1992; Baader *et al.*, 1992b].

1.4.2.3 Current generation Description Logic systems

In the current generation of DL-KRSs, the need for complete algorithms for expressive languages has been the focus of attention. The expressiveness of the DL language required for reasoning on data models and semistructured data has contributed to the identification of the most important extensions for practical applications.

The design of complete algorithms for expressive Description Logic has led to significant extensions of tableau-based techniques and to the introduction of several optimization techniques, partly borrowed from theorem proving and partly specifically developed for Description Logics. Recent systems that allow for expressive DL languages, while providing efficient implementations of reasoning are FACT [Horrocks, 1998b] and RACER [Haarslev and Möller, 2001e].

This research has also been influenced by newly discovered relationships between Description Logics and other logics, leading to exchanging benchmarks and experimental comparisons with other deduction systems.

The techniques that have been used in the implementation of very expressive Description Logics are addressed in detail in Chapter 9.

1.5 Applications developed with Description Logic systems

The third component in the picture of the development of Description Logics is the implementation of applications in different domains. Some of the applications created over the years may have only reached the level of prototype, but many of them have the completeness of industrial systems and have been deployed in production use.

A critical element in the development of applications based on Description Logics is the usability of the knowledge representation system. We have already emphasized that building a tool to be used in the design and implementation of knowledge-based applications requires significant work to make it suitable for interactive development, explanation and debugging, interface implementation, and so on. In addition, here we focus on the effectiveness of Description Logics as a modeling language. A modeling language should have intuitive semantics and the syntax must help convey the intended meaning. To this end, a somewhat different syntax than we have seen so far, closer to that of natural language, has often been adopted, and graphical interfaces that provide an operational view of the process of knowledge base construction have been developed. The issues arising in modeling application domains using Description Logics are dealt with in Chapter 10, and will be briefly addressed in the next subsection.

It is natural to expect that some classes of applications share similarities both in methodological patterns and in the design of specific structures or reasoning capabilities. Consequently, we identify several application domains in Subsection 1.5.2; these include software engineering, configuration, medicine, and digital libraries and Web-based information systems.

In Subsection 1.5.3 we consider several application areas where Description Logics play a major role; these include natural language processing and database management, where Description Logics can be used in several ways.

When addressing the design of applications it is also worth pointing out that there has been significant evolution in the way Description Logics have been used within complex applications. In particular, the DL-centered view that underlies the earliest generation of systems, wherein an application was developed in a single environment (the one provided by the DL system), was characterized by very loose interaction, if any, between the DL system and other applications. Later, an approach that viewed the Description Logic more as a component became evident; in this view the DL system acts as a component of a larger environment, typically leaving out functions, such those for data management, that are more effectively implemented by other technologies. The architecture where the component view is taken requires the definition of a clear interface between the components, possibly adopting different modeling languages, but focusing on Description Logics for the implementation of the reasoning services that can add powerful capabilities to the application. Obviously, the choice between the above architectural views depends upon the needs of the application at hand.

Finally, we have already stressed that research in Description Logics has benefited from tight interaction between language designers and developers of DL-KRSs. Thus, another major impact on the development of DL research was provided by the implementation of applications using DL-KRSs. Indeed, work on DL applications not only demonstrated the effectiveness of Description Logics and of DL-KRSs, but also provided mutual feedback within the DL community concerning the weaknesses of both the representation language and the features of an implemented DL-KRS.

1.5.1 Modeling with Description Logics

In order for designers to be able to use Description Logics to model their application domains, it is important for the DL constructs to be easily understandable; this helps facilitate the construction of convenient to use yet effective tools. To this end, the abstract notation that we have previously introduced and that is nowadays commonly used in the DL community is not fully satisfactory.

As already mentioned, there are at least two major alternatives for increasing the usability of Description Logics as a modeling language:

1. providing a syntax that resembles more closely natural language;
2. implementing interfaces where the user can specify the representation structures through graphical operations.

Before addressing the above two possibilities, one brief remark is in order.

While alternative ways of specifying knowledge, such as natural-language-style syntax, can be more appealing to the user, one should remember that Description Logics in part arose from a need to respond to the inadequacy – the lack of a formal semantic basis – of early semantic networks and frame systems. Those early systems often relied on an assumption of intuitive readings of natural-language-like constructs or graphical structures, which in the end made them unsatisfactory. Therefore, we need to keep in mind always the correspondence of the language used by the user and the abstract DL syntax, and consequently correspondences with the formal semantics should always be clear and available.

The option of a more readable syntax has been pursued in the majority of DL-KRSs. In particular, we refer to the concrete syntax proposed in [Patel-Schneider and Swartout, 1993], which is based on a LISP-like notation, where, for example, the concept of a female person is denoted by (and Person Female). Similarly, the concept $\forall$hasChild.Female would be written (all hasChild Female). In addition, there are shorthand expressions, such as (the hasChild Female), which indicates the existence of a unique female child, and can be phrased using qualified existential restriction and number restriction. In Chapter 10 this kind of syntax is discussed in detail and the possible sources for ambiguities in the natural language reading of the constructs are discussed.

The second option for providing the user with a concrete syntax is to rely on a graphical interface. Starting with the KL-ONE system, this possibility has been pursued by introducing a graphical notation for the representation of concepts and roles, as well as their relationships. More recently, Web-based interfaces for Description Logics have been proposed [Welty, 1996a]; in addition, an XML standard has been proposed [Bechhofer *et al.*, 1999; Euzenat, 2001], which is suitable not only for data interchange, but also for providing full-fledged Web interfaces to DL-KRSs or applications embodying them as components.

The modeling language is the vehicle for the expression of the modeling notions that are provided to the designers. Modeling in Description Logics requires the designer to specify the concepts of the domain of discourse and characterize their relationships to other concepts and to specific individuals. Concepts can be regarded as classes of individuals and Description Logics as an object-centered modeling language, since they allow one to introduce individuals (objects) and explicitly define their properties, as well as to express relationships among them. Concept definition, which provides for both necessary and sufficient conditions, is a characteristic feature of Description

Logics. The basic relationship between concepts is subsumption, which allows one to capture various kinds of subclassing mechanisms; however, other kinds of relationships can be modeled, such as grouping, materialization, and part–whole aggregation.

The model of a domain in Description Logics is embedded in a knowledge base. We have already addressed the TBox–ABox characterization of the knowledge base. We recall that the roles of TBox and ABox were motivated by the need to distinguish general knowledge about the domain of interest from specific knowledge about individuals characterizing a specific world or situation under consideration. Besides the TBox–ABox, other mechanisms for organizing a knowledge base such as *contexts* and *views* have been introduced in Description Logics. The use of the modeling notions provided by Description Logics and the organization of knowledge bases are addressed in greater detail in Chapter 10.

Finally, we recall that Description Logics as modeling languages overlap to a large extent with other modeling languages developed in fields such as programming languages and database management. While we shall focus on this relationship later, we recall here that, when compared to modeling languages developed in other fields, the characteristic feature of Description Logics is in the reasoning capabilities that are associated with them. In other words, we believe that, while modeling has general significance, the capability of exploiting the description of the model to draw conclusions about the problem at hand is a particular advantage of modeling using Description Logics.

1.5.2 Application domains

Description Logics have been used (and are being used) in the implementation of many systems that demonstrate their practical effectiveness. Some of these systems have found their way into production use, despite the fact that there was no real commercial platform that could be used for developing them.

1.5.2.1 Software engineering

Software engineering was one of the first application domains for Desciption Logics undertaken at AT&T, where the CLASSIC system was developed. The basic idea was to use a Description Logic to implement a *software information system*, i.e., a system that would support the software developer by helping him or her in finding out information about a large software system.

More specifically, it was found that the information of interest for software development was a combination of knowledge about the domain of the application and code-specific information. However, while the structure of the code can be determined automatically, the connection between code elements and domain concepts needs to be specified by the user.

One of the most novel applications of Description Logics is the LaSSIE system [Devanbu *et al.*, 1991], which allowed users to incrementally build a taxonomy of concepts relating domain notions to the code implementing them. The system could thereafter provide useful information in response to user queries concerning the code, such as, for example "the function to generate a dial tone". By exploiting the description of the domain, the information retrieval capabilities of the system went significantly beyond those of the standard tools used for software development. The LaSSIE system had considerable success but ultimately stumbled because of the difficulty of maintenance of the knowledge base, given the constantly changing nature of industrial software. Both the ideas of a software information system and the usage of Description Logics survived that particular application and have been subsequently used in other systems. The usage of Description Logics in applications for software engineering is described in Chapter 11.

1.5.2.2 Configuration

One very successful domain for knowledge-based applications built using Description Logics is *configuration*, which includes applications that support the design of complex systems created by combining multiple components.

The configuration task amounts to finding a proper set of components that can be suitably connected in order to implement a system that meets a given specification. For example, choosing computer components in order to build a home PC is a relatively simple configuration task. When the number, the type, and the connectivity of the components grow, the configuration task can become rather complex. In particular, computer configuration has been among the application fields of the first expert systems and can thus be viewed as a standard application domain for knowledge-based systems. Configuration tasks arise in many industrial domains, such as telecommunications, the automotive industry, building construction, etc.

DL-based knowledge representation systems meet the requirements for the development of configuration applications. In particular, they enable the object-oriented modeling of system components, which combines powerfully with the ability to reason from incomplete specifications and to automatically detect inconsistencies. Using Description Logics one can exploit the ability to classify the components and organize them within a taxonomy. In addition a DL-based approach supports incremental specification and modularity. Applications for configuration tasks require at least two features that were not in the original core of DL-KRSs: the representation of rules (together with a rule propagation mechanism), and the ability to provide explanations. However, extensions with so-called "active rules" are now very common in DL-KRSs, and a precise semantic account is given in Chapter 2; significant work on explanation capabilities of DL-KRSs has been developed in connection with the design of configuration applications [McGuinness and Borgida, 1995]. Chapter 12 is devoted to the applications developed in Description Logics for configuration tasks.

1.5.2.3 Medicine

Medicine is also a domain where expert systems have been developed since the 1980s; however, the complexity of the medical domain calls for a variety of uses for a DL-KRS. In practice, decision support for medical diagnosis is only one of the tasks in need of automation. One focus has been on the construction and maintenance of very large ontologies of medical knowledge, the subject of some large government initiatives. The need to deal with large-scale knowledge bases (hundreds of thousands of concepts) led to the development of specialized systems, such as GALEN [Rector *et al.*, 1993], while the requirement for standardization arising from the need to deal with several sources of information led to the adoption of the DL standard language KRSS [Patel-Schneider and Swartout, 1993] in projects like SNOMED [Spackman *et al.*, 1997].

In order to cope with the scalability of the knowledge base, the DL language adopted in these applications is often limited to a few basic constructs and the knowledge base turns out to be rather shallow, that is to say the taxonomy does not have very many levels of subconcepts below the top concepts. Nonetheless, there are several advanced language features that would be very useful in the representation of medical knowledge, such as, for example, specific support for PART-OF hierarchies (see Chapter 10), as well as defaults and modalities to capture lack of knowledge (see Chapter 6).

Obviously, since medical applications most often must be used by doctors, a formal logical language is not well-suited; therefore special attention is given to the design of the user interface; in particular, natural language processing (see Chapter 15) is important both in the construction of the ontology and in the operational interfaces.

Further, the DL component of a medical application usually operates within a larger information system, comprising several sources of information, which need to be integrated in order to provide a coherent view of the available data (on this topic see Chapter 16).

Finally, an important issue that arises in the medical domain is the management of ontologies, which not only requires common tools for project management, such as versioning systems, but also tools to support knowledge acquisition and re-use (on this topic see Chapter 8).

The use of Description Logics specifically in the design of medical applications is addressed in Chapter 13.

1.5.2.4 Digital libraries and Web-based information systems

The relationship between semantic networks and the linked structures implied by hypertext has motivated the development of DL applications for representing bibliographic information and for supporting classification and retrieval in digital libraries [Welty and Jenkins, 2000]. These applications have proven the effectiveness of Description Logics for representing the taxonomies that are commonly used in library classification schemes, and they have shown the advantage of subsumption reasoning for classifying and retrieving information. In these instances, a number of technical questions, mostly related to the use of individuals in the taxonomy, have motivated the use of more expressive Description Logics.

The possibility of viewing the World Wide Web as a semantic network has been considered since the advent of the Web itself. Even in the early days of the Web, thought was given to the potential benefits of enabling programs to handle not only simple unlabeled navigation structures, but also the information content of Web pages. The goal was to build systems for querying the Web "semantically", allowing the user to pose queries of the Web as if it were a database, roughly speaking. Based on the relationship between Description Logics and semantic networks, a number of proposals were developed that used Description Logics to model Web structures, allowing the exploitation of DL reasoning capabilities in the acquisition and management of information [Kirk *et al.*, 1995; De Rosa *et al.*, 1998].

More recently, there have been significant efforts based on the use of markup languages to capture the information content of Web structures. The relationship between Description Logics and markup languages, such as XML, has been precisely characterized [Calvanese *et al.*, 1999d], thus identifying DL language features for representing XML documents. Moreover, interest in the standardization of knowledge representation mechanisms for enabling knowledge exchange has led to the development of OWL (Ontology Web Language) [Bechhofer *et al.*, 2004; Patel-Schneider *et al.*, 2004;

Smith *et al.*, 2004] which is a product of the research on Description Logics, and the theoretical investigations on the computability and complexity of reasoning in Description Logics [Horrocks *et al.*, 2003]. The use of Description Logics in the design of digital libraries and Web applications is addressed in Chapter 14, with specific discussion on OWL and its standardization process.

1.5.2.5 Other application domains

The above list of application domains, while presenting some of the most relevant applications designed with DL-KRSs, is far from complete. There are many other domains that have been addressed by the DL community. Among the application areas that have resorted to Description Logics for useful functions are planning and data mining.

With respect to planning, many knowledge-based applications rely on the services of a planning component. While Description Logics do not provide such a component themselves, they have been used to implement several general-purpose planning systems. The basic idea is to represent plans and actions, as well as their constituent elements, as concepts. The system can thus maintain a taxonomy of plan types and provide several reasoning services, such as plan recognition, plan subsumption, plan retrieval, and plan refinement. Two examples of planning components developed in a DL-KRS are CLASP [Yen *et al.*, 1991b], developed on top of CLASSIC, and EXPECT [Swartout and Gil, 1996], developed on top of LOOM. In addition, the integration of Description Logics and other formalisms, such as constraint networks, has been proposed [Weida and Litman, 1992]. Planning systems based on Description Logics have been used in many application domains to support planning services in conjunction with a taxonomic representation of the domain knowledge. Such application domains include, among others, software engineering, medicine, campaign planning, and information integration.

It is worth mentioning that Description Logics have also been used to represent dynamic systems and to automatically generate plans based on such representations. However, in such cases the use of Description Logics is limited to the formalization of properties that characterize the states of the system, while plan generation is achieved through the use of a rule propagation mechanism [De Giacomo *et al.*, 1999]. Such use of Description Logics is inspired by the correspondence between Description Logics and Dynamic Logics described in Chapter 5.

Description Logics have also been used in data mining applications, where their inferences can help the process of analyzing large amounts of data. In this kind of application, DL structures can represent *views*, and DL systems can be used to store and classify such views. The classification mechanism can help in discovering interesting classes of items in the data. We address this type of application briefly in the next subsection on database management.

1.5.3 Application areas

From the beginning Description Logics have been considered general-purpose languages for knowledge representation and reasoning, and therefore suited for many applications. In particular, they were considered especially effective for those domains where the knowledge could be easily organized along a hierarchical structure, based on the "IS-A" relationship. The ability to represent and reason about taxonomies in Description Logics has motivated their use as a modeling language in the design and maintenance of large, hierarchically structured bodies of knowledge as well as their adoption as the representation language for formal ontologies [Welty and Guarino, 2001].

We now briefly look at some other research areas that have a more general relationship with Description Logics. Such a relationship exists either because Description Logics are viewed as a basic representation language, as in the case of natural language processing, or because they can be used in a variety of ways in concert with the main technology of the area, as in the field of database management.

1.5.3.1 Natural language

Description Logics, as well as semantic networks and frames, originally had natural language processing as a major field for application (see for example [Brachman, 1979]). In particular, when work on Description Logics began, not only was a large part of the DL community working on natural language applications, but Description Logics also bore a strong similarity to other formalisms used in natural language work, such as Feature Logics [Nebel and Smolka, 1991].

The use of Description Logics in natural language processing is mainly concerned with the representation of *semantic* knowledge that can be used to convey meanings of sentences. Such knowledge is typically concerned with the meaning of words (the lexicon), and with context, that is, a representation of the situation and domain of discourse.

A significant body of work has been devoted to the problem of disambiguating different syntactic readings of sentences, based on semantic knowledge, a process called *semantic interpretation*. Moreover, semantic knowledge expressed in Description Logics has also been used to support natural language generation.

Since the domain of discourse for a natural language application can be arbitrarily broad, work on natural language has also involved the construction of ontologies [Welty and Guarino, 2001]. In addition, the expressiveness of natural language has led also to investigations concerning extensions of Description Logics, such as default reasoning (see Chapter 6).

Several large projects for natural language processing based on the use of Description Logics have been undertaken, some reaching the level of industrially deployed applications. They are referenced in Chapter 15, where the role of Description Logics in natural language processing is addressed in more detail.

1.5.3.2 Database management

The relationship between Description Logics and databases is rather strong. In fact, there is often the need to build systems where both a DL-KRS and a DataBase Management System (DBMS) are present. DBMSs deal with persistence of data and with the management of large amounts of it, while a DL-KRS manages intensional knowledge, typically keeping the knowledge base in memory (possibly including assertions about individuals that correspond to data). While some of the applications created with DL-KRSs have developed *ad hoc* solutions to the problem of dealing with large amounts of persistent data, in a complex application domain it is very likely that a DL-KRSs and a DBMS would both be components of a larger system, and they would work together.

In addition, Description Logics provide a formal framework that has been shown to be rather close to the languages used in semantic data modeling, such as the Entity–Relationship model [Calvanese *et al.*, 1998g]. Description Logics are equipped with reasoning tools that can bring to the conceptual modeling phase significant advantages, as compared with traditional languages, whose role is limited to modeling. For instance, by using concept consistency one can verify at design time whether an entity can have at least one instance, thus clearly saving all the difficulties arising from discovering such a situation when the database is being populated [Borgida, 1995].

A second dimension of the enhancement of DBMSs with Description Logics involves the query language. By expressing the queries to a database in a Description Logic one gains the ability to classify them and therefore to deal with issues such as query processing and optimization. However, the basic DL machinery needs to be extended in order to deal with conjunctive queries; otherwise DL expressiveness with respect to queries is rather limited. In addition, Description Logics can be used to express constraints and intensional answers to queries.

A corollary of the relationship between Description Logics and DBMS query languages is the utility of Description Logics in reasoning with and about *views*. In the IMACS system [Brachman *et al.*, 1993], the CLASSIC language was used as a "lens" [Brachman, 1994] with which data in a conventional relational database could be viewed. The interface to the data was made significantly more appropriate for a data analyst, and views that were found to be productive could be saved; in fact, they were saved in a taxonomy and could be classified with respect to one another. In a sense, this allows the schema to be viewed and queried explicitly, something normally not available when using a raw DBMS directly.

A more recent use of Description Logics is concerned with so-called "semi-structured" data models [Calvanese *et al.*, 1998c], which are being proposed in order to overcome the difficulties in treating data that are not structured in a relational form, such as data on the Web, data in spreadsheets, etc. In this area Description Logics are sufficiently expressive to represent models and languages that are being used in practice, and they can offer significant advantages over other approaches because of the reasoning services they provide.

Another problem that has recently increased the applicability of Description Logics is information integration. As already remarked, data are nowadays available in large quantities and from a variety of sources. Information integration is the task of providing a unique coherent view of the data stored in the sources available. In order to create such a view, a proper relationship needs to be established between the data in the sources and the unified view of the data. Description Logics not only have the expressiveness needed in order to model the data in the sources, but their reasoning services can help in the selection of the sources that are relevant for a query of interest, as well as to specify the extraction process [Calvanese *et al.*, 2001c].

The uses of Description Logics with databases are addressed in more detail in Chapter 16.

1.6 Extensions of Description Logics

In this section we look at several types of extensions that have been proposed for Description Logics; these are addressed in more detail in Chapter 6. Such extensions are generally motivated by needs arising in applications. Unfortunately, some extended features in implemented DL-KRSs were created without precise, formal accounts; in some other cases, such accounts have been provided using a formal framework that is not restricted to first-order logic.

A first group of extensions has the purpose of adding to DL languages some representational features that were common in frame systems or that are relevant for certain classes of applications. Such extensions provide a representation of some novel epistemological notions and address the reasoning problems that arise in the extended framework.

Extensions of a second sort are concerned with reasoning services that are useful in the development of knowledge bases but are typically not provided by DL-KRSs. The implementation of such services relies on additional inference techniques that are considered non-standard, because they go beyond the basic reasoning services provided by DL-KRSs.

Below we first address the extensions of the knowledge representation framework and then non-standard inferences.

1.6.1 Language extensions

Some of the research associated with language extensions has investigated the semantics of the proposed extensions, but often the emphasis is only on finding reasoning procedures for the extended languages. Within these language extensions we find constructs for non-monotonic, epistemic, and temporal reasoning, and constructs for representing belief and uncertain and vague knowledge. In addition some constructs address reasoning in concrete domains.

1.6.1.1 Non-monotonic reasoning

When frame-based systems began to be formally characterized as fragments of first-order logic, it became clear that those frame-based systems as well as some DL-KRSs that were used in practice occasionally provided the user with constructs that could not be given a precise semantic characterization within the framework of first-order logic. Notable among the problematic constructs were those associated with the notion of defaults, which over time have been extensively studied in the field of non-monotonic reasoning [Brachman, 1985].

While one of the problems arising in semantic networks was the oft-cited so-called "Nixon diamond" [Reiter and Criscuolo, 1981], a whole line of research in non-monotonic reasoning was developed in trying to characterize the system behavior by studying structural properties of networks. For example, the general property that "birds fly" might not be inherited by a penguin, because a rule that penguins do not fly would give rise to an arc in the network that would block the default inference. But as soon as the network becomes relatively complex (see for example [Touretzky *et al.*, 1991]), we can see that attempts to provide semantic characterization in terms of network structure are inadequate.

Another approach that has been pursued in the formalization of non-monotonic reasoning in semantic networks is based on the use of default logic [Reiter, 1980; Etherington, 1987; Nado and Fikes, 1987]. Following a similar approach is the treatment of defaults in DL-based systems [Baader and Hollunder, 1995a], where formal tools borrowed from work on non-monotonic reasoning have been adapted to the framework of Description Logics. Such adaptation is non-trivial, however, because Description Logics are not, in general, propositional languages.

1.6.1.2 Modal representation of knowledge and belief

Modal logics have been widely studied to model a variety of features that in first-order logic would require the application of special constraints on certain elements of the formalization. For example, the notions of knowing something or believing that some sentence is true can be captured by introducing modal operators, which characterize properties that sentences have.

For instance the assertion

$$\mathbf{B}(\mathsf{Married}(\mathsf{ANNA}))$$

states a fact explicitly concerning the system's beliefs (the system believes that Anna is married), rather than asserting the truth of something about the world being modeled (the system could believe something to be true without firm knowledge about its truth in the world).

In general, by introducing a modal operator one gains the ability to model properties like knowledge, belief, time-dependence, obligation, and so on. On the one hand, extensions of Description Logics with modal operators can be viewed very much like the corresponding modal extensions of first-order logic. In particular, the semantic issues arising in the interpretation of quantified modal sentences (i.e., sentences with modal operators appearing inside the scope of quantifiers) are the same. On the other hand, the syntactic restrictions that are suited to a DL language lead to formalisms whose expressiveness and reasoning problems inherit some of the features of a specialized DL language. Extensions of Description Logics with modal operators including those for representing knowledge and belief are discussed in [Baader and Ohlbach, 1995].

1.6.1.3 Epistemic reasoning

It is not sufficient to provide a semantics for defaults to obtain a full semantic account of frame-based systems. Frame-based systems have included procedural rules as well as other forms of closure and epistemic reasoning that need to be covered by the semantics as well as by the reasoning algorithms. In particular, if one looks at the most widely-used systems based on Description Logics, such features are still present, possibly in new flavors, while their semantics is given informally and the consequences of reasoning sometimes not adequately explained.

Among the non-first-order features that are used in the practice of knowledge-based applications in both DL-based and frame-based systems we point out these:

- *procedural rules* (also called *trigger rules*), which are normally described as *if–then* statements and are used to infer new facts about known individuals;
- *default rules*, which enable default reasoning in inheritance hierarchies;
- *role closure*, which limits the reasoning involving role restrictions to the individuals explicitly in the knowledge base;
- *integrity constraints*, which provide consistency restrictions on admissible knowledge bases.

In Chapter 6, among other approaches an epistemic extension of Description Logics with a modal operator is addressed. In the resulting formalism [Donini *et al.*, 1998a] one can express epistemic queries and, by admitting a simple form of epistemic sentences in the knowledge base, one can formalize the aforementioned procedural rules. This characterization of procedural rules in terms of an epistemic operator has been widely accepted in the DL community and is thus also included in Chapter 2. The approach has been further extended to what have been called Autoepistemic Description Logics (ADLs) [Donini *et al.*, 1997b, 2002], where it is combined with default reasoning. This combination is achieved by relying on the non-monotonic modal logic *MKNF* [Lifschitz, 1991], thus introducing a second modal operator interpreted as autoepistemic assumption. The features mentioned above can be uniformly treated as epistemic sentences in the knowledge base, without the need to give them special status as in the case of procedural rules, defaults, and epistemic constraints on the knowledge base. This expressiveness does not come without making reasoning more difficult. An extension of the reasoning methods available for deduction in the propositional formalizations of non-monotonic reasoning to the fragment of first-order logic corresponding to Description Logics has nonetheless been shown to be decidable.

1.6.1.4 Temporal reasoning

One notion that is often required in the formalization of application domains is time. Temporal extensions of Description Logics have been treated as a special kind of modal extension. The first proposal for handling time in a DL framework [Schmiedel, 1990] was originated in the context of the DL system BACK. Later, following the standard approaches in the representation of time, both interval-based and point-based approaches have been studied, specifically focusing on the decidability and complexity of the reasoning problems (see [Artale and Franconi, 2001] for a survey the temporal extensions of Description Logics).

Time intervals can also be treated as a form of concrete domain (see below).

1.6.1.5 Representation of uncertain and vague knowledge

Another aspect of knowledge that is sometimes useful in representing and reasoning about application domains is uncertainty. As in other knowledge representation frameworks there are several approaches to the representation of uncertain knowledge in Description Logics. Two of them, namely probabilistic logic and fuzzy logic, have been proposed in the context of Description Logics. In the case of probabilistic Description Logics [Heinsohn, 1994; Jaeger, 1994] the knowledge about the domain is expressed in terms of probabilistic terminological axioms, which allow one to represent statistical information about the domain, and in terms of probabilistic assertions, which specify the degree of belief of asserted properties. The reasoning tasks aim at finding the probability bounds for subsumption relations and assertions. A more recent line of work tries to combine Description Logics with Bayesian networks.

In the case of fuzzy Description Logics [Yen, 1991] the goal is to characterize notions that cannot be properly defined with a "crisp" numerical bound. For example, the concept of living near Rome cannot be always defined with a crisp boundary on the map, but must be represented with a membership or degree function, which expresses closeness to the city in a continuous way.

Proposed approaches to fuzzy Description Logics not only define the semantics of assertions in terms of fuzzy sets, but also introduce new operators to express notions like "mostly", "very", etc. Reasoning algorithms are also provided for computing fuzzy subsumption within the framework of tableau-based methods.

1.6.1.6 Concrete domains

One of the limitations of basic Description Logics is related to the difficulty of integrating knowledge (and, consequently, performing reasoning) of specific domains, such as numbers or strings, which are needed in many applications. For example, in order to model the concept of a young person it seems rather natural to introduce the (functional) role *age* and to use a concrete value (or range of values) in the definition of the concept. In addition, one would like to be able to conclude that a person of school age is also a young person. Such a conclusion might require the use of properties of numbers to establish that the expected subsumption relation holds.

While for some time such extensions were designed in ad hoc ways, in [Baader and Hanschke, 1991a] a general method was established for integrating knowledge about concrete domains within a DL language. If a domain can be properly formalized, it is shown that the tableau-based reasoning technique can be suitably extended to handle the reasoning services in the extended language.

Concrete domains include not only data types such as numerical types, but also more elaborate domains, such as tuples of the relational calculus, spatial regions, or time intervals.

1.6.2 Additional reasoning services

Non-standard inference tasks can serve a variety of purposes, among them support in building and maintaining the knowledge base, as well as in obtaining information about the knowledge represented in it.

Among the more useful non-standard inference tasks in Description Logics we find the computation of the least common subsumer and the most specific concept, matching/unification, and concept rewriting.

1.6.2.1 Least common subsumer and most specific concept

The least common subsumer (*lcs*) of a set of concepts is the minimal concept that subsumes all of them. The minimality condition implies there is no other concept that subsumes all the concepts in the set and is less general (subsumed by) the lcs. This notion was first studied in [Cohen *et al.*, 1992] and it has subsequently been used for several tasks: inductive learning of concept description from examples; knowledge base vivification (as a way to represent disjunction in languages that do not admit it); and in the bottom-up construction of DL knowledge bases (starting from instances of the concepts).

The notion of lcs is closely related to that of most specific concept (*msc*) of an individual, i.e., the least concept description that the individual is an instance of, given the assertions in the knowledge base; the minimality condition is specified as before. More generally, one can define the msc of a set of assertions about individuals as the lcs of the msc associated with each individual. Based on the computation of the msc of a set of assertions about individuals one can incrementally construct a knowledge base [Baader and Küsters, 1999].

It interesting to observe that the techniques that have been proposed to compute the lcs and mcs rely on compact representations of concept expressions, which are built either following the structural subsumption approach, or through the definition of a well-suited normal form.

1.6.2.2 Unification and matching

Another tool to support the construction and maintenance of DL knowledge bases that goes beyond the standard inference services provided by DL-KRSs is the unification of concepts.

Concept unification [Baader and Narendran, 1998] is an operation that can be regarded as weakening the equivalence between two concept expressions. More precisely, two concept expressions unify if one can find a substitution of concept variables into concept expressions such that the result of applying the substitution gives equivalent concepts. The intuition is that, in order to find possible overlaps between concept definitions, one can treat certain concept names as variables and discover, via unification, that two concepts (possibly independently defined by distinct knowledge designers) are in fact equivalent. The knowledge base can consequently be simplified by introducing a single definition of the unifiable concepts.

As usual, matching is defined as a special case of unification, where variables occur only in one of the two concept expressions. In addition, in the framework of Description Logics, one can define matching and unification based on the subsumption relation instead of equivalence [Baader *et al.*, 1999a].

As with other non-standard inferences, the computation of matching and unification relies on the use of specialized representations for concept expressions, and it has been shown to be decidable for rather simple Description Logics.

1.6.2.3 Concept rewriting

Finally, there has been a significant body of work on the problem of concept rewriting. Given a concept expressed in a source language, concept rewriting amounts to finding a concept, possibly expressed in a target language, which is related to the given concept according to equivalence, subsumption, or some other relation.

In order to specify the rewriting, one can provide a suitable set of constraints between concepts in the source language and concepts in the target language. Concept rewriting can be applied to the translation of concepts from one knowledge base to another, or in the reformulation of concepts during the process of knowledge base construction and maintenance.

In addition, concept rewriting has been addressed in the context of the rewriting of queries using views, in database management (see also Chapter 16), and has recently been investigated in the framework of information integration. In this setting, one can apply concept rewriting techniques to automatically generate the queries that enable a system to gather information from a set of sources [Beeri *et al.*, 1997]. Given an initial specification of the query according to a common, global language, and a set of constraints expressing the relationship between the global schema and the individual sources where information is stored, the problem is to compute the queries to be posed to the local sources that provide answers, possibly approximate, to the original query [Calvanese *et al.*, 2000a].

1.7 Relationship to other fields of Computer Science

Description Logics were developed with the goals of providing formal, declarative meanings to semantic networks and frames, and of showing that such representation structures can be equipped with efficient reasoning tools. However, the underlying ideas of concept/class and hierarchical structure based upon the generality and specificity of a set of classes have appeared in many other fields of Computer Science, such as database management and programming languages. Consequently, there have been a number of attempts to find commonalities and differences among formalisms with similar underlying notions, but which were developed in different fields. Moreover, by looking at the syntactic form of Description Logics – logics that are restricted to unary and binary predicates and allow restricted forms of quantification – other logical formalisms that have strong relationships with Description Logics have been identified. In this section we briefly address such relationships; in particular, we focus our attention on the relationship of Description Logics to other class-based languages, and then we address the relationship between Description Logics and other logics. These topics are addressed in more detail in Chapter 4.

1.7.1 Description Logics and other class-based formalisms

As we have mentioned, Description Logics can, in principle, be related to other class-based formalisms. Before looking at other fields, it is worth relating Description Logics to other formalisms developed within the field of knowledge representation that share the intuitions underlying network-based representation structure. In [Lehmann, 1992] several languages aiming at structured representations of knowledge are reviewed. We have already discussed the relationship between Description Logics and semantic networks and frames, since they provided the basic motivations for developing Description Logics in the first place. Among others, *conceptual graphs* [Sowa, 1991] have been regarded as a way of representing conceptual structures very closely related to semantic networks (and consequently, to Description Logics). However, only recently has there been a detailed analysis of the relationship between conceptual graphs and Description Logics [Baader *et al.*, 1999c]. The outcome of this work makes it apparent that, although one can establish a relationship between simple conceptual graphs and a DL language, there are substantial differences between the two formalisms. The most significant one is that Description Logics are characterized by the universally quantified role restriction, which is not present in conceptual graphs. Consequently, the interpretation of the representation structures becomes substantially different.

In many other fields of Computer Science we find formalisms for the representation of objects and classes [Motschnig-Pitrik and Mylopoulous, 1992]. Such formalisms share the notion of a class that denotes a subset of the domain of discourse, and they allow one to express several kinds of relationships and constraints (e.g., subclass constraints) that hold among classes. Moreover, class-based formalisms aim at taking advantage of the class structure in order to provide various types of information, such as whether an element belongs to a class, whether a class is a subclass of another class, and more generally, whether a given constraint holds between two classes. In particular, formalisms that are built upon the notions of class and class-based hierarchies have been developed in the field of database management, in semantic data modeling (see for example [Hull and King, 1987]), in object-oriented languages (see for example [Kim and Lochovsky, 1989]), and more generally, in programming languages (see for example [Lenzerini *et al.*, 1991]).

There have been several attempts to establish relationships among the class-based formalisms developed in different fields. In particular, the common intuitions behind classes and concepts have stimulated several pieces of work aimed at establishing a precise relationship between class-based formalisms and Description Logics. However, it is difficult to find a common framework for carrying out a precise comparison.

In Chapter 4 a specific Description Logic is taken as a basis for identifying the common features of frame systems and object-oriented and semantic data models (see also [Calvanese *et al.*, 1999e]). Specifically, a precise correspondence between the chosen DL and the Entity–Relationship model [Chen, 1976], as well as with an object-oriented language in the style of [Abiteboul and Kanellakis, 1989], is presented there.

This kind of comparison shows that one can indeed identify a large common basis, but also that there are features that are currently missing in each formalism. For example, to capture semantic data models one needs a cyclic form of inclusion assertion, as well as the *inverses* of roles for modeling relationships that work in both directions, while DL roles have a directionality from one concept to another. Moreover, in order to make a comparison with frame-based systems, one has to leave out both the non-monotonic features of frames, such as defaults and closures (which are addressed among the extensions of Description Logics in the previous section) and their dynamic aspects such as daemons and and triggers (with the exception of trigger rules, which are also addressed in the previous section). Finally, with respect to object-oriented data models the main difference is that although Description Logics provide the expressiveness to model record and set structures, they are not explicitly available in Description Logics and thus their representation is a little cumbersome. On the other hand, semantic and object-oriented data models are typically not equipped with reasoning tools that are available with Description Logics. This issue is further developed in Chapter 16, where the applications of Description Logics in the field of database management are addressed. However, if the language is sufficiently expressive, as it needs to be in order to establish relationships among various class-based formalisms, one needs to distinguish between *finite model* reasoning, which is required for database languages that are designed to represent a closed domain of discourse, and *unrestricted* reasoning, which is typical of knowledge representation formalisms and, therefore, of Description Logics.

1.7.2 Relationships to other logics

The initial observation for addressing the relationship of Description Logics to other logics is the fact that Description Logics are subsets of first-order logic. This has been known since the earliest days of Description Logics, and has been thoroughly investigated in [Borgida, 1996]. In fact, the Description Logic $\mathcal{ALC}$ corresponds to the fragment of first-order logic obtained by restricting the syntax to formulas containing two variables. The importance of this and subsequent studies on this issue is related to finding adequate characterizations of the expressiveness of Description Logics.

Since Description Logics focus on a language formed by unary and binary predicates, it turned out that they are closely related to modal languages, if one regards roles as accessibility relations. In particular, Schild [1991] pointed out that some Description Logics are notational variants of certain propositional modal logics; specifically, the Description Logic $\mathcal{ALC}$ has a modal logic counterpart, namely the multi-modal version of the logic **K** (see [Halpern and Moses, 1992]). Actually, $\mathcal{ALC}$-concepts and formulas in multi-modal **K** can immediately be translated into each other. Moreover, an $\mathcal{ALC}$-concept is satisfiable if and only if the corresponding **K**-formula is satisfiable. Research in the complexity of the satisfiability problem for modal propositional logics was initiated quite some time before the complexity of Description Logics was investigated. Consequently, this relationship made it possible to borrow from modal logic complexity results, reasoning techniques, and language constructs that had not been previously considered in Description Logics. On the other hand, there are features of Description Logics that did not have counterparts in modal logics and therefore needed ad hoc extensions of the reasoning techniques developed for modal logics. In particular, number restrictions as well as the treatment of individuals in the ABox required specific treatments based on the idea of *reification*, which amounts to expressing the extensions through a special kind of axiom within the logic. Finally, we mention that recent work has pointed out a relationship between Description Logics and guarded fragments, which can be regarded as generalizations of modal logics. Most of the research on very expressive Description Logics, addressed in Chapter 5, has its roots in the correspondence with modal logic.

1.8 Conclusion

From their humble origins in the late 1970s as a remedy for logical and semantic problems in frame and semantic network representations, Description Logics have grown to be a unique and important keystone in the history of knowledge representation. DL formalisms certainly evoked interest in their earliest days, with the invention and application of the KL-ONE system, but international attention and research was given a significant boost in 1984 when Brachman and Levesque used the simple and intuitive structure of Description Logics as the basis for their observation about the tradeoff between knowledge representation language expressiveness and computational complexity of reasoning. The way Description Logics were able to separate out the structure of concepts and roles into simple term-forming operators opened the door to extensive analysis of a broad family of languages. One could add and subtract these operators to and from the language and explore both the computational ramifications and the relationship of the resulting language to other formal languages in Computer Science, such as modal logics and data models for database systems.

As a result, the family of Description Logic languages is probably the most thoroughly understood set of formalisms in all of knowledge representation. The computational space has been thoroughly mapped out, and a wide variety of systems have been built, testing out different styles of inference computation and being used in many applications.

Description Logics are responsible for many of the cornerstone notions used in knowledge representation and reasoning. They helped crystallize many of the ideas treated informally in earlier notations, such as concepts and roles. But they added many new important building blocks for later work in the field: the terminology/assertion distinction (TBox/ABox), number and value restrictions on roles, internal structure for concepts, Tell&Ask interfaces, and others. They have been the subject of a great deal of comparison and analysis with their cousins in other fields of Computer Science, and DL systems run the gamut from simple, restricted systems with provably advantageous computational properties to extremely expressive systems that can support very powerful applications. Perhaps the most important aspect of work on Description Logics has been the very tight coupling between theory and practice. The exemplary give-and-take between the formal, analytical side of the field and the pragmatic, implemented side – notable throughout the entire history of Description Logics – has been a role model for other areas of AI.

Acknowledgements

We are grateful to Franz Baader, Francesco M. Donini, Maurizio Lenzerini, and Riccardo Rosati for reading the manuscript and making suggestions for improving the final version of the chapter.

Part I
Theory

2

Basic Description Logics

Franz Baader
Werner Nutt

Abstract

This chapter provides an introduction to Description Logics as a formal language for representing knowledge and reasoning about it. It first gives a short overview of the ideas underlying Description Logics. Then it introduces syntax and semantics, covering the basic constructors that are used in systems or have been introduced in the literature, and the way these constructors can be used to build knowledge bases. Finally, it defines the typical inference problems, shows how they are interrelated, and describes different approaches for effectively solving these problems. Some of the topics that are only briefly mentioned in this chapter will be treated in more detail in subsequent chapters.

2.1 Introduction

As sketched in the previous chapter, Description Logics is the most recent name[1] for a family of knowledge representation (KR) formalisms that represent the knowledge of an application domain (the "world") by first defining the relevant concepts of the domain (its terminology), and then using these concepts to specify properties of objects and individuals occurring in the domain (the world description). As the name Description *Logics* indicates, one of the characteristics of these languages is that, unlike some of their predecessors, they are equipped with a formal, logic-based semantics. Another distinguished feature is the emphasis on reasoning as a central service: reasoning allows one to infer implicitly represented knowledge from the knowledge that is explicitly contained in the knowledge base.

---

[1] Previously used names are terminological knowledge representation languages, concept languages, term subsumption languages, and KL-ONE-based knowledge representation languages.

Description Logics support inference patterns that occur in many applications of intelligent information processing systems, and which are also used by humans to structure and understand the world: classification of concepts and individuals. Classification of concepts determines subconcept–superconcept relationships (called subsumption relationships in Description Logics) between the concepts of a given terminology, and thus allows one to structure the terminology in the form of a subsumption hierarchy. This hierarchy provides useful information on the connection between different concepts, and it can be used to speed up other inference services. Classification of individuals (or objects) determines whether a given individual is always an instance of a certain concept (i.e., whether this instance relationship is implied by the description of the individual and the definition of the concept). It thus provides useful information on the properties of an individual. Moreover, instance relationships may trigger the application of rules that insert additional facts into the knowledge base.

Because Description Logics are a KR formalism, and since in KR one usually assumes that a KR system should always answer the queries of a user in reasonable time, the reasoning procedures DL researchers are interested in are *decision procedures*, i.e., unlike first-order theorem provers, for example, these procedures should always terminate, both for positive and for negative answers. Since the guarantee of an answer in finite time need not imply that the answer is given in reasonable time, investigating the computational complexity of a given Description Logic with decidable inference problems is an important issue. Decidability and complexity of the inference problems depend on the expressive power of the Description Logic at hand. On the one hand, very expressive Description Logics are likely to have inference problems of high complexity, or they may even be undecidable. On the other hand, very weak Description Logics (with efficient reasoning procedures) may not be sufficiently expressive to represent the important concepts of a given application. As mentioned in the previous chapter, investigating this tradeoff between the expressivity of Description Logics and the complexity of their reasoning problems has been one of the most important issues in DL research.

Description Logics are descended from so-called "structured inheritance networks" [Brachman, 1977b, 1978], which were introduced to overcome the ambiguities of early semantic networks and frames, and which were first realized in the system KL-ONE [Brachman and Schmolze, 1985]. The following three ideas, first put forward in Brachman's work on structured inheritance networks, have largely shaped the subsequent development of Description Logics:

- The basic syntactic building blocks are atomic concepts (unary predicates), atomic roles (binary predicates), and individuals (constants).
- The expressive power of the language is restricted in that it uses a rather small set of (epistemologically adequate) constructors for building complex concepts and roles.
- Implicit knowledge about concepts and individuals can be inferred automatically with the help of inference procedures. In particular, subsumption relationships between concepts and instance relationships between individuals and concepts play an important role: unlike IS-A links in semantic networks, which are explicitly introduced by the user, subsumption relationships and instance relationships are inferred from the definition of the concepts and the properties of the individuals.

After the first logic-based semantics for KL-ONE-like KR languages were proposed, the inference problems like subsumption could also be provided with a precise meaning, which led to the first formal investigations of the computational properties of such languages. It has turned out that the languages used in early DL systems were too expressive, which led to undecidability of the subsumption problem [Schmidt-Schauß, 1989; Patel-Schneider, 1989b]. The first worst-case complexity results [Levesque and Brachman, 1987; Nebel, 1988] showed that the subsumption problem is intractable (i.e., not polynomially solvable) even for very inexpressive languages. As mentioned in the previous chapter, this work was the starting point of a thorough investigation of the worst-case complexity of reasoning in KL-ONE-like KR languages (see Chapter 3 for details).

Later on it has turned out, however, that intractability of reasoning (in the sense of being non-polynomial in the worst case) does not prevent a Description Logic from being useful in practice, provided that sophisticated optimization techniques are used when implementing a system based on such a Description Logic (see Chapter 9). When implementing a DL system, the efficient implementation of the basic reasoning algorithms is not the only issue, though. On the one hand, the derived system services (such as classification, i.e., constructing the subsumption hierarchy between all concepts defined in a terminology) must be optimized as well [Baader *et al.*, 1994]. On the other hand, one needs a good user and application programming interface (see Chapter 7 for more details). Most implemented DL systems provide for a rule language, which can be seen as a very simple, but effective, application programming mechanism (see Subsection 2.2.5 for details).

Section 2.2 introduces the basic formalism of Description Logics. By way of a prototypical example, it first introduces the formalism for describing concepts (i.e., the description language), and then defines the terminological (TBox) and the assertional (ABox) formalisms. Next, it introduces the basic

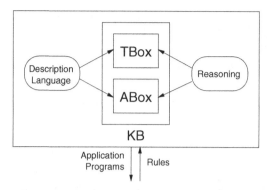

Fig. 2.1. Architecture of a knowledge representation system based on Description Logics.

reasoning problems and shows how they are related to each other. Finally, it defines the rule language that is available in many of the implemented DL systems.

Section 2.3 describes algorithms for solving the basic reasoning problems in Description Logics. After shortly sketching structural subsumption algorithms, it concentrates on tableau-based algorithms. Finally, it comments on the problem of reasoning w.r.t. terminologies.

Finally, Section 2.4 describes some additional language constructors that are not included in the prototypical family of description languages introduced in Section 2.2, but have been considered in the literature and are available in some DL systems.

2.2 Definition of the basic formalism

A KR system based on Description Logics provides facilities to set up knowledge bases, to reason about their content, and to manipulate them. Figure 2.1 sketches the architecture of such a system (see Chapter 8 for more information on DL systems).

A knowledge base (KB) comprises two components, the TBox and the ABox. The TBox introduces the *terminology*, i.e., the vocabulary of an application domain, while the ABox contains *assertions* about named individuals in terms of this vocabulary.

The vocabulary consists of *concepts*, which denote sets of individuals, and *roles*, which denote binary relationships between individuals. In addition to atomic concepts and roles (concept and role names), all DL systems allow their users to build complex descriptions of concepts and roles. The TBox can be used to assign names to complex descriptions. The language for building descriptions is a characteristic of each DL system, and different systems are distinguished by their description languages. The description language has a model-theoretic semantics. Thus, statements in the TBox and in the ABox can be identified with formulae in first-order logic or, in some cases, a slight extension of it.

A DL system not only stores terminologies and assertions, but also offers services that *reason* about them. Typical reasoning tasks for a terminology are to determine whether a description is *satisfiable* (i.e., non-contradictory), or whether one description is more general than another one, that is, whether the first *subsumes* the second. Important problems for an ABox are to find out whether its set of assertions is *consistent*, that is, whether it has a model, and whether the assertions in the ABox entail that a particular individual is an *instance* of a given concept description. Satisfiability checks of descriptions and consistency checks of sets of assertions are useful to determine whether a knowledge base is meaningful at all. With subsumption tests, one can organize the concepts of a terminology into a hierarchy according to their generality. A concept description can also be conceived as a query, describing a set of objects one is interested in. Thus, with instance tests, one can retrieve the individuals that satisfy the query.

In any application, a KR system is embedded into a larger environment. Other components interact with the KR component by querying the knowledge base and by modifying it, that is, by adding and retracting concepts, roles, and assertions. A restricted mechanism for adding assertions uses rules. Rules are an extension of the logical core formalism, which can still be interpreted logically. However, many systems, in addition to providing an application programming interface that consists of functions with a well-defined logical semantics, provide an escape hatch by which application programs can operate on the KB in arbitrary ways.

2.2.1 Description languages

We assume there are two kinds of symbols, which we call *atomic concepts* and *atomic roles*. In abstract notation, we use the letters A and B for atomic concepts and the letter R for atomic roles. We refer to atomic concepts and roles as *atomic symbols*. Atomic concepts and roles are elementary descriptions from which we inductively build complex descriptions by means of *concept constructors* and *role constructors*. In this chapter, we will mostly restrict the attention to concept constructors. Role constructors are introduced in Subsection 2.4.1. We use the letters C and D for arbitrary concept descriptions.

Description languages are distinguished by the constructors they provide. In the sequel we shall discuss various languages from the family of $\mathcal{AL}$-*languages*. The language $\mathcal{AL}$ (= attributive language) has been introduced in [Schmidt-Schauß and Smolka, 1991] as a minimal language that is of practical interest. The other languages of this family are extensions of $\mathcal{AL}$.

2.2.1.1 The basic description language $\mathcal{AL}$

Concept descriptions in $\mathcal{AL}$ are formed according to the following syntax rule:

$$
\begin{aligned}
C, D \longrightarrow \quad & A \mid && \text{(atomic concept)} \\
& \top \mid && \text{(universal concept)} \\
& \bot \mid && \text{(bottom concept)} \\
& \neg A \mid && \text{(atomic negation)} \\
& C \sqcap D \mid && \text{(intersection)} \\
& \forall R.C \mid && \text{(value restriction)} \\
& \exists R.\top && \text{(limited existential quantification).}
\end{aligned}
$$

Note that, in $\mathcal{AL}$, negation can only be applied to atomic concepts, and only the top concept is allowed in the scope of an existential quantification over a role. For historical reasons, the sublanguage of $\mathcal{AL}$ obtained by disallowing atomic negation is called $\mathcal{FL}^-$ and the sublanguage of $\mathcal{FL}^-$ obtained by disallowing limited existential quantification is called $\mathcal{FL}_0$.

To give examples of what can be expressed in $\mathcal{AL}$, we suppose that Person and Female are atomic concepts. Then Person $\sqcap$ Female and Person $\sqcap$ ¬Female are $\mathcal{AL}$-concepts describing, intuitively, those persons that are female, and those that are not female. If, in addition, we suppose that hasChild is an atomic role, we can form the concepts Person $\sqcap$ $\exists$hasChild.$\top$ and Person $\sqcap$ $\forall$hasChild.Female, denoting those persons that have a child, and those persons all of whose children are female. Using the bottom concept, we can also describe those persons without a child by the concept Person $\sqcap$ $\forall$hasChild.$\bot$.

In order to define a formal semantics of $\mathcal{AL}$-concepts, we consider *interpretations* $\mathcal{I}$ that consist of a non-empty set $\Delta^{\mathcal{I}}$ (the domain of the interpretation) and an interpretation function, which assigns to every atomic concept A a set $A^{\mathcal{I}} \subseteq \Delta^{\mathcal{I}}$ and to every atomic role R a binary relation $R^{\mathcal{I}} \subseteq \Delta^{\mathcal{I}} \times \Delta^{\mathcal{I}}$. The interpretation function is extended to concept descriptions by the following inductive definitions:

$$
\begin{aligned}
\top^{\mathcal{I}} &= \Delta^{\mathcal{I}} \\
\bot^{\mathcal{I}} &= \emptyset
\end{aligned}
$$

$$
\begin{aligned}
(\neg A)^{\mathcal{I}} &= \Delta^{\mathcal{I}} \setminus A^{\mathcal{I}} \\
(C \sqcap D)^{\mathcal{I}} &= C^{\mathcal{I}} \cap D^{\mathcal{I}} \\
(\forall R.C)^{\mathcal{I}} &= \{a \in \Delta^{\mathcal{I}} \mid \forall b.\ (a, b) \in R^{\mathcal{I}} \rightarrow b \in C^{\mathcal{I}}\} \\
(\exists R.\top)^{\mathcal{I}} &= \{a \in \Delta^{\mathcal{I}} \mid \exists b.\ (a, b) \in R^{\mathcal{I}}\}.
\end{aligned}
$$

We say that two concepts C, D are *equivalent*, and write $C \equiv D$, if $C^{\mathcal{I}} = D^{\mathcal{I}}$ for all interpretations $\mathcal{I}$. For instance, going back to the definition of the semantics of concepts, one easily verifies that $\forall$hasChild.Female $\sqcap$ $\forall$hasChild.Student and $\forall$hasChild.(Female $\sqcap$ Student) are equivalent.

2.2.1.2 The family of $\mathcal{AL}$-languages

We obtain more expressive languages if we add further constructors to $\mathcal{AL}$. The *union* of concepts (indicated by the letter $\mathcal{U}$) is written as $C \sqcup D$, and interpreted as

$$
(C \sqcup D)^{\mathcal{I}} = C^{\mathcal{I}} \cup D^{\mathcal{I}}.
$$

Full existential quantification (indicated by the letter $\mathcal{E}$) is written as $\exists R.C$, and interpreted as

$$
(\exists R.C)^{\mathcal{I}} = \{a \in \Delta^{\mathcal{I}} \mid \exists b.\ (a, b) \in R^{\mathcal{I}} \wedge b \in C^{\mathcal{I}}\}.
$$

Note that $\exists R.C$ differs from $\exists R.\top$ in that arbitrary concepts are allowed to occur in the scope of the existential quantifier.

Number restrictions (indicated by the letter $\mathcal{N}$) are written as $\geqslant n\, R$ (at-least restriction) and as $\leqslant n\, R$ (at-most restriction), where n ranges over the nonnegative integers. They are interpreted as

$$
(\geqslant n\, R)^{\mathcal{I}} = \left\{a \in \Delta^{\mathcal{I}} \ \middle|\ |\{b \mid (a, b) \in R^{\mathcal{I}}\}| \geq n\right\},
$$

and

$$
(\leqslant n\, R)^{\mathcal{I}} = \left\{a \in \Delta^{\mathcal{I}} \ \middle|\ |\{b \mid (a, b) \in R^{\mathcal{I}}\}| \leq n\right\},
$$

respectively, where "$|\cdot|$" denotes the cardinality of a set. From a semantic viewpoint, the coding of numbers in number restrictions is immaterial. However, for the complexity analysis of inferences it can matter whether a number n is represented in binary (or decimal) notation or by a string of length n, since binary (decimal) notation allows a more compact representation.

The *negation* of arbitrary concepts (indicated by the letter $\mathcal{C}$, for "complement") is written as $\neg C$, and interpreted as

$$
(\neg C)^{\mathcal{I}} = \Delta^{\mathcal{I}} \setminus C^{\mathcal{I}}.
$$

With the additional constructors, we can, for example, describe those persons that have either not more than one child or at least three children, one of whom is female:

$$\text{Person} \sqcap (\leqslant 1 \, \text{hasChild} \sqcup (\geqslant 3 \, \text{hasChild} \sqcap \exists \text{hasChild.Female})).$$

Extending $\mathcal{AL}$ by any subset of the above constructors yields a particular $\mathcal{AL}$-language. We name each $\mathcal{AL}$-language by a string of the form

$$\mathcal{AL}[\mathcal{U}][\mathcal{E}][\mathcal{N}][\mathcal{C}],$$

where a letter in the name stands for the presence of the corresponding constructor. For instance, $\mathcal{ALEN}$ is the extension of $\mathcal{AL}$ by full existential quantification and number restrictions (see the appendix on DL terminology for how to extend this naming scheme to more expressive Description Logics).

From the semantic point of view, not all these languages are distinct, however. The semantics enforces the equivalences $C \sqcup D \equiv \neg(\neg C \sqcap \neg D)$ and $\exists R.C \equiv \neg \forall R.\neg C$. Hence, union and full existential quantification can be expressed using negation. Conversely, the combination of union and full existential quantification gives us the ability to express negation of concepts (through their equivalent negation normal form, see Subsection 2.3.2). Therefore, we assume w.l.o.g. that union and full existential quantification are available in every language that contains negation, and vice versa. It follows that (modulo the equivalences mentioned above), all $\mathcal{AL}$-languages can be written using the letters $\mathcal{U}$, $\mathcal{E}$, $\mathcal{N}$ only. It is not hard to see that the eight languages obtained this way are indeed pairwise non-equivalent. In the sequel, we shall not distinguish between an $\mathcal{AL}$-language with negation and its counterpart that has union and full existential quantification instead. In the same vein, we shall use the letter $\mathcal{C}$ instead of the letters $\mathcal{UE}$ in language names. For instance, we shall write $\mathcal{ALC}$ instead of $\mathcal{ALUE}$ and $\mathcal{ALCN}$ instead of $\mathcal{ALUEN}$.

2.2.1.3 Description languages as fragments of predicate logic

The semantics of concepts identifies description languages as fragments of first-order predicate logic. Since an interpretation $\mathcal{I}$ respectively assigns to every atomic concept and role a unary and binary relation over $\Delta^{\mathcal{I}}$, we can view atomic concepts and roles as unary and binary predicates. Then, any concept C can be translated effectively into a predicate logic formula $\phi_C(x)$ with one free variable x such that for every interpretation $\mathcal{I}$ the set of elements of $\Delta^{\mathcal{I}}$ satisfying $\phi_C(x)$ is exactly $C^{\mathcal{I}}$: an atomic concept A is translated into the formula $A(x)$; the constructors intersection, union, and negation are translated into logical conjunction, disjunction, and negation, respectively; if C is already translated into $\phi_C(x)$ and R is an atomic role, then value restriction and existential quantification are captured by the formulae

$$
\begin{aligned}
\phi_{\exists R.C}(y) &= \exists x.\, R(y,x) \wedge \phi_C(x) \\
\phi_{\forall R.C}(y) &= \forall x.\, R(y,x) \to \phi_C(x),
\end{aligned}
$$

where y is a new variable; number restrictions are expressed by the formulae

$$
\phi_{\geqslant n\, R}(x) = \exists y_1, \ldots, y_n.\, R(x,y_1) \wedge \cdots \wedge R(x,y_n) \wedge \bigwedge_{i<j} y_i \neq y_j
$$

$$
\phi_{\leqslant n\, R}(x) = \forall y_1, \ldots, y_{n+1}.\, R(x,y_1) \wedge \cdots \wedge R(x,y_{n+1}) \to \bigvee_{i<j} y_i = y_j.
$$

Note that the equality predicate "=" is needed to express number restrictions, while concepts without number restrictions can be translated into equality-free formulae.

One may argue that, since concepts can be translated into predicate logic, there is no need for a special syntax. However, the above translations show that, in particular for number restrictions, the variable-free syntax of Description Logics is much more concise. As can be seen from Section 2.3, it also lends itself easily to the development of algorithms.

A more detailed analysis of the connection between fragments of first-order predicate logic and Description Logics can be found in Chapter 4.

2.2.2 Terminologies

We have seen how we can form complex descriptions of concepts to describe classes of objects. Now, we introduce *terminological axioms*, which make statements about how concepts or roles are related to each other. Then we single out *definitions* as specific axioms and identify *terminologies* as sets of definitions by which we can introduce atomic concepts as abbreviations or *names* for complex concepts. If the definitions in a terminology contain cycles, we may have to adopt *fixpoint semantics* to make them unequivocal. We discuss for which types of terminologies fixpoint models exist.

2.2.2.1 Terminological axioms

In the most general case, *terminological axioms* have the form

$$
C \sqsubseteq D \quad (R \sqsubseteq S) \qquad \text{or} \qquad C \equiv D \quad (R \equiv S),
$$

$$
\begin{aligned}
\text{Woman} &\equiv \text{Person} \sqcap \text{Female} \\
\text{Man} &\equiv \text{Person} \sqcap \neg\text{Woman} \\
\text{Mother} &\equiv \text{Woman} \sqcap \exists\text{hasChild.Person} \\
\text{Father} &\equiv \text{Man} \sqcap \exists\text{hasChild.Person} \\
\text{Parent} &\equiv \text{Father} \sqcup \text{Mother} \\
\text{Grandmother} &\equiv \text{Mother} \sqcap \exists\text{hasChild.Parent} \\
\text{MotherWithManyChildren} &\equiv \text{Mother} \sqcap \geqslant 3\, \text{hasChild} \\
\text{MotherWithoutDaughter} &\equiv \text{Mother} \sqcap \forall\text{hasChild.}\neg\text{Woman} \\
\text{Wife} &\equiv \text{Woman} \sqcap \exists\text{hasHusband.Man}
\end{aligned}
$$

Fig. 2.2. A terminology (TBox) with concepts about family relationships.

where C, D are concepts (and R, S are roles). Axioms of the first kind are called *inclusions*, while axioms of the second kind are called *equalities*. To simplify the exposition, we deal in the following only with axioms involving concepts.

The semantics of axioms is defined as one would expect. An interpretation $\mathcal{I}$ *satisfies* an inclusion $C \sqsubseteq D$ if $C^{\mathcal{I}} \subseteq D^{\mathcal{I}}$, and it satisfies an equality $C \equiv D$ if $C^{\mathcal{I}} = D^{\mathcal{I}}$. If $\mathcal{T}$ is a set of axioms, then $\mathcal{I}$ satisfies $\mathcal{T}$ iff $\mathcal{I}$ satisfies each element of $\mathcal{T}$. If $\mathcal{I}$ satisfies an axiom (resp. a set of axioms), then we say that it is a *model* of this axiom (resp. set of axioms). Two axioms or two sets of axioms are *equivalent* if they have the same models.

2.2.2.2 Definitions

An equality whose left-hand side is an atomic concept is a *definition*. Definitions are used to introduce *symbolic names* for complex descriptions. For instance, by the axiom

$$\text{Mother} \equiv \text{Woman} \sqcap \exists\text{hasChild.Person}$$

we associate to the description on the right-hand side the name Mother. Symbolic names may be used as abbreviations in other descriptions. If, for example, we have defined Father analogously to Mother, we can define Parent as

$$\text{Parent} \equiv \text{Mother} \sqcup \text{Father}.$$

A set of definitions should be unequivocal. We call a finite set of definitions $\mathcal{T}$ a *terminology* or *TBox* if no symbolic name is defined more than once, that is, if for every atomic concept A there is at most one axiom in $\mathcal{T}$ whose left-hand side is A. Figure 2.2 shows a terminology with concepts concerned with family relationships.

Suppose $\mathcal{T}$ is a terminology. We divide the atomic symbols occurring in $\mathcal{T}$ into two sets, the *name symbols* $\mathcal{N}_{\mathcal{T}}$ that occur on the left-hand side of some axiom and the *base symbols* $\mathcal{B}_{\mathcal{T}}$ that occur only on the right-hand side of axioms. Name symbols are often called *defined* concepts and base symbols *primitive* concepts and *primitive* roles.[2] We expect that the terminology *defines* the name symbols in terms of the base symbols, which now we make more precise.

A *base interpretation* for $\mathcal{T}$ is an interpretation that interprets only the base symbols. Let $\mathcal{J}$ be such a base interpretation. An interpretation $\mathcal{I}$ that interprets also the name symbols is an *extension* of $\mathcal{J}$ if it has the same domain as $\mathcal{J}$, i.e., $\Delta^{\mathcal{I}} = \Delta^{\mathcal{J}}$, and if it agrees with $\mathcal{J}$ for the base symbols. We say that $\mathcal{T}$ is *definitorial* if every base interpretation has exactly one extension that is a model of $\mathcal{T}$. In other words, if we know what the base symbols stand for, and $\mathcal{T}$ is definitorial, then the meaning of the name symbols is completely determined. Obviously, if a terminology is definitorial, then every equivalent terminology is also definitorial.

The question whether a terminology is definitorial or not is related to the question whether or not its definitions are cyclic. For instance, the terminology that consists of the the single axiom

$$\mathsf{Human'} \equiv \mathsf{Animal} \sqcap \forall \mathsf{hasParent.Human'} \tag{2.1}$$

contains a cycle because, intuitively, $\mathsf{Human'}$ is defined in terms of $\mathsf{Human'}$. We now give a technical definition of cycles in terminologies. Let A, B be atomic concepts occurring in $\mathcal{T}$. We say that A *directly uses* B in $\mathcal{T}$ if B appears on the right-hand side of the definition of A, and we define *uses* to be the transitive closure of the relation *directly uses*. Then $\mathcal{T}$ contains a *cycle* iff there exists an atomic concept in $\mathcal{T}$ that uses itself. Otherwise, $\mathcal{T}$ is called *acyclic*.

Unique extensions need not exist if a terminology contains cycles. Consider, for instance, the terminology that contains only Axiom (2.1). Here, $\mathsf{Human'}$ is a name symbol and Animal and $\mathsf{hasParent}$ are base symbols. For an interpretation where $\mathsf{hasParent}$ relates every animal to its progenitors, many extensions are possible to interpret $\mathsf{Human'}$ in a such a way that the axiom is satisfied: $\mathsf{Human'}$ can, among others, be interpreted as the set of all animals, as some species, or any other set of animals with the property that for each animal it contains also its progenitors.

In contrast, if a terminology $\mathcal{T}$ is acyclic, then it is definitorial. The reason is that we can expand through an iterative process the definitions in $\mathcal{T}$ by replacing each occurrence of a name on the right-hand side of a definition by the concepts that it stands for. Since there is no cycle in the set of definitions,

---

[2] Note that some papers use the notion "primitive concept" with a different meaning; e.g., synonymous with what we call atomic concepts, or to denote the (atomic) left-hand sides of concept inclusions.

$$
\begin{aligned}
\text{Woman} &\equiv \text{Person} \sqcap \text{Female} \\
\text{Man} &\equiv \text{Person} \sqcap \neg(\text{Person} \sqcap \text{Female}) \\
\text{Mother} &\equiv (\text{Person} \sqcap \text{Female}) \sqcap \exists \text{hasChild}.\text{Person} \\
\text{Father} &\equiv (\text{Person} \sqcap \neg(\text{Person} \sqcap \text{Female})) \sqcap \exists \text{hasChild}.\text{Person} \\
\text{Parent} &\equiv ((\text{Person} \sqcap \neg(\text{Person} \sqcap \text{Female})) \sqcap \exists \text{hasChild}.\text{Person}) \\
&\quad \sqcup ((\text{Person} \sqcap \text{Female}) \sqcap \exists \text{hasChild}.\text{Person}) \\
\text{Grandmother} &\equiv ((\text{Person} \sqcap \text{Female}) \sqcap \exists \text{hasChild}.\text{Person}) \\
&\quad \sqcap \exists \text{hasChild}.(((\text{Person} \sqcap \neg(\text{Person} \sqcap \text{Female})) \\
&\qquad\qquad \sqcap \exists \text{hasChild}.\text{Person}) \\
&\qquad \sqcup ((\text{Person} \sqcap \text{Female}) \\
&\qquad\qquad \sqcap \exists \text{hasChild}.\text{Person})) \\
\text{MotherWithManyChildren} &\equiv ((\text{Person} \sqcap \text{Female}) \sqcap \exists \text{hasChild}.\text{Person}) \sqcap \geqslant 3\,\text{hasChild} \\
\text{MotherWithoutDaughter} &\equiv ((\text{Person} \sqcap \text{Female}) \sqcap \exists \text{hasChild}.\text{Person}) \\
&\quad \sqcap \forall \text{hasChild}.(\neg(\text{Person} \sqcap \text{Female})) \\
\text{Wife} &\equiv (\text{Person} \sqcap \text{Female}) \\
&\quad \sqcap \exists \text{hasHusband}.(\text{Person} \sqcap \neg(\text{Person} \sqcap \text{Female}))
\end{aligned}
$$

Fig. 2.3. The expansion of the Family TBox in Figure 2.2.

the process eventually stops and we end up with a terminology $\mathcal{T}'$ consisting solely of definitions of the form $A \equiv C'$, where C' contains only base symbols and no name symbols. We call $\mathcal{T}'$ the *expansion* of $\mathcal{T}$. Note that the size of the expansion can be exponential in the size of the original terminology [Nebel, 1990b]. The Family TBox in Figure 2.2 is acyclic. Therefore, we can compute the expansion, which is shown in Figure 2.3.

Proposition 2.1 *Let $\mathcal{T}$ be an acyclic terminology and $\mathcal{T}'$ be its expansion. Then:*

1. *$\mathcal{T}$ and $\mathcal{T}'$ have the same name and base symbols;*
2. *$\mathcal{T}$ and $\mathcal{T}'$ are equivalent;*
3. *both $\mathcal{T}$ and $\mathcal{T}'$ are definitorial.*

Proof Let $\mathcal{T}_1$ be a terminology. Suppose $A \equiv C$ and $B \equiv D$ are definitions in $\mathcal{T}_1$ such that B occurs in C. Let C' be the concept obtained from C by replacing each occurrence of B in C by D, and let $\mathcal{T}_2$ be the terminology obtained from $\mathcal{T}_1$ by replacing the definition $A \equiv C$ by $A \equiv C'$. Then both terminologies have the same name and base symbols. Moreover, since $\mathcal{T}_2$ has been obtained from $\mathcal{T}_1$ by replacing equals by equals, both terminologies have the same models. Since $\mathcal{T}'$ is obtained from $\mathcal{T}$ by a sequence of replacement steps like the ones above, this proves claims 1 and 2.

Suppose now that $\mathcal{J}$ is an interpretation of the base symbols. We extend it to an interpretation $\mathcal{I}$ that covers also the name symbols by setting $A^{\mathcal{I}} = C'^{\mathcal{J}}$, if $A \equiv C'$ is the definition of A in $\mathcal{T}'$. Clearly, $\mathcal{I}$ is a model of $\mathcal{T}'$, and it is the only extension of $\mathcal{J}$ that is a model of $\mathcal{T}'$. This shows that

T' is definitorial. Moreover, T is definitorial as well, since it is equivalent to T'. □

It is characteristic of acyclic terminologies, in a sense to be made more precise, to uniquely define the name symbols in terms of the base symbols.

Of course, there are also terminologies *with* cycles that are definitorial. Consider for instance the one consisting of the axiom

$$A \equiv \forall R.B \sqcup \exists R.(A \sqcap \neg A), \tag{2.2}$$

which has a cycle. However, since $\exists R.(A \sqcap \neg A)$ is equivalent to the bottom concept, Axiom (2.2) is equivalent to the acyclic axiom

$$A \equiv \forall R.B. \tag{2.3}$$

This example is typical of the general situation.

Theorem 2.2 *Every definitorial $\mathcal{ALC}$-terminology is equivalent to an acyclic terminology.*

The theorem is a reformulation of Beth's Definability Theorem [Gabbay, 1972] for the modal propositional logic $\mathbf{K}_n$, which, as shown by Schild [1991], is a notational variant of $\mathcal{ALC}$.

2.2.2.3 Fixpoint semantics for terminological cycles

Under the semantics we have studied so far, which is essentially the semantics of first-order logic, terminologies have definitorial effect only if they are essentially acyclic. Following Nebel [1991], we shall call this semantics *descriptive* semantics to distinguish it from the fixpoint semantics introduced below. Fixpoint semantics are motivated by the fact that there are situations where intuitively cyclic definitions are meaningful and the intuition can be captured by least or greatest fixpoint semantics.

Example 2.3 Suppose that we want to specify the concept of a "man who has only male descendants", for short Momd. In particular, such a man is a Mos, that is, a "man who has only sons". A Mos can be defined without cycles as

$$\text{Mos} \equiv \text{Man} \sqcap \forall \text{hasChild.Man}.$$

For a Momd, however, we want to make a statement about the fillers of the transitive closure of the role hasChild. Here a recursive definition of Momd seems to be natural. A man having only male descendants is himself a man, and all his children are men having only male descendants:

$$\text{Momd} \quad \equiv \quad \text{Man} \sqcap \forall \text{hasChild.Momd.} \qquad (2.4)$$

In order to achieve the desired meaning, we have to interpret this definition under an appropriate fixpoint semantics. We shall show below that greatest fixpoint semantics captures our intuition here. ∎

Cycles also appear when we want to model recursive structures, e.g., binary trees.[3]

Example 2.4 We suppose that there is a set of objects that are Trees and a binary relation has-branch between objects that leads from a tree to its subtrees. Then the binary trees are the trees with at most two subtrees that are themselves binary trees:

$$\text{BinaryTree} \quad \equiv \quad \text{Tree} \sqcap \leqslant 2 \, \text{has-branch} \sqcap \forall \text{has-branch.BinaryTree.}$$

As with the definition of Momo, a fixpoint semantics will yield the desired meaning. However, for this example we have to use least fixpoint semantics. ∎

We now give a formal definition of fixpoint semantics. In a terminology $\mathcal{T}$, every name symbol A occurs exactly once as the left-hand side of an axiom $A \equiv C$. Therefore, we can view $\mathcal{T}$ as a mapping that associates to a name symbol A the concept description $\mathcal{T}(A) = C$. With this notation, an interpretation $\mathcal{I}$ is a model of $\mathcal{T}$ if, and only if, $A^{\mathcal{I}} = (\mathcal{T}(A))^{\mathcal{I}}$. This characterization has the flavor of a fixpoint equation. We exploit this similarity to introduce a family of mappings such that an interpretation is a model of $\mathcal{T}$ iff it is a fixpoint of such a mapping.

Let $\mathcal{T}$ be a terminology, and let $\mathcal{J}$ be a fixed base interpretation of $\mathcal{T}$. By $Ext_{\mathcal{J}}$ we denote the set of all extensions of $\mathcal{J}$. Let $\mathcal{T}_{\mathcal{J}} \colon Ext_{\mathcal{J}} \to Ext_{\mathcal{J}}$ be the mapping that maps the extension $\mathcal{I}$ to the extension $\mathcal{T}_{\mathcal{J}}(\mathcal{I})$ defined by $A^{\mathcal{T}_{\mathcal{J}}(\mathcal{I})} = (\mathcal{T}(A))^{\mathcal{I}}$ for each name symbol A.

Now, $\mathcal{I}$ is a fixpoint of $\mathcal{T}_{\mathcal{J}}$ iff $\mathcal{I} = \mathcal{T}_{\mathcal{J}}(\mathcal{I})$, i.e., iff $A^{\mathcal{I}} = A^{\mathcal{T}_{\mathcal{J}}(\mathcal{I})}$ for all name symbols. This means that, for every definition $A \equiv C$ in $\mathcal{T}$, we have $A^{\mathcal{I}} = A^{\mathcal{T}_{\mathcal{J}}(\mathcal{I})} = (\mathcal{T}(A))^{\mathcal{I}} = C^{\mathcal{I}}$, which means that $\mathcal{I}$ is a model of $\mathcal{T}$. This proves the following result.

Proposition 2.5 *Let $\mathcal{T}$ be a terminology, $\mathcal{I}$ be an interpretation, and $\mathcal{J}$ be the restriction of $\mathcal{I}$ to the base symbols of $\mathcal{T}$. Then $\mathcal{I}$ is a model of $\mathcal{T}$ if, and*

---

[3] The following example is taken from [Nebel, 1991].

only if, $\mathcal{I}$ is a fixpoint of $\mathcal{T}_{\mathcal{J}}$.

According to the preceding proposition, a terminology $\mathcal{T}$ is definitorial iff every base interpretation $\mathcal{J}$ has a unique extension that is a fixpoint of $\mathcal{T}_{\mathcal{J}}$.

Example 2.6 To get a feel for why cyclic terminologies are not definitorial, we discuss as an example the terminology $\mathcal{T}^{\mathsf{Momd}}$ that consists only of Axiom (2.4). Consider the base interpretation $\mathcal{J}$ defined by

$$
\begin{aligned}
\Delta^{\mathcal{J}} &= \{\textit{Charles}_1,\ \textit{Charles}_2, \ldots\} \cup \{\textit{James}_1, \ldots, \textit{James}_{Last}\} \\
\mathsf{Man}^{\mathcal{J}} &= \Delta^{\mathcal{J}} \\
\mathsf{hasChild}^{\mathcal{J}} &= \{(\textit{Charles}_i, \textit{Charles}_{(i+1)}) \mid i \geq 1\} \cup \\
&\quad\ \{(\textit{James}_i, \textit{James}_{(i+1)}) \mid 1 \leq i < Last\}.
\end{aligned}
$$

This means that the *Charles* dynasty does not die out, whereas there is a last member of the *James* dynasty.

We want to identify the fixpoints of $\mathcal{T}_{\mathcal{J}}^{\mathsf{Momd}}$. Note that an individual without children, i.e., without fillers of hasChild, is always in the interpretation of $\forall\mathsf{hasChild.Momd}$, no matter how Momd is interpreted. Therefore, if $\mathcal{I}$ is a fixpoint extension of $\mathcal{J}$, then $\textit{James}_{Last}$ is in $(\forall\mathsf{hasChild.Momd})^{\mathcal{I}}$, and thus in $\mathsf{Momd}^{\mathcal{I}}$. We conclude that every *James* is a Momd. Let $\mathcal{I}_1$ be the extension of $\mathcal{J}$ such that $\mathsf{Momd}^{\mathcal{I}_1}$ comprises exactly the *James* dynasty. Then it is easy to check that $\mathcal{I}_1$ is a fixpoint. If, in addition to the *James* dynasty, some *Charles* is a Momd, then all the members of the *Charles* dynasty before and after him must belong to the concept Momd. One can easily check that the extension $\mathcal{I}_2$ that interprets Momd as the entire domain is also a fixpoint, and that there is no other fixpoint. ∎

In order to give definitorial effect to a cyclic terminology $\mathcal{T}$, we must single out a particular fixpoint of the mapping $\mathcal{T}_{\mathcal{J}}$ if there are more than one. To this end, we define a partial ordering "$\preceq$" on the extensions of $\mathcal{J}$. We say that $\mathcal{I} \preceq \mathcal{I}'$ if $A^{\mathcal{I}} \subseteq A^{\mathcal{I}'}$ for every name symbol in $\mathcal{T}$. In the above example, Momd is the only name symbol. Since $\mathsf{Momd}^{\mathcal{I}_1} \subseteq \mathsf{Momd}^{\mathcal{I}_2}$, we have $\mathcal{I}_1 \preceq \mathcal{I}_2$.

A fixpoint $\mathcal{I}$ of $\mathcal{T}_{\mathcal{J}}$ is the *least fixpoint* (lfp) if $\mathcal{I} \preceq \mathcal{I}'$ for every other fixpoint $\mathcal{I}'$. We say that $\mathcal{I}$ is a *least fixpoint model* of $\mathcal{T}$ if $\mathcal{I}$ is the least fixpoint of $\mathcal{T}_{\mathcal{J}}$ for some base interpretation $\mathcal{J}$. Under *least fixpoint semantics* we only admit the least fixpoint models of $\mathcal{T}$ as intended interpretations. Greatest fixpoints (gfp), greatest fixpoint models, and greatest fixpoint semantics are defined analogously. In the Momd example, $\mathcal{I}_1$ is the least and $\mathcal{I}_2$ the greatest fixpoint of $\mathcal{T}_{\mathcal{J}}$.

2.2.2.4 Existence of fixpoint models

Least and greatest fixpoint models need not exist for every terminology.

Example 2.7 As a simple example, consider the axiom

$$A \equiv \neg A. \tag{2.5}$$

If $\mathcal{I}$ is a model of this axiom, then $A^{\mathcal{I}} = \Delta^{\mathcal{I}} \setminus A^{\mathcal{I}}$, which implies $\Delta^{\mathcal{I}} = \emptyset$, an absurdity.

A terminology containing Axiom (2.5) thus does not have any models, and therefore also no gfp (lfp) models.

There are also cases where models (i.e., fixpoints) exist, but there is neither a least one nor a greatest one. As an example, consider the terminology $\mathcal{T}$ with the single axiom

$$A \equiv \forall R.\neg A. \tag{2.6}$$

Let $\mathcal{J}$ be the base interpretation with $\Delta^{\mathcal{J}} = \{a, b\}$ and $R^{\mathcal{J}} = \{(a, b), (b, a)\}$. Then there are two fixpoint extensions $\mathcal{I}_1, \mathcal{I}_2$, defined by $A^{\mathcal{I}_1} = \{a\}$ and $A^{\mathcal{I}_2} = \{b\}$. However, they are not comparable with respect to "$\preceq$". ∎

In order to identify terminologies with the property that for every base interpretation there exists a least and a greatest fixpoint extension, we draw upon results from lattice theory. Recall that a lattice is *complete* if every family of elements has a least upper bound.

On $Ext_{\mathcal{J}}$ we have introduced the partial ordering "$\preceq$". For a family of interpretations $(\mathcal{I}_i)_{i \in I}$ in $Ext_{\mathcal{J}}$ we define $\mathcal{I}_0 = \bigsqcup_{i \in I} \mathcal{I}_i$ as the pointwise union of the $\mathcal{I}_i$s, that is, for every name symbol A we have $A^{\mathcal{I}_0} = \bigcup_{i \in I} A^{\mathcal{I}_i}$. Then $\mathcal{I}_0$ is the least upper bound of the $\mathcal{I}_i$s, which shows that $(Ext_{\mathcal{J}}, \preceq)$ is a complete lattice.

A function $f: L \to L$ on a lattice $(L, \preceq)$ is *monotone* if $f(x) \preceq f(y)$ whenever $x \preceq y$. Tarski's Fixpoint Theorem [Tarski, 1955] says that for a monotone function on a complete lattice the set of fixpoints is nonempty and itself forms a complete lattice. In particular, there is a least and a greatest fixpoint.

We define that a terminology $\mathcal{T}$ is *monotone* if the mapping $\mathcal{T}_{\mathcal{J}}$ is monotone for all base interpretations $\mathcal{J}$. By Tarski's theorem, such terminologies have greatest and least fixpoints.

Proposition 2.8 *If $\mathcal{T}$ is a monotone terminology and $\mathcal{J}$ a base interpretation, then there exist extensions of $\mathcal{J}$ that are an lfp-model and a gfp-model of $\mathcal{T}$, respectively.*

To find a syntactic criterion for monotonicity, we consider the operators of the $\mathcal{AL}$-languages that are applied to concepts, namely, "⊓", "⊔", "¬", "∀", and "∃".

These operators have as their natural counterparts operations on the subsets of some domain, say Δ. Clearly, intersection and union correspond to the set operations with the same names, while negation corresponds to complement with respect to the domain. Since "∀" and "∃" are applied to a role and a concept, we introduce, for every binary relation r on Δ, the unary operation A_r that maps a set $S \subseteq \Delta$ to

$$\mathsf{A}_r(S) = \{a \in \Delta \mid \forall b. \ (a, b) \in r \rightarrow b \in S\}$$

and the operation E_r that maps a set $S \subseteq \Delta$ to

$$\mathsf{E}_r(S) = \{a \in \Delta \mid \exists b. \ (a, b) \in r \wedge b \in S\}.$$

Then we see that all these operations, with the sole exception of complement, are monotone in the sense that if they are applied to larger arguments, then the results are larger, too. This is obvious for intersection and union. Also, one readily checks that $S \subseteq S'$ implies $\mathsf{A}_r(S) \subseteq \mathsf{A}_r(S')$ and $\mathsf{E}_r(S) \subseteq \mathsf{E}_r(S')$. Obviously, the analogous statement for negation does not hold.

We call a terminology *negation-free* if no negation sign occurs in it. Based on the above observations we can prove by induction a sufficient syntactic condition for an $\mathcal{ALCN}$-terminology to be monotone.

Proposition 2.9 *Every negation-free $\mathcal{ALCN}$-terminology is monotone.*

We can generalize this criterion by analyzing which negation signs in a terminology are potentially harmful for monotonicity. Clearly, a negation sign can only affect the monotonicity of a terminology if in its scope there is a name symbol. Moreover, intuitively, a negation sign is neutralized if it is in the scope of another negation. This motivates the following definition. We say a concept C is *syntactically monotone* if each name symbol in C occurs in the scope of an even number of negation signs. A terminology is *syntactically monotone* if every concept on the right-hand side of an equality is syntactically monotone.

Proposition 2.10 *Every syntactically monotone $\mathcal{ALCN}$-terminology is monotone.*

2.2.2.5 Terminologies with inclusion axioms

For certain concepts we may be unable to define them completely. In this case, we can still state necessary conditions for concept membership using an inclusion. We call an inclusion whose left-hand side is atomic a *specialization*.

For example, if a (male) knowledge engineer thinks that the definition of "woman" in our example TBox (Figure 2.2) is not satisfactory, but if he also feels that he is not able to define the concept "woman" in all detail, he can require that every woman is a person with the specialization

$$\text{Woman} \sqsubseteq \text{Person}. \tag{2.7}$$

If we also allow specializations in a terminology, then the terminology loses its definitorial effect, even if it is acyclic. A set of axioms $\mathcal{T}$ is a *generalized terminology* if the left-hand side of each axiom is an atomic concept and for every atomic concept there is at most one axiom where it occurs on the left-hand side.

We shall transform a generalized terminology $\mathcal{T}$ into a regular terminology $\bar{\mathcal{T}}$, containing definitions only, such that $\bar{\mathcal{T}}$ is equivalent to $\mathcal{T}$ in a sense that will be specified below. We obtain $\bar{\mathcal{T}}$ from $\mathcal{T}$ by choosing for every specialization $A \sqsubseteq C$ in $\mathcal{T}$ a new base symbol $\bar{A}$ and by replacing the specialization $A \sqsubseteq C$ with the definition $A \equiv \bar{A} \sqcap C$. The terminology $\bar{\mathcal{T}}$ is the *normalization* of $\mathcal{T}$.

If a TBox contains the specialization (2.7), then the normalization contains the definition

$$\text{Woman} \equiv \overline{\text{Woman}} \sqcap \text{Person}.$$

Intuitively, the additional base symbol $\overline{\text{Woman}}$ stands for the qualities that distinguish a woman among persons. Thus, normalization results in a TBox with a definition for Woman that is similar to the one in the Family TBox.

Proposition 2.11 *Let $\mathcal{T}$ be a generalized terminology and $\bar{\mathcal{T}}$ its normalization.*

- *Every model of $\bar{\mathcal{T}}$ is a model of $\mathcal{T}$.*
- *For every model $\mathcal{I}$ of $\mathcal{T}$ there is a model $\bar{\mathcal{I}}$ of $\bar{\mathcal{T}}$ that has the same domain as $\mathcal{I}$ and agrees with $\mathcal{I}$ on the atomic concepts and roles in $\mathcal{T}$.*

Proof The first claim holds because a model $\bar{\mathcal{I}}$ of $\bar{\mathcal{T}}$ satisfies $A^{\bar{\mathcal{I}}} = (\bar{A} \sqcap C)^{\bar{\mathcal{I}}}$ $= \bar{A}^{\bar{\mathcal{I}}} \cap C^{\bar{\mathcal{I}}}$, which implies $A^{\bar{\mathcal{I}}} \subseteq C^{\bar{\mathcal{I}}}$. Conversely, if $\mathcal{I}$ is a model of $\mathcal{T}$, then the extension $\bar{\mathcal{I}}$ of $\mathcal{I}$, defined by $\bar{A}^{\bar{\mathcal{I}}} = A^{\mathcal{I}}$, is a model of $\bar{\mathcal{T}}$, because $A^{\mathcal{I}} \subseteq C^{\mathcal{I}}$ implies $A^{\mathcal{I}} = A^{\mathcal{I}} \cap C^{\mathcal{I}} = \bar{A}^{\bar{\mathcal{I}}} \cap C^{\bar{\mathcal{I}}}$, and therefore $\bar{\mathcal{I}}$ satisfies $A \equiv \bar{A} \sqcap C$. $\square$

MotherWithoutDaughter(MARY)   Father(PETER)
hasChild(MARY, PETER)   hasChild(PETER, HARRY)
hasChild(MARY, PAUL)

Fig. 2.4. A world description (ABox).

Thus, in theory, inclusion axioms do not add to the expressivity of terminologies. However, in practice, they are a convenient means to introduce terms into a terminology that cannot be defined completely.

2.2.3 World descriptions

The second component of a knowledge base, in addition to the terminology or TBox, is the *world description* or *ABox*.

2.2.3.1 Assertions about individuals

In the ABox, one describes a specific state of affairs of an application domain in terms of concepts and roles. Some of the concept and role atoms in the ABox may be defined names of the TBox. In the ABox, one introduces individuals, by giving them names, and one asserts properties of these individuals. We denote individual names by a, b, c. Using concepts C and roles R, one can make assertions of the following two kinds in an ABox:

$$C(a), \qquad R(b, c).$$

By the first kind, called *concept assertions*, one states that a belongs to (the interpretation of) C. By the second kind, called *role assertions*, one states that c is a filler of the role R for b. For instance, if PETER, PAUL, and MARY are individual names, then Father(PETER) means that Peter is a father, and hasChild(MARY, PAUL) means that Paul is a child of Mary. An *ABox*, denoted by $\mathcal{A}$, is a finite set of such assertions. Figure 2.4 shows an example of an ABox.

In a simplified view, an ABox can be seen as an instance of a relational database with only unary or binary relations. However, contrary to the "closed-world semantics" of classical databases, the semantics of ABoxes is an "open-world semantics", since normally knowledge representation systems are applied in situations where one cannot assume that the knowledge in the KB is complete.[4] Moreover, the TBox imposes semantic relationships between the concepts and roles in the ABox that do not have counterparts in database semantics.

---

[4] We discuss implications of this difference in semantics in Subsection 2.2.4.4.

We give a semantics to ABoxes by extending interpretations to individual names. From now on, an interpretation $\mathcal{I} = (\Delta^{\mathcal{I}}, \cdot^{\mathcal{I}})$ not only maps atomic concepts and roles to sets and relations, but in addition maps each individual name a to an element $a^{\mathcal{I}} \in \Delta^{\mathcal{I}}$. We assume that distinct individual names denote distinct objects. Therefore, this mapping has to respect the *unique name assumption* (UNA), that is, if a, b are distinct names, then $a^{\mathcal{I}} \neq b^{\mathcal{I}}$. The interpretation $\mathcal{I}$ *satisfies* the concept assertion $C(a)$ if $a^{\mathcal{I}} \in C^{\mathcal{I}}$, and it *satisfies* the role assertion $R(a, b)$ if $(a^{\mathcal{I}}, b^{\mathcal{I}}) \in R^{\mathcal{I}}$. An interpretation *satisfies* the ABox $\mathcal{A}$ if it satisfies each assertion in $\mathcal{A}$. In this case we say that $\mathcal{I}$ is a *model* of the assertion or of the ABox. Finally, $\mathcal{I}$ *satisfies* an assertion α or an ABox $\mathcal{A}$ *with respect to* a TBox $\mathcal{T}$ if in addition to being a model of α or of $\mathcal{A}$, it is a model of $\mathcal{T}$. Thus, a model of $\mathcal{A}$ and $\mathcal{T}$ is an abstraction of a concrete world where the concepts are interpreted as subsets of the domain as required by the TBox and where the membership of the individuals to concepts and their relationships with one another in terms of roles respect the assertions in the ABox.

2.2.3.2 Individual names in the description language

Sometimes, it is convenient to allow *individual names* (also called *nominals*) not only in the ABox, but also in the description language. Some concept constructors employing individuals occur in systems and have been investigated in the literature. The most basic one is the "set" (or *one-of*) constructor, written

$$\{a_1, \ldots, a_n\},$$

where $a_1, \ldots, a_n$ are individual names. As one would expect, such a set concept is interpreted as

$$\{a_1, \ldots, a_n\}^{\mathcal{I}} \;=\; \{a_1^{\mathcal{I}}, \ldots, a_n^{\mathcal{I}}\}. \tag{2.8}$$

With sets in the description language one can for instance define the concept of permanent members of the UN security council as $\{\mathsf{CHINA}, \mathsf{FRANCE}, \mathsf{RUSSIA}, \mathsf{UK}, \mathsf{USA}\}$.

In a language with the union constructor "$\sqcup$", a constructor $\{a\}$ for singleton sets alone adds sufficient expressiveness to describe arbitrary finite sets since, according to the semantics of the set constructor in Equation (2.8), the concepts $\{a_1, \ldots, a_n\}$ and $\{a_1\} \sqcup \cdots \sqcup \{a_n\}$ are equivalent.

Another constructor involving individual names is the "fills" constructor

$$R : a,$$

for a role R. The semantics of this constructor is defined as

$$(R : a)^{\mathcal{I}} \;=\; \{d \in \Delta^{\mathcal{I}} \mid (d, a^{\mathcal{I}}) \in R^{\mathcal{I}}\}, \tag{2.9}$$

that is, $R : a$ stands for the set of those objects that have a as a filler of the role R. To a description language with singleton sets and full existential quantification, "fills" does not add anything new, since Equation (2.9) implies that $R : a$ and $\exists R.\{a\}$ are equivalent.

We note, finally, that "fills" allows one to express role assertions through concept assertions: an interpretation satisfies $R(a, b)$ iff it satisfies $(\exists R.\{b\})(a)$.

2.2.4 Inferences

A knowledge representation system based on Description Logics is able to perform specific kinds of reasoning. As said before, the purpose of a knowledge representation system goes beyond storing concept definitions and assertions. A knowledge base – comprising TBox and ABox – has a semantics that makes it equivalent to a set of axioms in first-order predicate logic. Thus, like any other set of axioms, it contains implicit knowledge that can be made explicit through inferences. For example, from the TBox in Figure 2.2 and the ABox in Figure 2.4 one can conclude that Mary is a grandmother, although this knowledge is not explicitly stated as an assertion.

The different kinds of reasoning performed by a DL system (see Chapter 8) are defined as logical inferences. In the following, we shall discuss these inferences, first for concepts, then for TBoxes and ABoxes, and finally for TBoxes and ABoxes together. It will turn out that there is one main inference problem, namely the consistency check for ABoxes, to which all other inferences can be reduced.

2.2.4.1 Reasoning tasks for concepts

When modeling a domain, a knowledge engineer constructs a terminology, say $\mathcal{T}$, by defining new concepts, possibly in terms of others that have been defined before. During this process, it is important to find out whether a newly defined concept makes sense or whether it is contradictory. From a logical point of view, a concept makes sense for us if there is some interpretation that satisfies the axioms of $\mathcal{T}$ (that is, a model of $\mathcal{T}$) such that the concept denotes a nonempty set in that interpretation. A concept with this property is said to be *satisfiable* with respect to $\mathcal{T}$ and *unsatisfiable* otherwise.

Checking satisfiability of concepts is a key inference. As we shall see, a number of other important inferences for concepts can be reduced to (un)satisfiability. For instance, in order to check whether a domain model is correct, or to optimize queries that are formulated as concepts, we may want to know whether some concept is more general than another one: this is the *subsumption problem*. A concept C *is subsumed* by a concept D if in every model of $\mathcal{T}$ the set denoted by C is a subset of the set denoted by D. Algorithms that check subsumption are also employed to organize the concepts of a TBox in a taxonomy according to their generality. Further interesting relationships between concepts are *equivalence* and *disjointness*.

These properties are formally defined as follows. Let $\mathcal{T}$ be a TBox.

Satisfiability A concept C is *satisfiable* with respect to $\mathcal{T}$ if there exists a model $\mathcal{I}$ of $\mathcal{T}$ such that $C^{\mathcal{I}}$ is nonempty. In this case we say also that $\mathcal{I}$ is a *model* of C.

Subsumption A concept C is *subsumed* by a concept D with respect to $\mathcal{T}$ if $C^{\mathcal{I}} \subseteq D^{\mathcal{I}}$ for every model $\mathcal{I}$ of $\mathcal{T}$. In this case we write $C \sqsubseteq_{\mathcal{T}} D$ or $\mathcal{T} \models C \sqsubseteq D$.

Equivalence Two concepts C and D are *equivalent* with respect to $\mathcal{T}$ if $C^{\mathcal{I}} = D^{\mathcal{I}}$ for every model $\mathcal{I}$ of $\mathcal{T}$. In this case we write $C \equiv_{\mathcal{T}} D$ or $\mathcal{T} \models C \equiv D$.

Disjointness Two concepts C and D are *disjoint* with respect to $\mathcal{T}$ if $C^{\mathcal{I}} \cap D^{\mathcal{I}} = \emptyset$ for every model $\mathcal{I}$ of $\mathcal{T}$.

If the TBox $\mathcal{T}$ is clear from the context, we sometimes drop the qualification "with respect to $\mathcal{T}$".

We also drop the qualification in the special case where the TBox is empty, and we simply write $\models C \sqsubseteq D$ if C is subsumed by D, and $\models C \equiv D$ if C and D are equivalent.

Example 2.12 With respect to the TBox in Figure 2.2, Person subsumes Woman, both Woman and Parent subsume Mother, and Mother subsumes Grandmother. Moreover, Woman and Man, and Father and Mother are disjoint. The subsumption relationships follow from the definitions because of the semantics of "$\sqcap$" and "$\sqcup$". That Man is disjoint from Woman is due to the fact that Man is subsumed by the negation of Woman. ■

Traditionally, the basic reasoning mechanism provided by DL systems checked the subsumption of concepts. This, in fact, is sufficient to implement also the other inferences, as can be seen by the following reductions.

Proposition 2.13 (Reduction to Subsumption) *For concepts C, D we have:*

1. *C is unsatisfiable* $\Leftrightarrow$ *C is subsumed by* $\perp$;
2. *C and D are equivalent* $\Leftrightarrow$ *C is subsumed by D and D is subsumed by C*;
3. *C and D are disjoint* $\Leftrightarrow$ $C \sqcap D$ *is subsumed by* $\perp$.

The statements also hold with respect to a TBox.

All description languages implemented in actual DL systems provide the intersection operator "$\sqcap$" and almost all of them contain an unsatisfiable concept. Thus, most DL systems that can check subsumption can perform all four inferences defined above.

If, in addition to intersection, a system allows one to form the negation of a description, one can reduce subsumption, equivalence, and disjointness of concepts to the satisfiability problem (see also Smolka [1988]).

Proposition 2.14 (Reduction to Unsatisfiability) *For concepts C, D we have:*

1. *C is subsumed by D* $\Leftrightarrow$ $C \sqcap \neg D$ *is unsatisfiable*;
2. *C and D are equivalent* $\Leftrightarrow$ *both* $(C \sqcap \neg D)$ *and* $(\neg C \sqcap D)$ *are unsatisfiable*;
3. *C and D are disjoint* $\Leftrightarrow$ $C \sqcap D$ *is unsatisfiable.*

The statements also hold with respect to a TBox.

The reduction of subsumption can easily be understood if one recalls that, for sets M, N, we have $M \subseteq N$ iff $M \setminus N = \emptyset$. The reduction of equivalence is correct because C and D are equivalent if, and only if, C is subsumed by D and D is subsumed by C. Finally, the reduction of disjointness is just a rephrasing of the definition.

Because of the above proposition, in order to obtain decision procedures for any of the four inferences we have discussed, it is sufficient to develop algorithms that decide the satisfiability of concepts, provided the language for which we can decide satisfiability supports conjunction as well as negation of arbitrary concepts.

In fact, this observation motivated researchers to study description languages in which, for every concept, one can also form the negation of that concept [Smolka, 1988; Schmidt-Schauß and Smolka, 1991; Donini *et al.*, 1991b; 1997a]. The approach that considers satisfiability checking as the principal inference gave rise to a new kind of algorithms for reasoning in Description Logics, which can be understood as specialized tableau calculi (see Section 2.3 in this chapter and Chapter 3). Also, the most recent generation of DL systems, like KRIS [Baader and Hollunder, 1991b], CRACK [Bresciani *et al.*, 1995], FACT [Horrocks, 1998b], DLP [Patel-Schneider, 1999], and RACE [Haarslev and Möller, 2001e], are based on satisfiability checking, and a considerable amount of research work is spent on the development of efficient implementation techniques for this approach [Baader *et al.*, 1994; Horrocks, 1998b; Horrocks and Patel-Schneider, 1999; Haarslev and Möller, 2001c].

In an $\mathcal{AL}$-language without full negation, subsumption and equivalence cannot be reduced to unsatisfiability in the simple way shown in Proposition 2.14 and therefore these inferences may be of different complexity.

As seen in Proposition 2.13, from the viewpoint of worst-case complexity, subsumption is the most general inference for any $\mathcal{AL}$-language. The next proposition shows that unsatisfiability is a special case of each of the other problems.

Proposition 2.15 (Reducing Unsatisfiability) *Let C be a concept. Then the following are equivalent:*

1. *C is unsatisfiable;*
2. *C is subsumed by $\bot$;*
3. *C and $\bot$ are equivalent;*
4. *C and $\top$ are disjoint.*

The statements also hold with respect to a TBox.

From Propositions 2.13 and 2.15 we see that, in order to obtain upper and lower complexity bounds for inferences on concepts in $\mathcal{AL}$-languages, it suffices to assess lower bounds for unsatisfiability and upper bounds for subsumption. More precisely, for each $\mathcal{AL}$-language, an upper bound for the complexity of the subsumption problem is also an upper bound for the complexity of the unsatifiability, the equivalence, and the disjointness problem. Moreover, a lower bound for the complexity of the unsatifiability problem is also a lower bound for the complexity of the subsumption, the equivalence, and the disjointness problem.

2.2.4.2 Eliminating the TBox

In applications, concepts usually come in the context of a TBox. However, for developing reasoning procedures it is conceptually easier to abstract from the TBox or, what amounts to the same, to assume that it is empty.

We show that, if $\mathcal{T}$ is an acyclic TBox, we can always reduce reasoning problems with respect to $\mathcal{T}$ to problems with respect to the empty TBox. As we have seen in Proposition 2.1, $\mathcal{T}$ is equivalent to its expansion $\mathcal{T}'$. Recall that in the expansion every definition is of the form $A \equiv D$ such that D contains only base symbols, not name symbols. Now, for each concept C we define the *expansion of C with respect to $\mathcal{T}$* as the concept C' that is obtained from C by replacing each occurrence of a name symbol A in C by the concept D, where $A \equiv D$ is the definition of A in $\mathcal{T}'$, the expansion of $\mathcal{T}$.

For example, we obtain the expansion of the concept

$$\textsf{Woman} \sqcap \textsf{Man} \qquad (2.10)$$

with respect to the TBox in Figure 2.2 by considering the expanded TBox in Figure 2.3, and replacing Woman and Man by the right-hand sides of their definitions in this expansion. This results in the concept

$$\textsf{Person} \sqcap \textsf{Female} \sqcap \textsf{Person} \sqcap \neg(\textsf{Person} \sqcap \textsf{Female}). \qquad (2.11)$$

We can readily deduce a number of facts about expansions. Since the expansion C' is obtained from C by replacing names by descriptions in such a way that both are interpreted in the same way in any model of $\mathcal{T}$, it follows that:

- $C \equiv_{\mathcal{T}} C'$.

Hence, C is satisfiable w.r.t. $\mathcal{T}$ iff C' is satisfiable w.r.t. $\mathcal{T}$. However, C' contains no defined names, and thus C' is satisfiable w.r.t. $\mathcal{T}$ iff it is satisfiable. This yields that:

- *C is satisfiable w.r.t. $\mathcal{T}$ iff C' is satisfiable.*

If D is another concept, then we have also $D \equiv_{\mathcal{T}} D'$. Thus, $C \sqsubseteq_{\mathcal{T}} D$ iff $C' \sqsubseteq_{\mathcal{T}} D'$, and $C \equiv_{\mathcal{T}} D$ iff $C' \equiv_{\mathcal{T}} D'$. Again, since C' and D' contain only base symbols, this implies:

- $\mathcal{T} \models C \sqsubseteq D$ iff $\models C' \sqsubseteq D'$;
- $\mathcal{T} \models C \equiv D$ iff $\models C' \equiv D'$.

By similar arguments we can show that:

- *C and D are disjoint w.r.t. $\mathcal{T}$ iff C' and D' are disjoint.*

Summing up, expanding concepts with respect to an acyclic TBox allows one to get rid of the TBox in reasoning problems. Going back to our example from above, this means that, in order to verify whether Man and Woman are disjoint with respect to the Family TBox, which amounts to checking whether Man ⊓ Woman is unsatisfiable, it suffices to check that the concept (2.11) is unsatisfiable.

Expanding concepts may be computationally costly, since in the worst case the size of $\mathcal{T}'$ is exponential in the size of $\mathcal{T}$, and therefore C' may be larger than C by a factor that is exponential in the size of $\mathcal{T}$. A complexity analysis of the difficulty of reasoning with respect to TBoxes shows that the expansion of definitions is a source of complexity that cannot always be avoided (see Subsection 2.3.3 of this chapter and Chapter 3).

2.2.4.3 Reasoning tasks for ABoxes

After a knowledge engineer has designed a terminology and has used the reasoning services of the DL system to check that all concepts are satisfiable and that the expected subsumption relationships hold, the ABox can be filled with assertions about individuals. We recall that an ABox contains two kinds of assertions, concept assertions of the form $C(a)$ and role assertions of the form $R(a, b)$. Of course, the representation of such knowledge has to be consistent, because otherwise – from the viewpoint of logic – one could draw arbitrary conclusions from it. If, for example, the ABox contains the assertions Mother(MARY) and Father(MARY), the system should be able to find out that, together with the Family TBox, these statements are inconsistent.

In terms of our model-theoretic semantics we can easily give a formal definition of consistency. An ABox $\mathcal{A}$ is *consistent with respect to a TBox* $\mathcal{T}$, if there is an interpretation that is a model of both $\mathcal{A}$ and $\mathcal{T}$. We simply say that $\mathcal{A}$ is *consistent* if it is consistent with respect to the empty TBox.

For example, the set of assertions {Mother(MARY), Father(MARY)} is consistent (with respect to the empty TBox), because without any further restrictions on the interpretation of Mother and Father, the two concepts can be interpreted in such a way that they have a common element. However, the assertions are not consistent with respect to the Family TBox, since in every model of it, Mother and Father are interpreted as disjoint sets.

Similarly as for concepts, checking the consistency of an ABox with respect to an acyclic TBox can be reduced to checking an expanded ABox. We define the *expansion* of $\mathcal{A}$ with respect to $\mathcal{T}$ as the ABox $\mathcal{A}'$ that is obtained from $\mathcal{A}$ by replacing each concept assertion $C(a)$ in $\mathcal{A}$ by the assertion $C'(a)$, where C' is the expansion of C with respect to $\mathcal{T}$.[5] In every model of $\mathcal{T}$, a

---

[5] We expand only concept assertions because the description language considered until now does not provide constructors for role descriptions and therefore we have not considered TBoxes with role definitions. If the description language is richer, and TBoxes contain also role definitions, then they clearly have to be taken into account in the definition of expansions.

concept C and its expansion C' are interpreted in the same way. Therefore, $\mathcal{A}'$ is consistent w.r.t. $\mathcal{T}$ iff $\mathcal{A}$ is so. However, since $\mathcal{A}'$ does not contain a name symbol defined in $\mathcal{T}$, it is consistent w.r.t. $\mathcal{T}$ iff it is consistent. We conclude:

- $\mathcal{A}$ *is consistent w.r.t.* $\mathcal{T}$ *iff*   *its expansion* $\mathcal{A}'$ *is consistent.*

A technique to check the consistency of $\mathcal{ALCN}$-ABoxes is discussed in Subsection 2.3.2.

Other inferences that we are going to introduce can also be defined with respect to a TBox or for an ABox alone. As in the case of consistency, reasoning tasks for ABoxes with respect to acyclic TBoxes can be reduced to reasoning on expanded ABoxes. For the sake of simplicity, we shall give only definitions of inferences with ABoxes alone, and leave it to the reader to formulate the appropriate generalization to inferences with respect to TBoxes and to verify that they can be reduced to inferences about expansions, provided the TBox is acyclic.

Over an ABox $\mathcal{A}$, one can pose queries about the relationships between concepts, roles and individuals. The prototypical ABox inference on which such queries are based is *instance checking*, or the check whether an assertion is entailed by an ABox. We say that an assertion α is *entailed* by $\mathcal{A}$ and we write $\mathcal{A} \models \alpha$, if every interpretation that satisfies $\mathcal{A}$, that is, every model of $\mathcal{A}$, also satisfies α. If α is a role assertion, instance checking is easy, since our description language does not contain constructors to form complex roles. If α is of the form $C(a)$, we can reduce instance checking to the consistency problem for ABoxes because there is the following connection:

- $\mathcal{A} \models C(a)$ *iff* $\mathcal{A} \cup \{\neg C(a)\}$ *is inconsistent.*

Also reasoning about concepts can be reduced to consistency checking. We have seen in Proposition 2.14 that the important reasoning problems for concepts can be reduced to that of deciding whether a concept is (un)satisfiable. Similarly, concept satisfiability can be reduced to ABox consistency because for every concept C we have:

- C *is satisfiable*   *iff* $\{C(a)\}$ *is consistent,*

where a is an arbitrarily chosen individual name. Conversely, Schaerf [1994b] has shown that ABox consistency can be reduced to concept satisfiability in languages with the "set" and the "fills" constructor. If these constructors are not available, however, then instance checking may be harder than the satisfiability and the subsumption problem [Donini *et al.*, 1994b].

For applications, more complex inferences than consistency and instance checking are usually required. If we consider a knowledge base as a means to store information about individuals, we may want to know all individuals that are instances of a given concept description C, that is, we use the description language to formulate queries. In our example, we may want to know from the system all parents that have at least two children – for instance, because they are entitled to a specific family tax break. The *retrieval problem* is, given an ABox $\mathcal{A}$ and a concept C, to find all individuals a such that $\mathcal{A} \models C(a)$. A non-optimized algorithm for a retrieval query can be realized by testing for each individual occurring in the ABox whether it is an instance of the query concept C.

The dual inference to retrieval is the *realization problem*: given an individual a and a set of concepts, find the *most specific concepts* C from the set such that $\mathcal{A} \models C(a)$. Here, the most specific concepts are those that are minimal with respect to the subsumption ordering $\sqsubseteq$. Realization can, for instance, be used in systems that generate natural language if terms are indexed by concepts and if a term as precise as possible is to be found for an object occurring in a discourse.

2.2.4.4 Closed- vs. open-world semantics

Often, an analogy is established between databases on the one hand and DL knowledge bases on the other hand (see also Chapter 16). The schema of a database is compared to the TBox and the database instance with the actual data is compared to the ABox. However, the semantics of ABoxes differs from the usual semantics of database instances. While a database instance represents exactly one interpretation, namely the one where classes and relations in the schema are interpreted by the objects and tuples in the instance, an ABox represents many different interpretations, namely all its models. As a consequence, absence of information in a database instance is interpreted as negative information, while absence of information in an ABox only indicates lack of knowledge.

For example, if the only assertion about Peter is hasChild(PETER, HARRY), then in a database this is understood as a representation of the fact that Peter has only one child, Harry. In an ABox, the assertion only expresses that, in fact, Harry is a child of Peter. However, the ABox has several models, some in which Harry is the only child and others in which he has brothers or sisters. Consequently, even if one also knows (by an assertion) that Harry is male, one cannot deduce that all of Peter's children are male. The only way of stating in an ABox that Harry is the only child is by doing so explicitly, that is by adding the assertion $(\leqslant 1\, \mathsf{hasChild})(\mathsf{PETER})$.

hasChild(JOCASTA, OEDIPUS)	hasChild(JOCASTA, POLYNEIKES)
hasChild(OEDIPUS, POLYNEIKES)	hasChild(POLYNEIKES, THERSANDROS)
Patricide(OEDIPUS)	¬Patricide(THERSANDROS)

Fig. 2.5. The Oedipus ABox $\mathcal{A}_{oe}$.

This means that, while the information in a database is always understood to be complete, the information in an ABox is in general viewed as being incomplete. The semantics of ABoxes is therefore sometimes characterized as an "open-world" semantics, while the traditional semantics of databases is characterized as a "closed-world" semantics.

This view has consequences for the way queries are answered. Essentially, a query is a description of a class of objects. In our setting, we assume that queries are concept descriptions. A database (in the sense introduced above) is a listing of a single finite interpretation. A finite interpretation, say $\mathcal{I}$, could be written up as a set of assertions of the form $A(a)$ and $R(b, c)$, where A is an atomic concept and R an atomic role. Such a set looks syntactically like an ABox, but is not an ABox because of the difference in semantics. Answering a query, represented by a complex concept C, over that database amounts to computing $C^{\mathcal{I}}$ as it was defined in Subsection 2.2.1. From a logical point of view this means that query evaluation in a database is not logical reasoning, but finite model checking (i.e., evaluation of a formula in a fixed finite model).

Since an ABox represents possibly infinitely many interpretations, namely its models, query answering is more complex: it requires nontrivial reasoning. Here we are only concerned with semantical issues (algorithmic aspects will be treated in Section 2.3). To illustrate the difference between a semantics that identifies a database with a single model, and the open-world semantics of ABoxes, we discuss the so-called Oedipus example, which has stimulated a number of theoretical developments in DL research.

Example 2.16 The example is based on the Oedipus story from ancient Greek mythology. In a nutshell, the story recounts how Oedipus killed his father, married his mother Jocasta, and had children with her, among them Polyneikes. Finally, Polyneikes also had children, among them Thersandros.

We suppose the ABox $\mathcal{A}_{oe}$ in Figure 2.5 represents some rudimentary facts about these events. For the sake of the example, our ABox asserts that Oedipus is a patricide and that Thersandros is not, which is represented using the atomic concept Patricide.

Suppose now that we want to know from the ABox whether Jocasta has a child that is a patricide and that itself has a child that is not a patricide.

This can be expressed as the entailment problem

$$\mathcal{A}_{oe} \models (\exists\mathsf{hasChild}.(\mathsf{Patricide} \sqcap \exists\mathsf{hasChild}.\neg\mathsf{Patricide}))(\mathsf{JOCASTA}) \ ?$$

One may be tempted to reason as follows. Jocasta has two children in the ABox. One, Oedipus, is a patricide. He has one child, Polyneikes. But nothing tells us that Polyneikes *is not* a patricide. So, Oedipus is not the child we are looking for. The other child is Polyneikes, but again, nothing tells us that Polyneikes *is* a patricide. So, Polyneikes is also not the child we are looking for. Based on this reasoning, one would claim that the assertion about Jocasta is not entailed.

However, the correct reasoning is different. All the models of $\mathcal{A}_{oe}$ can be divided into two classes, one in which Polyneikes is a patricide, and another one in which he is not. In a model of the first kind, Polyneikes is the child of Jocasta that is a patricide and has a child, namely Thersandros, that isn't. In a model of the second kind, Oedipus is the child of Jocasta that is a patricide and has a child, namely Polyneikes, that isn't. Thus, in all models Jocasta has a child that is a patricide and that itself has a child that is not a patricide (though this is not always the same child). This means that the assertion $(\exists\mathsf{hasChild}.(\mathsf{Patricide} \sqcap \exists\mathsf{hasChild}.\neg\mathsf{Patricide}))(\mathsf{JOCASTA})$ is indeed entailed by $\mathcal{A}_{oe}$. ∎

As this example shows, open-world reasoning may require case analyses. As will be explained in more detail in Chapter 3, this is one of the reasons why inferences in Description Logics are often more complex than query answering in databases.

2.2.5 Rules

The knowledge bases we have discussed so far consist of a TBox $\mathcal{T}$ and an ABox $\mathcal{A}$. We denote such a knowledge base as a pair $\mathcal{K} = (\mathcal{T}, \mathcal{A})$.

In some DL systems, such as CLASSIC [Brachman *et al.*, 1991] or LOOM [MacGregor, 1991a], in addition to terminologies and world descriptions, one can also use *rules* to express knowledge. The simplest variant of such rules is an expression of the form

$$C \Rightarrow D,$$

where C, D are concepts. The meaning of such a rule is "if an individual is proved to be an instance of C, then derive that it is also an instance of D". Such rules are often called *trigger rules*.

Operationally, the semantics of a finite set $\mathcal{R}$ of trigger rules can be described by a forward reasoning process. Starting with an initial knowledge base $\mathcal{K}$, a series of knowledge bases $\mathcal{K}^{(0)}, \mathcal{K}^{(1)}, \ldots$ is constructed, where $\mathcal{K}^{(0)} = \mathcal{K}$ and $\mathcal{K}^{(i+1)}$ is obtained from $\mathcal{K}^{(i)}$ by adding a new assertion $D(a)$ whenever $\mathcal{R}$ contains a rule $C \Rightarrow D$ such that $\mathcal{K}^{(i)} \models C(a)$ holds, but $\mathcal{K}^{(i)}$ does not contain $D(a)$. This process eventually halts because the initial knowledge base contains only finitely many individuals and there are only finitely many rules. Hence, there are only finitely many assertions $D(a)$ that can possibly be added. The result of the rule applications is a knowledge base $\mathcal{K}^{(n)}$ that has the same TBox as $\mathcal{K}^{(0)}$ and whose ABox is augmented by the membership assertions introduced by the rules. We call this final knowledge base the *procedural extension* of $\mathcal{K}$ and denote it by $\bar{\mathcal{K}}$. It is easy to see that this procedural extension is independent of the order of rule applications. Consequently, a set of trigger rules $\mathcal{R}$ uniquely specifies how to generate, for each knowledge base $\mathcal{K}$, an extended knowledge base $\bar{\mathcal{K}}$. The semantics of a knowledge base $\mathcal{K}$, augmented by a set of trigger rules, can thus be understood as the set of models of $\bar{\mathcal{K}}$.

This defines the semantics of trigger rules only operationally. It would be preferable to specify the semantics declaratively and then to prove that the extension computed with the trigger rules correctly represents this semantics. It might be tempting to use the declarative semantics of inclusion axioms as semantics for rules. However, this does not correctly reflect the operational semantics given above. An important difference between the trigger rule $C \Rightarrow D$ and the inclusion axiom $C \sqsubseteq D$ is that the trigger rule is not equivalent to its contrapositive $\neg D \Rightarrow \neg C$. In addition, when applying trigger rules one does not make a case analysis. For example, the inclusions $C \sqsubseteq D$ and $\neg C \sqsubseteq D$ imply that every object belongs to D, whereas neither of the trigger rules $C \Rightarrow D$ and $\neg C \Rightarrow D$ applies to an individual a for which neither $C(a)$ nor $\neg C(a)$ can be proven.

In order to capture the meaning of trigger rules in a declarative way, we must augment Description Logics by an operator $\mathbf{K}$, which does not refer to objects in the domain, but to what the knowledge base knows about the domain. Therefore, $\mathbf{K}$ is an *epistemic operator*. More information on epistemic operators in Description Logics can be found in Chapter 6.

To introduce the $\mathbf{K}$ operator, we enrich both the syntax and the semantics of description languages. Originally, the $\mathbf{K}$ operator was defined for $\mathcal{ALC}$ [Donini *et al.*, 1992b; 1998a]. In this subsection, we discuss only how to extend the basic language $\mathcal{AL}$. For other languages, one can proceed analogously (see also Chapter 6).

First, we add one case to the syntax rule in Subsection 2.2.1.1 that allows us to construct epistemic concepts:

$$C, D \longrightarrow \mathbf{K}C \qquad \text{(epistemic concept)}.$$

Intuitively, the concept $\mathbf{K}C$ denotes those objects for which the knowledge base knows that they are instances of C.

Next, using $\mathbf{K}$, we translate trigger rules $C \Rightarrow D$ into inclusion axioms

$$\mathbf{K}C \sqsubseteq D. \qquad (2.12)$$

Intuitively, the $\mathbf{K}$ operator in front of the concept C has the effect that the axiom is only applicable to individuals that appear in the ABox and for which ABox and TBox imply that they are instances of C. Such a restricted applicability prevents the inclusion axiom from influencing satisfiability or subsumption relationships between concepts. In the sequel, we will define a formal semantics for the operator $\mathbf{K}$ that has exactly this effect.

A *rule knowledge base* is a triple $\mathcal{K} = (\mathcal{T}, \mathcal{A}, \mathcal{R})$, where $\mathcal{T}$ is a TBox, $\mathcal{A}$ is an ABox, and $\mathcal{R}$ is a set of rules written as inclusion axioms of the form (2.12). The *procedural extension* of such a triple is the knowledge base $\bar{\mathcal{K}} = (\mathcal{T}, \bar{\mathcal{A}})$ that is obtained from $(\mathcal{T}, \mathcal{A})$ by applying the trigger rules as described above.

The semantics of epistemic inclusions will be defined in such a way that it applies only to individuals in the knowledge base that provably are instances of C, but not to arbitrary domain elements, which would be the case if we dropped $\mathbf{K}$. The semantics will go beyond first-order logic because we not only have to interpret concepts, roles and individuals, but also have to model the knowledge of a knowledge base. The fact that a knowledge base has knowledge about the domain can be understood in such a way that it considers only a subset $\mathcal{W}$ of the set of all interpretations as possible states of the world. Those individuals that are interpreted as elements of C under all interpretations in $\mathcal{W}$ are then "known" to be in C.

To make this formal, we modify the definition of ordinary (first-order) interpretations by assuming that:

1. there is a fixed countably infinite set Δ that is the domain of every interpretation (common domain assumption);
2. there is a mapping γ from the individuals to the domain elements that fixes the way individuals are interpreted (rigid term assumption).

The common domain assumption guarantees that all interpretations speak about the same domain. The rigid term assumption allows us to identify each individual symbol with exactly one domain element. These assumptions do not essentially reduce the number of possible interpretations. As a consequence, properties like satisfiability and subsumption of concepts are the same independently of whether we define them with respect to arbitrary interpretations or those that satisfy the above assumptions.

Now, we define an *epistemic interpretation* as a pair $(\mathcal{I}, \mathcal{W})$, where $\mathcal{I}$ is a first-order interpretation and $\mathcal{W}$ is a set of first-order interpretations, all satisfying the above assumptions. Every epistemic interpretation gives rise to a unique mapping $\cdot^{\mathcal{I}, \mathcal{W}}$ associating concepts and roles with subsets of Δ and $\Delta \times \Delta$, respectively. For $\top$, $\bot$, atomic concepts, negated atomic concepts, and atomic roles, $\cdot^{\mathcal{I}, \mathcal{W}}$ agrees with $\cdot^{\mathcal{I}}$. For intersections, value restrictions, and existential quantifications, the definition is similar to that of $\cdot^{\mathcal{I}}$:

$$
\begin{aligned}
(C \sqcap D)^{\mathcal{I}, \mathcal{W}} &= C^{\mathcal{I}, \mathcal{W}} \cap D^{\mathcal{I}, \mathcal{W}} \\
(\forall R.C)^{\mathcal{I}, \mathcal{W}} &= \{a \in \Delta \mid \forall b.\ (a, b) \in R^{\mathcal{I}, \mathcal{W}} \rightarrow b \in C^{\mathcal{I}, \mathcal{W}}\} \\
(\exists R.\top)^{\mathcal{I}, \mathcal{W}} &= \{a \in \Delta \mid \exists b.\ (a, b) \in R^{\mathcal{I}, \mathcal{W}}\}.
\end{aligned}
$$

For other constructors, $\cdot^{\mathcal{I}, \mathcal{W}}$ can be defined analogously. Note that for a concept C without an occurrence of **K**, the sets $C^{\mathcal{I}, \mathcal{W}}$ and $C^{\mathcal{I}}$ are identical. The set of interpretations $\mathcal{W}$ comes into play when we define the semantics of the epistemic operator:

$$
(\mathbf{K}C)^{\mathcal{I}, \mathcal{W}} = \bigcap_{\mathcal{J} \in \mathcal{W}} C^{\mathcal{J}, \mathcal{W}}.
$$

It would also be possible to allow the operator **K** to occur in front of roles and to define the semantics of role expressions of the form $\mathbf{K}R$ analogously. However, since epistemic roles are not needed to explain the semantics of rules, we restrict ourselves to epistemic concepts.

An epistemic interpretation $(\mathcal{I}, \mathcal{W})$ *satisfies* an inclusion $C \sqsubseteq D$ if $C^{\mathcal{I}, \mathcal{W}} \subseteq D^{\mathcal{I}, \mathcal{W}}$, and an equality $C \equiv D$ if $C^{\mathcal{I}, \mathcal{W}} = D^{\mathcal{I}, \mathcal{W}}$. It satisfies an assertion $C(a)$ if $a^{\mathcal{I}, \mathcal{W}} = \gamma(a) \in C^{\mathcal{I}, \mathcal{W}}$, and an assertion $R(a, b)$ if $(a^{\mathcal{I}, \mathcal{W}}, b^{\mathcal{I}, \mathcal{W}}) = (\gamma(a), \gamma(b)) \in R^{\mathcal{I}, \mathcal{W}}$. It satisfies a rule knowledge base $\mathcal{K} = (\mathcal{T}, \mathcal{A}, \mathcal{R})$ if it satisfies every axiom in $\mathcal{T}$, every assertion in $\mathcal{A}$, and every rule in $\mathcal{R}$.

An *epistemic model* for a rule knowledge base $\mathcal{K}$ is a *maximal* nonempty set $\mathcal{W}$ of first-order interpretations such that, for each $\mathcal{I} \in \mathcal{W}$, the epistemic interpretation $(\mathcal{I}, \mathcal{W})$ satisfies $\mathcal{K}$.

Note that, if $(\mathcal{T}, \mathcal{A})$ is first-order satisfiable, then the set of all first-order models of $(\mathcal{T}, \mathcal{A})$ is the only epistemic model of the rule knowledge base $\mathcal{K} = (\mathcal{T}, \mathcal{A}, \emptyset)$, whose rule set is empty. A similar statement holds for arbitrary rule knowledge bases. One can show that, if $\mathcal{W}_1$ and $\mathcal{W}_2$ are epistemic models, then the union $\mathcal{W}_1 \cup \mathcal{W}_2$ is one, too, which implies $\mathcal{W}_1 = \mathcal{W}_2$ because of the maximality of epistemic models.

Proposition 2.17 *Let $\mathcal{K} = (\mathcal{T}, \mathcal{A}, \mathcal{R})$ be a rule knowledge base such that $(\mathcal{T}, \mathcal{A})$ is first-order satisfiable. Then $\mathcal{K}$ has a unique epistemic model.*

Example 2.18 Let $\mathcal{R}$ consist of the rule

$$\mathsf{KStudent} \sqsubseteq \forall \mathsf{eats.JunkFood}. \tag{2.13}$$

The rule states that "those individuals that are known to be students eat only junk food".

We consider the rule knowledge base $\mathcal{K}_1 = (\emptyset, \mathcal{A}_1, \mathcal{R})$, where

$$\mathcal{A}_1 = \{\mathsf{Student}(\mathsf{PETER})\}.$$

Let us determine the epistemic model $\mathcal{W}$ of $\mathcal{K}_1$. Every first-order interpretation $\mathcal{I} \in \mathcal{W}$ must satisfy $\mathcal{A}_1$. Therefore, in every such $\mathcal{I}$, we have that $\mathsf{Student}(\mathsf{PETER})$ is true, and thus Peter is *known* to be a student. Since $\mathcal{W}$ satisfies Rule (2.13), the assertion $\forall \mathsf{eats.JunkFood}(\mathsf{PETER})$ also holds in every $\mathcal{I}$.

For any other domain element $a \in \Delta$, there is at least one interpretation in $\mathcal{W}$ where a is not a student. Thus, Peter is the only domain element to which the rule applies. Summing up, the epistemic model of $\mathcal{K}_1$ consists exactly of the first-order models of $\mathcal{A}_1 \cup \{\forall \mathsf{eats.JunkFood}(\mathsf{PETER})\}$.

Next we demonstrate with this example that the epistemic semantics for rules disallows contrapositive reasoning. We consider the rule knowledge base $\mathcal{K}_2 = (\emptyset, \mathcal{A}_2, \mathcal{R})$, where

$$\mathcal{A}_2 = \{\neg \forall \mathsf{eats.JunkFood}(\mathsf{PETER})\}.$$

In this case, $\neg \forall \mathsf{eats.JunkFood}(\mathsf{PETER})$ is true in every first-order interpretation of the epistemic model $\mathcal{W}$. However, because of the maximality of $\mathcal{W}$, there is at least *one* interpretation in $\mathcal{W}$ in which Peter *is* a student and *another one* where Peter *is not* a student. Therefore, Peter is *not known* to be a student. Thus, the epistemic model of $\mathcal{K}_2$ consists exactly of the first-order models of $\mathcal{A}_2$. The rule is satisfied because the antecedent is false. ∎

Clearly, the procedural extension of a rule knowledge base $\mathcal{K}$ contains only assertions that must be satisfied by the epistemic model of $\mathcal{K}$. It can be shown that the assertions added to $\mathcal{K}$ by the rule applications are in fact, as stated in the following proposition, a first-order representation of the information that is implicit in the rules (see [Donini *et al.*, 1998a] for a proof).

Proposition 2.19 *Let* $\mathcal{K} = (\mathcal{T}, \mathcal{A}, \mathcal{R})$ *be a rule knowledge base. If* $(\mathcal{T}, \mathcal{A})$ *is first-order satisfiable, then the epistemic model of* $\mathcal{K}$ *consists precisely of the first-order models of the procedural extension* $\bar{\mathcal{K}} = (\mathcal{T}, \bar{\mathcal{A}})$.

2.3 Reasoning algorithms

In Subsection 2.2.4 we have seen that all the relevant inference problems can be reduced to the consistency problem for ABoxes, provided that the Description Logic at hand allows conjunction and negation. However, the description languages of all the early and also of some of the present day DL systems do not allow negation. For such Description Logics, subsumption of concepts can usually be computed by so-called *structural subsumption algorithms*, i.e., algorithms that compare the syntactic structure of (possibly normalized) concept descriptions. In the first subsection, we will consider such algorithms in more detail. While they are usually very efficient, they are only complete for rather simple languages with little expressivity. In particular, Description Logics with (full) negation and disjunction cannot be handled by structural subsumption algorithms. For such languages, so-called *tableau-based algorithms* have turned out to be very useful. In the area of Description Logics, the first tableau-based algorithm was presented by Schmidt-Schauß and Smolka [1991] for satisfiability of $\mathcal{ALC}$-concepts. Since then, this approach has been employed to obtain sound and complete satisfiability (and thus also subsumption) algorithms for a great variety of Description Logics extending $\mathcal{ALC}$ (see, e.g., [Hollunder *et al.*, 1990; Hollunder and Baader, 1991a; Donini *et al.*, 1997a; Baader and Sattler, 1999] for languages with number restrictions; [Baader, 1991] for transitive closure of roles and [Sattler, 1996; Horrocks and Sattler, 1999] for transitive roles; and [Baader and Hanschke, 1991a; Hanschke, 1992; Haarslev *et al.*, 1999] for constructors that allow one to refer to concrete domains such as numbers). In addition, it has been extended to the consistency problem for ABoxes [Hollunder, 1990; Baader and Hollunder, 1991b; Donini *et al.*, 1994b; Haarslev and Möller, 2000], and to TBoxes allowing general sets of inclusion axioms and more [Buchheit *et al.*, 1993a; Baader *et al.*, 1996]. In the second subsection, we will first present a tableau-based satisfiability algorithm for $\mathcal{ALCN}$-concepts, then show how it can be extended to an algorithm for the consistency problem for ABoxes, and finally explain how general inclusion axioms can be taken into account. The third subsection is concerned with reasoning w.r.t. acyclic and cyclic terminologies.

Instead of designing new algorithms for reasoning in Description Logics, one can also try to reduce the problem to a known inference problem in logics (see also Chapter 4). For example, decidability of the inference problems for $\mathcal{ALC}$ and many other Description Logics can be obtained as a consequence of the known decidability result for the two-variable fragment of first-order predicate logic. The language $\mathcal{L}^2$ consists of all formulae of first-order predicate logic that can be built with the help of predicate symbols (including equality) and constant symbols (but without function symbols) using only the variables x, y. Decidability of $\mathcal{L}^2$ has been shown in [Mortimer, 1975]. It is easy to see that, by appropriately re-using variable names, any concept description of the language $\mathcal{ALC}$ can be translated into an $\mathcal{L}^2$-formula with one free variable (see [Borgida, 1996] for details). A direct translation of the concept description $\forall R.(\exists R.A)$ yields the formula $\forall y.(R(x, y) \rightarrow (\exists z.(R(y, z) \land A(z))))$. Since the subformula $\exists z.(R(y, z) \land A(z))$ does not contain x, this variable can be re-used: renaming the bound variable z to x yields the equivalent formula $\forall y.(R(x, y) \rightarrow (\exists x.(R(y, x) \land A(x))))$, which uses only two variables. This connection between $\mathcal{ALC}$ and $\mathcal{L}^2$ shows that any extension of $\mathcal{ALC}$ by constructors that can be expressed with the help of only two variables yields a decidable Description Logic. Number restrictions and composition of roles are examples of constructors that cannot be expressed within $\mathcal{L}^2$. Number restrictions can, however, be expressed in $\mathcal{C}^2$, the extension of $\mathcal{L}^2$ by counting quantifiers, which has recently been shown to be decidable [Grädel et al., 1997b; Pacholski et al., 1997]. It should be noted, however, that the complexity of the decision procedures obtained this way is usually higher than necessary: for example, the satisfiability problem for $\mathcal{L}^2$ is NExp-Time-complete, whereas satisfiability of $\mathcal{ALC}$-concept descriptions is "only" PSpace-complete.

Decision procedures with lower complexity can be obtained by using the connection between Description Logics and propositional modal logics. Schild [1991] was the first to observe that the language $\mathcal{ALC}$ is a syntactic variant of the propositional multi-modal logic **K**, and that the extension of $\mathcal{ALC}$ by transitive closure of roles [Baader, 1991] corresponds to Propositional Dynamic Logic (PDL). In particular, some of the algorithms used in propositional modal logics for deciding satisfiability are very similar to the tableau-based algorithms newly developed for Description Logics. This connection between Description Logics and modal logics has been used to transfer decidability results from modal logics to Description Logics [Schild, 1993; 1994; De Giacomo and Lenzerini, 1994a; 1994b] (see also Chapter 5). Instead of using tableau-based algorithms, decidability of certain propositional modal logics (and thus of the corresponding Description Logics) can also be shown by establishing the finite model property (see, e.g., [Fitting, 1993], Section 1.14) of the logic (i.e., showing that a formula or concept is satisfiable iff it is satisfiable in a finite interpretation) or by employing tree automata (see, e.g., [Vardi and Wolper, 1986]).

2.3.1 Structural subsumption algorithms

These algorithms usually proceed in two phases. First, the descriptions to be tested for subsumption are normalized, and then the syntactic structure of the normal forms is compared. For simplicity, we first explain the ideas underlying this approach for the small language $\mathcal{FL}_0$, which allows conjunction $(C \sqcap D)$ and value restrictions $(\forall R.C)$. Subsequently, we show how the bottom concept $(\bot)$, atomic negation $(\neg A)$, and number restrictions $(\leqslant n\,R$ and $\geqslant n\,R)$ can be handled. Evidently, $\mathcal{FL}_0$ and its extension by bottom and atomic negation are sublanguages of $\mathcal{AL}$, while adding number restrictions to the resulting language yields the Description Logic $\mathcal{ALN}$.

An $\mathcal{FL}_0$-concept description is in *normal form* iff it is of the form

$$A_1 \sqcap \cdots \sqcap A_m \sqcap \forall R_1.C_1 \sqcap \cdots \sqcap \forall R_n.C_n,$$

where $A_1, \ldots, A_m$ are distinct concept names, $R_1, \ldots, R_n$ are distinct role names, and $C_1, \ldots, C_n$ are $\mathcal{FL}_0$-concept descriptions in normal form. It is easy to see that any description can be transformed into an equivalent one in normal form, using associativity, commutativity and idempotence of $\sqcap$, and the fact that the descriptions $\forall R.(C \sqcap D)$ and $(\forall R.C) \sqcap (\forall R.D)$ are equivalent.

Proposition 2.20 *Let*

$$A_1 \sqcap \cdots \sqcap A_m \sqcap \forall R_1.C_1 \sqcap \cdots \sqcap \forall R_n.C_n$$

be the normal form of the $\mathcal{FL}_0$-concept description C, and

$$B_1 \sqcap \cdots \sqcap B_k \sqcap \forall S_1.D_1 \sqcap \cdots \sqcap \forall S_l.D_l$$

the normal form of the $\mathcal{FL}_0$-concept description D. Then $C \sqsubseteq D$ iff the following two conditions hold:

1. *for all i, $1 \leq i \leq k$, there exists j, $1 \leq j \leq m$ such that $B_i = A_j$;*
2. *for all i, $1 \leq i \leq l$, there exists j, $1 \leq j \leq n$ such that $S_i = R_j$ and $C_j \sqsubseteq D_i$.*

It is easy to see that this characterization of subsumption is sound (i.e., the "if" direction of the proposition holds) and complete (i.e., the "only if" direction of the proposition holds as well). This characterization yields an obvious recursive algorithm for computing subsumption, which can easily be shown to be of polynomial time complexity [Levesque and Brachman, 1987].

If we extend $\mathcal{FL}_0$ by language constructors that can express unsatisfiable concepts, then we must, on the one hand, change the definition of the normal form. On the other hand, the structural comparison of the normal forms must take into account that an unsatisfiable concept is subsumed by every concept. The simplest Description Logic where this occurs is $\mathcal{FL}_\perp$, the extension of $\mathcal{FL}_0$ by the bottom concept $\perp$.

An $\mathcal{FL}_\perp$-concept description is in *normal form* iff it is $\perp$ or of the form

$$A_1 \sqcap \cdots \sqcap A_m \sqcap \forall R_1.C_1 \sqcap \cdots \sqcap \forall R_n.C_n,$$

where $A_1, \ldots, A_m$ are distinct concept names different from $\perp$, $R_1, \ldots, R_n$ are distinct role names, and $C_1, \ldots, C_n$ are $\mathcal{FL}_\perp$-concept descriptions in normal form. Again, such a normal form can easily be computed. In principle, one just computes the $\mathcal{FL}_0$-normal form of the description (where $\perp$ is treated as an ordinary concept name): $B_1 \sqcap \cdots \sqcap B_k \sqcap \forall R_1.D_1 \sqcap \cdots \sqcap \forall R_n.D_n$. If one of the B_is is $\perp$, then replace the whole description by $\perp$. Otherwise, apply the same procedure recursively to the D_js. For example, the $\mathcal{FL}_0$-normal form of $\forall R.\forall R.B \sqcap A \sqcap \forall R.(A \sqcap \forall R.\perp)$ is

$$A \sqcap \forall R.(A \sqcap \forall R.(B \sqcap \perp)),$$

which yields the $\mathcal{FL}_\perp$-normal form

$$A \sqcap \forall R.(A \sqcap \forall R.\perp).$$

The structural subsumption algorithm for $\mathcal{FL}_\perp$ works just like the one for $\mathcal{FL}_0$, with the only difference that $\perp$ is subsumed by any description. For example, $\forall R.\forall R.B \sqcap A \sqcap \forall R.(A \sqcap \forall R.\perp) \sqsubseteq \forall R.\forall R.A \sqcap A \sqcap \forall R.A$ since the recursive comparison of their $\mathcal{FL}_\perp$-normal forms $A \sqcap \forall R.(A \sqcap \forall R.\perp)$ and $A \sqcap \forall R.(A \sqcap \forall R.A)$ finally leads to the comparison of $\perp$ and A.

The extension of $\mathcal{FL}_\perp$ by atomic negation (i.e., negation applied to concept names only) can be treated similarly. During the computation of the normal form, negated concept names are just treated like concept names. If, however, a name and its negation occur on the same level of the normal form, then $\perp$ is added, which can then be treated as described above. For example, $\forall R.\neg A \sqcap A \sqcap \forall R.(A \sqcap \forall R.B)$ is first transformed into $A \sqcap \forall R.(A \sqcap \neg A \sqcap \forall R.B)$, then into $A \sqcap \forall R.(\perp \sqcap A \sqcap \neg A \sqcap \forall R.B)$, and finally into $A \sqcap \forall R.\perp$. The structural comparison of the normal forms treats negated concept names just like concept names.

Finally, if we consider the language $\mathcal{ALN}$, the additional presence of number restrictions leads to a new type of conflict. On the one hand, as in the case of atomic negation, number restrictions may be in conflict with each other (e.g., $\geqslant 2\,R$ and $\leqslant 1\,R$). On the other hand, at-least restrictions $\geqslant n\,R$ for $n \geq 1$ are in conflict with value restrictions $\forall R.\bot$ that prohibit role successors. When computing the normal form, one can again treat number restrictions like concept names, and then take care of the new types of conflicts by introducing $\bot$ and using it for normalization as described above. During the structural comparison of normal forms, one must also take into account inherent subsumption relationships between number restrictions (e.g., $\geqslant n\,R \sqsubseteq \geqslant m\,R$ iff $n \geq m$). A more detailed description of a structural subsumption algorithm working on a graph-like data structure for a language extending $\mathcal{ALN}$ can be found in [Borgida and Patel-Schneider, 1994].

For larger Description Logics, structural subsumption algorithms usually fail to be complete. In particular, they cannot treat disjunction, full negation, and full existential restriction $\exists R.C$. For languages including these constructors, the tableau approach to designing subsumption algorithms has turned out to be quite useful.

2.3.2 Tableau algorithms

Instead of directly testing subsumption of concept descriptions, these algorithms use negation to reduce subsumption to (un)satisfiability of concept descriptions: as we have seen in Subsection 2.2.4, $C \sqsubseteq D$ iff $C \sqcap \neg D$ is unsatisfiable.

Before describing a tableau-based satisfiability algorithm for $\mathcal{ALCN}$ in more detail, we illustrate the underlying ideas by two simple examples. Let A, B be concept names, and let R be a role name.

As a first example, assume that we want to know whether $(\exists R.A) \sqcap (\exists R.B)$ is subsumed by $\exists R.(A \sqcap B)$. This means that we must check whether the concept description

$$C = (\exists R.A) \sqcap (\exists R.B) \sqcap \neg(\exists R.(A \sqcap B))$$

is unsatisfiable.

First, we push all negation signs as far as possible into the description, using De Morgan's rules and the usual rules for quantifiers. As a result, we obtain the description

$$C_0 = (\exists R.A) \sqcap (\exists R.B) \sqcap \forall R.(\neg A \sqcup \neg B),$$

which is in *negation normal form*, i.e., negation occurs only in front of concept names.

Then, we try to construct a finite interpretation $\mathcal{I}$ such that $C_0^{\mathcal{I}} \neq \emptyset$. This means that there must exist an individual in $\Delta^{\mathcal{I}}$ that is an element of $C_0^{\mathcal{I}}$.

The algorithm just generates such an individual, say b, and imposes the constraint $b \in C_0^{\mathcal{I}}$ on it. Since C_0 is the conjunction of three concept descriptions, this means that b must satisfy the following three constraints: $b \in (\exists R.A)^{\mathcal{I}}$, $b \in (\exists R.B)^{\mathcal{I}}$, and $b \in (\forall R.(\neg A \sqcup \neg B))^{\mathcal{I}}$.

From $b \in (\exists R.A)^{\mathcal{I}}$ we can deduce that there must exist an individual c such that $(b, c) \in R^{\mathcal{I}}$ and $c \in A^{\mathcal{I}}$. Analogously, $b \in (\exists R.B)^{\mathcal{I}}$ implies the existence of an individual d with $(b, d) \in R^{\mathcal{I}}$ and $d \in B^{\mathcal{I}}$. In this situation, one should not assume that $c = d$ since this would possibly impose too many constraints on the individuals newly introduced to satisfy the existential restrictions on b. Thus:

- *For any existential restriction the algorithm introduces a new individual as role filler, and this individual must satisfy the constraints expressed by the restriction.*

Since b must also satisfy the value restriction $\forall R.(\neg A \sqcup \neg B)$, and c, d were introduced as R-fillers of b, we obtain the additional constraints $c \in (\neg A \sqcup \neg B)^{\mathcal{I}}$ and $d \in (\neg A \sqcup \neg B)^{\mathcal{I}}$. Thus:

- *The algorithm uses value restrictions in interaction with already defined role relationships to impose new constraints on individuals.*

Now $c \in (\neg A \sqcup \neg B)^{\mathcal{I}}$ means that $c \in (\neg A)^{\mathcal{I}}$ or $c \in (\neg B)^{\mathcal{I}}$, and we must choose one of these possibilities. If we assume $c \in (\neg A)^{\mathcal{I}}$, this clashes with the other constraint $c \in A^{\mathcal{I}}$, which means that this search path leads to an obvious contradiction. Thus we must choose $c \in (\neg B)^{\mathcal{I}}$. Analogously, we must choose $d \in (\neg A)^{\mathcal{I}}$ in order to satisfy the constraint $d \in (\neg A \sqcup \neg B)^{\mathcal{I}}$ without creating a contradiction to $d \in B^{\mathcal{I}}$. Thus:

- *For disjunctive constraints, the algorithm tries both possibilities in successive attempts. It must backtrack if it reaches an obvious contradiction, i.e., if the same individual must satisfy constraints that are obviously conflicting.*

In the example, we have now satisfied all the constraints without encountering an obvious contradiction. This shows that C_0 is satisfiable, and thus $(\exists R.A) \sqcap (\exists R.B)$ is not subsumed by $\exists R.(A \sqcap B)$. The algorithm has generated an interpretation $\mathcal{I}$ as witness for this fact: $\Delta^{\mathcal{I}} = \{b, c, d\}$; $R^{\mathcal{I}} = \{(b, c), (b, d)\}$; $A^{\mathcal{I}} = \{c\}$ and $B^{\mathcal{I}} = \{d\}$. For this interpretation, $b \in C_0^{\mathcal{I}}$. This means that $b \in ((\exists R.A) \sqcap (\exists R.B))^{\mathcal{I}}$, but $b \notin (\exists R.(A \sqcap B))^{\mathcal{I}}$.

In our second example, we add a number restriction to the first concept of the above example, i.e., we now want to know whether $(\exists R.A) \sqcap (\exists R.B) \sqcap$

$\leqslant 1\,R$ is subsumed by $\exists R.(A \sqcap B)$. Intuitively, the answer should now be "yes" since $\leqslant 1\,R$ in the first concept ensures that the R-filler in A coincides with the R-filler in B, and thus there is an R-filler in $A \sqcap B$. The tableau-based satisfiability algorithm first proceeds as above, with the only difference that there is the additional constraint $b \in (\leqslant 1\,R)^{\mathcal{I}}$. In order to satisfy this constraint, the two R-fillers c, d of b must be identified with each other. Thus:

- *If an at-most number restriction is violated then the algorithm must identify different role fillers.*

In the example, the individual $c = d$ must belong to both $A^{\mathcal{I}}$ and $B^{\mathcal{I}}$, which together with $c = d \in (\neg A \sqcup \neg B)^{\mathcal{I}}$ always leads to a clash. Thus, the search for a counterexample to the subsumption relationship fails, and the algorithm concludes that $(\exists R.A) \sqcap (\exists R.B) \sqcap \leqslant 1\,R \sqsubseteq \exists R.(A \sqcap B)$.

2.3.2.1 A tableau-based satisfiability algorithm for $\mathcal{ALCN}$

Before we can describe the algorithm more formally, we need to introduce an appropriate data structure in which to represent constraints like "a belongs to (the interpretation of) C" and "b is an R-filler of a". The original paper by Schmidt-Schauß and Smolka [1991], and also many other papers on tableau algorithms for Description Logics, introduce the new notion of a constraint system for this purpose. However, if we look at the types of constraints that must be expressed, we see that they can actually be represented by ABox assertions. As we have seen in the second example above, the presence of at-most number restrictions may lead to the identification of different individual names. For this reason, we will not impose the unique name assumption on the ABoxes considered by the algorithm. Instead, we allow explicit *inequality assertions* of the form $x \not\doteq y$ for individual names x, y, with the obvious semantics that an interpretation $\mathcal{I}$ satisfies $x \not\doteq y$ iff $x^{\mathcal{I}} \neq y^{\mathcal{I}}$. These assertions are assumed to be symmetric, i.e., saying that $x \not\doteq y$ belongs to an ABox $\mathcal{A}$ is the same as saying that $y \not\doteq x$ belongs to $\mathcal{A}$.

Let C_0 by an $\mathcal{ALCN}$-concept in negation normal form. In order to test satisfiability of C_0, the algorithm starts with the ABox $\mathcal{A}_0 = \{C_0(x_0)\}$, and applies consistency-preserving transformation rules (see Figure 2.6) to the ABox until no more rules apply. If the "complete" ABox obtained this way does not contain an obvious contradiction (called clash), then $\mathcal{A}_0$ is consistent (and thus C_0 is satisfiable), and inconsistent (unsatisfiable) otherwise. The transformation rules that handle disjunction and at-most restrictions are *non-deterministic* in the sense that a given ABox is transformed into finitely many new ABoxes such that the original ABox is consistent iff *one*

The $\rightarrow_{\sqcap}$-rule
Condition $\mathcal{A}$ contains $(C_1 \sqcap C_2)(x)$, but it does not contain both $C_1(x)$ and $C_2(x)$.
Action $\mathcal{A}' = \mathcal{A} \cup \{C_1(x), C_2(x)\}$.

The $\rightarrow_{\sqcup}$-rule
Condition $\mathcal{A}$ contains $(C_1 \sqcup C_2)(x)$, but neither $C_1(x)$ nor $C_2(x)$.
Action $\mathcal{A}' = \mathcal{A} \cup \{C_1(x)\}$, $\mathcal{A}'' = \mathcal{A} \cup \{C_2(x)\}$.

The $\rightarrow_{\exists}$-rule
Condition $\mathcal{A}$ contains $(\exists R.C)(x)$, but there is no individual name z such that $C(z)$
          and $R(x, z)$ are in $\mathcal{A}$.
Action $\mathcal{A}' = \mathcal{A} \cup \{C(y), R(x, y)\}$ where y is an individual name not occurring in $\mathcal{A}$.

The $\rightarrow_{\forall}$-rule
Condition $\mathcal{A}$ contains $(\forall R.C)(x)$ and $R(x, y)$, but it does not contain $C(y)$.
Action $\mathcal{A}' = \mathcal{A} \cup \{C(y)\}$.

The $\rightarrow_{\geq}$-rule
Condition $\mathcal{A}$ contains $(\geq n\, R)(x)$, and there are no individual names $z_1, \ldots, z_n$ such
          that $R(x, z_i)$ $(1 \leq i \leq n)$ and $z_i \neq z_j$ $(1 \leq i < j \leq n)$ are contained in $\mathcal{A}$.
Action $\mathcal{A}' = \mathcal{A} \cup \{R(x, y_i) \mid 1 \leq i \leq n\} \cup \{y_i \neq y_j \mid 1 \leq i < j \leq n\}$, where $y_1, \ldots, y_n$
          are distinct individual names not occurring in $\mathcal{A}$.

The $\rightarrow_{\leq}$-rule
Condition $\mathcal{A}$ contains distinct individual names $y_1, \ldots, y_{n+1}$ such that $(\leq n\, R)(x)$
          and $R(x, y_1), \ldots, R(x, y_{n+1})$ are in $\mathcal{A}$, and $y_i \neq y_j$ is not in $\mathcal{A}$ for some $i \neq j$.
Action   For each pair y_i, y_j such that $i > j$ and $y_i \neq y_j$ is not in $\mathcal{A}$, the ABox
          $\mathcal{A}_{i,j} = [y_i/y_j]\mathcal{A}$ is obtained from $\mathcal{A}$ by replacing each occurrence of y_i by y_j.

Fig. 2.6. Transformation rules of the satisfiability algorithm.

of the new ABoxes is so. For this reason we will consider finite sets of ABoxes $\mathcal{S} = \{\mathcal{A}_1, \ldots, \mathcal{A}_k\}$ instead of single ABoxes. Such a set is *consistent* iff there is some i, $1 \leq i \leq k$, such that $\mathcal{A}_i$ is consistent. A rule of Figure 2.6 is applied to a given finite set of ABoxes $\mathcal{S}$ as follows: it takes an element $\mathcal{A}$ of $\mathcal{S}$, and replaces it by one ABox $\mathcal{A}'$, by two ABoxes $\mathcal{A}'$ and $\mathcal{A}''$, or by finitely many ABoxes $\mathcal{A}_{i,j}$.

The following lemma is an easy consequence of the definition of the transformation rules:

Lemma 2.21 (Soundness) *Assume that $\mathcal{S}'$ is obtained from the finite set of ABoxes $\mathcal{S}$ by application of a transformation rule. Then $\mathcal{S}$ is consistent iff $\mathcal{S}'$ is consistent.*

The second important property of the set of transformation rules is that the transformation process always terminates:

Lemma 2.22 (Termination) *Let C_0 be an $\mathcal{ALCN}$-concept description in negation normal form. There cannot be an infinite sequence of rule* *applications*

$$\{\{C_0(x_0)\}\} \rightarrow \mathcal{S}_1 \rightarrow \mathcal{S}_2 \rightarrow \cdots.$$

The main reasons for this lemma to hold are the following.[6]

Lemma 2.23 *Let $\mathcal{A}$ be an ABox contained in $\mathcal{S}_i$ for some $i \geq 1$.*

- *For every individual $x \neq x_0$ occurring in $\mathcal{A}$, there is a unique sequence $R_1, \ldots, R_l$ $(l \geq 1)$ of role names and a unique sequence $x_1, \ldots, x_{l-1}$ of individual names such that $\{R_1(x_0, x_1), R_2(x_1, x_2), \ldots, R_l(x_{l-1}, x)\} \subseteq \mathcal{A}$. In this case, we say that x occurs on level l in $\mathcal{A}$.*
- *If $C(x) \in \mathcal{A}$ for an individual name x on level l, then the maximal role depth of C (i.e., the maximal nesting of constructors involving roles) is bounded by the maximal role depth of C_0 minus l. Consequently, the level of any individual in $\mathcal{A}$ is bounded by the maximal role depth of C_0.*
- *If $C(x) \in \mathcal{A}$, then C is a subdescription of C_0. Consequently, the number of different concept assertions on x is bounded by the size of C_0.*
- *The number of different role successors of x in $\mathcal{A}$ (i.e., individuals y such that $R(x, y) \in \mathcal{A}$ for a role name R) is bounded by the sum of the numbers occurring in at-least restrictions in C_0 plus the number of different existential restrictions in C_0.*

Starting with $\{\{C_0(x_0)\}\}$, we thus obtain after a finite number of rule applications a set of ABoxes $\widehat{\mathcal{S}}$ to which no more rules apply. An ABox $\mathcal{A}$ is called *complete* iff none of the transformation rules applies to it. Consistency of a set of complete ABoxes can be decided by looking for obvious contradictions, called clashes. The ABox $\mathcal{A}$ contains a *clash* iff one of the following three situations occurs:

1. $\{\bot(x)\} \subseteq \mathcal{A}$ for some individual name x;
2. $\{A(x), \neg A(x)\} \subseteq \mathcal{A}$ for some individual name x and some concept name A;
3. $\{(\leqslant n\, R)(x)\} \cup \{R(x, y_i) \mid 1 \leq i \leq n+1\} \cup \{y_i \neq y_j \mid 1 \leq i < j \leq n+1\} \subseteq \mathcal{A}$ for individual names $x, y_1, \ldots, y_{n+1}$, a nonnegative integer n, and a role name R.

Obviously, an ABox that contains a clash cannot be consistent. Hence, if all the ABoxes in $\widehat{\mathcal{S}}$ contain a clash, then $\widehat{\mathcal{S}}$ is inconsistent, and thus by the soundness lemma $\{C_0(x_0)\}$ is inconsistent as well. Consequently, C_0 is unsatisfiable. If, however, one of the complete ABoxes in $\widehat{\mathcal{S}}$ is clash-free,

---

[6] A detailed proof of termination for a set of rules extending the one of Figure 2.6 can be found in [Baader and Sattler, 1999]. A termination proof for a slightly different set of rules has been given in [Donini *et al.*, 1997a].

then $\widehat{S}$ is consistent. By soundness of the rules, this implies consistency of $\{C_0(x_0)\}$, and thus satisfiability of C_0.

Lemma 2.24 (Completeness) *Any complete and clash-free ABox $\mathcal{A}$ has a model.*

This lemma can be proved by defining the *canonical interpretation $\mathcal{I}_\mathcal{A}$* induced by $\mathcal{A}$:

1. the domain $\Delta^{\mathcal{I}_\mathcal{A}}$ of $\mathcal{I}_\mathcal{A}$ consists of all the individual names occurring in $\mathcal{A}$;
2. for all atomic concepts A we define $A^{\mathcal{I}_\mathcal{A}} = \{x \mid A(x) \in \mathcal{A}\}$;
3. for all atomic roles R we define $R^{\mathcal{I}_\mathcal{A}} = \{(x,y) \mid R(x,y) \in \mathcal{A}\}$.

By definition, $\mathcal{I}_\mathcal{A}$ satisfies all the role assertions in $\mathcal{A}$. By induction on the structure of concept descriptions, it is easy to show that it satisfies the concept assertions as well. The inequality assertions are satisfied since $x \not\doteq y \in \mathcal{A}$ only if x, y are different individual names.

The facts stated in Lemma 2.23 imply that the canonical interpretation has the shape of a finite tree whose depth is linearly bounded by the size of C_0 and whose branching factor is bounded by the sum of the numbers occurring in at-least restrictions in C_0 plus the number of different existential restrictions in C_0. Consequently, $\mathcal{ALCN}$ has the *finite tree model property*, i.e., any satisfiable concept C_0 is satisfiable in a finite interpretation $\mathcal{I}$ that has the shape of a tree whose root belongs to C_0.

To sum up, we have seen that the transformation rules of Figure 2.6 reduce satisfiability of an $\mathcal{ALCN}$-concept C_0 (in negation normal form) to consistency of a finite set $\widehat{S}$ of complete ABoxes. In addition, consistency of $\widehat{S}$ can be decided by looking for obvious contradictions (clashes).

Theorem 2.25 *It is decidable whether or not an $\mathcal{ALCN}$-concept is satisfiable.*

2.3.2.2 Complexity issues

The tableau-based satisfiability algorithm for $\mathcal{ALCN}$ presented above may need exponential time and space. In fact, the size of the canonical interpretation built by the algorithm may be exponential in the size of the concept description. For example, consider the descriptions C_n $(n \geq 1)$, which are inductively defined as follows:

$$\begin{aligned} C_1 &= \exists R.A \sqcap \exists R.B \\ C_{n+1} &= \exists R.A \sqcap \exists R.B \sqcap \forall R.C_n. \end{aligned}$$

Obviously, the size of C_n grows linearly in n. However, given the input description C_n, the satisfiability algorithm introduced above generates a complete and clash-free ABox whose canonical model is the full binary tree of depth n, and thus consists of $2^{n+1} - 1$ individuals.

Nevertheless, the satisfiability algorithm can be modified such that it needs only polynomial space. The main reason is that different branches of the tree model to be generated by the algorithm can be investigated separately. Since the complexity class NPSPACE coincides with PSPACE [Savitch, 1970], it is sufficient to describe a non-deterministic algorithm using only polynomial space, i.e., for every non-deterministic rule we may simply assume that the algorithm chooses the correct alternative. In principle, the modified algorithm works as follows: it starts with $\{C_0(x_0)\}$ and:

1. applies the $\to_\sqcap$- and $\to_\sqcup$-rules as long as possible, and checks for clashes of the form $A(x_0)$, $\neg A(x_0)$ and $\bot(x_0)$;
2. generates all the necessary direct successors of x_0 using the $\to_\exists$- and the $\to_{\geq}$- rule;
3. generates the necessary identifications of these direct successors using the $\to_{\leq}$- rule, and checks for clashes caused by at-most restrictions;
4. successively handles the successors in the same way.

Since after identification the remaining successors can be treated separately, the algorithm needs to store only one path of the tree model to be generated, together with the *direct* successors of the individuals on this path and the information which of these successors must be investigated next. We already know that the length of the path is linear in the size of the input description C_0. Thus, the only remaining obstacle on our way to a PSPACE-algorithm is the fact that the number of direct successors of an individual on the path also depends on the numbers in the at-least restrictions. If we assumed these numbers to be written in base 1 representation (where the size of the representation coincides with the number represented), this would not be a problem. However, for bases larger than 1 (e.g., numbers in decimal notation), the number represented may be exponential in the size of the representation. For example, the representation of $10^n - 1$ requires only n digits in base 10 representation. Thus, we cannot introduce all the successors required by at-least restrictions while only using polynomial space in the size of the concept description if the numbers in this description are written in decimal notation.

It turns out, however, that most of the successors required by the at-least restrictions need not be introduced at all. If an individual x obtains at least one R-successor due to the application of the $\to_\exists$-rule, then the $\to_{\geq}$-rule need not be applied to x for the role R. Otherwise, we simply introduce *one* R-successor as representative. In order to detect inconsistencies due to conflicting number restrictions, we need to add a *new type of clash*: $\{(\leqslant n\, R)(x), (\geqslant m\, R)(x)\} \subseteq \mathcal{A}$ for nonnegative integers $n < m$. The canonical interpretation obtained by this modified algorithm need not satisfy the at-least restrictions in C_0. However, it can easily be modified to an interpretation that does, by duplicating R-successors (more precisely, the whole subtrees starting at these successors).

Theorem 2.26 *Satisfiability of $\mathcal{ALCN}$-concept descriptions is* PSPACE-*complete.*

The above argument shows that the problem is in PSPACE. The hardness result follows from the fact that the satisfiability problem is already PSPACE-hard for the sublanguage $\mathcal{ALC}$, which can be shown by a reduction from validity of Quantified Boolean Formulae [Schmidt-Schauß and Smolka, 1991]. Since subsumption and satisfiability of $\mathcal{ALCN}$-concept descriptions can be reduced to each other in linear time, this also shows that subsumption of $\mathcal{ALCN}$-concept descriptions is PSPACE-complete.

2.3.2.3 Extension to the consistency problem for ABoxes

The tableau-based satisfiability algorithm described in Subsection 2.3.2.1 can easily be extended to an algorithm that decides consistency of $\mathcal{ALCN}$-ABoxes. Let $\mathcal{A}$ be an $\mathcal{ALCN}$-ABox such that (w.l.o.g.) all concept descriptions in $\mathcal{A}$ are in negation normal form. To test $\mathcal{A}$ for consistency, we first add inequality assertions $a \neq b$ for every pair of distinct individual names a, b occurring in $\mathcal{A}$.[7] Let $\mathcal{A}_0$ be the ABox obtained this way. The consistency algorithm applies the rules of Figure 2.6 to the singleton set $\{\mathcal{A}_0\}$.

Soundness and completeness of the rule set can be shown as before. Unfortunately, the algorithm need not terminate, unless one imposes a specific strategy on the order of rule applications. For example, consider the ABox

$$\mathcal{A}_0 = \{R(a,a),\, (\exists R.A)(a),\, (\leqslant 1\, R)(a),\, (\forall R.\exists R.A)(a)\}.$$

By applying the $\rightarrow_\exists$-rule to a, we can introduce a new R-successor x of a:

$$\mathcal{A}_1 = \mathcal{A}_0 \cup \{R(a,x),\, A(x)\}.$$

The $\rightarrow_\forall$-rule adds the assertion $(\exists R.A)(x)$, which triggers an application of the $\rightarrow_\exists$-rule to x. Thus, we obtain the new ABox

$$\mathcal{A}_2 = \mathcal{A}_1 \cup \{(\exists R.A)(x),\, R(x,y),\, A(y)\}.$$

---

[7] This takes care of the UNA.

Since a has two R-successors in $\mathcal{A}_2$, the $\rightarrow_\leq$-rule is applicable to a. By replacing every occurrence of x by a, we obtain the ABox

$$\mathcal{A}_3 = \mathcal{A}_0 \cup \{A(a),\ R(a,y),\ A(y)\}.$$

Except for the individual names (and the assertion $A(a)$, which is, however, irrelevant), $\mathcal{A}_3$ is identical to $\mathcal{A}_1$. For this reason, we can continue as above to obtain an infinite chain of rule applications.

We can easily regain termination by requiring that generating rules (i.e., the rules $\rightarrow_\exists$ and $\rightarrow_\geq$) may only be applied if none of the other rules is applicable. In the above example, this strategy would prevent the application of the $\rightarrow_\exists$-rule to x in the ABox $\mathcal{A}_1 \cup \{(\exists R.A)(x)\}$ since the $\rightarrow_\leq$-rule is also applicable. After applying the $\rightarrow_\leq$-rule (which replaces x by a), the $\rightarrow_\exists$-rule is no longer applicable since a already has an R-successor that belongs to A.

Using a similar idea, one can reduce the consistency problem for $\mathcal{ALCN}$-ABoxes to satisfiability of $\mathcal{ALCN}$-concept descriptions [Hollunder, 1996]. In principle, this reduction works as follows. In a preprocessing step, one applies the transformation rules only to old individuals (i.e., individuals present in the original ABox). Subsequently, one can forget about the role assertions, i.e., for each individual name in the preprocessed ABox, the satisfiability algorithm is applied to the conjunction of its concept assertions (see [Hollunder, 1996] for details).

Theorem 2.27 *Consistency of $\mathcal{ALCN}$-ABoxes is* PSPACE-*complete.*

2.3.2.4 Extension to general inclusion axioms

In the above subsections, we have considered the satisfiability problem for concept descriptions and the consistency problem for ABoxes without an underlying TBox. In fact, for acyclic TBoxes one can simply expand the definitions (see Subsection 2.2.4). Expansion is, however, no longer possible if one allows general inclusion axioms of the form $C \sqsubseteq D$, where C and D may be complex descriptions. Instead of considering finitely many such axioms $C_1 \sqsubseteq D_1, \ldots, C_n \sqsubseteq D_n$, it is sufficient to consider the single axiom $\top \sqsubseteq \widehat{C}$, where

$$\widehat{C} = (\neg C_1 \sqcup D_1) \sqcap \cdots \sqcap (\neg C_n \sqcup D_n).$$

The axiom $\top \sqsubseteq \widehat{C}$ simply says that any individual must belong to the concept $\widehat{C}$. The tableau algorithm introduced above can easily be modified such that it takes this axiom into account: all individuals (both the original individuals and the ones newly generated by the $\rightarrow_\exists$-rule and the $\rightarrow_\geq$-

rule) are simply asserted to belong to $\widehat{C}$. However, this modification may obviously lead to nontermination of the algorithm. For example, consider what happens if this algorithm is applied to test consistency of the ABox $\mathcal{A}_0 = \{A(x_0), (\exists R.A)(x_0)\}$ w.r.t. the axiom $\top \sqsubseteq \exists R.A$: the algorithm generates an infinite sequence of ABoxes $\mathcal{A}_1, \mathcal{A}_2, \ldots$ and individuals $x_1, x_2, \ldots$ such that $\mathcal{A}_{i+1} = \mathcal{A}_i \cup \{R(x_i, x_{i+1}), A(x_{i+1}), (\exists R.A)(x_{i+1})\}$. Since all individuals x_i receive the same concept assertions as x_0, we may say that the algorithms has run into a cycle.

Termination can be regained by trying to detect such cyclic computations, and then blocking the application of generating rules: the application of the rules $\rightarrow_\exists$ and $\rightarrow_\geq$ to an individual x is *blocked* by an individual y in an ABox $\mathcal{A}$ iff $\{D \mid D(x) \in \mathcal{A}\} \subseteq \{D' \mid D'(y) \in \mathcal{A}\}$. The main idea underlying blocking is that the blocked individual x can use the role successors of y instead of generating new ones. For example, instead of generating a new R-successor for x_1 in the above example, one can simply use the R-successor of x_0. This yields an interpretation $\mathcal{I}$ with $\Delta^\mathcal{I} = \{x_0, x_1\}$, $A^\mathcal{I} = \Delta^\mathcal{I}$, and $R^\mathcal{I} = \{(x_0, x_1), (x_1, x_1)\}$. Obviously, $\mathcal{I}$ is a model of $\mathcal{A}_0$ and of the axiom $\top \sqsubseteq \exists R.A$.

To avoid cyclic blocking (of x by y and vice versa), we consider an enumeration of all individual names, and define that an individual x may only be blocked by individuals y that occur before x in this enumeration. This, together with some other technical assumptions, makes sure that an algorithm using this notion of blocking is sound and complete as well as terminating (see [Buchheit *et al.*, 1993a; Baader *et al.*, 1996] for details). Thus, consistency of $\mathcal{ALCN}$-ABoxes w.r.t. general inclusion axioms is decidable. It should be noted that the algorithm is no longer in PSPACE since it may generate role paths of exponential length before blocking occurs. In fact, even for the language $\mathcal{ALC}$, satisfiability w.r.t. a single general inclusion axiom is known to be EXPTIME-hard [Schild, 1994] (see also Chapter 3). The tableau-based algorithm sketched above is a NEXPTIME algorithm. However, using the translation technique mentioned at the beginning of this section, it can be shown [De Giacomo, 1995] that $\mathcal{ALCN}$-ABoxes and general inclusion axioms can be translated into PDL, for which satisfiability can be decided in exponential time. An EXPTIME tableau algorithm for $\mathcal{ALC}$ with general inclusion axioms was described by Donini and Massacci [2000].

Theorem 2.28 *Consistency of $\mathcal{ALCN}$-ABoxes w.r.t. general inclusion axioms is* EXPTIME-*complete.*

2.3.2.5 Extension to other language constructors

The tableau-based approach to designing concept satisfiability and ABox consistency algorithms can also be employed for languages with other concept and/or role constructors. In principle, each new constructor requires a new rule, and this rule can usually be obtained by simply considering the semantics of the constructor. Soundness of such a rule is often very easy to show. More problematic are completeness and termination since they must also take interactions between different rules into account. As we have seen above, termination can sometimes only be obtained if the application of rules is restricted by an appropriate strategy. Of course, one may only impose such a strategy if one can show that it does not destroy completeness.

2.3.3 Reasoning w.r.t. terminologies

Recall that terminologies (TBoxes) are sets of concept definitions (i.e., equalities of the form $A \equiv C$ where A is atomic) such that every atomic concept occurs at most once as a left-hand side. We will first comment briefly on the complexity of reasoning w.r.t. acyclic terminologies, and then consider in more detail reasoning w.r.t. cyclic terminologies.

2.3.3.1 Acyclic terminologies

As shown in Subsection 2.2.4, reasoning w.r.t. *acyclic* terminologies can be reduced to reasoning without terminologies by first expanding the TBox, and then replacing name symbols by their definitions in the terminology. Unfortunately, since the expanded TBox may be exponentially larger than the original one [Nebel, 1990b], this increases the complexity of reasoning. Nebel [1990b] also shows that this complexity can, in general, not be avoided: for the language $\mathcal{FL}_0$, subsumption between concept descriptions can be tested in polynomial time (see Subsection 2.3.1), whereas subsumption w.r.t. acyclic terminologies is coNP-complete (see also Subsection 2.3.3.2 below).

For more expressive languages, the presence of acyclic TBoxes may or may not increase the complexity of the subsumption problem. For example, subsumption of concept descriptions in the language $\mathcal{ALC}$ is PSPACE-complete, and so is subsumption w.r.t. acyclic terminologies [Lutz, 1999a]. Of course, in order to obtain a PSPACE-algorithm for subsumption in $\mathcal{ALC}$ w.r.t. acyclic TBoxes, one cannot first expand the TBox completely since this might need exponential space. The main idea is that one uses a tableau-based algorithm like the one described in Subsection 2.3.2, with the difference that it receives concept descriptions containing name symbols as input. Expansion is then done on demand: if the tableau-based algorithm encounters an assertion of the form $A(x)$, where A is a name occurring on the left-hand side of a definition $A \equiv C$ in the TBox, then it adds the assertion $C(x)$. However, it does not further expand C at this stage. It is not hard to show that this really yields a PSPACE-algorithm for satisfiability (and thus also for subsumption) of concepts w.r.t. acyclic TBoxes in $\mathcal{ALC}$ [Lutz, 1999a].

There are, however, extensions of $\mathcal{ALC}$ for which this technique no longer works. One such example is the language $\mathcal{ALCF}$, which extends $\mathcal{ALC}$ by functional roles as well as agreements and disagreements on chains of functional roles (see Section 2.4 below). Satisfiability of concepts is PSPACE-complete for this language [Hollunder and Nutt, 1990], but satisfiability of concepts w.r.t. acyclic terminologies is NEXPTIME-complete [Lutz, 1999a].

2.3.3.2 Cyclic terminologies

For cyclic terminologies, expansion is no longer possible since it would not terminate. If we use descriptive semantics, then cyclic terminologies are a special case of terminologies with general inclusion axioms. Thus, the tableau-based algorithm for handling general inclusion axioms introduced in Subsection 2.3.2.4 can also be used for cyclic $\mathcal{ALCN}$-TBoxes with descriptive semantics. For cyclic $\mathcal{ALC}$-TBoxes with fixpoint semantics, the connection between Description Logics and propositional modal logics turns out to be useful. In fact, syntactically monotone $\mathcal{ALC}$-TBoxes with least or greatest fixpoint semantics can be expressed within the propositional μ-calculus, which is an extension of the propositional multi-modal logic $\mathbf{K_m}$ by fixpoint operators (see [Schild, 1994; De Giacomo and Lenzerini, 1994b; 1997] and Chapter 5 for details). Since reasoning w.r.t. general inclusion axioms in $\mathcal{ALC}$ and reasoning in the propositional μ-calculus are both EXP-TIME-complete, these reductions yield an EXPTIME upper bound for reasoning w.r.t. cyclic terminologies in sublanguages of $\mathcal{ALC}$.

For less expressive Description Logics, more efficient algorithms can, however, be obtained with the help of techniques based on finite automata. Following [Baader, 1996b], we will sketch these techniques for the small language $\mathcal{FL}_0$. The results can, however, be extended to the language $\mathcal{ALN}$ [Küsters, 1998]. We will develop the results for $\mathcal{FL}_0$ in two steps, starting with an alternative characterization of subsumption between $\mathcal{FL}_0$-concept descriptions, and then extending this characterization to cyclic TBoxes with greatest fixpoint semantics. Baader [1996b] also considers cyclic $\mathcal{FL}_0$-TBoxes with descriptive and with least fixpoint semantics. For these semantics, the characterization of subsumption is more involved; in particular, the characterization of subsumption w.r.t. descriptive semantics depends on finite automata working on infinite words, so-called Büchi automata. Acyclic TBoxes can be seen as a special case of cyclic TBoxes, where all three types of semantics coincide.

In Subsection 2.3.1, the equivalence $(\forall R.C) \sqcap (\forall R.D) \equiv \forall R.(C \sqcap D)$ was used as a rewrite rule from left to right in order to compute the *structural subsumption normal form* of $\mathcal{FL}_0$-concept descriptions. If we use this rule in the opposite direction, we obtain a different normal form, which we call *concept-centered normal form* since it groups the concept description w.r.t. concept names (and not w.r.t. role names, as the structural subsumption normal form does). Using this rule, any $\mathcal{FL}_0$-concept description can be transformed into an equivalent description that is a conjunction of descriptions of the form $\forall R_1. \cdots \forall R_m.A$ for $m \geq 0$ (not necessarily distinct) role names $R_1, \ldots, R_m$ and a concept name A. We abbreviate $\forall R_1. \cdots \forall R_m.A$ by $\forall R_1 \cdots R_m.A$, where $R_1 \cdots R_m$ is viewed as a word over the alphabet Σ of all role names. In addition, instead of $\forall w_1.A \sqcap \cdots \sqcap \forall w_l.A$ we write $\forall L.A$ where $L = \{w_1, \ldots, w_l\}$ is a finite set of words over Σ. The term $\forall \emptyset.A$ is considered to be equivalent to the top concept $\top$, which means that it can be added to a conjunction without changing the meaning of the concept. Using these abbreviations, any pair of $\mathcal{FL}_0$-concept descriptions C, D containing the concept names $A_1, \ldots, A_k$ can be rewritten as

$$C \equiv \forall U_1.A_1 \sqcap \cdots \sqcap \forall U_k.A_k \quad \text{and} \quad D \equiv \forall V_1.A_1 \sqcap \cdots \sqcap \forall V_k.A_k,$$

where U_i, V_i are finite sets of words over the alphabet of all role names. This normal form provides us with the following *characterization of subsumption* of $\mathcal{FL}_0$-concept descriptions [Baader and Narendran, 1998]:

$$C \sqsubseteq D \quad \text{iff} \quad U_i \supseteq V_i \text{ for all } i, \ 1 \leq i \leq k.$$

Since the size of the concept-based normal forms is polynomial in the size of the original descriptions, and since the inclusion tests $U_i \supseteq V_i$ can also be realized in polynomial time, this yields a polynomial-time decision procedure for subsumption in $\mathcal{FL}_0$. In fact, as shown in [Baader et al., 1998a], the structural subsumption algorithm for $\mathcal{FL}_0$ can be seen as a special implementation of these inclusion tests.

This characterization of subsumption via inclusion of finite sets of words can be extended to cyclic TBoxes with greatest fixpoint semantics as follows. A given TBox $\mathcal{T}$ can be translated into a finite automaton[8] $\mathcal{A}_\mathcal{T}$ whose states are the concept names occurring in $\mathcal{T}$ and whose transitions are induced by

---

[8] Strictly speaking, we obtain a finite automaton with word transitions, i.e., transitions that may be labeled by a word over Σ rather than a letter of Σ.

$$A \equiv \forall R.A \sqcap \forall S.C$$
$$B \equiv \forall R.\forall S.C$$
$$C \equiv P \sqcap \forall S.C$$

Fig. 2.7. A TBox and the corresponding automaton.

the value restrictions occurring in $\mathcal{T}$ (see Figure 2.7 for an example and [Baader, 1996b] for the formal definition).

For a name symbol A and a base symbol P in $\mathcal{T}$, the language $L_{\mathcal{A}_{\mathcal{T}}}(A, P)$ is the set of all words labeling paths in $\mathcal{A}_{\mathcal{T}}$ from A to P. The languages $L_{\mathcal{A}_{\mathcal{T}}}(A, P)$ represent all the value restrictions that must be satisfied by instances of the concept A. With this intuition in mind, the following *characterization of subsumption w.r.t. cyclic $\mathcal{FL}_0$-TBoxes with greatest fixpoint semantics* should not be surprising:

$$A \sqsubseteq_{\mathcal{T}} B \quad \text{iff} \quad L_{\mathcal{A}_{\mathcal{T}}}(A, P) \supseteq L_{\mathcal{A}_{\mathcal{T}}}(B, P) \quad \text{for all base symbols } P.$$

In the example of Fig. 2.7, we have $L_{\mathcal{A}_{\mathcal{T}}}(A, P) = R^*SS^* \supset RSS^* = L_{\mathcal{A}_{\mathcal{T}}}(B, P)$, and thus $A \sqsubseteq_{\mathcal{T}} B$, but not $B \sqsubseteq_{\mathcal{T}} A$.

Obviously, the languages $L_{\mathcal{A}_{\mathcal{T}}}(A, P)$ are regular, and any regular language can be obtained as such a language. Since inclusion of regular languages is a PSPACE-complete problem [Garey and Johnson, 1979], this shows that subsumption w.r.t. cyclic $\mathcal{FL}_0$-TBoxes with greatest fixpoint semantics is PSPACE-complete [Baader, 1996b]. For an acyclic terminology $\mathcal{T}$, the automaton $\mathcal{A}_{\mathcal{T}}$ is acyclic as well. Since inclusion of languages accepted by acyclic finite automata is coNP-complete, this proves Nebel's result that subsumption w.r.t. acyclic $\mathcal{FL}_0$-TBoxes is coNP-complete [Nebel, 1990b].

2.4 Language extensions

In Section 2.2 we have introduced the language $\mathcal{ALCN}$ as a prototypical Description Logic. For many applications, the expressive power of $\mathcal{ALCN}$ is not sufficient. For this reason, various other language constructors have been introduced in the literature and are employed by systems. Roughly, these language extensions can be put into two categories, which (for lack of a better name) we will call "classical" and "nonclassical" extensions. Intuitively, a classical extension is one whose semantics can easily be defined within the model-theoretic framework introduced in Section 2.2, whereas defining the semantics of a nonclassical constructor is more problematic and requires an extension of the model-theoretic framework (such as the semantics of the epistemic operator **K** introduced in Subsection 2.2.5). In this section, we briefly introduce the most important classical extensions of Description Logics. Inference procedures for such expressive Description Logics are discussed in Chapter 5. Nonclassical extensions are the subject of Chapter 6.

In addition to constructors that can be used to build complex roles, we will introduce more expressive number restrictions, and constructors that allow one to express relationships between the role-filler sets of different (complex) roles.

2.4.1 Role constructors

Since roles are interpreted as binary relations, it is quite natural to employ the usual operations on binary relations (such as Boolean operators, composition, inverse, and transitive closure) as role-forming constructors. Syntax and semantics of these constructors can be defined as follows:

Definition 2.29 (Role constructors) Every role name is a role description (atomic role), and if R, S are role descriptions, then $R \sqcap S$ (intersection), $R \sqcup S$ (union), $\neg R$ (complement), $R \circ S$ (composition), R^+ (transitive closure), R^- (inverse) are also role descriptions.

A given interpretation $\mathcal{I}$ is extended to (complex) role descriptions as follows:

1. $(R \sqcap S)^{\mathcal{I}} = R^{\mathcal{I}} \cap S^{\mathcal{I}}$, $(R \sqcup S)^{\mathcal{I}} = R^{\mathcal{I}} \cup S^{\mathcal{I}}$, $(\neg R)^{\mathcal{I}} = \Delta^{\mathcal{I}} \times \Delta^{\mathcal{I}} \setminus R^{\mathcal{I}}$;
2. $(R \circ S)^{\mathcal{I}} = \{(a, c) \in \Delta^{\mathcal{I}} \times \Delta^{\mathcal{I}} \mid \exists b. \ (a, b) \in R^{\mathcal{I}} \wedge (b, c) \in S^{\mathcal{I}}\}$;
3. $(R^+)^{\mathcal{I}} = \bigcup_{i \geq 1} (R^{\mathcal{I}})^i$, i.e., $(R^+)^{\mathcal{I}}$ is the transitive closure of $(R^{\mathcal{I}})$;
4. $(R^-)^{\mathcal{I}} = \{(b, a) \in \Delta^{\mathcal{I}} \times \Delta^{\mathcal{I}} \mid (a, b) \in R^{\mathcal{I}}\}$.

For example, the union of the roles hasSon and hasDaughter can be used to define the role hasChild, and the transitive closure of hasChild expresses the role hasDescendants. The inverse of hasChild yields the role hasParent.

The complexity of satisfiability and subsumption of concepts in the language $\mathcal{ALCN}^{\sqcap}$ (also called $\mathcal{ALCNR}$ in the literature), which extends $\mathcal{ALCN}$ by intersection of roles, has been investigated in [Donini *et al.*, 1997a]. It is shown that these problems are still PSPACE-complete, provided that the numbers occurring in number restrictions are written in base 1 representation (where the size of the representation coincides with the number represented). Tobies [2001b] shows that this result also holds for non-unary coding of numbers. Decidability of the extension of $\mathcal{ALCN}$ by the three Boolean operators and the inverse operator is an immediate consequence of the fact that concepts of the extended language can be expressed in $\mathcal{C}^2$, i.e., first-order predicate logic with two variables and counting quantifiers, which is known to be decidable in NExpTime [Grädel *et al.*, 1997b; Pacholski *et al.*, 1997]. Lutz and Sattler [2000a] show that $\mathcal{ALC}$ extended by role complement is ExpTime-complete, whereas $\mathcal{ALC}$ extended by role intersection and (atomic) role complement is NExpTime-complete.

In [Baader, 1991], the Description Logic $\mathcal{ALC}_{trans}$, which extends $\mathcal{ALC}$ by transitive closure, composition, and union of roles, has been introduced, and subsumption and satisfiability of $\mathcal{ALC}_{trans}$-concepts has been shown to be decidable. Schild's observation [Schild, 1991] that $\mathcal{ALC}_{trans}$ is just a syntactic variant of Propositional Dynamic Logic (PDL) [Fischer and Ladner, 1979] yields the exact complexity of subsumption and satisfiability in $\mathcal{ALC}_{trans}$: they are ExpTime-complete [Fischer and Ladner, 1979; Pratt, 1979; 1980]. The extension of $\mathcal{ALC}_{trans}$ by the inverse constructor corresponds to converse PDL [Fischer and Ladner, 1979], which can also be shown to be decidable in deterministic exponential time [Vardi, 1985]. Whereas this extension of $\mathcal{ALC}_{trans}$ does not change the properties of the obtained Description Logic in a significant way, things become more complex if both number restrictions and the inverse of roles are added to $\mathcal{ALC}_{trans}$. Whereas $\mathcal{ALC}_{trans}$ and $\mathcal{ALC}_{trans}$ with inverse still have the finite model property, $\mathcal{ALC}_{trans}$ extended by inverse and number restrictions does not. Indeed, it is easy to see that the concept

$$\neg A \sqcap \exists R^-.A \sqcap (\leqslant 1\, R) \sqcap \forall (R^-)^+.(\exists R^-.A \sqcap (\leqslant 1\, R))$$

is satisfiable in an infinite interpretation, but not in a finite one. Nevertheless, this Description Logic still has an ExpTime-complete subsumption and satisfiability problem. In fact, in [De Giacomo, 1995], number restrictions, the inverse of roles, and Boolean operators on roles are added to $\mathcal{ALC}_{trans}$, and ExpTime-decidability is shown by a rather ingenious reduction to the decision problem for $\mathcal{ALC}_{trans}$. It should be noted, however, that in this work only atomic roles and their inverse may occur in number restrictions, and that the complement of roles is built with respect to a fixed role any, which must contain all other roles, but need not be interpreted as the universal role (i.e., $\Delta^\mathcal{I} \times \Delta^\mathcal{I}$). As we shall see below, allowing more complex roles inside number restrictions may easily cause undecidability.

2.4.2 Expressive number restrictions

There are three different ways in which the expressive power of number restrictions can be enhanced.

First, one can consider so-called *qualified number restrictions*, where the number restrictions are concerned with role fillers belonging to a certain concept. For example, given the role hasChild, the simple number restrictions introduced above can only state that the number of all children is within certain limits, such as in the concept $\geqslant 2\,\text{hasChild} \sqcap\, \leqslant 5\,\text{hasChild}$. Qualified number restrictions can also express that there are at least 2 sons and at most 5 daughters:

$$\geqslant 2\,\text{hasChild.Male} \sqcap\, \leqslant 5\,\text{hasChild.Female}.$$

Adding qualified number restrictions to $\mathcal{ALC}$ leaves the important inference problems (like subsumption and satisfiability of concepts, and consistency of ABoxes) decidable: the worst-case complexity is still PSPACE-complete. Membership in PSPACE was first shown for the case where numbers occurring in number restrictions are written in base 1 representation [Hollunder and Baader, 1991a; Hollunder, 1996]. More recently, this has been proved even for the case of binary (or, equivalently, decimal) representation of numbers [Tobies, 1999c; 2001b]. The language stays decidable if general sets of inclusion axioms are allowed [Buchheit *et al.*, 1993a].

Second, one can allow *complex role expressions inside number restrictions*. As already mentioned above, allowing the three Boolean operators and the inverse operator in number restrictions of $\mathcal{ALCN}$ leaves us within $\mathcal{C}^2$, which is known to be decidable. In [Baader and Sattler, 1996b; 1999], languages that allow composition of roles in number restrictions have been considered.[9] The extension of $\mathcal{ALC}$ by number restrictions involving composition has a decidable satisfiability and subsumption problem. On the other hand, if either number restrictions involving composition, union and inverse, or number restrictions involving composition and intersection are added, then satisfiability and subsumption become undecidable [Baader and Sattler, 1996b; 1999]. For $\mathcal{ALC}_{trans}$, the extension by number restrictions involving composition is already undecidable [Baader and Sattler, 1999].

Third, one can replace the explicit numbers n in number restrictions by variables α that stand for arbitrary nonnegative integers [Baader and Sattler, 1996a; 1999]. This allows one, for example, to define the concept of all persons having at least as many daughters as sons, without explicitly saying

---

[9] Note that composition cannot be expressed within $\mathcal{C}^2$.

how many sons and daughters the person has:

$$\text{Person} \sqcap \geqslant \alpha \text{ hasDaughter} \sqcap \leqslant \alpha \text{ hasSon}.$$

The expressive power of this language can further be increased by introducing explicit quantification of the numeric variables. For example, it is important to know whether the numeric variables are introduced before or after a value restriction. This is illustrated by the following concept

$$\text{Person} \sqcap \downarrow\alpha.(\forall\text{hasChild}.(\geqslant \alpha \text{ hasChild} \sqcap \leqslant \alpha \text{ hasChild})),$$

in which introducing the numerical variable before the universal value restriction makes sure that all the children of the person have the same number of children. Here, $\downarrow\alpha$ stands for an existential quantification of α. Universal quantification of numerical variables comes in via negation. In [Baader and Sattler, 1996a; 1999] it is shown that $\mathcal{ALCN}$ extended by such *symbolic number restrictions* with universal and existential quantification of numerical variables has an undecidable satisfiability and subsumption problem. If one restricts this language to existential quantification of numerical variables and negation on atomic concepts, then satisfiability becomes decidable, but subsumption remains undecidable.

2.4.3 Role-value-maps

Role-value-maps are a family of very expressive concept constructors, which were, however, available in the original KL-ONE system. They allow one to relate the sets of role fillers of role chains.

Definition 2.30 (Role-value-maps) A role chain is a composition $R_1 \circ \cdots \circ R_n$ of role names. If R, S are role chains, then $R \subseteq S$ and $R = S$ are concepts (role-value-maps). The former is called a *containment* role-value-map, while the latter is called an *equality* role-value-map.

A given interpretation $\mathcal{I}$ is extended to role-value-maps as follows:

1. $(R \subseteq S)^{\mathcal{I}} = \{a \in \Delta^{\mathcal{I}} \mid \forall b.\ (a,b) \in R^{\mathcal{I}} \rightarrow (a,b) \in S^{\mathcal{I}}\}$,
2. $(R = S)^{\mathcal{I}} = \{a \in \Delta^{\mathcal{I}} \mid \forall b.\ (a,b) \in R^{\mathcal{I}} \leftrightarrow (a,b) \in S^{\mathcal{I}}\}$.

For example, the concept

$$\text{Person} \sqcap (\text{hasChild} \circ \text{hasFriend} \subseteq \text{knows})$$

describes the persons knowing all the friends of their children, and

$$\text{Person} \sqcap (\text{marriedTo} \circ \text{likesToEat} = \text{likesToEat})$$

describes persons having the same favorite foods as their spouse.

Unfortunately, in the presence of role-value-maps, the subsumption problem is undecidable, even if the language allows only conjunction and value restriction as additional constructors [Schmidt-Schauß, 1989] (see also Chapter 3).

To avoid this problem, one may restrict attention to role chains of functional roles, also called *attributes* or *features* in the literature. An interpretation $\mathcal{I}$ interprets the role R as a *functional role* iff $\{(a,b),(a,c)\} \subseteq R^{\mathcal{I}}$ implies $b = c$. In the following, we assume that the set of role names is partitioned into the set of functional roles and the set of ordinary roles. Any interpretation must interpret the functional roles as such. Usually, we write functional roles with small letters f, g, possibly with index.

Definition 2.31 (Agreements) If f, g are role chains of functional roles, then $f \doteq g$ and $f \not\doteq g$ are concepts (agreement and disagreement).

A given interpretation $\mathcal{I}$ is extended to agreements and disagreements as follows:

1. $(f \doteq g)^{\mathcal{I}} = \{a \in \Delta^{\mathcal{I}} \mid \exists b.\ (a,b) \in f^{\mathcal{I}} \wedge (a,b) \in g^{\mathcal{I}}\}$,
2. $(f \not\doteq g)^{\mathcal{I}} = \{a \in \Delta^{\mathcal{I}} \mid \exists b_1, b_2.\ b_1 \neq b_2 \wedge (a,b_1) \in f^{\mathcal{I}} \wedge (a,b_2) \in g^{\mathcal{I}}\}$.

In the literature, the agreement constructor is sometimes also called the *same-as* constructor. Note that, since f, g are role chains between functional roles, there can be at most one role filler for a w.r.t. the respective role chain. Also note that the semantics of agreements and disagreements requires these role fillers to exist (and be equal or distinct) for a to belong to the concept.

For example, hasMother, hasFather, and hasLastName with their usual interpretation are functional roles, whereas hasParent and hasChild are not. The concept

$$\text{Person} \sqcap (\text{hasLastName} \doteq \text{hasMother} \circ \text{hasLastName})$$
$$\sqcap (\text{hasLastName} \not\doteq \text{hasFather} \circ \text{hasLastName})$$

describes persons whose last name coincides with the last name of their mother, but not with the last name of their father.

The restriction to functional roles makes reasoning in $\mathcal{ALC}$ extended by agreements and disagreements decidable [Hollunder and Nutt, 1990]. A structural subsumption algorithm for the language provided by the CLASSIC system, which includes the same-as constructor, can be found in [Borgida and Patel-Schneider, 1994]. However, if general inclusion axioms (or transitive closure of functional roles or cyclic definitions) are allowed, then agreements and disagreements between chains of functional roles again cause subsumption to become undecidable [Nebel, 1991; Baader *et al.*, 1993].

Additional types of role interaction constructors similar to agreements and role-value-maps are investigated in [Hanschke, 1992].

Acknowledgement

We would like to thank Maarten de Rijke for his pointers to the literature on Beth definability in modal logics.

3

Complexity of Reasoning

Francesco M. Donini

Abstract

We present lower bounds on the computational complexity of satisfiability and subsumption in several Description Logics. We interpret these lower bounds as coming from different "sources of complexity", which we isolate one by one. We consider both reasoning with simple concept expressions and reasoning with an underlying TBox. We discuss also complexity of instance checking in simple ABoxes. We have tried to enhance clarity and ease of presentation, sometimes sacrificing exhaustiveness for lack of space.

3.1 Introduction

Complexity of reasoning has been one of the major issues in the development of Description Logics. This is because such logics are conceived [Brachman and Levesque, 1984] as the formal specification of subsystems for representing knowledge, to be used in larger knowledge-based systems. Since using knowledge also means deriving implicit facts from the given ones, the implementation of derivation procedures should take into account the optimality of reasoning algorithms. The study of optimal algorithms starts from the elicitation of the computational complexity of the problem the algorithm should solve. Initially, studies about the complexity of reasoning problems in Description Logics were more focused on polynomial-time versus intractable (NP- or coNP-hard) problems. The idea was that a knowledge representation system based on a Description Logic with polynomial-time inference problems would guarantee timely answers to the rest of the system. However, once systems based on very expressive Description Logics with exponential-time reasoning problems were implemented [Horrocks, 1998b], it was recognized that knowledge bases of realistic size could be processed in reasonable time.

This shifted most of the complexity analysis to Description Logics whose reasoning problems are EXPTIME-hard, or worse.

This chapter presents some lower bounds on the complexity of basic reasoning tasks in simple Description Logics. The reasoning services taken into account are: first, satisfiability and subsumption of concept expressions alone (no TBox), then the same reasoning services considering a TBox also, and in the last part of the chapter, instance checking w.r.t. an ABox.

We show in detail some reductions from problems that are hard for complexity classes NP, CONP, PSPACE, EXPTIME, and from semidecidable problems to satisfiability/subsumption in various Description Logics. Then, we show how these reductions can be adapted to other Description Logics as well.

In several reductions, we use tableau expansions to prove the correctness of the reduction. Thus, a secondary aim in this chapter is to show how tableaux are useful not only in devising reasoning algorithms and complexity upper bounds – as seen in Chapter 2 – but also in finding complexity lower bounds. This is because tableaux untangle two different aspects of the computational complexity of reasoning in Description Logics:

- The first aspect is the structure of possible models of a concept. Such a structure is – in many Description Logics – a tree of individual names, linked by arcs labeled by roles. We consider such a tree an AND-tree, in the sense that all branches must be followed to obtain a candidate model. Following [Schmidt-Schauß and Smolka, 1991], we call each branch of such a tree a *trace*. Readers familiar with tableaux terminology should observe that traces are not tableau branches; in fact, they form a structure inside a single tableau branch.
- The second aspect is the structure of proofs or refutations. Clearly, if a trace contains an inconsistency – a *clash* in the terminology set up in Chapter 2 – the candidate models containing this trace can be discarded. When all candidate models are discarded this way, we obtain a proof of subsumption, or unsatisfiability. Hence, the structure of refutations is often best viewed as an OR-tree of traces containing clashes.

Here we have chosen to mark the nodes with AND, OR when considering a satisfiability problem; if either unsatisfiability or subsumption is considered, AND and OR labels should be exchanged. Before starting with the various results, we elaborate on this subject in the next subsection.

3.1.1 Intuition: sources of complexity

The deterministic version of the calculus for $\mathcal{ALCN}$ in Chapter 2 can be seen as exploring an AND–OR tree, where an AND-branching corresponds to the (independent) check of all successors of an individual, while an

OR-branching corresponds to the different choices of application of a non-deterministic rule.

Realizing that, one can see that the exponential-time behavior of the calculus is due to two independent origins: the AND-branching, responsible for the exponential size of a single candidate model, and the OR-branching, responsible for the exponential number of different candidate models. We call these two different combinatorial explosions *sources of complexity*.

3.1.1.1 OR-branching

The OR-branching is due to the presence of disjunctive constructors, which make a concept satisfiable by more than one model. The obvious disjunctive constructor is $\sqcup$; hence $\mathcal{ALU}$ is a good sublanguage to see this source of complexity. Recall that $\mathcal{ALU}$ allows one to form concepts using negation of concept names, conjunction $\sqcap$, disjunction $\sqcup$, universal role quantification $\forall R.C$, and unqualified existential role quantification $\exists R$. This source of complexity is the same that makes propositional satisfiability NP-hard: in fact, satisfiability in $\mathcal{ALU}$ can be trivially proved NP-hard by rewriting propositional letters as atomic concepts, $\wedge$ as $\sqcap$, and $\vee$ as $\sqcup$. Many proofs of coNP-hardness of subsumption were found by exploiting this source of complexity ([Levesque and Brachman, 1987; Nebel, 1988]), by reducing an NP-hard problem to non-subsumption. In Subsection 3.2.1, we show how disjunction can also be introduced by combining role restrictions and universal quantification, and in Subsection 3.2.2 by combining number restrictions and role intersection.

3.1.1.2 AND-branching

The AND-branching is more subtle. Its exponential behaviour is due to the interplay of qualified existential and universal quantifiers; hence $\mathcal{ALE}$ is now a minimal sublanguage of $\mathcal{ALCN}$ with these features. As mentioned in Chapter 2 one can see the effects of this source of complexity by expanding the tableau $\{D(x)\}$, when D is the following concept (whose pattern appears in many papers, from [Schmidt-Schauß and Smolka, 1991], to [Hemaspaandra, 1999]) – see Chapter 2 for its general form:

$$\exists P_1.\forall P_2.\forall P_3.C_{11} \sqcap$$
$$\exists P_1.\forall P_2.\forall P_3.C_{12} \sqcap$$
$$\forall P_1.(\exists P_2.\forall P_3.C_{21} \sqcap$$
$$\exists P_2.\forall P_3.C_{22} \sqcap$$
$$\forall P_2.(\exists P_3.C_{31} \sqcap$$
$$\exists P_3.C_{32})).$$

For each level l of nested quantifiers, we use a different role P_l (but using the same role R would produce the same results). The structure of the tableau for $\{D(x)\}$, which is the candidate model for D, is a binary tree of height 3: the nodes are the individual names, the arcs are given by the P_l-successor relation, and the branches are the traces in the tableau.

Each trace ends with an individual that belongs to C_{1i}, C_{2j}, C_{3k}, for $i, j, k \in \{1, 2\}$. Hence, a clash may be found independently in each trace, i.e., in each branch of the tree. To verify that this structure is indeed a model, one has to check every AND-branch of it; and branches can be exponentially many in the nesting of quantifiers.

This source of complexity causes an exponential number of possible *refutations* to be searched through (each refutation being a trace containing a clash).

This second source of complexity is not evident in propositional calculus, but a similar problem appears in predicate calculus – where the interplay of existential and universal quantifiers may lead to large models – and in Quantified Boolean Formulae.

Remark 3.1 For Description Logics that are not closed under negation, a source of complexity could be absent in satisfiability while it might appear in subsumption. This is because C is subsumed by D iff $C \sqcap \neg D$ is unsatisfiable, where $\neg D$ could belong to a Description Logic which is more expressive than the DL of C and D.   ∎

3.1.2 Overview of the chapter

We first present separately the effect of each source of complexity. In the next section, we discuss intractability results stemming from disjunction (OR-branching), which lead to coNP-hard lower bounds. We discuss both the case of plain logical disjunction (as the Description Logic $\mathcal{FL}$), and the case of disjunction arising from alternative identification of individuals ($\mathcal{ALEN}$). Then in Section 3.3 we present an NP lower bound stemming from AND-branching, namely a Description Logic in which concepts have one candidate model of exponential size.

A PSPACE lower bound combining the two sources of complexity is presented in Section 3.4, and then in Section 3.5 we show how axioms can combine in a succinct way the sources of complexity, leading to EXPTIME-hardness of satisfiability.

In Section 3.6 we examine one of the first undecidability results found for a Description Logic, using the powerful construct of role-value-maps – now recognized as very expressive, because of this result.

Finally, we analyze intractability arising from reasoning with individuals in ABoxes (Section 3.7), and add a final discussion (Section 3.8) about the significance of these results – beyond the initial study of theoretical complexity of reasoning – also for benchmark testing of implemented procedures.

Section 3.9, with a list of complexity results for satisfiability and subsumption, closes the chapter.

3.2 OR-branching: finding a model

When the number of candidate models is exponential in the size of the concepts involved, it is a combinatorial problem to find the right candidate model to check. In Description Logics, this may lead to NP-hardness of satisfiability, and coNP-hardness of subsumption.

3.2.1 Intractability in $\mathcal{FL}$

Brachman and Levesque [1984] (see also [Levesque and Brachman, 1987]) were the first to point out that a slight increase in the expressiveness of a Description Logic may result in a drastic change in the complexity of reasoning. They called this effect a "computational cliff" of structured knowledge representation languages. They considered the language $\mathcal{FL}$, which admits concept conjunction, universal role quantification, unqualified existential quantification, and role restriction. For readability, the syntax and semantics of $\mathcal{FL}$ are recalled in Table 3.1.

Role restriction allows one to construct a subrole of a role R, i.e., a role whose extension is a subset of the extension of R. For example, the role $\text{child}|_{\text{male}}$ may be used for the "son-of" relation. Observe two properties of role restriction, whose proofs easily follow from the semantics in Table 3.1:

1. for every role R, the role $R|_\top$ is equivalent to R;
2. for every role R, and concepts A, C, D, the concept $(\forall(R|_C).A) \sqcap (\forall(R|_D).A)$ is equivalent to $\forall(R|_{(C \sqcup D)}).A$.

The second property highlights that disjunction – although not explicitly present in the syntax of the language – arises from semantics.

Brachman and Levesque defined also the language $\mathcal{FL}^-$, derived from $\mathcal{FL}$ by omitting role restriction. They first showed that for $\mathcal{FL}^-$, subsumption can be decided by a structural algorithm, with polynomial-time complexity,

Table 3.1. *Syntax and semantics of the Description Logic* $\mathcal{FL}$. *For* $\mathcal{FL}^-$, *omit role restriction.*

	concept expressions	semantics
concept name	A	$\subseteq \Delta^{\mathcal{I}}$
concept intersection	$C \sqcap D$	$C^{\mathcal{I}} \cap D^{\mathcal{I}}$
limited exist. quant.	$\exists R$	$\{x \in \Delta^{\mathcal{I}} \mid \exists y.\,(x,y) \in R^{\mathcal{I}}\}$
value restriction	$\forall R.C$	$\{x \in \Delta^{\mathcal{I}} \mid \forall y.\,(x,y) \in R^{\mathcal{I}} \to y \in C^{\mathcal{I}}\}$

	role expressions	semantics
role name	P	$\subseteq \Delta^{\mathcal{I}} \times \Delta^{\mathcal{I}}$
role restriction	$R\vert_C$	$\{(x,y) \in \Delta^{\mathcal{I}} \times \Delta^{\mathcal{I}} \mid (x,y) \in R^{\mathcal{I}} \wedge y \in C^{\mathcal{I}}\}$

similar to the one shown in Chapter 2. Then they showed that subsumption in $\mathcal{FL}$ is coNP-hard, exhibiting the first "computational cliff" in Description Logics.

Since the original proof of coNP-hardness is somewhat complex, we give here a simpler proof, found by Calvanese [1990]. The proof is based on the observation that if $C_1 \sqcup \cdots \sqcup C_n \equiv \top$, then, given a role R and a concept A, we have

$$(\forall(R\vert_{C_1}).A) \sqcap \cdots \sqcap (\forall(R\vert_{C_n}).A) \;\equiv\; \text{(from 2)} \tag{3.1}$$
$$\forall R\vert_{(C_1 \sqcup \cdots \sqcup C_n)}.A \;\equiv\; \tag{3.2}$$
$$\forall R\vert_{\top}.A \;\equiv\; \text{(from 1)} \tag{3.3}$$
$$\forall R.A.$$

Moreover, observe that, for every role Q and every concept C, the disjunction $\exists Q \sqcup \forall Q.C$ is equivalent to the concept $\top$. Hence $\forall(R\vert_{\exists Q}).A \sqcap \forall(R\vert_{\forall Q.C}).A$ is equivalent to $\forall R.A$. These observations are the key to the reduction from tautology checking of propositional 3DNF formulae to subsumption in $\mathcal{FL}$.

Theorem 3.2 *Subsumption in* $\mathcal{FL}$ *is coNP-hard.*

Proof Given an alphabet of propositional variables $L = \{p_1, \ldots, p_k\}$, define a propositional formula $F = G_1 \vee \cdots \vee G_n$ in 3DNF over L, where each disjunct G_i is made of three literals $l_i^1 \wedge l_i^2 \wedge l_i^3$, and for every $i \in \{1, \ldots, n\}$, and $j \in \{1, 2, 3\}$, each literal l_i^j is either a variable $p \in L$, or its negation $\bar{p}$.

Given a set of role names $\{R, P_1, \ldots, P_k\}$ (one role P_i for each variable p_i) and a concept name A, define the concept $C_F = (\forall R|_{C_1}.A) \sqcap \cdots \sqcap (\forall R|_{C_n}.A)$ where, for each $i \in \{1, \ldots, n\}$, C_i is the conjunction of three concepts $D_i^1 \sqcap D_i^2 \sqcap D_i^3$, and each D_i^j is

$$D_i^j = \begin{cases} \forall P_h.A, & \text{if } l_i^j = p_h \\ \exists P_h, & \text{if } l_i^j = \overline{p_h} \end{cases} \quad \text{for } j \in \{1, 2, 3\}, \; i \in \{1, \ldots, n\}.$$

Then the claim follows from the following lemma. $\qquad\qquad\qquad\qquad$ $\square$

Lemma 3.3 F *is a tautology if and only if* $C_F \equiv \forall R.A$.

Proof The proof of the claim is straightforward; however, since it appears only in Calvanese's Master thesis (in Italian), we present it here in full.

Only if If F is a tautology, then $C_1 \sqcup \cdots \sqcup C_n \equiv \top$. This can be shown by contradiction: suppose $C_1 \sqcup \cdots \sqcup C_n$ is not equivalent to $\top$. Then, there exists an interpretation $\mathcal{I}$ in which there is an element $x \notin C_i^{\mathcal{I}}$, for every $i \in \{1, \ldots, n\}$. Since each $C_i = D_i^1 \sqcap D_i^2 \sqcap D_i^3$, it follows that for each i there is a $j \in \{1, 2, 3\}$ such that $x \notin D_i^j$. Define a truth assignment τ to L as follows. For each $h \in \{1, \ldots, k\}$:

- $\tau(p_h) = \textbf{false}$ iff $l_i^j = p_h$, and $x \notin D_i^j$
- $\tau(p_h) = \textbf{true}$ iff $l_i^j = \overline{p_h}$, and $x \notin D_i^j$.

Observe that we cannot have both $\tau(p_h) = \textbf{false}$ and $\tau(p_h) = \textbf{true}$ at the same time, since this would imply both $x \notin \exists P_h$ and $x \notin \forall P_h.A$, which is impossible since $\exists P_h \sqcup \forall P_h.A \equiv \top$. Evidently, τ assigns **false** to at least one literal for each disjunct of F, contradicting the hypothesis that F is a tautology. Therefore $C_1 \sqcup \cdots \sqcup C_n \equiv \top$.

The claim is now implied by equivalences (3.1)–(3.3).

If Suppose F is not a tautology. Then, there exists a truth assignment τ such that for each $i \in \{1, \ldots, n\}$, there exists a $j \in \{1, 2, 3\}$ such that $\tau(l_i^j) = \textbf{false}$.

Define an interpretation $(\Delta^{\mathcal{I}}, \cdot^{\mathcal{I}})$, with $\Delta^{\mathcal{I}}$ containing three elements x, y, z, such that $P_h^{\mathcal{I}} = (y, z)$ if $\tau(p_h) = \textbf{false}$, and $P_h^{\mathcal{I}} = \emptyset$ otherwise. Moreover, let $A^{\mathcal{I}} = \emptyset$, and $R^{\mathcal{I}} = \{x, y\}$.

Observe that in this way, $y \in (\exists P_h)^{\mathcal{I}}$ iff $\tau(p_h) = \textbf{false}$, and $y \in (\forall P_h.A)^{\mathcal{I}}$ iff $\tau(p_h) = \textbf{true}$. This implies that $x \notin (\forall R.A)^{\mathcal{I}}$. To prove the claim, we now show that $x \in C_F^{\mathcal{I}}$.

Observe that, for each $i \in \{1, \ldots, n\}$, there exists a $j \in \{1, 2, 3\}$ such that $\tau(l_i^j) = \mathbf{false}$. For such a j, we show by case analysis that $y \notin (D_i^j)^{\mathcal{I}}$:

- if $l_i^j = p_h$ then $D_i^j = \forall P_h.A$, and in this case, $\tau(p_h) = \mathbf{false}$, hence $y \notin (\forall P_h.A)^{\mathcal{I}}$;
- if $l_i^j = \overline{p_h}$ then $D_i^j = \exists P_h$, and in this case, $\tau(p_h) = \mathbf{true}$, hence $y \notin (\exists P_h)^{\mathcal{I}}$.

Therefore, for every $i \in \{1, \ldots, n\}$ we have $y \notin C_i^{\mathcal{I}}$. This implies that $(x, y) \notin R|_{(C_1 \sqcup \cdots \sqcup C_n)}^{\mathcal{I}}$, hence $x \in (\forall R|_{(C_1 \sqcup \cdots \sqcup C_n)}.A)^{\mathcal{I}}$, which is a concept equivalent to C_F. $\qquad\square$

The above proof shows only that subsumption in $\mathcal{FL}$ is coNP-hard. However, role restrictions could also be used to obtain qualified existential quantification, since $\exists R.C = \exists R|_C$. Hence, $\mathcal{FL}$ contains also the AND-branching source of complexity. Combining the two sources of complexity, Donini *et al.* [1997a] proved a PSPACE lower bound for subsumption in $\mathcal{FL}$, matching the upper bound found by Schmidt-Schauß and Smolka [1991].

3.2.2 Intractability in $\mathcal{FL}^-$ plus qualified existential quantification and number restrictions

As shown in Chapter 2, disjunction arises also from qualified existential quantification and number restrictions. This can be easily seen examining the construction of the tableau checking the satisfiability of the concept

$$(\exists R.A) \sqcap (\exists R.(\neg A \sqcap \neg B)) \sqcap (\exists R.B) \sqcap \leqslant 2\, R \qquad (3.4)$$

in which, once three objects are introduced to satisfy the existentials, one has to choose between three non-equivalent identifications of pairs of objects, where only one identification leads to a consistent tableau branch.

Remark 3.4 When a Description Logic includes number restrictions, then negation of concept names is included for free, at least from a computational viewpoint. In fact, a concept name A and its negation $\neg A$ can be coded as, say, $\geqslant 4\, R_A$ and $\leqslant 3\, R_A$ where R_A is a new role name introduced for A. Now these two concepts obey the same axioms as A and $\neg A$ – namely, their conjunction is $\bot$ and their union is $\top$. Hence, everything we say about computational properties of Description Logics including $\mathcal{FL}^-$ plus number restrictions holds also for $\mathcal{AL}$ plus number restrictions. $\qquad\blacksquare$

We now present a proof of intractability based on this property. The reduction was first published by Nebel [1988], who reduced the NP-complete problem of SET SPLITTING [Garey and Johnson, 1979, p. 221] to non-subsumption in the Description Logic of the BACK system, which included the basic $\mathcal{FL}^-$ plus intersection of roles and number restrictions. SET SPLITTING is the following problem:

Definition 3.5 (Set splitting) Given a collection $\mathcal{C}$ of subsets of a basic set S, decide if there exists a partition of S into two subsets S_1 and S_2 such that no subset of $\mathcal{C}$ is entirely contained in either S_1 or S_2.

We simplify the original reduction. We start from a variant of SET SPLITTING (still NP-complete) in which all $c \in \mathcal{C}$ have exactly three elements, and reduce it to satisfiability in $\mathcal{FL}^-$ plus qualified existential role quantification and number restrictions.[1] Since role intersection can simulate qualified existential role quantification (see next Subsection 3.2.2.1) this result implies the original one.

Theorem 3.6 *Satisfiability in $\mathcal{FL}^-\mathcal{EN}$ is NP-hard.*

Proof Let $S = \{1, \ldots, n\}$, and let $c_1, \ldots, c_k$ be the subsets of S. There exists a splitting of S iff the concept $D_1 \sqcap D_2 \sqcap D_3$ is satisfiable, where D_1, D_2, D_3 are defined as follows:

$$D_1 = \exists R.B_1 \sqcap \cdots \sqcap \exists R.B_n \tag{3.5}$$
$$D_2 = \forall R.(\leqslant 2\, Q_1 \sqcap \cdots \sqcap \leqslant 2\, Q_k) \tag{3.6}$$
$$D_3 = \leqslant 2\, R \tag{3.7}$$

where each concept B_i codes which subsets element i appears in, as follows:

$$B_i = \bigsqcap_{j \mid i \in c_j} \exists Q_j.A_i$$

and concepts $A_1, \ldots, A_n$ are defined in such a way that they are pairwise disjoint – say, for $i \in \{1, \ldots, n\}$ let $A_i = \geqslant i\, R \sqcap \leqslant i\, R$. Intuitively, when tableau rules dealing with $\sqcap$ and qualified existential quantification are applied to $D_1 \sqcap D_2 \sqcap D_3(x)$, one obtains a tableau whose tree structure of individual names can be visualized as in Figure 3.1. The rest of the proof strictly follows the original one [Nebel, 1988], hence we do not present it here. The intuition is that D_3 forces every ys generated by D_1 to be identified with one of only two successors of the root individual name x. Such identifications correspond to the sets S_1 and S_2. Then D_2 forces the split of each 3-subset, since it makes sure that neither of these successors has more

---

[1] From Remark 3.4, this DL has the same computational properties of $\mathcal{ALEN}$ [Donini *et al.*, 1997a]

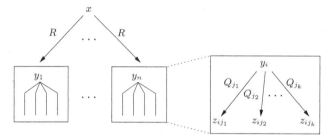

Fig. 3.1. The AND-tree structure of the tableau obtained by applying rules for $\sqcap$ and $\exists R.C$ to $D_1 \sqcap D_2 \sqcap D_3(x)$. Applying the rule for $\leqslant 2\, R(x)$ would lead to several OR-branches (as many as the possible identifications of ys).

than two Q_j-successors, and thus both have at least one Q_j-successor (since there are three of them). $\qquad\qquad\qquad\qquad\qquad\qquad\qquad\qquad\qquad$ $\square$

We clarify the construction and show its relevant properties by an example.

Example 3.7 Suppose $S = \{1, 2, 3, 4\}$, and let $c_1 = \{1, 2, 4\}$, $c_2 = \{2, 3, 4\}$, $c_3 = \{1, 3, 4\}$. Applying the tableau rules of Chapter 2 to D_1, one obtains the following tree of individual names (definitions of each B_i are expanded):

$$D_1(x) \begin{cases} R(x, y_1)\ B_1(y_1) \begin{cases} Q_1(y_1, z_{11})\ A_1(z_{11}) \\ Q_3(y_1, z_{13})\ A_1(z_{13}) \end{cases} \\ R(x, y_2)\ B_2(y_1) \begin{cases} Q_1(y_2, z_{21})\ A_2(z_{21}) \\ Q_2(y_2, z_{22})\ A_2(z_{22}) \end{cases} \\ R(x, y_3)\ B_3(y_1) \begin{cases} Q_2(y_3, z_{32})\ A_3(z_{32}) \\ Q_3(y_3, z_{33})\ A_3(z_{33}) \end{cases} \\ R(x, y_4)\ B_4(y_1) \begin{cases} Q_1(y_4, z_{41})\ A_4(z_{41}) \\ Q_2(y_4, z_{42})\ A_4(z_{42}) \\ Q_3(y_4, z_{43})\ A_4(z_{43}) \end{cases} \end{cases}$$

where the individual names $y_1, \ldots, y_4$ stand for the four elements of S, and each z_{ij} codes the fact that element i appears in subset c_j. Because of assertions $A_i(z_{ij})$, no two z's disagreeing on the first index – e.g., z_{32} and z_{42} – can be safely identified, since they must satisfy assertions on incompatible A's. This is the same as if the constraints $z_{ij} \neq z_{hj}$, for all $i, h \in \{1, \ldots, |S|\}$ with $i \neq h$, and all $j \in \{1, \ldots, |\mathcal{C}|\}$, were present.

Now D_3 states that $y_1, \ldots, y_4$ must be identified into only two individual names. Observe that identifying y_2, y_3, y_4 leads to an individual name (say, y_2) having among others, three unidentifiable Q_2-fillers z_{22}, z_{32}, z_{42}. But D_2 states that all R-fillers of x, including y_2, have no more than 2 fillers for Q_2.

This rules out the identification of y_2, y_3, y_4 in the tableau. Observe that this identification corresponds to a partition of S into $\{1\}$ and $\{2, 3, 4\}$, which is not a solution of SET SPLITTING because the subset c_2 is not split. Following the same line of reasoning, one could prove that the only identifications of all R-fillers into two individual names, leading to a satisfiable tableau, are one-to-one with solutions of SET SPLITTING. ∎

The same reduction works for non-subsumption, since $D_1 \sqcap D_2 \sqcap D_3$ is satisfiable iff $D_1 \sqcap D_2$ is not subsumed by $\neg D_3 \equiv \geqslant 3\, R$. This type of reduction has also been applied (see [Donini *et al.*, 1999]) to prove that subsumption in $\mathcal{ALNI}$ is coNP-hard, where $\mathcal{ALNI}$ is the Description Logic including $\mathcal{AL}$, number restrictions and inverse roles.

Observe that also $\mathcal{FL^-EN}$ contains the AND-branching source of complexity, since qualified existential restriction is present. With a more complex reduction from Quantified Boolean Formulae, combining the two sources of complexity, satisfiability and non-subsumption in $\mathcal{ALEN}$ has been proved PSPACE-complete by Hemaspaandra [1999].

Note that in the above proof of intractability, pairwise disjointness of $A_1, \ldots, A_n$ could be also expressed by conjoining $\log n$ concept names and their negations in all possible ways. Hence, the proof needs only the concept $\leqslant 2\, R$, and when qualified existentials are simulated by subroles, only $\geqslant 1\, R$ is used. This shows that the above proof of intractability is quite sharp: intractability arises independently of the size of the numbers involved. The computational cliff is evident if one moves to having 0 and 1 only in number restrictions, which leads to so-called *functional roles* – since the assertion $\leqslant 1\, R(x)$ forces R to be a partial function of x. In that case, the tractability of a Description Logic can usually be established, e.g., the Description Logic of the system CLASSIC [Borgida and Patel-Schneider, 1994]. The intuitive reason for tractability of functional roles can be found in the corresponding tableau rules, which for number restrictions of the form $\leqslant 1\, R(x)$ become *deterministic*: there is no choice in identifying individuals names $y_1, \ldots, y_k$ which are all R-fillers for x, but to collapse them all into one individual.

3.2.2.1 Simulating $\exists R.C$ with role conjunction

Donini *et al.* [1997a] showed that a concept D containing qualified existential role quantifications $\exists R.C$ is satisfiable iff the concept $\widetilde{D}$ is satisfiable, where in $\widetilde{D}$ each occurrence of a concept $\exists R.C$ is replaced by the concept $\exists (R \sqcap Q_C) \sqcap \forall (R \sqcap Q_C).C$, adding Q_C as a new role name (a different

Q_C for each occurrence of $\exists R.C$, to be used nowhere else). We call $\widetilde{D}$ an $\sqcap$-*simulation* of D in the rest of the chapter.

The proof that the simulation is correct can be easily given by referring to tableaux.

Example 3.8 Considering the concept D below on the left, and simulating qualified existential quantifications in D by role intersections, one obtains the concept $\widetilde{D}$ on the right,

$$D = \begin{cases} \exists R.A \sqcap \\ \exists R.B \sqcap \\ \forall R.C \end{cases} \qquad \widetilde{D} = \begin{cases} \exists (R \sqcap Q_A) \sqcap \forall (R \sqcap Q_A).A \sqcap \\ \exists (R \sqcap Q_B) \sqcap \forall (R \sqcap Q_B).B \sqcap \\ \forall R.C \end{cases}$$

where subscripts on new role names help to identify which existential they simulate. Applying the tableau rules of Chapter 2 to $\widetilde{D}(x)$, one obtains the model

$$\begin{array}{ll} R(x,y) & A(y) \\ Q_A(x,y) & C(y) \\ R(x,z) & B(z) \\ Q_B(x,z) & C(z) \end{array}$$

which satisfies both concepts. ∎

Proposition 3.9 *A concept D is satisfiable iff $\widetilde{D}$ is satisfiable.*

Proof The proof of the proposition follows the example. Namely, an open tableau branch for $\widetilde{D}$ is also an open tableau branch for D (ignoring assertions on new role names), and an open tableau branch for D can be transformed to an open tableau branch for $\widetilde{D}$ just by adding the assertions about new role names. □

As observed by Nebel [1990a], an acyclic role hierarchy in a Description Logic can be always simulated by conjunctions of existing roles and new role names. In the above example, using two role names Q_A, Q_B and the inclusions $Q_A \sqsubseteq R$, $Q_B \sqsubseteq R$ yields the same simulation.

Applying $\sqcap$-simulation, one could obtain from the reduction in Theorem 3.6 the original reduction by Nebel, proving that satisfiability (and non-subsumption) in $\mathcal{ALN}(\sqcap)$ is NP-hard. Using a more complex reduction, Donini *et al.* [1997a] proved that satisfiability in $\mathcal{ALN}(\sqcap)$ is in fact PSPACE-complete.

3.3 AND-branching: finding a clash

When candidate models of a concept have exponential size – as for the $\mathcal{ALE}$-concept of Subsection 3.1.1.2 – models cannot be guessed and checked in polynomial time. In this case, it is a combinatorial problem to find the clash – if any – in the candidate model. This leads to NP-hardness of *un*satisfiability and subsumption. However, for many Description Logics the AND-tree structure of a model is such that its traces (branches of the AND-tree) have polynomial size. A concept C is satisfiable iff there is no trace containing a clash; hence it is sufficient to guess such a trace to show that C is unsatisfiable. From this argument, Schmidt-Schauß and Smolka [1991] proved that satisfiability in $\mathcal{ALE}$ is in coNP.

3.3.1 Intractability of satisfiability in $\mathcal{ALE}$

We now report a proof that satisfiability in $\mathcal{ALE}$ is coNP-complete. The original proof was based on a polynomial-time reduction from a variant of the NP-complete problem ONE-IN-THREE 3SAT [Garey and Johnson, 1979, p. 259]. Here we present a proof based on the same idea, but with a slightly different construction, relying on a reduction from the NP-complete problem EXACT COVER (XC) [Garey and Johnson, 1979, p. 221]. Such a problem is defined as follows.

Definition 3.10 (Exact cover XC**)** Let $U = \{u_1, \ldots, u_n\}$ be a finite set, and let $\mathcal{M}$ be a family $M_1, \ldots, M_m$ of subsets of U. Decide if there are q mutually disjoint subsets $M_{i_1}, \ldots, M_{i_q}$ such that their union equals U, i.e., $M_{i_h} \cap M_{i_k} = \emptyset$ for $1 \le h < k \le q$, and $\bigcup_{k=1}^{q} M_{i_k} = U$.

The reduction consists in associating every instance of XC with an $\mathcal{ALE}$-concept $C_{\mathcal{M}}$, such that $\mathcal{M}$ has an exact cover if and only if $C_{\mathcal{M}}$ is *unsatisfiable*. It is important to note that, differently from the previous sections, here a solution of the NP-complete source problem is related to a proof of the *absence* of a model. In fact, exact covers of $\mathcal{M}$ are related to those traces of $\{C_{\mathcal{M}}(x)\}$ that contain a clash; hence proving the existence of a solution of an NP-complete problem is related to a refutation in the target Description Logic.

In the following we assume R to be a role name. We translate $\mathcal{M}$ into the concept

$$C_{\mathcal{M}} = C_1^1 \sqcap \cdots \sqcap C_1^m \sqcap D_1$$

where each concept C_1^j represents a subset M_j, and is inductively defined as

$$C_l^j = \begin{cases} \exists R.C_{l+1}^j, & \text{if either } l \le n,\ u_l \in M_j \text{ or } l > n,\ u_{l-n} \in M_j \\ \forall R.C_{l+1}^j, & \text{if either } l \le n,\ u_l \notin M_j \text{ or } l > n,\ u_{l-n} \notin M_j \end{cases}$$

$$\text{for } l \in \{1, \ldots, 2n\}$$

and by the base case $C_{2n+1}^j = \top$. The concept D_1 is defined by

$$D_1 = \underbrace{\forall R. \cdots \forall R.}_{2n} \bot$$

and each of $D_2, D_3, \ldots$ has one universal quantifier less than the previous one.

Intuitively, for every element u_l in U there are two corresponding levels $l, l + n$ in the concepts C_1^j's, where "level" refers to the nesting of quantifiers. The element u_l is present in M_j if and only if there is an existential quantifier in the concept C_1^j at level $l + n$ – which implies by construction that $\exists$ is also at level l. The concept D_1 is designed in such a way that a clash for $\{C_\mathcal{M}(x)\}$ can only occur in a trace containing at least $2n + 1$ individual names.

Example 3.11 Consider the following instance of XC: let $U = \{u_1, \ldots, u_3\}$, and

$$\mathcal{M} = \{M_1 = \{u_1, u_2\}, M_2 = \{u_2, u_3\}, M_3 = \{u_3\}\}.$$

The corresponding $\mathcal{ALE}$-concept $C_\mathcal{M}$ is given by the conjunction of C_1^1, C_1^2, C_1^3 and D_1, defined as follows:

		u_1	u_2	u_3	u_1	u_2	u_3
M_1	$\leftrightarrow$	$C_1^1 = \exists R.\exists R.\forall R.\exists R.\exists R.\forall R.\top$					
M_2	$\leftrightarrow$	$C_1^2 = \forall R.\exists R.\exists R.\forall R.\exists R.\exists R.\top$					
M_3	$\leftrightarrow$	$C_1^3 = \forall R.\forall R.\exists R.\forall R.\forall R.\exists R.\top$					
		$D_1 = \forall R.\forall R.\forall R.\forall R.\forall R.\forall R.\bot$					

where on the left we put the subset M_j corresponding to each C_1^j, and above we put the elements of U corresponding to each level of the concepts. Observe that the elements of U appear twice.   ∎

The conjunction of the above concepts is unsatisfiable if and only if the interplay of the various existential and universal quantifiers, represented by a trace, forces an individual name in the tableau for $\{C_\mathcal{M}(x)\}$ to belong to the extension of $\bot$. This reduction creates a correspondence between such a trace and an exact cover of U.

In order to formally characterize such a correspondence, we define the activeness of a concept in a trace. Let T be a trace and C be a concept. We say that C is *active in* T if C is of the form $\exists R.D$ and there are individual names y, z such that T contains $C(y)$, $R(y, z)$, and $D(z)$. Therefore, an existentially quantified concept $\exists R.D$ is active in T if the $\rightarrow_\exists$-rule has been applied to the assertion $\exists R.D(y)$ in T. Intuitively, if C_k^j is active in a trace of $\{C_{\mathcal{M}}(x)\}$ containing a clash, then u_k belongs to an exact cover of $\mathcal{M}$.

Lemma 3.12 ([Donini *et al.*, 1992a], Lemma 3.1) *Let T be a trace of $\{C_{\mathcal{M}}(x)\}$.*

1. *Suppose C_k^j is active in T. Then for all $l \in \{1, \ldots, k\}$ if the concept C_l^j is of the form $\exists R.C_{l+1}^j$, then it is active in T.*
2. *If T contains a clash, then for every $l \in \{1, \ldots, 2n\}$ there exists exactly one j such that C_l^j is active in T.*

Example 3.13 The reader can gain an insight into the importance of the above properties by constructing the tableau for the concept

$$(\exists R.\forall R.\exists R.A) \sqcap$$
$$(\exists R.\forall R.\exists R.B) \sqcap$$
$$(\forall R.\exists R.\top)$$

and verifying that the trace reaching the concept A has both existentials of the first line active (and neither existential of the second line), and vice versa for the trace reaching B. ∎

Example 3.14 (Example 3.11 Continued) Note that in Example 3.11 the two subsets M_1 and M_2 form a (non-exact) cover of U, and indeed, the tableau for $\{C_1^1 \sqcap C_2^1 \sqcap D_1(x)\}$ is satisfiable. Moreover, observe the importance of the two levels. If concepts were formed by just one level, the following concepts would be unsatisfiable (choose the highlighted existentials):

$$\overline{C_1^1} = \exists\mathbf{R}.\exists R.\forall R.\top$$
$$\overline{C_2^1} = \forall R.\exists\mathbf{R}.\exists\mathbf{R}.\top$$
$$\overline{D_1} = \forall R.\forall R.\forall R.\bot$$

corresponding to a cover by M_1 and M_2 which is non-exact. The second level ensures that once an existential is chosen, all nested existentials must be chosen too to form a trace. ∎

Theorem 3.15 *Unsatisfiability in $\mathcal{ALE}$ is* NP-*hard.*

Proof We show that an instance $(U, \mathcal{M})$ of XC has an exact cover if and only if $C_{\mathcal{M}}$ is unsatisfiable. Let $\mathcal{M} = \{M_1, \ldots, M_m\}$ be a set of subsets of U and $C_{\mathcal{M}} = C_1^1 \sqcap \cdots \sqcap C_1^m \sqcap D_1$ be the corresponding concept. Since this proof is the base for three others in the chapter, we present it in some detail.

Only if Let $M_{i_1}, \ldots, M_{i_q}$ be an exact cover of U. Let T be a trace of $\{C_{\mathcal{M}}(x_1)\}$ defined inductively as follows:

$$T_1 = \{C_1^j(x_1) \mid j \in \{1, \ldots, m\}\} \cup \{D_1(x_1)\}$$

$$T_{l+1} = T_l \cup \{R(x_l, x_{l+1})\} \cup \{C_{l+1}^j(x_{l+1}) \mid u_{l+1} \in M_j\} \cup \{D_{l+1}(x_{l+1})\}.$$

Obviously, $T = T_{2n+1}$ contains a clash, because $D_{2n+1} = \bot$. For each level l there is exactly one j such that $C_l^j = \exists R.C_{l+1}^j$. Using this fact, one can easily show that T is a trace by induction on l.

If If $C_{\mathcal{M}}$ is unsatisfiable, then there exists a trace T of $\{C_{\mathcal{M}}(x)\}$ such that T contains a clash. We show that the subsets in

$$\{M_j \mid \exists l \in \{1, \ldots, n\} : C_{n+l}^j \text{ is active in } T\}$$

form an exact cover of U. First of all, since T is a trace, for every level $l \in \{1, \ldots, 2n\}$ there exists a j such that C_l^j is active in T (Lemma 3.12(ii)). Hence the union of these subsets covers U.

We now prove that no two subsets overlap: in fact, suppose there are i, j such that M_i, M_j intersect non-trivially in an element u_l. Here we exploit the two-layered construction of $C_{\mathcal{M}}$. By definition, there are h, k such that C_{n+h}^i and C_{n+k}^j are active in T. Since u_l is in both M_i and M_j, by construction of $C_{\mathcal{M}}$ we have $C_l^i = \exists R.C_{l+1}^i$ and $C_l^j = \exists R.C_{l+1}^j$. From Lemma 3.12(i), we know that C_l^i and C_l^j are both active in T. Hence $i = j$ from Lemma 3.12(ii). $\qquad\square$

The above reduction works also for the special case of XC in which every subset has at most three elements, which corresponds to at most six nested existential quantifications in each concept C_1^j. Hence, bounding the number of nested existential quantifications by a constant $k \geq 6$ does not yield tractability. The original reduction from ONE-IN-THREE 3SAT shows moreover that bounding the number of existentials in each level by a constant $k \geq 3$ does not yield tractability.

Simulating qualified existential quantifications in $C_{\mathcal{M}}$ by role intersection (see Subsection 3.2.2.1), we conclude that unsatisfiability of concepts in $\mathcal{AL}(\sqcap)$ – $\mathcal{AL}$ plus role conjunction – is NP-hard, too.

Theorem 3.16 *Satisfiability and subsumption of concepts are* NP-*hard in* $\mathcal{AL}(\sqcap)$.

We note that this source of intractability is not due to the presence of the concept $\bot$, but to the interplay of universal and existential quantification. In fact, the above reduction works also for the Description Logic $\mathcal{FL}^-\mathcal{E}$, which is $\mathcal{FL}^-$ plus qualified existential quantification.

Theorem 3.17 *Subsumption is* NP-*hard in* $\mathcal{FL}^-\mathcal{E}$.

Proof The proof is based on the reduction given for $\mathcal{ALE}$. The $\mathcal{ALE}$-concept $C_\mathcal{M} = C_1^1 \sqcap \cdots \sqcap C_1^m \sqcap D_1$ in that reduction is unsatisfiable if and only if $C_1^1 \sqcap \cdots \sqcap C_1^m$ is subsumed by $\neg D_1$. Now $C_1^1 \sqcap \cdots \sqcap C_1^m$ is a concept in $\mathcal{FL}^-\mathcal{E}$ and $\neg D_1$ can be rewritten to the equivalent concept E, defined as

$$E = \underbrace{\exists R. \cdots \exists R.}_{2n} \top$$

i.e., a chain of $2n$ qualified existential quantifications terminating with the concept $\top$. Obviously, E is in $\mathcal{FL}^-\mathcal{E}$, hence subsumption in $\mathcal{FL}^-\mathcal{E}$ is NP-hard. $\square$

We now use the above construction to show that in three other Description Logics – extending $\mathcal{FL}^-$ with each pair of role constructs for role conjunction, role inverse, and role chain – subsumption is NP-hard. The fact that reductions can be easily re-used is a characteristic of Description Logics. It depends on the compositional semantics of constructs – hardness proofs obviously carry over to more general Description Logics – but also on the extensional semantics, that allows one to simulate a construct with others.

3.3.2 $\mathcal{FL}^-$ plus role conjunction and role inverse

We abbreviate this Description Logic as $\mathcal{FL}^-(\sqcap, ^-)$. We prove that $\mathcal{FL}^-(\sqcap, ^-)$ is hard for NP by an argument similar to that for $\mathcal{FL}^-\mathcal{E}$. One may be tempted to use $\sqcap$-simulation, defined in Subsection 3.2.2.1, which replaces qualified existential quantifications by role intersections. However, a direct $\sqcap$-simulation of the concepts used in the reduction for $\mathcal{FL}^-\mathcal{E}$ does not work. In fact, $\sqcap$-simulation preserves satisfiability, not subsumption; e.g., while $\exists R.C \sqcap D$ is subsumed by $\exists R.C$, its $\sqcap$-simulation $\exists(R \sqcap Q_1) \sqcap \forall Q_1.C \sqcap D$ is not subsumed by $\exists(R \sqcap Q_2) \sqcap \forall Q_2.C$.

To carry over the proof, it is useful to have a tableau rule for role inverse:

Condition $\mathcal{T}$ contains $R(x, y)$,
        where R is either a role name P or its inverse P^-;
Action $\mathcal{T}' = \mathcal{T} \cup \{R^-(y, x)\}$,
        where if $R = P^-$, then $R^- = P$.

Theorem 3.18 *Subsumption in* $\mathcal{FL}^-(\sqcap, ^-)$ *is* NP-*hard.*

Proof We refer to the concept $C_\mathcal{M}$ defined in the reduction given for $\mathcal{ALE}$. Let n be the cardinality of U in XC. First define the concept F as follows:

$$F = \underbrace{\forall R. \cdots \forall R.}_{2n} \underbrace{\forall(R^-). \cdots \forall(R^-).}_{2n} A$$

where A is a concept name (recall that $C_\mathcal{M}$ does not contain any concept name but $\top$ and $\bot$). F is a concept of $\mathcal{FL}^-(\sqcap, ^-)$.

Observe now that the $\mathcal{ALE}$-concept $C_\mathcal{M} = C_1^1 \sqcap \cdots \sqcap C_1^m \sqcap D_1$ is unsatisfiable if and only if $\widetilde{C}_1^1 \sqcap \cdots \sqcap \widetilde{C}_1^m \sqcap F$ is subsumed by A (where $\widetilde{C}$ is the $\sqcap$-simulation of C). In fact, the subsumption holds if and only if the complete tableau for $\{\widetilde{C}_1^1 \sqcap \cdots \sqcap \widetilde{C}_1^m \sqcap F(x), \neg A(x)\}$ contains the only possible clash $\{A(x), \neg A(x)\}$. This tableau contains a clash if and only if there is a trace of length $2n$ in the tableau, and such a trace is in one-to-one correspondence with the exact covers of the problem XC. Hence subsumption in $\mathcal{FL}^-(\sqcap, ^-)$ is NP-hard. $\qquad\square$

3.3.3 $\mathcal{FL}^-$ plus role conjunction and role chain

We abbreviate this Description Logic as $\mathcal{FL}^-(\sqcap, \circ)$.

Theorem 3.19 *Subsumption in* $\mathcal{FL}^-(\sqcap, \circ)$ *is* NP-*hard.*

Proof Again, we refer to the concept $C_\mathcal{M}$ defined in the reduction given for $\mathcal{ALE}$. Observe that the $\mathcal{ALE}$-concept $C_\mathcal{M} = C_1^1 \sqcap \ldots \sqcap C_1^m \sqcap D_1$ is unsatisfiable if and only if $\widetilde{C}_1^1 \sqcap \ldots \sqcap \widetilde{C}_1^m$ is subsumed by $\neg D_1$ (again, $\widetilde{C}$ is the $\sqcap$-simulation of C). The claim holds, since $\widetilde{C}_1^1 \sqcap \ldots \sqcap \widetilde{C}_1^m$ is in $\mathcal{FL}^-(\sqcap)$ and $\neg D_1$ can be expressed as the equivalent concept G, defined as follows:

$$G = \exists \underbrace{(R \circ \cdots \circ R)}_{2m}. \tag{3.8}$$

Obviously, G is in $\mathcal{FL}^-(\circ)$, hence subsumption in $\mathcal{FL}^-(\sqcap, \circ)$ is NP-hard. $\square$

We note that in the above reduction, subsumption is proved intractable by using only role conjunction in the subsumee (to simulate existential quantification), and only role chain in the subsumer. We will exploit the subsumer (3.8) also in Subsection 3.3.4.

3.3.4 $\mathcal{FL}^-$ plus role chain and role inverse

We abbreviate this Description Logic as $\mathcal{FL}^-(\circ, ^-)$. We first show that, similarly to Subsubsection 3.2.2.1, qualified existential quantifications in a concept D can be replaced by a combination of role chains and role inverses, obtaining a new concept $\widehat{D}$ that is satisfiable iff D is.

3.3.4.1 Simulating $\exists R.C$ via role chains and role inverses

Donini *et al.* [1991b; 1999] showed that a concept D containing qualified existential role quantifications $\exists R.C$ is satisfiable iff the concept $\widehat{D}$ is satisfiable, where in $\widehat{D}$ each occurrence of a concept $\exists R.C$ is replaced by the concept $\exists (R \circ Q_C) \sqcap \forall (R \circ Q_C \circ Q_C^-).C$, adding Q_C as a new role name (a different Q for each occurrence of $\exists R.C$, to be used nowhere else). We say that $\widehat{C}$ is a $\circ$-*simulation* of C.

This simulation too can be explained by referring to tableaux, through an example concept.

Example 3.20 Consider the concept D below on the left, and its $\circ$-simulation $\widehat{D}$ on the right:

$$D = \begin{cases} \exists R.A \sqcap \\ \exists R.B \sqcap \\ \forall R.C \end{cases} \qquad \widehat{D} = \begin{cases} \exists (R \circ Q_A) \sqcap \forall (R \circ Q_A \circ Q_A^-).A \sqcap \\ \exists (R \circ Q_B) \sqcap \forall (R \circ Q_B \circ Q_B^-).B \sqcap \\ \forall R.C \end{cases}$$

where subscripts on new role names help to identify which existential they simulate. Applying the tableau rules of Chapter 2 to $\widehat{D}(x)$, one obtains the model

$$\begin{array}{lll} R(x,y) & A(y) & Q_A(y, u_y) \\ & C(y) & \\ R(x,z) & B(z) & Q_B(z, u_z) \\ & C(z) & \end{array}$$

where subscripts on individuals u_y, u_z highlight that there is a new individual name for each individual name used to satisfy an existential quantification. That is, the number of individual names in the tableau for $\widehat{D}$ is at most twice that in the tableau for D. ■

Lemma 3.21 *Let D be an $\mathcal{ALE}$-concept and $\widehat{D}$ its ∘-simulation. Then D is satisfiable if and only if $\widehat{D}$ is satisfiable.*

Proof The proof extends the above example. In one direction, an open tableau for $\widehat{D}$ is also an open tableau for D (ignoring assertions on new role names). In the other direction, an open tableau for D can be transformed to an open tableau for $\widehat{D}$: to every role assertion $R(x, y)$ – added to satisfy an existential $\exists R.C$ in D – chain an assertion $Q_C(y, u_y)$. □

If C is an $\mathcal{ALE}$-concept, its ∘-simulation $\widehat{C}$ is a concept belonging to the language $\mathcal{AL}(\circ, ^-)$, that is, $\mathcal{AL}$ plus role inverses and role chains. Of course, ∘-simulations could be defined for concepts belonging to Description Logics more expressive than $\mathcal{ALE}$. For Description Logics in which every concept is satisfiable (like $\mathcal{FL}^-(\circ, ^-)$) this simulation can be interesting only in subsumptions.

We can now come back to subsumption in the Description Logic $\mathcal{FL}^-$ plus role inverses and role chains.

Theorem 3.22 *Subsumption in $\mathcal{FL}^-(\circ, ^-)$ is NP-hard.*

Proof For every $\mathcal{ALE}$-concept C, one can compute in quadratic time an ∘-simulation $\widehat{C}$. For a given instance $(U, \mathcal{M})$ of XC, $C_\mathcal{M}$ is unsatisfiable iff (by Lemma 3.21) $\widehat{C}_\mathcal{M}$ is satisfiable iff $\widehat{C}_1^1 \sqcap \cdots \sqcap \widehat{C}_1^m$ is subsumed by $\neg D_1$. Now the subsumee contains no negated concept, hence it belongs to $\mathcal{FL}^-(\circ, ^-)$. The subsumer is equivalent to the concept G in (3.8), which again is in $\mathcal{FL}^-(\circ, ^-)$. □

3.4 Combining sources of complexity

In a Description Logic containing both sources of complexity, one might expect to code any problem involving the exploration of polynomial-depth, rooted AND–OR graphs. The computational analog of such graphs is the class APTime (problems solved in polynomial time by an alternating Turing machine) which is equivalent to PSpace (e.g., see [Johnson, 1990, p. 98]). A well-known PSpace-complete problem is Validity of Quantified Boolean Formulae:

Definition 3.23 (Quantified Boolean Formulae QBF**)** Decide the validity of the (second-order logic) closed sentence

$$(Q_1 X_1)(Q_2 X_2) \cdots (Q_n X_n)[F(X_1, \ldots, X_n)],$$

where each Q_i is a quantifier (either $\forall$ or $\exists$) and $F(X_1, \ldots, X_n)$ is a Boolean formula with Boolean variables $X_1, \ldots, X_n$.

The problem remains PSPACE-complete if F is in 3CNF, i.e., conjunctive normal form with at most three literals per clause. We call the string of quantifiers the *prefix* of the quantified formula, and the 3CNF formula F its *matrix*.

This problem can be encoded in an AND–OR graph, using AND-nodes to encode $\forall$-quantifiers, and OR-nodes for $\exists$-quantifiers. In the leaves, there is the matrix F. We use this analogy to illustrate the reduction, taken from [Schmidt-Schauß and Smolka, 1991].

3.4.1 PSPACE *-hardness of satisfiability in $\mathcal{ALC}$*

Without loss of generality, we assume that each clause is non-tautological, i.e., a literal and its complement do not appear both in the same clause. Let $F = G_1 \wedge \cdots \wedge G_m$. The QBF $(Q_1 X_1) \cdots (Q_n X_n)[G_1 \wedge \cdots \wedge G_m]$ is valid iff the $\mathcal{ALC}$-concept

$$C = D \sqcap C_1^1 \sqcap \cdots \sqcap C_1^n \tag{3.9}$$

is satisfiable, where in C all concepts are formed using the concept name A and the atomic role name R. The concept D encodes the prefix, and is of the form $D_1 \sqcap \forall R.(D_2 \sqcap \forall R.(\ldots (D_{n-1} \sqcap \forall R.D_n) \ldots))$ where for $i \in \{1, \ldots, n\}$ each D_i corresponds to a quantifier of the QBF in the following way:

$$D_i = \begin{cases} (\exists R.A) \sqcap (\exists R.\neg A), & \text{if } Q_i = \forall \\ \exists R.\top, & \text{if } Q_i = \exists. \end{cases}$$

The concept C_1^i is obtained from the clause G_i using the concept name A when a Boolean variable occurs positively in G_i, $\neg A$ when it occurs negatively, and nesting l universal role quantifications to encode the variable X_l. In detail, let k be the maximum index of all Boolean variables appearing in G_i. Then, for $l \in \{1, \ldots, (k-1)\}$ one defines

$$C_l^i = \begin{cases} \forall R.(A \sqcup C_{l+1}^i), & \text{if } X_l \text{ appears positively in } G_i \\ \forall R.(\neg A \sqcup C_{l+1}^i), & \text{if } X_l \text{ appears negatively in } G_i \\ \forall R.C_{l+1}^i, & \text{if } X_l \text{ does not appear in } G_i \end{cases}$$

and the last concept of the sequence is defined as

$$C_k^i = \begin{cases} \forall R.A, & \text{if } X_k \text{ appears positively in } G_i \\ \forall R.\neg A, & \text{if } X_k \text{ appears negatively in } G_i. \end{cases}$$

It can be shown that each trace in a tableau branch for D corresponds to a truth assignment to the Boolean variables, and that all traces of a tableau branch correspond to a set of truth assignments consistent with the prefix. Therefore, Schmidt-Schauß and Smolka conclude that satisfiability in $\mathcal{ALC}$ is PSPACE-hard. Combining this result with the polynomial-space calculus given for $\mathcal{ALCN}$ in Chapter 2, one obtains that satisfiability (and subsumption) in $\mathcal{ALCN}$ are PSPACE-complete, and that the exponential-time behavior of the calculus cannot be improved unless PSPACE =PTIME. Satisfiability and subsumption are still in PSPACE if role conjunctions are added to $\mathcal{ALCN}$ [Donini et al., 1997a], or if inverse roles and transitive roles are added to $\mathcal{ALC}$ [Horrocks et al., 2000b].

Using ⊓-simulations, one can use the same reduction to prove that both satisfiability and subsumption in $\mathcal{ALU}(\sqcap)$ are PSPACE-hard (and thus PSPACE-complete). By a more complex reduction, Donini et al. [1991a] proved that satisfiability in $\mathcal{ALN}(\sqcap)$ is also PSPACE-hard. Hemaspaandra [1999] proved that satisfiability in $\mathcal{ALEN}$ is PSPACE-hard using a reduction from QBF, where the prefix was coded with a concept similar to D (more precisely, similar to the concept D in Subsubsection 3.1.1.2), and the matrix was coded in a more complex way. Also $\mathcal{FL}$ was proved PSPACE-hard in [Donini et al., 1997a]. Observe that all these Description Logics contain both sources of complexity.

3.4.2 A remark on reductions

Schild [1991] observed that $\mathcal{ALC}$ is a notational variant of multi-modal logic **K**, whose satisfiability was proved PSPACE-hard by Ladner [1977], using a different reduction from QBF. This gives us the occasion to point out a characteristic of reductions from a different, fairly experimental viewpoint.

The target modal formula in Ladner's reduction has size quadratic w.r.t. the given instance of QBF, while one can observe that the concept C in (3.9) has only linear size. From a theoretical perspective of the PSPACE reduction, this is irrelevant. However, QBF has also been studied from an experimental point of view (e.g., [Cadoli et al., 2000; Gent and Walsh, 1999]): trivial cases have been identified, easy–hard–easy patterns have been found, and one can use ratios of clauses/variables for which the probability that a random QBF is valid is around 0.5 – which have been proved experimentally to contain the "hard" instances. This experimental work can be transferred to Description

Logics, to compare the various algorithms and systems for reasoning in $\mathcal{ALC}$. This transfer yields the benefits that:

- concepts which are trivially (un)satifiable do not need to be isolated again;
- the translation of "hard" QBFs can be used to test reasoning algorithms for $\mathcal{ALC}$;
- the performance of algorithms for $\mathcal{ALC}$ can be compared with best known algorithms for solving QBF (see [Cadoli *et al.*, 2000; Rintanen, 1999; Giunchiglia *et al.*, 2001]), and optimizations can be carried over.

However, using Ladner's reduction to obtain "hard-to-reason" concepts, the quadratic blowup of the reduction soon makes the resulting concepts too big to be significantly tested. Using Schmidt-Schauß and Smolka linear reduction, instead, one can use a spectrum of "hard" concepts as wide as the original instances of QBF. Thus, experimental analysis might make significant differences between (theoretically equivalent) polynomial many-to-one transformations used in reductions [Donini and Massacci, 2000].

3.5 Reasoning in the presence of axioms

In this section we consider the impact of axioms on reasoning. Intuitively, axioms introduce new concept expressions in every individual generated in a tableau, so that simple arguments on termination and complexity based on the nesting of operators do not apply. We start with a comparison with Dynamic Logic, and then we show how axioms can encode a succinct representation of AND–OR graphs, leading to an ExpTime lower bound.

3.5.1 Results from Propositional Dynamic Logic

Propositional Dynamic Logic (PDL) [Harel *et al.*, 2000] is a formalism able to express propositional properties of programs. Instead of introducing yet another logical syntax, we will talk about PDL in terms of Description Logics. A precise correspondence between Description Logics and PDL can be found in Chapter 5.

The counterpart of PDL in Description Logics is $\mathcal{ALC}_{trans}$ [Baader, 1991], already defined in Chapter 2. We recall that $\mathcal{ALC}_{trans}$ is $\mathcal{ALC}$ plus a rich set of role constructors: union of roles, composition, and transitive closure. To be precise, PDL has also a role-forming constructor which is role identity, and the closure of a role is the reflexive–transitive one, denoted as R^*. Reflexive–transitive closure is defined similarly to transitive closure, but considering also every pair (a, a) to be in the interpretation of R^*. However, Schild [1991] showed that these are minor differences, as long as we are concerned with computational behavior only.

PDL and $\mathcal{ALC}_{trans}$ are relevant in this section about axioms, because using union and transitive closure of roles, one can "internalize" axioms in a concept in the following way [Baader, 1991; Schild, 1991]. Let C be an $\mathcal{ALC}$ concept, $\mathcal{T}$ a set of axioms of the form $C_i \sqsubseteq D_i$, $i \in \{1, \ldots, m\}$. Observe that every axiom can also be thought of as a concept $\neg C \sqcup D$ which every individual in a model must belong to. Let $R_1, \ldots, R_n$ be all the role names used in either C or $\mathcal{T}$. Then C is satisfiable w.r.t. $\mathcal{T}$ iff the following concept is satisfiable:

$$C \sqcap \forall (R_1 \sqcup \cdots \sqcup R_n)^*.((\neg C_1 \sqcup D_1) \sqcap \cdots \sqcap (\neg C_m \sqcup D_m)). \qquad (3.10)$$

The key property that makes this reduction correct is the connected model property [Streett, 1982]: if C has a model w.r.t. a set of axioms, then it has also a model in which one element $a \in \Delta^{\mathcal{I}}$ is in $C^{\mathcal{I}}$, and for every other element b in the model, there is a path of roles from a to b.

Concept (3.10) is just a syntactic variant of a PDL expression. Hence, every upper bound on complexity of satisfiability for PDL applies also to concept satisfiability in $\mathcal{ALC}$ w.r.t. axioms, including all role constructors of PDL. Namely, satisfiability in PDL was proved to be decidable in deterministic exponential time, first by Pratt [1979], and then by Vardi and Wolper [1986] using an embedding into tree automata. This upper bound holds also for $\mathcal{ALC}$ plus axioms. It is interesting to observe that the deterministic exponential time upper bound was nontrivial; simple nondeterministic upper bounds were proved by Fischer and Ladner [1979] for PDL and by Buchheit et al. [1993a] for Description Logics, using tableaux. Only recently a tableau with lemmas providing a deterministic exponential upper bound has been found [Donini and Massacci, 2000].

Regarding hardness, every lower bound on reasoning in $\mathcal{ALC}$ with axioms carries over to PDL. However, lower bounds for PDL were already known. Fischer and Ladner [1979] proved that PDL is ExpTime-hard using a reduction from Alternating Turing Machines working in polynomial space (recall that the complexity class Alternating Polynomial Space is the same as ExpTime [Johnson, 1990]). Van Emde Boas [1997] proved the same result using a reduction from alternating domino games. However, both hardness proofs use a very small part of PDL, and in particular, transitive closure on roles appears only in one expression of the form (3.10), so that proofs could be adapted to $\mathcal{ALC}$ concept satisfiability w.r.t. a set of inclusions, in a very simple way. Moreover, the proofs use $\forall R.C$ to code an AND-node, and $\exists R.C$ to code an OR-node. Hence, they follow the same intuition presented in the previous section, where we showed the correspondence between AND–OR trees and satisfiability of $\mathcal{ALC}$ without axioms.

Here, we want to present yet another proof, of a very different nature, that highlights the fact that concept inclusions can express a large structure in a succinct way.

3.5.2 Axioms and succinct representations of AND–OR graphs

We now need more precise definitions about AND–OR graphs. An AND–OR graph is a graph in which nodes are partitioned into AND-nodes and OR-nodes. An OR-node is reachable if one of its predecessors is reachable (as in ordinary graphs), while an AND-node is reachable only if all its predecessors are reachable.

Definition 3.24 (AND–OR graph Accessibility Problem (AGAP))
Given an AND–OR graph, a set of source nodes $S_1, \ldots, S_m$, and a target node T, is T reachable from $S_1, \ldots, S_m$?

Let n be the number of nodes of the graph, and d (a constant) the maximum number of predecessors of a node. It is well known that AGAP can be solved in time polynomial in n (e.g., it can be reduced to Monotone Circuit Value, which is PTIME-complete [Papadimitriou, 1994]). However, AGAP becomes ExpTime-complete when one considers its succinct version [Balcazar, 1996]. Let the out-degree of a node be bounded by a constant d. Let $\mathbf{C}$ be a Boolean circuit with $\log n$ inputs, and with $1 + d \log n$ outputs; when the input of $\mathbf{C}$ is the binary encoding of a node N, its outputs are the encodings of the type of N (AND/OR) and of the d predecessors of N (using a dummy node if there are fewer than d predecessors).

Definition 3.25 (Succinct AND–OR Graph Accessibility Problem (s(AGAP))) Given a circuit $\mathbf{C}$ representing an AND–OR graph, a set of source nodes $S_1, \ldots, S_m$, and a target node T, is T reachable from $S_1, \ldots, S_m$?

Now, s(AGAP) is ExpTime-complete [Balcazar, 1996]. The intuition for this exponential blowup in complexity is that there are many circuits which can encode graphs whose size is exponentially larger than the circuit size. This intuition applies to many other succinct representations of problems with circuits [Papadimitriou, 1994, p. 492] or with propositional formulae [Veith, 1997], yielding complete problems for high complexity classes.

We reduce s(AGAP) for graphs with in-degree $d = 2$ to unsatisfiability of an $\mathcal{ALC}$ concept C w.r.t. a set of inclusions $\mathcal{T}$. Intuitively, the axioms can succinctly encode either a proof of unsatisfiability for a concept, or a model for C w.r.t. $\mathcal{T}$. We note that, since we are coding reachability into unsatisfiability, we will use $\sqcap$ to code OR-nodes – a conjunction is unsatisfiable when at least one of its conjuncts is – and $\sqcup$ to code AND-nodes.

First of all, let $A_1, \ldots, A_{\log n}$ be a set of concept names one-to-one with the inputs of the circuit $\mathbf{C}$. Each node N in the graph is then mapped into a conjunction of As and their negations, denoted by $concept(N)$, depending on the code of N: if the ith bit in the code of N is 1, use A_i, if it is 0, use $\neg A_i$. For example, if N has code 1101 then $concept(N)$ is $A_1 \sqcap A_2 \sqcap \neg A_3 \sqcap A_4$.

Then, let $B_1^1, \ldots, B_{\log n}^1$ and $B_1^2, \ldots, B_{\log n}^2$ be two sets of concept names one-to-one with the outputs of $\mathbf{C}$. Conjunctions of Bs with negations code predecessor nodes.

Moreover, let two concept names AND, OR represent the type of a graph node. If $\mathbf{C}$ has k internal gates, we use also k concept names $W_1, \ldots, W_k$. For each gate, we use a concept equality that mimics the Boolean formula defining the gate. E.g., if $\mathbf{C}$ has an $\wedge$-gate $x_1 \wedge x_2 = x_3$, we use the equality $X_1 \sqcap X_2 = X_3$, where X_1, X_2, X_3 can either be concept names among $W_1, \ldots, W_k$ denoting input/output of internal gates, or be some of the As and Bs, denoting inputs/outputs of the whole circuit.

For the output of $\mathbf{C}$ encoding the type of the node, we use directly the two concept names AND, OR in the concept equality coding the output gate of $\mathbf{C}$. Moreover, to model the different interpretation of predecessors for the two type of nodes, we use the inclusions

$$AND \ \sqsubseteq \ \exists R^1.\top \sqcup \exists R^2.\top \tag{3.11}$$

$$OR \ \sqsubseteq \ \exists R^1.\top \sqcap \exists R^2.\top \tag{3.12}$$

where R^1 and R^2 are two role names (we use indices 1,2 to parallel indices of the Bs). Observe that concept AND implies a disjunction $\sqcup$, and concept OR implies a conjunction $\sqcap$. This is because we reduce reachability to unsatisfiability, as we said before. Moreover, observe that *predecessors* in the AND–OR graph are coded into role *successors* in the target Description Logic.

For the output of $\mathbf{C}$ encoding the predecessors of a node, we add the following inclusions for $i \in \{1, \ldots, \log n\}$:

$$B_i^1 \ \sqsubseteq \ \forall R^1.A_i \tag{3.13}$$

$$\neg B_i^1 \sqsubseteq \forall R^1.\neg A_i \qquad (3.14)$$

$$B_i^2 \sqsubseteq \forall R^2.A_i \qquad (3.15)$$

$$\neg B_i^2 \sqsubseteq \forall R^2.\neg A_i. \qquad (3.16)$$

We denote by $\mathcal{T}_\mathbf{C}$ the set of all of the above axioms.

We now give an example of what the axioms imply. Suppose $\mathbf{C}$ computes the two predecessors 1011 and 0110 for node 1101. Then, equalities coding $\mathbf{C}$ force $concept(1101) = A_1 \sqcap A_2 \sqcap \neg A_3 \sqcap A_4$ to be included in B_1^1, $\neg B_2^1$, B_3^1, B_4^1 (first predecessor) and $\neg B_1^2$, B_2^2, B_3^2, $\neg B_4^2$ (second predecessor). Then inclusions (3.13)–(3.16) say that every R^1-successor is included in A_1, $\neg A_2$, A_3, A_4 – which conjoined, make $concept(1011)$ – and that every R^2-successor is included in $\neg A_1$, A_2, A_3, $\neg A_4$ ($concept(0110)$). Moreover, if $\mathbf{C}$ computes an AND-type for node 1101, then axiom (3.11) implies that the corresponding concept is included in AND, and this implies that either an R^1-successor or an R^2-successor exists. For OR-type nodes, both successors exist.

Theorem 3.26 *Let $\mathbf{C}$ be a circuit, T be the target node, and $S_1, \ldots, S_m$ be the source nodes in an instance of $s(\text{AGAP})$. Then T is reachable from $S_1, \ldots, S_m$ iff $concept(T)$ is unsatisfiable in the TBox $\mathcal{T}_\mathbf{C} \cup \{concept(S_1) \sqsubseteq \perp\} \cup \cdots \cup \{concept(S_m) \sqsubseteq \perp\}$.*

Proof Most of the rationale of the proof has been informally given above. We sketch what is needed to complete the proof.

If Suppose T is unreachable from $S_1, \ldots, S_m$. We construct a model $(\mathcal{I}, \Delta^\mathcal{I})$ for $concept(T)$ satisfying the axioms as follows. Let $\Delta^\mathcal{I}$ be the set of all nodes in the graph which are unreachable from $S_1, \ldots, S_m$. Then, $(R^1)^\mathcal{I}$ is the set of pairs (a, b) of nodes in $\Delta^\mathcal{I}$, such that b is the first predecessor of a, and similarly for $(R^2)^\mathcal{I}$ (second predecessor). For $i \in \{1, \ldots, \log n\}$, $(A_i)^\mathcal{I}$ is the set of nodes in $\Delta^\mathcal{I}$ whose binary code has the ith bit equal to 1. The interpretation of the Bs, Ws, and AND, OR concepts is according to the 1-value of the circuit: node a is in their interpretation iff the output they correspond to is 1 when the code of a is the input of the circuit.

Then, $T \in (concept(T))^\mathcal{I}$, and moreover $(\mathcal{I}, \Delta^\mathcal{I})$ satisfies by construction all axioms in $\mathcal{T}_\mathbf{C}$; e.g., if an OR-node is unreachable, then both its predecessors are unreachable, hence both predecessors are in $\Delta^\mathcal{I}$, and axiom (3.12) is satisfied. Similarly for an AND-node.

Only if Let N be any node reachable from $S_1, \ldots, S_m$, and let $d(N)$ be the depth of the shortest hyperpath leading from $S_1, \ldots, S_m$ to N. We show by induction on $d(N)$ that $concept(N)$ is unsatisfiable in the TBox.

If $d(N) = 0$, the claim holds by construction. Let N be a reachable node, with $d(N) = k + 1$. If N is an OR-node, at least one of its predecessors – let it be the first predecessor, and call it M – is reachable with $d(M) = k$. Then *concept*(M) is unsatisfiable by inductive hypothesis. But axiom (3.12) implies that *concept*(N) is included in $\exists R^1.\top \sqcap \exists R^2.\top$, while (3.13)–(3.16) imply that *concept*(N) is included in $\forall R^1.$*concept*(M), that is, $\forall R^1.\bot$. Hence, also *concept*(N) is unsatisfiable. A similar proof holds in case N is an AND-node.

Then, the claim holds for $N = T$. □

Observe that in the above proof we did not use qualified existential quantification; hence, the proof works for the sublanguage of $\mathcal{ALC}$ called $\mathcal{ALU}$. Now, axioms coding the circuit can be propositionally rewritten without union. Moreover, the only other axiom in which union is needed is (3.11), which could be rewritten equivalently as $\forall R^1.\bot \sqcap \forall R^2.\bot \sqsubseteq \neg OR$, which is now in the language $\mathcal{AL}$.

Theorem 3.27 *Let C be a concept and $\mathcal{T}$ a set of inclusions in $\mathcal{AL}$, with at least two role names. Deciding whether C is unsatisfiable w.r.t. $\mathcal{T}$ is* EXPTIME-*hard.*

The above theorem sharpens a result by Calvanese [1996b], who proved EXPTIME-hardness for $\mathcal{ALU}$. McAllester *et al.* [1996] proved EXPTIME-hardness for a logic that includes $\mathcal{FL}^-\mathcal{E}$, and their proof can be rewritten to work with $\mathcal{ALU}$.

Remark 3.28 The above proof does not follow the correspondence used by Fischer and Ladner [1979] between AND-nodes and $\forall R.C$ concepts on one side, and OR-nodes and $\exists R.C$ concepts on the other side. There, quantifications $\exists R$ and $\forall R.C$ were used to code predecessors in the graph, node type was coded by $\sqcap$, $\sqcup$ constructors, while axioms were crucial to mimic the behavior of the circuit. ■

3.5.3 Syntax restrictions on axioms

In the proof, no restriction on axioms was imposed. A significant syntactic restriction is to allow only concept names on the left-hand side of axioms. In this case, a dependency graph induced by the axioms of a TBox $\mathcal{T}$ can be constructed, whose nodes are labeled by concept names. A node A is connected to a node B if the concept name B appears (also as a subconcept) in a concept C, and $A \sqsubseteq C$ is an axiom. Then, it makes sense to distinguish between *cyclic* axioms, in which the dependency graph contains a cycle, and *acyclic* axioms.

Acyclicity is significant, because if only acyclic axioms are allowed, then reasoning in $\mathcal{ALC}$ can be performed in PSPACE by expanding axioms when needed [Baader and Hollunder, 1991b; Calvanese, 1996b]. The only case for $\mathcal{ALC}$ (till now) in which acyclic axioms make reasoning EXPTIME-hard is when concrete domains are also added [Lutz, 2001b].

Also sublanguages of $\mathcal{ALC}$ can be considered. With regard to acyclic axioms in $\mathcal{AL}$, Buchheit *et al.* [1998] proved that subsumption in acyclic $\mathcal{AL}$ TBoxes is coNP-hard, and in PSPACE. Calvanese [1996b] proved that cyclic axioms in $\mathcal{AL}$ are PSPACE-complete, and other results for $\mathcal{ALE}$ and $\mathcal{ALU}$.

A second possible restriction is to allow axioms of the form $A \equiv C$, but in which a concept name can appear only *once* on the left-hand side. For axioms of this form in $\mathcal{ALN}$, Küsters [1998] proved that reasoning is PSPACE-complete when the TBox is cyclic, and NP-complete when it is acyclic.

3.6 Undecidability

One of the main reasons why satisfiability and subsumption in many Description Logics are decidable – although highly complex – is that most of the concept constructors can express only *local* properties about an element [Vardi, 1997; Libkin, 2000]. Let C be a concept in $\mathcal{ALC}$: recalling the tableau methods in Chapter 2, an assertion $C(x)$ states properties about x, and about elements which are linked to x by a chain of at most $|C|$ role assertions. Intuitively, this implies that a constraint regarding x will not "talk about" elements which are arbitrarily far (w.r.t. role links) from x. This also means that in $\mathcal{ALC}$, and in many Description Logics, an assertion on an individual cannot state properties about a whole structure satisfying it. However, not every Description Logic satisfies locality.

3.6.1 Undecidability of role-value-maps

The first notable non-local Description Logic is a subset of the language of the knowledge representation system KL-ONE, isolated by Schmidt-Schauß [1989], which we call[2] $\mathcal{FL}^-(\circ, =)$. It contains conjunction, universal quantification, role composition, and *equality role-value-maps* $R = Q$. A

---

[2] In his paper, Schmidt-Schauß used the name $\mathcal{ALR}$.

Table 3.2. *Syntax and semantics of the Description Logic* $\mathcal{FL}^-(\circ, \subseteq)$.

	concept expressions	semantics
concept name	A	$\subseteq \Delta^{\mathcal{I}}$
value restriction	$\forall R.C$	$\{x \in \Delta^{\mathcal{I}} \mid \forall y. \, (x,y) \in R^{\mathcal{I}} \rightarrow y \in C^{\mathcal{I}}\}$
concept intersection	$C \sqcap D$	$C^{\mathcal{I}} \cap D^{\mathcal{I}}$
role-value-map	$R \subseteq Q$	$\{x \in \Delta^{\mathcal{I}} \mid \forall y. \, (x,y) \in R^{\mathcal{I}} \rightarrow (x,y) \in Q^{\mathcal{I}}\}$

	role expressions	semantics
role name	P	$\subseteq \Delta^{\mathcal{I}} \times \Delta^{\mathcal{I}}$
role composition	$R \circ Q$	$\{(x,y) \in \Delta^{\mathcal{I}} \times \Delta^{\mathcal{I}} \mid \exists z. \, (x,z) \in R^{\mathcal{I}},$ $(z,y) \in Q^{\mathcal{I}}\}$

role-value-map allows one to express concepts like "persons whose co-workers coincide with their relatives", as it could be, e.g., a small family-based firm. Using two role names co-worker and relative, this concept would be expressed as (co-worker = relative ⊓ person).

The Description Logic proved undecidable by Schmidt-Schauß used equality role-value-maps. Here we present a simpler proof for a Description Logic using *containment* role-value-maps $R \subseteq Q$. We call this Description Logic $\mathcal{FL}^-(\circ, \subseteq)$. Clearly, $\mathcal{FL}^-(\circ, \subseteq)$ is (slightly) more expressive than $\mathcal{FL}^-(\circ, =)$, since $R = Q$ can be expressed by $(R \subseteq Q) \sqcap (Q \subseteq R)$, but not vice versa. Most of the original reduction is preserved, though.

Although all constructs of $\mathcal{FL}^-(\circ, \subseteq)$ have already been defined in different parts of Chapter 2, we recall for convenience their syntax and semantics in the single Table 3.2. Recall that $R \subseteq Q$ is a concept: namely, the concept of all elements whose set of fillers for role R is included in the set of fillers for role Q. To avoid many parentheses, we assume ∘ has always precedence over $\subseteq$.

Before giving the proof that subsumption in $\mathcal{FL}^-(\circ, \subseteq)$ is undecidable, let us consider an example illustrating why $\mathcal{FL}^-(\circ, \subseteq)$ is not local.

Example 3.29 Let Q, R, S, U, V be role names. Consider whether the concept $C = \forall S.\forall U.A \sqcap (R \circ Q \subseteq S) \sqcap \forall R.(Q \circ U \subseteq V)$ is subsumed by the concept $D = \forall R.\forall Q.\forall U.B$.

The answer is no: in fact, a model satisfying C and not satisfying D is shown in Fig. 3.2. This model can be obtained by trying to satisfy $\neg D = \exists R.\exists Q.\exists U.\neg B$ with individual x, y, z, w, and then adding role assertions satisfying C. Observe that a model of C cannot be a tree because of concepts like $(R \circ Q \subseteq S)$. Hence, any notion of "distance" between two

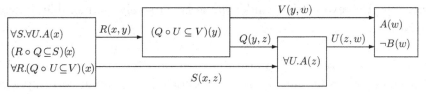

Fig. 3.2. A possible countermodel for $C \sqsubseteq D$ in Example 3.29. Boxes group assertions about an individual; arrows represent role assertions.

individuals in a model, as the number of role links connecting them, is ambiguous when a Description Logic has role-value-maps. Moreover, the satisfaction of the assertions $(R \circ Q \subseteq S)(x)$ and $\forall S.A(x)$ in an interpretation depends on the satisfaction of the assertion $A(z)$, for every individual z connected to x via a path of role fillers that can be composed according to role-value-maps. In fact, replacing B with A in D yields a concept D' which now subsumes C – and indeed, the previous model satisfies also D'.   ∎

These properties are crucial for the reduction from ground rewriting systems to subsumption in $\mathcal{FL}^-(\circ, \subseteq)$. For basics about rewriting systems, consult [Dershowitz and Jouannaud, 1990].

Definition 3.30 (Ground rewriting system) Let Σ be a finite alphabet $\{a, b, \ldots\}$. A *term* w on Σ is an element of Σ^*, i.e., a finite sequence of 0 or more letters from Σ. If v, w are terms, their *concatenation* is a term, denoted by vw. A ground *rewriting system* is a finite set of rewriting rules $\rho = \{s_i \to t_i\}_{i=1,\ldots,n}$, where for every $i \in \{1, \ldots, n\}$ both s_i and t_i are terms on Σ. The *rewriting relation* $\overset{*}{\to}$ induced by a set of rewriting rules ρ is the minimal relation which is reflexive, transitive, and satisfies the following conditions:

1. if $s \to t \in \rho$ then $s \overset{*}{\to} t$;
2. for every letter $a \in \Sigma$, if $p \overset{*}{\to} q$ then both $ap \overset{*}{\to} aq$ and $pa \overset{*}{\to} qa$.

The *rewriting problem* for ground rewriting systems is: Given a set of rewriting rules ρ and two terms v, w, decide whether $v \overset{*}{\to} w$.

Remark 3.31 In general, a single rewriting step of a term v consists in finding a substring of v which coincides with the antecedent s of a rewriting rule $s \to t$, and then substituting t for s in v. Hence, $v \overset{*}{\to} w$ if there exist n terms $u_1, \ldots, u_n$ such that $u_1 = v$, $u_n = w$, and for each $i \in \{1, \ldots, n-1\}$ the two terms u_i, u_{i+1} are such that for some terms p and q, we have $u_i = psq$, $u_{i+1} = ptq$, and $s \to t \in \rho$. This proves that the term problem is recursively enumerable. However, it is semidecidable (recursively enumerable, but non-recursive). ∎

We reduce this problem to subsumption in $\mathcal{FL}^-(\circ, \subseteq)$ as follows. First of all, observe that we can define the following one-to-one correspondence between terms and role chains:

- For every letter a in Σ, let P_a be a role name.
- For every term w, let R_w be the composition of the role names corresponding to the letters of w. For example, if $w = aab$, then $R_w = P_a \circ P_a \circ P_b$.

Now for each set of rewriting rules ρ, we define the concept C_ρ as

$$C_\rho = \bigsqcap\nolimits_{s \to t \in \rho} (R_s \subseteq R_t).$$

Let Q be a new atomic role: we define a concept C_Σ as

$$C_\Sigma = \bigsqcap\nolimits_{a \in \Sigma} (Q \circ P_a \subseteq Q).$$

Intuitively, if a model $\mathcal{I}$ satisfies $C_\Sigma(x)$, then for every term w, if $(Q \circ R_w)(x, z)$ holds in $\mathcal{I}$, then $Q(x, z)$ also holds, i.e., x is directly connected via Q to every other element z to which it is indirectly connected via $Q \circ R_w$.

If also $\mathcal{I} \models \forall Q.C_\rho(x)$, then $C_\rho(z)$ holds for every such z. This is a key property of the reduction.

Remark 3.32 The two concepts $\forall Q.C_\rho$ and C_Σ are a way to internalize simple axioms in a concept. Consider a TBox $\mathcal{T} = \{\top \sqsubseteq C_\rho\}$ which states that every individual in a model must satisfy concept C_ρ. One could prove that in $\mathcal{FL}^-(\circ, \subseteq)$ a concept C is subsumed by a concept D w.r.t. $\mathcal{T}$ iff $C_\Sigma \sqcap \forall Q.C_\rho \sqcap \forall Q.C$ is subsumed by $\forall Q.D$, where the latter is plain subsumption between concept expressions. ∎

Theorem 3.33 *Subsumption in $\mathcal{FL}^-(\circ, \subseteq)$ is undecidable.*

Let ρ be a set of rewriting rules, and v, w be two terms. Define the following two concepts:

$$C = C_\Sigma \sqcap \forall Q.C_\rho \tag{3.17}$$
$$D = \forall Q.(R_v \subseteq R_w). \tag{3.18}$$

We divide the proof in two lemmas.

Lemma 3.34 *If $v \xrightarrow{*} w$ then the concept C is subsumed by D.*

Proof We first prove that the claim holds for the base case of the inductive definition of $\stackrel{*}{\rightarrow}$ (Condition (i) in Definition 3.30). Then, we prove the claim for the two inductive cases (Condition (ii)). Finally, we prove that the proof carries over the closure conditions. In all cases, let $s \rightarrow t \in \rho$.

Base case The concept D is $\forall Q.(R_s \subseteq R_t)$. Observe that the concept $\forall Q.C_\rho$ is equivalent to $\bigsqcap_{s \rightarrow t \in \rho} \forall Q.(R_s \subseteq R_t)$. Hence, C is subsumed by D because D is one of the conjuncts of (an equivalent form of) C.

Inductive cases For the first inductive case, let $D = \forall Q.(P_a \circ R_p \subseteq P_a \circ R_q)$, and let the inductive hypothesis be that C is subsumed by $\forall Q.R_p \subseteq R_q$. For a contradiction, suppose C is not subsumed by D: then, there is a model $\mathcal{I}$ in which both $C(x)$ and $\neg D(x)$ hold. The latter constraint implies that there is an element y such that:

1. $\mathcal{I} \models Q(x, y)$
2. $\mathcal{I} \models (P_a \circ R_p)(y, z)$
3. $\mathcal{I} \not\models (P_a \circ R_q)(y, z)$.

From 2, there is an element y' such that both $P_a(y, y')$ and $R_p(y', z)$ hold. Now from $C_\Sigma(x)$, we must have $\mathcal{I} \models Q(x, y')$, and from the inductive hypothesis this implies $(R_p \subseteq R_q)(y')$. Then, $\mathcal{I} \models R_q(y', z)$ holds, hence $\mathcal{I} \models (P_a \circ R_q)(y, z)$, contradicting 3.

The second inductive case is simpler, since one does not need to consider $C_\Sigma(x)$. The interested reader can use it as an exercise.

We conclude the proof by showing that the reduction carries over the reflexive and transitive closure of $\stackrel{*}{\rightarrow}$.

First, from the semantics in Table 3.2 it follows that $R_w \subseteq R_w$ is equivalent to $\top$, which implies also that $D \equiv \top$. Hence the claim holds also for $w \stackrel{*}{\rightarrow} w$ (i.e., reflexivity).

For transitivity, the induction is easy: suppose $u \stackrel{*}{\rightarrow} v$ and $v \stackrel{*}{\rightarrow} w$: then by induction C is subsumed by D_1 and by D_2, where $D_1 = \forall Q.(R_u \subseteq R_v)$ and $D_2 = \forall Q.(R_v \subseteq R_w)$. Then C is subsumed also by $D_1 \sqcap D_2$ which is equivalent to $\forall Q.((R_u \subseteq R_v) \sqcap (R_v \subseteq R_w))$. This concept is subsumed by $\forall Q.(R_u \subseteq R_w)$, which is the claim. $\qquad\square$

We now prove the other direction of the reduction.

Lemma 3.35 *If $v \stackrel{*}{\not\rightarrow} w$, then the concept C is not subsumed by D.*

Proof We give the rule for constructing an infinite tableau branch $\mathcal{T}$ and show that it defines a model that satisfies C, and does not satisfy D. The tableau is one-to-one with an infinite automaton accepting the term v, and every other term into which v can be rewritten. Let $v[1], \ldots, v[n]$ denote the n letters of v ($v[i]$ is the ith letter of v).

Let x, y, z be individual names. Start from the set of assertions

$$\mathcal{T}_0 = P_{v[1]}(y, y_1), \ldots, P_{v[i+1]}(y_i, y_{i+1}), \ldots, P_{v[n]}(y_{n-1}, z).$$

Then add role assertions to $\mathcal{T}$ following the $\rightarrow_{\subseteq}$**-rule**:

Condition there is a rewriting rule $s \rightarrow t \in \rho$
> where $s = s[1] \cdots s[h]$ and $t = t[1] \cdots t[k]$;
> $\mathcal{T}$ contains $h + 1$ individuals $y_0, \ldots, y_h$ and h assertions
> $P_{s[i]}(y_{i-1}, y_i)$ for $i \in \{1, \ldots, h\}$
> $\mathcal{T}$ does not contain all assertions $P_{t[1]}(y_0, y_1'), \ldots, P_{t[k]}(y_{k-1}', y_h)$

Action $\mathcal{T}' = \mathcal{T} \cup \{P_{t[1]}(y_0, y_1'), \ldots, P_{t[k]}(y_{k-1}', y_h)\}$,
> where $y_1', \ldots, y_{k-1}'$, are $k - 1$ individual names not occurring in $\mathcal{T}$.

Intuitively, if there is in $\mathcal{T}$ a path of role assertions such that $R_s(y_0, y_h)$ holds, the $\rightarrow_{\subseteq}$-rule adds another path such that also $R_t(y_0, y_h)$ holds. Of course, $\mathcal{T}_\omega$ can have an infinite number of individuals and role assertions between them; this is reasonable, since its role paths from y to z are one-to-one with the possible transformations on v one can make using the rewriting rules. One can also think of $\mathcal{T}_\omega$ as an infinite-state automaton accepting $\overline{v} = \{u \mid v \xrightarrow{*} u\}$.

The $\rightarrow_{\subseteq}$-rule always adds new assertions to $\mathcal{T}$, and its application given some premises does not destroy other premises of application of the $\rightarrow_{\subseteq}$-rule itself, since we keep in $\mathcal{T}$ all the rewritten terms. Therefore, the construction is monotonic over the $\subseteq$-lattice of all tableaux with a countable number of individuals and role assertions between individuals. Hence there exists a fixpoint $\mathcal{T}_\omega$. In building $\mathcal{T}_\omega$, however, a *fair strategy* must be adopted. That is, if at a given stage $\mathcal{T}_i$ of the construction, the $\rightarrow_{\subseteq}$-rule is applicable for individuals $y_0, \ldots, y_h$, then for some finite k, in $\mathcal{T}_{i+k}$ the $\rightarrow_{\subseteq}$-rule has been applied for those premises – i.e., a possible rule application is not indefinitely deferred. This could be achieved by, e.g., inserting possible rule applications in a queue.

Proposition 3.36 *Let $\mathcal{T}_\omega$ be constructed using the $\rightarrow_{\subseteq}$-rule, and a fair strategy. For every term $u = u[1] \cdots u[k]$, $v \xrightarrow{*} u$ iff in $\mathcal{T}_\omega$ there are $k - 1$ individual names $y_1, \ldots, y_{k-1}$ and k assertions $P_{u[1]}(y, y_1), \ldots, P_{u[k]}(y_{k-1}, z)$.*

Proof If $v \xrightarrow{*} u$, then there are a minimum finite number n of applications of rewriting rules in ρ transforming v into u. By induction on such n, the premises of the $\rightarrow_{\subseteq}$-rule are fulfilled, and since $\mathcal{T}_\omega$ is built adopting a fair strategy, from some finite stage of its construction onwards, $R_u(y, z)$ must hold. For the other direction, if $R_u(y, z)$ holds in $\mathcal{T}_\omega$, then for each $\rightarrow_\sqsubseteq$-rule application leading to $R_u(y, z)$ one can apply a rewriting rule to v, leading to u. $\qquad\square$

We can now define the model $\mathcal{I}$ satisfying C and not satisfying D. Let N be the set of individual names of $\mathcal{T}_\omega$. $\mathcal{I}$ has domain $\{x\} \cup N$. Let $\mathcal{I} = \mathcal{T}_\omega \cup \{Q(x, y) | y \in N\}$. Then $\mathcal{I}$ satisfies $C(x)$ straightforwardly; moreover, it does not satisfy D from Proposition 3.36. $\qquad\square$

To prove that subsumption is undecidable in the less expressive Description Logic $\mathcal{FL}^-(\circ, =)$, Schmidt-Schauß [1989] started from the word problem for groups. Starting from the Post correspondence problem, with a more complex construction, Patel-Schneider [1989b] proved that subsumption is also undecidable in the more expressive Description Logic $\mathcal{FL}^-(\circ, \sqsubseteq)$ plus role inverses, functional roles, and role restrictions.

Starting from the *word problem* – which is less general than the term rewriting problem, but still semidecidable – Baader [1998] showed that subsumption in $\mathcal{FL}^-(\circ, \sqsubseteq)$ is undecidable without referring to tableaux. We report here the second part of his proof (corresponding to Lemma 3.35), since it is quite short and elegant, and shows a different way of proving the only-if direction, namely, giving a direct definition of an infinite structure satisfying the concepts.

The word problem follows Definition 3.30, but considers the reflexive-symmetric-transitive closure $\overset{*}{\leftrightarrow}$ of rewriting rules. This is also known as the word problem for semigroups, or Thue systems. In this case, *ground term* and *word* are synonyms. Of course, $\overset{*}{\leftrightarrow}$ is an equivalence relation on words; let $[v]$ denote the $\overset{*}{\leftrightarrow}$-equivalence classes. Note that $[u] = [v]$ iff $u \overset{*}{\leftrightarrow} v$. There is a natural multiplication on these classes induced by concatenation: $[u][v] = [uv]$ (since $\overset{*}{\leftrightarrow}$ is even a congruence, this is well-defined).

Taking the equivalence classes plus one distinguished element x as the domain of the model $\mathcal{I}$, the roles can be interpreted as

$$Q^\mathcal{I} = \{(x, [u]) | u \in \Sigma^*\} \tag{3.19}$$
$$(P_a)^\mathcal{I} = \{([u], [ua]) | a \in \Sigma, u \in \Sigma^*\}. \tag{3.20}$$

Then, it can be shown that if $v \overset{*}{\not\leftrightarrow} w$, then x belongs to $C^\mathcal{I}$ but not to $D^\mathcal{I}$, as follows:

1. x belongs to $C^\mathcal{I}$: from (3.20), for every word u we have $(x, [u]) \in Q^\mathcal{I}$ and $([u], [ua]) \in (P_a)^\mathcal{I}$; but also from (3.19), $(x, [ua]) \in Q^\mathcal{I}$, hence $C_\Sigma(x)$ is

satisfied by $\mathcal{I}$. Regarding $\forall Q.C_\rho(x)$, suppose $([u], [w]) \in (R_s)^{\mathcal{I}}$, where $s \rightarrow t \in \rho$. Then $[w] = [us]$ by definition of $(P_a)^{\mathcal{I}}$. Moreover, from $s \rightarrow t \in \rho$ it follows that $us \overset{*}{\leftrightarrow} ut$, hence $[us] = [ut]$. Consequently, $([u], [w]) = ([u], [ut]) \in (R_t)^{\mathcal{I}}$ from (3.20).

2. x does not belong to $D^{\mathcal{I}}$: for the empty word ϵ, $[\epsilon]$ is a Q-filler of x; however, $[\epsilon]$ does not satisfy the concept $R_v \sqsubseteq R_w$. In fact, $([\epsilon], [v]) \in (R_v)^{\mathcal{I}}$; but $([\epsilon], [v]) \notin (R_w)^{\mathcal{I}}$, since $[w]$ is the only R_w-filler of $[\epsilon]$ but $[v] \neq [w]$ from the assumption that $v \overset{*}{\not\rightarrow} w$.

3.7 Reasoning about individuals in ABoxes

When an ABox is considered, the reasoning problem of *instance checking* arises: Given an ABox $\mathcal{A}$, an individual a and a concept C, decide whether $\mathcal{A} \models C(a)$. For the instance check problem, the size of the input is formed by the size of the concept expression C plus the size of $\mathcal{A}$. Since the size of one input may be much larger than the other in real applications, it makes sense to distinguish the complexity w.r.t. the two inputs – as is usually done in databases with data complexity and query complexity [Vardi, 1982].

A common intuition [Schmolze and Lipkis, 1983] about instance checking was that it could be performed via subsumption, using the so-called most specific concept (msc) method.

Definition 3.37 (Most specific concepts) Let $\mathcal{A}$ be an ABox in a given Description Logic, and let a be an individual in $\mathcal{A}$. A concept C is the *most specific concept* of a in $\mathcal{A}$, written $msc(\mathcal{A}, a)$, if, for every concept D in the given Description Logic, $\mathcal{A} \models D(a)$ implies $C \sqsubseteq D$.

Recall from Chapter 2 a slightly different definition of msc in the *realization problem*: given an individual a and an ABox $\mathcal{A}$, find the most specific concepts C (w.r.t. subsumption) such that $\mathcal{A} \models C(a)$ [Nebel, 1990a, p. 104]. Since conjunction is always available in every Description Logic, the two definitions are equivalent (just conjoin all specific concepts of realization into one msc).

Clearly, once $msc(\mathcal{A}, a)$ is known, to decide whether a is an instance of a concept D it should be sufficient to check whether $msc(\mathcal{A}, a)$ is subsumed by D, turning instance checking into subsumption. Moreover, when a TBox is present, off-line classification of all msc's in the TBox may provide a way to pre-compute many instance checks, providing an on-line speed-up.

The intuition about how to compute $msc(\mathcal{A}, a)$ was to gather the concepts/properties explicitly stated for a in $\mathcal{A}$. However, this approach is quite sensitive to the Description Logic chosen to express $msc(\mathcal{A}, a)$ and the queries. In fact, most specific concepts can be easily computed for simple Description Logics, like $\mathcal{AL}$. However, it may not be possible when slightly more expressive languages are considered.

Example 3.38 A simple example (simplified from [Baader and Küsters, 1998]) is the ABox made just by the assertion $R(a, a)$. If $\mathcal{FL}^-$ is used for most specific concepts and queries, then $msc(\{R(a, a)\}, a) = \exists R$. However, if qualified existential quantification is allowed for most specific concepts, then each of the concepts $\exists R$, $\exists R.\exists R$, $\exists R.\exists R.\exists R$, $\ldots$, is more specific than the previous one. Using this argument, it is possible to prove that $msc(\{R(a, a)\}, a)$ has no finite representation, unless transitive closure on roles is also allowed. Using the axiom $A \sqsubseteq \exists R.A$ in an ad hoc TBox, $msc(\{R(a, a)\}, a) = A$ for the simple ABox of this example – but this does not simplify instance checking. An alternative approach would be to raise individuals in the language to express concepts, through the concept constructor $\{\ldots\}$ that enumerates the individuals belonging to it (called "one-of" in CLASSIC). In that case, $msc(\{R(a, a)\}, a) = \exists R.\{a\}$ (see [Donini *et al.*, 1990]). But this "solution" to instance checking becomes now a problem for subsumption, which must take individuals into account (for a treatment of Description Logics with one-of, see [Schaerf, 1994a]). ∎

The msc method makes an implicit assumption: to work well, the size of $msc(\mathcal{A}, a)$ should be comparable with the size of the whole ABox, and in most cases much shorter. However, consider the Description Logic $\mathcal{ALE}$, in which subsumption is in NP. Then, solving instance checking by means of subsumption in polynomial space and time would imply that instance checking was in NP, too. However, suppose that we prove that instance checking is hard for coNP. Then, solving instance checking by subsumption implies that either coNP $\subseteq$ NP, or $msc(\mathcal{A}, a)$, if ever exists, has superpolynomial size w.r.t. $\mathcal{A}$. The former conclusion is unlikely to hold, while the latter would make unfeasible the entire method of msc's.

In general, this argument works whenever subsumption in a Description Logic belongs to a complexity class $\mathcal{C}$, while instance checking is proved hard for a different complexity class $\mathcal{C}'$, for which $\mathcal{C}' \subseteq \mathcal{C}$ is believed to be false. We present here a proof using this argument, found by Schaerf [1993; 1994b; 1994a].

We first start with a simple example highlighting the construction.

Example 3.39 Let f, c_1, c_2, x, y, z be individuals, R, P, N be role names, and A be a concept name. Let $\mathcal{A}$ be the following ABox, whose structure we highlight by means of arrows between assertions:

$$f \begin{array}{c} \nearrow R(f, c_1) \\ \searrow R(f, c_2) \end{array} \begin{array}{c} \nearrow P(c_1, x) \quad A(x) \\ \searrow N(c_1, y) \\ \nearrow P(c_2, y) \\ \searrow N(c_2, z) \quad \neg A(z). \end{array}$$

The query $\exists R.(\exists P.A \sqcap \exists N.\neg A)(f)$ is entailed by $\mathcal{A}$. That is, one among c_1 and c_2 has its P-filler in A and its N-filler in $\neg A$. This can be verified by *case analysis* on y: in every model either $A(y)$ or $\neg A(y)$ must be true. For models in which $A(y)$ holds, c_2 is the R-filler of f satisfying the query; for models in which $\neg A(y)$ holds, c_1 is. Observe that if $\mathcal{ALE}$ is used to express most specific concepts, the best approximation we can find for $msc(\mathcal{A}, f)$, by collecting assertions along the role paths starting from f, is the concept $C = \exists R.(\exists P.A \sqcap \exists N) \sqcap \exists R.(\exists P \sqcap \exists N.\neg A)$, in which the fact that the *same* individual y is both the N-filler of $\exists N$ and the P-filler of $\exists P$ is lost. Indeed, C is *not* subsumed by the query, as one can see by constructing an open tableau for $C \sqcap \neg \exists R.(\exists P.A \sqcap \exists N.\neg A)(f)$.   ∎

The above example can be extended to a proof that deciding $\mathcal{A} \models C(a)$, where C is an $\mathcal{ALE}$-concept, is coNP-hard. Observe that this is a different source of complexity w.r.t. unsatisfiability in $\mathcal{ALE}$. In fact, a concept C is unsatisfiable iff $\{C(a)\} \models \bot(a)$. This problem is NP-complete when C is a concept in $\mathcal{ALE}$ (Subsection 3.3.1).

The source coNP-complete problem is the complement of 2+2-SAT, which is the following problem.

Definition 3.40 (2+2-SAT) Given a 4CNF propositional formula F, in which every clause has exactly two positive literals and two negative ones, decide whether F is satisfiable.

The problem 2+2-SAT is a simple variant of the well-known 3-SAT. Indeed, for 3-literal clauses mixing both positive and negative literals, add a fourth disjunct, constantly false; e.g., $X \vee Y \vee \neg Z$ is transformed into the 2+2-clause $X \vee Y \vee \neg Z \vee \neg\mathbf{true}$. Unmixed clauses can be replaced by two mixed ones using a new variable (see [Schaerf, 1994a, Theorem 4.2.6]).

Given an instance of 2+2-SAT $F = C_1 \wedge C_2 \wedge \cdots \wedge C_n$, where each clause $C_i = L_{1+}^i \vee L_{2+}^i \vee \neg L_{1-}^i \vee \neg L_{2-}^i$, we construct an ABox $\mathcal{A}_F$ as follows. $\mathcal{A}_F$ has one individual l for each variable L in F, one individual c_i for each clause

C_i, one individual f for the whole formula F, plus two individuals *true* and *false* for the corresponding propositional constants.

The roles of $\mathcal{A}_F$ are Cl (for Clause), P_1, P_2 (for positive literals), N_1, N_2 (for negative literals), and the only concept name is A. Finally, $\mathcal{A}_F$ is given by (we group role assertions on first individual to ease reading):

$$
Cl(f, c_1) \begin{cases} P_1(c_1, l^1_{1+}) \\ P_2(c_1, l^1_{2+}) \\ N_1(c_1, l^1_{1-}) \\ N_2(c_1, l^1_{2-}) \end{cases}
$$

$$
\vdots \qquad\qquad \vdots \qquad\qquad A(true), \quad \neg A(false).
$$

$$
Cl(f, c_n) \begin{cases} P_1(c_n, l^n_{1+}) \\ P_2(c_n, l^n_{2+}) \\ N_1(c_n, l^n_{1-}) \\ N_2(c_n, l^n_{2-}) \end{cases}
$$

Now let D be the following, fixed, query concept:

$$
D = \exists Cl.((\exists P_1.\neg A) \sqcap (\exists P_2.\neg A) \sqcap (\exists N_1.A) \sqcap (\exists N_2.A)).
$$

Intuitively, an individual name l is in the extension of A or $\neg A$ iff the propositional variable L is assigned **true** or **false**, respectively. Then, checking whether $\mathcal{A}_F \models D(f)$ corresponds to checking that in every truth assignment for F there exists a clause whose positive literals are interpreted as false, and whose negative literals are interpreted as true – i.e., a clause that is not satisfied. If one applies the above idea to translate the two clauses (having just two literals each) **false** $\vee \neg Y$, $Y \vee \neg$**true**, one obtains exactly the ABox of Example 3.39.

The correctness of this reduction was proved by Schaerf [1993; 1994a]. We report here only the concluding lemma.

Lemma 3.41 *A 2+2-CNF formula F is unsatisfiable if and only if $\mathcal{A}_F \models D(f)$.*

Hence, instance checking in $\mathcal{ALE}$ is coNP-hard. This implies that instance check in $\mathcal{ALE}$ cannot be efficiently solved by subsumption, unless coNP $\subseteq$ NP. We remark that only the size of $\mathcal{A}_F$ depends on the source formula F, while D is fixed. Hence, instance checking in $\mathcal{ALE}$ is coNP-hard with respect to *knowledge base* complexity – and it is also NP-hard from Subsection 3.3.1. The upper bound for knowledge base complexity of instance checking in $\mathcal{ALE}$ is in Π^p_2, but it is still not known whether the problem is Π^p_2-complete. Regarding combined complexity – that is, neither the size of the ABox nor that of the query is fixed – in [Schaerf, 1994a; Donini *et al.*, 1994b] it was proved that instance checking in $\mathcal{ALE}$ is PSPACE-complete.

Since the above reduction makes use of negated concept names, it may seem that coNP-hardness arises from the interaction between qualified existential quantification and negated concept names. However, all that is needed are two concepts whose union covers all possible cases. We saw in Subsection 3.2.1 that $\exists R$ and $\forall R.B$ have this property. Therefore, if we replace A and $\neg A$ in $\mathcal{A}_F$ with $\exists R$ and $\forall R.B$, respectively (where R is a *new* role name and B is a *new* concept name), we obtain a new reduction for which Lemma 3.41 still holds. Hence, instance checking in $\mathcal{FL}^-\mathcal{E}$ (i.e., $\mathcal{ALE}$ without negation of concept names) is coNP-hard too, thus confirming that coNP-hardness is originated by qualified existential quantification alone. In other words, intractability arises from a query language containing both qualified existential quantification, and pairs of concepts whose union is equivalent to $\top$. Hence, for languages containing these constructs, the msc method is not effective.

Regarding the expressivity of the language for assertions in the ABox, coNP-hardness of instance checking arises already when assertions in the ABox involve just concept and role names. However, note that a key point in the reduction is the fact that two individuals in the ABox can be linked via different role paths, as f and y were in Example 3.39.

3.8 Discussion

In this chapter we analyzed various lower bounds on the complexity of reasoning about simple concept expressions in Description Logics. Our presentation appealed to the intuitive notions of exploring AND–OR trees, in the special case when the tree is derived from a tableau.

We remark that an alternative approach to reasoning is to reduce it to the emptiness test for automata (e.g., [Vardi, 1996]), which has been quite successfully applied to temporal logics, and propositional logics of programs. However, till now such techniques have been used to obtain upper bounds in reasoning, while in order to obtain lower bounds one would need a way to reduce problems on automata to unsatisfiability/subsumption in Description Logic. The only example of this reduction is [Nebel, 1990b], for a very simple Description Logic, which we have omitted in this chapter for lack of space.

We end the chapter with a perspective on the significance of the NP, coNP, and PSPACE complexity lower bounds we have presented. Present reasoning systems in Description Logics (see Chapter 8) can now cope with reasonable size EXPTIME-complete problems. Hence the computational complexity of the problems now reachable is above PSPACE. However, in our opinion, for implemented systems the significance of a reduction lies not just in the theoretical lower bound obtained, but also in the reduction itself. In fact, when experimenting with algorithms for subsumption, satisfiability, etc. [Baader *et al.*, 1992b; Hustadt and Schmidt, 1997] on an implemented system, one can exploit already known "hard" cases of a source problem like 3-SAT, 2+2-SAT, SET SPLITTING, or QBF validity to obtain "hard" instances for the algorithm under test. These instances isolate the influence of each source of combinatorial explosion on the performance of the overall reasoning system, and can be used to optimize reasoning algorithms in a piecewise fashion [Horrocks and Patel-Schneider, 1999], separately for the various sources of complexity. In this respect, the issue of finding "efficient" reductions (w.r.t. the size of the resulting concepts) is still open, and can make the difference when concepts to be tested scale up (see [Donini and Massacci, 2000]).

3.9 A list of complexity results for subsumption and satisfiability

Many names have been invented for languages of different Description Logics, e.g., $\mathcal{FL}$ for Frame Language, $\mathcal{ALC}$ for Attributive Descriptions Language with Complement, etc. Although suggestive, these names are not very explicit about which constructs are in the named language. This makes the huge mass of results about complexity of reasoning in Description Logics often difficult to screen by non-experts in the field. To clarify the constructs each language is equipped with, we use two lists of constructors: the first one for concept constructors, and the second one for role constructors. For example, the pair of lists $(\sqcap, \exists R, \forall R.C)$ $(\sqcap, \circ)$ denotes a language whose concept constructors are conjunction $\sqcap$, unqualified existential quantification $\exists R$, and universal role quantification $\forall R.C$, and whose role constructors are conjunction $\sqcap$ and composition $\circ$. Many combinations of concept constructors have been given a name which is now commonly used. For instance, the first list of the above example is known as $\mathcal{FL}^-$. In these cases, we follow a syntax first proposed in [Baader and Sattler, 1996b], and write just $\mathcal{FL}^-(\sqcap, \circ)$ – that is, $\mathcal{FL}^-$ augmented with role conjunction and composition – to make it immediately recognizable by researchers in the field.

3.9.1 Notation

In the following catalog, satisfiability and subsumption refer to the problems with plain concept expressions. When satisfiability and subsumption are w.r.t. a set of axioms, we state it explicitly. Moreover, when the constructs of the Description Logic allow one to reduce subsumption between C and D to satisfiability of $C \sqcap \neg D$, we mention only satisfiability.

In the lists, we have tried to use the symbol of the DL construct whenever possible. We have abbreviated some constructs, however: unqualified number restrictions $\geqslant nR$, $\leqslant nR$ are denoted by $\lessgtr R$, while qualified number restrictions $\geqslant n\,R.C$, $\leqslant nR.C$ are $\lessgtr R.C$. When a construct is allowed only for names (either concept names in the first list, or role names in the second one) we apply the construct to the word *name*.

3.9.2 *Subsumption in* PTIME

To the best of the author's knowledge, no proof of PTIME-hardness has been given for any Description Logic so far. Therefore the following results refer only to membership in PTIME.

- $(\sqcap, \exists R, \forall R.C)$ () known as $\mathcal{FL}^-$ [Levesque and Brachman, 1987].
- $(\sqcap, \exists R, \forall R.C, \neg(name))$ () known as $\mathcal{AL}$ [Schmidt-Schauß and Smolka, 1991].
- $(\sqcap, \exists R, \forall R.C, \lessgtr R)$ () known as $\mathcal{ALN}$ [Donini *et al.*, 1997a].
- $\mathcal{AL}(\circ), \mathcal{AL}(^-)$ [Donini *et al.*, 1999].
- $\mathcal{FL}^-(\sqcap)$ [Donini *et al.*, 1991a].
- $(\sqcap, \exists R.C, \{individual\})$ $(\sqcap, ^-)$ known as $\mathcal{ELIRO}^1$ [Baader *et al.*, 1998b].

3.9.3 NP *and* CONP

- $(\sqcap, \exists R.C, \forall R.C, \neg(name))$ () (known as $\mathcal{ALE}$) subsumption and unsatisfiability are NP-complete [Donini *et al.*, 1992a] (see Subsection 3.3.1).
- $\mathcal{AL}(\sqcap)$, $\mathcal{ALE}(\sqcap)$, and $(\sqcap, \exists R.C, \forall R.C)$ () (known as $\mathcal{ALR}$, $\mathcal{ALER}$ and $\mathcal{FL}^-\mathcal{E}$ respectively) subsumption and unsatisfiability are NP-complete [Donini *et al.*, 1997a] (see Theorems 3.16, 3.17 for hardness, and [Donini *et al.*, 1992a] for membership).
- $(\sqcap, \sqcup, \exists R, \forall R.C, \neg(name))$ () (known as $\mathcal{ALU}$) subsumption and unsatisfiability are CONP-complete [Donini *et al.*, 1997a] (see Subsection 3.1.1.1).
- $\mathcal{ALN}(^-)$ subsumption is CONP-complete, while satisfiability is decidable in polynomial time [Donini *et al.*, 1999].
- $\mathcal{FL}^-(\sqcap, ^-)$, $\mathcal{FL}^-(\sqcap, \circ)$, and $\mathcal{FL}^-(\circ, ^-)$ [Donini *et al.*, 1999] (see Subsections 3.3.2, 3.3.3, and 3.3.4).
- $\mathcal{AL}()$, satisfiability w.r.t. a set of *acyclic* axioms is CONP-hard [Buchheit *et al.*, 1994a; Calvanese, 1996b; Buchheit *et al.*, 1998] (CONP-complete for $\mathcal{ALE}()$ [Calvanese, 1996b]).

3.9.4 PSPACE

- $(\sqcap, \sqcup, \neg, \exists R.C, \forall R.C)$ () (known as $\mathcal{ALC}$) [Schmidt-Schauß and Smolka, 1991] (see Subsection 3.4.1).
- $(\sqcap, \neg(name), \exists R.C, \forall R.C, \leqslant R)$ () (known as $\mathcal{ALEN}$) [Hemaspaandra, 1999].
- $\mathcal{FL}^-(R|_C)$ (known as $\mathcal{FL}$), $\mathcal{ALN}(\sqcap)$, $\mathcal{ALU}(\sqcap)$, $(\sqcap, \exists R.C, \forall R.C, \neg, \leqslant R)$ ($\sqcap$) (known as $\mathcal{ALCNR}$) [Donini *et al.*, 1997a].
- $\mathcal{ALC}(\sqcap, \sqcup, \circ)$ satisfiability [Massacci, 2001]. Membership is nontrivial.
- $\mathcal{ALE}()$ satisfiability w.r.t. a set of cyclic axioms is PSPACE-complete [Calvanese, 1996b].
- $\mathcal{ALN}()$ satisfiability w.r.t. a set of cyclic axioms of the form $A \equiv C$, where each concept name A can appear only once on the left-hand side, is PSPACE-complete [Küsters, 1998].

3.9.5 EXPTIME

- $\mathcal{AL}$ w.r.t. a set of axioms (see Section 3.5 for hardness).
- $(\sqcap, \sqcup, \neg, \exists R.C, \forall R.C)$ $(\sqcup, \circ, ^*, id(), ^-)$ which includes $\mathcal{ALC}_{trans}$ [Baader, 1991; Schild, 1991]. Membership is nontrivial, and was proved by Pratt [1979] without inverse, and by Vardi and Wolper [1986] for *converse*-PDL, reducing the problem to emptiness of tree automata.
- $(\sqcap, \sqcup, \neg, \exists R.C, \forall R.C, \leqslant name.C, \leqslant name^-.C)$ $(\sqcup, \circ, ^*, ^-, id())$, known as $\mathcal{ALCQI}_{reg}$ (see Chapter 5). Membership is nontrivial.
- $(\sqcap, \sqcup, \neg, \exists R.C, \forall R.C, \mu x.C[x], \{individual\})$ $(^-)$, where $\mu x.C[x]$ denotes the least fixpoint of x [Sattler and Vardi, 2001]. Membership is nontrivial.

3.9.6 NEXPTIME

- adding concrete domains (see [Baader and Hanschke, 1991a]), satisfiability in $\mathcal{ALC}$ w.r.t. a set of acyclic axioms, and $\mathcal{ALC}(^-)$ [Lutz, 2001a].
- $\mathcal{ALC}(\sqcap, \sqcup, \neg)$ satisfiability [Lutz and Sattler, 2001].
- $(\sqcap, \sqcup, \exists R.C, \forall R.C, \neg, \{individual\}, \leqslant R.C)$ () satisfiability [Tobies, 2001b].
- $(\sqcap, \sqcup, \neg, \exists R.C, \forall R.C, \leq \geq R)$ ($\sqcap$) (known as $\mathcal{ALCNR}$) satisfiability w.r.t. a set of axioms (only membership was proved) in [Buchheit *et al.*, 1993a]).

3.9.7 Undecidability results

- $\mathcal{FL}^-(\circ, =)$, which is a subset of the language of the knowledge representation system KL-ONE [Schmidt-Schauß, 1989] (see Subsection 3.6.1 for undecidability of $\mathcal{FL}^-(\circ, \subseteq)$).
- $\mathcal{FL}^-(\circ, \subseteq, ^-, functionality, R|_C)$, which is a subset of the language of the knowledge representation system NIKL [Patel-Schneider, 1989a].

- $()$, $(\sqcap, \circ, \neg)$ (known as U) [Schild, 1989].
- $\mathcal{ALCN}(\circ, \sqcup, ^-)$, $\mathcal{ALCN}(\circ, \sqcap)$ satisfiability w.r.t. a set of axioms [Baader and Sattler, 1999].

Acknowledgements

I thank Franz Baader for useful and stimulating discussions on the proofs of Lemmas 3.34, 3.35, and many other comments and help. I am indebted to Maurizio Lenzerini, Daniele Nardi, Werner Nutt and Andrea Schaerf, co-authors of many papers containing results presented in this chapter. I thank also Fabio Massacci for involving me in the experimental evaluation of reasoning algorithms. Giuseppe De Giacomo spent some time discussing automata with me, and Diego Calvanese made helpful comments on an early draft; I thank them both.

The work has been supported by the Italian CNR (projects LAICO, De-MAnD, "Metodi di Ragionamento Automatico nella modellazione ed analisi di dominio"), and the Italian MURST (project MOSES).

4

Relationships with other Formalisms

Ulrike Sattler
Diego Calvanese
Ralf Molitor

Abstract

In this chapter, we are concerned with the relationship between Description Logics and other formalisms, regardless of whether they were designed for knowledge representation issues or not. We concentrate on those representation formalisms that either (1) had or have a strong influence on Description Logics (e.g., modal logics), (2) are closely related to Description Logics for historical reasons (e.g., semantic networks and structured inheritance networks), or (3) have similar expressive power (e.g., semantic data models). There are far more knowledge representation formalisms than those mentioned in this chapter. For example, "verb-centered" graphical formalisms like those introduced by Simmons [1973] are not mentioned since we believe that their relationship with Description Logics is too weak.

4.1 AI knowledge representation formalisms

In artificial intelligence (AI), various "non-logical" knowledge representation formalisms were developed, motivated by the belief that classical logic is inadequate for knowledge representation in AI applications. This belief was mainly based upon cognitive experiments carried out with human beings and the wish to have representational formalisms that are close to the representations in human brains. In this section, we discuss some of these formalisms, namely semantic networks, frame systems, and conceptual graphs. The first two formalisms are mainly presented for historical reasons since they can be regarded as ancestors of Description Logics. In contrast, the third formalism can be regarded as a "sibling" of Description Logics since both have similar ancestors and live in the same time.

149

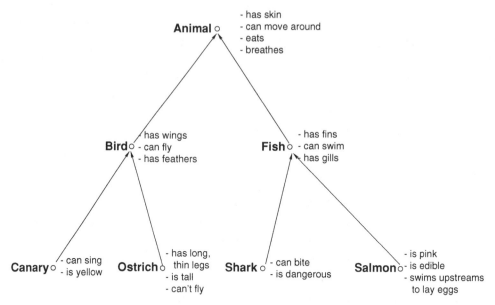

Fig. 4.1. A semantic network describing animals.

4.1.1 Semantic networks

Semantic networks originate in Quillian's *semantic memory models* [Quillian, 1967], a graphical formalism designed to represent "word concepts" in a definitorial way, i.e., similar to the one that can be found in an encyclopedia definition. This formalism is based on labeled graphs with different kinds of edges and nodes. Besides others, Quillian's networks allow *subclass–superclass* edges, *and* and *or* edges, and *subject–object* edges between nodes.

Following Quillian's memory models, a great variety of *semantic network* formalisms were proposed; an overview of their history can be found in [Brachman, 1979]. In general, semantic networks distinguish between *concepts* (denoted by *generic nodes*) and *individuals* (denoted by *individual nodes*), and between *subclass–superclass edges* and *property edges*. Using subclass–superclass links, concepts can be organised in a specialization hierarchy. Using property edges, properties can be associated to concepts, that is, to the individuals belonging to the concept the properties are associated with. Figure 4.1 contains a hierarchy of animals, birds, fishes, etc. Interestingly, the cognitive adequacy of this approach was proven empirically [Collins and Quillian, 1970].

The two kinds of edges interact with each other: a property is *inherited* along subclass–superclass edges – if not modified in a more specific class. For example, birds are equipped with skin because animals are equipped with skin, and birds inherit this property because of the subclass–superclass edge between birds and animals. In contrast, although ostriches are birds, they do not inherit the property "can fly" from birds because this property is "modified" for ostriches.

Intuitively, it should be possible to translate subclass–superclass edges into concept definitions, for example,[1]

$$\text{Shark} \equiv \text{Fish} \sqcap \text{CanBite} \sqcap \text{IsDangerous}.$$

According to Brachman [1985], the above translation is not always intended. Subclass–superclass edges can also be read as *primitive* concept definitions, that is, they impose only necessary properties but not sufficient ones. Hence the above translation might better be

$$\text{Shark} \sqsubseteq \text{Fish} \sqcap \text{CanBite} \sqcap \text{IsDangerous}.$$

Due to the lack of a precise semantics, there are even more readings of subclasssuperclass edges, which are discussed in [1975; 1977b; 1985]. A prominent reading is that of *inheritance by default*, which can be specified in different ways, thus leading to misunderstandings and to the question which of these specifications is the "right" one (see also Chapter 6).

As a consequence of this ambiguity, new formalisms mainly evolved along two lines: (1) To capture inheritance by default, various non-monotonic inheritance systems, respectively various ways of reasoning in non-monotonic inheritance systems, were investigated [Touretzky *et al.*, 1987; 1991; Selman and Levesque, 1993]. (2) To capture the monotonic aspects of semantic networks, a new graphical formalism, *structured inheritance networks*, was introduced and implemented in the system KL-ONE [Brachman, 1979; Brachman and Schmolze, 1985]. It was designed to cover the declarative, monotonic aspects of semantic networks, and hence did not specify the way in which (non-monotonic multiple) inheritance was supposed to function in conflicting situations. Brachman and Schmolze [1985] argue that KL-ONE does not allow cancellation or inheritance by default because such mechanisms would make taxonomies meaningless. Indeed, all properties of a given concept could be canceled, so that it would fit everywhere in the taxonomy. Their proposition is to make a strict separation of default assertions and conceptual descriptions.

Brachman and Schmolze [1985], besides pointing out the computation of the taxonomy as a core system service, describe the meaning of various concept constructors that were implemented in KL-ONE, for example conjunction, universal value restrictions, role hierarchies, role-value-maps, etc.

---

[1] In the following, we use standard Description Logics as defined in Chapter 2.

Moreover, we find a clear distinction between individuals and concepts, and between a terminological and an assertional formalism.

Later [Levesque and Brachman, 1987], KL-ONE was provided with a well-defined "Tarski-style" semantics which fixed the precise meaning of its graphical constructs and led to the definition of the first *Description Logic* [Levesque and Brachman, 1987], at that time also called terminological languages, concept languages, or KL-ONE-based languages. Besides giving a precise meaning to semantic networks, this formalization allowed the investigation of inference algorithms with respect to their soundness, completeness, and computational complexity. For example, it turned out that subsumption in KL-ONE is undecidable, mainly due to role-value-maps [Schmidt-Schauß, 1989].

4.1.2 Frame systems

Minsky [1981] introduced frame systems as an alternative to logic-oriented approaches to knowledge representation, which he thought were not adequate to "simulate common-sense thinking" for various reasons. His system provides record-like data structures to represent prototypical knowledge concerning situations and objects and includes defaults, multiple perspectives, and analogies. Nowadays, semantic networks and frame systems are often viewed as the same family of formalisms. However, in standard semantic networks, properties are restricted to primitive, atomic ones, whereas, in general, properties in frame systems can be complex concepts described by frames.

One goal of the frame approach was to gather all relevant knowledge about a situation (e.g., entering a restaurant) in one object instead of distributing this knowledge across various axioms. Roughly speaking, a situation (or an object) is described in one *frame*. A frame contains *slots*, similar to entries in a record, to represent properties of the situation described by the frame. Reasoning comes in two shapes: (1) Using a "partial matching", more specific frames are embedded into more general ones, thus giving, for example, meaning to a new situation or classifying an object as a kind of, say, bird. (2) Searching for slot *fillers* to collect more information concerning a specific situation. A variety of expert systems [Fikes and Kehler, 1985; Christaller *et al.*, 1992; Gen, 1995; Flex, 1999] are based on a frame-based formalism and are further enhanced with rules, triggers, daemons, etc.

Despite the fact that frame systems were designed as an alternative to logic, the monotonic, declarative part of this formalism could be shown to be captured using first-order predicate logic [Hayes, 1977; 1979]. To our knowledge, no precise semantics could be given for the non-declarative, non-logical, or non-monotonic aspects of frame systems. Hence neither their expressive power nor the quality of the corresponding reasoning algorithms and services can be compared with other formalisms.

In the remainder of this section, we show how the monotonic part of a frame-based knowledge base can be translated into an $\mathcal{ALUN}$ TBox [Calvanese *et al.*, 1994].[2] Since there is no standard syntax for frame systems, we have chosen to use basically the notation adopted by Fikes and Kehler [1985], which is used also in the KEE[3] system.

A *frame definition* is of the form **Frame** : F **in KB** $\mathcal{F}$ E, where F is a *frame name* and E is a *frame expression*, i.e., an expression formed according to the following syntax:

$$
\begin{aligned}
E \longrightarrow\ &\textbf{SuperClasses}:\ F_1,\ldots,F_h \\
&\textbf{MemberSlot}:\ S_1 \\
&\quad\textbf{ValueClass}:\ H_1 \\
&\quad\textbf{Cardinality.Min}:\ m_1 \\
&\quad\textbf{Cardinality.Max}:\ n_1 \\
&\quad\cdots \\
&\textbf{MemberSlot}:\ S_k \\
&\quad\textbf{ValueClass}:\ H_k \\
&\quad\textbf{Cardinality.Min}:\ m_k \\
&\quad\textbf{Cardinality.Max}:\ n_k.
\end{aligned}
$$

F_i denotes a frame name, S_j denotes a slot name, m_j and n_j denote positive integers, and H_j denotes slot constraints. A *slot constraint* can be specified as follows:

$$
\begin{aligned}
H \longrightarrow\ &F\ | \\
&(\text{INTERSECTION } H_1\ H_2)\ | \\
&(\text{UNION } H_1\ H_2)\ | \\
&(\text{NOT } H).
\end{aligned}
$$

A *frame knowledge base* $\mathcal{F}$ is a set of frame definitions.

For example, Figure 4.2 shows a simple KEE knowledge base describing courses in a university. Cardinality restrictions are used to impose a minimum and maximum number of students that may be enrolled in a course, and to express that each course is taught by exactly one individual. The frame AdvCourse represents courses which enroll only graduate students,

---

[2] Not only the translation but also the example are by Calvanese *et al.* [1994].

[3] KEE is a trademark of Intellicorp. Note that KEE users do not directly specify their knowledge base in this notation, but are allowed to define frames interactively via the graphical system interface.

Frame: Course **in KB** University
  MemberSlot: enrolls
    ValueClass: Student
    Cardinality.Min: 2
    Cardinality.Max: 30
  MemberSlot: taughtby
    ValueClass: (UNION GradStudent
                   Professor)
    Cardinality.Min: 1
    Cardinality.Max: 1

Frame: AdvCourse **in KB** University
  SuperClasses: Course
  MemberSlot: enrolls
    ValueClass: (INTERSECTION
             GradStudent
             (NOT Undergrad))
    Cardinality.Max: 20

Frame: BasCourse **in KB** University
  SuperClasses: Course
  MemberSlot: taughtby
    ValueClass: Professor

Frame: Professor **in KB** University

Frame: Student **in KB** University

Frame: GradStudent **in KB** University
  SuperClasses: Student
  MemberSlot: degree
    ValueClass: String
    Cardinality.Min: 1
    Cardinality.Max: 1

Frame: Undergrad **in KB** University
  SuperClasses: Student

Fig. 4.2. A KEE knowledge base.

i.e., students who already have a degree. Basic courses, on the other hand, may be taught only by professors.

Hayes [1979] gives a semantics to frame definitions by translating them to first-order formulae in which frame names are translated to unary predicates, and slots are translated to binary predicates.

In order to translate frame knowledge bases to $\mathcal{ALUN}$ knowledge bases, we first define the function Ψ that maps each frame expression into an $\mathcal{ALUN}$ concept expression as follows: Each frame name F is mapped onto an atomic concept $\Psi(F)$, each slot name S onto an atomic role $\Psi(S)$, and each slot constraint H onto the corresponding Boolean combination $\Psi(H)$ of concepts. Then, every frame expression of the form

$$
\begin{aligned}
&\textbf{SuperClasses}: \ F_1, \ldots, F_h \\
&\textbf{MemberSlot}: \ S_1 \\
&\quad \textbf{ValueClass}: \ H_1 \\
&\quad \textbf{Cardinality.Min}: \ m_1 \\
&\quad \textbf{Cardinality.Max}: \ n_1 \\
&\quad \cdots \\
&\textbf{MemberSlot}: \ S_k \\
&\quad \textbf{ValueClass}: \ H_k \\
&\quad \textbf{Cardinality.Min}: \ m_k \\
&\quad \textbf{Cardinality.Max}: \ n_k
\end{aligned}
$$

Course	$\sqsubseteq$	$\forall$enrolls.Student $\sqcap \geqslant 2$ enrolls $\sqcap \leqslant 30$ enrolls $\sqcap$
		$\forall$taughtby.(Professor $\sqcup$ GradStudent) $\sqcap = 1$ taughtby
AdvCourse	$\sqsubseteq$	Course $\sqcap \forall$enrolls.(GradStudent $\sqcap \neg$Undergrad) $\sqcap \leqslant 20$ enrolls
BasCourse	$\sqsubseteq$	Course $\sqcap \forall$taughtby.Professor
GradStudent	$\sqsubseteq$	Student $\sqcap \forall$degree.String $\sqcap = 1$ degree
Undergrad	$\sqsubseteq$	Student

Fig. 4.3. The $\mathcal{ALUN}$ knowledge base corresponding to the KEE knowledge base in Figure 4.2.

is mapped into the concept

$$\Psi(F_1) \sqcap \cdots \sqcap \Psi(F_h) \sqcap$$
$$\forall\Psi(S_1).\Psi(H_1) \sqcap \geqslant m_1 \, \Psi(S_1) \sqcap \leqslant n_1 \, \Psi(S_1) \sqcap$$
$$\cdots$$
$$\forall\Psi(S_k).\Psi(H_k) \sqcap \geqslant m_k \, \Psi(S_k) \sqcap \leqslant n_k \, \Psi(S_k).$$

Making use of the mapping Ψ, we obtain the $\mathcal{ALUN}$ knowledge base $\Psi(\mathcal{F})$ corresponding to a frame knowledge base $\mathcal{F}$, by introducing in $\Psi(\mathcal{F})$ an inclusion assertion $\Psi(F) \sqsubseteq \Psi(E)$ for each frame definition **Frame :** F **in KB** $\mathcal{F}$ E in $\mathcal{F}$.

The $\mathcal{ALUN}$ knowledge base corresponding to the KEE knowledge base given in Figure 4.2 is shown in Figure 4.3.

The correctness of the translation follows from the correspondence between the set-theoretic semantics of $\mathcal{ALUN}$ and the first-order interpretation of frames [Hayes, 1979; Borgida, 1996; Donini *et al.*, 1996b]. Consequently:

- verifying whether a frame F is satisfiable in a knowledge base and
- identifying which of the frames are more general than a given frame

are captured by concept satisfiability and concept subsumption in $\mathcal{ALUN}$ knowledge bases. Hence reasoning for the monotonic, declarative part of frame systems can be reduced to concept satisfiability and concept subsumption in $\mathcal{ALUN}$ knowledge bases.

4.1.3 Conceptual graphs

Besides Description Logics, conceptual graphs [Sowa, 1984] can be viewed as descendants of frame systems and semantic networks. Conceptual graphs (CGs) are a rather popular (especially in natural language processing) and expressive formalism for representing knowledge about an application domain in a graphical way. They are given a formal semantics, e.g., by translating them into (first-order) formulae.

In the CG formalism, one is, just as for Description Logics, not only interested in *representing* knowledge, but also in *reasoning* about it.

Reasoning services for CGs are, for example, deciding whether a given graph is *valid*, i.e., whether the corresponding formula is valid, or whether a graph g is *subsumed by* a graph h, i.e., whether the formula corresponding to g implies the formula corresponding to h. Since CGs can express all of first-order predicate logic [Sowa, 1984], these reasoning problems are undecidable for general CGs. In the literature [Sowa, 1984; Wermelinger, 1995; Kerdiles and Salvat, 1997] one can find complete calculi for validity of CGs, but implementations of these calculi may not terminate for formulae that are not valid. An approach to overcoming this problem, which has also been employed in the area of Description Logics, is to identify decidable fragments of the formalism. The most prominent decidable fragment of CGs is the class of *simple conceptual graphs* (SGs) [Sowa, 1984], which corresponds to the conjunctive, positive, and existential fragment of first-order predicate logic (i.e., existentially quantified conjunctions of atoms). Even for this simple fragment, however, subsumption is still an NP-complete problem [Chein and Mugnier, 1992].[4]

Although Description Logics and CGs are employed in very similar applications, precise comparisons were published, to our knowledge, only recently [Coupey and Faron, 1998; Baader *et al.*, 1999c]. These comparisons are based on translations of CGs and DL concepts into first-order formulae. It turned out that the two formalisms are quite different for several reasons:

1. CGs are translated into *closed* first-order formulae, whereas DL concepts are translated into formulae in one free variable;
2. since Description Logics use a variable-free syntax, certain identifications of variables expressed by cycles in SGs and by co-reference links in CGs cannot be expressed in Description Logics;
3. in contrast to CGs, most Description Logics considered in the literature only allow unary and binary relations and not relations of arity greater than 2;
4. SGs are interpreted by existential sentences, whereas almost all Description Logics considered in the literature allow for universal quantification.

Possibly as a consequence of these differences, so far no natural fragment of CGs that corresponds to a Description Logic has been identified. In the sequel, we will illustrate the main aspects of the correspondence result presented by Baader *et al.* [1999c], which strictly extends the one proposed by Coupey and Faron [1998].

---

[4] Since SGs are equivalent to conjunctive queries (see also Chapter 16), the NP-completeness of subsumption of SGs is also an immediate consequence of NP-completeness of containment of conjunctive queries [Chandra and Merlin, 1977].

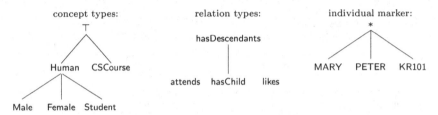

Fig. 4.4. An example of a support.

Simple conceptual graphs

Simple conceptual graphs (SGs) as introduced by Sowa [1984] are the most prominent decidable fragment of CGs. They are defined with respect to a so-called *support*. Roughly speaking, the support is a partially ordered signature that can be used to fix the a primitive ontology of a given application domain. It introduces a set of *concept types* (unary predicates), a set of *relation types* (n-ary predicates), and a set of *individual markers* (constants). As an example, consider the support S shown in Figure 4.4, where $\top$ is the most general concept type representing the entire domain. The partial ordering on the individual markers is flat, i.e., all individual markers are pairwise incomparable and the so-called *generic marker* $*$ is more general than all individual markers. In this example, all relation types are assumed to have arity 2 and to be pairwise incomparable except for hasDescendants, which is more general than hasChild. The partial orderings on the types yield a fixed specialization hierarchy for these types that must be taken into account when computing subsumption relations between SGs. For binary relation types, this partial ordering resembles a role hierarchy in Description Logics.

An *SG over the support* S is a labeled bipartite graph of the form $g = (C, R, E, \ell)$, where C is a set of *concept nodes*, R is a set of *relation nodes*, $E \subseteq C \times R$ is the edge relation L, and ℓ is a *labeling* of concept nodes. As an example, consider the SGs depicted in Figure 4.5: the SG g describes a woman Mary having a child who likes its grandfather Peter and who attends the computer science course number KR101; the node d_0 in the SG h describes all mothers having a child who likes one of its grandparents.

Each concept node is labeled by ℓ with a concept type (such as **Female**) and a *referent*, i.e., an individual marker (such as **MARY**) or the generic marker $*$. A concept node is called *generic* if its referent is the generic marker; otherwise, it is called an *individual concept node*. Each relation node is labeled with a relation type r (such as **hasChild**), and its outgoing edges are labeled with indices according to the arity of r. For example, for the binary relation **hasChild**, there is one edge labeled with 1 (leading to the parent), and one edge labeled with 2 (leading to the child).

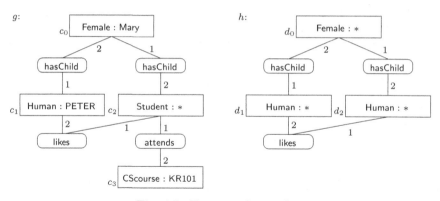

Fig. 4.5. Two simple graphs.

Simple graphs are given a formal semantics in first-order predicate logic (FOL) by the operator Φ [Sowa, 1984]: each generic concept node is related to a unique variable, and each individual concept node is related to its individual marker. Concept types and relation types are translated into atomic formulae, and the whole SG g is translated into the existentially closed conjunction of all atoms obtained from the nodes in g.

In our example, this operator yields

$$\Phi(g) \;=\; \exists x_1.(\mathsf{Female}(\mathsf{MARY}) \wedge \mathsf{Human}(\mathsf{PETER}) \wedge \mathsf{Student}(x_1) \wedge$$
$$\mathsf{CScourse}(\mathsf{KR101}) \wedge \mathsf{hasChild}(\mathsf{PETER}, \mathsf{MARY}) \wedge$$
$$\mathsf{hasChild}(\mathsf{MARY}, x_1) \wedge \mathsf{likes}(x_1, \mathsf{PETER}) \wedge \mathsf{attends}(x_1, \mathsf{KR101})),$$
$$\Phi(h) \;=\; \exists x_0 x_1 x_2.(\mathsf{Female}(x_0) \wedge \mathsf{Human}(x_1) \wedge \mathsf{Human}(x_2) \wedge$$
$$\mathsf{hasChild}(x_1, x_0) \wedge \mathsf{hasChild}(x_0, x_2) \wedge \mathsf{likes}(x_2, x_1)),$$

where x_1 in $\Phi(g)$ is (resp. x_0, x_1, and x_2 in $\Phi(h)$ are) introduced for the generic concept node c_2 (resp. the generic concept nodes d_0, d_1, and d_2).

In general, there are three different ways of expressing conjunction of concept types. For example, suppose we want to express that Mary is both female and a student. This can be expressed by an SG containing one individual concept node for each statement (see Figure 4.6(1)).[5] A second possibility is to introduce a new concept type in the support for a common specialization of $\mathsf{Female}(\mathsf{MARY})$ and $\mathsf{Student}(\mathsf{MARY})$ (see Figure 4.6(2)). Finally, such a conjunction can be represented by labeling the corresponding concept node with a *set* of concept types instead of a single concept type (see Figure 4.6(3); for details on how to handle SGs labeled with sets of concept types see [Baader *et al.*, 1999c]).

---

[5] Note that this solution could not be applied if the individual marker MARY were replaced by the generic marker $*$, because the two resulting generic concept nodes would be interpreted by different variables.

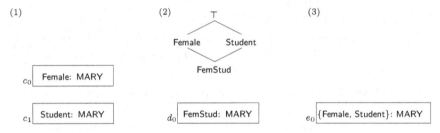

Fig. 4.6. Expressing conjunction of concept types in SGs.

Subsumption with respect to a support $\mathcal{S}$ for two SGs g, h is defined by a so-called *projection* from h to g [Sowa, 1984; Chein and Mugnier, 1992]: g is *subsumed by* h w.r.t. $\mathcal{S}$ iff there exists a mapping from h to g that (1) maps concept nodes (resp. relation nodes) in h onto more specific (w.r.t. the partial ordering in $\mathcal{S}$) concept nodes (resp. relation nodes) in g and that (2) preserves adjacency.

In our example (Figure 4.5), it is easy to see that g is subsumed by h, since mapping d_i onto c_i for $0 \leq i \leq 2$ yields a projection w.r.t. $\mathcal{S}$ from h to g.

Subsumption for SGs is an NP-complete problem [Chein and Mugnier, 1992]. In the restricted case where the subsumer h is a tree, subsumption can be decided in polynomial time [Mugnier and Chein, 1992].

Concept descriptions and simple graphs

In order to determine a Description Logic corresponding to (a fragment of) SGs, one must take into account the differences between Description Logics and CGs mentioned before.

- Most Description Logics only allow role terms corresponding to binary relations and concept descriptions describing connected structures. Thus, Baader *et al.* [1999c] and Coupey and Faron [1998] restrict their attention to connected SGs over a support $\mathcal{S}$ containing only unary and binary relation types.
- Due to the different semantics of SGs and concept descriptions (closed formulae vs. formulae in one free variable), Coupey and Faron restrict their attention to SGs that are trees. Baader *et al.* introduce so-called *rooted* SGs, i.e., SGs that have one distinguished node called the *root*. An adaption of the operator Φ yields a translation of a rooted SG g into an FO formula $\Phi(g)(x_0)$ with one free variable x_0.
- Since all Description Logics considered in the literature allow conjunction of concepts, Baader *et al.* allow concept nodes labeled with a set of concept types instead of a single concept type in order to express conjunction of atomic

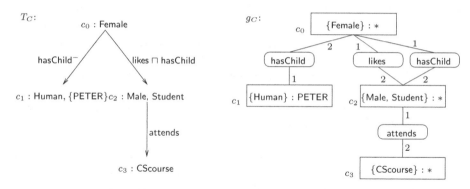

Fig. 4.7. Translating concept descriptions into simple graphs.

concepts in SGs. Coupey and Faron avoid the problem of expressing conjunction of atomic concepts: they just do not allow (1) conjunctions of atomic concepts in concept descriptions, and (2) individual concept nodes in SGs.

The Description Logic considered by Baader *et al.*, denoted by $\mathcal{ELIRO}_1$, allows *existential restrictions* and *intersection of concept descriptions* ($\mathcal{EL}$), *inverse roles* ($\mathcal{I}$), *intersection of roles* ($\mathcal{R}$), and *unary one-of concepts* ($\mathcal{O}_1$). For the constants occurring in the one-of concepts the *unique name assumption* applies, i.e., all constants are interpreted as different objects. Coupey and Faron only consider a fragment of the Description Logic $\mathcal{ELI}$.

In both papers, the correspondence result is based on translating concept descriptions into syntax trees. For example, consider the $\mathcal{ELIRO}_1$-concept

$$C = \text{Female} \sqcap \exists \text{hasChild}^-.(\text{Human} \sqcap \{\text{PETER}\}) \sqcap$$
$$\exists(\text{hasChild} \sqcap \text{likes}).(\text{Male} \sqcap \text{Student} \sqcap \exists \text{attends}.\text{CScourse})$$

describing all daughters of Peter who have a fond child that is a student attending a computer science course. The syntax tree corresponding to C is depicted on the left-hand side of Figure 4.7.

One can show [Baader *et al.*, 1999c] that, if concept descriptions C are restricted to *contain at most one unary one-of concept in each conjunction*, the corresponding syntax tree T_C can be easily translated into an equivalent rooted SG g_C that is a tree[6] (see Figure 4.7). Conversely, every rooted SG g that is a tree and that contains only binary relation types can be translated into an equivalent $\mathcal{ELIRO}_1$-concept description C_g. There are, however, rooted SGs that can be translated into equivalent $\mathcal{ELIRO}_1$-concept descriptions though they are not trees. For example, the rooted SG g depicted in Figure 4.5 is equivalent to the concept

---

[6] In this context, a tree may contain more than one relation between two adjacent concept nodes.

description

$$C_g \ = \ \{\text{MARY}\} \sqcap \text{Female} \sqcap \exists \text{hasChild}^-.(\text{Human} \sqcap \{\text{PETER}\}) \sqcap$$
$$\exists \text{hasChild}.(\text{Student} \sqcap \exists \text{attends}.(\{\text{KR101}\} \sqcap \text{CScourse}) \sqcap \exists \text{likes}.\{\text{PETER}\}).$$

In general, the above correspondence result can be strengthened as follows [Baader *et al.*, 1999c]: every rooted SG g containing only binary relation types can be transformed into an equivalent rooted SG that is a tree if each cycle in g with more than two concept nodes contains at least one individual concept node. Hence, each such rooted SG can be translated into an equivalent $\mathcal{ELIRO}_1$-concept description.

Note that the SG h with root d_0 in Figure 4.5 cannot be translated into an equivalent $\mathcal{ELIRO}_1$-concept description C_h because, in $\mathcal{ELIRO}_1$, one cannot express that the grandparent (represented by the concept node d_1) and the human liked by the child (represented by the concept node d_2) must be the same person.

The correspondence result between $\mathcal{ELIRO}_1$ and rooted SGs allows the tractability result for subsumption between SGs that are trees to be transferred to $\mathcal{ELIRO}_1$. Furthermore, the characterization of subsumption based on projections between graphs was adapted to $\mathcal{ELIRO}_1$ and other Description Logics, e.g., $\mathcal{ALE}$, and is used in the context of inference problems like matching and computing least common subsumers [Baader and Küsters, 1999; Baader *et al.*, 1999b]. Conversely, the correspondence result can be used as a basis for determining more expressive fragments of conceptual graphs, for which validity and subsumption are decidable. Based on an appropriate characterization of a fragment of conceptual graphs corresponding to a more expressive Description Logic (like $\mathcal{ALC}$), one could use algorithms for these Description Logics to decide validity or subsumption of graphs in this fragment.

4.2 Logical formalisms

In this section, we will investigate the relationship between Description Logics and other logical formalisms.

Traditionally, the semantics of Description Logics is given in a Tarskistyle model-theoretic way. Alternatively, it can be given by a translation into predicate logic, where it depends on the Description Logic whether this translation yields first-order formulae or whether it goes beyond first-order, as is the case for Description Logics that allow, e.g., the transitive closure of roles or fixpoints. Due to the variable-free syntax of Description Logics and the fact that concepts denote sets of individuals, the translation of concepts yields formulae in one free variable. Following the definition by Borgida [1996], a concept C and its translation $\pi(C)(x)$ are said to be *equivalent* if and only if, for all interpretations[7] $\mathcal{I} = (\Delta^{\mathcal{I}}, \cdot^{\mathcal{I}})$ and all $a \in \Delta^{\mathcal{I}}$, we have

$$a \in C^{\mathcal{I}} \text{ iff } \mathcal{I} \models \pi(C)(a).$$

A Description Logic $\mathcal{DL}$ is said to be *less expressive* than a logic $\mathcal{L}$ if there is a translation that translates all $\mathcal{DL}$-concepts into equivalent $\mathcal{L}$ formulae. Such a translation is called *preserving*.

Note that there are various other ways in which equivalence of formulae and logics being "less expressive than" others could have been defined [Baader, 1996a; Kurtonina and de Rijke, 1997; Areces and de Rijke, 1998]. For example, a less strict definition is the one that only asks the translation to preserve satisfiability.

To start with, we give a translation π that translates $\mathcal{ALC}$-concepts into predicate logic and which will be useful in the remainder of this section. For those familiar with modal logics, note that this translation parallels the one from propositional modal logic [van Benthem, 1983; 1984]; the close relationship between modal logic and Description Logic will be discussed in Subsection 4.2.2. For $\mathcal{ALC}$, the translation of concepts into predicate logic formulae can be defined in such a way that the resulting formulae involve only two variables, say x, y, and only unary and binary predicates. In the following, $\mathcal{L}^k$ denotes the first-order predicate logic over unary and binary predicates with k variables.

The translation is given by two mappings π_x and π_y from $\mathcal{ALC}$-concepts into $\mathcal{L}^2$ formulae in one free variable. Each concept name A is also viewed as a unary predicate symbol, and each role name R is viewed as a binary predicate symbol. For $\mathcal{ALC}$-concepts, the translation is inductively defined as follows:

$$
\begin{aligned}
\pi_x(A) &= A(x) & \pi_y(A) &= A(y) \\
\pi_x(C \sqcap D) &= \pi_x(C) \wedge \pi_x(D) & \pi_y(C \sqcap D) &= \pi_y(C) \wedge \pi_y(D) \\
\pi_x(C \sqcup D) &= \pi_x(C) \vee \pi_x(D) & \pi_y(C \sqcup D) &= \pi_y(C) \vee \pi_y(D) \\
\pi_x(\exists R.C) &= \exists y. R(x, y) \wedge \pi_y(C) & \pi_y(\exists R.C) &= \exists x. R(y, x) \wedge \pi_x(C) \\
\pi_x(\forall R.C) &= \forall y. R(x, y) \supset \pi_y(C) & \pi_y(\forall R.C) &= \forall x. R(y, x) \supset \pi_x(C).
\end{aligned}
$$

Other concept and role constructors that can easily be translated into first-order predicate logic without involving more than two variables are inverse roles, conjunction, disjunction, and negation on roles, and one-of.[8]

---

[7] In the following, we view interpretations both as DL and predicate logic interpretations.
[8] In this case, the translation is to $\mathcal{L}^2$ with constants.

If a Description Logic allows number restrictions $\geqslant n\,R$, $\leqslant n\,R$, the translation involves either *counting quantifiers* $\exists^{\geq n}$, $\exists^{\leq n}$ (and still involves only two variables) or equality (and involves an unbounded number of variables):

$$\pi_x(\geqslant n\,R) = \exists^{\geq n} y.R(x,y) = \exists y_1,\ldots,y_n.\bigwedge_{i\neq j} y_i \neq y_j \wedge \bigwedge_i R(x,y_i)$$
$$\pi_x(\leqslant n\,R) = \exists^{\leq n} y.R(x,y) = \forall y_1,\ldots,y_{n+1}.\bigwedge_{i\neq j} y_i \neq y_j \supset \bigvee_i \neg R(x,y_i).$$

For qualified number restrictions, the translations can easily be modified with the same effect on the number of variables involved.

So far, all Description Logics have been less expressive than first-order predicate logic (possibly with equality or counting quantifiers). In contrast, the expressive power of a Description Logic including the transitive closure of roles goes beyond first-order logic: First, it is easy to see that expressing transitivity $(\rho^+(x,y) \wedge \rho^+(y,z)) \supset \rho^+(x,z)$ involves at least three variables. To express that a relation ρ^+ is the transitive closure of ρ, we first need to enforce that ρ^+ is a transitive relation including ρ – which can easily be axiomatized in first-order predicate logic. Secondly, we must enforce that ρ^+ is *the smallest* transitive relation including ρ – which, as a consequence of the Compactness Theorem, cannot be expressed in first-order logic.

Internalization of Knowledge Bases: So far, we have been concerned with preserving translations of concepts into logical formulae, and thus could reduce satisfiability of concepts to satisfiability of formulae in the target logic. In Description Logics, however, we are also concerned with concept consistency and logical implication w.r.t. a TBox, and with ABox consistency w.r.t. a TBox.

Furthermore, TBoxes differ in whether they are restricted to be acyclic, allow cyclic definitions, or allow general concept inclusion axioms (see Chapter 2 for details). In first-order logic, the equivalent to a TBox assertion is simply a universally quantified formula, and thus it is not necessary to make the above-mentioned distinction between, for example, pure concept satisfiability and satisfiability with respect to a TBox – provided that cyclic TBoxes are read with descriptive semantics [Baader, 1990a; Nebel, 1991] (cyclic TBoxes read with least or greatest fixpoint semantics go beyond the expressive power of first-order predicate logic). In the following, we consider only the most expressive form of TBoxes, namely those allowing general concept inclusion axioms. Given a preserving translation π from DL concepts into first-order formulae and a TBox $\mathcal{T} = \{C_i \sqsubseteq D_i \mid 1 \leq i \leq n\}$, we define

$$\pi(\mathcal{T}) = \forall x. \bigwedge_{i=1}^{n} (\pi_x(C_i) \supset \pi_x(D_i)).$$

Then it is easy to show that:

- A concept C is satisfiable with respect to $\mathcal{T}$ iff the formula $\pi_x(C) \wedge \pi(\mathcal{T})$ is satisfiable.
- A concept C is subsumed by a concept D with respect to $\mathcal{T}$ iff the formula $\pi_x(C) \wedge \neg\pi_x(D) \wedge \pi(\mathcal{T})$ is unsatisfiable.
- Given two index sets I, J, an ABox $\{R_k(a_i, a_j) \mid \langle i, j, k \rangle \in I\} \cup \{C_j(a_i) \mid \langle i, j \rangle \in J\}$ is consistent with $\mathcal{T}$ iff the formula

$$\bigwedge_{\langle i,j,k \rangle \in I} R_k(a_i, a_j) \wedge \bigwedge_{\langle i,j \rangle \in J} \pi_x(C_j)(a_i) \wedge \pi(\mathcal{T})$$

is satisfiable, where the a_i-s in the formula are constants corresponding to the individuals in the ABox.

Observe that, if all concepts in a TBox $\mathcal{T}$ can be translated to $\mathcal{L}^2$ (resp. $\mathcal{C}^2$), then the translation $\pi(\mathcal{T})$ of $\mathcal{T}$ is also a formula of $\mathcal{L}^2$ (resp. $\mathcal{C}^2$).

Hence in first-order logic, reasoning with respect to a knowledge base (consisting of a TBox and possibly an ABox) is not more complex than reasoning about concept expressions alone – in contrast to the complexity of reasoning for most Description Logics, where considering even acyclic TBoxes can make a considerable difference (for example, see [Calvanese, 1996b; Lutz, 1999a]). This gap is not surprising since first-order predicate logic is far more complex than most Description Logics, namely undecidable.

In the following, we investigate logics that are more closely related to Description Logics, namely restricted variable fragments, modal logics, and guarded fragments.

4.2.1 Restricted variable fragments

One way to define decidable fragments of first-order logic is to restrict the set of variables which are allowed inside formulae and the arity of relation symbols. As mentioned in the previous section, we use $\mathcal{L}^k$ to denote first-order predicate logic over unary and binary predicates with at most k variables. Analogously, $\mathcal{C}^k$ denotes first-order predicate logic over unary and binary predicates with at most k variables and counting quantifiers $\exists^{\geq n}$, $\exists^{\leq n}$.

With the exception of the Description Logics introduced by Calvanese *et al.* [1998a] and Lutz *et al.* [1999], the translation of DL concepts into predicate logic formulae involves predicates of arity at most 2.

From the translations in the previous section, it follows immediately that:

- $\mathcal{ALCR}$ is less expressive than $\mathcal{L}^2$ and that
- $\mathcal{ALCNR}$ is less expressive than $\mathcal{C}^2$.

As we have shown above, general TBox assertions can be translated into $\mathcal{L}^2$ formulae. These facts together with the linearity of the translation yield upper bounds for the complexity of $\mathcal{ALCR}$ and $\mathcal{ALCNR}$ (even though these bounds are far from being tight): $\mathcal{L}^2$ and $\mathcal{C}^2$ are known to be NExpTime-complete [Grädel *et al.*, 1997a; Pacholski *et al.*, 2000] (for $\mathcal{C}^2$, this is true only if numbers in counting quantifiers are assumed to be coded in unary, an assumption often made in Description Logics); hence satisfiability and subsumption with respect to a (possibly cyclic) TBox are in NExpTime for $\mathcal{ALCR}$ and $\mathcal{ALCNR}$.

However, both $\mathcal{L}^2$ and $\mathcal{C}^2$ are far more expressive than $\mathcal{ALCR}$ and $\mathcal{ALCNR}$, respectively. For example, both logics allow the negation of binary predicates, i.e., subformulae of the form $\neg R(x, y)$. In Description Logics, this corresponds to negation of roles, an operator that is rarely considered in Description Logics, except in the weakened form of difference[9] [De Giacomo, 1995; Calvanese *et al.*, 1998a] (exceptions are the work by Mameide and Montero [1993] and Lutz and Sattler [2000b], which deal with genuine negation of roles). Moreover, $\mathcal{L}^2$ and $\mathcal{C}^2$ allow "global" quantification, i.e., formulae of the form $\exists x.\Phi(x)$ or $\forall x.\Psi(x)$ that talk about the whole interpretation domain. In contrast, quantification in Description Logics is, in general, "local", e.g., concepts of the form $\forall R.C$ only constrain all R-successors of an individual.

Borgida [1996] presents a variety of results stating that a certain Description Logic is less expressive than, or as expressive as, a certain fragment of first-order logic. We mention only the most important ones:

- $\mathcal{ALC}$ extended with

  (role constructors) full Boolean operators on roles, inverse roles, cross-product of two concepts, an identity role *id*, and

  (concept constructors) individuals ("one-of"),

  is as expressive as $\mathcal{L}^2$ (and therefore decidable and, more precisely, NExpTime-complete).
- A further extension of this logic with all sorts of role-value-maps is as expressive as $\mathcal{L}^3$ (and therefore undecidable).

---

[9] Difference of roles is easier to deal with than genuine negation, since it does not destroy "locality" of quantification.

Since both extensions include full Boolean operators on roles, they can simulate a universal role using the complex role $R \sqcup \neg R$, and thus general TBox assertions can be internalized (see Chapter 5). Thus, for these two extensions, reasoning with respect to (possibly cyclic) TBoxes can be reduced to pure concept reasoning – i.e., the TBox can be internalized – and the above complexity results include both sorts of reasoning problems.

Later, a second Description Logic was presented that is as expressive as $\mathcal{L}^2$ [Lutz *et al.*, 2001a]. In contrast to the logic in [Borgida, 1996], this logic does not allow a role to be built as the cross-product of two concepts, and it does not provide individuals. However, using the identity role *id* (with $id^{\mathcal{I}} = \{(x,x) \mid x \in \Delta^{\mathcal{I}}\}$ for all interpretations $\mathcal{I}$), we can guarantee that (the atomic concept) N is interpreted as an individual, i.e., a singleton set, using the following TBox axiom:

$$\top \sqsubseteq \exists (R \sqcup \neg R).(N \sqcap \forall \neg id.\neg N).$$

4.2.2 Modal logics

Modal logics and Description Logics have a very close relationship, which was first described in [Schild, 1991]. In a nutshell, Schild [1991] points out that $\mathcal{ALC}$ can be seen as a notational variant of the multi-modal logic $\mathbf{K_m}$. Later, a similar relationship was observed between more expressive modal logics and Description Logics [De Giacomo and Lenzerini, 1994a; Schild, 1994], namely between (extensions of) Propositional Dynamic Logic PDL and (extensions of) $\mathcal{ALC}_{reg}$, i.e., $\mathcal{ALC}$ extended with regular roles. Following and exploiting these observations, various (complexity) results for Description Logics were found by translating results from modal or propositional dynamic logics and the μ-calculus to Description Logics [De Giacomo and Lenzerini, 1994a; 1994b; Schild, 1994; De Giacomo, 1995]. Moreover, upper bounds for the complexity of satisfiability problems were tightened considerably, mostly in parallel with the development of decision procedures suitable for implementations and optimization techniques for these procedures [De Giacomo and Lenzerini, 1995; De Giacomo, 1995; Horrocks *et al.*, 1999]. In the following, we will describe the relation between modal logics and Description Logics in more detail.

We start by introducing the basic modal logic $\mathbf{K}$; for a nice introduction and overview see [Halpern and Moses, 1992; Blackburn *et al.*, 2001]. Given a set of *propositional letters* $p_1, p_2, \ldots$, the set of formulae of the modal logic $\mathbf{K}$ is the smallest set that:

• contains $p_1, p_2, \ldots$,

- is closed under Boolean connectives $\wedge$, $\vee$, and $\neg$, and
- if it contains ϕ, then it also contains $\Box\phi$ and $\Diamond\phi$.

The semantics of modal formulae is given by so-called *Kripke structures* $M = \langle S, \pi, \mathcal{K} \rangle$, where S is a set of so-called *states* or *worlds* (which correspond to individuals in Description Logics), π is a mapping from the set of propositional letters into sets of states (i.e., $\pi(p_i)$ is the set of states in which p_i holds), and $\mathcal{K}$ is a binary relation on the states S, the so-called *accessibility relation* (which can be seen as the interpretation of a single role). The semantics is then given as follows, where, for a modal formula ϕ and a state $s \in S$, the expression $M, s \models \phi$ is read as "ϕ holds in M in state s".

$M, s \models p_i$	iff	$s \in \pi(p_i)$
$M, s \models \phi_1 \wedge \phi_2$	iff	$M, s \models \phi_1$ and $M, s \models \phi_2$
$M, s \models \phi_1 \vee \phi_2$	iff	$M, s \models \phi_1$ or $M, s \models \phi_2$
$M, s \models \neg\phi$	iff	$M, s \not\models \phi$
$M, s \models \Diamond\phi$	iff	there exists $s' \in S$ with $(s, s') \in \mathcal{K}$ and $M, s' \models \phi$
$M, s \models \Box\phi$	iff	for all $s' \in S$, if $(s, s') \in \mathcal{K}$, then $M, s' \models \phi$.

In contrast to many other modal logics, **K** does not impose any restrictions on the Kripke structures. For example, the modal logic **S4** is obtained from **K** by restricting the Kripke structures to those where the accessibility relation $\mathcal{K}$ is reflexive and transitive. Other modal logics restrict $\mathcal{K}$ to be symmetric, well-founded, an equivalence relation, etc. Moreover, the number of accessibility relations may be different from one. Then we are talking about *multi-modal logics*, where each accessibility relation $\mathcal{K}_i$ can be thought to correspond to one *agent*, and is quantified using the multi-modal operators $\Box_i$ and $\Diamond_i$ (or, alternatively $[i]$ and $\langle i \rangle$). For example, $\mathbf{K_m}$ stands for the multi-modal logic **K** with m agents.

To establish the correspondence between the modal logic $\mathbf{K_m}$ and the Description Logic $\mathcal{ALC}$, Schild [1991] gave the following translation f from $\mathcal{ALC}$-concepts using role names $R_1, \ldots, R_m$ to $\mathbf{K_m}$:

$$
\begin{aligned}
f(A) &= A \\
f(C \sqcap D) &= f(C) \wedge f(D) \\
f(C \sqcup D) &= f(C) \vee f(D) \\
f(\neg(C)) &= \neg(f(C)) \\
f(\forall R_i.C) &= \Box_i(f(C)) \\
f(\exists R_i.C) &= \Diamond_i(f(C)).
\end{aligned}
$$

Now, Kripke structures can easily be viewed as DL interpretations and vice versa. Then, from the semantics of $\mathbf{K_m}$ and $\mathcal{ALC}$, it follows immediately that

a is an instance of an $\mathcal{ALC}$-concept C in an interpretation $\mathcal{I}$ iff its translation $f(C)$ holds in a in the Kripke structure corresponding to $\mathcal{I}$. Obviously, we can define an analogous translation from $\mathbf{K_m}$ formulae into $\mathcal{ALC}$.

There exists a large variety of modal logics for a variety of applications. In the following, we will sketch some of them together with their relation to Description Logics.

Propositional Dynamic Logics are designed for reasoning about the behavior of programs. *Propositional Dynamic Logic* (PDL) was introduced by Fischer and Ladner [1979], and proven to have an EXPTIME-complete satisfiability problem by Fischer and Ladner [1979] and Pratt [1979]; for an overview, see [Harel *et al.*, 2000]. PDL was designed to describe the (dynamic) behavior of programs: complex programs can be built starting from atomic programs by using non-deterministic choice ($\cup$), composition (;), and iteration ($\cdot^*$). PDL formulae can be used to describe the properties that should hold in a state after the execution of a complex program. For example, the following PDL formula holds in a state if the following condition is satisfied: whenever program α or β is executed, a state is reached where p holds, and there is a sequence of alternating executions of α and β such that a state is reached where $\neg p \wedge q$ holds:

$$[\alpha \cup \beta]p \wedge \langle (\alpha; \beta)^* \rangle (\neg p \wedge q).$$

Its DL counterpart, $\mathcal{ALC}_{reg}$, was introduced independently by Baader [1991]. $\mathcal{ALC}_{reg}$ is the extension of $\mathcal{ALC}$ with regular expressions over roles[10] and can be seen as a notational variant of Propositional Dynamic Logic. For this correspondence, see the work by Schild [1991] and De Giacomo and Lenzerini [1994a], and Chapter 5. There exist a variety of extensions of PDL (or $\mathcal{ALC}_{reg}$), for example with inverse roles, counting, or difference of roles, most of which still have an EXPTIME satisfiability problem; see, e.g., [Kozen and Tiuryn, 1990; De Giacomo, 1995; De Giacomo and Lenzerini, 1996] and Chapter 5.

The μ-calculus can be viewed as a generalization of dynamic logic, with similar applications, and was introduced by Pratt [1981] and Kozen [1983]. It is obtained from multi-modal $\mathbf{K_m}$ by allowing (least and greated) fixpoint operators to be used on propositional letters. For example, for μ the least fixpoint operator and X a variable for propositional letters,

---

[10] Regular expressions over roles are built using union ($\sqcup$), composition ($\circ$), and the Kleene operator ($\cdot^*$) on roles and can be used in $\mathcal{ALC}_{reg}$-concepts in the place of atomic roles (see Chapter 5).

the formula $\mu X.p \vee \langle \alpha \rangle X$ describes the states with a (possibly empty) chain of α edges into a state in which p holds. In PDL, this formula is written $\langle \alpha^* \rangle p$, and its $\mathcal{ALC}_{reg}$ counterpart is $\exists R_\alpha^*.p$. However, the μ-calculus is strictly more expressive than PDL or $\mathcal{ALC}_{reg}$: for example, the μ-calculus can express *well-foundedness* of a program (binary relation), i.e., there is a μ-calculus formula that has only models in which α is interpreted as a well-founded relation (that is, a relation without any infinite chains). In [De Giacomo and Lenzerini, 1994b; 1997; Calvanese *et al.*, 1999c], this additional expressive power is shown to be useful in a variety of DL applications. The DL counterpart of the μ-calculus extended with number restrictions [De Giacomo and Lenzerini, 1994b; 1997] and additionally with inverse roles [Calvanese *et al.*, 1999c] is proven to have an EXPTIME-complete satisfiability problem.

There are two other classes of Description Logics with other forms of fixpoints: in Description Logics, fixpoints first came in through (1) the transitive closure operator [Baader, 1991], which is naturally defined using a least fixpoint, and (2) terminological cycles [Baader, 1990a], which have a different meaning according to whether a greatest, least, or arbitrary fixpoint semantics is employed [Nebel, 1991; Baader, 1996b; Küsters, 1998].

Temporal logics are designed for reasoning about time-dependent information. They have applications in databases, automated verification of programs, hardware, distributed systems, natural language processing, planning, etc. and come in various shapes; for a survey of temporal logics, see, e.g., [Gabbay *et al.*, 1994]. Firstly, they can differ in whether the basic temporal entities are time *points* or time *intervals*. Secondly, they differ in whether they are based on a linear or on a branching temporal structure. In the latter structures, the flow of time might "branch" into various succeeding future times. Finally, they differ in the underlying logic (e.g., Boolean logic or first-order predicate logic) and in the operators provided to speak about the past and the future (e.g., operators that refer to the next time point, to all future time points, to a future time point and all its respective future time points, etc.).

In contrast to some other modal logics, temporal logics do not have very close Description Logic relatives. However, they are mentioned here because they are used to "temporalize" Description Logics; for a survey on temporal Description Logics, see [Artale and Franconi, 2001] and Chapter 6. When speaking of the "temporalization" of a logic, e.g., $\mathcal{ALC}$, one usually refers to a logic with two-dimensional interpretations. One dimension refers to the flow of time, and each state in this flow of time comprises an interpretation of the underlying logic, e.g., an $\mathcal{ALC}$ interpretation. Obviously, the logic obtained depends on the temporal logic chosen for the temporal dimension and on the underlying (description) logic. Moreover, one has the choice of requiring that the interpretation domain of each time point is the same for all states ("constant domain assumption") or that it is a subset of the domains of the interpretations underlying future states. Examples of temporalized Description Logics can be found in [Wolter and Zakharyaschev, 1999d; Sturm and Wolter, 2002; Artale *et al.*, 2001; Schild, 1993; Lutz *et al.*, 2001b]. An alternative to this temporalization is to extend a Description Logic with a temporal concrete domain [Baader and Hanschke, 1991a]. This yields a "two-sorted" interpretation domain, consisting of abstract individuals on the one hand and time points or intervals on the other hand. Abstract individuals are then related to the temporal structure using features (functional roles) and the standard concrete domain constructs. An example of such a logic is described by Lutz [2001a].

Hybrid logics extend standard modal logics with the ability to refer to single states (individuals in the interpretation domain) using so-called *nominals* (see, e.g., [Blackburn and Seligman, 1995; Areces *et al.*, 2000; Areces, 2000] for hybrid logics related to Description Logics). Nominals are simply special propositional variables which hold in exactly one state. Hybrid logics enjoy a variety of "nice" properties whose description goes beyond the scope of this article; for a summary, see [Areces, 2000]. In Description Logics, there are three standard ways to refer to individuals: (1) we can use ABox individuals in ABoxes, (2) we can use the "one-of" concept constructor $\{o_1, \ldots, o_k\}$ which can be applied to individual names o_i and which is present in only a few Description Logics (e.g., in the Description Logic described in [Bresciani *et al.*, 1995]), and (3) we can use nominals in a similar way as in hybrid logics (e.g., [De Giacomo, 1995; Tobies, 2000; Horrocks and Sattler, 2001]), namely as special atomic concepts that are interpreted as singleton sets. For most Description Logics, there is a direct mapping between nominals and the "one-of" constructor and back: let o_i stand for individual names and, at the same time, nominals. Then we can extend the translation f mentioned above to the "one-of" constructor as follows – provided that we make the *unique name assumption* (see Chapter 2) either for both the individual names and the nominals or for neither of them:

$$f(\{o_1, \ldots, o_k\}) = f(\{o_1\} \sqcup \cdots \sqcup \{o_k\}) = o_1 \vee \cdots \vee o_k.$$

ABox individuals can be viewed as a restricted form of nominals, and each ABox in a Description Logic $\mathcal{L}$ can be translated into a single concept of (the extension of) $\mathcal{L}$ with conjunction, existential restriction, and "one-of": first, translate each assertion of the form

$$C(a) \quad \text{into } \{a\} \sqcap C \text{ and}$$
$$R(a,b) \quad \text{into } \{a\} \sqcap \exists R.\{b\}.$$

Next, for $C_1, \ldots, C_m$ the resulting concepts of this translation and U a role name not occurring in any C_i, define $C = \underset{1 \leq i \leq m}{\bigsqcap} \exists U.C_i$. Then each model of C is a model of the original ABox – provided, again, that the unique name assumption holds either for both individual names and nominals or for neither. Vice versa, each model of the original ABox can easily be extended to a model of C.

So far, we have only mentioned the weakest way in which nominals occur in hybrid logics. The next stronger form is formulae of the form $\varphi @ o_i$ which describes, intuitively, that φ holds in the state o_i. For U a universal role and C_φ the translation of φ, this formula corresponds to the concept $\exists U.(o_i \sqcap C_\varphi)$. Finally, we only point out that there are even more expressive ways of talking about nominals in hybrid logics using, for example, variables for nominals and quantification over them.

So much for the relation between certain modal logics and certain Description Logics. In the remainder of this section, the relationship between standard DL constructors and their counterpart in modal logics is discussed.

Number restrictions: In modal logics, the equivalent to qualified number restrictions $\geq n\,R.C$ and $\leq n\,R.C$ [Hollunder and Baader, 1991b] is known as *graded modalities* [Fine, 1972; Van der Hoek and de Rijke, 1995], whereas no equivalent to the standard, weaker form of number restrictions, $\geq n\,R$ and $\leq n\,R$, has been considered explicitly.

Number restrictions can be said to play a central role in Description Logics: they are present in almost all knowledge representation systems based on Description Logics, several variants have been investigated with respect to their computational complexity (e.g., see [Tobies, 1999c] for qualified number restrictions, [Baader and Sattler, 1999] for symbolic number restrictions and number restrictions on complex roles), and it was proved by De Giacomo and Lenzerini [1994a] that reasoning with respect to (possibly cyclic) TBoxes for the DL equivalent to *converse*-PDL extended with qualified number restrictions (on atomic and inverse atomic roles) is ExpTime-complete.

In contrast, they play a minor role in modal and dynamic logics. A more prominent role in dynamic logics is played by *deterministic* programs, i.e., programs that are to be interpreted as *functional* relations (see Chapter 2). Ben-Ari *et al.* [1982] and Parikh [1981] show that validity (and hence satisfiability) of DPDL (i.e., the logic that is obtained from PDL by restricting programs to be deterministic) is ExpTime-complete. Moreover, Parikh [1981] has shown that PDL formulae can be linearly translated into DPDL formulae, and this translation was used by De Giacomo and Lenzerini [1994a] to code qualified number restrictions into DPDL formulae. As a consequence, we have that satisfiability and subsumption with respect to (possibly cyclic) TBoxes in $\mathcal{ALC}$ extended with regular expressions over roles and qualified number restrictions is in ExpTime.

Transitivity: In modal logics and Description Logics, transitivity comes in (at least) two different shapes, as transitive roles (or frames whose accessibility relation is transitive, as in $\mathbf{K4_m}$) and as the transitive closure operator on roles (or the Kleene star operator on programs in PDL). Interestingly, these two sorts of transitivity differ in their complexity.

Fischer and Ladner [1979] prove that satisfiability in PDL is ExpTime-complete. However, the only operator on programs (or roles) used in the hardness proof is the transitive closure operator. Translated to Description Logics, this yields ExpTime-completeness of satisfiability in $\mathcal{ALC}$ extended with the transitive closure operator on roles.

In contrast, $\mathbf{K4_m}$ is known to be of the same complexity as $\mathbf{K_m}$ (or $\mathcal{ALC}$), namely PSpace-complete [Halpern and Moses, 1992], while providing transitivity: $\mathbf{K4_m}$ is obtained from $\mathbf{K_m}$ by restricting Kripke structures to those where the accessibility relations are transitive. Translated into Description Logics, this means that concept satisfiability in $\mathcal{ALC}$ extended with transitive roles (i.e., the ability to say that certain roles are interpreted as transitive relations) is in PSpace [Sattler, 1996]. An extension of this Description Logic with role hierarchies was implemented in the Description Logic system FaCT [Horrocks, 1998a]. Although pure concept satisfiability of this extension is ExpTime-hard, its highly optimized implementation behaves quite well [Horrocks, 1998b].

Inverse roles: Without the converse operator on programs/time (or the inverse operator on roles), binary relations are restricted to be used asymmetrically: for example, one is restricted to modeling either "into the future" or "into the past", or one must decide whether to use a role "has-child" or "is-child-of", but may not use both and relate them in the proper way. Hence in both modal and Description Logics, the converse/inverse operator plays an important role since it overcomes this asymmetry, and a variety of logics allowing this operator have been investigated [Streett, 1982; Vardi, 1985; De Giacomo and Massacci, 1996; Calvanese, 1996a; De Giacomo, 1996; Horrocks *et al.*, 1999].

4.2.3 Guarded fragments

Andréka *et al.* [1996] introduce guarded fragments as natural generalizations of modal logics to relations of arbitrary arity. Their definition and investigation was motivated by the question why modal logics have such "nice" properties, e.g., finite axiomatizability, Craig interpolation, and decidability. Guarded fragments are obtained from first-order logic by allowing the use of quantified variables only if these variables are *guarded* by appropriate atoms[11] before they are used in the body of a formula. More precisely, quantifiers are restricted to appear only in the form

$\exists \mathbf{y}(P(\mathbf{x}, \mathbf{y}) \wedge \Phi(\mathbf{y}))$ or $\forall \mathbf{y}(P(\mathbf{x}, \mathbf{y}) \supset \Phi(\mathbf{y}))$ (First Guarded Fragment)

$\exists \mathbf{y}(P(\mathbf{x}, \mathbf{y}) \wedge \Phi(\mathbf{x}, \mathbf{y}))$ or $\forall \mathbf{y}(P(\mathbf{x}, \mathbf{y}) \supset \Phi(\mathbf{x}, \mathbf{y}))$ (Guarded Fragment)

for atoms P, vectors of variables $\mathbf{x}$ and $\mathbf{y}$, and (first) guarded fragment formulae Φ with free variables in $\mathbf{y}$ and $\mathbf{x}$ (resp. in $\mathbf{y}$). The *loosely* guarded fragment further allows a restricted form of conjunction as guards.

Obviously, the translation $(\exists y.R(x, y) \wedge \varphi(y))(x)$ of the **K** formula $\Diamond \varphi$ (or of the $\mathcal{ALC}$ concept $\exists R.C_\varphi$) is a formula in the first guarded fragment since the quantified variable y is "guarded" by R. A more complex guarded fragment formula is

$\exists z_1, z_2.(\mathsf{parents}(x, z_1, z_2) \wedge (\mathsf{married}(z_1, z_2) \wedge (\forall y.\mathsf{parents}(y, z_1, z_2) \supset \mathsf{rich}(y))))$

in one free variable x, a guard atom parents, and describing all those persons that have married parents and whose siblings (including oneself) are rich.

All guarded fragments have been shown to be decidable [Andréka *et al.*, 1996]. Grädel [1999] proves that satisfiability of the guarded fragment is in EXPTIME – provided that the arity of the predicates is bounded – and 2EXPTIME-complete for unbounded signatures. Interestingly, the guarded fragment was shown to remain in 2EXPTIME when extended with fixpoints [Grädel and Walukiewicz, 1999]. These "nice" properties together with their close relationship to modal logics and Description Logics suggest that they are a good starting point for the development of a Description Logic with n-ary predicates [Grädel, 1998]: in [Lutz *et al.*, 1999], a restriction of the

---

[11] Atoms are formulae $P(x_1, \ldots, x_k)$ where P is a k-ary predicate symbol and x_i are variables.

guarded fragment was proven to be PSPACE-complete, where the restriction concerns the way in which variables are used in guard atoms. Roughly speaking, each predicate A comes with a two-fold arity (i, j) and, when A is used as a guard, either all first i variables are quantified and none of the last j are or, symmetrically, all last j variables are quantified and none of the first i are. Hence one might think of the predicates as having two-fold "groupings". A similar logic, the so-called action-guarded fragment AGF, is proposed in [Gonçalvès and Grädel, 2000]: it comes with a similar grouping of variables in predicates (which is, when extended with "inverse actions", the same as the grouping in [Lutz *et al.*, 1999]) and, additionally, it divides predicates into those allowed as guards and those allowed in the body of formulae. From a DL perspective, this should not be too severe a restriction since it parallels the distinction between role and concept names. Interestingly, the extension of AGF with counting quantifiers (the first-order counterpart of number restrictions), inverse actions, and fixpoints yields an EXPTIME logic – provided that the arity of the predicates is bounded and that numbers in counting quantifiers are coded unarily [Gonçalvès and Grädel, 2000]. This result is even more interesting when we note that the guarded fragment, when extended with number restrictions, functional restrictions, *or* transitivity (i.e., statements saying that certain binary relations are to be interpreted as transitive relations) becomes undecidable [Grädel, 1999].

To the best of our knowledge, the only other n-ary Description Logics with sound and complete inference algorithms are $\mathcal{DLR}$ [Calvanese *et al.*, 1998a] and $\mathcal{DLR}_\mu$ [Calvanese *et al.*, 1999c], which seem to be orthogonal to the guarded fragment. An exact description of the relationship between $\mathcal{DLR}$ (resp. $\mathcal{DLR}_\mu$) and the guarded fragment (resp. its extension with fixpoints) is missing so far.

4.3 Database models

In this section we will describe the relationship between Description Logics and data models used in databases. We will consider both traditional data models used in the conceptual modeling of an application domain, such as semantic and object-oriented data models, and more recently introduced formalisms for representing semistructured data and data on the web. We will concentrate on the relationship between the formalisms and refer to Chapter 16 for a more detailed discussion on the use of Description Logics in data management [Borgida, 1995].

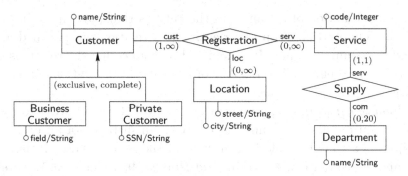

Fig. 4.8. An Entity–Relationship schema.

4.3.1 Semantic data models

Semantic data models were introduced primarily as formalisms for database schema design [Abrial, 1974; Chen, 1976], and are currently adopted in most of the database and information system design methodologies and Computer Aided Software Engineering (CASE) tools [Hull and King, 1987; Batini *et al.*, 1992]. In semantic data models, classes provide an explicit representation of objects with their attributes and their relationships to other objects, and subtype–supertype relationships are used to specify the inheritance of properties. Here, we concentrate on the *Entity–Relationship* (ER) model [Chen, 1976; Teorey, 1989; Batini *et al.*, 1992; Thalheim, 1993], which is one of the most widespread semantic data models. However, the considerations we make hold also for other formalisms for conceptual modeling, such as UML class diagrams [Rumbaugh *et al.*, 1998; Jacobson *et al.*, 1998].

4.3.1.1 Formalization

The basic elements of the ER model are entities, relationships, and attributes, which are used to model the domain of interest by means of an *ER schema*.

Figure 4.8 shows a simple ER schema representing the registration of customers for (telephone) services provided by departments (e.g., of a telephone company). The schema is drawn using the standard graphical ER notation, in which entities are represented as boxes, and relationships as diamonds. An attribute is shown as a circle attached to the entity for which it is defined. An *entity type* (or simply *entity*) denotes a set of objects, called its *instances*, with common properties. Elementary properties are modeled through *attributes*, whose values belong to one of several predefined *domains*, such as Integer, String, Boolean, etc. Relationships between instances of different entities are modeled through *relationship types* (or simply *relationships*). A relationship denotes a set of tuples, each one representing an association among a combination of instances of the entities that participate in the relationship. The participation of an entity in a relationship is called an *ER role* and has a unique name. It is depicted by connecting the relationship to the participating entity. The number of ER roles for a relationship is called its *arity*.

Cardinality constraints can be attached to an ER role in order to restrict the minimum or maximum number of times an instance of an entity may participate via that ER role in instances of the relationship [Abrial, 1974; Grant and Minker, 1984; Lenzerini and Nobili, 1990; Ferg, 1991; Ye *et al.*, 1994; Thalheim, 1992; Calvanese and Lenzerini, 1994b]. Minimal and maximal cardinality constraints can be arbitrary non-negative integers. However, typical values for minimal cardinality constraints are 0, denoting no constraint, and 1, denoting mandatory participation of the entity in the relationship; typical values for maximal cardinality constraints are 1, denoting functionality, and ∞, denoting no constraint. In Figure 4.8, cardinality constraints are used to impose that each customer must be registered for at least one service. Also, each service is provided by exactly one department, which in turn may not provide more than 20 different services.

To represent inclusions between the sets of instances of two entities or two relationships, so called *IS-A* relations are used. An IS-A relation states the inheritance of properties from a more general entity (resp. relationship) to a more specific one. A *generalization* is a set of IS-A relations which share the more general entity (resp. relationship). Multiple generalizations can be combined in a *generalization hierarchy*. A generalization can be *mutually exclusive*, meaning that all the specific entities (resp. relationships) are mutually disjoint, or *complete*, meaning that the union of the more specific entities (resp. relationships) completely covers the more general entity (resp. relationship). In Figure 4.8, a mutually exclusive and complete generalization is used to represent the fact that customers are partitioned into private and business customers.

Additionally, *keys* are used to represent the fact that an instance of an entity is uniquely identified by a certain set of attributes, or that an instance of a relationship is uniquely identified by a set of instances of the entities participating in the relationship.

Although we do not provide a formal definition here, the semantics of an ER schema can be given by specifying which database states are consistent with the information structure represented by the schema; for details see e.g., [Calvanese *et al.*, 1999e].

Traditionally, the ER model has been used in the design phase of commercial applications, and modern CASE tools usually provide sophisticated schema editing facilities and automatic generation of code for the interaction with the database management system. However, these tools do not provide any support beyond the graphical user interface, for dealing with the complexity of schemas. In particular, the designer is responsible for checking schemas for important properties such as consistency and redundancy. This may be a complex and time-consuming task if performed by hand. By translating an ER schema into a DL knowledge base in such a way that the verification of schema properties corresponds to traditional DL reasoning tasks, the reasoning facilities of a DL system can be profitably exploited to support conceptual database design.

4.3.1.2 Correspondence with Description Logics

Both in Description Logics and in the ER model, the domain of interest is modeled through classes and relationships, and various proposals have been made for establishing a correspondence between the two formalisms. Bergamaschi and Sartori [1992] provide a translation of ER schemas into acyclic $\mathcal{ALN}$ knowledge bases. However, due to the limited expressiveness of the target language, several features of the ER model and desired reasoning tasks could not fully be captured by the proposed translation. Indeed, when relating the ER model to Description Logics, one has to take into account the following aspects:

1. The ER model allows relations of arbitrary arity, while in traditional Description Logics only unary and binary relations are considered.
2. The assumption of acyclicity is unrealistic in an ER schema, while it is common in DL knowledge bases.
3. Database states are considered to be finite structures, while no assumption on finiteness is usually made on the interpretation domain of a DL knowledge base.

Before discussing these issues in more detail, we show in Figure 4.9 part of the $\mathcal{ALUNI}$ knowledge base corresponding to the ER schema in Figure 4.8, derived according to the translation proposed by Calvanese *et al.* [1994; 1999e]. We have omitted the part corresponding to the translation of most attributes, showing as an example only the translation of the attribute name of the entity Customer.

Due to point 1, when translating ER schemas into knowledge bases of a traditional Description Logic, it becomes necessary to *reify* relationships,

Fig. 4.9. Part of the knowledge base corresponding to the Entity–Relationship schema in Figure 4.8.

i.e., to translate each relationship into a concept whose instances represent the tuples of the relationship. Each entity is also translated into a concept, while each ER role is translated into a Description Logic role. Then, using functional roles, one can enforce that each instance of the atomic concept C corresponding to a relationship R represents a tuple of R, i.e., for each role representing an ER role of R, the instance of C is connected to exactly one instance of the entity associated to the ER role.

There is, however, one condition, which is implicit in the semantics of the ER model, but which does not necessarily hold once relationships are reified, and which can also not be enforced in Description Logics on the models of a knowledge base: the condition is that the extension of a relationship R does not contain some tuple twice. After reification this corresponds to the fact that there are no two instances of the concept corresponding to R that are connected through all roles of R exactly to the same instances of the entities associated to the roles. However, it can be shown that, when reasoning on a knowledge base corresponding to an ER schema, nothing is lost by ignoring this condition. Indeed, given an arbitrary model of such a knowledge base, one can always find a model in which the condition holds, and thus one that corresponds directly to a legal database state [Calvanese et al., 1994; De Giacomo, 1995; Calvanese et al., 1999e].

Cardinality constraints are translated using number restrictions on the inverse of the roles connecting relationships to entities. To avoid the need for qualified number restrictions, in the translation in Figure 4.9 we have disambiguated the roles by appending to their name the name of the relationship they belong to. An alternative would be to allow the same role to appear in several places, and use qualified number restrictions instead of unqualified ones. While considerably complicating the language, this makes it possible to translate also IS-A relations between relationships, which cannot be captured using the translation proposed by Calvanese *et al.* [1999e]. Also more general forms of cardinality constraints have been proposed for the ER model [Thalheim, 1992], allowing one, e.g., to limit the number of locations a customer may be registered for, independently of the service. To the best of our knowledge, such types of cardinality constraints cannot be captured in Description Logics in general. Borgida and Weddell [1997] have studied reasoning in Description Logics in the presence of functional dependencies that are more general than unary ones, and which allow one to represent keys of relations. Decidability of reasoning in a very expressive Description Logic augmented with non-unary key constraints has been shown by Calvanese *et al.* [2000b], and Calvanese *et al.* [2001a] have shown that also general functional dependencies can be added without losing EXPTIME-completeness.

IS-A relations are simply translated using concept inclusion assertions. Generalization hierarchies additionally require negation, if they are mutually disjoint, and union, if they are complete.

With respect to point 2, we observe that the translation of an ER schema containing cycles obviously gives rise to a cyclic DL knowledge base. However, due to the necessity of properly relating a relationship via an ER role to an entity, even when translating an acyclic ER schema, the resulting knowledge base contains cycles. On the other hand, it is sufficient to use inclusion assertions rather than equivalence, since the former naturally correspond to the semantics of ER schemas.

With respect to point 3, we observe that one cannot simply ignore it and adopt algorithms that reason with respect to arbitary models. Indeed, the ER model itself does not have the *finite model property* [Cosmadakis *et al.*, 1990; Calvanese and Lenzerini, 1994b], which states that, if a knowledge base (resp. schema) has an arbitrary, possibly infinite model (resp. database state), then it also has a finite one (see also Chapter 5 for more details). A further confirmation comes from the fact that, for correctly capturing ER schemas in Description Logics, possibly cyclic knowledge bases expressed in a Description Logic including functional restrictions and inverse roles are required, and such knowledge bases do not have the finite model property [Calvanese *et al.*, 1994; 1999e]. Therefore one must resort to techniques for finite model reasoning. Calvanese *et al.* [1994] show that reasoning w.r.t. finite models in $\mathcal{ALUNI}$ knowledge bases containing only inclusion assertions is EXPTIME-complete, and Calvanese [1996a] presents a 2EXPTIME algorithm for reasoning in $\mathcal{ALCQI}$ knowledge bases with general inclusion assertions.

4.3.1.3 Applications of the correspondence

The study of the correspondence between Description Logics and semantic data models has led to significant advantages in both fields. On the one hand, the richness of constructs that is typical of Description Logics makes it possible to add them to semantic data models and take them fully into account when reasoning on a schema [Calvanese *et al.*, 1998g]. Notable examples are:

- the ability to specify not only IS-A and generalization hierarchies, but also arbitrary Boolean combinations of entities or relationships, which can correspond to forms of negative and incomplete knowledge [Di Battista and Lenzerini, 1993];
- the ability to refine properties along an IS-A hierarchy, such as restricting the numeric range for cardinality constraints, or refining the participation in relationships using universal quantification over roles;
- the ability to define classes by means of equality assertions, and not only to state necessary properties for them.

The correspondence between semantic data models and Description Logics has been recently exploited to add such advanced capabilities to CASE tools. A notable example is the I●COM tool [Franconi and Ng, 2000] for conceptual modeling, which combines a user-friendly graphical interface with the ability to automatically infer properties of a schema (e.g., inconsistency of a class, or implicit IS-A relations) by invoking the FACT Description Logic reasoner [Horrocks, 1998a; 1999].

On the other hand, the basic ideas behind the translation of semantic data models into Description Logics, namely reification and the fact that one can restrict the attention to models in which distinct instances of a reified relation correspond to distinct tuples, have led to the development of Description Logics in which relations of arbitrary arity are first class citizens [De Giacomo and Lenzerini, 1994c; Calvanese *et al.*, 1997; 1998a]. Using such Description Logics, the translation of an ER schema is immediate, since now relationships of arbitrary arity also have their direct counterpart. For example, using $\mathcal{DLR}$ [Calvanese *et al.*, 1998a], the part of the schema in Figure 4.8 relative to the ternary relation Registration can be translated as follows:

$$\text{Registration} \sqsubseteq (\$1\colon \text{Customer}) \sqcap (\$2\colon \text{Location}) \sqcap (\$3\colon \text{Service})$$
$$\text{Customer} \sqsubseteq \exists[\$1]\text{Registration}.$$

We refer to Chapter 16, Subsection 16.2.2 for the details of the translation.

Description Logics could also be considered as expressive variants of semantic data models with incorporated reasoning facilities. This is of particular importance in the context of information integration, where a high expressiveness is required to capture in the best possible way the complex relationships that hold between data in different information sources [Levy *et al.*, 1995; Calvanese *et al.*, 1998d; 1998e].

4.3.2 Object-oriented data models

Object-oriented data models have been proposed recently with the goal of devising database formalisms that could be integrated with object-oriented programming systems [Abiteboul and Kanellakis, 1989; Kim, 1990; Cattell and Barry, 1997; Rumbaugh *et al.*, 1998]. Object-oriented data models rely on the notion of *object identifier* at the extensional level (as opposed to traditional data models which are value-oriented) and on the notion of *class* at the intensional level. The structure of the classes is specified by means of *typing* and *inheritance*. Since we aim at discussing the relationship with Description Logics, which are well-suited to describe structural rather than dynamic properties, we restrict our attention to the structural component of object-oriented models. Hence we do not consider all those aspects that are related to the specification of the behavior and evolution of objects, which nevertheless constitute an important part of these data models. Although in our discussion we do not refer to any specific formalism, the model we use is inspired by the one presented by Abiteboul and Kanellakis [1989], and embodies the basic features of the static part of the ODMG standard [Cattell and Barry, 1997].

4.3.2.1 Formalization

An *object-oriented schema* is a finite set of class declarations, which impose constraints on the instances of the classes that are used to model the application domain. A *class declaration* for a class C has the form

$$\underline{\text{class }} C \underline{\text{ is-a }} C_1, \ldots, C_k \underline{\text{ type-is }} T,$$

where the is-a part, which is optional, specifies inclusions between the sets of instances of the classes involved, while the type-is part specifies through the *type expression* T the structure assigned to the objects that are instances of the class. We consider *union, set,* and *record types*, built according to the following syntax, where the letter A is used to denote *attributes*:

$$
\begin{aligned}
T \longrightarrow\ & C \mid \\
& \underline{\text{union }} T_1, \ldots, T_k \underline{\text{ end }} \mid \\
& \underline{\text{set-of }} T \mid \\
& \underline{\text{record }} A_1 \colon T_1, \ldots, A_k \colon T_k \underline{\text{ end}}.
\end{aligned}
$$

Figure 4.10 shows part of an object-oriented schema modeling the same

```
class Customer type-is                     class Registration type-is
   union BusinessCustomer, PrivateCustomer    record
end                                             cust: Customer,
                                                regis: set-of record
class PrivateCustomer is-a Customer type-is                 serv: Service
   record                                                   loc: Location
      SSN: String                                        end
end                                        end

class Service type-is
   record
      code: Integer,
      suppliedBy: Department
end
```

Fig. 4.10. Part of an object-oriented schema.

reality as the Entity–Relationship schema of Figure 4.8. Notice that now registrations are represented as a class and grouped according to the customer, since all registrations related to one customer are collected in the set-valued attribute regis.

The meaning of an object-oriented schema is given by specifying the characteristics of a database state for the schema. The definition of a *database state* makes use of the notions of *object identifier* and *value*. Starting from a finite set $\mathcal{O}^{\mathcal{J}}$ of object identifiers, the set of complex values over $\mathcal{O}^{\mathcal{J}}$ is built inductively by grouping values into finite sets and records. A *database state* $\mathcal{J}$ for a schema is constituted by the set of object identifiers, a mapping $\pi^{\mathcal{J}}$ assigning to each class a subset of $\mathcal{O}^{\mathcal{J}}$, and a mapping $\rho^{\mathcal{J}}$ assigning to each object in $\mathcal{O}^{\mathcal{J}}$ a value over $\mathcal{O}^{\mathcal{J}}$.

Notice that, although the set of values that can be constructed from a set $\mathcal{O}^{\mathcal{J}}$ of object identifiers is infinite, for a database state one only needs to consider the finite subset $\mathcal{V}_{\mathcal{J}}$ of values assigned by $\rho^{\mathcal{J}}$ to the elements of $\mathcal{O}^{\mathcal{J}}$, including the values that are not explicitly associated with object identifiers, but are used to form other values.

The interpretation of type expressions in a database state $\mathcal{J}$ is defined through an *interpretation function* $\cdot^{\mathcal{J}}$ that assigns to each type expression T a set $T^{\mathcal{J}}$ of values in $\mathcal{V}_{\mathcal{J}}$ as follows:

- if T is a class C, then $T^{\mathcal{J}} = \pi^{\mathcal{J}}(C)$;
- if T is a union type union $T_1, \ldots, T_k$ end, then $T^{\mathcal{J}} = T_1^{\mathcal{J}} \cup \cdots \cup T_k^{\mathcal{J}}$;
- it T is a record type (resp. set type), then $T^{\mathcal{J}}$ is the set of record values (resp. set values) compatible with the structure of T. For records we are using an open semantics, meaning that the records that are instances of a record type may have more components than those explicitly specified in the type [Abiteboul and Kanellakis, 1989].

A database state $\mathcal{J}$ for an object-oriented schema $\mathcal{S}$ is said to be *legal* (with respect to $\mathcal{S}$) if for each declaration

$$\underline{\text{class}}\ C\ \underline{\text{is-a}}\ C_1, \ldots, C_n\ \underline{\text{type-is}}\ T$$

in $\mathcal{S}$, we have (1) $C^{\mathcal{J}} \subseteq C_i^{\mathcal{J}}$ for each $i \in \{1, \ldots, n\}$, and (2) $\rho^{\mathcal{J}}(C^{\mathcal{J}}) \subseteq T^{\mathcal{J}}$. Therefore, for a legal database state, the type expressions that are present in the schema determine the (finite) set of values that must be considered. The construction of such values is limited by the depth of type expressions.

4.3.2.2 Correspondence with Description Logics

When establishing a correspondence between an object-oriented model such as the one presented above, and Description Logics, one must take into account that the interpretation domain for a DL knowledge base consists of atomic objects, whereas each object of an object-oriented schema is assigned a possibly structured value. Therefore one needs to explicitly represent in Description Logics the type structure of classes [Calvanese *et al.*, 1994; 1999e; Artale *et al.*, 1996a]. We describe now the translation proposed by Calvanese *et al.* [1994; 1999e], that overcomes this difficulty by introducing into the DL knowledge base concepts and roles with a specific meaning: the concepts AbstractClass, RecType, and SetType are used to denote instances of classes, record values, and set values, respectively. The associations between classes and types induced by the class declarations, as well as the basic characteristics of types, are modeled by means of specific roles: the functional role value models the association between classes and types, and the role member is used for specifying the type of the elements of a set. Moreover, the concepts representing types are assumed to be mutually disjoint, and disjoint from the concepts representing classes. These constraints are expressed by the following inclusion assertions, which are always part of the knowledge base that is obtained from an object-oriented schema:

$$
\begin{aligned}
\mathsf{AbstractClass} &\sqsubseteq\ =1\,\mathsf{value} \\
\mathsf{RecType} &\sqsubseteq\ \forall\mathsf{value}.\bot \\
\mathsf{SetType} &\sqsubseteq\ \forall\mathsf{value}.\bot \sqcap \neg\mathsf{RecType}.
\end{aligned}
$$

The translation from object-oriented schemas to Description Logic knowledge bases is defined through a mapping Γ, which maps each type expression to a concept expression as follows:

- Each class C is mapped to an atomic concept $\Gamma(C)$.
- Each type expression $\underline{\text{union}}\ T_1, \ldots, T_k\ \underline{\text{end}}$ is mapped to $\Gamma(T_1) \sqcup \cdots \sqcup \Gamma(T_k)$.
- Each type expression $\underline{\text{set-of}}\ T$ is mapped to $\mathsf{SetType} \sqcap \forall\mathsf{member}.\Gamma(T)$.

$$
\begin{aligned}
\text{Customer} &\sqsubseteq \text{AbstractClass} \sqcap \forall \text{value.}(\text{BusinessCustomer} \sqcup \text{PrivateCustomer}) \\
\text{PrivateCustomer} &\sqsubseteq \text{AbstractClass} \sqcap \text{Customer} \sqcap \forall \text{value.}(\text{RecType} \sqcap = 1\,\text{SSN} \sqcap \forall \text{SSN.String}) \\
\text{Service} &\sqsubseteq \text{AbstractClass} \sqcap \\
&\quad \forall \text{value.}(\text{RecType} \sqcap = 1\,\text{code} \sqcap \forall \text{code.Integer} \sqcap \\
&\qquad = 1\,\text{suppliedBy} \sqcap \forall \text{suppliedBy.Department}) \\
\text{Customer} &\sqsubseteq \text{AbstractClass} \sqcap \\
&\quad \forall \text{value.}(\text{RecType} \sqcap = 1\,\text{cust} \sqcap \forall \text{cust.Customer} \sqcap \\
&\qquad = 1\,\text{regis} \sqcap \forall \text{regis.}(\text{SetType} \sqcap \\
&\qquad\qquad \forall \text{member.}(\text{RecType} \sqcap \\
&\qquad\qquad\qquad = 1\,\text{serv} \sqcap \forall \text{serv.Service} \sqcap \\
&\qquad\qquad\qquad = 1\,\text{loc} \sqcap \forall \text{loc.Location})))
\end{aligned}
$$

Fig. 4.11. The specific part of the knowledge base corresponding to the object-oriented schema in Figure 4.10.

- Each attribute A is mapped to an atomic role $\Gamma(A)$, and each type expression record $A_1 : T_1, \ldots, A_k : T_k$ end is mapped to

$$
\begin{aligned}
\text{RecType} \;\sqcap\; &\forall \Gamma(A_1).\Gamma(T_1) \sqcap = 1\,\Gamma(A_1) \sqcap \cdots \sqcap \\
&\forall \Gamma(A_k).\Gamma(T_k) \sqcap = 1\,\Gamma(A_k).
\end{aligned}
$$

Then, the knowledge base $\Gamma(\mathcal{S})$ corresponding to an object-oriented schema $\mathcal{S}$ is obtained by taking for each class declaration

$$
\underline{\text{class}}\ C\ \underline{\text{is-a}}\ C_1, \ldots, C_n\ \underline{\text{type-is}}\ T
$$

an inclusion assertion

$$
\Gamma(C) \;\sqsubseteq\; \text{AbstractClass} \sqcap \Gamma(C_1) \sqcap \cdots \sqcap \Gamma(C_n) \sqcap \forall \text{value.}\Gamma(T).
$$

We show in Figure 4.11 the knowledge base resulting from the translation of the fragment of object-oriented schema shown in Figure 4.10.

Analogously to the ER model, it is sufficient to use inclusion assertions instead of equivalence assertions to capture the semantics of object-oriented schemas. A translation to an acyclic knowledge base is possible under the assumption that no class in the schema refers to itself, either directly in its type or indirectly via the class declarations[12] [Artale *et al.*, 1996a]. However, since this assumption represents a rather strong limitation in expressiveness, cycles are typically present in object-oriented schemas, and in this case the resulting DL knowledge base will contain cyclic assertions. No inverse roles are needed for the translation, since in object-oriented models the inverse of an attribute is rarely considered. Furthermore, the use of number restrictions is limited to functionality, since all attributes are implicitly functional.

To establish the correctness of the transformation, and thus ensure that the reasoning tasks on an object-oriented schema can be reduced to reasoning tasks on its translation into Description Logics, we would like to establish

---

[12] Note that cyclic references cannot appear directly in a type, which is constructed inductively, but only through the class declarations.

a one-to-one correspondence between database states legal for the schema and models of the knowledge base resulting from the translation. However, as for the ER model, the knowledge base may have models that do not correspond directly to legal database states. In this case, this is due to the fact that, while values have a treelike structure, the corresponding individuals in a model of the Description Logic knowledge base may be part of cyclic substructures. One way of ruling out such cyclic substructures would be to adopt a specific constructor that allows one to impose well-foundedness [Calvanese *et al.*, 1995], or even exploit general fixed points on concepts [Schild, 1994; De Giacomo and Lenzerini, 1994a; 1997; Calvanese *et al.*, 1999c]. However, it turns out that, in this case, it is not necessary to explicitly enforce such a condition. Indeed, due to the finite depth of nesting of types in a schema, it can be shown that each model of the translation of the schema can be unfolded into one that directly corresponds to a legal database state (more details are provided by Calvanese *et al.* [1999e]).

4.3.2.3 Applications of the correspondence

Similarly to the ER model, the existence of property-preserving transformations from object-oriented schemas into DL knowledge bases makes it possible to exploit the reasoning capabilities of a DL system for checking relevant schema properties, such as consistency and redundancy [Bergamaschi and Nebel, 1994; Artale *et al.*, 1996a; Calvanese *et al.*, 1998g]. Additionally, several extensions of the object-oriented formalism that are useful for the purpose of conceptual modeling can be considered:

- Not only IS-A, but also disjointness, and, more generally, Boolean combinations of classes can be used.
- Class definitions can be used to specify not only necessary but also necessary and sufficient properties for an object to be an instance of a class [Bergamaschi and Nebel, 1994].
- Cardinality constraints and not only implicit functionality can be imposed on attributes. Having attributes with multiple values could in some cases be a useful alternative to set-valued attributes.
- By admitting also the use of inverse roles in the language, one gains the ability to impose constraints using a relation in both directions, as is customary in semantic data models. The increase in expressiveness that one obtains this way has indeed been recognized as extremely important by the database community [Albano *et al.*, 1991], and has been included in the recent ODMG standard [Cattell and Barry, 1997].

The basic characteristics of object-oriented data models have also been included in the structural part of the Unified Modeling Language (UML)

[Rumbaugh *et al.*, 1998; Jacobson *et al.*, 1998], which is becoming the standard language for the analysis phase of software and information system development. Additionally, UML allows the definition of generic recursive data structures (both inductive and co-inductive) such as lists and trees, and their specialization to specific types. In order to capture also these aspects of UML in Description Logics and take them fully into account when reasoning over a schema, the Description Logic must provide the ability to represent and reason over data structures. In particular, to represent UML schemas, it is necesary to resort to very expressive Description Logics including number restrictions, inverse roles or *n*-ary relations, and fixpoint constructs on concepts [Calvanese *et al.*, 1999c]. Also in this case, the reasoning services provided by a DL system can be integrated into CASE tools and profitably exploited to support the designer in the analysis phase [Franconi and Ng, 2000].

4.3.3 Semistructured data models and XML

In recent application areas such as data integration, access to data on the web, and digital libraries, the structure of the data is usually not rigid, as in conventional databases, and thus it is difficult to describe it using traditional data models. Therefore, so called *semistructured data models* have been proposed, which are graph-based data models that provide flexible structuring mechanisms, and thus allow one to represent data that is neither raw nor strictly typed [Abiteboul *et al.*, 2000; Abiteboul, 1997; Buneman *et al.*, 1997; Mendelzon *et al.*, 1997]. The *Extensible Markup Language* (XML) [Bray *et al.*, 1998; Abiteboul *et al.*, 2000], which has been introduced as a mechanism for representing structured documents on the Web, can in fact also be considered a model for semistructured data. Indeed, XML is by now the most popular model for data on the Web, and there is a tremendous effort related to XML and the associated standards,[13] both in the research community and in industry.

Description Logics have traditionally been used to describe and organize data in a more flexible way than is done in databases, basically using graph-like structures. Hence it seems natural to adopt Description Logics and the associated reasoning services for representing and reasoning on semistructured data and XML as well. In the following, we discuss the (rather few) proposals made in the literature. What these proposals have in common is the necessity to resort to fixpoints, either by adopting fixpoint semantics [Nebel, 1991; Baader, 1991], or by using reflexive–transitive closure or

---

[13] http://www.w3.org/

explicit fixpoint constructs [De Giacomo and Lenzerini, 1997] (see also Chapter 5).

For the recent extensive work on the use of Description Logics to provide a semantically richer representation of data on the Web we refer to Chapter 14.

4.3.3.1 Relationship between semistructured data and Description Logics

Michaeli *et al.* [1997] propose to extend a semistructured data model that is an abstraction of the OEM model [Abiteboul *et al.*, 1997] with a layer of classes, representing objects with common properties. Class expressions correspond to DL concepts and the properties for the classes are specified by a set of *classification rules*, which provide sufficient conditions for class membership and are interpreted under a least fixpoint semantics. By a reduction to reasoning in a Description Logic with fixpoint operators [De Giacomo and Lenzerini, 1997; Calvanese *et al.*, 1999c], it is shown that determining class satisfiability and containment under a set of rules is ExpTime-decidable (and in fact ExpTime-complete).

In the following, we discuss in more detail the use of Description Logics to represent and reason on semistructured data, on the example of one typical representative for semistructured data models. In semistructured data models, data is organized in the form of a graph, and information on both the values and the schema for the data is attached to the edges of the graph. In the formalism proposed by Buneman *et al.* [1997], the labels of edges in a schema are formulae of a complete first-order theory, and the *conformance* of a database to a schema is defined in terms of a special relation, called *simulation*. The notion of simulation is less rigid than the usual notion of satisfaction, and suitably reflects the need for dealing with less strict data structures. In order to capture in Description Logics the notion of simulation, it is necessary on the one hand to express the local conditions that a node must satisfy, and on the other hand to deal with the fact that the simulation relation is the greatest relation satisfying the local conditions. Since semistructured data schemas may contain cycles, the local conditions may depend on each other in a cyclic way. Therefore, while the local conditions can be encoded by means of suitable inclusion assertions in $\mathcal{ALU}$, the maximality condition on the simulation relation can only be captured correctly by resorting to a greatest fixpoint semantics [Calvanese *et al.*, 1998c; 1998b]. Then, using a Description Logic with fixpoint constructs, such as $\mu\mathcal{ALCQ}$ [De Giacomo and Lenzerini, 1994b; 1997] (see also Chapter 5), a so-called *characteristic concept* for a semistructured data schema can be constructed, which captures exactly the properties of the schema. Subsumption

```
<?xml version="1.0"?>                      <?xml version="1.0"?>
<!DOCTYPE Customers SYSTEM "services.dtd">  <!DOCTYPE Services SYSTEM "services.dtd">

<Customers>                                <Services>
  <Customer type="business">                 <Department name="standard-services">
    <Name>FIAT</Name>                          <Service code="522">
    <Field>manufacturing</Field>                 <Name>call-back when busy</Name>
    <Registered service="522">                   <Cost>...</Cost>
      <Location><City>Torino</City>              ...
              <Address>...</Address>           </Service>
      </Location>                              <Service code="214">
      <Location>...</Location>                    <Name>three-party call</Name>
    </Registered>                              </Service>
    <Registered service="612">               </Department>
      <Location>...</Location>
    </Registered>                            <Department name="business-services">
  </Customer>                                  <Service code="612">
                                                 <Name>conference call</Name>
  <Customer type="private">                    </Service>
    <Name>...</Name>                            ...
    <SSN>...</SSN>                            </Department>
    <Registered service="214">             </Services>
      <Location>...</Location>
    </Registered>
  </Customer>
  ...
</Customers>
```

Fig. 4.12. Two XML documents specifying respectively customers and services.

between two schemas, which is the task of deciding whether every semistructured database conforming to one schema also conforms to another schema [Buneman *et al.*, 1997], can be decided by checking subsumption between the characteristic concepts of the schemas [Calvanese *et al.*, 1998c].

The correspondence with Description Logics can again be exploited to enrich semistructured data models, without losing the ability to check schema subsumption. Indeed, the requirement already raised by Buneman *et al.* [1997], to extend semistructured data models with several types of constraints, has been addressed by Calvanese *et al.* [1998b], who propose several types of constraints, such as existence and cardinality constraints, which are naturally derived from DL constructs. Reasoning in the presence of constraints is done by encoding also the constraints in the characteristic concept of a schema. Calvanese *et al.* deal also with the presence of incomplete information in the theory describing the properties of edge labels, by proposing the use of a theory expressed in $\mu\mathcal{ALCQ}$, instead of a complete first order theory.

4.3.3.2 Relationship between XML and Description Logics

XML [Bray *et al.*, 1998] is a formalism for representing documents that are structured by means of nested tags. Recently, XML has gained

```
<!-- File: services.dtd -->

<!ELEMENT Customers  (Customer)+ >
<!ELEMENT Customer   (Name, (Field|SSN), Registered+) >
<!ELEMENT Registered (Location)+ >
...
<!ELEMENT Services   (Department)+ >
<!ELEMENT Department (Service)* >
<!ELEMENT Service    (Name, Cost?, ...) >
<!ELEMENT Name       #PCDATA >
...

<!ATTLIST Customer   type     (business|private) "private">
<!ATTLIST Registered service  IDREF              #REQUIRED>
<!ATTLIST Department name     CDATA              #REQUIRED>
<!ATTLIST Service    code     ID                 #REQUIRED>
...
```

Fig. 4.13. Part of the Document Type Declaration S for the XML documents in Figure 4.12.

popularity also as a formalism for representing (semistructured) data and exchanging it over the Web. Figure 4.12 shows two example XML documents containing respectively data about customers and their registration to services provided by various departments (e.g., of a telephone company). A part of an XML document consisting of a *start tag* (e.g., <Customer>), the matching *end tag* (e.g., </Customer>), and everything in between is called an *element*. Elements can be arbitrarily nested, and can have associated *attributes*, specified by means of attribute–value pairs inside the start tag (e.g., type="business"). Intuitively, each XML document can be viewed as a finite ordered unranked tree,[14] where each element represents a node, and the children of an element are those elements directly contained in it. How XML documents are viewed as trees is defined, together with an API for accessing and manipulating such trees/XML-documents, by the *Document Object Model*,[15] which defines, besides element nodes, other types of nodes, such as attributes, comments, etc.

In XML, it is possible to impose a structure on documents by means of a *Document Type Declaration* (DTD) [Bray *et al.*, 1998]. A DTD consists of a set of declarations: For each *element type* used in the XML document, the DTD must contain a declaration that specifies, by means of a regular expression, how elements can be nested within elements of that type. The keyword #PCDATA is used to specify that the *element content* (i.e., the part enclosed by the tags) is free text without nested elements. For each attribute

---

[14] In an *unranked* tree each node can have an arbitrary finite number of child nodes. The tree is *ordered* since the order among children of the same node matters.
[15] http://www.w3.org/DOM/

appearing in the XML document, the DTD must contain a declaration specifying the name of the attribute, the type of the elements it is associated to, and additional properties (e.g., the type and whether the attribute is optional or mandatory). Figure 4.13 shows part of the DTD for the XML documents in Figure 4.12. We refer to [Bray *et al.*, 1998] for a precise definition of the syntax and semantics of XML DTDs.

We illustrate the method for encoding XML DTDs into DL knowledge bases proposed in [Calvanese *et al.*, 1999d]. For simplicity, we do not consider XML attributes, although they can easily be dealt with by introducing suitable roles. Due to the presence of regular expressions, to encode DTDs into Description Logics, it is necessary to resort to a Description Logic equipped with constructs for building regular expressions over roles (see Chapter 5). Notice that the encoding of DTDs into DL knowledge bases must allow for representing unranked trees and at the same time for preserving the order of the children of a node. For example, the DTD in Figure 4.13 enforces that the content of a `Customer` element consists of a `Name` element, followed by (in DTDs, *concatenation* is denoted by ",") either a `Field` or an `SSN` element (*alternative* is denoted by "|"), followed by an arbitrary number (but at least one) of `Registered` elements (*transitive closure* is denoted by "+"). To overcome these difficulties, Calvanese *et al.* [1999d] propose to represent XML documents (i.e., ordered unranked trees) by means of binary trees, and provide an encoding of DTDs in Description Logics that exploits such a representation. Figure 4.14 shows the binary tree corresponding to one of the XML documents in Figure 4.12.

Figure 4.15 shows part of the axioms encoding the DTD in Figure 4.13. The two roles f and r are used to encode binary trees, and such roles are globally functional (axiom (4.1)). Moreover, the *well-founded* construct (see Chapter 5) $wf(f \sqcup r)$ is used to express that there can be no infinite chain of objects, each one connected to the next by means of $f \sqcup r$. Such a condition turns out to be necessary to correctly capture the fact that XML documents correspond to trees that are *finite*. For each element type E, the atomic concepts $\mathsf{Start}E$ and $\mathsf{End}E$ represent respectively the start tags (4.2) and end tags (4.3) for E, and such tags are leaves of the tree (4.4). The remaining leaves of the tree are free text, represented by the atomic concept PCDATA (4.5). Using such concepts and roles, one can introduce for each element type E appearing in a DTD D an atomic concept E_D, and encode the regular expression specifying the structure of elements of type E in a suitable complex role, exploiting constructs for regular expressions over roles (including the $id(\cdot)$ construct). This is illustrated in Figure 4.15 for part of

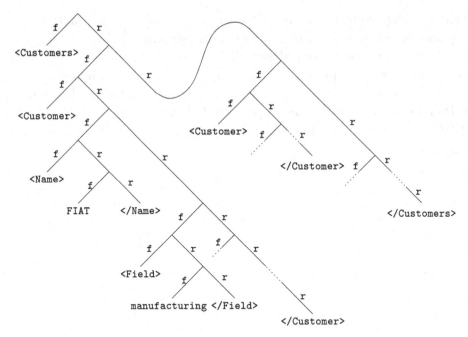

Fig. 4.14. The binary tree corresponding to the XML document on the left-hand side of Figure 4.12.

$$\top \;\equiv\; \leqslant 1\,f \sqcap \leqslant 1\,r \sqcap \mathit{wf}\,(f \sqcup r) \tag{4.1}$$
$$\mathsf{Start}E \;\sqsubseteq\; \mathsf{Tag} \qquad \text{for each element type } E \tag{4.2}$$
$$\mathsf{End}E \;\sqsubseteq\; \mathsf{Tag} \qquad \text{for each element type } E \tag{4.3}$$
$$\mathsf{Tag} \;\sqsubseteq\; \forall (f \sqcup r).\bot \tag{4.4}$$
$$\mathsf{PCDATA} \;\sqsubseteq\; \forall (f \sqcup r).\bot \sqcap \neg\mathsf{Tag} \tag{4.5}$$
$$\mathsf{Customers}_S \;\equiv\; \exists f.\mathsf{StartCustomers} \sqcap \exists (r \circ (\mathit{id}\,(\exists f.\mathsf{Customer}_S) \circ r)^+).\mathsf{EndCustomers}$$
$$\mathsf{Customer}_S \;\equiv\; \exists f.\mathsf{StartCustomers} \sqcap \exists (r \circ \mathit{id}\,(\exists f.\mathsf{Name}_S) \circ r$$
$$\circ\,(\mathit{id}\,(\exists f.\mathsf{Field}_S) \sqcup \mathit{id}\,(\exists f.\mathsf{SSN}_S)) \circ r$$
$$\circ\,(\mathit{id}\,(\exists f.\mathsf{Registered}_S) \circ r)^+).\mathsf{EndCustomer}$$
$$\mathsf{Name}_S \;\equiv\; \exists f.\mathsf{StartName} \sqcap \exists (r \circ \mathit{id}\,(\exists f.\mathsf{PCDATA}) \circ r).\mathsf{EndName}$$
$$\vdots$$

Fig. 4.15. Part of the encoding of the DTD S in Figure 4.13 into a DL knowledge base.

the element types of the DTD in Figure 4.13. We refer to [Calvanese *et al.*, 1999d] for the precise definition of the encoding.

The encoding of DTDs into Description Logics can be exploited to verify different kinds of properties on DTDs, namely *inclusion, equivalence,* and *disjointness* between the sets of documents conforming respectively to two DTDs. Such reasoning tasks come in different forms. For *strong* inclusion (resp. equivalence, disjointness) both the document structure *and* the actual tag names are of importance when comparing documents, while for *structural* inclusion (resp. equivalence, disjointness) one abstracts away from the actual tag names, and considers only the document structure [Wood, 1995]. *Parametric* inclusion (resp. equivalence, disjointness) generalizes both notions, by considering an equivalence relation between tag names, and comparing documents modulo such an equivalence relation. By exploiting the encoding of DTDs into Description Logics presented above, all forms of inference on DTDs can be carried out in deterministic exponential time [Calvanese *et al.*, 1999d].

5

Expressive Description Logics

Diego Calvanese
Giuseppe De Giacomo

Abstract

This chapter covers extensions of the basic Description Logics introduced
in Chapter 2 by very expressive constructs that require advanced reasoning
techniques. In particular, we study reasoning in description logics that include general inclusion axioms, inverse roles, number restrictions, reflexive–
transitive closure of roles, fixpoint constructs for recursive definitions, and
relations of arbitrary arity. The chapter will also address reasoning w.r.t.
knowledge bases including both a TBox and an ABox, and discuss more
general ways to treat objects. Since the logics considered in the chapter lack
the finite model property, finite model reasoning is of interest and will also
be discussed. Finally, we mention several extensions to description logics
that lead to undecidability, confirming that the expressive description logics
considered in this chapter are close to the boundary between decidability
and undecidability.

5.1 Introduction

Description Logics have been introduced with the goal of providing a formal reconstruction of frame systems and semantic networks. Initially, the
research has concentrated on subsumption of concept expressions. However,
for certain applications, it turns out that it is necessary to represent knowledge by means of inclusion axioms without limitation on cycles in the TBox.
Therefore, recently there has been a strong interest in the problem of reasoning over knowledge bases of a general form. See Chapters 2, 3, and 4 for
more details.

When reasoning over general knowledge bases, it is not possible to gain tractability by limiting the expressive power of the description logic, because the power of arbitrary inclusion axioms in the TBox alone leads to high complexity in the inference mechanisms. Indeed, logical implication is ExpTime-hard even for the very simple language $\mathcal{AL}$ (see Chapter 3). This has led to the investigation of very powerful languages for expressing concepts and roles, for which the property of interest is no longer tractability of reasoning, but rather decidability. Such logics, called here *expressive description logics*, have the following characteristics:

1. The language used for building concepts and roles comprises all classical concept-forming constructs, plus several role-forming constructs such as inverse roles and reflexive–transitive closure.
2. No restriction is posed on the axioms in the TBox.

The goal of this chapter is to provide an overview of the results and techniques for reasoning in expressive description logics. The chapter is organized as follows. In Section 5.2, we outline the correspondence between expressive description logics and Propositional Dynamic Logics, which has given the basic tools to study reasoning in expressive description logics. In Section 5.3, we exploit automata-theoretic techniques developed for variants of Propositional Dynamic Logics to address reasoning in expressive description logics with functionality restrictions on roles. In Section 5.4 we illustrate the basic technique of *reification* for reasoning with expressive variants of number restrictions. In Section 5.5, we show how to reason with knowledge bases composed of a TBox and an ABox, and discuss extensions to deal with *names* (one-of construct). In Section 5.6, we introduce description logics with explicit fixpoint constructs, which are used to express in a natural way inductively and coinductively defined concepts. In Section 5.7, we study description logics that include relations of arbitrary arity, which overcome the limitations of traditional description logics of modeling only binary links between objects. This extension is particularly relevant for the application of description logics to databases. In Section 5.8, the problem of finite model reasoning in description logics is addressed. Indeed, for expressive description logics, reasoning w.r.t. finite models differs from reasoning w.r.t. unrestricted models, and requires specific methods. Finally, in Section 5.9, we discuss several extensions to description logics that lead in general to undecidability of the basic reasoning tasks. This shows that the expressive description logics considered in this chapter are close to the limit of undecidability, and are carefully designed in order to retain decidability.

5.2 Correspondence between Description Logics and Propositional Dynamic Logics

In this section, we focus on expressive description logics that, besides the standard $\mathcal{ALC}$ constructs, include regular expressions over roles and possibly inverse roles [Baader, 1991; Schild, 1991]. It turns out that such description logics correspond directly to Propositional Dynamic Logics, which are modal logics used to express properties of programs. We first introduce the syntax and semantics of the description logics we consider, then introduce Propositional Dynamic Logics, and finally discuss the correspondence between the two formalisms.

5.2.1 Description Logics

We consider the description logic $\mathcal{ALCI}_{reg}$, in which concepts and roles are formed according to the following syntax:

$$C, C' \longrightarrow A \mid \neg C \mid C \sqcap C' \mid C \sqcup C' \mid \forall R.C \mid \exists R.C$$
$$R, R' \longrightarrow P \mid R \sqcup R' \mid R \circ R' \mid R^* \mid id(C) \mid R^-$$

where A and P denote respectively atomic concepts and atomic roles, and C and R denote respectively arbitrary concepts and roles.

In addition to the usual concept-forming constructs, $\mathcal{ALCI}_{reg}$ provides constructs to form regular expressions over roles. Such constructs include *role union, role composition, reflexive–transitive closure,* and *role identity.* Their meaning is straightforward, except for role identity $id(C)$ which, given a concept C, allows one to build a role which connects each instance of C to itself. As we shall see in the next section, there is a tight correspondence between these constructs and the operators on programs in Propositional Dynamic Logics. The presence in the language of the constructs for regular expressions is specified by the subscript "*reg*" in the name.

$\mathcal{ALCI}_{reg}$ also includes the *inverse role* construct, which allows one to denote the inverse of a given relation. One can, for example, state with $\exists \mathsf{child}^-.\mathsf{Doctor}$ that someone has a parent who is a doctor, by making use of the inverse of the role child. It is worth noticing that, in a language without inverse of roles, in order to express such a constraint one must use two distinct roles (e.g., child and parent) that cannot be put in the proper relation to each other. We use the letter $\mathcal{I}$ in the name to specify the presence of inverse roles in a description logic; by dropping inverse roles from $\mathcal{ALCI}_{reg}$, we obtain the description logic $\mathcal{ALC}_{reg}$.

From the semantic point of view, given an interpretation $\mathcal{I}$, concepts are interpreted as subsets of the domain $\Delta^{\mathcal{I}}$, and roles as binary relations over

$\Delta^{\mathcal{I}}$, as follows:[1]

$$
\begin{aligned}
A^{\mathcal{I}} &\subseteq \Delta^{\mathcal{I}} \\
(\neg C)^{\mathcal{I}} &= \Delta^{\mathcal{I}} \setminus C^{\mathcal{I}} \\
(C \sqcap C')^{\mathcal{I}} &= C^{\mathcal{I}} \cap C'^{\mathcal{I}} \\
(C \sqcup C')^{\mathcal{I}} &= C^{\mathcal{I}} \cup C'^{\mathcal{I}} \\
(\forall R.C)^{\mathcal{I}} &= \{o \in \Delta^{\mathcal{I}} \mid \forall o'. (o, o') \in R^{\mathcal{I}} \sqsupset o' \in C^{\mathcal{I}}\} \\
(\exists R.C)^{\mathcal{I}} &= \{o \in \Delta^{\mathcal{I}} \mid \exists o'. (o, o') \in R^{\mathcal{I}} \wedge o' \in C^{\mathcal{I}}\} \\
P^{\mathcal{I}} &\subseteq \Delta^{\mathcal{I}} \times \Delta^{\mathcal{I}} \\
(R \sqcup R')^{\mathcal{I}} &= R^{\mathcal{I}} \cup R'^{\mathcal{I}} \\
(R \circ R')^{\mathcal{I}} &= R^{\mathcal{I}} \circ R'^{\mathcal{I}} \\
(R^*)^{\mathcal{I}} &= (R^{\mathcal{I}})^* \\
id(C)^{\mathcal{I}} &= \{(o, o) \in \Delta^{\mathcal{I}} \times \Delta^{\mathcal{I}} \mid o \in C^{\mathcal{I}}\} \\
(R^-)^{\mathcal{I}} &= \{(o, o') \in \Delta^{\mathcal{I}} \times \Delta^{\mathcal{I}} \mid (o', o) \in R^{\mathcal{I}}\}.
\end{aligned}
$$

We consider the most general form of TBoxes constituted by general inclusion axioms of the form $C \sqsubseteq C'$, without any restriction on cycles. We use $C \equiv C'$ as an abbreviation for the pair of axioms $C \sqsubseteq C'$ and $C' \sqsubseteq C$. We adopt the usual descriptive semantics for TBoxes (see Chapter 2).

Example 5.1 The following $\mathcal{ALCI}_{reg}$ TBox $\mathcal{T}_{file}$ models a file system constituted by file-system elements (FSelem), each of which is either a Directory or a File. Each FSelem has a name, a Directory may have children while a File may not, and Root is a special directory which has no parent. The parent relationship is modeled through the inverse of the role child.

$$
\begin{aligned}
\text{FSelem} &\sqsubseteq \exists \text{name.String} \\
\text{FSelem} &\equiv \text{Directory} \sqcup \text{File} \\
\text{Directory} &\sqsubseteq \neg \text{File} \\
\text{Directory} &\sqsubseteq \forall \text{child.FSelem} \\
\text{File} &\sqsubseteq \forall \text{child.}\bot \\
\text{Root} &\sqsubseteq \text{Directory} \\
\text{Root} &\sqsubseteq \forall \text{child}^-.\bot.
\end{aligned}
$$

The axioms in $\mathcal{T}_{file}$ imply that in a model every object connected by a chain of role child to an instance of Root is an instance of FSelem. Formally, $\mathcal{T}_{file} \models \exists (\text{child}^-)^*.\text{Root} \sqsubseteq \text{FSelem}$. To verify that the implication holds, suppose that

---

[1] We use $\mathcal{R}^*$ to denote the reflexive–transitive closure of the binary relation $\mathcal{R}$, and $\mathcal{R}_1 \circ \mathcal{R}_2$ to denote the chaining of the binary relations $\mathcal{R}_1$ and $\mathcal{R}_2$.

there exists a model in which an instance o of $\exists(\text{child}^-)^*.\text{Root}$ is not an instance of FSelem. Then, reasoning by induction on the length of the chain from the instance of Root to o, one can derive a contradiction. Observe that induction is required, and hence such reasoning is not first-order. ∎

In the following, when convenient, we assume, without loss of generality, that $\sqcup$ and $\forall R.C$ are expressed by means of $\neg$, $\sqcap$, and $\exists R.C$. We also assume that the inverse operator is applied to atomic roles only. This can again be done without loss of generality, since the following equivalences hold: $(R_1 \circ R_2)^- = R_2^- \circ R_1^-$, $(R_1 \sqcup R_2)^- = R_1^- \sqcup R_2^-$, $(R^*)^- = (R^-)^*$, and $(id(C))^- = id(C)$.

5.2.2 *Propositional Dynamic Logics*

Propositional Dynamic Logics (PDLs) are modal logics specifically developed for reasoning about computer programs [Fischer and Ladner, 1979; Kozen and Tiuryn, 1990; Harel *et al.*, 2000]. In this subsection, we provide a brief overview of PDLs, and illustrate the correspondence between description logics and PDLs.

Syntactically, a PDL is constituted by expressions of two sorts: *programs* and *formulae*. Programs and formulae are built by starting from *atomic programs* and *propositional letters*, and applying suitable operators. We denote propositional letters by A, arbitrary formulae by ϕ, atomic programs by P, and arbitrary programs by r, all possibly with subscripts. We focus on *converse*-PDL [Fischer and Ladner, 1979] which, as it turns out, corresponds to $\mathcal{ALCI}_{reg}$. The abstract syntax of *converse*-PDL is as follows:

$$\phi, \phi' \longrightarrow \top \mid \bot \mid A \mid \phi \wedge \phi' \mid \phi \vee \phi' \mid \neg\phi \mid \langle r \rangle \phi \mid [r]\phi$$
$$r, r' \longrightarrow P \mid r \cup r' \mid r; r' \mid r^* \mid \phi? \mid r^-.$$

The basic Propositional Dynamic Logic PDL [Fischer and Ladner, 1979] is obtained from *converse*-PDL by dropping converse programs r^-.

The semantics of PDLs is based on the notion of (Kripke) structure, defined as a triple $\mathcal{M} = (\mathcal{S}, \{\mathcal{R}_P\}, \Pi)$, where $\mathcal{S}$ denotes a non-empty set of states, $\{\mathcal{R}_P\}$ is a family of binary relations over $\mathcal{S}$, each of which denotes the state transitions caused by an atomic program P, and Π is a mapping from $\mathcal{S}$ to propositional letters such that $\Pi(s)$ determines the letters that are true in state s. The basic semantical relation is "a formula ϕ holds at a state s of a structure $\mathcal{M}$", written $\mathcal{M}, s \models \phi$, and is defined by induction on the formation of ϕ:

$$
\begin{aligned}
\mathcal{M}, s &\models A && \text{iff} && A \in \Pi(s) \\
\mathcal{M}, s &\models \top && \text{always} \\
\mathcal{M}, s &\models \bot && \text{never} \\
\mathcal{M}, s &\models \phi \wedge \phi' && \text{iff} && \mathcal{M}, s \models \phi \text{ and } \mathcal{M}, s \models \phi' \\
\mathcal{M}, s &\models \phi \vee \phi' && \text{iff} && \mathcal{M}, s \models \phi \text{ or } \mathcal{M}, s \models \phi' \\
\mathcal{M}, s &\models \neg\phi && \text{iff} && \mathcal{M}, s \not\models \phi \\
\mathcal{M}, s &\models \langle r \rangle \phi && \text{iff} && \text{there is } s' \text{ such that } (s, s') \in \mathcal{R}_r \text{ and } \mathcal{M}, s' \models \phi \\
\mathcal{M}, s &\models [r]\phi && \text{iff} && \text{for all } s', (s, s') \in \mathcal{R}_r \text{ implies } \mathcal{M}, s' \models \phi
\end{aligned}
$$

where the family $\{\mathcal{R}_P\}$ is systematically extended so as to include, for every program r, the corresponding relation $\mathcal{R}_r$ defined by induction on the formation of r:

$$
\begin{aligned}
\mathcal{R}_P &\subseteq \mathcal{S} \times \mathcal{S} \\
\mathcal{R}_{r \cup r'} &= \mathcal{R}_r \cup \mathcal{R}_{r'} \\
\mathcal{R}_{r;r'} &= \mathcal{R}_r \circ \mathcal{R}_{r'} \\
\mathcal{R}_{r^*} &= (\mathcal{R}_r)^* \\
\mathcal{R}_{\phi?} &= \{(s, s) \in \mathcal{S} \times \mathcal{S} \mid \mathcal{M}, s \models \phi\} \\
\mathcal{R}_{r^-} &= \{(s_1, s_2) \in \mathcal{S} \times \mathcal{S} \mid (s_2, s_1) \in \mathcal{R}_r\}.
\end{aligned}
$$

If, for each atomic program P, the transition relation $\mathcal{R}_P$ is required to be a function that assigns to each state a unique successor state, then we are dealing with the *deterministic* variants of PDLs, namely DPDL and *converse-*DPDL [Ben-Ari *et al.*, 1982; Vardi and Wolper, 1986].

It is important to understand, given a formula ϕ, which are the formulae that play some role in establishing the truth-value of ϕ. In simpler modal logics, these formulae are simply all the subformulae of ϕ, but due to the presence of reflexive–transitive closure this is not the case for PDLs. Such a set of formulae is given by the *Fischer–Ladner closure* of ϕ [Fischer and Ladner, 1979].

To be concrete we now illustrate the Fischer–Ladner closure for *converse-*PDL. However, the notion of Fischer–Ladner closure can be easily extended to other PDLs. Let us assume, without loss of generality, that $\vee$ and $[\cdot]$ are expressed by means of $\neg$, $\wedge$, and $\langle \cdot \rangle$. We also assume that the converse operator is applied to atomic programs only. This can again be done without loss of generality, since the following equivalences hold: $(r \cup r')^- = r^- \cup r'^-$, $(r; r')^- = r'^-; r^-$, $(r^*)^- = (r^-)^*$, and $(\phi?)^- = \phi?$.

The Fischer–Ladner closure of a *converse*-PDL formula ψ, denoted $CL(\psi)$, is the least set F such that $\psi \in F$ and such that:

if $\phi \in F$	then $\neg\phi \in F$	(if ϕ is not of the form $\neg\phi'$)
if $\neg\phi \in F$	then $\phi \in F$	
if $\phi \wedge \phi' \in F$	then $\phi, \phi' \in F$	
if $\langle r \rangle \phi \in F$	then $\phi \in F$	
if $\langle r \cup r' \rangle \phi \in F$	then $\langle r \rangle \phi, \langle r' \rangle \phi \in F$	
if $\langle r; r' \rangle \phi \in F$	then $\langle r \rangle \langle r' \rangle \phi \in F$	
if $\langle r^* \rangle \phi \in F$	then $\langle r \rangle \langle r^* \rangle \phi \in F$	
if $\langle \phi'? \rangle \phi \in F$	then $\phi' \in F$.	

Note that $CL(\psi)$ includes all the subformulae of ψ, but also formulae of the form $\langle r \rangle \langle r^* \rangle \phi$ derived from $\langle r^* \rangle \phi$, which are in fact bigger than the formula they derive from. On the other hand, both the number and the size of the formulae in $CL(\psi)$ are linearly bounded by the size of ψ [Fischer and Ladner, 1979], exactly like the set of subformulae. Note also that, by definition, if $\phi \in CL(\psi)$, then $CL(\phi) \subseteq CL(\psi)$.

A structure $\mathcal{M} = (\mathcal{S}, \{\mathcal{R}_P\}, \Pi)$ is called a *model* of a formula ϕ if there exists a state $s \in \mathcal{S}$ such that $\mathcal{M}, s \models \phi$. A formula ϕ is *satisfiable* if there exists a model of ϕ, otherwise the formula is *unsatisfiable*. A formula ϕ is *valid* in a structure $\mathcal{M}$ if for all $s \in \mathcal{S}$, $\mathcal{M}, s \models \phi$. Formulae that are used to select the interpretations of interest are called *axioms*. Formally, a structure $\mathcal{M}$ is a model of an axiom ϕ, if ϕ is valid in $\mathcal{M}$. A structure $\mathcal{M}$ is a model of a finite set of axioms Γ if $\mathcal{M}$ is a model of all axioms in Γ. An axiom is satisfiable if it has a model, and a finite set of axioms is satisfiable if it has a model. We say that a finite set Γ of axioms *logically implies* a formula ϕ, written $\Gamma \models \phi$, if ϕ is valid in every model of Γ.

It is easy to see that satisfiability of a formula ϕ as well as satisfiability of a finite set of axioms Γ can be reformulated by means of logical implication, as $\emptyset \not\models \neg\phi$ and $\Gamma \not\models \bot$ respectively.

Interestingly, logical implication can, in turn, be reformulated in terms of satisfiability, by making use of the following theorem (see [Kozen and Tiuryn, 1990]).

Theorem 5.2 (Internalization of axioms) *Let Γ be a finite set of* converse-PDL *axioms, and ϕ a* converse-PDL *formula. Then $\Gamma \models \phi$ if and only if the formula*

$$\neg\phi \wedge [(P_1 \cup \cdots \cup P_m \cup P_1^- \cup \cdots \cup P_m^-)^*]\Gamma'$$

is unsatisfiable, where $P_1, \ldots, P_m$ are all atomic programs occurring in $\Gamma \cup \{\phi\}$ and Γ' is the conjunction of all axioms in Γ.

Such a result exploits the power of program constructs (union, reflexive–transitive closure) and the *connected model property* (i.e., if a formula has a model, it has a model which is connected) of PDLs in order to represent axioms. The connected model property is typical of modal logics and it is enjoyed by all PDLs. As a consequence, a result analogous to Theorem 5.2 holds for virtually all PDLs.

Reasoning in PDLs has been thoroughly studied from the computational point of view, and the results for the PDLs considered here are summarized in the following theorem [Fischer and Ladner, 1979; Pratt, 1979; Ben-Ari *et al.*, 1982; Vardi and Wolper, 1986]:

Theorem 5.3 *Satisfiability in* PDL *is* ExpTime-*hard. Satisfiability in* PDL, *in* converse-PDL, *and in* converse-DPDL *can be decided in deterministic exponential time.*

5.2.3 The correspondence

The correspondence between description logics and PDLs was first published by Schild [1991].[2] In the work by Schild, it was shown that $\mathcal{ALCI}_{reg}$ can be considered a notational variant of *converse*-PDL. This observation allowed the results on *converse*-PDL to be exploited for instantly closing long-standing issues regarding the decidability and complexity of both satisfiability and logical implication in $\mathcal{ALC}_{reg}$ and $\mathcal{ALCI}_{reg}$.[3] The paper was very influential for the research in expressive description logics in the following decade, since thanks to the correspondence between PDLs and description logics, first results but especially formal techniques and insights could be shared by the two communities. The correspondence between PDLs and description logics has been extensively used to study reasoning methods for expressive description logics. It has also led to a number of interesting extensions of PDLs in terms of those constructs that are typical of description logics and have never been considered in PDLs. In particular, there is a tight relation between qualified number restrictions and graded modalities in modal logics [Van der Hoek, 1992; Van der Hoek and de Rijke, 1995; Fattorosi-Barnaba and De Caro, 1985; Fine, 1972].

The correspondence is based on the similarity between the interpretation structures of the two logics: at the extensional level, individuals (members

---

[2] In fact, the correspondence was first noticed by Levesque and Rosenschein at the beginning of the 1980s, but never published. In those days Levesque just used it in seminars to show the intractability of certain description logics.

[3] In fact, the decidability of $\mathcal{ALC}_{reg}$ without the $id(C)$ construct was independently established by Baader [1991].

of $\Delta^{\mathcal{I}}$) in description logics correspond to states in PDLs, and links between two individuals correspond to state transitions. At the intensional level, concepts correspond to propositions, and roles correspond to programs. Formally, the correspondence is realized through a one-to-one and onto mapping τ from $\mathcal{ALCI}_{reg}$ concepts to *converse*-PDL formulae, and from $\mathcal{ALCI}_{reg}$ roles to *converse*-PDL programs. The mapping τ is defined inductively as follows:

$$
\begin{aligned}
\tau(A) &= A & \tau(P) &= P \\
\tau(\neg C) &= \neg\tau(C) & \tau(R^-) &= \tau(R)^- \\
\tau(C \sqcap C') &= \tau(C) \wedge \tau(C') & \tau(R \sqcup R') &= \tau(R) \cup \tau(R') \\
\tau(C \sqcup C') &= \tau(C) \vee \tau(C') & \tau(R \circ R') &= \tau(R); \tau(R') \\
\tau(\forall R.C) &= [\tau(R)]\tau(C) & \tau(R^*) &= \tau(R)^* \\
\tau(\exists R.C) &= \langle\tau(R)\rangle\tau(C) & \tau(id(C)) &= \tau(C)?
\end{aligned}
$$

Axioms in TBoxes of description logics correspond in the obvious way to axioms in PDLs. Moreover all forms of reasoning (satisfiability, logical implication, etc.) have their natural counterpart.

One of the most important contributions of the correspondence is obtained by rephrasing Theorem 5.2 in terms of description logics. It says that every TBox can be "internalized" into a single concept, i.e., it is possible to build a concept that expresses all the axioms of the TBox. In doing so we rely on the ability to build a "universal" role, i.e., a role linking all individuals in a (connected) model. Indeed, a universal role can be expressed by using regular expressions over roles, and in particular the union of roles and the reflexive–transitive closure. The possibility of internalizing the TBox when dealing with expressive description logics tells us that for such description logics reasoning with TBoxes, i.e., logical implication, is no harder than reasoning with a single concept.

Theorem 5.4 *Concept satisfiability and logical implication in $\mathcal{ALC}_{reg}$ are* ExpTime-*hard. Concept satisfiability and logical implication in $\mathcal{ALC}_{reg}$ and $\mathcal{ALCI}_{reg}$ can be decided in deterministic exponential time.*

Observe that for description logics that do not allow the expression of a universal role, there is a sharp difference between reasoning techniques used in the presence of TBoxes, and techniques used to reason on concept expressions. The profound difference is reflected by the computational properties of the associated decision problems. For example, the logic $\mathcal{AL}$ admits simple structural algorithms for deciding reasoning tasks not involving axioms, and these algorithms are sound and complete and work in polynomial time. However, if general inclusion axioms are considered, then reasoning

becomes ExpTime-complete (see Chapter 3), and the decision procedures
that have been developed include suitable termination strategies [Buchheit
et al., 1993a]. Similarly, for the more expressive logic $\mathcal{ALC}$, reasoning tasks
not involving a TBox are PSpace-complete [Schmidt-Schauß and Smolka,
1991], while those that do involve one are ExpTime-complete.

5.3 Functional restrictions

We have seen that the logics $\mathcal{ALC}_{reg}$ and $\mathcal{ALCI}_{reg}$ correspond to standard
PDL and *converse*-PDL respectively, which are both well-studied. In this section we show how the correspondence can also be used to deal with constructs that are typical of description logics, namely functional restrictions,
by exploiting techniques developed for reasoning in PDLs. In particular, we
will adopt automata-based techniques, which have been very successful in
studying reasoning for expressive variants of PDL and characterizing their
complexity.

Functional restrictions are the simplest form of number restrictions considered in description logics, and allow one to specify local functionality of
roles, i.e., that instances of certain concepts have unique role fillers for a
given role. By adding functional restrictions on atomic roles and their inverse to $\mathcal{ALCI}_{reg}$, we obtain the Description Logic $\mathcal{ALCFI}_{reg}$. The PDL
corresponding to $\mathcal{ALCFI}_{reg}$ is a PDL that extends *converse*-DPDL [Vardi
and Wolper, 1986] with determinism of both atomic programs and their inverse, and such that determinism is no longer a global property, but one
that can be imposed locally.

Formally, $\mathcal{ALCFI}_{reg}$ is obtained from $\mathcal{ALCI}_{reg}$ by adding *functional restrictions* of the form $\leqslant 1\,Q$, where Q is a *basic role*, i.e., either an atomic role
or the inverse of an atomic role. Such a functional restriction is interpreted
as follows:

$$(\leqslant 1\,Q)^{\mathcal{I}} \;=\; \{o \in \Delta^{\mathcal{I}} \mid |\{o' \in \Delta^{\mathcal{I}} \mid (o,o') \in Q^{\mathcal{I}}\}| \leq 1\}.$$

We show that reasoning in $\mathcal{ALCFI}_{reg}$ is in ExpTime, and, since reasoning
in $\mathcal{ALC}_{reg}$ is already ExpTime-hard, is in fact ExpTime-complete. Without loss of generality we concentrate on concept satisfiability. We exploit
the fact that $\mathcal{ALCFI}_{reg}$ has the *tree model property*, which states that if an
$\mathcal{ALCFI}_{reg}$ concept C is satisfiable then it is satisfied in an interpretation
which has the structure of a (possibly infinite) tree with bounded branching
degree (see later). This allows us to make use of techniques based on automata on infinite trees. In particular, we make use of *two-way alternating
automata on infinite trees* (2ATAs) introduced by Vardi [1998]. 2ATAs were
used by Vardi [1998] to derive a decision procedure for modal μ-calculus

with backward modalities. We first introduce 2ATAs and then show how they can be used to reason in $\mathcal{ALCFI}_{reg}$.

5.3.1 Automata on infinite trees

Infinite trees are represented as prefix-closed (infinite) sets of words over $\mathbb{N}$ (the set of positive natural numbers). Formally, an *infinite tree* is a set of words $T \subseteq \mathbb{N}^*$, such that if $x \cdot c \in T$, where $x \in \mathbb{N}^*$ and $c \in \mathbb{N}$, then also $x \in T$. The elements of T are called *nodes*, the empty word ε is the *root* of T, and for every $x \in T$, the nodes $x \cdot c$, with $c \in \mathbb{N}$, are the *successors* of x. By convention we take $x \cdot 0 = x$, and $x \cdot i \cdot -1 = x$. The *branching degree* $d(x)$ of a node x denotes the number of successors of x. If the branching degree of all nodes of a tree is bounded by k, we say that the tree has branching degree k. An *infinite path* P of T is a prefix-closed set $P \subseteq T$ such that for every $i \geq 0$ there exists a unique node $x \in P$ with $|x| = i$. A *labeled tree* over an alphabet Σ is a pair (T, V), where T is a tree and $V : T \to \Sigma$ maps each node of T to an element of Σ.

Alternating automata on infinite trees are a generalization of nondeterministic automata on infinite trees, introduced by Muller and Schupp [1987]. They allow an elegant reduction of decision problems for temporal and program logics [Emerson and Jutla, 1991; Bernholtz *et al.*, 1994]. Let $\mathcal{B}(I)$ be the set of positive Boolean formulae over I, built inductively by applying $\wedge$ and $\vee$ starting from **true**, **false**, and elements of I. For a set $J \subseteq I$ and a formula $\varphi \in \mathcal{B}(I)$, we say that J *satisfies* φ if and only if assigning **true** to the elements in J and **false** to those in $I \setminus J$ makes φ true. For a positive integer k, let $[k] = \{-1, 0, 1, \ldots, k\}$. A *two-way alternating automaton* over infinite trees with branching degree k is a tuple $\mathbf{A} = \langle \Sigma, Q, \delta, q_0, F \rangle$, where Σ is the input alphabet, Q is a finite set of states, $\delta : Q \times \Sigma \to \mathcal{B}([k] \times Q)$ is the transition function, $q_0 \in Q$ is the initial state, and F specifies the acceptance condition.

The transition function maps a state $q \in Q$ and an input letter $\sigma \in \Sigma$ to a positive Boolean formula over $[k] \times Q$. Intuitively, if $\delta(q, \sigma) = \varphi$, then each pair (c, q') appearing in φ corresponds to a new copy of the automaton going to the direction suggested by c and starting in state q'. For example, if $k = 2$ and $\delta(q_1, \sigma) = ((1, q_2) \wedge (1, q_3)) \vee ((-1, q_1) \wedge (0, q_3))$, when the automaton is in the state q_1 and is reading the node x labeled by the letter σ, it proceeds either by sending off two copies, in the states q_2 and q_3 respectively, to the first successor of x (i.e., $x \cdot 1$), or by sending off one copy in the state q_1 to the predecessor of x (i.e., $x \cdot -1$) and one copy in the state q_3 to x itself (i.e., $x \cdot 0$).

A *run* of a 2ATA $\mathbf{A}$ over a labeled tree (T, V) is a labeled tree (T_r, r) in which every node is labeled by an element of $T \times Q$. A node in T_r labeled by (x, q) describes a copy of **A** that is in the state q and reads the node x of T. The labels of adjacent nodes have to satisfy the transition function of **A**. Formally, a run (T_r, r) is a $T \times Q$-labeled tree satisfying:

1. $\varepsilon \in T_r$ and $r(\varepsilon) = (\varepsilon, q_0)$.
2. Let $y \in T_r$, with $r(y) = (x, q)$ and $\delta(q, V(x)) = \varphi$. Then there is a (possibly empty) set $S = \{(c_1, q_1), \ldots, (c_n, q_n)\} \subseteq [k] \times Q$ such that:
   - S satisfies φ and
   - for all $1 \leq i \leq n$, we have that $y{\cdot}i \in T_r$, $x{\cdot}c_i$ is defined, and $r(y{\cdot}i) = (x{\cdot}c_i, q_i)$.

A run (T_r, r) is *accepting* if all its infinite paths satisfy the acceptance condition.[4] Given an infinite path $P \subseteq T_r$, let $inf(P) \subseteq Q$ be the set of states that appear infinitely often in P (as second components of node labels). We consider here *Büchi* acceptance conditions. A Büchi condition over a state set Q is a subset F of Q, and an infinite path P satisfies F if $inf(P) \cap F \neq \emptyset$.

The non-emptiness problem for 2ATAs consists in determining, whether a given 2ATA accepts a nonempty set of trees. The results by Vardi [1998] provide the following complexity characterization of non-emptiness of 2ATAs.

Theorem 5.5 ([Vardi, 1998]) *Given a 2ATA **A** with n states and an input alphabet with m elements, deciding non-emptiness of **A** can be done in time exponential in n and polynomial in m.*

5.3.2 Reasoning in $\mathcal{ALCFI}_{reg}$

The (Fischer–Ladner) *closure* for $\mathcal{ALCFI}_{reg}$ extends immediately the analogous notion for *converse*-PDL (see Subsection 5.2.2), treating functional restrictions as atomic concepts. In particular, the closure $CL(C_0)$ of an $\mathcal{ALCFI}_{reg}$ concept C_0 is defined as the smallest set of concepts such that $C_0 \in CL(C_0)$ and such that (assuming $\sqcup$ and $\forall$ to be expressed by means of $\sqcap$ and $\exists$, and the inverse operator applied only to atomic roles):[5]

if $C \in CL(C_0)$	then	$\neg C \in CL(C_0)$ (if C is not of the form $\neg C'$)
if $\neg C \in CL(C_0)$	then	$C \in CL(C_0)$
if $C \sqcap C' \in CL(C_0)$	then	$C, C' \in CL(C_0)$
if $\exists R.C \in CL(C_0)$	then	$C \in CL(C_0)$
if $\exists (R \sqcup R').C \in CL(C_0)$	then	$\exists R.C, \exists R'.C \in CL(C_0)$
if $\exists (R \circ R').C \in CL(C_0)$	then	$\exists R.\exists R'.C \in CL(C_0)$
if $\exists R^*.C \in CL(C_0)$	then	$\exists R.\exists R^*.C \in CL(C_0)$
if $\exists id(C).C' \in CL(C_0)$	then	$C \in CL(C_0)$.

The cardinality of $CL(C_0)$ is linear in the length of C_0.

---

[4] No condition is imposed on the finite paths of the run.
[5] We recall that C and C' stand for arbitrary concepts, and R and R' stand for arbitrary roles.

It can be shown, following the lines of the proof in [Vardi and Wolper, 1986] for *converse*-DPDL, that $\mathcal{ALCFI}_{reg}$ enjoys the *tree model property*, i.e., every satisfiable concept has a model that has the structure of a (possibly infinite) tree with branching degree linearly bounded by the size of the concept. More precisely, we have the following result.

Theorem 5.6 *Every satisfiable $\mathcal{ALCFI}_{reg}$ concept C_0 has a tree model with branching degree k_{C_0} equal to twice the number of elements of $CL(C_0)$.*

This property allows us to check satisfiability of an $\mathcal{ALCFI}_{reg}$ concept C_0 by building a 2ATA that accepts the (labeled) trees that correspond to tree models of C_0. Let $\mathcal{A}$ be the set of atomic concepts appearing in C_0, and $\mathcal{B} = \{Q_1, \ldots, Q_n\}$ the set of atomic roles appearing in C_0 and their inverses. We construct from C_0 a 2ATA $\mathbf{A}_{C_0}$ that checks that C_0 is satisfied at the root of the input tree. We represent in each node of the tree the information about which atomic concepts are true in the node, and about the basic role that connects the predecessor of the node to the node itself (except for the root). More precisely, we label each node with a pair $\sigma = (\alpha, q)$, where α is the set of atomic concepts that are true in the node, and $q = Q$ if the node is reached from its predecessor through the basic role Q. That is, if Q stands for an atomic role P, then the node is reached from its predecessor through P, and if Q stands for P^-, then the predecessor is reached from the node through P. In the root, $q = P_{dum}$, where P_{dum} is a new symbol representing a dummy role.

Given an $\mathcal{ALCFI}_{reg}$ concept C_0, we construct an automaton $\mathbf{A}_{C_0}$ that accepts trees that correspond to tree models of C_0. For technical reasons, it is convenient to consider concepts in *negation normal form* (i.e., negations are pushed inside as much as possible). It is easy to check that the transformation of a concept into negation normal form can be performed in linear time in the size of the concept. Below, we denote by $nnf(C)$ the negation normal form of C, and by $CL_{nnf}(C_0)$ the set $\{nnf(C) \mid C \in CL(C_0)\}$. The automaton $\mathbf{A}_{C_0} = (\Sigma, S, \delta, s_{ini}, F)$ is defined as follows:

- The alphabet is $\Sigma = 2^{\mathcal{A}} \times (\mathcal{B} \cup \{P_{dum}\})$, i.e., the set of pairs whose first component is a set of atomic concepts, and whose second component is a basic role or the dummy role P_{dum}. This corresponds to labeling each node of the tree with a truth assignment to the atomic concepts, and with the role used to reach the node from its predecessor.
- The set of states is $S = \{s_{ini}\} \cup CL_{nnf}(C_0) \cup \{Q, \neg Q \mid Q \in \mathcal{B}\}$, where s_{ini} is the initial state, $CL_{nnf}(C_0)$ is the set of concepts (in negation normal form) in the closure of C_0, and $\{Q, \neg Q \mid Q \in \mathcal{B}\}$ are states used to check whether a basic role

labels a node. Intuitively, when the automaton in a state $C \in CL_{nnf}(C_0)$ visits a node x of the tree, this means that the automaton has to check that C holds in x.

- The transition function δ is defined as follows:

1. For each $\alpha \in 2^{\mathcal{A}}$, there is a transition from the initial state

$$\delta(s_{ini}, (\alpha, P_{dum})) = (0, nnf(C_0)).$$

Such a transition checks that the root of the tree is labeled with the dummy role P_{dum}, and moves to the state that verifies C_0 in the root itself.

2. For each $(\alpha, q) \in \Sigma$ and each atomic concept $A \in \mathcal{A}$, there are transitions

$$\delta(A, (\alpha, q)) = \begin{cases} \textbf{true}, & \text{if } A \in \alpha \\ \textbf{false}, & \text{if } A \notin \alpha \end{cases}$$

$$\delta(\neg A, (\alpha, q)) = \begin{cases} \textbf{true}, & \text{if } A \notin \alpha \\ \textbf{false}, & \text{if } A \in \alpha. \end{cases}$$

Such transitions check the truth value of atomic concepts and their negations in the current node of the tree.

3. For each $(\alpha, q) \in \Sigma$ and each basic role $Q \in \mathcal{B}$, there are transitions

$$\delta(Q, (\alpha, q)) = \begin{cases} \textbf{true}, & \text{if } q = Q \\ \textbf{false}, & \text{if } q \neq Q \end{cases}$$

$$\delta(\neg Q, (\alpha, q)) = \begin{cases} \textbf{true}, & \text{if } q \neq Q \\ \textbf{false}, & \text{if } q = Q. \end{cases}$$

Such transitions check through which role the current node is reached.

4. For the concepts in $CL_{nnf}(C_0)$ and each $\sigma \in \Sigma$, there are transitions

$$\delta(C \sqcap C', \sigma) = (0, C) \wedge (0, C')$$
$$\delta(C \sqcup C', \sigma) = (0, C) \vee (0, C')$$
$$\delta(\forall Q.C, \sigma) = ((0, \neg Q^-) \vee (-1, C)) \wedge \bigwedge_{1 \leq i \leq k_{C_0}} ((i, \neg Q) \vee (i, C))$$

$$\delta(\forall (R \sqcup R').C, \sigma) = (0, \forall R.C) \wedge (0, \forall R'.C)$$
$$\delta(\forall (R \circ R').C, \sigma) = (0, \forall R.\forall R'.C)$$
$$\delta(\forall R^*.C, \sigma) = (0, C) \wedge (0, \forall R.\forall R^*.C)$$
$$\delta(\forall id(C).C', \sigma) = (0, nnf(\neg C)) \vee (0, C')$$
$$\delta(\exists Q.C, \sigma) = ((0, Q^-) \wedge (-1, C)) \vee \bigvee_{1 \leq i \leq k_{C_0}} ((i, Q) \wedge (i, C))$$
$$\delta(\exists (R \sqcup R').C, \sigma) = (0, \exists R.C) \vee (0, \exists R'.C)$$
$$\delta(\exists (R \circ R').C, \sigma) = (0, \exists R.\exists R'.C)$$
$$\delta(\exists R^*.C, \sigma) = (0, C) \vee (0, \exists R.\exists R^*.C)$$
$$\delta(\exists id(C).C', \sigma) = (0, C) \wedge (0, C').$$

All such transitions, except for those involving $\forall R^*.C$ and $\exists R^*.C$, inductively decompose concepts and roles, and move to appropriate states of the automaton and nodes of the tree. The transitions involving $\forall R^*.C$ treat $\forall R^*.C$ as the equivalent concept $C \sqcap \forall R.\forall R^*.C$, and the transitions involving $\exists R^*.C$ treat $\exists R^*.C$ as the equivalent concept $C \sqcup \exists R.\exists R^*.C$.

5. For each concept of the form $\leqslant 1\,Q$ in $CL_{nnf}(C)$ and each $\sigma \in \Sigma$, there is a transition

$$\delta(\leqslant 1\,Q, \sigma) \;=\; ((0, Q^-) \;\wedge\; \bigwedge_{1 \leq i \leq k_{C_0}} (i, \neg Q)) \;\vee$$
$$((0, \neg Q^-) \;\wedge\; \bigwedge_{1 \leq i < j \leq k_{C_0}} ((i, \neg Q) \vee (j, \neg Q))).$$

Such transitions check that, for a node x labeled with $\leqslant 1\,Q$, there exists at most one node (among the predecessor and the successors of x) reachable from x through Q.

6. For each concept of the form $\neg \leqslant 1\,Q$ in $CL_{nnf}(C)$ and each $\sigma \in \Sigma$, there is a transition

$$\delta(\neg \leqslant 1\,Q, \sigma) \;=\; ((0, Q^-) \;\wedge\; \bigvee_{1 \leq i \leq k_{C_0}} (i, Q)) \;\vee$$
$$\bigvee_{1 \leq i < j \leq k_{C_0}} ((i, Q) \wedge (j, Q)).$$

Such transitions check that, for a node x labeled with $\neg \leqslant 1\,Q$, there exist at least two nodes (among the predecessor and the successors of x) reachable from x through Q.

- The set F of final states is the set of concepts in $CL_{nnf}(C_0)$ of the form $\forall R^*.C$. Observe that concepts of the form $\exists R^*.C$ are not final states, and this is sufficient to guarantee that such concepts are satisfied in all accepting runs of the automaton.

A run of the automaton $\mathbf{A}_{C_0}$ on an infinite tree starts in the root, checking that C_0 holds there (item 1 above). It does so by inductively decomposing $nnf(C_0)$ while appropriately navigating the tree (items 3 and 4) until it arrives at atomic concepts, functional restrictions, and their negations. These are checked locally (items 2, 5, and 6). Concepts of the form $\forall R^*.C$ and $\exists R^*.C$ are propagated using the equivalent concepts $C \sqcap \forall R.\forall R^*.C$ and $C \sqcup \exists R.\exists R^*.C$, respectively. It is only the propagation of such concepts that may generate infinite branches in a run. Now, a run of the automaton may contain an infinite branch in which $\exists R^*.C$ is always resolved by choosing the disjunct $\exists R.\exists R^*.C$, without ever choosing the disjunct C. This infinite branch in the run corresponds to an infinite path in the tree where R is iterated forever and in which C is never fulfilled. However, the semantics of $\exists R^*.C$ requires that C is fulfilled after a finite number of iterations of R. Hence such an infinite path cannot be used to satisfy $\exists R^*.C$. The acceptance condition of the automaton, which requires that each infinite branch in a run contains a state of the form $\forall R^*.C$, rules out such infinite branches in accepting runs. Indeed, a run always deferring the fulfillment of C will contain an infinite branch where all states have the form $\exists R_1. \cdots \exists R_n. \exists R^*.C$, with $n \geq 0$ and $R_1 \circ \cdots \circ R_n$ a postfix of R. Observe that the only remaining infinite branches in a run are those that arise by propagating concepts of the form $\forall R^*.C$ indefinitely often. The acceptance condition allows for such branches.

Given a labeled tree $\mathcal{T} = (T, V)$ accepted by $\mathbf{A}_{C_0}$, we define an interpretation $\mathcal{I}_\mathcal{T} = (\Delta^\mathcal{I}, \cdot^\mathcal{I})$ as follows. First, we define for each atomic role P, a relation $\mathcal{R}_P$ as follows: $\mathcal{R}_P = \{(x, xi) \mid xi \in T$ and $V(xi) = (\alpha, P)$ for some $\alpha \in 2^\mathcal{A}\} \cup \{(xi, x) \mid xi \in T$ and $V(xi) = (\alpha, P^-)$ for some $\alpha \in 2^\mathcal{A}\}$. Then, using such relations, we define:

- $\Delta^\mathcal{I} = \{ x \mid (\varepsilon, x) \in (\bigcup_P (\mathcal{R}_P \cup \mathcal{R}_P^-))^* \}$;
- $A^\mathcal{I} = \Delta^\mathcal{I} \cap \{x \mid V(x) = (\alpha, q)$ and $A \in \alpha$, for some $\alpha \in 2^\mathcal{A}$ and $q \in \mathcal{B} \cup \{P_{dum}\} \}$, for each atomic concept A;
- $P^\mathcal{I} = (\Delta^\mathcal{I} \times \Delta^\mathcal{I}) \cap \mathcal{R}_P$, for each atomic role P.

Lemma 5.7 *If a labeled tree $\mathcal{T}$ is accepted by $\mathbf{A}_{C_0}$, then $\mathcal{I}_\mathcal{T}$ is a model of C_0.*

Conversely, given a tree model $\mathcal{I}$ of C_0 with branching degree k_{C_0}, we can obtain a labeled tree $\mathcal{T}_\mathcal{I} = (T, V)$ (with branching degree k_{C_0}) as follows:

- $T = \Delta^\mathcal{I}$;
- $V(\varepsilon) = (\alpha, P_{dum})$, where $\alpha = \{A \mid \varepsilon \in A^\mathcal{I}\}$;
- $V(xi) = (\alpha, Q)$, where $\alpha = \{A \mid xi \in A^\mathcal{I}\}$ and $(x, xi) \in Q^\mathcal{I}$.

Lemma 5.8 *If $\mathcal{I}$ is a tree model of C_0 with branching degree k_{C_0}, then $\mathcal{T}_\mathcal{I}$ is a labeled tree accepted by $\mathbf{A}_{C_0}$.*

From the lemmas above and the tree model property of $\mathcal{ALCFI}_{reg}$ (Theorem 5.6), we get the following result.

Theorem 5.9 *An $\mathcal{ALCFI}_{reg}$ concept C_0 is satisfiable if and only if the set of trees accepted by $\mathbf{A}_{C_0}$ is not empty.*

From this theorem, it follows that we can use algorithms for non-emptiness of 2ATAs to check satisfiability in $\mathcal{ALCFI}_{reg}$. It turns out that such a decision procedure is indeed optimal w.r.t. the computational complexity. The 2ATA $\mathbf{A}_{C_0}$ has a number of states that is linear in the size of C_0, while the alphabet is exponential in the number of atomic concepts occurring in C_0.

By Theorem 5.5 we get an upper bound for reasoning in $\mathcal{ALCFI}_{reg}$ that matches the EXPTIME lower bound.

Theorem 5.10 *Concept satisfiability (and hence logical implication) in* $\mathcal{ALCFI}_{reg}$ *is* EXPTIME-*complete.*

Functional restrictions, in the context of expressive description logics that include inverse roles and TBox axioms, were originally studied in [De Giacomo and Lenzerini, 1994a; De Giacomo, 1995] using the so called *axiom schema instantiation* technique. The technique is based on the idea of devising an axiom schema corresponding to the property of interest (e.g., functional restrictions) and instantiating such a schema to a finite (polynomial) number of concepts. A nice illustration of this technique is the reduction of *converse*-PDL to PDL in [De Giacomo, 1996]. Axiom schema instantiation can be used to show that reasoning w.r.t. TBoxes is EXPTIME-complete in significant subcases of $\mathcal{ALCFI}_{reg}$ (such as reasoning w.r.t. $\mathcal{ALCFI}$ TBoxes [Calvanese *et al.*, 2001b]). However, it is still open whether it can be applied to show EXPTIME-completeness of $\mathcal{ALCFI}_{reg}$. The attempt in this direction presented in [De Giacomo and Lenzerini, 1994a; De Giacomo, 1995] turned out to be incomplete [Zakharyaschev, 2000].

5.4 Qualified number restrictions

Next we deal with *qualified number restrictions*, which are the most general form of number restrictions, and allow one to specify arbitrary cardinality constraints on roles with role fillers belonging to a certain concept. In particular we will consider qualified number restrictions on basic roles, i.e., atomic roles and their inverse. By adding such constructs to $\mathcal{ALCI}_{reg}$ we obtain the description logic $\mathcal{ALCQI}_{reg}$. The PDL corresponding to $\mathcal{ALCQI}_{reg}$ is an extension of *converse*-PDL with "graded modalities" [Fattorosi-Barnaba and De Caro, 1985; Van der Hoek and de Rijke, 1995; Tobies, 1999c] on atomic programs and their converse.

Formally, $\mathcal{ALCQI}_{reg}$ is obtained from $\mathcal{ALCI}_{reg}$ by adding *qualified number restrictions* of the form $\leqslant n\,Q.C$ and $\geqslant n\,Q.C$, where n is a nonnegative integer, Q is a basic role, and C is an $\mathcal{ALCQI}_{reg}$ concept. Such constructs are interpreted as follows:

$$(\leqslant n\,Q.C)^{\mathcal{I}} = \{o \in \Delta^{\mathcal{I}} \mid |\{o' \in \Delta^{\mathcal{I}} \mid (o,o') \in Q^{\mathcal{I}} \wedge o' \in C^{\mathcal{I}}\}| \leq n\}$$
$$(\geqslant n\,Q.C)^{\mathcal{I}} = \{o \in \Delta^{\mathcal{I}} \mid |\{o' \in \Delta^{\mathcal{I}} \mid (o,o') \in Q^{\mathcal{I}} \wedge o' \in C^{\mathcal{I}}\}| \geq n\}.$$

Reasoning in $\mathcal{ALCQI}_{reg}$ is still EXPTIME-complete under the standard assumption in description logics, that numbers in number restrictions are represented in unary.[6] This could be shown by extending the automata-theoretic techniques introduced in Section 5.3 to deal also with qualified number restrictions. Here we take a different approach and study reasoning in $\mathcal{ALCQI}_{reg}$ by exhibiting a reduction from $\mathcal{ALCQI}_{reg}$ to $\mathcal{ALCFI}_{reg}$ [De Giacomo and Lenzerini, 1995; De Giacomo, 1995]. Since the reduction is polynomial, we get as a result ExpTime-completeness of $\mathcal{ALCQI}_{reg}$. The reduction is based on the notion of *reification*. Such a notion plays a major role in dealing with Boolean combinations of (atomic) roles [De Giacomo and Lenzerini, 1995; 1994c], as well as in extending expressive Description Logics with relations of arbitrary arity (see Section 5.7).

5.4.1 Reification of roles

Atomic roles are interpreted as binary relations. Reifying a binary relation means creating for each pair of individuals (o_1, o_2) in the relation an individual which is connected by means of two special roles V_1 and V_2 to o_1 and o_2, respectively. The set of such individuals represents the set of pairs forming the relation. However, the following problem arises: in general, there may be two or more individuals all connected by means of V_1 and V_2 to o_1 and o_2 respectively, and thus all representing the same pair (o_1, o_2). Obviously, in order to have a correct representation of a relation, such a situation must be avoided.

Given an atomic role P, we define its *reified form* to be the role

$$V_1^- \circ id(A_P) \circ V_2$$

where A_P is a new atomic concept denoting individuals representing the tuples of the relation associated with P, and V_1 and V_2 denote two functional roles that connect each individual in A_P respectively to the first and the second component of the tuple represented by the individual. Observe that there is a clear symmetry between the role $V_1^- \circ id(A_P) \circ V_2$ and its inverse $V_2^- \circ id(A_P) \circ V_1$.

Definition 5.11 Let C be an $\mathcal{ALCQI}_{reg}$ concept. The *reified counterpart* $\xi_1(C)$ of C is the conjunction of two concepts, $\xi_1(C) = \xi_0(C) \sqcap \Theta_1$, where:

- $\xi_0(C)$ is obtained from the original concept C by (i) replacing every atomic role P by the complex role $V_1^- \circ id(A_P) \circ V_2$, where V_1 and V_2 are new atomic roles

---

[6] In [Tobies, 2001a] techniques for dealing with qualified number restrictions with numbers coded in binary are presented, and are used to show that even under this assumption reasoning over $\mathcal{ALCQI}$ knowledge bases can be done in ExpTime.

(the only ones present after the transformation) and A_P is a new atomic concept;
(ii) and then re-expressing every qualified number restriction

$$
\begin{array}{lll}
\leqslant n\,(V_1^- \circ id(A_P) \circ V_2).D & \text{as} & \leqslant n\,V_1^-.(A_P \sqcap \exists V_2.D) \\
\geqslant n\,(V_1^- \circ id(A_P) \circ V_2).D & \text{as} & \geqslant n\,V_1^-.(A_P \sqcap \exists V_2.D) \\
\leqslant n\,(V_2^- \circ id(A_P) \circ V_1).D & \text{as} & \leqslant n\,V_2^-.(A_P \sqcap \exists V_1.D) \\
\geqslant n\,(V_2^- \circ id(A_P) \circ V_1).D & \text{as} & \geqslant n\,V_2^-.(A_P \sqcap \exists V_1.D)
\end{array}
$$

- $\Theta_1 = \forall(V_1 \sqcup V_2 \sqcup V_1^- \sqcup V_2^-)^*.(\leqslant 1\,V_1 \sqcap \leqslant 1\,V_2)$.

The next theorem guarantees that, without loss of generality, we can restrict our attention to models of $\xi_1(C)$ that correctly represent relations associated with atomic roles, i.e., models in which each tuple of such relations is represented by a single individual.

Theorem 5.12 *If the concept $\xi_1(C)$ has a model $\mathcal{I}$ then it has a model $\mathcal{I}'$ such that for each $(o, o') \in (V_1^- \circ id(A_{P_i}) \circ V_2)^{\mathcal{I}'}$ there is exactly one individual $o_{oo'}$ such that $(o_{oo'}, o) \in V_1^{\mathcal{I}'}$ and $(o_{oo'}, o') \in V_2^{\mathcal{I}'}$. That is, for all $o_1, o_2, o, o' \in \Delta^{\mathcal{I}'}$ such that $o_1 \neq o_2$ and $o \neq o'$, the following condition holds:*

$$
o_1, o_2 \in A_{P_i}^{\mathcal{I}'} \supset \neg((o_1, o) \in V_1^{\mathcal{I}'} \wedge (o_2, o) \in V_1^{\mathcal{I}'} \wedge (o_1, o') \in V_2^{\mathcal{I}'} \wedge (o_2, o') \in V_2^{\mathcal{I}'}).
$$

The proof of Theorem 5.12 exploits the *disjoint union model property*: let C be an $\mathcal{ALCQI}_{reg}$ concept and $\mathcal{I} = (\Delta^{\mathcal{I}}, \cdot^{\mathcal{I}})$ and $\mathcal{J} = (\Delta^{\mathcal{J}}, \cdot^{\mathcal{J}})$ be two models of C, then also the interpretation $\mathcal{I} \uplus \mathcal{J} = (\Delta^{\mathcal{I}} \uplus \Delta^{\mathcal{J}}, \cdot^{\mathcal{I}} \uplus \cdot^{\mathcal{J}})$, which is the disjoint union of $\mathcal{I}$ and $\mathcal{J}$, is a model of C. We remark that most description logics have such a property, which is, in fact, typical of modal logics. Without going into details, we just mention that the model $\mathcal{I}'$ is constructed from $\mathcal{I}$ as the disjoint union of several copies of $\mathcal{I}$, in which the extension of role V_2 is modified by exchanging, in those instances that cause a wrong representation of a role, the second component with a corresponding individual in one of the copies of $\mathcal{I}$.

By using Theorem 5.12 we can prove the result below.

Theorem 5.13 *An $\mathcal{ALCQI}_{reg}$ concept C is satisfiable if and only if its reified counterpart $\xi_1(C)$ is satisfiable.*

5.4.2 Reducing $\mathcal{ALCQI}_{reg}$ to $\mathcal{ALCFI}_{reg}$

By Theorem 5.13, we can concentrate on the reified counterparts of $\mathcal{ALCQI}_{reg}$ concepts. Note that these are themselves $\mathcal{ALCQI}_{reg}$ concepts, but their special form allows us to convert them into $\mathcal{ALCFI}_{reg}$ concepts.

Intuitively, we represent the role V_i^-, $i = 1, 2$ (recall that V_i is functional while V_i^- is not), by the role $F_{V_i} \circ F_{V_i}'^*$, where F_{V_i} and F_{V_i}' are new functional roles.[7] The main point of such a transformation is that it is easy to express qualified number restrictions as constraints on the chain of $(F_{V_i} \circ F_{V_i}'^*)$-successors of an individual. Formally, we define the $\mathcal{ALCFI}_{reg}$-counterpart of an $\mathcal{ALCQI}_{reg}$ concept as follows.

Definition 5.14 Let C be an $\mathcal{ALCQI}_{reg}$ concept and $\xi_1(C) = \xi_0(C) \sqcap \Theta_1$ its reified counterpart. The $\mathcal{ALCFI}_{reg}$-counterpart $\xi_2(C)$ of C is the conjunction of two concepts, $\xi_2(C) = \xi_0'(C) \wedge \Theta_2$, where:

- $\xi_0'(C)$ is obtained from $\xi_0(C)$ by simultaneously replacing:[8]
  - every occurrence of role V_i in constructs different from qualified number restrictions by $(F_{V_i} \circ F_{V_i}'^*)^-$, where F_{V_i} and F_{V_i}' are new atomic roles;
  - every $\leqslant n\, V_i^-.D$ by $\forall (F_{V_i} \circ F_{V_i}'^* \circ (id(D) \circ F_{V_i}'^+)^n).\neg D$;
  - every $\geqslant n\, V_i^-.D$ by $\exists (F_{V_i} \circ F_{V_i}'^* \circ (id(D) \circ F_{V_i}'^+)^{n-1}).D$.
- $\Theta_2 = \forall(\bigsqcup_{i=1,2}(F_{V_i} \sqcup F_{V_i}' \sqcup F_{V_i}^- \sqcup F_{V_i}'^-))^*.(\theta_1 \sqcap \theta_2)$, with θ_i of the form:

$$\leqslant 1\, F_{V_i} \sqcap\; \leqslant 1\, F_{V_i}' \sqcap\; \leqslant 1\, F_{V_i}^- \sqcap\; \leqslant 1\, F_{V_i}'^- \sqcap \neg(\exists F_{V_i}^-.\top \sqcap \exists F_{V_i}'^-.\top).$$

Observe that Θ_2 constrains each model $\mathcal{I}$ of $\xi_2(C)$ so that the relations $F_{V_i}^{\mathcal{I}}$, $F_{V_i}'^{\mathcal{I}}$, $(F_{V_i}^-)^{\mathcal{I}}$, and $(F_{V_i}'^-)^{\mathcal{I}}$ are partial functions, and each individual cannot be linked to other individuals by both $(F_{V_i}^-)^{\mathcal{I}}$ and $(F_{V_i}'^-)^{\mathcal{I}}$. As a consequence, we get that $((F_{V_i} \circ F_{V_i}'^*)^-)^{\mathcal{I}}$ is a partial function. This allows us to reconstruct the extension of V_i, as required.

We illustrate the basic relationships between a model of an $\mathcal{ALCQI}_{reg}$ concept and the models of its reified counterpart and $\mathcal{ALCFI}_{reg}$-counterpart by means of an example.

Example 5.15 Consider the concept

$$C_0 = \exists P.(= 2\, P^-.(= 2\, P.\top))$$

and consider the model $\mathcal{I}$ of C_0 depicted in Figure 5.1, in which $a \in C_0^{\mathcal{I}}$. Such a model corresponds to a model $\mathcal{I}'$ of the reified counterpart $\xi_1(C_0)$ of C_0, shown in Figure 5.2. The model $\mathcal{I}'$ of $\xi_1(C_0)$ in turn corresponds to a model $\mathcal{I}''$ of the $\mathcal{ALCFI}_{reg}$-counterpart $\xi_2(C_0)$ of C_0, shown in Figure 5.3. Notice that from $\mathcal{I}''$ we can easily reconstruct $\mathcal{I}'$, and from $\mathcal{I}'$ the model $\mathcal{I}$ of the original concept. ∎

---

[7] The idea of expressing nonfunctional roles by means of chains of functional roles is due to Parikh [1981], who used it to reduce standard PDL to DPDL.
[8] Here R^+ stands for $R \circ R^*$ and R^n stands for $R \circ \cdots \circ R$ (n times).

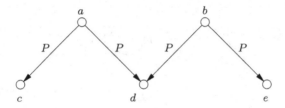

Fig. 5.1. A model of the $\mathcal{ALCQI}_{reg}$ concept $C_0 = \exists P.(\geq 2\,P^-.(\geq 2\,P.\top))$.

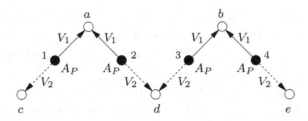

Fig. 5.2. A model of the reified counterpart $\xi_1(C_0)$ of C_0.

It can be shown that $\xi_1(C)$ is satisfiable if and only if $\xi_2(C)$ is satisfiable. Since, as it is easy to see, the size of $\xi_2(C)$ is polynomial in the size of C, we get the following characterization of the computational complexity of reasoning in $\mathcal{ALCQI}_{reg}$.

Theorem 5.16 *Concept satisfiability (and hence logical implication) in* $\mathcal{ALCQI}_{reg}$ *is* ExpTime-*complete.*

5.5 Objects

In this section, we review results involving knowledge about individuals expressed in terms of membership assertions. Given an alphabet $\mathcal{O}$ of symbols for individuals, a *(membership) assertion* has one of the following forms:

$$C(a) \qquad\qquad P(a_1, a_2)$$

where C is a concept, P is an atomic role, and a, a_1, a_2 belong to $\mathcal{O}$. An interpretation $\mathcal{I}$ is extended so as to assign to each $a \in \mathcal{O}$ an element $a^{\mathcal{I}} \in \Delta^{\mathcal{I}}$ in such a way that the *unique name assumption* is satisfied, i.e., different elements are assigned to different symbols in $\mathcal{O}$. $\mathcal{I}$ *satisfies* $C(a)$ if $a^{\mathcal{I}} \in C^{\mathcal{I}}$, and $\mathcal{I}$ *satisfies* $P(a_1, a_2)$ if $(a_1^{\mathcal{I}}, a_2^{\mathcal{I}}) \in P^{\mathcal{I}}$. An *ABox* $\mathcal{A}$ is a finite set of membership assertions, and an interpretation $\mathcal{I}$ is called a *model of* $\mathcal{A}$ if $\mathcal{I}$ satisfies every assertion in $\mathcal{A}$.

A *knowledge base* is a pair $\mathcal{K} = (\mathcal{T}, \mathcal{A})$, where $\mathcal{T}$ is a TBox, and $\mathcal{A}$ is an ABox. An interpretation $\mathcal{I}$ is called a *model of* $\mathcal{K}$ if it is a model of

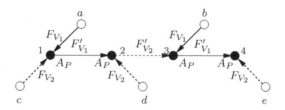

Fig. 5.3. A model of the $\mathcal{ALCFI}_{reg}$-counterpart $\xi_2(C_0)$ of C_0.

both $\mathcal{T}$ and $\mathcal{A}$. $\mathcal{K}$ is *satisfiable* if it has a model, and $\mathcal{K}$ *logically implies* an assertion β, denoted $\mathcal{K} \models \beta$, where β is either an inclusion or a membership assertion, if every model of $\mathcal{K}$ satisfies β. Logical implication can be reformulated in terms of unsatisfiability: e.g., $\mathcal{K} \models C(a)$ iff $\mathcal{K} \cup \{\neg C(a)\}$ is unsatisfiable; similarly $\mathcal{K} \models C_1 \sqsubseteq C_2$ iff $\mathcal{K} \cup \{(C_1 \sqcap \neg C_2)(a')\}$ is unsatisfiable, where a' does not occur in $\mathcal{K}$. Therefore, we only need a procedure for checking satisfiability of a knowledge base.

Next we illustrate the technique for reasoning on $\mathcal{ALCQI}_{reg}$ knowledge bases [De Giacomo and Lenzerini, 1996]. The basic idea is as follows: checking the satisfiability of an $\mathcal{ALCQI}_{reg}$ knowledge base $\mathcal{K} = (\mathcal{T}, \mathcal{A})$ is polynomially reduced to checking the satisfiability of an $\mathcal{ALCQI}_{reg}$ knowledge base $\mathcal{K}' = (\mathcal{T}', \mathcal{A}')$, whose ABox $\mathcal{A}'$ is made of a single membership assertion of the form $C(a)$. In other words, the satisfiability of $\mathcal{K}$ is reduced to the satisfiability of the concept C w.r.t. the TBox $\mathcal{T}'$ of the resulting knowledge base. The latter reasoning service can be realized by means of the method presented in Section 5.4, and, as we have seen, is EXPTIME-complete. Thus, by means of the reduction, we get an EXPTIME algorithm for satisfiability of $\mathcal{ALCQI}_{reg}$ knowledge bases, and hence for all standard reasoning services on $\mathcal{ALCQI}_{reg}$ knowledge bases.

Definition 5.17 Let $\mathcal{K} = (\mathcal{T}, \mathcal{A})$ be an $\mathcal{ALCQI}_{reg}$ knowledge base. The *reduced form* of $\mathcal{K}$ is the $\mathcal{ALCQI}_{reg}$ knowledge base $\mathcal{K}' = (\mathcal{T}', \mathcal{A}')$ defined as follows. We introduce a new atomic role *create*, and also for each individual a_i, $i = 1, \ldots, m$, occurring in $\mathcal{A}$, a new atomic concept A_i. Then:

$$\mathcal{A}' = \{(\exists create.A_1 \sqcap \cdots \sqcap \exists create.A_m)(g)\},$$

where g is a new individual (the only one present in $\mathcal{A}'$), and $\mathcal{T}' = \mathcal{T} \cup \mathcal{T}_\mathcal{A} \cup \mathcal{T}_{aux}$, where:

- $\mathcal{T}_\mathcal{A}$ is constituted by the following inclusion axioms:
  - for each membership assertion $C(a_i) \in \mathcal{A}$, one inclusion axiom

$$A_i \sqsubseteq C$$

– for each membership assertion $P(a_i, a_j) \in \mathcal{A}$, two inclusion axioms

$$A_i \sqsubseteq \exists P.A_j \sqcap \leqslant 1\, P.A_j$$
$$A_j \sqsubseteq \exists P^-.A_i \sqcap \leqslant 1\, P^-.A_i$$

– for each pair of distinct individuals a_i and a_j occurring in $\mathcal{A}$, one inclusion axiom

$$A_i \sqsubseteq \neg A_j$$

- $\mathcal{T}_{aux}$ is constituted by one inclusion axiom (U stands for $(P_1 \sqcup \cdots \sqcup P_n \sqcup P_1^- \sqcup \cdots \sqcup P_n^-)^*$, where $P_1, \ldots, P_n$ are all atomic roles in $\mathcal{T} \cup \mathcal{T}_{\mathcal{A}}$):

$$A_i \sqcap C \sqsubseteq \forall U.(\neg A_i \sqcup C)$$

for each A_i occurring in $\mathcal{T} \cup \mathcal{T}_{\mathcal{A}}$ and each $C \in CL_{ext}(\mathcal{T} \cup \mathcal{T}_{\mathcal{A}})$, where $CL_{ext}(\mathcal{T} \cup \mathcal{T}_{\mathcal{A}})$ is a suitably extended syntactic closure[9] of $\mathcal{T} \cup \mathcal{T}_{\mathcal{A}}$ whose size is polynomially related to the size of $\mathcal{T} \cup \mathcal{T}_{\mathcal{A}}$ [De Giacomo and Lenzerini, 1996].

To understand how the reduced form $\mathcal{K}' = (\mathcal{T}', \mathcal{A}')$ relates to the original knowledge base $\mathcal{K} = (\mathcal{T}, \mathcal{A})$, first observe that the ABox $\mathcal{A}'$ is used to force the existence of the only individual g connected by the role *create* to one instance of each A_i. It can be shown that this allows us to restrict our attention to models of $\mathcal{K}'$ that represent a graph connected to g, i.e., models $\mathcal{I} = (\Delta^{\mathcal{I}}, \cdot^{\mathcal{I}})$ of $\mathcal{K}'$ such that $\Delta^{\mathcal{I}} = \{g\} \cup \{s' \mid (g, s') \in create^{\mathcal{I}} \circ (\bigcup_P (P^{\mathcal{I}} \cup P^{\mathcal{I}^-})^*)\}$.

The TBox $\mathcal{T}'$ consists of three parts $\mathcal{T}$, $\mathcal{T}_{\mathcal{A}}$, and $\mathcal{T}_{aux}$. $\mathcal{T}$ is the original inclusion axioms. $\mathcal{T}_{\mathcal{A}}$ is what we may call a "naive encoding" of the original ABox $\mathcal{A}$ as inclusion axioms. Indeed, each individual a_i is represented in $\mathcal{T}_{\mathcal{A}}$ as a new atomic concept A_i (disjoint from the other A_j's), and the membership assertions in the original ABox $\mathcal{A}$ are represented as inclusion axioms in $\mathcal{T}_{\mathcal{A}}$ involving such new atomic concepts. However $\mathcal{T} \cup \mathcal{T}_{\mathcal{A}}$ alone does not suffice to represent faithfully (w.r.t. the reasoning services we are interested in) the original knowledge base, because an individual a_i in $\mathcal{K}$ is represented by the set of instances of A_i in $\mathcal{K}'$. In order to reduce the satisfiability of $\mathcal{K}'$ to the satisfiability of $\mathcal{K}$, we must be able to single out, for each A_i, one instance of A_i representative of a_i. For this purpose, we need to include in $\mathcal{T}'$ a new part, called $\mathcal{T}_{aux}$, which contains inclusion axioms of the form

$$A_i \sqcap C \sqsubseteq \forall U.(\neg A_i \sqcup C).$$

---

[9] The syntactic closure of a TBox is the syntactic closure of the concept obtained by internalizing the axioms of the TBox.

Intuitively, such axioms say that, if one instance of A_i is also an instance of C, then every instance of A_i is an instance of C. Observe that, if we could add an infinite set of axioms of this form, one for each possible concept of the language (i.e., an axiom schema), we could safely restrict our attention to models of $\mathcal{K}'$ with just one instance for every concept A_i, since there would be no way in the logic to distinguish two instances of A_i one from the other. What is shown by De Giacomo and Lenzerini [1996] is that in fact we do need only a polynomial number of such inclusion axioms (as specified by $\mathcal{T}_{aux}$) in order to be able to identify, for each i, an instance of A_i as representative of a_i. This allows us to prove that the existence of a model of $\mathcal{K}'$ implies the existence of a model of $\mathcal{K}$.

Theorem 5.18 *Knowledge base satisfiability (and hence every standard reasoning service) in $\mathcal{ALCQI}_{reg}$ is* ExpTime-*complete.*

Using a similar approach, De Giacomo and Lenzerini [1994a] and De Giacomo [1995] extend $\mathcal{ALCQ}_{reg}$ and $\mathcal{ALCI}_{reg}$ by adding special atomic concepts A_a, called *nominals*, having exactly one single instance a, i.e., the individual they name. Nominals may occur in concepts exactly as atomic concepts, and hence they constitute one of the most flexible ways to express knowledge about single individuals.

By using nominals we can capture the "one-of" construct, having the form $\{a_1, \ldots, a_n\}$, denoting the concept made of exactly the enumerated individuals $a_1, \ldots, a_n$.[10] We can also capture the "fills" construct, having the form $R : a$, denoting those individuals having the individual a as a role filler of R.[11] (See [Schaerf, 1994b] and references therein for further discussion on these constructs.)

Let us denote by $\mathcal{ALCQO}_{reg}$ and $\mathcal{ALCIO}_{reg}$ the description logics resulting from adding nominals to $\mathcal{ALCQ}_{reg}$ and $\mathcal{ALCI}_{reg}$ respectively. De Giacomo and Lenzerini [1994a] and De Giacomo [1995] polynomially reduce satisfiability in $\mathcal{ALCQO}_{reg}$ and $\mathcal{ALCIO}_{reg}$ knowledge bases to satisfiability of $\mathcal{ALCQ}_{reg}$ and $\mathcal{ALCI}_{reg}$ concepts respectively, hence showing decidability and ExpTime-completeness of reasoning in these logics. ExpTime-completeness does not hold for $\mathcal{ALCQIO}_{reg}$, i.e., $\mathcal{ALCQI}_{reg}$ extended with nominals. Indeed, a result by Tobies [1999a; 1999b] shows that reasoning in such a logic is NExpTime-hard. Its decidability remains an open problem.

---

[10] Actually, nominals and the one-of construct are essentially equivalent, since a name A_a is equivalent to $\{a\}$ and $\{a_1, \ldots, a_n\}$ is equivalent to $A_{a_1} \sqcup \cdots \sqcup A_{a_n}$.
[11] The "fills" construct $R : a$ is captured by $\exists R.A_a$.

The notion of nominal introduced above has a correspondent in modal logic [Prior, 1967; Bull, 1970; Blackburn and Spaan, 1993; Gargov and Goranko, 1993; Blackburn, 1993]. Nominals have also been studied within the setting of PDLs [Passy and Tinchev, 1985; Gargov and Passy, 1988; Passy and Tinchev, 1991]. The results for $\mathcal{ALCQO}_{reg}$ and $\mathcal{ALCIO}_{reg}$ are immediately applicable also in the setting of PDLs. In particular, the PDL corresponding to $\mathcal{ALCQO}_{reg}$ is standard PDL augmented with nominals and graded modalities (qualified number restrictions). It is an extension of *deterministic combinatory PDL*, DcPDL, which is essentially DPDL augmented with nominals. The decidability of DcPDL is established by Passy and Tinchev [1985], who also prove that satisfiability can be checked in nondeterministic double exponential time. This is tightened by the result above on ExpTime-completeness of $\mathcal{ALCQO}_{reg}$, which says that DcPDL is in fact ExpTime-complete, thus closing the previous gap between the upper bound and the lower bound. The PDL corresponding to $\mathcal{ALCIO}_{reg}$ is *converse*-PDL augmented with nominals, which is also called *converse combinatory PDL*, CcPDL [Passy and Tinchev, 1991]. Such a logic was not known to be decidable [Passy and Tinchev, 1991]. Hence the results mentioned above allow us to establish the decidability of CcPDL and to precisely characterize the computational complexity of satisfiability (and hence of logical implication) as ExpTime-complete.

5.6 Fixpoint constructs

Decidable description logics equipped with explicit fixpoint constructs have been devised in order to model inductive and coinductive data structures such as lists, streams, trees, etc. [De Giacomo and Lenzerini, 1994d; Schild, 1994; De Giacomo and Lenzerini, 1997; Calvanese *et al.*, 1999c]. Such logics correspond to extensions of the *propositional μ-calculus* [Kozen, 1983; Streett and Emerson, 1989; Vardi, 1998], a variant of PDL with explicit fixpoints that is used to express temporal properties of reactive and concurrent processes [Stirling, 1996; Emerson, 1996]. Such logics can also be viewed as a well-behaved fragment of first-order logic with fixpoints [Park, 1970; 1976; Abiteboul *et al.*, 1995].

Here, we concentrate on the description logic $\mu\mathcal{ALCQI}$ studied by Calvanese *et al.* [1999c]. Such a description logic is derived from $\mathcal{ALCQI}$ by adding *least and greatest fixpoint constructs*. The availability of explicit fixpoint constructs allows *inductive* and *coinductive* concepts to be expressed in a natural way.

Example 5.19 Consider the concept Tree, representing trees, inductively defined as follows:

1. An individual that is an EmptyTree is a Tree.
2. If an individual is a Node, has at most one parent, has some children, and all children are Trees, then such an individual is a Tree.

In other words, Tree is the concept with the smallest extension among those satisfying the assertions 1 and 2. Such a concept is naturally expressed in $\mu\mathcal{ALCQI}$ by making use of the least fixpoint construct $\mu X.C$:

$$\mathsf{Tree} \;\equiv\; \mu X.(\mathsf{EmptyTree} \sqcup (\mathsf{Node} \sqcap\, \leqslant 1\,\mathsf{child}^- \sqcap\, \exists\mathsf{child}.\top \sqcap \forall\mathsf{child}.X)).$$

∎

Example 5.20 Consider the well-known linear data structure, called stream. Streams are similar to lists except that, while lists can be considered as finite sequences of nodes, streams are infinite sequences of nodes. Such a data structure is captured by the concept **Stream**, coinductively defined as follows:

1. An individual that is a Stream, is a Node and has a single successor which is a Stream.

In other words, Stream is the concept with the largest extension among those satisfying condition 1. Such a concept is naturally expressed in $\mu\mathcal{ALCQI}$ by making use of the greatest fixpoint construct $\nu X.C$:

$$\mathsf{Stream} \equiv \nu X.(\mathsf{Node} \sqcap\, \leqslant 1\,\mathsf{succ} \sqcap\, \exists\mathsf{succ}.X).$$

∎

Let us now introduce $\mu\mathcal{ALCQI}$ formally. We make use of the standard first-order notions of *scope*, *bound* and *free occurrences* of variables, *closed formulae*, etc., treating μ and ν as quantifiers.

The primitive symbols in $\mu\mathcal{ALCQI}$ are *atomic concepts*, *(concept) variables*, and *atomic roles*. Concepts and roles are formed according to the following syntax:

$$\begin{aligned} C &\longrightarrow A \;\mid\; \neg C \;\mid\; C_1 \sqcap C_2 \;\mid\; \geqslant n\,R.C \;\mid\; \mu X.C \;\mid\; X \\ R &\longrightarrow P \;\mid\; P^- \end{aligned}$$

where A denotes an atomic concept, P an atomic role, C an arbitrary $\mu\mathcal{ALCQI}$ concept, R an arbitrary $\mu\mathcal{ALCQI}$ role (i.e., either an atomic role or the inverse of an atomic role), n a natural number, and X a variable.

The concept C in $\mu X.C$ must be *syntactically monotone*, that is, every free occurrence of the variable X in C must be in the scope of an even number of negations [Kozen, 1983]. This restriction guarantees that the concept C denotes a monotonic operator and hence both the least and the greatest fixpoints exist and are unique (see later).

In addition to the usual abbreviations used in $\mathcal{ALCQI}$, we introduce the abbreviation $\nu X.C$ for $\neg\mu X.\neg C[X/\neg X]$, where $C[X/\neg X]$ is the concept obtained by replacing all free occurrences of X by $\neg X$.

The presence of free variables prevents us from extending the interpretation function $\cdot^{\mathcal{I}}$ directly to every concept of the logic. For this reason we introduce valuations. A *valuation* ρ on an interpretation $\mathcal{I}$ is a mapping from variables to subsets of $\Delta^{\mathcal{I}}$. Given a valuation ρ, we denote by $\rho[X/\mathcal{E}]$ the valuation identical to ρ except that $\rho[X/\mathcal{E}](X) = \mathcal{E}$.

Let $\mathcal{I}$ be an interpretation and ρ a valuation on $\mathcal{I}$. We assign meaning to concepts of the logic by associating to $\mathcal{I}$ and ρ an *extension function* $\cdot^{\mathcal{I}}_{\rho}$, mapping concepts to subsets of $\Delta^{\mathcal{I}}$, as follows:

$$
\begin{aligned}
X^{\mathcal{I}}_{\rho} &= \rho(X) \subseteq \Delta^{\mathcal{I}} \\
A^{\mathcal{I}}_{\rho} &= A^{\mathcal{I}} \subseteq \Delta^{\mathcal{I}} \\
(\neg C)^{\mathcal{I}}_{\rho} &= \Delta^{\mathcal{I}} \setminus C^{\mathcal{I}}_{\rho} \\
(C_1 \sqcap C_2)^{\mathcal{I}}_{\rho} &= (C_1)^{\mathcal{I}}_{\rho} \cap (C_2)^{\mathcal{I}}_{\rho} \\
\geqslant n\, R.C^{\mathcal{I}}_{\rho} &= \{ s \in \Delta^{\mathcal{I}} \mid |\{ s' \mid (s, s') \in R^{\mathcal{I}} \text{ and } s' \in C^{\mathcal{I}}_{\rho} \}| \geq n \} \\
(\mu X.C)^{\mathcal{I}}_{\rho} &= \bigcap \{ \mathcal{E} \subseteq \Delta^{\mathcal{I}} \mid C^{\mathcal{I}}_{\rho[X/\mathcal{E}]} \subseteq \mathcal{E} \}.
\end{aligned}
$$

Observe that $C^{\mathcal{I}}_{\rho[X/\mathcal{E}]}$ can be seen as an operator from subsets $\mathcal{E}$ of $\Delta^{\mathcal{I}}$ to subsets of $\Delta^{\mathcal{I}}$, and that, by the syntactic restriction enforced on variables, such an operator is guaranteed to be monotonic w.r.t. set inclusion. $\mu X.C$ denotes the *least fixpoint* of the operator. Observe also that the semantics assigned to $\nu X.C$ is

$$
(\nu X.C)^{\mathcal{I}}_{\rho} = \bigcup \{ \mathcal{E} \subseteq \Delta^{\mathcal{I}} \mid \mathcal{E} \subseteq C^{\mathcal{I}}_{\rho[X/\mathcal{E}]} \}.
$$

Hence $\nu X.C$ denotes the *greatest fixpoint* of the operator.

In fact, we are interested in closed concepts, whose extension is independent of the valuation. For closed concepts we do not need to consider the valuation explicitly, and hence the notions of concept satisfiability, logical implication, etc. extend straightforwardly.

Exploiting a recent result on EXPTIME decidability of modal μ-calculus with converse [Vardi, 1998], and exploiting a reduction technique for qualified number restrictions similar to the one presented in Section 5.4, Calvanese *et al.* [1999c] have shown that the same complexity bound holds also for reasoning in $\mu\mathcal{ALCQI}$.

Theorem 5.21 *Concept satisfiability (and hence logical implication) in $\mu\mathcal{ALCQI}$ is* EXPTIME-*complete.*

For certain applications, variants of $\mu\mathcal{ALCQI}$ that allow for *mutual fixpoints*, denoting least and greatest solutions of *mutually* recursive equations, are of interest [Schild, 1994; Calvanese *et al.*, 1998c; 1999b]. Mutual fixpoints can be re-expressed by suitably nesting the kind of fixpoints considered here (see, for example, [de Bakker, 1980; Schild, 1994]). It is interesting to notice that, although the resulting concept may be exponentially large in the size of the original concept with mutual fixpoints, the number of (distinct) subconcepts of the resulting concept is polynomially bounded by the size of the original one. By virtue of this observation, and using the reasoning procedure of Calvanese *et al.* [1999c], we can strengthen the above result.

Theorem 5.22 *Checking satisfiability of a closed $\mu\mathcal{ALCQI}$ concept C can be done in deterministic exponential time w.r.t. the number of (distinct) subconcepts of C.*

Although $\mu\mathcal{ALCQI}$ does not have the rich variety of role constructs of $\mathcal{ALCQI}_{reg}$, it is actually an extension of $\mathcal{ALCQI}_{reg}$, since any $\mathcal{ALCQI}_{reg}$ concept can be expressed in $\mu\mathcal{ALCQI}$ using the fixpoint constructs in a suitable way. To express concepts involving complex role expressions, it suffices to resort to the following equivalences:

$$\begin{aligned}
\exists(R_1 \circ R_2).C &= \exists R_1.\exists R_2.C \\
\exists(R_1 \sqcup R_2).C &= \exists R_1.C \sqcup \exists R_2.C \\
\exists R^*.C &= \mu X.(C \sqcup \exists R.X) \\
\exists id(D).C &= C \sqcap D.
\end{aligned}$$

Note that, according to such equivalences, we have also that

$$\forall R^*.C = \nu X.(C \sqcap \forall R.X).$$

Calvanese *et al.* [1995] advocate a further construct corresponding to an implicit form of fixpoint, the so called *well-founded* concept construct *wf* (R). Such a construct is used to impose well-foundedness of chains of roles, and thus allows one to correctly capture inductive structures. Using explicit fixpoints, *wf* (R) is expressed as $\mu X.(\forall R.X)$.

We remark that, in order to gain the ability to express inductively and coinductively defined concepts, it has been proposed to adopt ad hoc semantics for interpreting knowledge bases, specifically the *least fixpoint semantics* for expressing inductive concepts and the *greatest fixpoint semantics* for expressing coinductive ones (see Chapter 2 and also [Nebel, 1991; Baader, 1990a; 1991; Dionne *et al.*, 1992; Küsters, 1998; Buchheit *et al.*, 1998]). Logics equipped with fixpoint constructs allow statements interpreted according to the least and greatest fixpoint semantics to be mixed in the same knowledge base [Schild, 1994; De Giacomo and Lenzerini, 1997], and thus can be viewed as a generalization of these approaches.

Recently, using techniques based on alternating two-way automata, it has been shown that the propositional μ-calculus with converse programs remains ExpTime-decidable when extended with nominals [Sattler and Vardi, 2001]. This logic corresponds to a description logic which could be called $\mu\mathcal{ALCIO}$.

5.7 Relations of arbitrary arity

A limitation of traditional description logics is that only binary relationships between instances of concepts can be represented, while in some real world situations it is required to model relationships among more than two objects. Such relationships can be captured by making use of relations of arbitrary arity instead of (binary) roles. Various extensions of description logics with relations of arbitrary arity have been proposed [Schmolze, 1989; Catarci and Lenzerini, 1993; De Giacomo and Lenzerini, 1994c; Calvanese *et al.*, 1997; 1998a; Lutz *et al.*, 1999].

We concentrate on the description logic $\mathcal{DLR}$ [Calvanese *et al.*, 1997; 1998a], which represents a natural generalization of traditional description logics towards n-ary relations. The basic elements of $\mathcal{DLR}$ are *atomic relations* and *atomic concepts*, denoted by $\mathbf{P}$ and A respectively. Arbitrary *relations*, of given *arity* between 2 and n_{max}, and arbitrary *concepts* are formed according to the following syntax:

$$\mathbf{R} \longrightarrow \top_n \mid \mathbf{P} \mid (\$i/n{:}C) \mid \neg\mathbf{R} \mid \mathbf{R}_1 \sqcap \mathbf{R}_2$$
$$C \longrightarrow \top_1 \mid A \mid \neg C \mid C_1 \sqcap C_2 \mid \exists[\$i]\mathbf{R} \mid \leqslant k\,[\$i]\mathbf{R}$$

where i denotes a component of a relation, i.e., an integer between 1 and n_{max}, n denotes the arity of a relation, i.e., an integer between 2 and n_{max}, and k denotes a nonnegative integer. Concepts and relations must be *well-typed*, which means that only relations of the same arity n can be combined to form expressions of type $\mathbf{R}_1 \sqcap \mathbf{R}_2$ (which inherit the arity n), and $i \leq n$ whenever i denotes a component of a relation of arity n.

The semantics of $\mathcal{DLR}$ is specified through the usual notion of *interpretation* $\mathcal{I} = (\Delta^{\mathcal{I}}, \cdot^{\mathcal{I}})$, where the *interpretation function* $\cdot^{\mathcal{I}}$ assigns to each concept C a subset $C^{\mathcal{I}}$ of $\Delta^{\mathcal{I}}$, and to each relation $\mathbf{R}$ of arity n a subset $\mathbf{R}^{\mathcal{I}}$ of $(\Delta^{\mathcal{I}})^n$, such that the following conditions are satisfied:

$$
\begin{aligned}
\top_n^{\mathcal{I}} &\subseteq (\Delta^{\mathcal{I}})^n \\
\mathbf{P}^{\mathcal{I}} &\subseteq \top_n^{\mathcal{I}} \\
(\neg \mathbf{R})^{\mathcal{I}} &= \top_n^{\mathcal{I}} \setminus \mathbf{R}^{\mathcal{I}} \\
(\mathbf{R}_1 \sqcap \mathbf{R}_2)^{\mathcal{I}} &= \mathbf{R}_1^{\mathcal{I}} \cap \mathbf{R}_2^{\mathcal{I}} \\
(\$i/n\!:C)^{\mathcal{I}} &= \{(d_1, \ldots, d_n) \in \top_n^{\mathcal{I}} \mid d_i \in C^{\mathcal{I}}\} \\[4pt]
\top_1^{\mathcal{I}} &= \Delta^{\mathcal{I}} \\
A^{\mathcal{I}} &\subseteq \Delta^{\mathcal{I}} \\
(\neg C)^{\mathcal{I}} &= \Delta^{\mathcal{I}} \setminus C^{\mathcal{I}} \\
(C_1 \sqcap C_2)^{\mathcal{I}} &= C_1^{\mathcal{I}} \cap C_2^{\mathcal{I}} \\
(\exists[\$i]\mathbf{R})^{\mathcal{I}} &= \{d \in \Delta^{\mathcal{I}} \mid \exists (d_1, \ldots, d_n) \in \mathbf{R}^{\mathcal{I}}. d_i = d\} \\
(\leqslant k\,[\$i]\mathbf{R})^{\mathcal{I}} &= \{d \in \Delta^{\mathcal{I}} \mid |\{(d_1, \ldots, d_n) \in \mathbf{R}_1^{\mathcal{I}} \mid d_i = d\}| \leq k\}
\end{aligned}
$$

where $\mathbf{P}$, $\mathbf{R}$, $\mathbf{R}_1$, and $\mathbf{R}_2$ have arity n. Observe that $\top_1$ denotes the interpretation domain, while $\top_n$, for $n > 1$, does *not* denote the n-cartesian product of the domain, but only a subset of it, that covers all relations of arity n that are introduced. As a consequence, the "$\neg$" construct on relations expresses *difference of relations* rather than complement.

The construct ($\$i/n\!:C$) denotes all tuples in $\top_n$ that have an instance of concept C as their ith component, and therefore represents a kind of selection. Existential quantification and number restrictions on relations are a natural generalization of the corresponding constructs using roles. This can be seen by observing that, while for roles the "direction of traversal" is implicit, for a relation one needs to explicitly say which component is used to "enter" a tuple and which component is used to "exit" it.

$\mathcal{DLR}$ is in fact a proper generalization of $\mathcal{ALCQI}$. The traditional DL constructs can be re-expressed in $\mathcal{DLR}$ as follows:

$$
\begin{aligned}
\exists P.C &\quad \text{as} \quad \exists[\$1](P \sqcap (\$2/2\!:C)) \\
\exists P^-.C &\quad \text{as} \quad \exists[\$2](P \sqcap (\$1/2\!:C)) \\
\forall P.C &\quad \text{as} \quad \neg\exists[\$1](P \sqcap (\$2/2\!:\neg C)) \\
\forall P^-.C &\quad \text{as} \quad \neg\exists[\$2](P \sqcap (\$1/2\!:\neg C)) \\
\leqslant k\,P.C &\quad \text{as} \quad \leqslant k\,[\$1](P \sqcap (\$2/2\!:C)) \\
\leqslant k\,P^-.C &\quad \text{as} \quad \leqslant k\,[\$2](P \sqcap (\$1/2\!:C)).
\end{aligned}
$$

Observe that the constructs using direct and inverse roles are represented in $\mathcal{DLR}$ by using binary relations and explicitly specifying the direction of traversal.

A TBox in $\mathcal{DLR}$ is a finite set of inclusion axioms on both concepts and relations of the form

$$C \sqsubseteq C' \qquad\qquad \mathbf{R} \sqsubseteq \mathbf{R}'$$

where $\mathbf{R}$ and $\mathbf{R}'$ are two relations of the same arity. The notions of an interpretation *satisfying* an assertion, and of *model* of a TBox are defined as usual.

The basic technique used in $\mathcal{DLR}$ to reason on relations is *reification* (see Subsection 5.4.1), which allows one to reduce logical implication in $\mathcal{DLR}$ to logical implication in $\mathcal{ALCQI}$. Reification for n-ary relations is similar to reification of roles (see Definition 5.11): a relation of arity n is reified by means of a new concept and n functional roles $f_1, \ldots, f_n$. Let the $\mathcal{ALCQI}$ TBox $\mathcal{T}'$ be the *reified counterpart* of a $\mathcal{DLR}$ TBox $\mathcal{T}$. A tuple of a relation $\mathbf{R}$ in a model of $\mathcal{T}$ is represented in a model of $\mathcal{T}'$ by an instance of the concept corresponding to $\mathbf{R}$, which is linked through $f_1, \ldots, f_n$ respectively to n individuals representing the components of the tuple. In this case reification is further used to encode Boolean constructs on relations into the corresponding constructs on the concepts representing relations.

As for reification of roles (see Subsection 5.4.1), performing the reification of relations requires some care, since the semantics of a relation rules out that there may be two identical tuples in its extension, i.e., two tuples constituted by the same components in the same positions. In the reified counterpart, on the other hand, one cannot explicitly rule out (e.g., by using specific axioms) the existence of two individuals o_1 and o_2 "representing" the same tuple, i.e., that are connected through $f_1, \ldots, f_n$ to exactly the same individuals denoting the components of the tuple. A model of the reified counterpart $\mathcal{T}'$ of $\mathcal{T}$ in which this situation occurs may not correspond directly to a model of $\mathcal{T}$, since by collapsing the two equivalent individuals into a tuple, axioms may be violated (e.g., cardinality constraints). However, also in this case the analog of Theorem 5.12 holds, ensuring that from any model of $\mathcal{T}'$ one can construct a new one in which no two individuals represent the same tuple. Therefore one does not need to take this constraint explicitly into account when reasoning on the reified counterpart of a knowledge base with relations. Since reification is polynomial, from EXPTIME-decidability of logical implication in $\mathcal{ALCQI}$ (and EXPTIME-hardness of logical implication in $\mathcal{ALC}$) we get the following characterization of the computational complexity of reasoning in $\mathcal{DLR}$ [Calvanese *et al.*, 1997].

Theorem 5.23 *Logical implication in $\mathcal{DLR}$ is* EXPTIME-*complete.*

$\mathcal{DLR}$ can be extended to include regular expressions built over projections of relations on two of their components, thus obtaining $\mathcal{DLR}_{reg}$. Such a logic, which represents a generalization of $\mathcal{ALCQI}_{reg}$, allows the internalization of a TBox. ExpTime-decidability (and hence completeness) of $\mathcal{DLR}_{reg}$ can again be shown by exploiting reification of relations and reducing logical implication to concept satisfiability in $\mathcal{ALCQI}_{reg}$ [Calvanese et al., 1998a]. Recently, $\mathcal{DLR}_{reg}$ has been extended to $\mathcal{DLR}_{\mu}$, which includes explicit fixpoint constructs on concepts, like those introduced in Section 5.6. The ExpTime-decidability result extends to $\mathcal{DLR}_{\mu}$ as well [Calvanese et al., 1999c].

Recently it has been observed that guarded fragments of first-order logic [Andréka et al., 1996; Grädel, 1999] (see Subsection 4.2.1), which include n-ary relations, share with description logics the "locality" of quantification. This makes them of interest as extensions of description logics with n-ary relations [Grädel, 1998; Lutz et al., 1999]. Such description logics are incomparable in expressive power with $\mathcal{DLR}$ and its extensions: On the one hand the description logics corresponding to guarded fragments allow one to refer, by the use of explicit variables, to components of relations in a more flexible way than is possible in $\mathcal{DLR}$. On the other hand such description logics lack number restrictions, and extending them with number restrictions leads to undecidability of reasoning. Also, reasoning in the guarded fragments is in general NExpTime-hard [Grädel, 1998; 1999] and thus more difficult than in $\mathcal{DLR}$ and its extensions, although PSpace-complete fragments have been identified [Lutz et al., 1999].

5.7.1 Boolean constructs on roles and role inclusion axioms

Observe also that $\mathcal{DLR}$ (and $\mathcal{DLR}_{reg}$) allows Boolean constructs on relations (with negation interpreted as difference) as well as relation inclusion axioms $\mathbf{R} \sqsubseteq \mathbf{R'}$. In fact, $\mathcal{DLR}$ (resp. $\mathcal{DLR}_{reg}$) can be viewed as a generalization of $\mathcal{ALCQI}$ (resp. $\mathcal{ALCQI}_{reg}$) extended with Boolean constructs on atomic and inverse atomic roles. Such extensions of $\mathcal{ALCQI}$ were first studied in [De Giacomo and Lenzerini, 1994c; De Giacomo, 1995], where logical implication was shown to be ExpTime-complete by a reduction to $\mathcal{ALCQI}$ (resp. $\mathcal{ALCQI}_{reg}$). The logics above do not allow atomic roles to be combined with inverse roles in Boolean combinations and role inclusion axioms. Tobies [2001a] shows that, for $\mathcal{ALCQI}$ extended with arbitrary Boolean combinations of atomic and inverse atomic roles, logical implication remains in

EXPTIME. Note that, in all logics above, negation on roles is interpreted as difference. For results on the impact of full negation on roles see [Lutz and Sattler, 2001; Tobies, 2001a].

Horrocks *et al.* [2000b] investigate reasoning in $\mathcal{SHIQ}$, which is $\mathcal{ALCQI}$ extended with roles that are transitive and with role inclusion axioms on arbitrary roles (direct, inverse, and transitive). $\mathcal{SHIQ}$ does not include reflexive–transitive closure. However, transitive roles and role inclusions allow a universal role to be expressed (in a connected model), and hence allow TBoxes to be internalized. Satisfiability and logical implication in $\mathcal{SHIQ}$ are EXPTIME-complete [Tobies, 2001a]. The importance of $\mathcal{SHIQ}$ lies in the fact that it is the logic implemented by the current state-of-the-art DL-based systems (see Chapters 8 and 9).

5.7.2 Structured objects

An alternative way to overcome the limitations that result from the restriction to binary relationships between concepts, is to consider the interpretation domain as being constituted by objects with a complex structure, and extend the description logics with constructs that allow one to specify such a structure [De Giacomo and Lenzerini, 1995]. This approach is in the spirit of object-oriented data models used in databases [Lecluse and Richard, 1989; Bancilhon and Khoshafian, 1989; Hull, 1988], and has the advantage, with respect to introducing relationships, that all aspects of the domain to be modeled can be represented in a uniform way, as concepts whose instances have certain structures. In particular, objects can either be unstructured or have the structure of a *set* or of a *tuple*. For objects having the structure of a set, a particular role allows one to refer to the members of the set, and similarly each component of a tuple can be referred to by means of the (implicitly functional) role that labels it.

In general, reasoning over structured objects can have a very high computational complexity [Kuper and Vardi, 1993]. However, reasoning over a significant fragment of structuring properties can be reduced in polynomial time to reasoning in traditional Description Logics, again by exploiting reification to deal with tuples and sets. Thus, for such a fragment, reasoning can be done in EXPTIME [De Giacomo and Lenzerini, 1995]. An important aspect in exploiting Description Logics for reasoning over structured objects is being able to limit the depth of the structure of an object to avoid infinite nesting of tuples or sets. This requires the use of a well-founded construct, which is a restricted form of fixpoint (see Section 5.6).

5.8 Finite model reasoning

For expressive description logics, in particular for those containing inverse roles and functionality, a TBox may admit only models with an infinite domain [Cosmadakis *et al.*, 1990; Calvanese *et al.*, 1994]. Similarly, there may be TBoxes in which a certain concept can be satisfied only in an infinite model. This is illustrated in the following example by Calvanese [1996c].

Example 5.24 Consider the TBox

$$\mathsf{FirstGuard} \sqsubseteq \mathsf{Guard} \sqcap \forall \mathsf{shields}^-.\bot$$
$$\mathsf{Guard} \sqsubseteq \exists \mathsf{shields} \sqcap \forall \mathsf{shields}.\mathsf{Guard} \sqcap \leqslant 1\,\mathsf{shields}^-.$$

In a model of this TBox, an instance of FirstGuard can have no shields-predecessor, while each instance of Guard can have at most one. Therefore, the existence of an instance of FirstGuard implies the existence of an infinite sequence of instances of Guard, each one connected through the role shields to the following one. This means that FirstGuard can be satisfied in an interpretation with a domain of arbitrary cardinality, but not in interpretations with a finite domain.   ∎

Note that the TBox above is expressed in a very simple description logic, in particular $\mathcal{AL}$ (see Chapter 2) extended with inverse roles and functionality.

A logic is said to have the *finite model property* if every satisfiable formula of the logic admits a *finite model*, i.e., a model with a finite domain. The example above shows that virtually all description logics including functionality, inverse roles, and TBox axioms (or having the ability to internalize them) lack the finite model property. The example shows also that to lose the finite model property, functionality in only one direction is sufficient. In fact, it is well known that *converse*-DPDL, which corresponds to a fragment of $\mathcal{ALCFI}_{reg}$, lacks the finite model property [Kozen and Tiuryn, 1990; Vardi and Wolper, 1986].

For all logics that lack the finite model property, reasoning with respect to unrestricted and finite models are fundamentally different tasks, and this needs to be taken explicitly into account when devising reasoning procedures. Restricting reasoning to finite domains is not common in knowledge representation. However, it is typically of interest in databases, where one assumes that the data available are always finite [Calvanese *et al.*, 1994; 1999e].

When reasoning w.r.t. finite models, some properties that are essential for the techniques developed for unrestricted model reasoning in expressive description logics fail. In particular, all reductions exploiting the tree model property (or similar properties that are based on "unraveling" structures) [Vardi, 1997] cannot be applied since this property does not hold when only finite models are considered. An intuitive justification can be given by observing that, whenever a (finite) model contains a cycle, the unraveling of such a model into a tree generates an infinite structure. Therefore alternative techniques have been developed.

In this section, we study decidability and computational complexity of finite model reasoning over TBoxes expressed in various sublanguages of $\mathcal{ALCQI}$. Specifically, by using techniques based on reductions to linear programming problems, we show that finite concept satisfiability w.r.t. to $\mathcal{ALUNI}$ TBoxes[12] constituted by inclusion axioms only is EXPTIME-complete [Calvanese *et al.*, 1994], and that finite model reasoning in arbitrary $\mathcal{ALCQI}$ TBoxes can be done in deterministic double exponential time [Calvanese, 1996a].

5.8.1 Finite model reasoning using linear inequalities

A procedure for finite model reasoning must specifically address the presence of number restrictions, since it is only in their presence that the finite model property fails. We discuss a method which is indeed based on an encoding of number restrictions into linear inequalities, and which generalizes the one developed by Lenzerini and Nobili [1990] for the Entity–Relationship model with disjoint classes and relationships (hence without IS-A). We first describe the idea underlying the reasoning technique in a simplified case. In the next subsection we show how to apply the technique to various expressive description logics [Calvanese and Lenzerini, 1994b; 1994a; Calvanese *et al.*, 1994; Calvanese, 1996a].

Consider an $\mathcal{ALNI}$ TBox[13] $\mathcal{T}$ containing the following axioms: for each pair of distinct atomic concepts A and A', an axiom $A \sqsubseteq \neg A'$; and for each atomic role P, an axiom of the form $\top \sqsubseteq \forall P.A_2 \sqcap \forall P^-.A_1$, for some atomic concepts A_1 and A_2 (not necessarily distinct). Such axioms enforce that in all models of $\mathcal{T}$ the following hold:

P_1: The atomic concepts have pairwise disjoint extensions.

P_2: Each role is "typed", which means that its domain is included in the extension of an atomic concept A_1, and its codomain is included in the extension of an atomic concept A_2.

---

[12] $\mathcal{ALUNI}$ is the description logic obtained by extending $\mathcal{ALUN}$ (see Chapter 2) with inverse roles.
[13] $\mathcal{ALNI}$ is the description logic obtained by extending $\mathcal{ALN}$ (see Chapter 2) with inverse roles.

Assume further that the only additional axioms in $\mathcal{T}$ are used to impose cardinality constraints on roles and inverse roles, and are of the form

$$\top \sqsubseteq \; \geqslant m_1 P \sqcap \leqslant n_1 P$$
$$\top \sqsubseteq \; \geqslant m_2 P^- \sqcap \leqslant n_2 P^-$$

where m_1, n_1, m_2, and n_2 are positive integers with $m_1 \leq n_1$ and $m_2 \leq n_2$.

Due to the fact that properties P_1 and P_2 hold, the local conditions imposed by number restrictions on the number of successors of each individual are reflected into global conditions on the total number of instances of atomic concepts and roles. Specifically, it is not difficult to see that, for a model $\mathcal{I}$ of such a TBox, and for each P, A_1, A_2, m_1, m_2, n_1, and n_2 as above, the cardinalities of $P^{\mathcal{I}}$, $A_1^{\mathcal{I}}$, and $A_2^{\mathcal{I}}$ must satisfy the following inequalities:

$$m_1 \cdot |A_1^{\mathcal{I}}| \;\leq\; |P^{\mathcal{I}}| \;\leq\; n_1 \cdot |A_1^{\mathcal{I}}|$$
$$m_2 \cdot |A_2^{\mathcal{I}}| \;\leq\; |P^{\mathcal{I}}| \;\leq\; n_2 \cdot |A_2^{\mathcal{I}}|.$$

On the other hand, consider the system $\Psi_{\mathcal{T}}$ of linear inequalities containing for each atomic role P typed by A_1 and A_2 the inequalities

$$m_1 \cdot \mathrm{Var}(A_1) \;\leq\; \mathrm{Var}(P) \;\leq\; n_1 \cdot \mathrm{Var}(A_1)$$
$$m_2 \cdot \mathrm{Var}(A_2) \;\leq\; \mathrm{Var}(P) \;\leq\; n_2 \cdot \mathrm{Var}(A_2) \tag{5.1}$$

where we denote by $\mathrm{Var}(A)$ and $\mathrm{Var}(P)$ the unknowns, ranging over the non-negative integers, corresponding to the atomic concept A and the atomic role P respectively.

It can be shown that, if the only axioms in $\mathcal{T}$ are those mentioned above, then certain non-negative integer solutions of $\Psi_{\mathcal{T}}$ (called *acceptable* solutions) can be put into correspondence with finite models of $\mathcal{T}$. More precisely, for each acceptable solution $\mathcal{S}$, one can construct a model of $\mathcal{T}$ in which the cardinality of each concept or role X is equal to the value assigned by $\mathcal{S}$ to $\mathrm{Var}(X)$ [Lenzerini and Nobili, 1990; Calvanese *et al.*, 1994; Calvanese, 1996c]. Moreover, given $\Psi_{\mathcal{T}}$, it is possible to verify, in time polynomial in its size, whether it admits an acceptable solution.

This property can be exploited to check finite satisfiability of an atomic concept A w.r.t. a TBox $\mathcal{T}$ as follows:

1. Construct the system $\Psi_{\mathcal{T}}$ of inequalities corresponding to $\mathcal{T}$.
2. Add to $\Psi_{\mathcal{T}}$ the inequality $\mathrm{Var}(A) > 0$, which enforces that the solutions correspond to models in which the cardinality of the extension of A is positive.
3. Check whether $\Psi_{\mathcal{T}}$ admits an acceptable solution.

Observe that for simple TBoxes of the form described above, this method works in polynomial time, since (i) Ψ_T is of size polynomial in the size of T, and can also be constructed in polynomial time, and (ii) checking the existence of acceptable solutions of Ψ_T can be done in time polynomial in its size. Notice also that the applicability of the technique heavily relies on conditions P_1 and P_2, which ensure that, from an acceptable solution of Ψ_T, a model of T can be constructed.

5.8.2 Finite model reasoning in expressive Description Logics

The method we have presented above is not directly applicable to more complex languages or TBoxes not respecting the particular form above. In order to extend it to more general cases we make use of the following observation: Linear inequalities capture global constraints on the total number of instances of concepts and roles. So we have to represent local constraints expressed by number restrictions by means of global constraints. This can be done only if P_1 and the following generalization of P_2 hold:

P_2': For each atomic role P and each concept expression C appearing in T, the domain of P is either included in the extension of C or disjoint from it. Similarly for the codomain of P.

This condition guarantees that, in a model, all instances of a concept "behave" in the same way, and thus the local constraints represented by number restrictions are indeed correctly captured by the global constraints represented by the system of inequalities.

It is possible to enforce conditions P_1 and P_2' for expressive description logics, by first transforming the TBox, and then deriving the system of inequalities from the transformed version. We briefly sketch the technique to decide finite concept satisfiability in $\mathcal{ALUNI}$ TBoxes consisting of *specializations*, i.e., inclusion axioms in which the concept on the left-hand side is atomic. A detailed account of the technique and an analysis of its computational complexity has been presented by Calvanese [1996c].

First of all, it is easy to see that, by introducing at most a linear number of new atomic concepts and TBox axioms, we can transform the TBox into an equivalent one in which the nesting of constructs is eliminated. Specifically, in such a TBox the concept on the right-hand side of an inclusion axiom is of the form L, $L_1 \sqcup L_2$, $\forall R.L$, $\geqslant n\, R$, or $\leqslant n\, R$, where L is an atomic or negated atomic concept. For example, given the axiom

$$A \sqsubseteq C_1 \sqcup C_2$$

where C_1 and C_2 do not have the form above, we introduce two new atomic concepts A_{C_1} and A_{C_2}, and replace the axiom above by the following ones:

$$
\begin{aligned}
A &\sqsubseteq A_{C_1} \sqcup A_{C_2} \\
A_{C_1} &\sqsubseteq C_1 \\
A_{C_2} &\sqsubseteq C_2.
\end{aligned}
$$

Then, to ensure that conditions P_1 and P'_2 are satisfied, we use instead of atomic concepts, sets of atomic concepts, called *compound concepts*[14] and instead of atomic roles, so called *compound roles*. Each compound role is a triple $(P, \widehat{C}_1, \widehat{C}_2)$ consisting of an atomic role P and two compound concepts $\widehat{C}_1$ and $\widehat{C}_2$. Intuitively, the instances of a compound concept $\widehat{C}$ are all those individuals of the domain that are instances of all concepts in $\widehat{C}$ and are not instances of any concept not in $\widehat{C}$. A compound role $(P, \widehat{C}_1, \widehat{C}_2)$ is interpreted as the restriction of role P to the pairs whose first component is an instance of $\widehat{C}_1$ and whose second component is an instance of $\widehat{C}_2$.

This means that two different compound concepts have necessarily disjoint extensions, and hence that the property corresponding to P_1 holds. The same observation holds for two different compound roles $(P, \widehat{C}_1, \widehat{C}_2)$ and $(P, \widehat{C}'_1, \widehat{C}'_2)$ that correspond to the same role P. Moreover, for compound roles, the property corresponding to property P_2 holds by definition, and, considering that the TBox contains only specializations and that nesting of constructs has been eliminated, P'_2 also holds.

We first consider the set $\mathcal{T}'$ of axioms in the TBox that do not involve number restrictions. Such axioms force certain compound concepts and compound roles to be *inconsistent*, i.e., have an empty extension in all interpretations that satisfy $\mathcal{T}'$. For example, the axiom $A_1 \sqsubseteq \neg A_2$ makes all compound concepts that contain both A_1 and A_2 inconsistent. Similarly, the axiom $A_1 \sqsubseteq \forall P.A_2$ makes all compound roles $(P, \widehat{C}_1, \widehat{C}_2)$ such that $\widehat{C}_1$ contains A_1 and $\widehat{C}_2$ does not contain A_2 inconsistent. Checking whether a given compound concept is inconsistent essentially amounts to evaluating a propositional formula in a given propositional model (the one corresponding to the compound concept), and hence can be done in time polynomial in the size of the TBox. Similarly, one can check in time polynomial in the size of the TBox whether a given compound role is inconsistent. Observe, however, that since the total number of compound concepts and roles is exponential in the number of atomic concepts in the TBox, doing the check for all compound concepts and roles takes in general exponential time.

---

[14] A similar technique, called *atomic decomposition* there, was used by Ohlbach and Koehler [1999].

Once the consistent compound concepts and roles have been determined, we can introduce for each of them an unknown in the system of inequalities (the inconsistent compound concepts and roles are discarded). The axioms in the TBox involving number restrictions are taken into account by encoding them into suitable linear inequalities. Such inequalities are derived in a way similar to inequalities (5.1), except that now each inequality involves one unknown corresponding to a compound concept and a sum of unknowns corresponding to compound roles.

Then, to check finite satisfiability of an atomic concept A, we can add to the system the inequality

$$\sum_{\widehat{C} \subseteq 2^A \mid A \in \widehat{C}} \text{Var}(\widehat{C}) \geq 1$$

which forces the extension of A to be nonempty. Again, if the system admits an acceptable solution, then we can construct from such a solution a finite model of the TBox in which A is satisfied; if no such solution exists, then A is not finitely satisfiable. To check finite satisfiability of an arbitrary concept C, we can introduce a new concept name A, add to the TBox the axiom $A \sqsubseteq C$, and then check the satisfiability of A. Indeed, if A is finitely satisfiable, then so is C. Conversely, if the original TBox admits a finite model $\mathcal{I}$ in which C has a nonempty extension, then we can simply extend $\mathcal{I}$ to A by interpreting A as $C^{\mathcal{I}}$, thus obtaining a finite model of the TBox plus the additional axiom in which A is satisfied.

The system of inequalities can be effectively constructed in time exponential in the size of the TBox, and checking for the existence of acceptable solutions is polynomial in the size of the system [Calvanese *et al.*, 1994; Calvanese, 1996a]. Moreover, since verifying concept satisfiability is already EXPTIME-hard for TBoxes consisting of specializations only and expressed in the much simpler language $\mathcal{ALU}$ [Calvanese, 1996b], the above method provides a computationally optimal reasoning procedure.

Theorem 5.25 *Finite concept satisfiability in $\mathcal{ALUNI}$ TBoxes consisting of specializations only is EXPTIME-complete.*

The method can be extended to decide finite concept satisfiability for a wider class of TBoxes, in which a negated atomic concept and, more generally, an arbitrary Boolean combination of atomic concepts may appear on the left-hand side of axioms. In particular, this makes it possible to deal also with knowledge bases containing definitions of concepts that are Boolean combinations of atomic concepts, and to reason on such knowledge bases in deterministic exponential time. Since $\mathcal{ALUNI}$ is not closed under negation, we cannot immediately reduce logical implication to concept satisfiability. However, the technique presented above can be adapted in specific cases to decide also finite logical implication in deterministic exponential time [Calvanese, 1996c].

A further extension of the above method can be used to decide logical implication in $\mathcal{ALCQI}$. The technique uses two successive transformations on the TBox, each of which introduces a worst-case exponential blowup, and a final polynomial encoding into a system of linear inequalities [Calvanese, 1996c; 1996a].

Theorem 5.26 *Logical implication w.r.t. finite models in $\mathcal{ALCQI}$ can be decided in worst-case deterministic double exponential time.*

For more expressive description logics, and in particular for all those description logics containing the construct for reflexive–transitive closure of roles, the decidability of finite model reasoning is still an open problem. Decidability of finite model reasoning for $\mathcal{C}^2$, i.e., first-order logic with two variables and counting quantifiers (see also Chapter 4, Section 4.2) was shown recently [Grädel *et al.*, 1997b]. $\mathcal{C}^2$ is a logic that is strictly more expressive than $\mathcal{ALCQI}$ TBoxes, since it allows one, for example, to impose cardinality restrictions on concepts [Baader *et al.*, 1996] or to use the full negation of a role. However, apart from decidability, no complexity bound is known for finite model reasoning in $\mathcal{C}^2$.

Techniques for finite model reasoning have also been studied in databases. In the relational model, the interaction between inclusion dependencies and functional dependencies causes the loss of the finite model property, and finite implication of dependencies under various assumptions has been investigated by Cosmadakis *et al.* [1990]. A method for finite model reasoning has been presented by Calvanese and Lenzerini [1994b; 1994a] in the context of a semantic and an object-oriented database model, respectively. The reasoning procedure, which represents a direct generalization of the one discussed above to relations of arbitrary arity, does not exploit reification to handle relations (see Section 5.7) but directly encodes the constraints on them into a system of linear inequalities.

5.9 Undecidability results

Several additional DL constructs besides those discussed in the previous sections have been proposed in the literature. In this section we present the most important of these extensions, discussing how they influence decidability, and what modifications to the reasoning procedures are needed to take them into account. In particular, we discuss Boolean constructs on roles, variants of role-value-maps or role agreements, and number restrictions on complex roles. Most of these constructs lead to undecidability of reasoning, if used in an unrestricted way. Roughly speaking, this is mainly due to the fact that the tree model property is lost [Vardi, 1997].

5.9.1 Boolean constructs on complex roles

In those Description Logics that include regular expressions over roles, such as $\mathcal{ALCQI}_{reg}$, since regular languages are closed under intersection and complementation, the intersection of roles and the complement of a role are already expressible, if we consider them applied to the set of role expressions. Here we consider the more common approach in PDLs, namely to regard Boolean operators as applied to the binary relations denoted by complex roles. The logics thus obtained are more expressive than traditional PDL [Harel, 1984] and reasoning is usually harder. We notice that the semantics immediately implies that intersection of roles can be expressed by means of union and complementation.

Satisfiability in PDL augmented with intersection of arbitrary programs is decidable in deterministic double exponential time [Danecki, 1984], and so is satisfiability in $\mathcal{ALC}_{reg}$ augmented with intersection of complex roles, even though these logics have neither the tree model nor the finite model property. On the other hand, satisfiability in PDL augmented with complementation of programs is undecidable [Harel, 1984], and so is reasoning in $\mathcal{ALC}_{reg}$ augmented with complementation of complex roles. Also, DPDL augmented with intersection of complex roles is highly undecidable [Harel, 1985; 1986], and since global functionality of roles (which corresponds to determinism of programs) can be expressed by means of local functionality, the undecidability carries over to $\mathcal{ALCF}_{reg}$ augmented with intersection of roles.

These proofs of undecidability make use of a general technique based on the reduction from the unbounded *tiling* (or *domino*) *problem* [Berger, 1966; Robinson, 1971], which is the problem of checking whether a quadrant of the integer plane can be tiled using a finite set of tile type – i.e., square tiles with a color on each side – in such a way that adjacent tiles have the same color on the sides that touch.[15] We sketch the idea of the proof using the terminology

---

[15] In fact the reduction is from the Π_1^1-complete – and thus highly undecidable – recurring tiling problem [Harel, 1986], where one additionally requires that a certain tile occurs infinitely often on the x-axis.

of description logics, instead of that of PDLs. The reduction uses two roles right and up which are globally functional (i.e., $\leqslant 1$ right, $\leqslant 1$ up) and denote pairs of tiles that are adjacent in the x and y directions, respectively. By means of intersection of roles, right and up are constrained to effectively define a two-dimensional grid. This is achieved by imposing for each point of the grid (i.e., reachable through rightand up) that by following right $\circ$ up one reaches a point reached also by following up $\circ$ right:

$$\forall(\text{right} \sqcup \text{up})^*.\exists((\text{right} \circ \text{up}) \sqcap (\text{up} \circ \text{right})).$$

To enforce this condition, the use of intersection of compositions of atomic roles is essential. Reflexive–transitive closure (i.e., $\forall(\text{right} \sqcup \text{up})^*.C$) is then also exploited to impose the required constraints on all tiles of the grid. Observe that, in the above reduction, one can use TBox axioms instead of reflexive–transitive closure to enforce the necessary conditions in every point of the grid.

The question arises whether decidability can be preserved if one restricts Boolean operations to basic roles, i.e., atomic roles and their inverse. This is indeed the case if complementation of basic roles is used only to express difference of roles, as demonstrated by the EXPTIME decidability of $\mathcal{DLR}$ and its extensions, in which intersection and difference of relations are allowed (see Section 5.7).

5.9.2 Role-value-maps

Another construct, which stems from frame systems, and which provides an additional useful means to specify structural properties of concepts, is the so called *role-value-map* [Brachman and Schmolze, 1985], which comes in two forms: An *equality role-value-map*, denoted $R_1 = R_2$, represents the individuals o such that the set of individuals that are connected to o via role R_1 equals the set of individuals connected to o via role R_2. The second form of role-value-map is *containment role-value-map*, denoted $R_1 \subseteq R_2$, whose semantics is defined analogously, using set inclusion instead of set equality. Using these constructs, one can denote, for example, by means of owns $\circ$ made_in $\subseteq$ lives_in the set of all persons that own only products manufactured in the country they live in.

When role-value-maps are added, the logic loses the tree model property, and this construct leads immediately to undecidability of reasoning when applied to *role chains* (i.e., compositions of atomic roles). For $\mathcal{ALC}_{reg}$, this can be shown by a reduction from the tiling problem in a similar way to that used in [Harel, 1985] for DPDL with intersection of roles. In this case, the concept right ∘ up = up ∘ right involving role-value-map can be used instead of role intersection to define the constraints on the grid. The proof is slightly more involved than that for DPDL, since one needs to take into account that the roles right and up are not functional (while in DPDL all programs/roles are functional). However, undecidability holds already for concept subsumption (with respect to an empty TBox) in $\mathcal{AL}$ (in fact $\mathcal{FL}^-$) augmented with role-value-maps, where the roles involved are compositions of atomic roles [Schmidt-Schauß, 1989] – see Chapter 3 for the details of the proof.

As for role intersection, in order to show undecidability, it is necessary to apply role-value-maps to compositions of roles. Indeed, if the application of role-value-maps is restricted to Boolean combinations of basic roles, it can be added to $\mathcal{ALCQI}_{reg}$ without influencing decidability and worst-case complexity of reasoning. This follows directly from the decidability results for the extension with Boolean constructs on atomic and inverse atomic roles (captured by $\mathcal{DLR}$). Indeed, $R_1 \sqsubseteq R_2$ is equivalent to $\forall(R_1 \sqcap \neg R_2).\bot$, and thus can be expressed using difference of roles. We observe also that *universal* and *existential role agreements* introduced in [Hanschke, 1992], which allow one to define concepts by posing various types of constraints that relate the sets of fillers of two roles, can be expressed by means of intersection and difference of roles. Thus reasoning in the presence of role agreements is decidable, provided these constructs are applied only to basic roles.

5.9.3 Number restrictions on complex roles

In $\mathcal{ALCFI}_{reg}$, the use of (qualified) number restrictions is restricted to atomic and inverse atomic roles, which guarantees that the logic has the tree model property. This property is lost, together with decidability, if functional restrictions may be imposed on arbitrary roles. The reduction to show undecidability is analogous to the one used for intersection of roles, except that now functionality of a complex role (i.e., $\leqslant 1\,(\text{right} \circ \text{up}) \sqcup (\text{up} \circ \text{right})$) is used instead of role intersection to define the grid.

An example of decidable logic that does not have the tree model property is obtained by allowing the use of role composition (but not transitive closure) inside number restrictions. Let us denote by $\mathcal{N}(X)$, where X is a subset of $\{\sqcup, \sqcap, \circ, {}^-\}$, unqualified number restrictions on roles that are obtained by applying the role constructs in X to atomic roles. Let us denote by $\mathcal{ALCN}(X)$ the description logic obtained by extending $\mathcal{ALC}$ (see Chapter 2) with number restrictions in $\mathcal{N}(X)$. As shown by Baader and Sattler [1999], concept satisfiability is decidable for the logic $\mathcal{ALCN}(\circ)$, even when extended with number restrictions on union and intersection of role chains of the same length. Notice that decidability for $\mathcal{ALCN}(\circ)$ holds only for reasoning on concept expressions and is lost if one considers reasoning with respect to a TBox (or alternatively adds transitive closure of roles) [Baader and Sattler, 1999]. Reasoning even with respect to the empty TBox is undecidable if one adds to $\mathcal{ALCN}$ number restrictions on more complex roles. In particular, this holds for $\mathcal{ALCN}(\sqcap, \circ)$ (if no constraints on the lengths of the role chains are imposed) and for $\mathcal{ALCN}(\sqcup, \circ, {}^-)$ [Baader and Sattler, 1999]. The reductions again exploit the tiling problem, and make use of number restrictions on complex roles to simulate a universal role that is used for imposing local conditions on all points of the grid.

Summing up, we can state that the borderline between decidability and undecidability of reasoning in the presence of number restrictions on complex roles has been traced quite precisely, although there are still some open problems. E.g., it is not known whether concept satisfiability in $\mathcal{ALCN}(\sqcup, \circ)$ is decidable (although logical implication is undecidable) [Baader and Sattler, 1999].

6

Extensions to Description Logics

Franz Baader
Ralf Küsters
Frank Wolter

Abstract

This chapter considers, on the one hand, extensions of Description Logics by features not available in the basic framework, but considered important for using Description Logics as a modeling language. In particular, it addresses the extensions concerning: concrete domain constraints; modal, epistemic, and temporal operators; probabilities and fuzzy logic; and defaults.

On the other hand, it considers non-standard inference problems for Description Logics, i.e., inference problems that – unlike subsumption or instance checking – are not available in all systems, but have turned out to be useful in applications. In particular, it addresses the non-standard inference problems: least common subsumer and most specific concept; unification and matching of concepts; and rewriting.

6.1 Introduction

Chapter 2 introduces the language $\mathcal{ALCN}$ as a prototypical Description Logic, defines the most important reasoning tasks (like subsumption, instance checking, etc.), and shows how these tasks can be realized with the help of tableau-based algorithms. For many applications, the expressive power of $\mathcal{ALCN}$ is not sufficient to express the relevant terminological knowledge of the application domain. Some of the most important extensions of $\mathcal{ALCN}$ by concept and role constructs have already been briefly introduced in Chapter 2; these and other extensions have then been treated in more detail in Chapter 5. All these extensions are "classical" in the sense that their semantics can easily be defined within the model-theoretic framework introduced in Chapter 2. Although combinations of these constructs may lead to very expressive Description Logics (the unrestricted combination even to undecidable ones), all the Description Logics obtained this way can only be used to represent time-independent, objective, and certain knowledge. In addition, they do not allow "built-in data structures" like numerical domains.

The "nonclassical" language extensions considered in the first part of this chapter try to overcome some of these deficiencies. The extension by *concrete domains* allows us to integrate numerical and other domains in a schematic way into Description Logics. The extension of Description Logics by *modal operators* allows the representation of time-dependent and subjective knowledge (e.g., knowledge about knowledge and belief of intelligent agents). Description Logics that can explicitly represent *time* have also been introduced outside the modal framework. The extension by *epistemic operators* provides a model-theoretic semantics for rules; it can be used to impose "local" closed world assumptions, and to integrate integrity constraints into Description Logics. In order to represent *vague and uncertain knowledge*, different approaches based on probabilistic, possibilistic, and fuzzy logics have been proposed. Finally, non-monotonic Description Logics are obtained by the integration of *defaults* into Description Logics.

When building and maintaining large DL knowledge bases, inference services like subsumption and satisfiability are very helpful, but in general not quite sufficient for an adequate support of the knowledge engineer. For this reason, some DL systems (e.g., CLASSIC) provide their users with additional system services, which can formally be reconstructed as new types of inference problems. In the second part of this chapter we will motivate and introduce the most prominent of these "non-standard" inference problems, and try to give an intuition on how they can be solved.

6.2 Language extensions

The extensions introduced in this section are "nonclassical" in the sense that defining their semantics is not obvious and requires an extension of the model-theoretic framework considered until now; for many (but not all) of these extensions, nonclassical logics (such as modal and non-monotonic logics) are employed to provide the right framework.

6.2.1 Concrete domains

A drawback that all Description Logics introduced until now share is that all the knowledge must be represented on the abstract logical level. In many applications, one would like to be able to refer to concrete domains and predefined predicates on these domains when defining concepts. An example of such a concrete domain could be the set of nonnegative integers, with predicates such as $\geq$ (greater or equal) or $<$ (less than). For example, assume that we want to give an adequate definition of the concept Woman. The first idea could be to use the concept description Human $\sqcap$ Female for this purpose. However, a newborn female baby would probably not be called a woman, and neither would a three-year-old toddler. Thus, as an additional property, one could require that a female human being should be old enough (e.g., at least 18) to be called a woman. In order to express this property, one would like to introduce a new (functional) role has-age, and define Woman by an expression of the form Human $\sqcap$ Female $\sqcap$ $\exists$has-age.$\geq_{18}$. Here $\geq_{18}$ stands for the unary predicate $\{n \mid n \geq 18\}$ of all nonnegative integers greater than or equal to 18.

Stating such properties directly with reference to a given numerical domain seems to be easier and more natural than encoding them somehow into abstract concept expressions. In addition, such a direct representation makes it possible to use existing reasoners for the concrete domain. For example, we could have also decided to introduce a new atomic concept AtLeast18 to express the property of being at least 18 years old. However, if for some reason we also need the property of being at least 21 years old, we must make sure that the appropriate subsumption relationship between AtLeast18 and AtLeast21 is asserted as well. While this could still be done by adding appropriate inclusion axioms, it does not appear to be an elegant solution, and it would still not take care of other relationships, e.g., the fact that AtLeast18 $\sqcap$ AtMost16 is unsatisfiable. In contrast, an appropriate reasoner for intervals of nonnegative integers would automatically take care of these relationships.

The need for such a language extension was already evident to the designers of early DL systems such as MESON [Edelmann and Owsnicki, 1986; Patel-Schneider *et al.*, 1990], K-REP [Mays *et al.*, 1988; 1991a], andCLASSIC [Brachman *et al.*, 1991; Borgida and Patel-Schneider, 1994]: in addition to abstract individuals, these systems also allow one to refer to "concrete" individuals such as numbers and strings. Both the CLASSIC and the K-REP reasoner can deal correctly with intervals, whereas in MESON the user had to supply the adequate relationships between the concrete predicates in a separate hierarchy. All these approaches are, however, ad hoc in the sense that they are restricted to a specific collection of concrete objects.

In contrast, Baader and Hanschke [1991a] propose a scheme for integrating (almost) arbitrary concrete domains into Description Logics. This extension was designed such that:

- it still has a formal declarative semantics that is very close to the usual semantics employed for Description Logics;
- it is possible to combine the tableau-based algorithms available for Description Logics with existing reasoning algorithms in the concrete domain in order to obtain the appropriate algorithms for the extension;
- it provides a scheme for extending Description Logics by various concrete domains rather than constructing a single ad hoc extension for a specific concrete domain.

In the following, we will first introduce the original proposal by Baader and Hanschke, and then describe two extensions of this proposal [Hanschke, 1992; Haarslev *et al.*, 1999].

6.2.1.1 The family of Description Logics $\mathcal{ALC}(\mathcal{D})$

Before we can define the members of this family of Description Logics, we must formalize the notion of a concrete domain.

Definition 6.1 A *concrete domain* $\mathcal{D}$ consists of a set $\Delta^{\mathcal{D}}$, the domain of $\mathcal{D}$, and a set $pred(\mathcal{D})$, the predicate names of $\mathcal{D}$. Each predicate name $P \in pred(\mathcal{D})$ is associated with an arity n, and an n-ary predicate $P^{\mathcal{D}} \subseteq (\Delta^{\mathcal{D}})^n$.

Let us illustrate this definition by examples of interesting concrete domains. Let us start with some numerical ones:

- The concrete domain $\mathcal{N}$, which we have employed in our introductory example, has the set $\mathbb{N}$ of all nonnegative integers as its domain, and $pred(\mathcal{N})$ consists of the binary predicate names $<, \leq, \geq, >$ and the unary predicate names $<_n, \leq_n, \geq_n, >_n$ for $n \in \mathbb{N}$, which are interpreted by predicates on $\mathbb{N}$ in the obvious way.
- The concrete domain $\mathcal{R}$ has the set $\mathbb{R}$ of all real numbers as its domain, and the predicates of $\mathcal{R}$ are given by formulae that are built by first-order means (i.e., by using Boolean connectives and quantifiers) from equalities and inequalities between integer polynomials in several indeterminates. For example, $x + z^2 = y$ is an equality between the polynomials $p(x, z) = x + z^2$ and $q(y) = y$; and $x > y$ is an inequality between very simple polynomials. From these equalities and inequalities one can for instance build the formulae $\exists z.(x + z^2 = y)$ and $\exists z.(x + z^2 = y) \lor (x > y)$. The first formula yields a predicate name of arity 2 (since it has two free variables), and it is easy to see that the associated predicate is $\{(r, s) \mid r$ and s are real numbers and $r \leq s\}$. Consequently, the predicate associated to the second formula is $\{(r, s) \mid r$ and s are real numbers$\} = \mathbb{R} \times \mathbb{R}$.
- The concrete domain $\mathcal{Z}$ is defined just like $\mathcal{R}$, with the only difference that $\Delta^{\mathcal{Z}}$ is the set of all integers instead of all real numbers.

In addition to numerical domains, Definition 6.1 also captures more abstract domains:

- A given (fixed) relational database DB can be seen as a concrete domain $\mathcal{DB}$, whose domain is the set of atomic values occurring in DB, and whose predicates are the relations that can be defined over DB using a query language (such as SQL).
- One can also consider Allen's interval calculus [Allen, 1983] as concrete domain $\mathcal{IC}$. Here $\Delta^{\mathcal{IC}}$ consists of time intervals, and the predicates are built from Allen's basic interval relations (such as before, after, ...) with the help of Boolean connectives.
- Instead of time intervals one can also consider spatial regions (e.g., in $\mathbb{R} \times \mathbb{R}$), and use as predicates Boolean combinations of the basic relations of the Region Connection Calculus RCC-8 [Randell *et al.*, 1992; Bennett, 1997].

Although the syntax and semantics of Description Logics extended by concrete domains could be defined with the general notion of a concrete domain introduced in Definition 6.1, the requirement that the extended language should still have decidable reasoning problems adds some additional restrictions.

To be able to compute the negation normal form of concepts in the extended language, we must require that the set of predicate names of the concrete domain is *closed under negation*, i.e., if P is an n-ary predicate name in $pred(\mathcal{D})$ then there has to exist a predicate name Q in $pred(\mathcal{D})$ such that $Q^{\mathcal{D}} = (\Delta^{\mathcal{D}})^n \setminus P^{\mathcal{D}}$. We will refer to this predicate name by $\overline{P}$. In addition, we need a unary predicate name that denotes the predicate $\Delta^{\mathcal{D}}$. The domain $\mathcal{N}$ from above satisfies these two properties since, e.g., $\overline{<_n} = \geq_n$ and $(\geq_0)^{\mathcal{N}} = \mathbb{N}$.

Let us now clarify what kind of reasoning mechanisms are required in the concrete domain. Let $P_1, \ldots, P_k$ be k (not necessarily different) predicate names in $pred(\mathcal{D})$ of arities $n_1, \ldots, n_k$. We consider the conjunction

$$\bigwedge_{i=1}^{k} P_i(\underline{x}^{(i)}).$$

Here $\underline{x}^{(i)}$ stands for an n_i-tuple $(x_1^{(i)}, \ldots, x_{n_i}^{(i)})$ of variables. It is important to note that neither all variables in one tuple nor those in different tuples are assumed to be distinct. Such a conjunction is said to be *satisfiable* iff there exists an assignment of elements of $\Delta^{\mathcal{D}}$ to the variables such that the conjunction becomes true in $\mathcal{D}$. We will call the problem of deciding satisfiability of finite conjunctions of this form the *satisfiability problem* for $\mathcal{D}$.

Definition 6.2 The concrete domain $\mathcal{D}$ is called *admissible* iff (i) the set of its predicate names is closed under negation and contains a name $\top_{\mathcal{D}}$ for $\Delta^{\mathcal{D}}$, and (ii) the satisfiability problem for $\mathcal{D}$ is decidable.

With the exception of $\mathcal{Z}$, all the concrete domains introduced above are admissible. For example, decidability of the satisfiability problem for $\mathcal{R}$ is a consequence of Tarski's decidability result for real arithmetic [Tarski, 1951; Collins, 1975]. In contrast, the undecidability of the satisfiability problem for $\mathcal{Z}$ is a consequence of the undecidability of Hilbert's 10th problem [Matiyasevich, 1971; Davis, 1973].

In the following, we will take the language $\mathcal{ALC}$ as the (prototypical) starting point of our extension.[1] In the following, let $\mathcal{D}$ be an arbitrary (but fixed) concrete domain. The interface between $\mathcal{ALC}$ and the concrete domain is inspired by the agreement construct between chains of functional roles (see Chapter 2, Subsection 2.4.3). With this construct one can, for example, express the concept of all women whose father and husband are of the same age by the expression Woman $\sqcap$ has-father $\circ$ has-age $\doteq$ has-husband $\circ$ has-age. However, one cannot express that the husband is even older than the father. This becomes possible if we take the concrete domain $\mathcal{N}$. Then we can simply write

$$\text{Woman} \sqcap \exists(\text{has-father} \circ \text{has-age}, \text{has-husband} \circ \text{has-age}).<.$$

More generally, our extension, called $\mathcal{ALC}(\mathcal{D})$, will allow us to state that a tuple of chains of functional roles satisfies a (not necessarily binary) predicate, which is provided by the concrete domain in question.

Thus, $\mathcal{ALC}(\mathcal{D})$ extends $\mathcal{ALC}$ in two respects. First, the set of role names is now assumed to be partitioned into a set of functional roles and a set of ordinary roles. Both types of roles are allowed to occur in value restrictions and in the existential quantification construct. In addition, there is a new constructor, called *existential predicate restriction*, which is defined by adding to the syntax rules for $\mathcal{ALC}$ the rule

$$C, D \longrightarrow \exists(u_1, \ldots, u_n).P,$$

where P is an n-ary predicate of $\mathcal{D}$ and $u_1, \ldots, u_n$ are chains of functional roles. When considering $\mathcal{ALC}(\mathcal{D})$-ABoxes, one must distinguish between names for abstract and for concrete individuals. Concrete predicates $P \in$

---

[1] All the definitions would, of course, also work for any other concept description language. The approach for combining the reasoning algorithms will work for many other languages, but not for all of them.

pred($\mathcal{D}$) give rise to additional ABox assertions of the form $P(x_1, \ldots, x_n)$, where $x_1, \ldots, x_n$ are names for concrete individuals.

Definition 6.3 An *interpretation* $\mathcal{I}$ for $\mathcal{ALC}(\mathcal{D})$ consists of a set $\Delta^{\mathcal{I}}$, the abstract domain of the interpretation, and an interpretation function. The abstract domain and the given concrete domain must be disjoint, i.e., $\Delta^{\mathcal{D}} \cap \Delta^{\mathcal{I}} = \emptyset$. As before, the interpretation function associates with each concept name a subset of $\Delta^{\mathcal{I}}$ and with each ordinary role name a binary relation on $\Delta^{\mathcal{I}}$. The new feature is that the functional roles are now interpreted by partial functions from $\Delta^{\mathcal{I}}$ into $\Delta^{\mathcal{I}} \cup \Delta^{\mathcal{D}}$. If $u = f_1 \circ \cdots \circ f_n$ is a chain of functional roles, then $u^{\mathcal{I}}$ denotes the composition $f_1^{\mathcal{I}} \circ \cdots \circ f_n^{\mathcal{I}}$ of the partial functions $f_1^{\mathcal{I}}, \ldots, f_n^{\mathcal{I}}$.

The semantics of the usual $\mathcal{ALC}$-constructors is defined as before. In particular, this means that complex concept descriptions are always interpreted as subsets of the abstract domain $\Delta^{\mathcal{I}}$. The existential predicate restriction is interpreted as follows:

$$(\exists(u_1, \ldots, u_n).P)^{\mathcal{I}} = \{x \in \Delta^{\mathcal{I}} \mid \text{there exist } r_1, \ldots, r_n \in \Delta^{\mathcal{D}} \text{ such that } \\ u_1^{\mathcal{I}}(x) = r_1, \ldots, u_n^{\mathcal{I}}(x) = r_n \text{ and } (r_1, \ldots, r_n) \in P^{\mathcal{D}}\}.$$

Above, we have already seen two examples of concepts of $\mathcal{ALC}(\mathcal{N})$. The following $\mathcal{ALC}(\mathcal{R})$-concepts describe rectangles and squares in $\mathbb{R} \times \mathbb{R}$:

$$\text{Rectangle} = \exists(\text{x}, \text{y}, \text{b}, \text{h}).\text{rectangle-cond},$$
$$\text{Square} = \text{Rectangle} \sqcap \exists(\text{b}, \text{h}).\text{equal},$$

where the concrete predicates rectangle-cond and equal are defined as $\text{equal}(x, y) \Leftrightarrow x = y$ and $\text{rectangle-cond}(x, y, b, h) \Leftrightarrow b > 0 \wedge h > 0$. In rectangle-cond, the first two arguments are assumed to express the x and y coordinates of the lower left corner of the rectangle, while the third and fourth argument express the breadth and height of the rectangle. We leave it to the reader to define the concept "pairs of rectangles" where the first component is a square that is contained in the second component.

A tableau-based algorithm for deciding consistency of $\mathcal{ALC}(\mathcal{D})$-ABoxes for admissible $\mathcal{D}$ was introduced in [Baader and Hanschke, 1991b]. The algorithm has an additional rule that treats existential predicate restrictions according to their semantics. The main new feature is that, in addition to the usual "abstract" clashes, there may be concrete ones, i.e., one must test whether the given combination of concrete predicate assertions is non-contradictory. This is the reason why we must require that the satisfiability problem for $\mathcal{D}$ is decidable. As described in [Baader and Hanschke,

1991b], the algorithm is not in PSPACE. Using techniques similar to the ones employed for $\mathcal{ALC}$ it can be shown, however, that the algorithm can be modified such that it needs only polynomial space [Lutz, 1999b], provided that the satisfiability procedure for $\mathcal{D}$ is in PSPACE. In the presence of acyclic TBoxes, reasoning in $\mathcal{ALC}(\mathcal{D})$ may become NEXPTIME-hard even for rather simple concrete domains with a polynomial satisfiability problem [Lutz, 2001b].

This technique of combining a tableau-based algorithm for the Description Logics with a satisfiability procedure for the concrete domain can be extended to more expressive Description Logics (e.g., $\mathcal{ALCN}$ and $\mathcal{ALCN}$ with agreements and disagreements). However, this is not true for arbitrary Description Logics with tableau-based decision procedures. For example, the technique does not work if the tableau-based algorithm requires some sort of blocking (see Chapter 2, Subsection 2.3.2.4) to ensure termination. Technically, the problem is that concrete predicates can be used to state properties concerning different individuals in the ABox, and that blocking, which is concerned only with the properties of a single individual, cannot take this into account. The main idea underlying an undecidability proof for such a logic is that elements of the concrete domain (e.g., $\mathcal{R}$) can encode configurations of a Turing machine and that one can define a concrete predicate stating that one configuration is a direct successor of the other. Finally, the Description Logic must provide some means of representing sequences of configurations of arbitrary length, which is usually the case for Description Logics requiring blocking. More concretely, it was shown in [Baader and Hanschke, 1992] (by reduction from Post's correspondence problem) that satisfiability of concepts becomes undecidable if transitive closure (of a single functional role) is added to $\mathcal{ALC}(\mathcal{R})$. Post's correspondence problem can also be used to show undecidability of $\mathcal{ALC}(\mathcal{R})$ with general inclusion axioms, although one cannot use exactly the same reduction as for transitive closure (see [Haarslev et al., 1998] for a similar reduction). A notable exception to the rule of thumb that concrete domains together with general inclusion axioms lead to undecidability has recently been shown by Lutz [2001a], who combines $\mathcal{ALC}$ with the concrete domain of rational numbers with equality and inequality predicates.

6.2.1.2 Predicate restrictions on role chains

The role chains occurring in predicate restrictions of $\mathcal{ALC}(\mathcal{D})$ are restricted to chains of functional roles. In [Hanschke, 1992] this restriction was removed. To be more precise, the syntax rules for $\mathcal{ALC}$ are extended by the two rules

$$C, D \longrightarrow \exists(u_1, \ldots, u_n).P \mid \forall(u_1, \ldots, u_n).P,$$

where P is an n-ary predicate of $\mathcal{D}$ and $u_1, \ldots, u_n$ are chains of (not necessarily functional) roles.

In this setting, ordinary roles are also allowed to have fillers in the concrete domain, i.e., both functional and ordinary roles are interpreted as subsets of $\Delta^{\mathcal{I}} \times (\Delta^{\mathcal{I}} \cup \Delta^{\mathcal{D}})$. Of course, functional roles must still be be interpreted as partial functions. The extension of the predicate restrictions is defined as

$$(\exists(u_1, \ldots, u_n).P)^{\mathcal{I}} = \{x \in \Delta^{\mathcal{I}} \mid \text{there exist } r_1, \ldots, r_n \in \Delta^{\mathcal{D}} \text{ such that} \\ (x, r_1) \in u_1^{\mathcal{I}}, \ldots, (x, r_n) \in u_n^{\mathcal{I}} \text{ and } (r_1, \ldots, r_n) \in P^{\mathcal{D}}\},$$

$$(\forall(u_1, \ldots, u_n).P)^{\mathcal{I}} = \{x \in \Delta^{\mathcal{I}} \mid \text{for all } r_1, \ldots, r_n: (x, r_1) \in u_1^{\mathcal{I}}, \ldots, (x, r_n) \in u_n^{\mathcal{I}} \\ \text{implies } (r_1, \ldots, r_n) \in P^{\mathcal{D}}\}.$$

Using the universal predicate restriction one can, for example, define the concept of parents all of whose children are younger than 4 by the description

$$\text{Parent} \sqcap \forall \text{has-child} \circ \text{has-age.} \leq_4 .$$

Hanschke [1992] shows that an extension of the Description Logic we have just introduced still has a decidable ABox consistency problem, provided that the concrete domain $\mathcal{D}$ is admissible.

6.2.1.3 Predicate restrictions defining roles

In [Haarslev et al., 1998; 1999], $\mathcal{ALC}(\mathcal{D})$ was extended in a different direction: predicate restrictions can now also be used to define new roles. To be more precise, if P is a predicate of $\mathcal{D}$ of arity $n + m$, and $u_1, \ldots, u_n$ and $v_1, \ldots, v_m$ are chains of functional roles, then

$$\exists(u_1, \ldots, u_n)(v_1, \ldots, v_m).P$$

is a complex role. These complex roles may be used both in value restrictions and in the existential quantification construct. The semantics of complex roles is defined as

$$(\exists(u_1, \ldots, u_n)(v_1, \ldots, v_m).P)^{\mathcal{I}} = \\ \{(x, y) \in \Delta^{\mathcal{I}} \times \Delta^{\mathcal{I}} \mid \text{there exist } r_1, \ldots, r_n, s_1, \ldots, s_m \in \Delta^{\mathcal{D}} \text{ such that} \\ u_1^{\mathcal{I}}(x) = r_1, \ldots, u_n^{\mathcal{I}}(x) = r_n, v_1^{\mathcal{I}}(y) = s_1, \ldots, v_m^{\mathcal{I}}(y) = s_m \\ \text{and } (r_1, \ldots, r_n, s_1, \ldots, s_m) \in P^{\mathcal{D}}\}.$$

For example, the complex role $\exists(\text{has-age})(\text{has-age}).>$ consists of all pairs of individuals having an age such that the first is older than the second.

Unfortunately, it has turned out that the full logic obtained by this extension has an undecidable satisfiability problem [Haarslev et al., 1998]. To overcome this problem, Haarslev *et al.* [1999] define syntactic restrictions on concepts such that the restricted language (i) is closed under negation, and (ii) has a decidable ABox consistency problem. Consequently, the subsumption and the instance problem are also decidable. The complexity of reasoning in this Description Logic is investigated in [Lutz, 2001b]. As in the case of acyclic TBoxes, rather simple concrete domains can already make reasoning NEXPTIME-hard.

An approach for integrating arithmetic reasoning into Description Logics that considerably differs from the concrete domain approach described above was proposed by Ohlbach and Koehler [1999].

6.2.2 Modal extensions

Although the Description Logics discussed so far provide a wide choice of constructors, usually they are intended to represent only static knowledge and are not able to express various dynamic aspects such as time-dependence, beliefs of different agents, obligations, etc. For example, in every standard description language we can define a concept "good car" as, say, a car with an air-conditioner:

$$\mathsf{GoodCar} \equiv \mathsf{Car} \sqcap \exists \mathsf{part.Airconditioner.} \qquad (6.1)$$

However, we have no means to represent the subtler knowledge that only John believes (6.1) to be the case, while Mary does not think so:

$$[\textit{John believes}](6.1) \wedge \neg[\textit{Mary believes}](6.1).$$

Nor can we express the fact that (6.1) holds now, but in the future the notion of a good car may change (since, for instance, all cars will have air conditioners):

$$(6.1) \wedge \langle \textit{eventually} \rangle \neg (6.1).$$

A way to bridge this gap seems quite clear and will be discussed in this and the next section: one can simply combine a Description Logic with a suitable modal language treating belief, temporal, deontic or some other intensional operators. However, there are a number of parameters that determine the design of a modal extension of a given Description Logic.

(**I**) First, modal operators can be applied to different kinds of well-formed expressions of the Description Logic.

One may apply them only to conceptual and assertional axioms, thereby forming new axioms of the form

$$[John\ believes](\mathsf{GoodCar} \equiv \mathsf{Car} \sqcap \exists\mathsf{part.Airconditioner}),$$

$$[Mary\ believes]\ \langle eventually \rangle\ (\mathsf{Rich(JOHN)}).$$

Modal operators may also be applied to concepts in order to form new ones:

$$[John\ believes]\mathsf{expensive}$$

i.e., the concept of all objects John believes to be expensive, or

$$\mathsf{HumanBeing} \sqcap \exists\mathsf{child}.[Mary\ believes]\ \langle eventually \rangle\ \mathsf{GoodStudent}$$

i.e., the concept of all human beings with a child that Mary believes will eventually be a good student. By allowing applications of modal operators to both concepts and axioms we obtain expressions of the form

$$[John\ believes](\mathsf{GoodCar} \equiv [Mary\ believes]\mathsf{GoodCar})$$

i.e., John believes that a car is good if and only if Mary thinks so.

Finally, one can supplement the options above with modal operators applicable to roles. For example, using the temporal operator [*always*] (in future) and the role loves, we can form the new role [*always*]loves (which is understood as a relation between objects x and y that holds if and only if x will always love y) to say

$$(\exists[always]\mathsf{loves.Woman})(\mathsf{JOHN})$$

i.e., John will always love the very same woman (but perhaps not only her), which is not the same as $([always]\exists\mathsf{loves.Woman})(\mathsf{JOHN})$.

(II) All these languages are interpreted with the help of the possible worlds semantics, in which the accessibility relations between worlds (or points in time, ...) treat the modal operators, and the worlds themselves are Description Logic interpretations.

The properties of the modal operators are determined by the conditions we impose on the corresponding accessibility relations. For example, by imposing no condition at all we obtain what is known as the minimal normal modal logic **K** – although of definite theoretical interest, it does not have the properties required to model operators like [*agent A knows*], $\langle eventually \rangle$, etc. In the *temporal* case, depending on the application domain we may assume time to be linear and discrete (for example, the usual strict ordering of the natural numbers), or branching, or dense, etc. (see [Gabbay *et al.*, 1994; van Benthem, 1996]). Moreover, we have the possibility to work with intervals instead of points in time (see Subsection 6.2.4). In *epistemic logic*, transitivity of the accessibility relation for agent A's knowledge means what is called *positive introspection* (A knows what A knows), euclideanness corresponds to *negative introspection* (A knows what A does not know), and reflexivity means that everything known by A is true; see Subsection 6.2.3 for a formulation of these principles in terms of Description Logics. For more information and further references consult [Fagin *et al.*, 1995; Meyer and van der Hoek, 1995].

(III) When connecting worlds – that is, ordinary interpretations of the pure description language – by accessibility relations, we are faced with the problem of connecting their objects. Depending on the particular application, we may assume worlds to have arbitrary domains (the *varying domain assumption*), or we may assume that the domain of a world accessible from a world w contains the domain of w (the *expanding domain assumption*), or that all the worlds share the same domain (the *constant domain assumption*); see [van Benthem, 1996] for a discussion in the context of first-order temporal logic. Consider, for instance, the following axioms:

$$\neg[agent\ A\ knows](\mathsf{Unicorn} \equiv \bot)$$
$$([agent\ A\ knows]\neg\mathsf{Unicorn}) \equiv \top.$$

The former means that agent A does not know that unicorns do not exist, while according to the latter, for every existing object, A knows that it is not a unicorn. Such a situation can be modeled under the expanding domain assumption, but these two formulas cannot be simultaneously satisfied in a model with constant domains.

(IV) Finally, one should take into account the difference between *global* (or *rigid*) and *local* (or *flexible*) symbols. In our context, the former are the symbols which have the same extension in every world in the model under consideration, while the latter are those whose interpretation is not fixed. Again the choice between these depends on the application domain: if the knowledge base is talking about employees of a company then the name *John Smith* should probably denote the same person no matter what world we consider, while *President of the company* may refer to different persons in different worlds. For a more detailed discussion consult, e.g., [Fitting, 1993; Kripke, 1980].

To describe the syntax and semantics more precisely we briefly introduce the modal extension $\mathcal{L}^n_{\mathcal{ALC}}$ of $\mathcal{ALC}$ with n unary modal operators $\Box_1, \ldots, \Box_n$, and their duals $\Diamond_1, \ldots, \Diamond_n$.

Definition 6.4 (Concepts, roles, axioms) *Concepts* and *roles* of $\mathcal{L}^n_{\mathcal{ALC}}$ are defined inductively as follows: all concept names are concepts, and if C,

D are concepts, R is a role, and $\Diamond_i$ is a modal operator, then $C \sqcap D$, $\neg C$, $\Diamond_i C$, and $\exists R.C$ are concepts.[2] All role names are roles, and if R is a role, then $\Box_i R$ and $\Diamond_i R$ are roles.

Let C and D be concepts, R a role, and a, b object names. Then expressions of the form $C \equiv D$, $R(a, b)$, and $C(a)$ are axioms. If φ and ψ are axioms then so are $\Diamond_i \varphi$, $\neg \varphi$, and $\varphi \wedge \psi$.

We remind the reader that models of a propositional modal language are based on Kripke frames, i.e., structures of the form $\mathfrak{F} = \langle W, \lhd_1, \ldots, \lhd_n \rangle$ in which each $\lhd_i$ is a binary (accessibility) relation on the set of worlds W. What is going on inside the worlds is of no importance in the propositional framework (see, e.g., [Chagrov and Zakharyaschev, 1997] for more information on propositional modal logics). Models of $\mathcal{L}^n_{\mathcal{ALC}}$ are also constructed on Kripke frames; however, in this case their worlds come equipped with interpretations of $\mathcal{ALC}$.

Definition 6.5 (model) A *model* of $\mathcal{L}^n_{\mathcal{ALC}}$ based on a frame $\mathfrak{F} = \langle W, \lhd_1, \ldots, \lhd_n \rangle$ is a pair $\mathfrak{M} = \langle \mathfrak{F}, I \rangle$ in which I is a function associating with each $w \in W$ an $\mathcal{ALC}$-interpretation

$$I(w) = \langle \Delta^{I,w}, \cdot^{I,w} \rangle.$$

$\mathfrak{M}$ has constant domain iff $\Delta^{I(v)} = \Delta^{I(w)}$, for all $v, w \in W$. $\mathfrak{M}$ has expanding domains iff $\Delta^{I(v)} \subseteq \Delta^{I(w)}$ whenever $v \lhd_i w$, for some i.

Definition 6.6 For a model $\mathfrak{M} = \langle \mathfrak{F}, I \rangle$ and a world w in it, the *extensions* $C^{I,w}$ and $R^{I,w}$, and the *satisfaction relation* $w \models \varphi$ (φ an axiom) are defined inductively. The interesting new steps of the definition are:

1. $x \in (\Diamond_i C)^{I,w}$ iff $\exists v.\, v \rhd_i w$ and $x \in C^{I,v}$;
2. $(x, y) \in (\Diamond_i R)^{I,w}$ iff $\exists v.\, v \rhd_i w$ and $(x, y) \in R^{I,v}$;
3. $w \models \Diamond_i \varphi$ iff $\exists v.\, v \rhd_i w$ and $v \models \varphi$.

An axiom φ (resp. a concept C) is *satisfiable* in a class of models $\mathcal{M}$ if there is a model $\mathfrak{M} \in \mathcal{M}$ and a world w in $\mathfrak{M}$ such that $w \models \varphi$ (resp. $C^{I,w} \neq \emptyset$).

Given a class of frames $\mathcal{K}$, the satisfiability problems for axioms and concepts in $\mathcal{K}$ are the most important reasoning tasks; others are reducible to them (see [Wolter and Zakharyaschev, 1998; 1999b]). Notice that the satisfiability

---

[2] Note that value restrictions (the modal box operators $\Box_i$) need not explicitly be included here since they can be expressed using negation and existential restrictions (the modal diamond operators $\Diamond_i$).

problem for concepts is reducible to that for axioms since $\neg(C \equiv \bot)$ is satisfiable iff C is satisfiable. Also, the satisfiability problem for models with expanding or varying domain is reducible to that for models with constant domain (see [Wolter and Zakharyaschev, 1998]).

We are now going to survey briefly the state of the art in the field. We will restrict ourselves first to modal Description Logics which are not temporal logics. The latter will be considered in Subsection 6.2.4. Chronologically, the first investigations of modal Description Logics are [Laux, 1994; Gräber *et al.*, 1995; Baader and Laux, 1995; Baader and Ohlbach, 1993; 1995]. The papers [Laux, 1994; Gräber *et al.*, 1995] construct multi-agent epistemic Description Logics in which the belief operators apply only to axioms; the accessibility relations are transitive, serial, and euclidean. The decidability of the satisfiability problem for axioms follows immediately from the decidability of both the propositional fragment of the logic and $\mathcal{ALC}$, because in languages without modalized concepts and roles there is no interaction between the modal operators and role quantification (see [Finger and Gabbay, 1992]). Baader and Laux [1995] introduce a Description Logic in which modal operators can be applied to both axioms and concepts (but not to roles); it is interpreted in models with arbitrary accessibility relations under the expanding domain assumption. The decidability of the satisfiability problem for axioms is proved by constructing a complete tableau calculus. This tableau calculus was modified and extended for checking satisfiability in models with constant domain in [Lutz *et al.*, 2002]. It decides satisfiability in constant domain models in NEXPTIME, which matches the lower bound established in [Mosurovic and Zakharyaschev, 1999] (see also [Gabbay *et al.*, 2003]).

The papers [Wolter and Zakharyaschev, 1998; 1999a; 1999c; 1999b; Wolter, 2000; Mosurovic and Zakharyaschev, 1999] investigate the decision problem for various families of modal Description Logics in detail. For example, in [Wolter and Zakharyaschev, 1999c; 1999b] it is shown that the satisfiability problem for arbitrary axioms (possibly containing modalized roles) is decidable in the class of all frames and in the class of polymodal **S5**-frames – frames in which all accessibility relations are equivalence relations – based on constant, expanding, and varying domains. It becomes undecidable, however, if common-knowledge epistemic operators (in the sense of [Fagin *et al.*, 1995]) are added to the language or if the class of frames consists of the flow of time $\langle \mathbb{N}, < \rangle$. In [Wolter and Zakharyaschev, 1999a; 1998] it is shown that for expressive modal languages – like logics with common knowledge operators or Propositional Dynamic Logics – the satisfiability problem for axioms becomes decidable when modalized roles are not included. Wolter [2000] shows that the satisfiability problem for concepts interpreted in frames with global (i.e., world-independent) roles is decidable for expressive modal logics based on $\mathcal{ALC}$ while the satisfiability problem for axioms is undecidable for them. However, even the complexity of the satisfiability problem for concepts becomes non-elementary for these logics [Gabbay *et al.*, 2003]. In fact, for various decidable modal Description Logics only computationally non-elementary decision procedures are known and the precise complexity has not yet been determined (consult [Gabbay *et al.*, 2003] for further results).

The papers [Baader and Ohlbach, 1993; 1995] introduce a multi-dimensional description language that is even more expressive than $\mathcal{L}^n_{\mathcal{ALC}}$ (but without object names). Roughly, in this approach each dimension (object, time, belief, etc.) is represented by a set D_i (of objects, moments of time, possible worlds, etc.), concepts are interpreted as subsets of the cartesian product $\prod_{i=1}^n D_i$, and roles of dimension i as binary relations between n-tuples that may differ only in the ith coordinate. One can quantify over both roles and concepts, *in any dimension*. Thus, in contrast to $\mathcal{L}^n_{\mathcal{ALC}}$ arbitrarily many dimensions are considered and no dimension is labeled as the "modal" or "$\mathcal{ALC}$"-one. This language has turned out to be extremely expressive. The satisfiability problem for the full language is known to be undecidable and even for natural fragments no sound and complete reasoning procedures have appeared. Baader and Ohlbach [1995] provide only a sound satisfiability-checking algorithm for such a fragment.

6.2.3 Epistemic operators

The systems CLASSIC and LOOM make it possible for their users to include *procedural rules* into knowledge bases (see also Chapter 2, Subsection 2.2.5). Such rules take the form

$$C \Rightarrow D,$$

where C and D are concepts. The meaning of a procedural rule is different from the meaning of an inclusion axiom: while $C \sqsubseteq D$ represents conceptual knowledge and says that – no matter what is known about individuals – the concept D subsumes C, the rule $C \Rightarrow D$ represents the incidental fact that "if an individual is known to be an instance of C, then we can conclude that it is an instance of D". Consider the following example: suppose a knowledge base Φ consists of

$$\textsf{GreatLogician} \sqsubseteq \textsf{Professor}, \quad \neg\textsf{Professor}(a).$$

Obviously we can derive $\neg\textsf{GreatLogician}(a)$ from Φ. In this representation we assume a conceptual relation between the terms 'professor' and 'great logician'. More appropriate, however, seems to be the weaker claim that people who are known to be great logicians are professors: let Φ' be the knowledge base which results from Φ when $\textsf{GreatLogician} \sqsubseteq \textsf{Professor}$ is replaced with

$$\textsf{GreatLogician} \Rightarrow \textsf{Professor}.$$

The assertion $\neg\textsf{GreatLogician}(a)$ turns out not to be derivable from Φ'. The *procedural* explanation for this phenomenon is this: in the knowledge base Φ' we do not find an individual belonging to the concept $\textsf{GreatLogician}$. Therefore the rule $\textsf{GreatLogician} \Rightarrow \textsf{Professor}$ does not "fire" and nothing new about the world is derivable by using it. However, Description Logic is aiming at an extensional semantics for frame-based systems, hence it would be desirable to have a precise model-theoretic explanation of the behavior of procedural rules as well.

It turns out that adding an *epistemic operator* together with a possible worlds semantics interpreting it provides us with the required models. Integrating the operator $\mathbf{K}$ – 'the knowledge base knows that' – into $\mathcal{ALC}$ will allow us to rephrase the rule $\textsf{GreatLogician} \Rightarrow \textsf{Professor}$ by the inclusion axiom $\mathbf{K}\textsf{GreatLogician} \sqsubseteq \textsf{Professor}$, which says that all objects that are *known* to be great logicians are professors. Actually, it will turn out that extensions of Description Logics by means of epistemic operators are useful in other contexts as well. We postpone their discussion until we have introduced some technical prerequisites. We will follow [Donini *et al.*, 1992b; 1998a], where the extension of $\mathcal{ALC}$ by epistemic operators was introduced and investigated.

Formulated in terms of Subsection 6.2.2, we consider the language $\mathcal{L}^1_{\mathcal{ALC}}$ in which the modal operator $\Box_1$ (now denoted by $\mathbf{K}$) can be applied to concepts and roles but not to axioms. Following [Donini *et al.*, 1998a] we call this language $\mathcal{ALCK}$. The following principles are assumed to govern the epistemic operator (we formulate them here for $\mathbf{K}$ applied to concepts; the formulation for roles is similar):

- $\mathbf{K}C \sqsubseteq C$ (only true facts are known: if an object is known to be an instance of C, then it is an instance of C);
- $\mathbf{K}C \sqsubseteq \mathbf{KK}C$ (positive introspection: if it is known that an object is an instance of C, then this is known);
- $\neg\mathbf{K}C \sqsubseteq \mathbf{K}\neg\mathbf{K}C$ (negative introspection: if it is not known whether an object is an instance of C, then this is known).

These principles are valid in all models based on a Kripke frame $\mathfrak{F} = \langle W, \lhd \rangle$ iff $\mathfrak{F}$ is an **S5**-frame, or, equivalently, if $\lhd$ is the universal relation on W, i.e., $\lhd = W \times W$. So, we consider frames of the form $\langle W, W \times W \rangle$ only.

We assume also that:

- it is known which object an object name denotes (so, object names are assumed to be global (or rigid) designators),
- the set of existing objects Δ is known and countably infinite (so, we adopt the constant domain assumption).

These assumptions together allow us to simplify the possible worlds semantics considerably: we can identify the set of worlds W with a set of interpretations $\mathcal{M}$ (all having the same countably infinite domain Δ and the same interpretation of the object names) and the accessibility relation is implicitly given as the universal relation on $\mathcal{M}$. Hence, we call any set of interpretations $\mathcal{M}$ satisfying these constraints a *model* (for $\mathcal{ALCK}$) and can define the *extensions* $C^{\mathcal{I},\mathcal{M}}$ and $R^{\mathcal{I},\mathcal{M}}$ of a concept C and a role R in an interpretation $\mathcal{I}$ in $\mathcal{M}$ as follows:

$$
\begin{aligned}
A^{\mathcal{I},\mathcal{M}} &= A^{\mathcal{I}} \text{ for atomic concepts } A \\
P^{\mathcal{I},\mathcal{M}} &= P^{\mathcal{I}} \text{ for atomic roles } P \\
(\neg C)^{\mathcal{I},\mathcal{M}} &= \Delta \setminus C^{\mathcal{I},\mathcal{M}} \\
(C_1 \sqcap C_2)^{\mathcal{I},\mathcal{M}} &= C_1^{\mathcal{I},\mathcal{M}} \cap C_2^{\mathcal{I},\mathcal{M}} \\
(\exists R.C)^{\mathcal{I},\mathcal{M}} &= \{a \in \Delta \mid \exists b. (a,b) \in R^{\mathcal{I},\mathcal{M}} \wedge b \in C^{\mathcal{I},\mathcal{M}}\} \\
(\mathbf{K}C)^{\mathcal{I},\mathcal{M}} &= \bigcap_{\mathcal{J} \in \mathcal{M}} C^{\mathcal{J},\mathcal{M}} \; (= \{a \in \Delta \mid \forall \mathcal{J} \in \mathcal{M}. \, a \in C^{\mathcal{J},\mathcal{M}}\}) \\
(\mathbf{K}R)^{\mathcal{I},\mathcal{M}} &= \bigcap_{\mathcal{J} \in \mathcal{M}} R^{\mathcal{J},\mathcal{M}} \; (= \{(a,b) \in \Delta \mid \forall \mathcal{J} \in \mathcal{M}. \, (a,b) \in R^{\mathcal{J},\mathcal{M}}\}).
\end{aligned}
$$

So, $\mathbf{K}C$ comprises the set of all objects that are instances of C in every world regarded as possible.

An $\mathcal{ALCK}$-*knowledge base* Φ consists of a set of inclusion axioms and ABox assertions whose concepts and roles are in $\mathcal{ALCK}$. A model $\mathcal{M}$ *satisfies* Φ (is a Φ-model) iff all inclusion and membership assertions of Φ are true in every $\mathcal{I} \in \mathcal{M}$.

So far, we have introduced a rather simple version of the epistemic extensions of $\mathcal{ALC}$ discussed in Subsection 6.2.2. In the present subsection, however, we are not interested in the satisfiability of epistemic knowledge bases, but in a relation $\models$ between knowledge bases and assertions such that $\Phi \models \varphi$ iff a knowledge base knows φ under the assumption that "all the knowledge base knows is Φ". For example, if Φ is empty (the knowledge base knows nothing), then both $\neg\mathbf{K}C(a)$ and $\neg\mathbf{K}\neg C(a)$ should be derivable, since the knowledge base does not know whether a is an instance of C or not. On the semantic level this means that we are not interested in arbitrary models satisfying Φ but only in those Φ-models that refute as many $\mathcal{ALC}$-assertions as possible. In other words, we consider Φ-models only with as many worlds as possible (corresponding to the intuition that more worlds are regarded as possible if less is known). For example, if Φ is empty, then the intended models comprise *all* interpretations (with a fixed domain and interpretation of the object names), since all interpretations are regarded as possible by an empty knowledge base. Here are the precise definitions:

Definition 6.7 An *epistemic model* for Φ is a *maximal* non-empty set of interpretations $\mathcal{M}$ satisfying Φ. The knowledge base Φ *logically implies* an assertion φ, written $\Phi \models \varphi$, if every epistemic model $\mathcal{M}$ for Φ satisfies φ.

Consequently, $\models$ is a *non-monotonic* consequence relation: although $\emptyset \models (\neg\mathbf{K}C \wedge \neg\mathbf{K}\neg C)(a)$, we have $C(a) \models \mathbf{K}C(a)$. On the propositional level, this type of reasoning is known as *ground non-monotonic* **S5** (see [Donini *et al.*, 1995; 1997c; Nardi and Rosati, 1995]).

Reasoning with arbitrary $\mathcal{ALCK}$-knowledge-bases has not been investigated. In fact, all applications considered in the literature require only very small fragments of $\mathcal{ALCK}$. In what follows, we shall briefly introduce two such fragments and some of their applications.

6.2.3.1 $\mathcal{ALCK}$ as a query language

We first confine ourselves to knowledge bases that are ordinary $\mathcal{ALC}$-ABoxes. Hence, the epistemic operator $\mathbf{K}$ can be used only in queries. Recall that concept languages can be applied as query languages in a straightforward manner: the answer set of a query consisting of a concept C to a knowledge base Φ comprises the set of individuals a with $\Phi \models C(a)$. Queries with epistemic operators enable us to extract the knowledge which the knowledge base has about its own knowledge. Consider, for example, the knowledge base $\Phi = \{\exists\mathsf{friend.Male}(\mathsf{SUSAN})\}$, which contains incomplete information about Susan. Applications of $\mathbf{K}$ to different concepts and roles in $\exists\mathsf{friend.Male}$ enable us to form a variety of different queries:

- $\exists\mathsf{friend.Male}$; clearly, the answer to this query is $\{\mathsf{SUSAN}\}$.
- $\exists\mathsf{friend.K Male}$; the answer set is empty, since no *known* male is a friend of Susan.
- $\exists\mathbf{K}\mathsf{friend.Male}$; the answer set is empty since we do not find a male individual who is *known* to be a friend of Susan.

- **K**∃friend.Male; the answer set is {SUSAN} since the knowledge base *knows* that Susan has a friend who is male.

Observe that, for $\Phi' = \Phi \cup \{\mathsf{friend(SUSAN, BOB), Male(BOB)}\}$, the answer set would consist of SUSAN in all four cases. We refer the reader to [Donini *et al.*, 1992b; 1998a] for more examples.

Epistemic queries can also be used to formulate *integrity constraints*. Recall that integrity constraints can be viewed as epistemic sentences that state what a knowledge base must know about the world [Reiter, 1990]. For example, suppose that we want to rule out those knowledge bases that are uncertain about whether a given course is a course for undergraduates or graduates. This can be expressed using the query

$$\neg\mathbf{K}\,\mathsf{Course} \sqcup (\mathbf{K}\,\mathsf{Undergraduate} \sqcup \mathbf{K}\,\mathsf{Graduate}). \tag{6.2}$$

A knowledge base satisfies the integrity constraint iff it logically implies the assertion (6.2)(a), for every object name a appearing in it. Observe, by the way, that the query ¬Course ⊔ (Undergraduate ⊔ Graduate) has a different meaning: although $\emptyset \models (6.2)(a)$, for all a (corresponding to the intention), $\emptyset \not\models (\neg\mathsf{Course} \sqcup (\mathsf{Undergraduate} \sqcup \mathsf{Graduate}))(a)$. We refer the reader to [Levesque, 1984; Lifschitz, 1991; Reiter, 1990] for a discussion of the use of epistemic queries in general.

What is the computational complexity of querying $\mathcal{ALC}$-ABoxes by means of $\mathcal{ALCK}$-concepts? The following result is proved in [Donini *et al.*, 1992b; 1998a]:

Theorem 6.8 *There is an algorithm for deciding, given an $\mathcal{ALC}$-ABox Σ, an object name a, and an $\mathcal{ALCK}$-concept C, whether $\Sigma \models C(a)$. More precisely, the problem $\Sigma \models C(a)$ is PSPACE-complete (w.r.t. the size of C and Σ).*

Recall that querying $\mathcal{ALC}$-ABoxes with $\mathcal{ALC}$-concepts is PSPACE-complete as well [Hollunder, 1996]. Thus, the additional epistemic operators in queries do not cause any increase of the computational complexity.

6.2.3.2 Semantics for procedural rules

To capture the meaning of procedural rules as discussed above (and in Chapter 2, Section 2.2.5), we must admit assertions of the form $\mathbf{K}C \sqsubseteq D$ in the knowledge base. A *rule ABox* consists of an $\mathcal{ALC}$-ABox and a set of sentences of the form

$$\mathbf{K}C \sqsubseteq D,$$

where C, D are $\mathcal{ALC}$-concepts and C is not equivalent to $\top$ (the reason for this technical condition will be discussed below).

Fortunately, the additional inclusion axioms again do not lead to any increase of the complexity [Donini *et al.*, 1992b; 1998a].

Theorem 6.9 *There is an algorithm for deciding, given a rule $\mathcal{ALC}$-ABox Σ, an object name a, and an $\mathcal{ALCK}$-concept C, whether $\Sigma \models C(a)$. More precisely, the problem $\Sigma \models C(a)$ is* PSPACE-*complete (w.r.t. the size of C and Σ).*

Observe that this result does not extend to the language with inclusion axioms of the form $\mathbf{K}C \sqsubseteq D$, where C is equivalent to $\top$. In this case $\mathbf{K}C$ would be equivalent to $\top$ as well, and so $\mathbf{K}C \sqsubseteq D$ would be equivalent to $D \equiv \top$. However, for knowledge bases with axioms of this type instance checking is known to be ExpTime-complete [Schild, 1994]. Notice that in applications a rule of the form $\top \Rightarrow C$ does not make sense.

6.2.3.3 An extension of $\mathcal{ALCK}$

The non-monotonic logic *MKNF* is an expressive extension of ground non-monotonic **S5**, which can simulate in a natural manner Default Logic, Autoepistemic Logic, and Circumscription (see [Lifschitz, 1994]). This is achieved by adding to classical logic not only the operator $\mathbf{K}$ (of ground non-monotonic **S5**) but also a second epistemic operator $\mathbf{A}$, which is interpreted in terms of autoepistemic assumption. The papers [Donini *et al.*, 1997b; Rosati, 1998] study the corresponding bimodal extension of $\mathcal{ALC}$ by means of $\mathbf{K}$ and $\mathbf{A}$, called $\mathcal{ALCB}$ in what follows.

We first consider the two operators $\mathbf{K}$ and $\mathbf{A}$ separately: the consequence relation $\models$ for assertions containing $\mathbf{K}$ only is still the one introduced above. On the other side, for assertions containing $\mathbf{A}$ ('it is assumed that') only we are interested in a consequence relation $\models^{AE}$ such that[3] $\Phi \models^{AE} \varphi$ iff φ belongs to every stable expansion of Φ, i.e., iff φ belongs to every reasonable theory[4] about the world which a rational agent who assumes only the assertions in Φ can have. In particular, it is assumed that agents are capable of introspection. Consider, for example, an agent assuming precisely $\Phi = \{\mathbf{A}C \equiv \top\}$ ("the set of all objects I assume to be in C comprises all existing objects"). We still assume that agents know which objects exist (the

---

[3] AE indicates that autoepistemic propositional logic in the sense of [Moore, 1985] is extended here to $\mathcal{ALC}$.

[4] In terms of propositional logic a theory T is called reasonable iff the following conditions hold: (0) T is closed under classical reasoning, (1) if $P \in T$, then $\mathbf{A}P \in T$, (2) if $P \notin T$, then $\neg \mathbf{A}P \in T$.

constant domain assumption). Hence Φ can be rephrased as "I assume that all objects belong to C". Now, according to the autoepistemic approach such an agent cannot have a coherent theory about the world, for then she would have to assume as well that $C \equiv \top$ from the very beginning.

From the "possible worlds" viewpoint the relation $\models^{AE}$ can be captured as follows. Firstly, the extension of $\mathcal{ALC}$ by $\mathbf{A}$ is interpreted in pairs $(\mathcal{I}, \mathcal{M})$ in precisely the same manner as $\mathcal{ALCK}$. However, now we allow that the actual world $\mathcal{I}$ is not in $\mathcal{M}$ – corresponding to the idea that assumptions (in contrast to known assertions) are not always true. Thus we may have $(\mathbf{A}C)^{\mathcal{I},\mathcal{M}} = \top$ but $C^{\mathcal{I},\mathcal{M}} \neq \top$, which is not possible for $\mathbf{K}$. The intended models are called AE-models in what follows.

Definition 6.10 An *AE-model* for a set of assertions Φ is a set of interpretations $\mathcal{M}$ that satisfies Φ and such that, for every interpretation $\mathcal{I} \notin \mathcal{M}$, Φ is refuted in $(\mathcal{I}, \mathcal{M})$. Now put $\Phi \models^{AE} \varphi$ iff φ is satisfied in all AE-models for Φ.

So, we do not maximize the set of possible worlds, but we exclude the case that Φ is true in an actual world that is not regarded as possible (i.e., is not a member of $\mathcal{M}$). The consequence relation $\models^{AE}$ is also non-monotonic since $\emptyset \models^{AE} \neg \mathbf{A}C(a)$ but $C(a) \models \mathbf{A}C(a)$. Observe that $\models$ and $\models^{AE}$ are different: while $\mathbf{A}C \equiv \top$ has no AE-models, $\mathbf{K}C \equiv \top$ has the epistemic model consisting of all interpretations in which $C \equiv \top$.

How should one interpret the combined language $\mathcal{ALCB}$ and define a consequence relation? Following Lifschitz [1994], the intended models (called $\mathcal{ALCB}$-models) are defined as follows.

Definition 6.11 The $\mathcal{ALCB}$-*models* for a set of $\mathcal{ALCB}$-assertions Φ are those models $\mathcal{M}$ satisfying Φ and the following maximality condition: if a non-empty set of new worlds $\mathcal{N}$ is added to $\mathcal{M}$, $\mathbf{K}$ is interpreted in the model $\mathcal{M} \cup \mathcal{N}$, and $\mathbf{A}$ is interpreted in the old model $\mathcal{M}$, then Φ is refuted in some interpretation from $\mathcal{N}$. Now Φ *logically implies* φ, in symbols $\Phi \models \varphi$, iff φ is satisfied in every $\mathcal{ALCB}$-model satisfying Φ.

Thus, roughly speaking, we still maximize the set of worlds, but now we require that any larger set of possible worlds contains a world at which Φ is refuted under the interpretation of $\mathbf{A}$ by means of the original set of possible worlds. But this corresponds, for the operator $\mathbf{A}$, to the definition of AE-models. Clearly, the new consequence relation is a conservative extension of the one defined for $\mathcal{ALCK}$ above (and of $\models^{AE}$ as well). Hence using the same symbol for both does not cause any ambiguity.

The new logic is considerably more expressive than $\mathcal{ALCK}$. Donini *et al.*, [1997b] show that Default Logic can be embedded into $\mathcal{ALCB}$ more naturally than into $\mathcal{ALCK}$. They also consider the formalization of integrity constraints *in* knowledge bases, which cannot be expressed in $\mathcal{ALCK}$, and they discuss how role and concept closure can be formalized in $\mathcal{ALCB}$. Here we confine ourselves to a brief discussion of the formalization of integrity constraints in $\mathcal{ALCB}$. Above we have seen that the query (6.2) can be used to express the constraint that every course known to the knowledge base should be known to be for undergraduates or graduates. Sometimes it is more useful not to formalize integrity constraints as queries, but as part of the knowledge base (see [Donini *et al.*, 1997b]). However, the addition of constraints should not change the content of the knowledge base, but just force the knowledge base to be inconsistent iff the constraint is violated. How can this be achieved in $\mathcal{ALCK}$? The naive idea is to add the assertion $(6.2) \equiv \top$ to the knowledge base in order to express the constraint. Unfortunately, this does not work: consider the knowledge base Φ consisting of $\mathsf{Course}(a)$, which does not satisfy the integrity constraint. However, the knowledge base obtained from Φ by adding $(6.2) \equiv \top$ does not tell us that the constraint is violated in Φ since the extended knowledge base is still consistent: the set $\mathcal{M}$ consisting of all interpretations $\mathcal{J}$ (with a fixed domain and interpretation of a) satisfying $a^{\mathcal{J}} \in \mathsf{Course}^{\mathcal{J}} \cap \mathsf{Graduate}^{\mathcal{J}}$ is an epistemic model for the extended knowledge base. In fact, there is no way to formulate the required constraint within $\mathcal{ALCK}$. On the other hand, by adding the $\mathcal{ALCB}$-assertion

$$\mathbf{K}\,\mathsf{Course} \sqsubseteq \mathbf{A}\,\mathsf{Graduate} \sqcup \mathbf{A}\,\mathsf{Undergraduate}$$

to Φ, we obtain a knowledge base without $\mathcal{ALCB}$-models, as required. Note, for example, that the model $\mathcal{M}$ introduced above is not an $\mathcal{ALCB}$-model for this knowledge base because any set of worlds $\mathcal{N} = \{\mathcal{I}\}$ with $\mathcal{I} \notin \mathcal{M}$ and $a^{\mathcal{I}} \in \mathsf{Course}^{\mathcal{I}}$ refutes the maximality condition.

Donini *et al.* [1997b] present a number of decidability results for reasoning with $\mathcal{ALCB}$ knowledge bases.

6.2.4 Temporal extensions

Temporal extensions are a special form of modal extensions of Description Logics. However, because of the intended interpretation in flows of time they have a specific flavor, which is slightly different from general modal logic.

Chronologically, the first example of a "modalized" Description Logic was the temporal Description Logic of Schmiedel [1990]. The papers [Bettini, 1997; Artale and Franconi, 1994; 1998] introduce and investigate variants of Schmiedel's formalism. The papers mentioned so far employ an *interval-based* approach to the semantics of temporal operators. *Point-based* temporal Description Logics have been introduced by Schild [1993] and further investigated by Wolter and Zakharyaschev [1999e].

For simplicity, let us first consider propositional temporal logic and then see how it can be extended to temporal Description Logic. In what follows we assume that a *flow of time* $\mathfrak{T} = \langle T, < \rangle$ consists of a set of points in time T and a precedence relation $<$ between points in time which is assumed to be a strict linear order. This corresponds to the intuition that, for any two moments $t_1, t_2 \in T$, either t_1 precedes t_2, t_2 precedes t_1, or t_1 equals t_2.

How should one define a satisfiability relation $\models$ between entities in a flow of time and formulae? There exist (at least) two different ways to select the entities at which formulas are evaluated: points in time and intervals. While in the first case we are considering a relation $t \models \varphi$ between time-points t and formulas φ, in the second case we have a relation $[u, v] \models \varphi$ between intervals $[u, v] = \{z \in T \mid u \leq z \leq v\}$, where $u \leq v$, in $\mathfrak{T}$ and formulae φ. Denote by $\mathfrak{T}^*$ the set of all intervals in $\mathfrak{T}$. Both point- and interval-based temporal logics are special instances of modal logics: in the former the worlds of Kripke frames are interpreted as time-points while in the latter they are interpreted as intervals. Both point- and interval-based temporal models are easily extended to temporal $\mathcal{ALC}$-models:

Definition 6.12 A *point-based temporal* $\mathcal{ALC}$-model $\mathfrak{M} = \langle \mathfrak{T}, I \rangle$ consists of a flow of time $\mathfrak{T}$ and a function I which associates with every $t \in T$ an interpretation

$$I(t) = \langle \Delta^{I,t}, \cdot^{I,t} \rangle.$$

An *interval-based temporal* $\mathcal{ALC}$-model $\mathfrak{M} = \langle \mathfrak{T}, I \rangle$ consists of a flow of time $\mathfrak{T}$ and a function I which associates with every interval $i \in \mathfrak{T}^*$ an interpretation

$$I(i) = \langle \Delta^{I,i}, \cdot^{I,i} \rangle.$$

We can now evaluate $\mathcal{ALC}$-concepts and axioms in point- and interval-based temporal models. For example:

- $(\mathfrak{M}, t) \models \mathsf{Alive}(a)$ iff $a^{I,t} \in \mathsf{Alive}^{I,t}$, i.e., a is alive at moment t
- $(\mathfrak{M}, i) \models \mathsf{Sleep}(a)$ iff $a^{I,i} \in \mathsf{Sleep}^{I,i}$, i.e., a is sleeping in the interval i.

We now add temporal operators and quantifiers to $\mathcal{ALC}$, which enable us to relate different moments and intervals to each other.

For the point-based approach we have discussed appropriate operators already: we can form the language $\mathcal{L}^1_{\mathcal{ALC}}$ and interpret the operator $\square = \square_1$ as "*always in the future*". Thus, $t \models \square(C \equiv D)$ iff $t' \models C \equiv D$ for all $t' > t$, (always in the future of t, C and D are interpreted as the same set), and $x \in (\diamond C)^{I,t}$ iff there exists $t' > t$ such that $x \in C^{I,t'}$ (eventually x is an instance of C). Often, however, more expressive temporal operators are required. The operator $\mathcal{U}$ (until), for example, is a binary temporal operator with the following truth-conditions, for all concepts C, D and axioms φ, ψ:

1. $x \in (C\mathcal{U}D)^{I,t}$ iff there exists $t' > t$ such that $x \in D^{I,t'}$ and, for all t'' with $t < t'' < t'$, $x \in C^{I,t''}$,
2. $t \models \varphi\mathcal{U}\psi$ iff there exists $t' > t$ such that $t' \models \psi$ and, for all t'' with $t < t'' < t'$, $t'' \models \varphi$.

In this language we can define a mortal as, say, a living being that is alive until it dies:

$$\mathsf{Mortal} \equiv \mathsf{LivingBeing} \sqcap (\mathsf{LivingBeing}\ \mathcal{U}\ \square\neg\mathsf{LivingBeing}).$$

This language, interpreted in the flow of time $\langle \mathbb{N}, < \rangle$, was first considered by Schild [1993], who showed that the satisfiability problem for concepts (without modalized or global roles) is decidable. Wolter [2000] proves the decidability for concepts with global roles (but without modalized roles). However, the complexity of the decision problem for this language is non-elementary [Gabbay *et al.*, 2003]. Wolter and Zakharyaschev [1999e] prove that even for axioms the satisfiability problem is decidable, provided that they do not contain modalized or global roles. Tableau calculi (running in double-exponential time) for the case of expanding and constant domains were developed in [Sturm and Wolter, 2002; Lutz *et al.*, 2001b]. The satisfiability problem for axioms in the full language with the flow of time $\langle \mathbb{N}, < \rangle$ is undecidable.

For the interval-based approach we find both languages that extend $\mathcal{ALC}$ by means of temporal operators which are interpreted by accessibility relations between intervals [Bettini, 1997] and languages that allow explicit quantification over intervals [Schmiedel, 1990; Artale and Franconi, 1994; 1998].

We start the discussion with the temporal operators approach. Bettini [1997] extends the propositional interval-based temporal logic of [Halpern and Shoham, 1991] to $\mathcal{ALC}$ (and weaker Description Logics). Thus, given a concept C, we can now form new concepts like $\langle starts \rangle C$ and

⟨*finishes*⟩ C. They are interpreted in interval-based models ⟨$\mathfrak{T}, I$⟩ as follows:

- $x \in (\langle starts \rangle\, C)^{I,[u,v]}$ iff $\exists t \in T.\ u \leq t < v \wedge x \in C^{I,[u,t]}$
  (x is an instance of ⟨*starts*⟩ C in the interval $[u, v]$ iff x is an instance of C in some interval starting $[u, v]$),
- $x \in (\langle finishes \rangle\, C)^{I,[u,v]}$ iff $\exists t \in T.\ u < t \leq v \wedge x \in C^{I,[t,v]}$.

In other words, the modal operators ⟨*starts*⟩ and ⟨*finishes*⟩ are interpreted in the standard "possible worlds manner" by means of the accessibility relations "*starts*" and "*finishes*", respectively, where $(i, j) \in$ *starts* iff j starts i and $(i, j) \in$ *finishes* if j finishes i. By adding the converse operators of ⟨*starts*⟩ and ⟨*finishes*⟩ to the language, we obtain a language that can express all the thirteen Allen relations between intervals [Allen, 1983]. Here is a definition of Mortal in this language:

$$\text{Mortal} \equiv \text{LivingBeing} \sqcap \langle after \rangle\, \neg\text{LivingBeing}.$$

Unfortunately, for the full language based on $\mathcal{ALC}$ the satisfiability problem for concepts is undecidable in all interesting flows of time. This follows from the fact that propositional interval-based temporal logic is undecidable already in ⟨$\mathbb{R}, <$⟩, ⟨$\mathbb{Q}, <$⟩, ⟨$\mathbb{N}, <$⟩, etc. (see [Halpern and Shoham, 1991]). However, there are numerous open decision problems when Description Logics weaker than $\mathcal{ALC}$ and different notions of intervals are considered (see [Bettini, 1997; Artale and Franconi, 2000; 2001]).

Now, let us consider interval-based temporal extensions of Description Logics that allow explicit quantification over intervals. Schmiedel [1990] develops an expressive formalism[5] in which we have two quantifiers $\square(i)$ ("for all intervals i") and $\lozenge(i)$ ("there exists an interval i"), where i is a variable ranging over intervals. The language does not contain negation so that the quantifiers are not mutually definable. The quantifiers are relativized (alias bounded or guarded) by so-called *time nets*, which can, for example, be some relations like *starts* or *finishes* between intervals (metric and granularity constraints are admitted as well). An operator @ specifies the interval at which a concept applies to an object and ♯ denotes a reference interval. The following concept can be regarded as a definition of the concept Mortal in Schmiedel's language:

$$\text{LivingBeing} \sqcap (\lozenge(i)(\text{after } i\ \sharp)(\neg\text{LivingBeing} @ i)).$$

Here (after i ♯) is the time net which relativizes the quantifier $\lozenge(i)$ by means of the constraint expressing that i must be after the reference interval denoted by ♯. According to this definition, an object x is an instance of Mortal

---

[5] Here and in what follows we use the notation of [Artale and Franconi, 1998].

at the reference interval ♯ iff x is living at ♯ and there exists an interval i that is after ♯, and at which x is not living.

Schmiedel [1990] does not address computational problems for his language. However, it is not difficult to see that, in the presence of negation, this language is more expressive than that of Bettini [1997] considered above – and thus subsumption is undecidable for all interesting flows of time. The decision problem for the language without negation appears to be open.

A brief remark concerning the relation between interval-based temporal logic with and without explicit quantification over intervals is in order. Of course, explicit quantification provides more expressive power. Using the temporal operators introduced above, it is not possible to represent relations between more than two intervals because referring to a fixed reference interval is impossible. On the other hand, variable-free languages are much closer in spirit to pure Description Logics and therefore seem to be more natural candidates for temporalizations of Description Logics; we refer the reader to [Artale and Franconi, 2000; 2001] for a detailed discussion.

The papers [Artale and Franconi, 1994; 1998] present a number of languages weaker than Schmiedel's with a decidable subsumption problem. Among others, they define a temporal extension of a Description Logic extending $\mathcal{ALC}$ with functional roles. They show decidability of concept subsumption and PSPACE-completeness of satisfiability w.r.t. an empty KB in an unbounded and dense flow of time. The main reason for the decidability is that the language does not admit universal quantification over intervals and that the constructors of the underlying Description Logic cannot be applied to the temporalized part of the language. In particular, the negation of the underlying Description Logic cannot be used to define the universal quantifier by means of the existential one. The authors show by means of a number of examples that their formalism still has enough expressive power to represent non-trivial actions and plans.

An interesting feature of the subsumption algorithm presented by Artale and Franconi [1998] is that it consists of two parts: firstly, a normalization procedure is employed to reduce the subsumption problem for the temporalized Description Logic to that problem for the pure Description Logic, which can then be solved with known algorithms [Hollunder and Nutt, 1990].

For a more detailed survey of the state of art in temporal Description Logic we refer the reader to [Artale and Franconi, 2000; 2001], where one can also find an introduction to the work of Weida and Litman [1992], who propose a loose hybrid integration between Description Logics and constraint networks with the aim of reasoning about plans.

6.2.5 *Representing uncertain and vague knowledge*

Description Logics whose semantics is based on classical first-order logic cannot express vague or uncertain knowledge. To overcome this deficiency, approaches for integrating probabilistic logic and fuzzy logic into Description Logics have been proposed. Although both types of approaches assign numerical values to entries in the knowledge base, they are quite different, not only from a technical point of view, but also w.r.t. the basic phenomena they are trying to model. We talk about uncertainty if we deal with propositions that are either true or false, but due to a lack of information we do not know for certain which is the case. This gives rise to statements about the probability with which a proposition is assumed to be true. In contrast, vagueness means that the propositions themselves are only true to a certain degree. This vagueness is not caused by incomplete knowledge; it is due to the fact that fuzzy notions, i.e., notions without crisp boundaries (e.g., tall person) are modeled.

In the following, we will restrict our attention to the probabilistic extensions of Description Logics introduced in [Heinsohn, 1994; Jaeger, 1994; Koller *et al.*, 1997; Yelland, 2000] and the fuzzy extensions of Description Logics introduced in [Yen, 1991; Tresp and Molitor, 1998; Straccia, 1998; 2001]. The possibilistic extension by Hollunder [1994b] can be viewed as lying between these two approaches: possibilistic logic is mainly used to model uncertainty, but its formal semantics is defined in terms of fuzzy sets of interpretations.

6.2.5.1 *Probabilistic extensions*

Let us first concentrate on how to extend the terminological (TBox) formalism. In classical Description Logics, one has very restricted means of expressing (and testing for) relationships between concepts. Given two concepts C and D, subsumption tells us whether C is contained in D, and the satisfiability test (applied to $C \sqcap D$) tells us whether C and D are disjoint. Relationships that are in between (e.g., 90% of all Cs are Ds) can neither be expressed nor be derived.

This deficiency is overcome in [Heinsohn, 1994; Jaeger, 1994] by allowing *probabilistic terminological axioms* of the form[6]

$$P(C|D) = p,$$

where C, D are concept descriptions and $0 < p < 1$ is a real number. Such an axiom states that the conditional probability for an object known to be

---

[6] Actually, Heinsohn uses a different notation and allows more expressive axioms stating that $P(C|D)$ belongs to an interval $[p_l, p_u]$, where $0 \le p_l \le p_u \le 1$.

in D to belong to C is p. A given *finite* interpretation $\mathcal{I}$ satisfies $\mathrm{P}(C|D) = p$ iff

$$\frac{|(C \sqcap D)^{\mathcal{I}}|}{|D^{\mathcal{I}}|} = p.$$

More generally, the formal semantics of the extended language is defined in terms of probability measures on the set of all concept descriptions (modulo equivalence).

Given a knowledge base $\mathcal{P}$ consisting of probabilistic terminological axioms, the main *inference task* is then to derive optimal bounds for additional conditional probabilities. Intuitively,

$$\mathcal{P} \models \mathrm{P}(C|D) \in [p, q]$$

iff in all probability measures satisfying $\mathcal{P}$ the conditional probability $\mathrm{P}(C|D)$ belongs to the interval $[p, q]$. Given $\mathcal{P}, C, D$, one is interested in finding the maximal p and minimal q such that $\mathcal{P} \models \mathrm{P}(C|D) \in [p, q]$ is true.

Heinsohn [1994] introduces local inference rules that can be used to derive bounds for conditional probabilities, but these rules are not complete, that is, in general they are not sufficient to derive the optimal bounds.

Jaeger [1994] only describes a naive method for computing optimal bounds. A more sophisticated version of that method reduces the inference problem to a linear optimization problem. In the following, we will sketch the main idea underlying this reduction. Assume that $C_1, \ldots, C_m$ are the concept descriptions occurring in $\mathcal{P}$ and $\mathrm{P}(C|D)$, and consider all conjunctions $D_1 \sqcap \cdots \sqcap D_m$, where D_i is either C_i or $\neg C_i$. Let $\mathfrak{A}$ be the set of those conjunctions that are satisfiable. Given a probability measure on all concept descriptions, the value of this measure on $C_1, \ldots, C_m$ is uniquely determined by the value on $\mathfrak{A}$. To be more precise, its value for C_i can be obtained as the sum of the values for those elements of $\mathfrak{A}$ that are subsumed by C_i (i.e., the ones where C_i occurs positively). The idea is to introduce a numerical variable x_t (ranging over the real interval $(0, 1)$) for each element $t \in \mathfrak{A}$. For example, if C_1, C_2 are two concept names, then $\mathfrak{A}$ consists of the four elements $t_0 = \neg C_1 \sqcap \neg C_2$, $t_1 = \neg C_1 \sqcap C_2$, $t_2 = C_1 \sqcap \neg C_2$, and $t_3 = C_1 \sqcap C_2$, for which we introduce the variables x_0, x_1, x_2, x_3, respectively. Thus, the probability associated with $C_1 \sqcap C_2$ is x_3 and the one for C_2 is $x_1 + x_3$. Consequently, the probabilistic terminological axiom $\mathrm{P}(C_1|C_2) = 0.7$ can be represented by the (linear) constraint $x_3 = 0.7(x_1 + x_3)$.

We have to find the maximal and minimal values that $\mathrm{P}(C|D)$ attains on the set of values $(x_0, \ldots, x_n)$ satisfying the linear constraints induced by $\mathcal{P}$.

The value of the function $P(C|D)$ (in terms of the variables x_t) is given by

$$\frac{\sum \{x_t \mid t \in \mathfrak{A} \wedge t \sqsubseteq C \sqcap D\}}{\sum \{x_t \mid t \in \mathfrak{A} \wedge t \sqsubseteq D\}}.$$

By a simple transformation, this *fractional optimization problem* can be transformed into a linear optimization problem [Amarger *et al.*, 1991].

Jaeger [1994] also extends the assertional formalism by allowing *probabilistic assertions* of the form

$$P(C(a)) = p,$$

where C is a concept description, a an individual name, and p a real number between 0 and 1. It should be noted that this kind of probabilistic statement is quite different from the one introduced by the terminological formalism. Whereas probabilistic terminological axioms state *statistical information*, which is usually obtained by observing a large number of objects, probabilistic assertions express a *degree of belief* in assertions for specific individuals. The formal semantics of probabilistic assertions is again defined with the help of probability measures on the set of all concept descriptions, one for each individual name. Intuitively, the measure for a tells us for each concept C how likely it is (believed to be) that a belongs to C.

Given a knowledge base $\mathcal{P}$ consisting of probabilistic terminological axioms and assertions, the main *inference task* is now to derive optimal bounds for additional probabilistic assertions. However, if the probabilistic terminological axioms are supposed to have an impact on this inference problem, the semantics as sketched so far is not sufficient. In fact, to date there is no connection between the probability measure used for the terminological part and the measures for the assertional part. Intuitively, one wants the measures for the assertional part to "most closely resemble" the measure for the terminological part, while not violating the probabilistic assertions. Jaeger [1994] uses *cross entropy minimization* in order to give a formal meaning to this intuition. To date, there is no algorithm for computing optimal bounds for $P(C(a))$, given a knowledge base consisting of probabilistic terminological axioms and assertions.

The work reported in [Koller *et al.*, 1997], which is restricted to the terminological component, has a focus that is quite different from the one in [Heinsohn, 1994; Jaeger, 1994]. In the latter work, the probabilistic terminological axioms provide constraints on the set of admissible probability measures. However, these constraints may still be satisfied by a large set of distributions, and hence the optimal interval entailed for the probabilities of interest can be fairly large. In contrast, Koller *et al.* [1997] present a framework for the specification of a unique probability distribution on the set of all concept descriptions (modulo equivalence). Since there are infinitely many such descriptions, providing such a (finite) specification is a nontrivial task. The basic idea is to specify a distribution on concepts of role-depth 0, and then to specify how to extend a distribution on concepts of role-depth n to one on concepts of role-depth $n + 1$. Koller *et al.* [1997] employ Bayesian networks as the basic representation language for the required probabilistic specifications. The probability $P(C)$ of a concept description C can then be computed by using inference algorithms developed for Bayesian networks. The complexity of this computation is linear in the length of C. Under certain restrictions on the Bayesian networks used in the specification, it is polynomial in the size of that specification.

Yelland [2000] also combines Bayesian networks and Description Logics. In contrast to [Koller *et al.*, 1997], this work extends Bayesian networks by DL features rather than the other way round. The Description Logic used in [Yelland, 2000] is rather inexpressive, but this allows the author to avoid restrictions on the network that had to be imposed by Koller *et al.* [1997].

6.2.5.2 Fuzzy extensions

The concepts in Description Logics are interpreted as crisp sets, i.e., an individual either belongs to the set or not. However, many "real-life" concepts are vague in the sense that they do not have precisely defined membership criteria. Consider, for example, the concept of a tall person. It does not make sense to fix an exact boundary such that persons of height larger than this boundary are tall and others are not. In fact, what about a person whose height is 1 millimeter below the boundary? It is more sensible to say that an individual belongs to the concept "tall person" only to a certain degree $n \in [0, 1]$, which depends on the height of the individual. This is exactly what fuzzy logic allows one to do.

The main idea underlying the fuzzy extensions of Description Logics proposed in [Yen, 1991; Tresp and Molitor, 1998; Straccia, 1998; 2001] is to leave the syntax as it is, but to use fuzzy logic for defining the semantics. Thus, an interpretation now assigns fuzzy sets to concepts and roles, i.e., concept names A are interpreted by membership degree functions of the form $A^{\mathcal{I}} : \Delta^{\mathcal{I}} \to [0, 1]$, and role names R by membership degree functions of the form $R^{\mathcal{I}} : \Delta^{\mathcal{I}} \times \Delta^{\mathcal{I}} \to [0, 1]$. The interpretation of the Boolean operators and the quantifiers must then be extended from $\{0, 1\}$ to the interval $[0, 1]$. Fuzzy logics provide different options for such an extension. In [Yen, 1991; Tresp and Molitor, 1998; Straccia, 1998; 2001], the usual interpretation of conjunction as minimum, disjunction as maximum, negation as $\lambda x.(1 - x)$, universal quantifier as infimum, and existential quantifier as supremum is considered. For example,

$$(\forall R.C)^{\mathcal{I}}(d) = \inf\{\max\{1 - R^{\mathcal{I}}(d, e), C^{\mathcal{I}}(d, e)\} \mid e \in \Delta^{\mathcal{I}}\},$$

since $\forall R.C$ corresponds to the formula $\forall x.(\neg R(x, y) \vee C(y))$.

Tresp and Molitor [1998] also propose an extension of the syntax by so-called manipulators, which are unary operators that can be applied to concepts. Examples of manipulators could be "mostly", "more or less", or "very". For example, if Tall is a concept (standing for the fuzzy set of all tall persons), then VeryTall, which is obtained by applying the manipulator Very to the concept Tall, is a new concept (standing for the fuzzy set of all very tall persons). Intuitively, the manipulators modify the membership degree functions of the concepts they are applied to appropriately. In our example, the membership function for VeryTall should have its largest values at larger heights than the membership function for Tall. Formally, the semantics of a manipulators is defined by a function that maps membership degree functions to membership degree functions. The manipulators considered in [Tresp and Molitor, 1998] are, however, of a very restricted form.

Lets us now consider what kind of inference problems are of interest in this context. Yen [1991] considers crisp subsumption of fuzzy concepts, i.e., given two concepts C, D defined in the fuzzy Description Logic, he is interested in the question whether $C^{\mathcal{I}}(d) \leq D^{\mathcal{I}}(d)$ for all fuzzy interpretations $\mathcal{I}$ and $d \in \Delta^{\mathcal{I}}$. Thus, the subsumption relationship itself is not fuzzified. He describes a structural subsumption algorithm for a rather small fuzzy Description Logic, which is almost identical to the subsumption algorithm for the corresponding classical Description Logic. In contrast, Tresp and Molitor [1998] are interested in determining fuzzy subsumption between fuzzy concepts, i.e., given concepts C, D, they want to know to what degree C is a subset of D. In [Straccia, 1998; 2001] and [Molitor and Tresp, 2000], also ABoxes are considered, where the ABox assertions are equipped with a degree. In this context one wants to find out to what degree other assertions follow from the ABox.

Both [Straccia, 1998; 2001] and [Tresp and Molitor, 1998] contain complete algorithms for solving these inference problems in the respective fuzzy extension of $\mathcal{ALC}$. Although both algorithms are extensions of the usual tableau-based algorithm for $\mathcal{ALC}$, they differ considerably. For example, the algorithm in [Tresp and Molitor, 1998] introduces numerical variables for the degrees, and produces a linear optimization problem, which must be solved in place of the usual clash test. In contrast, Straccia deals with the membership degrees within his tableau-based algorithm.

6.2.6 Extensions by default rules

In Description Logics, inclusion axioms of the form $C \sqsubseteq D$ are interpreted as universal statements, i.e., *all* instances of C also belong to D. The same is true for inferred subsumption relationships. In commonsense reasoning, however, one often wants to state and infer relationships that are only "normally" true, but may have exceptions. The most prominent example from the non-monotonic reasoning community is the statement that all birds fly; but of course penguins and other non-flying birds are exceptions. Allowing such *default* statements has a strong impact both on the semantics and the reasoning capabilities of Description Logics. Instead of basing the semantics on classical first-order logic, one must employ a non-monotonic logic [Ginsberg, 1987]. In fact, conclusions drawn from a given knowledge base with defaults may ultimately turn out to be false when additional knowledge is added, and thus must be withdrawn.

Since most of the classical Description Logics can be seen as fragments of first-order predicate logic, an obvious approach for extending Description Logics by non-monotonic reasoning capabilities is to take one of the well-known non-monotonic logics, and restrict the first-order version of this logic to the Description Logic in question. This approach was employed in [Baader and Hollunder, 1995a], where Reiter's default logic [Reiter, 1980] is integrated into Description Logics. In addition to terminological axioms in the TBox and assertions in the ABox, Baader and Hollunder allow *terminological defaults* of the form

$$\frac{C(x) : D(x)}{E(x)},$$

where C, D, E are concept descriptions (viewed as first-order formulae with one free variable x). Intuitively, such a default rule can be applied to an ABox individual a, i.e., $E(a)$ is added to the current set of beliefs, if its prerequisite $C(a)$ is already believed for this individual and its justification $D(a)$ is consistent with the set of beliefs. Formally, the consequences of a *terminological default theory* (consisting of a TBox, an ABox, and a set of terminological defaults) are defined with reference to the notion of an *extension*, which is a set of deductively closed first-order formulae defined by a fixpoint construction (see [Reiter, 1980]). In general, a default theory may have more than one extension, or even no extension. Depending on whether one wants to employ *skeptical* or *credulous* reasoning, an assertion $F(a)$ is a *consequence of a default theory* iff it is in all extensions or if it is in at least one extension of the theory.

It should be noted that in this setting the application of default rules is restricted to individuals explicitly present in the ABox.[7] For example, assume that the ABox consists of the fact that Tom has a child that is a doctor, i.e., $\mathcal{A} = \{(\exists\text{has-child}.\text{Doctor})(\text{TOM})\}$, and that by default we assume that doctors are usually rich:

$$\frac{\text{Doctor}(x) : \text{Rich}(x)}{\text{Rich}(x)}.$$

Intuitively, one might expect that $(\exists\text{has-child}.\text{Rich})(\text{TOM})$ is a default consequence of this terminological default theory. However, since the ABox does not contain a name for Tom's child, the default cannot be applied to this "implicit" individual, and thus one cannot conclude that Tom has a rich child by default. Baader and Hollunder [1995a] give two reasons that justify restricting the application of defaults to explicit individuals. From a semantic point of view, adapting Reiter's treatment of implicit individuals via skolemization is quite unsatisfactory, since semantically equivalent (but syntactically different) ABoxes may lead to different default consequences. From the algorithmic point of view, the application of defaults to implicit individuals is problematic since it may lead to an undecidable default consequence relation, even though the Description Logic employed is decidable. In contrast, the restriction of default application to explicit individuals ensures that reasoning in terminological default theories stays decidable whenever reasoning in the underlying Description Logic is decidable.

A major drawback, which terminological default logic inherits from general default logic, is that it does not take precedence of more specific defaults over more general ones into account. For example, assume that we have a default that says that doctors are usually rich, and another one that says that general practitioners are usually not rich, and that classification shows that general practitioners are doctors. Intuitively, for any general practitioner the more specific second default should be preferred, which means that there should be only one default extension, in which the general practitioner is not rich. However, in default logic the second default has no priority over the first one, which means that one also gets a second extension where the general practitioner is rich. This behavior has already been criticized in the general context of default logic, but it is all the more problematic in the terminological case where the emphasis lies on the hierarchical organization of concepts. To overcome this problem, Baader and Hollunder [1995b] first define a prioritized version of Reiter's default logic, where priorities

---

[7] This agrees with the semantics given to (monotonic) rules in Description Logics (see Subsection 6.2.3 and Chapter 2, Subsection 2.2.5).

are given by an arbitrary partial order on defaults. In the terminological case, the priority is induced by the subsumption relationship between prerequisites of defaults. A similar approach is proposed in [Straccia, 1993], with the main difference that in that paper the defaults also influence the priority order. In addition, Straccia also allows defaults of the form

$$\frac{A(x) \wedge r(x, y) : C(y)}{C(y)},$$

where A is an atomic concept, r a role name, and C a concept description. Such a default can, for example, be used to say that usually a child of a doctor is again a doctor.

A quite different proposal for how to treat defaults in Description Logics can be found in [Quantz and Royer, 1992]. There, preference semantics [Shoham, 1987] is employed to define the semantics of default assertions $C \rightsquigarrow D$, which are intuitively interpreted as saying: "whenever an object is an instance of C, it is also an instance of D, unless this is in conflict with other knowledge". Though on this intuitive level the meaning of the default $C \rightsquigarrow D$ coincides with that of the terminological default $C(x) : D(x)/D(x)$, the formal semantics (and thus also the default consequences) differ significantly. The semantics proposed by Quantz and Royer is based on a preference relation on models, which tries to minimize the exceptions to defaults while maximizing the number of defaults that have been fired. In contrast to the work mentioned above, Quantz and Royer do not restrict reasoning with defaults to the derivation of concept assertions of the form $C(a)$. They also consider *default subsumption* between concepts. However, default subsumption is reduced to reasoning about individuals. The subsumption relationship $C \sqsubseteq D$ follows by default from the knowledge base iff the knowledge base extended by $C(a)$ implies $D(a)$ by default, where a is a new individual name. Designing reasoning methods for such a model-based approach to non-monotonic reasoning is rather hard. Quantz and Royer only provide some ideas for how to obtain a sound but incomplete procedure.

Default subsumption is also considered in [Padgham and Zhang, 1993], where non-monotonic inheritance networks [Horty *et al.*, 1987] are extended in the direction of Description Logics, though the Description Logic employed is of a very limited expressive power.

6.3 Non-standard inference problems

All DL systems provide their users with standard inference services like computing the subsumption hierarchy and testing ABox consistency. In some applications it has turned out, however, that these services are not quite sufficient for providing an optimal support when building and maintaining large DL knowledge bases. For this reason, some DL systems (e.g., CLASSIC) provide their users with additional system services, which can formally be reconstructed as new types of inference problems.

First, the standard inferences can be applied *after* a new concept has been defined to find out whether the concept is non-contradictory or whether its place in the taxonomy coincides with the intuition of the knowledge engineer; however, these inferences do not directly support the process of actually defining the new concept. To overcome this problem, the non-standard inference services of computing the *least common subsumer* and the *most specific concept* have been proposed.

Second, if a knowledge base is maintained by different knowledge engineers, one needs support for detecting multiple definitions of the same intuitive concept. Since different knowledge engineers might use different names for the "same" primitive concept, the standard equivalence test may not be adequate to check whether different descriptions refer to the same notion. The non-standard inference service *unification of concept descriptions* tackles this problem by allowing concept names to be replaced by appropriate concept descriptions before testing for equivalence. *Matching* is a special case of unification, which has, for example, been used for pruning irrelevant parts of large concept descriptions before displaying them to the user.

Third, and very abstractly speaking, *rewriting* of concept descriptions allows one to transform a given concept description C into a "better" description D, which satisfies certain optimality criteria (e.g., small size) and is in a certain relationship (e.g., equivalence or subsumption) with the original description C.

Before describing the different non-standard inferences in more detail, we start with some general remarks on how these new problems have until now been tackled in the literature. An overview of the state of the art in this field and detailed proofs of several of the results mentioned below can be found in [Küsters, 2001].

6.3.1 Techniques for solving non-standard inferences – a general remark

Approaches for solving the new inference problems are usually based on an appropriate characterization of subsumption, which can be used to obtain a structural subsumption algorithm. First, the concept descriptions are turned into a certain normal form, in which implicit facts have been made explicit.

Second, the structure of the normal forms is compared appropriately. This is one of the reasons why most of the results on non-standard inferences are restricted to languages that can be treated by structural subsumption algorithms.

One can distinguish two kinds of normal forms proposed in the literature. In one approach, called *language-based* approach in the sequel, the normal form of a concept description is given in terms of certain finite or regular sets of words over the alphabet of all role names. Then, subsumption can be characterized via the inclusion of these sets (see Chapter 2, Subsection 2.3.3.2). The second approach, called *graph-based* in the following, turns concept descriptions into so-called description graphs. Here, subsumption of concept descriptions is characterized via the existence of certain homomorphisms between the corresponding description graphs. The structural subsumption algorithm introduced in Chapter 2, Subsection 2.3.1, can be represented in this way (although this was not explicitly done in Chapter 2).

For the sublanguage $\mathcal{ALN}$ of Classic, the graph-based approach can be seen as a special implementation of the language-based approach [Baader *et al.*, 1998a]. In general, however, either the language-based or the graph-based approach may turn out to be more appropriate, depending on the Description Logic under consideration. On the one hand, the language-based approach is particularly useful for characterizing subsumption between cyclic concept descriptions, i.e., descriptions defined by means of cyclic terminologies in $\mathcal{FL}_0$ and $\mathcal{ALN}$ [Baader, 1996b; Küsters, 1998]. On the other hand, the graph-based approach can be employed to handle full Classic [Borgida and Patel-Schneider, 1994] as well as $\mathcal{ALE}$ [Baader *et al.*, 1999b], which extends $\mathcal{FL}_0$ by primitive negation and existential restrictions. Although Borgida and Patel-Schneider did not explicitly characterize subsumption in terms of homomorphisms between description graphs, their subsumption algorithm does in fact check for the existence of an appropriate homomorphism.

The known approaches for solving non-standard inference problems are usually based on one of the two approaches for characterizing subsumption, depending on the Description Logic of choice. In the sequel, we will give an idea of how to solve the inference problems by mainly looking at the language-based approach for the Description Logic $\mathcal{FL}_0$. We will also briefly comment on how to treat extensions of $\mathcal{FL}_0$.

6.3.2 Least common subsumer and most specific concept

Intuitively, the least common subsumer of a given collection of concept descriptions is a description that represents the properties that all the elements of the collection have in common. More formally, it is the most specific concept description that subsumes the given descriptions:

Definition 6.13 Let $\mathcal{L}$ be a description language. A concept description E of $\mathcal{L}$ is the *least common subsumer* (lcs) of the concept descriptions $C_1, \ldots, C_n$ in $\mathcal{L}$ ($lcs(C_1, \ldots, C_n)$ for short) iff it satisfies:

1. $C_i \sqsubseteq E$ for all $i = 1, \ldots, n$, and
2. E is the least $\mathcal{L}$-concept description satisfying (i), i.e., if E' is an $\mathcal{L}$-concept description satisfying $C_i \sqsubseteq E'$ for all $i = 1, \ldots, n$, then $E \sqsubseteq E'$.

As an easy consequence of this definition, the lcs is unique up to equivalence. In fact, if E_1 and E_2 are both least common subsumers of the same collection of concepts, then $E_1 \sqsubseteq E_2$ (since E_2 satisfies (i) and E_1 is the least concept description satisfying (i)). The subsumption relationship $E_2 \sqsubseteq E_1$ can be derived analogously. It should be noted, however, that the lcs need not always exist. This can have two different reasons: (a) there may be several subsumption incomparable minimal concept descriptions satisfying (i) of the definition; (b) there may be an infinite chain of more and more specific descriptions satisfying (i). It is easy to see, however, that for Description Logics allowing conjunction of descriptions (a) cannot occur.

The lcs was first introduced by Cohen *et al.* [1992] as a new inference task that is useful for a number of different reasons. First, finding the most specific concept that generalizes a set of examples is a common operation in inductive learning, called learning from examples. Cohen and Hirsh [1994a] as well as Frazier and Pitt [1994] investigate the learnability of sublanguages of CLASSIC with regard to the PAC learning model proposed by Valiant [1984]. The lcs-computation is used as a subprocedure in their learning algorithms. Experimental results concerning the learnability of concepts based on computing the lcs can be found in [Cohen and Hirsh, 1994b].

Another motivation for considering the lcs is to use it as an alternative to disjunction. The idea is to replace disjunctions like $C_1 \sqcup \cdots \sqcup C_n$ by the lcs of $C_1, \ldots, C_n$. In [Cohen *et al.*, 1992; Borgida and Etherington, 1989], this operation is called *knowledge base vivification*. Although, in general, the lcs is not equivalent to the corresponding disjunction, it is the best approximation of the disjunctive concept within the available Description Logic. The use of such an approximation is motivated by the fact that, in many cases, adding disjunction would increase the complexity of reasoning. Observe that, if the Description Logic already allows disjunction, we have $lcs(C_1, \ldots, C_n) \equiv C_1 \sqcup \cdots \sqcup C_n$. In particular, this means that, for such Description Logics, the lcs is not really of interest.

Finally, as proposed in [Baader and Küsters, 1998; Baader *et al.*, 1999b], the lcs operation can be used to support the "bottom-up" construction of DL knowledge bases. In contrast to the usual "top-down" approach, where the knowledge engineer first defines the terminology of the application domain in the TBox and then uses this terminology when describing individuals in the ABox, the "bottom-up" approach proceeds as follows. The knowledge engineer first specifies some "typical" examples of a concept to be defined using individuals in the ABox. Then, in a second step, these individuals are generalized to their most specific concept, i.e., a concept description that (i) has all the individuals as instances, and (ii) is the most specific description satisfying property (i). Finally, the knowledge engineer inspects and possibly modifies the concept description obtained this way.

Let us now define the most specific concept of an ABox individual in more detail.

Definition 6.14 A concept description E in some description language $\mathcal{L}$ is the *most specific concept* (msc) of the individuals $a_1, \ldots, a_n$ defined in an ABox $\mathcal{A}$ ($msc(a_1, \ldots, a_n)$ for short) iff:

1. $\mathcal{A} \models E(a_i)$ for all $i = 1, \ldots, n$, and
2. E is the least concept satisfying (i), i.e., if E' is an $\mathcal{L}$-concept description satisfying $\mathcal{A} \models E'(a_i)$ for all $i = 1, \ldots, n$, then $E \sqsubseteq E'$.

The task of computing the msc can be split into two subtasks: computing the most specific concept of a single individual, and computing the least common subsumer of a given finite number of concepts. In fact, it is easy to see that $msc(a_1, \ldots, a_n) \equiv lcs(msc(a_1), \ldots, msc(a_n))$.

6.3.2.1 Computing the lcs and the msc

We will now give an intuition on how to compute the lcs for the Description Logic $\mathcal{FL}_0$ and an extension, and briefly comment on the problems that arise when considering the msc. As mentioned above, the first step towards an algorithm for computing the lcs is to characterize subsumption of concept descriptions. For the Description Logic $\mathcal{FL}_0$, we will present such a characterization using the language-based approach.

The normal form of $\mathcal{FL}_0$-concept descriptions employed in the language-based approach is the so-called *concept-centered normal form* (CCNF), which has already been introduced in Chapter 2, Subsection 2.3.3.2. For example, using the equivalence $\forall R.(C \sqcap D) \equiv \forall R.C \sqcap \forall R.D$ and commutativity of concept conjunction, the $\mathcal{FL}_0$-concept description $C = \forall R.(\forall S.A \sqcap \forall R.B) \sqcap \forall S.\forall S.A$ can be transformed into CCNF as follows:

$$C \equiv \forall R.\forall S.A \sqcap \forall S.\forall S.A \sqcap \forall R.\forall R.B$$
$$\equiv \forall\{RS, SS\}.A \sqcap \forall\{RR\}.B.$$

Recall that $\forall\{RS, SS\}.A$ has been introduced in Chapter 2, Subsection 2.3.3.2 as an abbreviation for $\forall R.\forall S.A \sqcap \forall S.\forall S.A$. Similarly, $\forall\{RR\}.B$ abbreviates $\forall R.\forall R.B$.

In general, if N_C is a finite set of atomic concepts and N_R is a finite set of role names, then the CCNF of a concept C built using only these names is of the form

$$C \equiv \bigsqcap_{A \in N_C} \forall U_A.A,$$

where U_A is a finite set of words over the alphabet of role names, i.e., $U_A \subseteq N_R^*$. Note that $\forall\emptyset.A$ represents the universal concept $\top$, and $\forall\{\varepsilon\}.A$ for the empty word ε is equivalent to A.

If the CCNF of D is $\bigsqcap_{A \in N_C} \forall V_A.A$, then subsumption of C by D can be characterized as follows:

Proposition 6.15 $C \sqsubseteq D$ *iff* $V_A \subseteq U_A$ *for all* $A \in N_C$.

As an easy consequence, we obtain

Corollary 6.16 $lcs(C, D) \equiv \bigsqcap_{A \in N_C} \forall(U_A \cap V_A).A$.

By Proposition 6.15, this concept description obviously subsumes C and D. Moreover, $U_A \cap V_A$ is the largest set contained in both U_A and V_A, and thus $\bigsqcap_{A \in N_C} \forall(U_A \cap V_A).A$ is in fact the least concept subsuming both C and D. As an example consider the concept C specified above and $D \equiv \forall\{RS, RR\}.A \sqcap \forall\{RR, SR\}.B$. Then, $lcs(C, D) \equiv \forall\{RS\}.A \sqcap \forall\{RR\}.B$.

For Description Logics extending $\mathcal{FL}_0$ by constructs that can express unsatisfiable concepts, like $\bot$, the language-based approach can still be applied. However, in order to characterize subsumption, we need to consider certain infinite regular languages instead of finite ones. The reason is that $\bot$ is subsumed by an infinite number of concept descriptions. For example, although $\forall\{R, RSR\}.\bot \sqsubseteq \forall\{RR\}.\bot$, we do *not* have $V_\bot = \{RR\} \subseteq \{R, RSR\} =: U_\bot$. However, we know that $\forall\{R\}.\bot$ is subsumed by $\forall\{Rw\}.\bot$ for any word w of the alphabet N_R. Consequently, we must use $U_\bot \cdot N_R^* = \{vw \mid v \in U_\bot \text{ and } w \in N_R^*\}$ in place of $U_\bot$ in the inclusion test. For this reason, the lcs must also be described in terms of possibly infinite regular languages. As a simple example, consider the concept descriptions $C \equiv \forall \{R, SR\}.\bot$ and $D \equiv \forall \{RS, S\}.\bot$. Then,

$$\begin{aligned} lcs(C, D) &\equiv \forall (\{R, SR\} \cdot N_R^* \cap \{RS, S\} \cdot N_R^*).\bot \\ &\equiv \forall (\{RS, SR\} \cdot N_R^*).\bot \\ &\equiv \forall \{RS, SR\}.\bot. \end{aligned}$$

A detailed description of how to compute the lcs in $\mathcal{ALN}$, which extends $\mathcal{FL}_0$ by $\bot$, atomic complement, and number restrictions, is given in [Baader and Küsters, 1998]. Moreover, Baader and Küsters investigate cyclic $\mathcal{ALN}$-concept descriptions, which are defined in terms of cyclic terminologies with greatest fixpoint semantics. In this context, the languages U_A introduced above can be arbitrary regular languages (see also Chapter 2, Subsection 2.3.3.2).

Cyclic descriptions become necessary if one wants to guarantee the existence of the msc. Consider, for example, the ABox consisting only of the assertion $R(a, a)$. Then, we know that $msc(a) \sqsubseteq \forall R. \cdots \forall R.(\leqslant 1\, R)$ for arbitrarily deep nesting of value restrictions. Baader and Küsters show that there does not exist an acyclic $\mathcal{ALN}$-concept description presenting the msc of a. However, the msc of individuals described in $\mathcal{ALN}$-ABoxes can always be represented by a cyclic $\mathcal{ALN}$-concept description. In our example, $msc(a)$ can be represented by the concept A defined by $A \equiv (= 1\, R) \sqcap \forall R.A$, if this definition is interpreted with greatest fixpoint semantics.

Using the graph-based approach, the lcs can be computed for the Description Logic that extends $\mathcal{FL}_0$ by the same-as construct [Cohen and Hirsh, 1994a; Frazier and Pitt, 1994; Küsters and Borgida, 2001], for the language $\mathcal{ALE}$, which extends $\mathcal{FL}_0$ by full existential quantification and primitive negation [Baader *et al.*, 1999b], and for the language $\mathcal{ALEN}$, which extends $\mathcal{ALE}$ by number restrictions [Küsters and Molitor, 2001b]. On the one hand, it is not clear how to handle these languages with the language-based approach. On the other hand, up to now the graph-based approach cannot deal with cyclic concept descriptions, which are needed for computing the msc. Consequently, for the extensions of $\mathcal{FL}_0$ treated with the help of the graph-based approach, the msc can currently only be approximated [Cohen and Hirsh, 1994b; Küsters and Molitor, 2001a].

6.3.3 Unification and matching

Unification and matching are non-standard inferences that allow us to replace certain concept names by concept descriptions before testing for equivalence or subsumption. This capability turns out to be useful when maintaining (large) knowledge bases. In this subsection, we will first introduce unification and matching and mention the main motivations for considering these new inference tasks. We will then review the results available in the literature, and give an intuition on how unification problems in the small language $\mathcal{FL}_0$ can be solved.

6.3.3.1 Unification

Unification of concepts was first introduced by Baader and Narendran [1998], motivated by the following application problem. If several knowledge engineers are involved in defining new concepts, and if this knowledge acquisition process takes rather long (several years), it happens that the same (intuitive) concept is introduced several times, often with slightly differing descriptions. Testing for equivalence of concepts is not always sufficient to find out whether, for a given concept description, there already exists another concept description in the knowledge base describing the same notion. As an example, let us ask whether the following two $\mathcal{FL}_0$-concept descriptions might denote the same (intuitive) concept.

$$\forall\text{has-child}.\forall\text{has-child}.\text{Rich} \sqcap \forall\text{has-child}.\text{Rmr},$$

$$\text{Acr} \sqcap \forall\text{has-child}.\text{Acr} \sqcap \forall\text{has-child}.\forall\text{has-spouse}.\text{Rich}.$$

The answer is yes, since replacing the concept name Rmr by the description Rich $\sqcap$ $\forall$has-spouse.Rich and Acr by $\forall$has-child.Rich yields the descriptions

$$\forall\text{has-child}.\forall\text{has-child}.\text{Rich} \sqcap \forall\text{has-child}.(\text{Rich} \sqcap \forall\text{has-spouse}.\text{Rich}),$$

$$\forall\text{has-child}.\text{Rich} \sqcap \forall\text{has-child}.\forall\text{has-child}.\text{Rich} \sqcap \forall\text{has-child}.\forall\text{has-spouse}.\text{Rich},$$

which are obviously equivalent. Thus, under the assumption that Rmr stands for "Rich and married rich" and Acr for "All children are rich", we can conclude that both descriptions are meant to express the concept "All grandchildren are rich and all children are rich and married rich".

A substitution of concept descriptions for concept names that makes two concept descriptions C, D equivalent is called a *unifier* of C and D. Of course, before testing for unifiability, one must decide which of the concept names the unifier is allowed to replace. These names are then called *concept variables* to distinguish them from the usual concept names, which cannot be replaced. In the above example, the strange acronyms Acr and Rmr were considered to be variables, whereas Rich was treated as a (non-replaceable) concept name. Concept descriptions containing variables are called concept patterns. More precisely, $\mathcal{FL}_0$-*concept patterns* are defined by means of the following syntax rules:

$$C, D \longrightarrow X \mid A \mid \forall R.C \mid C \sqcap D$$

where X stands for concept variables.

Now, a *substitution* in $\mathcal{FL}_0$ is a mapping from the concept variables into the set of $\mathcal{FL}_0$-concept descriptions. An example is the substitution {Rmr $\mapsto$ Rich $\sqcap$ $\forall$has-spouse.Rich, Acr $\mapsto$ $\forall$has-child.Rich} used in our example. The application of a substitution can be extended from variables to $\mathcal{FL}_0$-concept patterns in the usual way (as exemplified above).

Definition 6.17 Let C, D be $\mathcal{FL}_0$-concept patterns. Then, a substitution σ is a *unifier* of the unification problem $C \equiv^? D$ iff $\sigma(C) \equiv \sigma(D)$.

Of course, it is not necessarily the case that concept descriptions that are unifiable in this way are really meant to represent the same notion. A unifiability test can, however, suggest to the knowledge engineer possible candidate descriptions.

6.3.3.2 Matching

Matching can be seen as a special case of unification, where one of the two expressions to be unified does not contain variables [Baader and Narendran, 1998; 2001]. Thus, a matching problem is of the form $C \equiv^? D$ where C is a concept description and D a concept pattern. A substitution σ is a *matcher* of this problem iff $C \equiv \sigma(D)$.

Borgida and McGuinness [1996] have introduced a different notion of matching, which we call *matching modulo subsumption* to distinguish it from *matching modulo equivalence*, as introduced above. A matching problem modulo subsumption is of the form $C \sqsubseteq^? D$, where C is a concept description and D is a concept pattern. Such a problem asks for a substitution σ such that $C \sqsubseteq \sigma(D)$.

Since σ is a solution of $C \sqsubseteq^? D$ iff σ solves $C \equiv^? C \sqcap D$, matching modulo subsumption can be reduced to matching modulo equivalence, and thus to unification. However, in the context of matching modulo subsumption, one is interested in finding "minimal" solutions of $C \sqsubseteq^? D$, i.e., σ should satisfy the property that there does not exist another substitution δ such that $C \sqsubseteq \delta(D) \sqsubset \sigma(D)$. In addition, Baader *et al.* [1999a] introduce side conditions of the form $X \sqsubseteq E$ and $X \sqsubset E$, with X a variable and E a concept pattern, to further restrict possible substitutions for the variables occurring in the matching problem.

The original reason for introducing matching modulo equivalence was (i) to help filter out unimportant aspects of complicated concepts appearing in large knowledge bases, and (ii) to specify patterns for explaining proofs carried out by Description Logic systems [McGuinness and Borgida, 1995]. For example, matching the concept pattern

$$D = \forall\text{research-interests}.X$$

against the description

$$C = \forall\text{pets}.\text{Cat} \sqcap \forall\text{research-interests}.\text{AI} \sqcap \forall\text{hobbies}.\text{Gardening}$$

yields the minimal matcher $\sigma = \{X \mapsto \text{AI}\}$, and thus finds the scientific interest described in the concept, filtering out the other aspects described by C.

Another motivation for matching as well as unification can be found in the area of integrating data or knowledge base schemas represented in some Description Logic. An integrated schema can be viewed as the union of the local schemas along with some interschema assertions satisfying certain conditions. Finding such interschema assertions can be supported by solving matching or unification problems. Borgida and Küsters [2000] propose a formal framework for schema integration, and provide initial theoretical as well as experimental results concerning this application of unification and matching.

6.3.3.3 Results on matching and unification

As with computing the lcs, the algorithms for matching that can be found in the literature follow either the language-based or the graph-based approach. Matching modulo subsumption for a description language containing most of the constructs available in CLASSIC has been considered in [Borgida and McGuinness, 1996]. Borgida and McGuinness describe a polynomial-time matching algorithm, which follows the graph-based approach. However, this algorithm cannot be applied to arbitrary patterns, and it is not complete. Using the language-based approach, complete and polynomial-time algorithms for matching modulo equivalence and matching modulo subsumption in $\mathcal{FL}_0$ were presented in [Baader and Narendran, 1998; 2001]. This result was extended to the language $\mathcal{ALN}$ by Baader *et al.* [1999a] and its extension $\mathcal{ALN}_{\text{reg}}$ by the role constructors union, composition, and transitive closure by Küsters [2001]. Baader *et al.* [2001] consider matching under side conditions in more detail. Basically, subsumption conditions of the form $X \sqsubseteq E$ leave the complexity of matching in $\mathcal{ALN}$ polynomial, whereas strict subsumption conditions $X \sqsubset E$ cause NP-hardness. Matching in $\mathcal{ALE}$ based on the characterization of subsumption by homomorphism between graphs has been investigated in [Baader and Küsters, 2000]. It is shown that matching modulo equivalence is NP-complete, and that appropriate matchers can be computed in exponential time. Finally, complete algorithms for matching in CLASSIC are provided by Küsters [2001].

For unification, the only results available to date are for the small Description Logic $\mathcal{FL}_0$ and its extension $\mathcal{FL}_{reg}$ by the role constructors union, composition, and transitive closure. In [Baader and Narendran, 1998; 2001] it is shown that deciding unifiability of $\mathcal{FL}_0$-patterns is an EXPTIME-complete problem, and in [Baader and Küsters, 2001] this result is extended to $\mathcal{FL}_{reg}$. In the remainder of this subsection, we will try to give a flavor of how to solve unification problems in $\mathcal{FL}_0$.

As an immediate consequence of Proposition 6.15, equivalence of $\mathcal{FL}_0$-concept descriptions $C = \bigsqcap_{A \in N_C} \forall U_A.A$ and $D = \bigsqcap_{A \in N_C} \forall V_A.A$ in CCNF can be characterized as follows:

$$C \equiv D \text{ iff } U_A = V_A \text{ for all } A \in N_C. \tag{6.3}$$

This fact can be used to turn $\mathcal{FL}_0$-unification problems into certain formal language equations, which then can be solved using tree automata.

Let us illustrate this by the example from Subsection 6.3.3.1. There, we considered the unification problem[8]

$$\forall\{cc\}.R \sqcap \forall\{c\}.X \equiv^? \forall\{\varepsilon, c\}.Y \sqcap \forall\{cs\}.R.$$

As an easy consequence of (6.3), a substitution σ of the form

$$\{X \mapsto \forall U_X.R, \ Y \mapsto \forall U_Y.R\},$$

where U_X, U_Y are sets of words over the alphabet $\{c, s\}$, is a unifier of this problem iff the assignment $X = U_X$ and $Y = U_Y$ solves the formal language equation

$$\{cc\} \cup \{c\}\cdot X = \{cs\} \cup \{\varepsilon, c\}\cdot Y.$$

For example, the unifier $\{X \mapsto R \sqcap \forall s.R, \ Y \mapsto \forall c.R\}$ corresponds to the solution $X = \{\varepsilon, s\}, Y = \{c\}$ of the above formal language equation. In general, unification problems correspond to systems of formal language equations of the form

$$S_0 \cup S_1\cdot X_1 \cup \cdots \cup S_n\cdot X_n = T_0 \cup T_1\cdot X_1 \cup \cdots \cup T_n\cdot X_n,$$

where the S_i, T_i are given finite sets of words and the X_i are variables ranging over finite sets of words. In [Baader and Narendran, 1998;

---

[8] To increase readability, has-spouse is replaced by s, has-child by c, Rich by R, and Rmr, Acr by the variables X, Y. In addition, we have already transformed the patterns into their CCNF.

2001] it is shown that solvability of such a system of equations can be reduced (in exponential time) to the emptiness problem for automata on finite trees. This yields an EXPTIME-decision procedure for unification in $\mathcal{FL}_0$. For unification in $\mathcal{FL}_{\mathrm{reg}}$, the S_i, T_i are regular languages, and to test the equation for solvability one must employ automata working on infinite trees.

6.3.4 Concept rewriting

A general framework for rewriting concepts using terminologies has been proposed in Baader *et al.* [2000]. Assume that $\mathcal{L}_1, \mathcal{L}_2$, and $\mathcal{L}_3$ are three description languages, and let C be an $\mathcal{L}_1$-concept description and $\mathcal{T}$ an $\mathcal{L}_2$-TBox. We are interested in rewriting (i.e., transforming) C into an $\mathcal{L}_3$-concept description D such that C and D are in a certain relationship (e.g., equivalence, subsumption w.r.t. $\mathcal{T}$) and such that D satisfies certain optimality criteria (e.g., being of minimal size).

This very general framework has several interesting instances. In the following, we will discuss the three most promising ones.

The first instance is the *translation of concept descriptions* from one Description Logic into another. Here, we assume that $\mathcal{L}_1$ and $\mathcal{L}_3$ are different description languages, and that the TBox $\mathcal{T}$ is empty. By trying to rewrite an $\mathcal{L}_1$-concept C into an *equivalent* $\mathcal{L}_3$-concept D, one can find out whether C is expressible in $\mathcal{L}_3$. In many cases, such an exact rewriting may not exist. In this case, one can try to approximate C by an $\mathcal{L}_3$-concept from above (below), i.e., find a minimal (maximal) concept description D in $\mathcal{L}_3$ such $C \sqsubseteq D$ ($D \sqsubseteq C$). An inference service that can compute such rewritings could, for example, support the transfer of knowledge bases between different systems. First results in this direction for the case where $\mathcal{L}_1$ is $\mathcal{ALC}$ and $\mathcal{L}_3$ is $\mathcal{ALE}$ can be found in [Brandt *et al.*, 2001].

The second instance comes from the database area, where the problem of *rewriting queries using views* is a well-known research topic [Beeri *et al.*, 1997]. The aim is to optimize the runtime of queries by using cached views, which allows one to minimize the (more expensive) access to source relations. In the context of the above framework, views can be regarded as TBox definitions and queries as concept descriptions. Beeri *et al.* [1997] investigate the instance where $\mathcal{L}_1 = \mathcal{L}_2 = \mathcal{ALCNR}$ and $\mathcal{L}_3 = \{\sqcap, \sqcup\}$. More precisely, they are interested in maximally contained total rewritings, i.e., D should be subsumed by C, contain only concept names defined in the TBox, and be a maximal concept (w.r.t. subsumption) satisfying these properties. They show that such a rewriting is computable (whenever it exists).

The third instance of the general framework, which was first proposed in [Baader and Molitor, 1999], tries to increase the readability of large concept descriptions by using concepts defined in a TBox. The motivation comes from the experiences made with non-standard inferences (like lcs, msc and matching) in applications. The concept descriptions produced by these services are usually unfolded (i.e., do not use defined names), and are thus often very large and hard to read and comprehend. Therefore, one is interested in automatically generating an equivalent concept description of minimal length that employs the concept names defined in the underlying terminology. Referring to the framework, one thus considers the case where $\mathcal{L} = \mathcal{L}_1 = \mathcal{L}_2 = \mathcal{L}_3$ and the TBox is nonempty. For a given concept description C and a TBox $\mathcal{T}$ in $\mathcal{L}$ one is interested in an $\mathcal{L}$-concept description D (containing concept names defined in $\mathcal{T}$) such that $C \equiv_{\mathcal{T}} D$ and the size of D is minimal. Rewriting in this sense has been investigated for the languages $\mathcal{ALN}$ and $\mathcal{ALE}$ [Baader and Molitor, 1999; Baader *et al.*, 2000]. Rewritings can be computed by a nondeterministic polynomial algorithm that uses an oracle for deciding subsumption. The corresponding decision problem (i.e., the question whether there exists a rewriting of size $\leq k$ for a given number k) is NP-hard for both languages.

Acknowledgement

We would like to thank Jochen Heinsohn and Manfred Jaeger for helpful discussions regarding the treatment of uncertain and vague knowledge and Riccardo Rosati regarding the treatment of epistemic operators.

Part II

Implementation

7

From Description Logic Provers
to Knowledge Representation Systems

Deborah L. McGuinness
Peter F. Patel-Schneider

Abstract

A DL-based knowledge representation system is more than an inference engine for a particular Description Logic. A knowledge representation system must provide a number of services to human users, including presentation of the information stored in the system in a manner palatable to users and justification of the inferences performed by the system. If human users cannot understand what the system is doing, then the development of knowledge bases is made much more difficult or even impossible. A knowledge representation system must also provide a number of services to application programs, including access to the basic information stored in the system but also including access to the machinations of the system. If programs cannot easily access and manipulate the information stored in the system, then the development of applications is made much more difficult or even impossible.

7.1 Introduction

A DL-based knowledge representation system does not live in a vacuum. It has to be prepared to interact with several sorts of other entities. One class of entities consists of human users who develop knowledge bases using the system. If the system cannot effectively interact with these users then it will be difficult to create knowledge bases in the system, and the system will not be used. Another class of entities consists of programs that use the services of the system to provide information to support applications. If the system cannot effectively interact with these programs then it will be difficult to create applications using the system, and the system will not be used.

However, before one can talk about effective interaction, there has to be basic interaction between the knowledge representation system and applications or users. This basic interaction has to do with the mechanics of telling information to the system and retrieving information from it. At this level the system just maintains what it was told and responds to the queries by running an inference procedure for the logic it implements.

The basic interface is not sufficient for effective access to the system. On the application side there is need for a treatment of exceptional conditions, wider interface to applications, remote interfaces, and concurrent access, among others. There is also need for responsive reaction by the system. On the human side there is need for better presentation of the results of queries, particularly the suppression of irrelevant detail; explanation of the inferences performed by the system; better support for the creation of large DL knowledge bases, particularly by several people working in collaboration.

Even if all the above are present in a system, it will still not be complete. There is also a need to have effective information about the system widely available. This information has to be in various forms, including the obvious user manuals, but also including interactive tutorials and demonstration systems.

A system that does not include all of the above services is not a complete knowledge representation system.

Our discussion of the services that need to be provided will mostly be described in terms of an arbitrary DL knowledge representation system. However, some of our examples will be given in the context of the CLASSIC family of knowledge representation systems developed at AT&T [Borgida *et al.*, 1989; Brachman *et al.*, 1991; Patel-Schneider *et al.*, 1991], as CLASSIC has had the longest-lived and most extensive industrial application history of any DL knowledge representation system. The CLASSIC application that we will refer to the most is the configuration of transmissions equipment – an application developed within AT&T [Wright *et al.*, 1993; McGuinness *et al.*, 1995; McGuinness and Wright, 1998b; McGuinness *et al.*, 1998].

In a typical configuration problem, a user is interested in entering a small number of constraints and obtaining a complete, correct, and consistent parts list. Given a configuration application's domain knowledge and the base DL inference system, the application can determine if the user's constraints are consistent. It can then calculate the deductive closure of the user-stated knowledge and the background domain knowledge to generate a more complete description of the final parts list. For example, in a home theater demonstration configuration system [McGuinness *et al.*, 1995], user input is solicited on the quality a user is willing to pay for and the typical use (audio only, home theater only, or combination), and then the application deduces all applicable consequences. This typically generates descriptions for 6–20 subcomponents which restrict properties such as price range, television diagonal, power rating, etc. A user might then inspect any of the individual components possibly adding further requirements to it which may, in turn, cause further constraints to appear on other components of the system. Also, a user may ask the system to "complete" the configuration task, completely specifying each component so that a parts list is generated and an order may be completed.

This home theater configurator example is fairly simple but it is motivated by real-world application uses in configuring very large pieces of transmission equipment where objects may have thousands of parts and subparts and one decision can easily have hundreds of ramifications. It was complicated applications such as these that drove our work on access to information. More information can be found on Description Logics for configuration in this book in Chapter 12. Another example application that drove our work on information access and presentation needs was a simple DL backend system supporting knowledge-enhanced search for the web called FINDUR [McGuinness, 1998; McGuinness *et al.*, 1997] which is also described in Chapter 14.

7.2 Basic access

Basic access to a DL knowledge base consists of simple mechanisms to create DL knowledge bases and to query them. The foundational aspects of this basic interaction have been well-studied. For example, Levesque [1984] proposed that the basic interface to any knowledge representation system consist of two kinds of interactions – one to *tell* information to the system and one to *ask* whether information follows from what was previously told to the system.

Many frame-oriented knowledge representation systems embody such distinctions, such as the Generic Frame Protocol [Chaudhri *et al.*, 1997], and OKBC (Open Knowledge Base Connectivity) [Chaudhri *et al.*, 1998a]. In the DL community, this basic interaction was standardized into an interface specification that defined a number of Tell&Ask operations that a DL knowledge representation system should implement [Patel-Schneider and Swartout, 1993]. This specification is commonly known as the KRSS

Table 7.1. *Syntax and semantics of making definitions.*

Program Syntax	Abstract Syntax	Semantics
(define-concept CN C)	$CN \equiv C$	$CN^{\mathcal{I}} = C^{\mathcal{I}}$
(define-primitive-concept CN C)	$CN \sqsubseteq C$	$CN^{\mathcal{I}} \subseteq C^{\mathcal{I}}$
(define-role RN R)	$RN \equiv R$	$RN^{\mathcal{I}} = R^{\mathcal{I}}$
(define-primitive-role RN R)	$RN \sqsubseteq R$	$RN^{\mathcal{I}} \subseteq R^{\mathcal{I}}$
(define-attribute AN A)	$AN \equiv A$	$AN^{\mathcal{I}} = A^{\mathcal{I}}$
(define-primitive-attribute AN R)	$AN \sqsubseteq R$	$AN^{\mathcal{I}} \subseteq R^{\mathcal{I}}$

specification.[1] The description of a minimal DL knowledge representation system interface given here will generally follow this KRSS specification. The KRSS specification incorporates the DFKI standardized syntax and semantics [Baader *et al.*, 1991]. Examples given here follow the syntax of Chapter 2, for the abstract syntax, and the syntax of KRSS for a LISP-like syntax that can actually be used from within a computer.

One problem with defining a Tell&Ask interface for a DL knowledge representation system is that even a minimal interface depends on the expressive power of the logic. As an example, if the Description Logic implemented by the system does not include individuals then of course there is no need to include any facilities for making statements about individuals. To overcome this difficulty this chapter will describe the interfaces required for a system that implements a typical Description Logic with both concepts and individuals.

Such a system has to have a method for creating a terminology of concepts. A syntax for creating such a terminology, taken directly from the KRSS specification, is given in Table 7.1. A terminological knowledge base, or TBox, is then a set of such definitions perhaps with the condition that every concept, role, and attribute name has at most one definition. There may also be the side condition that there are no recursive definitions.

Some representation systems may have other definitions allowable or other restrictions. For example, some systems allow the definition of transitive roles, via a define-transitive-role definition. Other systems prohibit non-primitive roles.

If the underlying Description Logic allows recursive definitions, then it may be easier to provide an even more basic interface to define concepts. Table 7.2 shows a minimal interface for a system that employs arbitrary concept inclusions as its means of defining concepts.

---

[1] The KRSS specification also incorporates a number of operations that fall under the advanced interface that will be discussed later.

Table 7.2. *Inclusion syntax and semantics.*

Program Syntax	Abstract Syntax	Semantics
(included C D)	$C \sqsubseteq D$	$C^{\mathcal{I}} \subseteq D^{\mathcal{I}}$

Table 7.3. *Assertion syntax and semantics.*

Program Syntax	Abstract Syntax	Semantics
(instance IN C)	$IN \in C$	$IN^{\mathcal{I}} \in C^{\mathcal{I}}$
(related IN I R)	$\langle IN, I \rangle \in R$	$\langle IN^{\mathcal{I}}, I^{\mathcal{I}} \rangle \in R^{\mathcal{I}}$

Table 7.4. *Query syntax and semantics.*

Query	Meaning
(concept-subsumes? C1 C2)	$C_1^{\mathcal{I}} \subseteq C_2^{\mathcal{I}}$
(role-subsumes? R1 R2)	$R_1^{\mathcal{I}} \subseteq R_2^{\mathcal{I}}$
(individual-instance? IN C)	$IN^{\mathcal{I}} \in C^{\mathcal{I}}$
(individual-related? IN I R)	$\langle IN^{\mathcal{I}}, I^{\mathcal{I}} \rangle \in R^{\mathcal{I}}$

If the system incorporates individual reasoning, then it has to have a mechanism for adding information about these individuals. One such method is via the assertions in Table 7.3. An assertional knowledge base, or ABox, is then a set of such assertions.

Once information has been told to the system, there has to be a mechanism for determining what follows from this information. A minimal mechanism for this is via a set of queries, such as those given in Table 7.4. The system answers a quary by determining if the meaning of the query is implied by the information that has been told to the system.

The interface described above is sufficient for determining the contents of a knowledge base but only in the theoretical sense. For reasonable access to the information in a knowledge base a richer interface is required. One part of this richer access even really belongs in the basic interface, namely retrievals of taxonomy information. The interface in Table 7.5 provides a simple interface to the taxonomy information implicit in a DL knowledge base. The meaning of the calls should be obvious from their description, except perhaps the "**-direct-**" versions, which return the concepts,

Table 7.5. *Taxonomy retrieval*
syntax.

```
(concept-descendants C)
(concept-children C)
(concept-ancestors C)
(concept-parents C)
(concept-instances C)
(concept-direct-instances C)
(role-descendants R)
(role-children R)
(role-ancestors R)
(role-parents R)
(individual-types IN)
(individual-direct-types IN)
(individual-fillers IN R)
```

individuals, or roles that are directly related to the query, i.e., that have no intervening concept or role.

Another basic service that is missing from above interface is the ability to remove information from the knowledge base. This is not the ability to perform arbitrary changes to the implicit information represented by the knowledge base. Instead it is just the ability to "un-tell" information that had been previously told to the system. A basic interface for this purpose is given in Table 7.6. There may be restrictions on what can be un-told, such as requiring that concepts that are currently mentioned in the definition of other concepts cannot be removed from the knowledge base.

7.3 Advanced application access

The basic interface described above provides only minimal access to a DL knowledge base. Effective access requires a number of augmentations to the basic interface.

One of the most important augmentations has to do with defining a complete application programming interface (API). The basic interface assumes that the system is implemented in a language like LISP, where there is a simple way of creating descriptions and other values for the various operations and there is a mechanism for returning values of any type. This was acceptable when systems and applications were all implemented in LISP, but this is no longer the case.

A complete API must then provide a syntax for creating all the types of values that need to be passed to the representation system. Further, it

Table 7.6. *UnTell syntax.*

```
(undefine-concept CN)
(undefine-role RN)
(undefine-attribute AN)
(un-tell-instance IN C)
(un-tell-related IN I R)
```

needs to provide or define mechanisms for returning values, particularly compound values such as the sets of concepts that are returned by the taxonomic retrieval operations.

7.3.1 Efficiency

Because the operations of the representation system may represent the largest resource consumption of an application, it is often necessary to know how expensive various operations of the system may be. For example, it is often necessary to know the usual resource consumption of the most frequently called operations of the knowledge representation system or those operations that are called at critical time in the operation of the whole system.

The CLASSIC family has been particularly aggressive in ensuring that queries to the system are fast, working under the assumption that the most common operations are queries. Most queries in CLASSIC are simply retrievals of data stored by the system, as CLASSIC responds to the addition of knowledge by computing most of its consequences. Further, the performance of the addition of knowledge to the system is optimized over the retraction or change of knowledge.

CLASSIC achieves these characteristics of fastest queries, fast additions, and slower retractions and changes by retaining data structures that record the current set of consequences and also record, on a fairly granular level, which knowledge affects other knowledge. This is not full truth-maintenance data, which would be prohibitively expensive to compute (and store), but is just enough to make additions cheap. It also serves to make retractions and changes somewhat cheaper than they otherwise would be, but this effect is much less than the gain in speed of adding knowledge.

7.3.2 Wide application programming interface

In the vast majority of applications, the knowledge representation system has to serve as a tightly integrated component of a much larger overall system. For this to be workable, the knowledge representation system must provide a full-featured interface for the use of the rest of the system.

The NEOCLASSIC system, which is programmed in C++, and is designed to be part of a larger C++ program, provides a very wide application programming interface. In addition to the above interface, there is a large interface that lets the rest of the system receive and process the actual data structures used inside NEOCLASSIC to represent knowledge, but without allowing these structures to be modified outside of NEOCLASSIC.[2] This interface allows much faster access to the knowledge stored by NEOCLASSIC, as many accesses just retrieve fields from a data structure. Further, direct access to data structures allows the rest of the system to keep track of knowledge from NEOCLASSIC without having to keep track of a "name" for the knowledge querying using this name. (In fact, it is in this way possible to dispense with any notion of querying by name.)

There are also ways to obtain the data structures that are used by NEOCLASSIC for other purposes, including explanation. We have used this facility to write graphical user interfaces to present explanations and other information.

An additional interface that is provided by both LISP CLASSIC and NEOCLASSIC is a notification mechanism, or hooks. This mechanism allows programmers to write functions that are called when particular changes are made in the knowledge stored in the system or when the system infers new knowledge from other knowledge. Hooks for the retraction of knowledge from the system are also provided. These hooks allow, among other things, the creation of a graphical user interface that mirrors (some portion or view of) the knowledge stored in the representation system.

Others in the knowledge representation community have recognized the need for common APIs, (e.g., the Generic Frame Protocol [Chaudhri *et al.*, 1997] and the Open Knowledge Base Connectivity [Chaudhri *et al.*, 1998a]). Some systems embrace the notion of loading many different forms of knowledge bases and accept wrapper specifications for other source formats and APIs. For example, ONTOLINGUA has implemented capability for loading a number of formats including CLASSIC, OKBC, ANSI KIF, KIF 3.0, CML, CLIPS, ONTOLINGUA, PROTÉGÉ, SNARK, and DAML+OIL. It also provides the ability to dump frames in multiple formats such as OKBC,

---

[2] Of course, as C++ does not have an inviolable type system, there are mechanisms to modify these structures. It is just that any well-typed access cannot.

CLASSIC, CLOS, CML, ONTOLINGUA, and DAML+OIL and it has also been made interoperable with at least two reasoners including one in LISP and one in Java.

7.3.3 Remote and concurrent access

The standard computing environment is becoming more and more distributed. If a DL knowledge representation system is to be part of this environment it must allow effective remote access. There are several mechanisms for allowing remote access, including applications that run on the same machine as the DL knowledge representation system but themselves provide a remote access mechanism. Examples of such applications are the wines [Brachman *et al.*, 1991] and stereo configuration demonstration systems [McGuinness *et al.*, 1995] mentioned later in this chapter.

The DL knowledge representation system itself can also directly provide a remote access mechanism. This can be as simple as providing the system with a pipe-like interface where clients can send a sequence of commands to the system from remote machines, and receive responses via the same pipe. NEOCLASSIC provides this sort of simple remote access mechanism.

A more complicated remote access mechanism would be to provide a CORBA interface to the system. This kind of access was proposed by Bechhofer *et al.* [1999]. Their interface gives a CORBA layering around a Tell&Ask interface. Providing a wider CORBA access to DL knowledge representation systems, such as providing CORBA access to the actual data structures of the system, is more difficult, as the CORBA mechanism for dealing with recursive objects is annoying. Nevertheless, an effective remote access mechanism should provide the same functionality as is desired for local access.

If remote access to a DL knowledge representation system is provided, then the issue of concurrent access becomes vital. (This is not to say that concurrent access is not of interest if the system does not allow remote access.) The interesting issues with respect to concurrent access involve simultaneous access to the same repository of knowledge. Most of the issues with respect to concurrent access are the same as concurrent access to databases, including locking and providing transactions. In fact, there have been informal proposals to use a database system to store the information in a DL knowledge representation system like CLASSIC just so as to piggyback on the facilities for concurrent access provided by the database system.

The remote interface proposal mentioned above provides a limited form of transactions, basically allowing clients to batch up a collection of updates to a knowledge base and apply them all at once as an atomic transaction. This interface, however, does not provide any mechanism to abort transactions or to provide a local view of the knowledge base during the execution of a transaction.

At least one other knowledge representation system has dealt with the notion of concurrent access by leveraging the notion of sessions. ONTOLINGUA allows users to log into a particular session that may already be opened by a previous user. All users logged into the same session see the same version of the knowledge base. A more sophisticated approach to concurrent access and knowledge base editing is embodied in ONTOBUILDER [Das *et al.*, 2001]. In this system, users can not only do something similar to sharing a session, but the implementation also facilitates collaboration through dialog with other users currently signed on to the same ontology and allows locking of concepts for updates.

7.3.4 Platforms

Another important access aspect concerns the platforms on which the knowledge representation system runs. This encompasses not only the machines and operating systems, but also the language in which the system is written (if it is visible), the version of the libraries that the system uses, and the mechanism for linking to the system. Many applications have needs for a particular operating system or language, and cannot utilize tools not available in this context.

Some Description Logics like CLASSIC have been made available on a reasonable number of platforms. The underlying language of a member of the CLASSIC family is visible, not just because of the API which is, of necessity, language-specific, but also because programmers can write functions to extend the expressive power of the system, and these functions have to be written in the underlying language of the system.

CLASSIC is currently available in two different languages: LISP and C++. The C++ member is the more recent, and the reimplementation used C++ precisely to make CLASSIC available for a larger number of applications. This was done even though C++ is not the ideal language in which to write a representation system.

The members of the CLASSIC family have also been written in a platform-independent manner. This has required not using some of the nicer capabilities of the underlying language or of particular operating systems. For example, NEOCLASSIC does not use C++ exceptions, partly because few C++ compilers supported this extension to the language. LISP-CLASSIC runs on various LISP implementations and on various operating systems, including most versions of Unix, MacOS, and Windows. NEOCLASSIC runs under four C++ compilers and on both Unix and Windows NT.

With the influence of the web and more distributed development environments, it may be expected that more Description Logics may be made available on multiple platforms and may be integrated into more hybrid environments. One example of another knowledge representation system that found a need to do this is the CHIMAERA Ontology Evolution Environment [McGuinness *et al.*, 2000b]. This system has been connected to ONTOLINGUA for ontology editing and simple inference, a LISP-based reasoner for some diagnostics, and a hybrid Java-based reasoning environment that supports both first-order logic reasoning as well as special-purpose reasoning for the DAML+OIL Description Logic.

7.4 Advanced human access

7.4.1 Explanation

Many research areas which focus on deductive systems (such as expert systems and theorem proving) have determined that explanation modules are required for even simple deductive systems to be usable by people other than their designers. Description Logics have at least as great a need for explanation as other deductive systems since they typically provide similar inferences to those found in other fields and also support added inferences particular to Description Logics. They provide a wide array of inferences [Borgida, 1992b] which can be strung together to provide complicated chains of inferences. Thus conclusions may be puzzling even to experts in Description Logics when application domains are unfamiliar or when chains of inference are long. Additionally, naive users may require explanations for deductions which may appear simple to knowledgeable users. Both sets of needs became evident in work on a family of configuration applications and necessitated an automatic explanation facility.

The main inference in Description Logics is subsumption – determining when membership in one class necessitates membership in another class. For example, Person is subsumed by Mammal since anything that is a member of the class Person must be a member of the class Mammal. Almost every inference in Description Logics can be rewritten using subsumption relationships and thus subsumption explanation forms the foundation of an explanation module [McGuinness and Borgida, 1995].

Although subsumption in most implemented Description Logics is calculated procedurally, it is preferable to provide a declarative presentation of the deductions because a procedural trace typically is very long and is littered with details of the implementation. A declarative explanation mechanism which relies on a proof-theoretic representation of deductions may be used as a framework. Such a mechanism has been specified [McGuinness, 1996] and implemented for CLASSIC and later specified for $\mathcal{ALN}$ [Baader *et al.*, 1999a].

All the inferences in a DL system can be represented declaratively by proof rules which state some (optional) antecedent conditions and deduce some consequent relationship. The subsumption rules may be written so that they have a single subsumption relationship in the denominator. For example, if **Person** is subsumed by **Mammal**, then it follows that something that has all of its children restricted to be **Persons** must be subsumed by something that has all of its children restricted to be **Mammals**. This can be written more generally (with C representing **Person**, D representing **Mammal**, and R representing `child`) as the $\forall$ restriction rule below:

$$\text{All restriction} \qquad \frac{\vdash C \sqsubseteq D}{\vdash \forall R.C \sqsubseteq \forall R.D}.$$

Using a set of proof rules that represent DL inferences, it is possible to give a declarative explanation of subsumption conclusions in terms of proof rule applications and appropriate antecedent conditions. This basic foundation can be applied to all of the inferences in Description Logics, including all of the inferences for handling constraint propagation and other individual inferences. There is a wealth of techniques that one can employ to make this basic approach more manageable and meaningful for users [McGuinness and Borgida, 1995; McGuinness, 1996].

Expressive DL-based systems may require a large number of proof rules. If one is interested in limiting both explanation implementation work and also the size of explanations, it is beneficial to prune the number of inferences to be explained. In one configuration family of applications [McGuinness and Wright, 1998b] the help desk logs were analyzed to determine the most frequent questions that related to explanation. These inferences included inheritance (if A is an instance of B and B is a subclass of C, then A "inherits" all the properties of C), propagation (if A fills a role R on B, and B is an instance of something which is known to restrict all of its fillers for the R role to be instances of D, then A is an instance of D), rule firing (if a is an instance of E and E has a rule associated with it that says that anything that is an E must also be an F, then a is an instance of F), and contradiction detection (e.g., I cannot be an instance of something that has at least 3 children and at most 2 children). In the initial development version, explanation was only provided for these inferences in an effort to minimize development costs, resulting in a quite useful explanation mechanism with much less effort than a full explanation system. (The two current implementations of explanation in CLASSIC contain complete explanation.) One demonstration system [McGuinness *et al.*, 1995] incorporates special handling for the most heavily used inferences providing natural language templates for presentations of explanations aimed at lay people.

7.4.2 Error handling

Since one common usage of deductive systems is for contradiction detection, handling error reporting and explanation is critical to usability. This usage is common in applications where object descriptions can easily become over-constrained. For example, in the home theater system application, one could generate a non-contradictory request for a high quality stereo system that costs under a certain amount. The description could later become inconsistent as more information is added. For example, a required high quality, expensive speaker set could violate a low total price constraint. Understanding evolving contradictions such as this challenges many users and leads them to request special error explanation support. Informal studies with internal users and external academic users indicate that adequate error support is crucial to the usability of the system.

Error handling could be viewed simply as a special case of inference where the conclusion is that some object is found to be described by a special concept typically called bottom or nothing. For example, a concept is incoherent if it has conflicting bounds on some role:

$$\text{Bounds Conflict} \quad \frac{\vdash C \sqsubseteq (\geqslant m\, r) \quad \vdash C \sqsubseteq (\leqslant n\, r) \quad n < m}{\vdash C \sqsubseteq \bot}.$$

If an explanation system is already implemented to explain proof-theoretic inference rules, then explaining error conditions is *almost* a special case of explaining any inference. There are two issues that are worth noting, however. The first is that information added to one object in the knowledge base may cause another object to become inconsistent. In fact, information about one object may impact another series of objects before a contradiction is discovered at some distant point along an inference chain. Typical DL systems require consistent knowledge bases; thus whenever they discover a contradiction, they use some form of truth maintenance to revert to a consistent state of knowledge, removing conclusions that depend on the information removed from the knowledge base. Thus, it is possible, if not typical, for an error condition to depend upon some conclusion that was later removed. A simple minded explanation based solely on information that is currently in the knowledge base would not be able to refer to these removed conclusions. Thus, any explanation system capable of explaining errors will need access to the inconsistent state of the knowledge base as well as to its current state.

Because of the added complexity resulting from the distinction between the current (consistent) state and the inconsistent state of the knowledge base and because of the importance of error explanation, we believe system designers will want to support special handling of error conditions. For example, in a number of situations surveyed, users typically asked for explanations of a particular object property or relationships between objects. Under error conditions, users had more trouble identifying an appropriate query to ask. This suggests that special error support should be introduced. In CLASSIC, for example, an automatic error explanation option is generated upon contradiction detection. This way the user requires no knowledge (other than the error explanation command name) in order to ask for help.

Another issue of importance to error handling is the completeness or incompleteness of the system. If a system is incomplete then it may miss deductions. Thus, it is possible that an object is inconsistent – if all of the logically implied deductions were to be made – but, because the system is incomplete, it misses some of these deductions and thus the object remains consistent in the knowledge base. In order for users to be able to use a system that is incomplete, they may need to be able to explain not only error deductions but deductions that were missed because of incomplete reasoning. An approach that completes the reasoning with respect to a particular aspect of an object is described in [McGuinness, 1996, Chapter 5]. Given the completed information, the system can then explain missed deductions.

7.4.3 Pruning

If a knowledge representation system makes it easy to generate and reason with complicated objects, users may find naive object presentations to be much too complex to handle. In order to make a system more usable, there needs to be some way of limiting the amount of information presented about complicated objects. For example, in the stereo demonstration application, a typical stereo system description may generate four pages of printout. The information contained in the description may be clearly meaningful information such as price ranges and model numbers for components but it may also contain descriptions of where the component might be displayed in the rack and which superconcepts are related to the object. In certain contexts it is desirable to print just model numbers and prices, and in other contexts it is desirable to print price ranges of components. We believe it is critical to provide support for encoding domain independent and domain dependent information which can be used along with contextual information to determine what information to print or explain. As one example, we consider some of the knowledge bases written for the DARPA High Performance Knowledge Base project. This project includes a very general upper level ontology with many slots defined on many of the classes. Most objects in the system inherit a large number of slots from upper ontology classes and it is not uncommon for normalized objects to have hundreds of slots associated with them even though they only have a couple of properties defined on them in the local knowledge bases.

Knowledge representation systems faced with information overload need to take some approach to filtering. One of the simplest approaches allows a specification on roles concerning whether they should be displayed on objects or not. This may work for homogeneous knowledge bases where role information is uniformly interesting or uninteresting. Our experience is, however, that context needs to be taken into account in more heterogeneous knowledge base applications. One example implementation that allows context and domain dependent information to be considered along with domain independent information is implemented in CLASSIC. A meta-language is defined for describing what is interesting to either print or explain on a class by class basis. Any subclass or instance of the class will then inherit the meta-description and thus will inherit "interestingness" properties from its parent classes. The meta-language essentially captures the expressive power of the base Description Logic with some carefully chosen epistemic operators to allow contextual information (such as known fillers or closed roles) to impact decisions on what to print.

The meta-language has been used to reduce object presentation and explanation by an order of magnitude in at least one application [McGuinness *et al.*, 1995]. This reduction was required for the application to be able to include object presentation. The algorithms of the basic approach are included in [McGuinness, 1996]; the theory of a generalized approach is presented in [Borgida and McGuinness, 1996] and further analyzed in [Baader *et al.*, 1999a].

7.4.4 Knowledge acquisition

If an application is expected to have a long life-cycle, then acquisition and maintenance of knowledge become major issues for usability. There are two kinds of knowledge acquisition which are worth considering: (i) acquisition of additional knowledge once a knowledge base is in place, and (ii) acquisition of original domain knowledge. A complete environment will address both concerns; however, the original acquisition of knowledge is a much more general and difficult problem and, conveniently enough, is not the activity that many users will find themselves doing repeatedly while maintaining a project.

We observe that with knowledge of the domain and appropriate analysis of evolution, it is possible to build a knowledge evolution environment suitable for non-experts to use for extending knowledge bases. One such project considered the evolution support environment for configurators. The specific domain and usage patterns were analyzed, and it was found that only certain classes had new subclasses added to them as product knowledge evolved. It was also found that instances were typically populated in particular patterns. A special purpose interface was developed for a family of configurators that exploited these findings and supported new configurator application development by non-experts [McGuinness and Wright, 1998b]. Also, in related work, Gil and Melz [1996] have analyzed planning-based uses of another DL-based system that systematically supports knowledge base evolution with respect to the known plan usage.

A more general problem that does not rely on domain or reasoning knowledge has been addressed in the editor work [Paley *et al.*, 1997] for the general frame protocol and also in editor work for collaborative generation and maintenance of ontologies by non-experts in the Collaborative Topic Builder component of FINDUR [McGuinness, 1998] and recently in CHIMAERA work [McGuinness *et al.*, 2000b] for merging, analyzing, and maintaining ontologies. The general work, of course, is broader yet shallower with respect to reasoning implications. In the FINDUR collaborative topic builder environment, simple hierarchies of node names (with role filler and value restriction information) are used to support query expansion to provide more intelligent web searching. In order to deploy this broadly, a web-based distributed ontology editor was required to allow non-experts to input, modify, and maintain background ontologies. The basic functionality for this interface follows the same requirements specified in Section 7.2 although this particular implementation limited some of the interface specifications according to expected usage patterns. For example, in the medical deployments

[McGuinness, 1999] of FINDUR, it was expected that all of the roles that were to be used had been defined and thus pulldown lists of these roles were hardcoded into the interface and new role specification was not one of the exposed functionalities in the GUI. FINDUR also allows importing of seed ontologies and supports contradiction detection from ontology input. CHIMAERA's environment takes the analysis task to a much more detailed level and it provides a number of different ways of detecting not only explicit contradictions but also possible contradictions and possible term merges.

7.5 Other technical concerns

The computer science concerns that affect the suitability of a knowledge representation system have to do with the behavior of the system as a computer program or routine, ignoring its status as a representer of knowledge. The most-studied aspect of this collection of concerns has to do with the computational analysis of the basic algorithms embodied in the system, in particular their worst-case complexity. Because this worst-case complexity has been so well studied, we will not say anything about it further, except to state that it *is* important in determining the suitability of a knowledge representation system for particular task, notably tasks that need a performance *guarantee*.

7.6 Public relations concerns

Researchers sometimes underestimate the varied public relations aspects involved with making a system usable. Barriers to usability come in many forms: potential users who are unaware of a system's existence will not use it; potential users who do not understand how a system can meet the their needs are unlikely to use it; potential users who do not have enough understanding to visualize an abstract solution to their problem using a new system are unlikely to depend on the new system over tools they understand and can predict; and finally potential users who have a limited set of approved tools which does not include the new system are unlikely go to the effort of getting the new system approved for their internal use. In order to address these issues, DL system designers need to devise ways to make their systems known to likely users, educate those users about the possible uses, provide support for teaching users how to use them for some standard and leverageable uses, and either obtain approval for their systems or provide ammunition for users to gain approval.

In experiences with CLASSIC, the following tools have been employed to overcome the above stated barriers to usability.

Beyond the standard research papers, users demand usage guidelines aimed at non-PhD researchers. A paper that provides a running (executable) example on how to use the system is most desirable: an example is [Brachman *et al.*, 1991]. That paper also tries to provide guidance on when a DL-based system might be useful, what its limitations are, and how one might go about using one in a simple application. That paper was used as the basis of a tutorial on building ontologies in other knowledge representation systems including PROTÉGÉ and ONTOLINGUA [Noy and McGuinness, 2000].

A demonstration system is also of great utility as it helps users understand a simple reasoning paradigm and provides a prototyping domain for showing off novel functionality which exploits the strengths of the underlying system. In the CLASSIC project a number of demonstration systems were developed, including a simple application that captures "typical" reasoning patterns in an accessible domain. This one system has been used in dozens of universities as a pedagogical tool and test system. While this application was appropriate for many students, an application more closely resembling some actual applications was needed to (i) give more meaningful demonstrations internally and to (ii) provide concrete suggestions of new functionality that developers might consider using in their applications. This led to a more complex application with a fairly serious graphical interface [McGuinness *et al.*, 1995]. Both of these applications have been adapted for the web.[3] It was only when a demonstration system that was clearly isomorphic to the developer's applications was available that there could be effective providing of clear descriptions and implemented examples of the functionality that we believed should be incorporated into development applications.

Interactive courses are also of benefit in training potential users in how to use a DL-based knowledge representation system. Several courses [McGuinness *et al.*, 1994; Abrahams *et al.*, 1996] on how to use CLASSIC have been developed, including one from a university for course use, which includes a set of five running assignments to help students gain experience using the system. Other general DL courses can be found on the DL web site at `http://www.dl.kr.org/`.

For a system to be used in the business community, it has to satisfy their demand for common standard implementation languages, reasonable support, and standard platform toolkits. Some DL implementations, such as

---

[3] The web version of the wines demonstration system was provided by Chris Welty and is available at `http://untangle.cs.vassar.edu/wine-demo/index.html`.

CLASSIC, attempted to meet this need by providing an implementation in C while still maintaining the LISP research version. This later proved problematic to maintain and the decision was made to provide an implementation in C++ that was to meet both developers' and implementers' needs. Interestingly enough, years later, it is the LISP version that appears to be most heavily used. More details of the evolution of the usability of that system can be found in [Brachman *et al.*, 1999].

7.7 Summary

Although a knowledge representation system must have sufficient expressive power and appropriate computational complexity to be considered for use in applications, there are many other issues that also determine whether it will be used. These issues involve access to the knowledge stored in the system, such as explanation and presentation of the knowledge, other technical issues, such as efficiency and programming interfaces, and non-technical issues, such as publicity and demos. If these issues are not addressed appropriately, a knowledge representation system will not be used in real applications.

8

Description Logic Systems

Ralf Möller
Volker Haarslev

Abstract

This chapter discusses implemented DL systems that have played or play an important role in the field. It first presents several earlier systems that, although not based on Description Logics, have provided important ideas. These systems include KL-ONE, KRYPTON, NIKL, and KANDOR. Then, successor systems are described by classifying them along the characteristics discussed in the previous chapters, addressing the following systems: CLASSIC ("almost" complete, fast); BACK, LOOM (expressive, incomplete); KRIS, CRACK (expressive, complete). Finally, a new optimized generation of very expressive but sound and complete DL systems is also introduced. In particular, we focus on the systems DLP, FaCT, and RACER and explain what they can and cannot do.

8.1 New light through old windows?

In this chapter a description of the goals behind the development of different DL systems is given from a historical perspective. The description of DL systems allows important insights into the development of the knowledge representation research field as a whole. The design decisions behind the well-known systems which we discuss in this chapter not only reflect the trends in different knowledge representation research areas but also characterize the point of view on knowledge representation that different researchers advocate. The chapter discusses general capabilities of the systems and gives an analysis of the main language features and design decisions behind system architectures. The analysis of current systems in the light of a historical perspective might lead to new ideas for the development of even more powerful DL systems in the future. References to previous descriptions of DL systems (e.g., in [MacGregor, 1991a; Woods and Schmolze, 1992; Horrocks, 1997a]) or publications on DL theory that also contain discussions about DL systems (e.g., [Patel-Schneider, 1987a; Nebel, 1990a; Schmidt, 1991]) are included where appropriate. For references to other systems not mentioned here see also [Woods and Schmolze, 1992] and [Nebel, 1990b, pp. 46f., pp. 63f.].

Basic concept and role constructors have already been introduced in Chapter 2 (see also the Appendix for a summary of syntax and semantics of DL constructors). However, before starting the discussion about DL systems it is appropriate to introduce some notation for language constructors in order to keep this chapter self-contained. It is assumed that the reader is familiar with the basic Description Logics $\mathcal{AL}$ and $\mathcal{ALC}$. In a similar way as in Chapter 2, further language features are indicated by different letters. The letter $\mathcal{N}$ is used for simple number restrictions and the letter $\mathcal{Q}$ is used for qualified number restrictions. $\mathcal{H}$ is used for role hierarchies with multiple parents whereas h is used for role hierarchies with single inheritance only. In some languages, no role hierarchies but role conjunctions are provided. Role conjunctions are indicated with the letter $\mathcal{R}$ in the following. In addition, the abbreviations $\mathcal{F}$ and f are used for features with and without equality for feature chains (i.e., agreements), respectively. The index R^+ is used to indicate support for transitive roles. Language constructors for an extensional specification of concepts using nominals (or individuals) are denoted by the letters $\mathcal{O}$ and $\mathcal{B}$ (see Chapter 2 or the Appendix for details). If inverse roles are supported by a DL system, this is indicated either by a superscript $^{-1}$ or by the letter $\mathcal{I}$. The latter variant is used in order to allow a convenient pronunciation of the DL language.

8.2 The first generation

Inspired by research on human cognitive behavior, proposals for knowledge representation languages were first discussed in the late 1960s. For example, [Quillian, 1967] is one of the first publications of the languages called "semantic networks" (see also [Quillian, 1968]). Originally, *semantic network formalisms* were seen as alternatives to first-order logic. In a similar spirit, [Minsky, 1981] introduced the initial notion of a *frame system*. The motivation of these representation formalisms was to mimic human reasoning in the sense of achieving "cognitive adequacy". Thus, the idea was to support problem solving with appropriate representation structures that somehow "resemble" representation structures assumed in human information processing. The exploitation of inheritance was a predominant idea in frame systems. The specification of knowledge bases should be simple and the use of the representation structures should be intuitive ("epistemological adequacy"). However, as pointed out by [Woods, 1975], it was not at all simple to specify what an inference system was supposed to actually compute. The late 1970s saw initial research on the relation of frame systems and first-order logic [Hayes, 1977; 1979] which revealed that some aspects of frame-based systems can be considered as special "instantiations" of first-order reasoning. Hayes argued that frame-based reasoning was not an entirely new way of knowledge representation with particular advantages over first-order reasoning. Specific features of frame systems beyond first-order reasoning (e.g., defaults) were not very well understood at that time. The consequence of these publications was that many researchers no longer considered frame systems and semantic network systems as possible alternatives to logic-based approaches.

The criticisms of early frame systems and semantic network formalisms stimulated research on the development of mathematical structures and techniques for defining the semantics of representational constructs supported by different representation languages. For instance, in early frame systems there was no clear distinction between constructs for representing "generic" knowledge about sets of individuals and knowledge about "specific" individuals. Furthermore, frames were often used as data structures in procedural programs. For these programs a formal specification of what they were expected to compute was rarely provided. Rather than interpreting frame structures as data structures, [Woods, 1975] suggested using a formal semantics to clearly specify what is to be computed by inference algorithms.

KL-ONE

Inspired by critics such as [Woods, 1975], Brachman started to develop a new representation system (called KL-ONE) that inherently included the notion of inferring implicit knowledge from given declarations [Brachman, 1977b; 1979]. Although the initial approach was not logic-based, KL-ONE started the era of logic-based representation systems which can be used to formalize application problems as inference problems over the constructs supported by the representation language. One of the prevailing inference patterns is centered around inheritance [Brachman, 1983]. The final report on the KL-ONE language is published in [Brachman and Schmolze, 1985].

One of the core ideas behind KL-ONE as a representation language for the "epistemological level" resulted from problems with languages offering built-in primitives for general representation purposes (e.g., CD theory [Schank, 1975]). Rather than providing general built-in primitives, in KL-ONE, for a specific representation problem a set of adequate primitives was defined by the user. The primitives were denoted by so-called *concept names*. The next idea was to use *concept-forming operators* to build new concepts from basic concepts. These compound concepts were also referred to as "concepts", "concept terms" or "concept descriptions". *Generic concepts* were intended to denote classes of individuals and *individual concepts* were intended to denote individuals (see also [Nebel, 1990a, p. 42]). Individuals were related by so-called *roles* which, in turn, could be primitive roles (role names) or roles described with role constructors [Brachman and Schmolze, 1985].

In KL-ONE, concepts and roles are the building blocks for representational purposes. The main idea behind concepts and concept constructors in KL-ONE is that the *meaning of a concept* is derived only from the meaning of its superconcepts and other restrictions associated with a concept [Brachman and Schmolze, 1985]. A KL-ONE generic concept consists of a set of superconcept names, a set of role descriptions, and a set of structural descriptions [Patel-Schneider, 1987a, pp. 58f.].[1] Roles can be viewed as potential relationships between an individual of a certain class and other individuals in the world [Nebel, 1990a, p. 42].

Role descriptions could be either restrictions or differentiations. The former restricted the class of permitted fillers (value restrictions) or the number of fillers (number restrictions). Role differentiations were used to describe a subrole with possible value or number restrictions. So-called structural descriptions were used to state relationships between the fillers of roles (see also [Patel-Schneider, 1987a, pp. 58f.]). Descriptions for individual concepts consisted simply of a set of values for roles plus a set of generic concepts. Individual concepts were seen as *instances* of these generic concepts, i.e., an individual concept had to satisfy all restrictions (and differentiations) inherited by the generic concepts. On the other hand, individual concepts were also *subsumed* by their generic concepts. However, the semantics of individuals was never completely worked out (see [Schmolze and Brachman, 1982, pp. 23–31] cited after [Nebel, 1990a, p. 64]).

The representation structures offered by KL-ONE were similar to those offered by semantic networks or frames. Although, initially, the structures offered by KL-ONE were called "structural inheritance networks" [Brach-

---

[1] Note that, in KL-ONE-like languages, there are specific syntactic constructs for specifying superconcepts. These specific constructs are no longer present in logic-based concept languages of the 1990s.

man, 1977b; 1979], in [Brachman and Levesque, 1984] the authors talk of
"frame structures".[2] In accordance with [Nebel, 1990a, p. 45] we argue that
in contrast to, e.g., CD theory [Schank, 1975], providing a (large) set of
primitive representation structures (names) for all kinds of representation
purposes was not the development goal of KL-ONE. As Nebel points out
[Nebel, 1990a, p. 45], more important and unique to KL-ONE is the core idea
of proving ways to specify *concept definitions*, i.e., the ability to let a knowledge engineer declare the relation of "high-level concepts" to "lower-level
primitives".

A concept definition was an assignment of a (unique) name to a concept
term. In KL-ONE the well-known distinction between the two kinds of concept definitions, definitions with necessary and sufficient conditions and definitions with only necessary conditions (so-called primitive definitions), was
investigated for knowledge representation purposes for the first time.[3] In the
original approach no cycles were allowed in the set of concept definitions.[4]
The most important consequence of the introduction of concept definitions
with necessary and sufficient conditions was that reasoning about the relationships between concepts became important. In KL-ONE there is still the
notion of a "told subsumer" syntactically being explicitly mentioned in a list
of so-called superconcepts but, according to the semantics, there are also additional *computed* subsumers which are concept names (direct subsumers or
direct superconcepts). Note that inferences in KL-ONE were based on the
open-world assumption. Hence, unlike frame systems, where the names as
superconcepts are always given explicitly, KL-ONE introduced the idea that
the set of direct superconcepts (i.e., concept names) for a given concept must
be inferred.

Direct superconcept–subconcept relationships (also called parent–children
relationships) are dependent on the concept terms used in the definitions of
a TBox. In particular, the notion of defined concepts (with necessary and
sufficient conditions) led to the idea of *classifying* a TBox. The idea was

---

[2] There are large differences between frame systems and DL systems: if for i the restriction $\forall R.C$
holds, and we set i into relation to j via the role R, then every KL-ONE-based system concludes
that j is an instance of C. In standard frame-based systems, j can only be set into relation to
i via R if it is already known that j is an instance of C. Otherwise, in frame systems at least
a warning is issued or even an error is signaled.

[3] In the literature, some authors use the word "definition" as a synonym for concept terms
themselves (e.g., [Schmidt, 1991], see also [Woods, 1991, p. 65]). In this case, "primitive"
concepts with only necessary conditions were introduced with a specific marker to be used in
concept terms.

[4] The semantics of cycles was analyzed in [Baader, 1990b; 1991; Nebel, 1990a; 1991]. The so-
called *descriptive semantics* provided many advantages over so-called *fixpoint semantics*. For
details see [Nebel, 1990a]. One of the first publications of an expressive Description Logic
supporting cyclic axioms with a descriptive semantics and a sound and complete calculus is
[Buchheit *et al.*, 1993a]. Cyclic axioms are usually not considered as concept definitions.

to compute the subsumption hierarchy (sometimes also called "inheritance hierarchy") of parents and children for each concept name mentioned in a TBox during a so-called *classification* process. The intention was that a model for a specific application domain could be verified by a knowledge engineer based on the subsumption hierarchy. Considering the subsumption hierarchy, i.e., the lattice of direct superconcepts, the idea was also that concept *terms* could be automatically "inserted" between named concepts in the hierarchy. Hence, concept terms could be set into relation to "predefined" concept names (and, indirectly, other concept terms). This feature has been used in many projects for implementing application functionality.

The first development of an algorithm for computing the subsumption hierarchy of a TBox (the "classifier") is described in [Schmolze and Lipkis, 1983]. Another inference component called "realizer" computes for each individual mentioned in an ABox the most specific atomic concepts (or concept names) of which the individual is an instance. One of the first algorithms for computing the realization of an ABox is described in [Mark, 1982]. Initial KL-ONE systems were implemented in INTERLISP [Lipkis, 1982] and Smalltalk [Fikes, 1982]. The Consul project [Kaczmarek *et al.*, 1986] was one of the first projects in which classifier and realizer inference services were exploited.

First investigations about defaults and exceptions were published in [Brachman, 1985]. Nowadays, the semantical theory of defaults in Description Logics is much clearer, see [Baader and Hollunder, 1992; 1993; Baader and Schlechta, 1993; Padgham and Zhang, 1993; Padgham and Nebel, 1993; Baader and Hollunder, 1995a; 1995b; Donini *et al.*, 1997b].

At the first KL-ONE workshop [Schmolze and Brachman, 1982] it became clear that the informal specification of the semantics of KL-ONE concept and role constructors led to serious problems. The development of the classifier [Schmolze and Lipkis, 1983] was based on the intuitive meaning of the KL-ONE formalism [Nebel, 1990a, p. 46]. Attempts to logically reconstruct the representation constructs, e.g., [Schmolze and Israel, 1983; Israel and Brachman, 1984], resulted in a deeper understanding of the formalism. Given the formal semantics, implemented algorithms for classification and realization were shown to be incomplete. Later investigations revealed that KL-ONE (with the formal semantics given in the logical reconstruction approaches) is undecidable (e.g., this holds for the combination of conjunction, value restrictions and role-value-maps [Schmidt-Schauß, 1989]). In [Brachman and Levesque, 1984] the first thoughts about tractability of subsumption for sublanguages are discussed. Terminological reasoning with concept definitions even for sublanguages with low expressiveness were shown to be inherently intractable in the worst case [Nebel, 1990b, p. 28, pp. 71f.]. Proposals for a semantics based on many-valued logics (e.g., [Patel-Schneider, 1986; 1987a; 1987b; 1989a]) ensure tractable algorithms concerning concept consistency reasoning but also result in a weak expressiveness: many intuitive inferences are not sanctioned by this semantics (see also [Nebel, 1990a]).

Another result of [Schmolze and Brachman, 1982] was that the semantics of individual concepts was not quite clear (e.g., concerning coreference and unique name assumption). Thus, at the first KL-ONE workshop [Schmolze and Brachman, 1982], the notions of a *hybrid* reasoning system consisting of a TBox (a set of concept definitions) and an ABox (a set of assertions concerning individuals) were made more precise. The change of the view on KL-ONE spelled out in [Schmolze and Brachman, 1982, pp. 8–17] (see also [Nebel, 1990a, p. 46]) can be summarized as follows: It is not the *names* of representation structures that are important but the functionality, i.e., the declaration and inference services which the system provides. It was first pointed out that inferences have to be formally defined based on the semantics of the representation formalism. This view led to the development of the functional view of knowledge representation as pursued with the development of the system KRYPTON.

KRYPTON

The knowledge representation system KRYPTON [Brachman *et al.*, 1983a; 1983b; 1985] can be seen as the first attempt at defining a new language of the KL-ONE family with a formal, Tarskian semantics. Furthermore, the goal was to overcome the problems with individual concepts in KL-ONE [Nebel, 1990a, p. 63]. The hybrid representation approach with a TBox and an ABox was first implemented in the KRYPTON system (see also [MacGregor, 1991a, p. 391]). As in KL-ONE, the distinction between primitive and defined concepts and the computation of the most specific atomic concepts which instantiate individuals is one of the core ideas of KRYPTON.

KRYPTON offered a concept language with low expressiveness. While the initial approach [Brachman *et al.*, 1983b] was too expressive to be tractable (see also [MacGregor, 1991a, p. 390]), in a revised version [Brachman *et al.*, 1985] the concept constructors of KRYPTON were defined as conjunction, value restrictions and role chains. Thus, subsumption checking was polynomial [Patel-Schneider, 1987a, p. 75]. For the ABox a full-fledged resolution-based FOPL theorem prover [Stickel, 1982] was proposed, i.e., the ABox reasoner of KRYPTON was incomplete. Another perspective is that KRYPTON started with a first-order logic theorem prover and augmented it with a special-purpose inference system for terminological reasoning to cut out some of the combinatorial search [Vilain, 1985]. KRYPTON can be regarded as one of the first efforts in combining knowledge representation and theorem-proving techniques but was not used for industrial applications [Nebel, 1990a, pp. 63f.].

Rather than dealing with specific representation structures and operations on them, KRYPTON offers a so-called "functional approach". Using the interface functions "tell" and "ask", a knowledge base can be defined and queries can be answered about it. In this sense, a "functional approach" means that a formal representation system does not necessarily have to maintain, for instance, frame structures, the subsumption hierarchy, or even an ABox as a graph structure. If, for internal implementation purposes, graph structures are indeed used, they are nevertheless hidden from the user in order to avoid "procedural" operations being carried out with internal record structures. Arbitrary procedural operations are usually not related to the semantics of the representation formalism, so that, in this case, it is hard to characterize what is actually represented and what is computed as solutions to inference problems. Thus, the focus of KRYPTON was not on the structures to be maintained by the system but was centered around the question about what the system should do for the user, i.e., what services should be made available. In other publications this idea was described as the "knowledge level" [Newell, 1982]. In KRYPTON, inference services for concept terms are checks for concept consistency, disjointness, and subsumption. For a TBox, the most specific subsumers (parent–children relation) can be computed, whereas for an ABox, consistency, instance checking, realization (direct types) and instance retrieval are offered as inference services. KRYPTON pioneered the idea that the user should only know, at some level not dependent on implementation details, what questions the system is capable of answering and what operations are permitted that allow new information to be provided to it. For instance, it is not important how the association between an individual and a certain role filler is actually represented in terms of memory arrangements (called the symbol level). What counted for the underlying implementation was what operations must be supported in order to answer queries at the semantical level. This view about KL-ONE-based representation systems was one of the major achievements of the KRYPTON project.

NIKL, PENNI, KL-TWO

At the same time as KRYPTON, the knowledge representation system NIKL was developed as a successor of KL-ONE. NIKL was a New Implementation of KL-ONE [Schmolze and Israel, 1983; Schmolze, 1985; Schmolze and Mark, 1991]. As discussed in [Kaczmarek *et al.*, 1986], in

NIKL, roles are also ordered with respect to subsumption (see also [Schmidt, 1991, p. 13]).

The assertional components of KL-ONE were initially discarded in the NIKL system (see the NIKL user guide [Robins, 1986]). Compared to the initial KL-ONE implementation, the algorithms in the NIKL classifier were faster in the average case because "obvious" information was exploited to a larger degree (see [MacGregor, 1988, p. 405] or [MacGregor, 1991a, p. 392]). However, the subsumption algorithm of NIKL was incomplete and it was hard to characterize which inferences were omitted [Schmolze and Israel, 1983] (see also [Patel-Schneider, 1987a, p. 74]).

Later, an assertional reasoning component was added with the system PENNI which is based on RUP [McAllester, 1982]. The resulting system was called KL-TWO [Vilain, 1985] (see also [Schmidt, 1991, p. 15]). In KL-TWO a propositional reasoner with equality (the PENNI subsystem) was augmented with a so-called quantificational reasoning component (the NIKL subsystem). For the propositional part in the PENNI component, incremental additions and retractions were supported due to the facilities provided by RUP. However, as shown in [Patel-Schneider, 1989b] the concept language of NIKL contained concept and role constructs that rendered the satisfiability problem for NIKL concept terms undecidable (see also [Schmidt-Schauß, 1989]).

Concerning hybrid reasoning, i.e., the systematic integration of TBox and ABox reasoning, there were shortcomings as well. Because in RUP different constants do not necessarily denote different objects, the unique name assumption was not built into the assertional component PENNI. Thus, number restrictions imposed by NIKL concepts often did not have the intended effects concerning hybrid reasoning. Other sources of incompleteness were pointed out (see also the analysis of "inferential gaps" in [Nebel, 1990a, pp. 63f.]). The research on the KL-TWO system demonstrated that hybrid reasoning is not just a matter of integrating reasoning subsystems at the software level. Hybrid reasoning requires a dedicated architecture implementing a sound and complete calculus which, in turn, can be developed only after a deep analysis of the semantics of the representation constructs. Nevertheless, the principal idea of exploiting subsumption information for resolution-based first-order reasoning has been integrated into many theorem-proving systems.

KANDOR

Research on KANDOR [Patel-Schneider, 1984] was influenced by the KRYPTON architecture and the performance problems of the NIKL approach. The goal of KANDOR was to increase the expressive power of the terminological representation component in such a way that an efficient subsumption algorithm could be developed. Basically, KANDOR supported conjunction, value restriction and number restrictions as concept-forming operators. In minimum number restrictions, range-restricted roles could be used (hence, qualified minimum number restrictions were allowed, see also [Patel-Schneider, 1987a, p. 76]). In order to provide effective inference algorithms (e.g., for information retrieval scenarios) in the KANDOR approach the expressiveness of the assertional component was cut down to a representation system comparable to a database (without revision mechanisms). Subsumption in KANDOR was shown to be coNP-complete (see [Nebel, 1988] and [Nebel, 1990a, p. 90] for details). The initially proposed subsumption algorithm with polynomial runtime must have been incomplete.

KANDOR was called a frame-based system (which might be reasonable because of the expressiveness offered by the ABox language). A frame in KANDOR was essentially a specification of conditions for describing how an individual can be an instance of it (in terms of superframes and restrictions). KANDOR supported defined frames and primitive frames in the spirit of KL-ONE. The system adopted the "small interfaces" approach of KRYPTON, i.e., models were built using the declaration interface (tell interface), and application services were realized with the query interface (ask interface). Although called a frame system, frames were not treated as record structures to be manipulated by procedural programs. The authors of KANDOR argued for a small knowledge representation system that could be used as part of larger systems with different subcomponents. The main achievement of KANDOR was the introduction of a small-can-be-beautiful approach which, finally, led to the design of the system CLASSIC which will be discussed in detail in the next section.

8.3 Second generation Description Logic systems

Whereas the prototypical implementations of first generation systems were used to study knowledge representation problems, second generation DL systems have been more extensively used in serious applications. The implementations discussed in this section are not only not prototypes but are much more stable. In addition, since the beginning of the 1990s, the systems have been called DL systems. We first discuss systems for (almost) tractable languages based on (almost) complete algorithms and investigate systems for expressive Description Logics afterwards.

CLASSIC

The basic CLASSIC system supported the logic $\mathcal{ALNFh}^{-1}$ with TBoxes and ABoxes plus facilities for dealing with numbers [Borgida *et al.*, 1989]. We use the lowercase letter h to indicate that CLASSIC supports role inclusion but not role conjunction, i.e., CLASSIC supports "single-inheritance" role hierarchies. CLASSIC is available for research purposes. Implementation languages for CLASSIC are COMMONLISP [Steele, 1990] and C. The interfaces are described in [Resnick *et al.*, 1995]. Full CLASSIC also contained the concept constructors $\mathcal{O}$ and $\mathcal{B}$ for referring to individuals in concept terms.

Subsumption in full CLASSIC was initially assumed to be polynomial [Borgida *et al.*, 1989]. Problems with individuals in full CLASSIC were recognized in [Patel-Schneider *et al.*, 1991]. At the same time, subsumption in CLASSIC was shown to be coNP complete [Lenzerini and Schaerf, 1991]. In the modified semantics for the concept constructors $\mathcal{O}$ and $\mathcal{B}$ (see [Borgida and Patel-Schneider, 1994]) the interpretation function maps individuals in concept terms to disjoint sets of domain objects. With this semantics concerning individuals the inference algorithms of the CLASSIC system could be shown to be complete [Borgida and Patel-Schneider, 1994]. However, given the non-standard semantics for the concept constructors $\mathcal{O}$ and $\mathcal{B}$, the same effect can be achieved with existential quantifications and disjunctions w.r.t. atomic concepts:[5] For each individual I a new atomic concept A_I can be introduced. Note that atomic concepts are also mapped to sets of individuals. Additionally, since CLASSIC imposes the unique name assumption, a set of axioms ensures that the new atomic concepts are disjoint. Now every term of the form $\exists R.I$ can be replaced by $\exists R.A_I$. Terms of the form $\{I_1, \ldots, I_n\}$ can be replaced by $A_{I_1} \sqcup \cdots \sqcup A_{I_n}$. In an ABox, for each individual I a concept assertion is added to ensure that the individual is an instance of the associated atomic concept A_I. Thus, only in an ABox, can a real coreference between roles be enforced. On the one hand, we can call the CLASSIC system "almost" complete. "Almost" refers to non-standard semantics w.r.t. individuals being supported by current system implementations. On the other hand, the transformation makes clear that in CLASSIC nevertheless a limited kind of disjunction (with concept names for which no definitions exist) can be expressed while retaining polynomial inference algorithms.

The recommended techniques for knowledge-based system development with CLASSIC are outlined in [Brachman *et al.*, 1991]. As Brachman [Brachman, 1992, p. 256] points out, a tractable Description Logic does not guarantee that a system is useful in practice. Therefore, the CLASSIC system

---

[5] Note that these concept constructors are not directly provided by CLASSIC.

was also carefully designed to meet practical requirements and to guarantee predictable system behavior. The context in which the system was expected to be used required that many queries were given to knowledge bases which rarely changed. The architectural design of CLASSIC supports a precomputation of index structures such that queries can be answered quickly (mostly by simple storage retrieval). The architecture is made possible by a careful selection of the concept and role constructors for the DL language. Inference services for the Description Logic supported by CLASSIC can be implemented by transforming concept expressions into a normal form ("structural subsumption"). Once the normal form is computed, queries can be answered by inspecting the data structures used to encode the normal form. It should be noted that, in CLASSIC, retraction of told information is possible but not optimized.

Another facility offered by CLASSIC is a rule system. Rules are applied to individuals explicitly named in the ABox. Furthermore, rules are applied in a forward-chaining way. Basically, a rule has a precondition (a concept) and a conclusion (also a concept). If it can be shown that an individual mentioned in the ABox is an instance of the precondition concept, a concept assertion for stating the membership of the individual in the conclusion concept is added to the ABox. In order to provide support for modeling, the rule base is statically checked for inconsistencies. For instance, if there are two rules whose preconditions subsume each other, the conclusions must not be disjoint.

Furthermore, CLASSIC provides simple support for closed-world reasoning ([Resnick *et al.*, 1995], see also [Weida, 1996]). Closing a role for an individual means adding an appropriate maximum number restriction for the role. The maximum number of fillers is restricted to the largest integer such that the minimum number restriction with this integer (and the corresponding role) is entailed by the knowledge base. The problem with role closing is that in combination with rules, the exact sequence of several closing operations determines what actually holds in the resulting ABox. These and other problems concerning different closing operations have to be considered with default reasoning as the theoretical background [Baader and Hollunder, 1995a; 1995b; Donini *et al.*, 1997b; Rosati, 1998]. For a specific approach concerning the integration of defaults into the CLASSIC system see also [Wahlöf, 1996; Lambrix *et al.*, 1998].

CLASSIC is one of the first systems that provided support for incorporating inferences over other domains. Consistency and subsumption checking for expressions of another domain (e.g., the reals) can be integrated into the CLASSIC system via an extension interface [Borgida *et al.*, 1996].

CLASSIC was one of the first DL systems designed with respect to users who are not experts in DL theory. An important lesson learned by the CLASSIC approach and its applications was the importance of explanation and output pruning facilities [McGuinness and Borgida, 1995; McGuinness, 1996; Borgida and McGuinness, 1996]. Moreover, CLASSIC was the first system capable of supporting some reasonable form of error reporting [Brachman, 1992]. However, in the current state of the art there is hardly an adequate measure for the quality of these indispensable services [Brachman, 1992, p. 253].

Although CLASSIC was a very successful DL modeling environment, the low expressiveness of the CLASSIC Description Logic made it hard to use the system in many kinds of applications. In many cases, users wanted more expressiveness [Patel-Schneider *et al.*, 1990]. In the following sections we discuss systems for (more) expressive Description Logics. As can be expected, increases in expressiveness came at a certain price. The predictability of the behavior of CLASSIC in terms of performance could not be reached by systems implementing complete algorithms for more expressive DLs. On the other hand, incomplete algorithms have the problem that results computed by a system cannot be trusted in general. Thus, the complete–incomplete debate for expressive DL systems started at the end of the 1980s and the beginning of the 1990s. First, we describe the systems LOOM and BACK, which are based on incomplete algorithms. Afterwards, initial research on DL systems based on complete algorithms is summarized with a discussion of the systems KRIS and CRACK.

LOOM

The LOOM architecture [MacGregor and Bates, 1987; MacGregor, 1991b] offers TBox and ABox reasoning facilities for a Description Logic that can be characterized by the name $\mathcal{ALCQRIFO}$ plus additional constructs for dealing with real numbers (see also [Brill, 1994] or [Horrocks, 1997a, p. 43]). LOOM is based on KL-ONE, i.e., concept definitions with necessary or with necessary and sufficient conditions play an important role in domain modeling with LOOM. It should be emphasized that truth maintenance facilities for revision were built into the LOOM architecture right from the beginning and have influenced the design of the whole system [MacGregor, 1988; MacGregor and Brill, 1992]. While the first LOOM versions were based on Description Logics [MacGregor and Brill, 1992], in later versions an attempt was made to develop a "description classifier for the Predicate Calculus" [MacGregor, 1994]. For instance, facilities for dealing with definitions for

relations were added. The current version of LOOM is implemented in COM-
MONLISP and is available for research purposes. A new system (called POW-
ERLOOM) for COMMONLISP as well as C- and Java-based platforms can be
licensed as well.

A distinguishing design goal of LOOM was the incorporation of an expressive query language for retrieving ABox individuals. Another design goal of
LOOM was to support rule-based programming [Yen *et al.*, 1991b; 1991a;
MacGregor and Burstein, 1991]. Based on the rule system, it is possible to
specify additional necessary conditions for individuals which (i) are explicitly
mentioned in the ABox and (ii) are derived to be instances of a certain defined concept. The additional necessary conditions are called "implications"
in LOOM [MacGregor, 1988]. The additional necessary conditions specified
by rules are not exploited, for instance, for TBox reasoning. Note that an
"implication" $A \rightarrow B$ stated by a LOOM rule does not mean that $\neg B \rightarrow \neg A$
holds, i.e., rule-based "implications" are not to be confused with true logi-
cal implications as provided by generalized concept inclusions that are now
standard in newer systems (see below).

In order to meet the performance requirements of the applications for
which LOOM was developed (e.g., natural language and image interpretation), incomplete algorithms for concept consistency and subsumption are
implemented. Concerning ABox reasoning, LOOM applications required specific strategies to avoid the computation of unused results. Rather than
employing the usual forward-chaining strategy of computing the most specific atomic concepts of which the ABox individuals are instances, LOOM
uses a scheme that considers the queries being posed to the system. Thus,
backward-chaining strategies for query answering are used in the implementation [MacGregor and Brill, 1992]. However, for the rule system, it is
important to detect whether an individual is an instance of a concept that is
used as a precondition of a rule. In this case, forward-chaining techniques are
exploited [MacGregor, 1991b; MacGregor and Brill, 1992]. The combination
of forward-chaining and backward-chaining inferences can be specified for
a certain application problem by "marking" concepts accordingly. The user
can control the inference process by these means but is also responsible for
estimating the effects of these declarations.

The arguments for the LOOM approach can be summarized as follows:
The intractability of the representation language can hardly be avoided if
the requirements of users are to be fulfilled. Therefore, the idea is to support
the features in one system rather than as a set of application-specific ad hoc
supplements ("Where resides the scruffiness?" [MacGregor, 1991a, p. 396]).
Obviously, incompleteness is no problem as long as the answers of the

inference system are interpreted in the right way (i.e., "no" answers should not be trusted). Several researchers argued that there is always the inherent danger that non-expert users either do not know this or might not recognize this as a potential danger (cf. the work on complete systems [Baader and Hollunder, 1991a; 1991b] discussed below). However, if a combinatorial explosion occurs in a complete algorithm, in practice, no result is available at all. Concerning incomplete algorithms for decidable Description Logics, arguments similar to those for other modeling environments based on first-order logic can be mentioned: If, in a certain application, concept terms are checked for consistency and combinatorial explosions occur in complete algorithms, incomplete algorithms at least might provide some support, e.g., for building a TBox. Just signaling a timeout during the execution of a complete algorithm that runs into a combinatorial explosion might result in less information. In this case, an incomplete algorithm might succeed in finding at least some inconsistencies. Note however, that in modern inference system technologies supporting complete reasoning, incomplete reasoners are used as "preprocessors" in order to speed up inferences (see the next chapter).

LOOM supports different kinds of individuals (classified instances, light instances, CLOS instances). For different kinds of instances different levels of inference services are supported, e.g., for classified instances, the set of most specific atomic concepts of which the classified individual is an instance is computed once new assertions are specified. Thus, for classified instances, the rule-based forward-chaining engine is triggered, possibly adding new assertions to an ABox (for details see [MacGregor and Brill, 1992]).

A problem with the LOOM approach is that from a user perspective it is hard to characterize the source of the incompleteness of the LOOM reasoning algorithms (see the discussion in [Horrocks, 1997a, p. 42]). Although the inference techniques used in LOOM are characterized in [MacGregor, 1991b, p. 90], once a system is incomplete there is no adequate measure for the "quality of service" in terms of an implementation-independent characterization. For instance, in CLASSIC the characterization of the incompleteness of the inference system concerning individual reasoning was given in terms of a weak semantics for the offered representation constructs (see above). It should be noted that specifying the incompleteness on the semantic level is by no means a trivial task. Not only incompleteness issues are important in this context. For instance, the theoretical background for giving a semantics for rule-based computations was only investigated recently [Donini et al., 1992b; 1994a; 1998a].

Incomplete reasoning facilities might lead to unexpected behavior. We demonstrate by an example that incomplete inference algorithms can have effects in situations a user might not be aware of. LOOM also supports closed-world reasoning. The strategy for closing a role for an individual is to count the number of known role fillers. However, in addition to the individuals explicitly mentioned in the ABox, existential quantifications and minimum number restrictions have to be considered. Assuming too few of these individuals might result in an inconsistency. This is demonstrated by a simple knowledge base example with the following ABox: $\{(\exists R.A \sqcap \exists R.B \sqcap \exists R.C)(i),\ R(i,j)\}$. Let us assume that in the TBox there exist axioms such that A is *implicitly* declared as disjoint from both concepts, B and C. In the LOOM system, specific reasoning techniques (e.g., a technique called "conditioning" [MacGregor, 1991b]) are implemented to compute the number of necessary fillers. Closing the role R for i by adding $(\leq 1\,R)(i)$ makes the ABox inconsistent. However, since LOOM is incomplete, it might be the case that the disjointness of A and B as well as A and C is not detected and, therefore, too few fillers are assumed to exist in the closing process. Thus, the added maximum number restriction might be too restrictive, i.e., the system is unsound if closed-world reasoning is employed. Note that the semantic basis of automatic closing of roles as offered by LOOM is hard to characterize for expressive representation languages. Obviously, closing the role R for i with $(\leq 2\,R)(i)$ might be a candidate. However, closing the role R for i with $(\leq 3\,R)(i)$ might also be possible. In this case we have more individuals but with less specific constraints.

BACK *and* FLEX

Research on BACK (Berlin Advanced Computational Knowledge representation system) started in 1985, approximately at the same time as work on the LOOM system was initiated. BACK was also called a knowledge representation environment [Quantz and Kindermann, 1990; Peltason, 1991; Hoppe *et al.*, 1993].

The Description Logic of the initial BACK system can be called $\mathcal{ALQR}^{-1}$. There was also support for reasoning with numbers and attribute sets. Research on the inference algorithms for the basic BACK language stimulated the development of theoretical results on the complexity of concept consistency reasoning (e.g., [Nebel, 1988; 1990a]) and the semantics of cycles [Nebel, 1991]. Additionally, not only was terminological reasoning considered but an investigation was made into the development of a hybrid architecture consisting of a TBox and an ABox. Issues of integration and balancing in hybrid knowledge representation systems, namely balanced expressiveness and tight coupling in hybrid systems, were analyzed in [Nebel and von Luck, 1987; 1988]. Research on the BACK system helped to shape the current view on balanced representation schemes with TBox and ABox. In order to provide an hybrid representation language, BACK was one of the first systems in which TBox concept terms could also be used in an ABox to assert, e.g., disjunctive information about individuals. In addition, distinct individuals were assumed to denote distinct objects. Hence, the number of role fillers could be counted and compared against number restrictions (this was also done in KRYPTON as pointed out by [Woods and Schmolze, 1992, p. 165]). The algorithms used in BACK for instance checking and instance retrieval are described in [Nebel and von Luck, 1987; 1988; Kindermann and Randi, 1990]. In general, the discussion of the problems of incomplete algorithms that was sketched in the account of LOOM also applies to the BACK system because the inference algorithms used in BACK are also known to be incomplete.

In order to provide a knowledge representation environment, the BACK architecture was designed to support incremental additions to the ABox. BACK was one of the first attempts to implement algorithms for reasoning about retractions of ABox assertions. BACK supported retraction of told information, also called literal retraction [Nebel, 1990a; Kindermann, 1992]. This is also supported in the LOOM system. ABox assertions can be retrieved from a database by automatically computing SQL queries [Schmiedel, 1993]. For the applications considered in the BACK project, reasoning about time was important. Therefore, an integration of temporal reasoning and terminological reasoning was investigated by several project members. Investigations into how to incorporate temporal reasoning into terminological reasoning are reported in [Schmiedel, 1988; 1990; Schild, 1993; Fischer, 1992; Neuwirth, 1993].

In the successor system FLEX [Quantz et al., 1995], incomplete algorithms were implemented for the Description Logic $\mathcal{ALCQRIFO}$. Additionally, reasoning about equations and inequalities concerning integers was supported. Furthermore, the FLEX system served as a testbed for investigating so-called weighted defaults [Quantz and Royer, 1992]. The initial implementation of FLEX was developed in Prolog. FLEX++ was a reimplementation in C++. The implementation was faster, but for application knowledge bases the performance was not sufficient. Appropriate optimization techniques (see the next chapter) had not been investigated in the context of Description Logics at the time of the development of the FLEX implementation.

In general, it is quite difficult to compare different systems and knowledge representation environments because the services being offered and the representation languages are not standardized (see [Patel-Schneider and Swartout, 1993] for a proposal on standardizing representation languages and inference services). Experiences with system implementations indicated that either limited expressiveness or incompleteness of reasoning could possibly lead to problems in applications. Therefore, other researchers investigated the implementation of systems based on sound and complete algorithms (published at the end of the 1980s and beginning of the 1990s). One can consider [Schmidt-Schauß and Smolka, 1991] as a starting point of this development (see also [Donini *et al.*, 1991a]). Based on tableau calculi, practical DL implementations were developed. We discuss the architectures of the systems KRIS and CRACK.

KRIS

The development of sound and complete reasoning systems for more expressive Description Logics started at the end of the 1980s. One of the main developments in this direction was the system KRIS. The approach of KRIS was to implement sound and complete algorithms for an expressive Description Logic and to develop optimization techniques for TBox reasoning so that, in practice, reasonable performance could be expected. The Description Logic of KRIS is $\mathcal{ALCNF}$ [Baader and Hollunder, 1991a; 1991b]. As an addition, KRIS provides enumerated types ($\mathcal{O}$ operator) and an experimental interface for reasoning about so-called concrete domains [Baader and Hanschke, 1991a; 1991b; 1992] (e.g., linear inequalities over the reals). Role conjunctions were supported with a prototype implementation. The focus of the work in the KRIS project was on TBox classification. Nevertheless, KRIS was one of the first systems also supporting sound and complete ABox reasoning in expressive Description Logics. Even multiple ABoxes could be handled. The implementation language of KRIS was COMMONLISP (see [Hollunder *et al.*, 1991] for a User's Guide and [Achilles *et al.*, 1991] for a description of the graphical user interface).

The idea behind optimizing TBox classification was to exploit "obvious" information concerning "told" superconcepts and primitive concepts. In many concept definitions of application knowledge bases the right-hand side is a conjunction with concept names and concept terms. The conjuncts which are concept names on the right-hand side are defined as the "told" subsumers. Another important point was to avoid recomputation of subsumption relations found in preceding computation steps. Thus, caching and propagation techniques were implemented. The idea was that information can be propagated in the subsumption lattice such that expensive subsumption tests can be avoided where possible. KRIS was the first system for which systematic empirical tests were carried out. The algorithms evaluated in [Baader et al., 1992b; 1994] are still in use in modern DL systems (see below). Extensions such as defaults were investigated as well (see also [Baader and Hollunder, 1992; 1993; Hollunder, 1994a]) but have not been implemented in KRIS.

Although the benchmarks considered in [Baader et al., 1994] revealed that the performance of KRIS for TBox reasoning was comparable to that of other systems of that time, the more or less direct implementation of *nondeterministic* tableau algorithms that were developed for proving the decidability of problems in the field of theoretical computer science with chronological backtracking as in KRIS led to performance problems for many applications. One of the main results of the KRIS project was that sound and complete inference algorithms are an important starting point for research on optimized sound and complete algorithms for practical system development.

CRACK

One of the main research goals of the system CRACK was to implement sound and complete algorithms for dealing with inferences about individuals in concept terms. Rather than providing a non-standard semantics as in CLASSIC (individuals are mapped onto sets of domain objects), in CRACK, individuals are mapped to elements of the domain. Thus, coreferences also have to be considered in concept terms. CRACK supports the Description Logic $\mathcal{ALCRIFO}$ [Bresciani et al., 1995]. The implementation of CRACK is based on COMMONLISP. CRACK provided a web interface.

In a similar way as in KRIS, obvious information is exploited in the architecture to some extent but, nevertheless, CRACK is a direct implementation of the tableau rules of the underlying calculus. At the beginning of the 1990s it became clear that sound and complete reasoning is needed for many applications but the inference techniques employed, which had been developed for (manually) deriving decidability results, e.g., with tableau algorithms, were not suited for direct implementation. Thus, it was realized that there is a long way to go from a decidability proof to a working system that has good performance in the average case.

Other systems

The list of systems we have discussed in this chapter is certainly incomplete. The large number of projects involved in the development of knowledge representation systems shows the importance of this area. Usually DL systems are built around a core engine which is a consistency checker. However, there are other services to be supplied which are also important to make the systems usable in larger application projects. We present an overview of some additional systems with interesting features developed at the beginning of the 1990s.

Among other points, the graphical manipulation of representations was investigated in the SB-ONE project [Allgayer, 1990; Kobsa, 1991b; 1991a]. The implementation language was COMMONLISP. Techniques for graphical interfaces to support knowledge base development with SB-ONE are described in [Kalmes, 1988; 1990] (see also [Abrett and Burstein, 1987] for a description of the KREME system). Furthermore, in SB-ONE the use of contexts (also called partitions) was explored for user modeling applications in natural language generation.

Another important point for DL inference systems is persistence and transaction management. We have already discussed the BACK approach [Schmiedel, 1993] (see also [Borgida, 1995]). Additional investigations were also made with the K-REP system [Mays *et al.*, 1991a; 1991b].

Summary: standard inference services of Description Logics systems

Before discussing successors of the second generation systems presented in this section it is appropriate to summarize the main inference problems that are now assumed as standard for DL systems. The inference services provided by DL systems for concept consistency and TBox reasoning can be summarized as follows:

- *Concept consistency* (w.r.t. a TBox).
- *Concept subsumption* (w.r.t. a TBox).
- Another important inference service for practical knowledge representation is to check whether a certain concept name is inconsistent w.r.t. a TBox. Usually, inconsistent concept names are the consequence of modeling errors. Checking the consistency of all concept names mentioned in a TBox without computing the parents and children is called a TBox *coherence check*.
- The problem of computing the most specific concept names mentioned in a TBox that subsume a certain concept is known as computing the *parents* of a concept. The *children* are the most general concept names mentioned in a TBox that are subsumed by a certain concept. We use the name *concept ancestors* (*concept descendants*) for the transitive closure of the parents (children) relation. The computation of the parents and children of every concept name is also called

classification of the TBox. This inference is needed to build a hierarchy of concept names w.r.t. specificity and is known as TBox classification.

If a system supports ABox reasoning, the following inference services are provided:

- *ABox consistency* (w.r.t. a TBox).
- *Instance checking* w.r.t. a TBox and an ABox.
- The most specific concept names mentioned in a TBox $\mathcal{T}$ of which an individual is an instance are called the *direct types* of the individual w.r.t. a TBox and an ABox.
- The *retrieval* inference problem is to find all individuals mentioned in an ABox that are an instance of a given concept C w.r.t. a TBox.
- The set of *fillers* of a role R for an individual i w.r.t. a TBox $\mathcal{T}$ and an ABox $\mathcal{A}$ is defined as $\{x \mid (\mathcal{T}, \mathcal{A}) \models (i, x) : R\}$ where $(\mathcal{T}, \mathcal{A}) \models ax$ means that all models of $\mathcal{T}$ and $\mathcal{A}$ are also models of ax.
- The set of *roles* between two individuals i and j w.r.t. a knowledge base $(\mathcal{T}, \mathcal{A})$ is defined as $\{R \mid (\mathcal{T}, \mathcal{A}) \models (i, j) : R\}$.

In many DL systems, there are some auxiliary queries supported: retrieval of the concept names or individuals mentioned in a knowledge base, retrieval of the set of roles, retrieval of the role parents and children (defined analogously to the concept parents and children, see above), retrieval of the set of individuals in the domain and in the range of a role, etc. As we have discussed in this section, DL systems of the second generation offer most if not all of these inference services. An exception is a language for specifying retrieval queries that goes beyond the simple retrieval inference problem mentioned above (see e.g., the discussion about LOOM).

8.4 The next generation: FACT, DLP and RACER

The declarative nature of DL modeling is even more important when problems are treated for which languages are required that are no longer tractable. Inspired by theoretical advances – e.g., for handling number restrictions, role conjunctions, generalized concept inclusions and cyclic axioms with descriptive semantics ($\mathcal{ALCNR}$ [Buchheit *et al.*, 1993a]); transitive roles ($\mathcal{ALC}_{R^+}$ [Sattler, 1996]); role hierarchies and features ($\mathcal{ALCHf}_{R^+}$ [Horrocks, 1998b]); and inverse roles, qualified number restrictions, and role hierarchies ($\mathcal{SHIQ}$ [Horrocks *et al.*, 1999] also called $\mathcal{ALCQHI}_{R^+}$, pronounced ALC-choir) – the development of another generation of sound and complete DL systems was started at the end of the 1990s.

FACT

Initially, research on practical implementations of DL systems for expressive Description Logics started with a focus on concept and TBox reasoning. However, rather than directly implementing the tableau calculus used for the theoretical decidability proofs and complexity analyses, a rigorous investigation into methods for informed search was made for developing the next generation of DL systems. In particular, average-case optimization techniques have been investigated with the system FACT ([Horrocks, 1997a; 1998b; Horrocks and Patel-Schneider, 1999] see also the subsequent chapter for details). At the time of this writing, two versions of FACT are available. One version supports TBox reasoning for the Description Logic $\mathcal{ALCH}f_{R^+}$ [Horrocks, 1997a; 1998b]. Furthermore, a newer version of FACT also supports TBox reasoning with inverse roles and qualified number restrictions ($\mathcal{SHIQ}$ [Horrocks, 1999; Horrocks *et al.*, 1999]). At the time of this writing, FACT does not support ABoxes.

It was the FACT system that first demonstrated the usefulness of expressive Description Logics for developing practical applications. It was shown that, although runtime behavior can be exponential in the worst case, in practical contexts, optimization techniques can be found that prevent a DL system from running into combinatorial explosion. Nevertheless, the algorithms are still sound and complete. Indeed, after several years of experience with less expressive systems such as CLASSIC, research on FACT stimulated many research activities for developing optimized DL system implementations for expressive Description Logics.

The system FACT is implemented in COMMONLISP and can be downloaded with source code for research purposes. A CORBA interface guarantees seamless integration into network-aware applications. Various input formats are supported by FACT (e.g., for XML-based notations of TBoxes). The graphical interface OILED for developing TBoxes in the spirit of frame systems is described in [Bechhofer *et al.*, 2001b].

DLP

Based on similar techniques to FACT, the system DLP utilizes extended techniques for optimizations [Horrocks and Patel-Schneider, 1998c; 1998d; Patel-Schneider, 1999]. DLP supports concept consistency reasoning for the Description Logic $\mathcal{ALCN}_{reg}$. From a modal logic perspective, $\mathcal{ALCN}_{reg}$ can also be called Propositional Dynamic Logic (PDL) with a restricted form of graded modalities, i.e., simple number restrictions.

DLP has succeeded in many performance competitions [Horrocks, 1998a; Horrocks and Patel-Schneider, 1998c; Patel-Schneider, 1999]. It was shown that tableau-based approaches can be implemented such that the performance for satisfiability testing for $\mathcal{ALC}$ or modal logic K_m is comparable to traditional approaches used in the community [Giunchiglia and Sebastiani, 1996b; Giunchiglia et al., 1999].

However, in the current version of DLP TBox classification is not provided as an inference service. In particular, no generalized concept inclusions and no TBoxes with forward references are supported (i.e., algorithms for dealing with generalized concept inclusions are not implemented in DLP). ABoxes are not supported either. DLP is implemented in SML.

RACER

For many applications, besides concept consistency and TBox reasoning, ABox reasoning is also important. Calculi for ABox consistency have been presented for the above-mentioned representation constructs: $\mathcal{ALCNR}$ [Buchheit et al., 1993b], $\mathcal{ALCNH}_{R^+}$ [Haarslev and Möller, 2000], $\mathcal{ALCQHI}_{R^+}$ ($\mathcal{SHIQ}$) [Horrocks et al., 2000c]. Based on theoretical results, a practical implementation of ABox calculi was developed with the full TBox and ABox DL system RACER [Haarslev and Möller, 1999; 2001e]. RACER supports all optimization techniques that are incorporated into FACT. Some new optimization techniques investigated with the RACER system (e.g., for dealing with number restrictions and ABoxes) are mentioned in the next chapter. In RACER, the unique name assumption for ABox individuals is imposed. In order to demonstrate the usefulness of DL systems for practical applications, high performance reasoning for large TBoxes is discussed in [Haarslev and Möller, 2001c].

Initial versions of the RACER system supported the logic $\mathcal{ALCNH}_{R^+}$. In later versions reasoning was extended to ABox reasoning with the logic $\mathcal{ALCQHI}_{R^+}$ ($\mathcal{SHIQ}$). In addition, RACER supports concrete domains without so-called feature chains (see [Baader and Hanschke, 1991a] and the discussion of the KRIS system). In particular, predicates representing linear inequalities about the reals are handled by RACER (see [Haarslev et al., 2001; Haarslev and Möller, 2001b] for details).

RACER dynamically selects appropriate optimization techniques based on a static analysis of input TBoxes, ABoxes and queries. As a distinguishing feature, which is important for many applications, it should also be mentioned that RACER supports multiple TBoxes and ABoxes (see also the KRIS system). Assertions can be added to ABoxes after queries have been answered. In addition, for instance, RACER also provides support for retraction of assertions.

RACER can be downloaded for research purposes as a server program for standard operating systems with no additional licenses. A socket-based network version with Java interface is available. The implementation language of RACER is COMMONLISP.

8.5 Lessons learned

Considering the evolving technology of DL systems it becomes clear that since the end of the 1990s there has been an enormous interest in DL reasoning systems. This is demonstrated by the quite large number of system implementations. Currently, all modern DL systems are based on sound and complete algorithms. Thus, system developers can really rely on all answers computed by a DL system. This positive trend has been initiated by the development of optimization techniques that ensure stable runtimes for average-case inputs for real-world problems even if the worst-case complexity is exponential (see also below). The trend has been initiated by the landmark system FACT.

The original idea of the Tell&Ask interface of KRYPTON is still realized in modern systems. However, at the time of this writing, the systems support only some kind of batch-oriented behavior. A knowledge base (TBox and ABox) is passed to the systems (tell interface). Afterwards, queries can be answered (ask interface). But, no incremental additions to the knowledge base are possible after the first query is answered. The difficulty is that complex transformations on the knowledge bases are necessary in order to compute an internal representation that can be used for relatively fast query answering (see the discussion on optimization techniques in subsequent chapters). The price to pay is that algorithms for appropriately handling incremental additions to a knowledge base are not yet known. Other features, e.g., explanation facilities, retraction, etc., still have to be developed for expressive DLs as well.

As a second and quite important lesson one can see that Description Logics with more expressiveness and sound and complete algorithms impose a different view in modeling. Concept definitions as known from, for instance, CLASSIC are no longer the central modeling device if generalized concept inclusions (representing cyclic implications or equalities) are available.[6]

A third lesson we can learn from considering DL systems and their de-

---

[6] Nevertheless, Description Logics can still be called object-based representation formalisms, although there are some approaches to deal with *n*-ary relations [Schmolze, 1989; Calvanese *et al.*, 1998d] as well.

velopment is that speed depends much more on the expressiveness of the Description Logic than it does on the implementation language. What really counts is the set of optimization strategies, the implementation of index data structures and the selection of clever heuristics. There are first attempts at providing a distributed implementation of a DL system. However, performance problems in network communication lead to server-based solutions, i.e., a knowledge base is being processed at a single workstation computer (but may be accessed from different clients). Benchmark generators and standardized application knowledge bases are used for metering system performance. Thus, different system implementations can be compared.

With RACER we have discussed a state-of-the-art DL system that also supports ABoxes and concrete domains. However, only simple query languages are currently available. For Description Logics without inverse roles and number restrictions (i.e., $\mathcal{ALCHf}_{R^+}$), Tessaris [2001] developed the basic techniques for supporting the so-called conjunctive queries in DL systems. However, for Description Logics as expressive as $\mathcal{SHIQ}$ much less is known from an implementation standpoint.

Another lesson is that the development of techniques for practically incorporating facilities for the representation of space and time into Description Logics is still an open issue. The necessity of a semantics-based integration of temporal and terminological reasoning has been emphasized in first investigations in the BACK project. However, early approaches (e.g., [Schmiedel, 1990]) have been shown to be undecidable [Halpern and Shoham, 1991; Schild, 1993]. In the context of planning, the opportunities of an integrated environment combining temporal and terminological reasoning were clearly demonstrated with the RHET system [Allen, 1991]. It has been shown that spatial reasoning (e.g., about topological relations) induces non-obvious subsumption relationships between concepts [Haarslev *et al.*, 1998; 1999]. The work presented in [Artale *et al.*, 2001] demonstrates that the decidability barrier is reached if temporal operators are integrated into expressive Description Logics. Nevertheless, [Artale *et al.*, 2001] identify a fragment that allows a limited kind of practical modeling. Initial experiments concerning an implementation of a Description Logic that supports operators for linear time temporal reasoning are discussed in [Günsel and Wittmann, 2001].

9

Implementation and Optimization Techniques

Ian Horrocks

Abstract

This chapter will discuss the implementation of the reasoning services which form the core of DL-based knowledge representation systems. To be useful in realistic applications, such systems need both expressive logics and fast reasoners. As expressive logics inevitably have high worst-case complexities, this can only be achieved by employing highly optimized implementations of suitable reasoning algorithms. Systems based on such implementations have demonstrated that they can perform well with problems that occur in realistic applications, including problems where unoptimized reasoning is hopelessly intractable.

9.1 Introduction

The usefulness of Description Logics in applications has been hindered by the basic conflict between expressiveness and tractability. Realistic applications typically require both expressive logics, with inevitably high worst-case complexities for their decision procedures, and acceptable performance from the reasoning services. Although the definition of acceptable may vary widely from application to application, early experiments with Description Logics indicated that, in practice, performance was a serious problem, even for logics with relatively limited expressive powers [Heinsohn et al., 1992].

On the other hand, theoretical work has continued to extend our understanding of the boundaries of decidability in Description Logics, and has led to the development of sound and complete reasoning algorithms for much more expressive logics. The expressive power of these logics goes a long way towards addressing the criticisms leveled at Description Logics in traditional applications such as ontological engineering [Doyle and Patil, 1991] and is sufficient to suggest that they could be useful in several exciting new application domains, for example reasoning about database schemas and queries [Calvanese *et al.*, 1998f; 1998a] and providing reasoning support for the so-called Semantic Web [Decker *et al.*, 2000; Bechhofer *et al.*, 2001b]. However, the worst-case complexity of their decision procedures is invariably (at least) exponential with respect to problem size.

This high worst-case complexity initially led to the conjecture that expressive Description Logics might be of limited practical applicability [Buchheit *et al.*, 1993c]. However, although the theoretical complexity results are discouraging, empirical analyses of real applications have shown that the kinds of construct which lead to worst-case intractability rarely occur in practice [Nebel, 1990b; Heinsohn *et al.*, 1994; Speel *et al.*, 1995], and experiments with the KRIS system showed that applying some simple optimization techniques could lead to a significant improvement in the empirical performance of a DL system [Baader *et al.*, 1992a]. More recently the FaCT, DLP and RACER systems have demonstrated that, even with very expressive logics, highly optimized implementations can provide acceptable performance in realistic applications [Horrocks and Patel-Schneider, 1999; Haarslev and Möller, 2001c].[1]

In this chapter we will study the implementation of DL systems, examining in detail the wide range of optimization techniques that can be used to improve performance. Some of the techniques that will be discussed are completely independent of the logical language supported by the Description Logic and the kind of algorithm used for reasoning; many others would be applicable to a wide range of languages and implementation styles, particularly those using search-based algorithms. However, the detailed descriptions of implementation and optimization techniques will assume, for the most part, reasoning in an expressive DL based on a sound and complete tableau algorithm.

9.1.1 Performance analysis

Before designing and implementing a DL-based knowledge representation system, the implementor should be clear about the goals that they are trying to meet and against which the performance of the system will ultimately be measured. In this chapter it will be assumed that the primary goal is utility in realistic applications, and that this will normally be assessed by empirical analysis.

---

[1] It should be pointed out that experience in this area is still relatively limited.

Unfortunately, as DL systems with very expressive logics have only recently become available [Horrocks, 1998a; Patel-Schneider, 1998; Haarslev and Möller, 2001e], there are very few applications that can be used as a source for test data.[2] One application that has been able to provide such data is the European GALEN project, part of which has involved the construction of a large DL knowledge base describing medical terminology [Rector *et al.*, 1993]. Reasoning performance with respect to this knowledge base has been used for comparing DL systems [Horrocks and Patel-Schneider, 1998b], and we will often refer to it when assessing the effectiveness of optimization techniques.

As few other suitable knowledge bases are available, the testing of DL systems has often been supplemented with the use of randomly generated or hand crafted test data [Giunchiglia and Sebastiani, 1996b; Heuerding and Schwendimann, 1996; Horrocks and Patel-Schneider, 1998b; Massacci, 1999; Donini and Massacci, 2000]. In many cases the data was originally developed for testing propositional modal logics, and has been adapted for use with Description Logics by taking advantage of the well-known correspondence between the two formalisms [Schild, 1991]. Tests using this kind of data, in particular the test suites from the Tableaux'98 comparison of modal logic theorem provers [Balsiger and Heuerding, 1998] and the DL'98 comparison of DL systems [Horrocks and Patel-Schneider, 1998b], will also be referred to in assessments of optimization techniques.

9.2 Preliminaries

This section will introduce the syntax and semantics of Description Logics (full details of which can be found in Chapter 2) and discuss the reasoning services which would form the core of a DL-based knowledge representation system. It will also discuss how, through the use of *unfolding* and *internalization*, these reasoning services can often be reduced to the problem of determining the satisfiability of a single concept.

9.2.1 Syntax and semantics

Description Logics are formalisms that support the logical description of concepts and roles. Arbitrary concept and role descriptions (from now on referred to simply as concepts and roles) are constructed from atomic concept and role names using a variety of concept- and role-forming operators,

---

[2] This situation is changing rapidly, however, with the increasing use of Description Logics in database and ontology applications.

the range of which is dependent on the particular logic. In the following discussion we will use C and D to denote arbitrary concepts, R and S to denote arbitrary roles, A and P to denote atomic concept and role names, and n to denote a nonnegative integer.

For concepts, the available operators usually include some or all of the standard logical connectives, *conjunction* (denoted $\sqcap$), *disjunction* (denoted $\sqcup$) and *negation* (denoted $\neg$). In addition, the universal concept *top* (denoted $\top$, and equivalent to $A \sqcup \neg A$) and the incoherent concept *bottom* (denoted $\bot$, and equivalent to $A \sqcap \neg A$) are often pre-defined. Other commonly supported operators include restricted forms of quantification called *existential role restrictions* (denoted $\exists R.C$) and *universal role restrictions* (denoted $\forall R.C$). Some Description Logics also support *qualified number restrictions* (denoted $\leqslant n.PC$ and $\geqslant n.PC$), operators that place cardinality restrictions on the roles relating instances of a concept to instances of some other concept. Cardinality restrictions are often limited to the forms $\leqslant n.P\top$ and $\geqslant n.P\top$, when they are called *unqualified number restrictions*, or simply *number restrictions*, and are often abbreviated to $\leqslant n$ P and $\geqslant nP$. The roles that can appear in cardinality restriction concepts are usually restricted to being atomic, as allowing arbitrary roles in such concepts is known to lead to undecidability [Baader and Sattler, 1996b].

Role-forming operators may also be supported, and in some very expressive logics roles can be regular expressions formed using *union* (denoted $\sqcup$), *composition* (denoted $\circ$), *reflexive–transitive closure* (denoted *) and *identity* operators (denoted *id*), possibly augmented with the *inverse* (also known as *converse*) operator (denoted $^-$) [De Giacomo and Lenzerini, 1996]. In most implemented systems, however, roles are restricted to being atomic names.

Concepts and roles are given a standard Tarski-style model-theoretic semantics, their meaning being given by an interpretation $\mathcal{I} = (\Delta^{\mathcal{I}}, \cdot^{\mathcal{I}})$, where $\Delta^{\mathcal{I}}$ is the domain (a set) and $^{\mathcal{I}}$ is an interpretation function. Full details of both syntax and semantics can be found in Chapter 2.

In general, a DL knowledge base (KB) consists of a set $\mathcal{T}$ of *terminological axioms*, and a set $\mathcal{A}$ of *assertional axioms*. The axioms in $\mathcal{T}$ state facts about concepts and roles while those in $\mathcal{A}$ state facts about individual instances of concepts and roles. As in this chapter we will mostly be concerned with terminological reasoning, that is reasoning about concepts and roles, a KB will usually be taken to consist only of the terminological component $\mathcal{T}$.

A terminological KB $\mathcal{T}$ usually consists of a set of axioms of the form $C \sqsubseteq D$ and $C \equiv D$, where C and D are concepts. An interpretation $\mathcal{I}$ satisfies $\mathcal{T}$ if for every axiom $(C \sqsubseteq D) \in \mathcal{T}$, $C^{\mathcal{I}} \subseteq D^{\mathcal{I}}$, and for every axiom $(C \equiv D) \in \mathcal{T}$,

$C^{\mathcal{I}} = D^{\mathcal{I}}$; $\mathcal{T}$ is satisfiable if there exists some non-empty interpretation that satisfies it. Note that $\mathcal{T}$ can, without loss of generality, be restricted to contain only inclusion axioms or only equality axioms, as the two forms can be reduced one to the other using the following equivalences:

$$C \sqsubseteq D \iff \top \equiv D \sqcup \neg C$$
$$C \equiv D \iff C \sqsubseteq D \text{ and } D \sqsubseteq C.$$

A concept C is *subsumed* by a concept D with respect to $\mathcal{T}$ (written $\mathcal{T} \models C \sqsubseteq D$) if $C^{\mathcal{I}} \subseteq D^{\mathcal{I}}$ in every interpretation $\mathcal{I}$ that satisfies $\mathcal{T}$, a concept C is *satisfiable* with respect to $\mathcal{T}$ (written $\mathcal{T} \models C \not\sqsubseteq \bot$) if $C^{\mathcal{I}} \neq \emptyset$ in some $\mathcal{I}$ that satisfies $\mathcal{T}$, and a concept C is *unsatisfiable* (not satisfiable) with respect to $\mathcal{T}$ (written $\mathcal{T} \models \neg C$) if $C^{\mathcal{I}} = \emptyset$ in every $\mathcal{I}$ that satisfies $\mathcal{T}$. Subsumption and (un)satisfiability are closely related. If $\mathcal{T} \models C \sqsubseteq D$, then in all interpretations $\mathcal{I}$ that satisfy $\mathcal{T}$, $C^{\mathcal{I}} \subseteq D^{\mathcal{I}}$ and so $C^{\mathcal{I}} \cap (\neg D)^{\mathcal{I}} = \emptyset$. Conversely, if C is not satisfiable with respect to $\mathcal{T}$, then in all $\mathcal{I}$ that satisfy $\mathcal{T}$, $C^{\mathcal{I}} = \emptyset$ and so $C^{\mathcal{I}} \subseteq \bot^{\mathcal{I}}$. Subsumption and (un)satisfiability can thus be reduced one to the other using the following equivalences:

$$\mathcal{T} \models C \sqsubseteq D \iff \mathcal{T} \models \neg(C \sqcap \neg D)$$
$$\mathcal{T} \models \neg C \iff \mathcal{T} \models C \sqsubseteq \bot.$$

In some Description Logics $\mathcal{T}$ can also contain axioms that define a set of transitive roles $\mathbf{R}_+$ and/or a subsumption partial ordering on roles [Horrocks and Sattler, 1999]. An axiom $R \in \mathbf{R}_+$ states that R is a transitive role while an axiom $R \sqsubseteq S$ states that R is subsumed by S. An interpretation $\mathcal{I}$ satisfies the axiom $R \in \mathbf{R}_+$ if $R^{\mathcal{I}}$ is transitively closed (i.e., $(R^{\mathcal{I}})^+ = R^{\mathcal{I}}$), and it satisfies the axiom $R \sqsubseteq S$ if $R^{\mathcal{I}} \subseteq S^{\mathcal{I}}$.

9.2.2 Reasoning services

Terminological reasoning in a DL-based knowledge representation system is based on determining subsumption relationships with respect to the axioms in a KB. As well as answering specific subsumption and satisfiability queries, it is often useful to compute and store (usually in the form of a directed acyclic graph) the subsumption partial ordering of all the concept names appearing in the KB, a procedure known as *classifying* the KB [Patel-Schneider and Swartout, 1993]. Some systems may also be capable of dealing with *assertional* axioms, those concerning instances of concepts and roles, and performing reasoning tasks such as *realization* (determining the concepts instantiated by a given individual) and *retrieval* (determining the set of individuals that instantiate a given concept) [Baader *et al.*, 1991]. However, we will mostly concentrate on terminological reasoning because it has been more widely used in DL applications. Moreover, given a sufficiently expressive Description Logic, assertional reasoning can be reduced to terminological reasoning [De Giacomo and Lenzerini, 1996].

In practice, many systems use subsumption-testing algorithms that are not capable of determining subsumption relationships with respect to an arbitrary KB. Instead, they restrict the kinds of axiom that can appear in the KB so that dependency-eliminating substitutions (known as *unfolding*) can be performed prior to evaluating subsumption relationships. These restrictions require that all axioms are *unique, acyclic definitions*. An axiom is called a definition of A if it is of the form $A \sqsubseteq D$ or $A \equiv D$, where A is an atomic name, it is unique if the KB contains no other definition of A, and it is acyclic if D does not refer either directly or indirectly (via other axioms) to A. A KB that satisfies these restrictions will be called an *unfoldable* KB.

Definitions of the form $A \sqsubseteq D$ are sometimes called *primitive* or *necessary*, as D specifies a necessary condition for instances of A, while those of the form $A \equiv D$ are sometimes called *non-primitive* or *necessary and sufficient* as D specifies conditions that are both necessary and sufficient for instances of A. In order to distinguish non-definitional axioms, they are often called *general* axioms [Buchheit *et al.*, 1993a]. Restricting the KB to definition axioms makes reasoning much easier, but significantly reduces the expressive power of the DL. However, even with an unrestricted (or *general*) KB, definition axioms and unfolding are still useful ideas, as they can be used to optimize the reasoning procedures (see Subsection 9.4.3).

9.2.3 Unfolding

Given an unfoldable KB $\mathcal{T}$, and a concept C whose satisfiability is to be tested with respect to $\mathcal{T}$, it is possible to eliminate from C all concept names occurring in $\mathcal{T}$ using a recursive substitution procedure called unfolding. The satisfiability of the resulting concept is independent of the axioms in $\mathcal{T}$ and can therefore be tested using a decision procedure that is only capable of determining the satisfiability of a single concept (or equivalently, the satisfiability of a concept with respect to an empty KB).

For a non-primitive concept name A, defined in $\mathcal{T}$ by an axiom $A \equiv D$, the procedure is simply to replace A with D wherever it occurs in C, and then to recursively unfold D. For a primitive concept name A, defined in $\mathcal{T}$ by an axiom $A \sqsubseteq D$, the procedure is slightly more complex. Wherever A occurs in C it is replaced with the concept $\mathsf{A}' \sqcap D$, where A' is a new concept name not occurring in $\mathcal{T}$ or C, and D is then recursively unfolded. The concept A' represents the "primitiveness" of A – the unspecified characteristics that differentiate it from D. We will use $\mathsf{Unfold}(C, \mathcal{T})$ to denote the concept C unfolded with respect to a KB $\mathcal{T}$.

A decision procedure that tries to find a satisfying interpretation $\mathcal{I}$ for the unfolded concept can now be used, as any such interpretation will also satisfy $\mathcal{T}$. This can easily be shown by applying the unfolding procedure to all of the concepts forming the right-hand side of axioms in $\mathcal{T}$, so that they are constructed entirely from concept names that are not defined in $\mathcal{T}$, and are thus independent of the other axioms in $\mathcal{T}$. The interpretation of each defined concept in $\mathcal{T}$ can then be taken to be the interpretation of the unfolded right-hand side concept, as given by $\mathcal{I}$ and the semantics of the concept and role forming operators.

Subsumption reasoning can be made independent of $\mathcal{T}$ using the same technique. Given two concepts C and D, determining if C is subsumed by D with respect to $\mathcal{T}$ is the same as determining if $\mathsf{Unfold}(C, \mathcal{T})$ is subsumed by $\mathsf{Unfold}(D, \mathcal{T})$ with respect to an empty KB:

$$\mathcal{T} \models C \sqsubseteq D \iff \emptyset \models \mathsf{Unfold}(C, \mathcal{T}) \sqsubseteq \mathsf{Unfold}(D, \mathcal{T}).$$

Unfolding would not be possible, in general, if the axioms in $\mathcal{T}$ were not unique acyclic definitions. If $\mathcal{T}$ contained multiple definition axioms for some concept A, for example $\{(\mathsf{A} \equiv C), (\mathsf{A} \equiv D)\} \subseteq \mathcal{T}$, then it would not be possible to make a substitution for A that preserved the meaning of both axioms. If $\mathcal{T}$ contained cyclic axioms, for example $(\mathsf{A} \sqsubseteq \exists R.\mathsf{A}) \in \mathcal{T}$, then trying to unfold A would lead to non-termination. If $\mathcal{T}$ contained general axioms, for example $\exists R.C \sqsubseteq D$, then it could not be guaranteed that an interpretation satisfying the unfolded concept would also satisfy these axioms.

9.2.4 Internalization

While it is possible to design an algorithm capable of reasoning with respect to a general KB [Buchheit *et al.*, 1993a], with more expressive logics, in particular those allowing the definition of a *universal role*, a procedure called *internalization* can be used to reduce the problem to that of determining the satisfiability of a single concept [Baader, 1991]. A truly universal role is one whose interpretation includes every pair of elements in the domain of interpretation (i.e., $\Delta^{\mathcal{I}} \times \Delta^{\mathcal{I}}$). However, a role U is universal w.r.t. a terminology $\mathcal{T}$ if it is defined such that U is transitively closed and $\mathsf{P} \sqsubseteq U$

for all role names P occurring in $\mathcal{T}$. For a logic that supports the union and transitive reflexive closure role-forming operators, this can be achieved simply by taking U to be

$$(\mathsf{P}_1 \sqcup \cdots \sqcup \mathsf{P}_n \sqcup \mathsf{P}_1^- \sqcup \cdots \sqcup \mathsf{P}_n^-)^*,$$

where $\mathsf{P}_1, \ldots, \mathsf{P}_n$ are all the roles names occurring in $\mathcal{T}$. For a logic that supports transitively closed roles and role inclusion axioms, this can be achieved by adding the axioms

$$(U \in \mathbf{R}_+), (\mathsf{P}_1 \sqsubseteq U), \ldots, (\mathsf{P}_n \sqsubseteq U), (\mathsf{P}_1^- \sqsubseteq U), \ldots, (\mathsf{P}_n^- \sqsubseteq U)$$

to $\mathcal{T}$, where $\mathsf{P}_1, \ldots, \mathsf{P}_n$ are all the roles names occurring in $\mathcal{T}$ and U is a new role name not occurring in $\mathcal{T}$. Note that in either case, the inverse role components are only required if the logic supports the inverse role operator.

The concept axioms in $\mathcal{T}$ can be reduced to axioms of the form $\top \sqsubseteq C$ using the equivalences:

$$A \equiv B \iff \top \sqsubseteq (A \sqcup \neg B) \sqcap (\neg A \sqcup B)$$
$$A \sqsubseteq B \iff \top \sqsubseteq \neg A \sqcup B.$$

These axioms can then be conjoined to give a single axiom $\top \sqsubseteq C$, where

$$C = \bigsqcap_{(A_i \equiv B_i) \in \mathcal{T}} ((A_i \sqcup \neg B_i) \sqcap (\neg A_i \sqcup B_i)) \sqcap \bigsqcap_{(A_j \sqsubseteq B_j) \in \mathcal{T}} (\neg A_j \sqcup B_j).$$

Because the interpretation of $\top$ is equal to the domain ($\top^{\mathcal{I}} = \Delta^{\mathcal{I}}$), this axiom states that every element in the domain must satisfy C. When testing the satisfiability of a concept D with respect to $\mathcal{T}$, this constraint on possible interpretations can be imposed by testing the satisfiability of $D \sqcap C \sqcap \forall U.C$ (or simply $D \sqcap \forall U.C$ in the case where U is transitively reflexively closed). This relies on the fact that satisfiable DL concepts always have an interpretation in which every element is connected to every other element by some sequence of roles (the collapsed model property) [Schild, 1991].

9.3 Subsumption-testing algorithms

The use of unfolding and internalization means that, in most cases, terminological reasoning in a DL-based Knowledge Representation System can be reduced to subsumption or satisfiability reasoning. There are several algorithmic techniques for computing subsumption relationships, but they divide into two main families: structural and logical.

9.3.1 Structural subsumption algorithms

Structural algorithms were used in early DL systems such as KL-ONE [Brachman and Schmolze, 1985], NIKL [Kaczmarek *et al.*, 1986] and KRYP-TON [Brachman *et al.*, 1983a], and are still used in systems such as CLASSIC [Patel-Schneider *et al.*, 1991], LOOM [MacGregor, 1991b] and GRAIL [Rector *et al.*, 1997]. To determine if one concept subsumes another, structural algorithms simply compare the (normalized) syntactic structure of the two concepts (see Chapter 2).

Although such algorithms can be quite efficient [Borgida and Patel-Schneider, 1994; Heinsohn *et al.*, 1994], they have several disadvantages:

- Perhaps the most important disadvantage of this type of algorithm is that while it is generally easy to demonstrate the soundness of the structural inference rules (they will never infer an invalid subsumption relationship), they are usually incomplete (they may fail to infer all valid subsumption relationships).
- It is difficult to extend structural algorithms in order to deal with more expressive logics, in particular those supporting general negation, or to reason with respect to an arbitrary KB. This lack of expressive power makes the DL system of limited value in traditional ontological engineering applications [Doyle and Patil, 1991], and completely useless in database schema reasoning applications [Calvanese *et al.*, 1998f].
- Although accepting some degree of incompleteness is one way of improving the performance of a DL reasoner, the performance of incomplete reasoners is highly dependent on the degree of incompleteness, and this is notoriously difficult to quantify [Borgida, 1992a].

9.3.2 Logical algorithms

These kinds of algorithm use a refutation-style proof: C is subsumed by D if it can be shown that the existence of an individual x that is in the extension of C ($x \in C^{\mathcal{I}}$) but not in the extension of D ($x \notin D^{\mathcal{I}}$) is logically inconsistent. As we have seen in Subsection 9.2.2, this corresponds to testing the logical (un)satisfiability of the concept $C \sqcap \neg D$ (i.e., $C \sqsubseteq D$ iff $C \sqcap \neg D$ is not satisfiable). Note that forming this concept obviously relies on having full negation in the logic.

Various techniques can be used to test the logical satisfiability of a concept. One obvious possibility is to exploit an existing reasoner. For example, the LOGICSWORKBENCH [Balsiger *et al.*, 1996], a general-purpose propositional modal logic reasoning system, could be used simply by exploiting the well-known correspondences between description and modal logics [Schild, 1991]. First-order logic theorem provers can also be used via appropriate traslations of Description Logics into first-order logic. Examples of this approach can be seen in systems developed by Hustadt and Schmidt [1997], using the SPASS theorem prover, and Paramasivam and Plaisted [1998], using the CLIN-S theorem prover. An existing reasoner could also be used as a component of a more powerful system, as in KSAT/*SAT [Giunchiglia and Sebastiani, 1996a; Giunchiglia *et al.*, 2002], where a propositional satisfiability (SAT) tester is used as the key component of a propositional modal satisfiability reasoner.

There are advantages and disadvantages to the "re-use" approach. On the positive side, it should be much easier to build a system based on an existing reasoner, and performance can be maximized by using a state-of-the-art implementation such as SPASS (a highly optimized first-order theorem prover) or the highly optimized SAT testing algorithms used in KSAT and *SAT (the use of a specialized SAT tester allows *SAT to outperform other systems on classes of problem that emphasize propositional reasoning). The translation (into first-order logic) approach has also been shown to be able to deal with a wide range of expressive Description Logics, in particular those with complex role-forming operators such as negation or identity [Hustadt and Schmidt, 2000].

On the negative side, it may be difficult to extend the reasoner to deal with more expressive logics, or to add optimizations that take advantage of specific features of the Description Logic, without reimplementing the reasoner (as has been done, for example, in more recent versions of the *SAT system).

Most, if not all, implemented DL systems based on logical reasoning have used custom designed tableau decision procedures. These algorithms try to prove that D subsumes C by starting with a single individual satisfying $C \sqcap \neg D$, and demonstrating that any attempt to extend this into a complete interpretation (using a set of *tableau expansion rules*) will lead to a logical contradiction. If a complete and non-contradictory interpretation is found, then this represents a counterexample (an interpretation in which some element of the domain is in $C^{\mathcal{I}}$ but not in $D^{\mathcal{I}}$) that disproves the conjectured subsumption relationship.

This approach has many advantages and has dominated recent DL research:

- It has a sound theoretical basis in first-order logic [Hollunder *et al.*, 1990].
- It can be relatively easily adapted to allow for a range of logical languages by changing the set of tableau expansion rules [Hollunder *et al.*, 1990; Bresciani *et al.*, 1995].
- It can be adapted to deal with very expressive logics, and to reason with respect

to an arbitrary KB, by using more sophisticated control mechanisms to ensure termination [Baader, 1991; Buchheit *et al.*, 1993c; Sattler, 1996].
- It has been shown to be optimal for a number of DL languages, in the sense that the worst-case complexity of the algorithm is no worse than the known complexity of the satisfiability problem for the logic [Hollunder *et al.*, 1990].

In the remainder of this chapter, detailed descriptions of implementation and optimization techniques will assume the use of a tableau decision procedure. However, many of the techniques are independent of the subsumption-testing algorithm or could easily be adapted to most logic-based methods. The reverse is also true, and several of the described techniques have been adapted from other logical decision procedures, in particular those that try to optimize the search used to deal with non-determinism.

9.3.2.1 Tableau algorithms

Tableau algorithms try to prove the satisfiability of a concept D by constructing a *model*, an interpretation $\mathcal{I}$ in which $D^{\mathcal{I}}$ is not empty. A *tableau* is a graph which represents such a model, with nodes corresponding to individuals (elements of $\Delta^{\mathcal{I}}$) and edges corresponding to relationships between individuals (elements of $\Delta^{\mathcal{I}} \times \Delta^{\mathcal{I}}$).

A typical algorithm will start with a single individual satisfying D and try to construct a tableau, or some structure from which a tableau can be constructed, by inferring the existence of additional individuals or of additional constraints on individuals. The inference mechanism consists of applying a set of expansion rules which correspond to the logical constructs of the language, and the algorithm terminates either when the structure is complete (no further inferences are possible) or when obvious contradictions have been revealed. Non-determinism is dealt with by searching different possible expansions: the concept is unsatisfiable if every expansion leads to a contradiction and is satisfiable if any possible expansion leads to the discovery of a complete non-contradictory structure.

Theoretical presentations of tableau algorithms use a variety of notational styles including constraints [Hollunder *et al.*, 1990], prefixes [De Giacomo and Massacci, 1996] and labeled graphs [Sattler, 1996]. We will use the labeled graph notation as it has an obvious correspondence with standard implementation techniques. In its basic form, this notation describes the construction of a directed graph (usually a tree) in which each node x is labeled with a set of concepts ($\mathcal{L}(x) = \{C_1, \ldots, C_n\}$), and each edge $\langle x, y \rangle$ is labeled with a role ($\mathcal{L}(\langle x, y \rangle) = R$). When a concept C is in the label of a node x ($C \in \mathcal{L}(x)$), it represents a model in which the individual

⊓-rule   if 1. $(C \sqcap D) \in \mathcal{L}(x)$
            2. $\{C, D\} \nsubseteq \mathcal{L}(x)$
         then $\mathcal{L}(x) \longrightarrow \mathcal{L}(x) \cup \{C, D\}$

⊔-rule   if 1. $(C \sqcup D) \in \mathcal{L}(x)$
            2. $\{C, D\} \cap \mathcal{L}(x) = \emptyset$
         then   *either* $\mathcal{L}(x) \longrightarrow \mathcal{L}(x) \cup \{C\}$
                or $\mathcal{L}(x) \longrightarrow \mathcal{L}(x) \cup \{D\}$

∃-rule   if 1. $\exists R.C \in \mathcal{L}(x)$
            2.   there is no y s.t. $\mathcal{L}(\langle x, y \rangle) = R$ and $C \in \mathcal{L}(y)$
         then   create a new node y and edge $\langle x, y \rangle$
                with $\mathcal{L}(y) = \{C\}$ and $\mathcal{L}(\langle x, y \rangle) = R$

∀-rule   if 1. $\forall R.C \in \mathcal{L}(x)$
            2.   there is some y s.t. $\mathcal{L}(\langle x, y \rangle) = R$ and $C \notin \mathcal{L}(y)$
         then $\mathcal{L}(y) \longrightarrow \mathcal{L}(y) \cup \{C\}$

Fig. 9.1. Tableau expansion rules for $\mathcal{ALC}$.

corresponding with x is in the interpretation of C. When an edge $\langle x, y \rangle$ is labeled R ($\mathcal{L}(\langle x, y \rangle) = R$), it represents a model in which the tuple corresponding with $\langle x, y \rangle$ is in the interpretation of R. A node y is called an R-successor of a node x if there is an edge $\langle x, y \rangle$ labeled R, x is called the predecessor of y if y is an R-successor of x, and x is called an ancestor of y if x is the predecessor of y or there exists some node z such that z is the predecessor of y and x is an ancestor of z. A contradiction or *clash* is detected when $\{C, \neg C\} \subseteq \mathcal{L}(x)$ for some concept C and some node x.

To test the satisfiability of a concept D, a basic algorithm initializes a tree to contain a single node x (called the *root* node) with $\mathcal{L}(x) = \{D\}$, and then expands the tree by applying rules that either extend node labels or add new leaf nodes. A set of expansion rules for the $\mathcal{ALC}$ Description Logic is shown in Figure 9.1, where C and D are concepts, and R is a role. Note that:

- Concepts are assumed to be in *negation normal form*, that is with negations only applying to concept names. Arbitrary $\mathcal{ALC}$ concepts can be converted to negation normal form by pushing negations inwards using a combination of De Morgan's laws and the equivalences $\neg(\exists R.C) \Longleftrightarrow (\forall R.\neg C)$ and $\neg(\forall R.C) \Longleftrightarrow (\exists R.\neg C)$. This procedure can be extended to more expressive logics by using additional equivalences such as $\neg(\leqslant n\, R) \Longleftrightarrow (\geqslant (n+1)R)$.
- Disjunctive concepts $(C \sqcup D) \in \mathcal{L}(x)$ give rise to non-deterministic expansion. In practice this is usually dealt with by search: trying each possible expansion in turn until a fully expanded and clash-free tree is found, or all possibilities have been shown to lead to contradictions. In more expressive logics other constructs, such as maximum number restrictions $(\leqslant n\, \mathsf{R})$, also lead to non-deterministic expansion. Searching non-deterministic expansions is the main cause of intractability in tableau subsumption testing algorithms.

- Existential role restriction concepts $\exists R.C \in \mathcal{L}(x)$ cause the creation of new R-successor nodes, and universal role restriction concepts $\forall R.C \in \mathcal{L}(x)$ extend the labels of R-successor nodes.

The tree is fully expanded when none of the expansion rules can be applied. If a fully expanded and clash-free tree can be found, then the algorithm returns *satisfiable*; otherwise it returns *unsatisfiable*.

More expressive logics may require several extensions to this basic formalism. For example, with logics that include both role inclusion axioms and some form of cardinality restriction, it may be necessary to label edges with sets of role names instead of a single role name [Horrocks, 1998b]. It may also be necessary to add cycle detection (often called *blocking*) to the preconditions of some of the inference rules in order to guarantee termination [Buchheit *et al.*, 1993a; Baader *et al.*, 1996], the general idea being to stop the expansion of a branch whenever the same node label recurs in the branch. Blocking can also lead to a more complex correspondence between the structure created by the algorithm and a model of a satisfiable concept, as the model may contain cycles or even be infinite [Horrocks and Sattler, 1999].

9.4 Theory versus practice

So far, what we have seen is typical of theoretical presentations of tableau-based decision procedures. Such a presentation is sufficient for soundness and completeness proofs, and is an essential starting point for the implementation of a reliable subsumption-testing algorithm. However, there often remains a considerable gap between the theoretical algorithm and an actual implementation. Additional points which may need to be considered are:

- the efficiency of the algorithm, in the theoretical (worst-case) sense;
- the efficiency of the algorithm, in a practical (typical-case) sense;
- how to use the algorithm for reasoning with unfoldable, general and cyclical KBs;
- optimizing the (implementation of the) algorithm to improve the typical-case performance.

In the remainder of this section we will consider the first three points, while in the following section we will consider implementation and optimization techniques in detail.

9.4.1 Worst-case complexity

When considering an implementation, it is sensible to start with an algorithm that is known to be theoretically efficient, even if the implementation

∃∀-rule   if 1. $\exists R.C \in \mathcal{L}(x)$
           2.   there is no y s.t. $\mathcal{L}(\langle x, y \rangle) = R$ and $C \in \mathcal{L}(y)$
           3.   neither the ⊓-rule nor the ⊔-rule is applicable to $\mathcal{L}(x)$
      then   create a new node y and edge $\langle x, y \rangle$
            with $\mathcal{L}(y) = \{C\} \cup \{D \mid \forall R.D \in \mathcal{L}(x)\}$ and $\mathcal{L}(\langle x, y \rangle) = R$

Fig. 9.2. Combined ∃∀-rule for $\mathcal{ALC}$.

subsequently departs from the theory to some extent. Theoretically efficient is taken to mean that the complexity of the algorithm is equal to the complexity of the satisfiability problem for the logic, where this is known, or at least that consideration has been given to the worst-case complexity of the algorithm. This is not always the case, as the algorithm may have been designed to facilitate a soundness and completeness proof, with little consideration having been given to worst-case complexity, much less implementation.

Apart from establishing an upper bound for the "hardness" of the problem, studies of theoretical complexity can suggest useful implementation techniques. For example, a study of the complexity of the satisfiability problem for $\mathcal{ALC}$ concepts with respect to a general KB has demonstrated that caching of intermediate results is required in order to stay in EXPTIME [Donini *et al.*, 1996a], while studying the complexity of the satisfiability problem for $\mathcal{SIN}$ concepts has shown that a more sophisticated labeling and blocking strategy can be used in order to stay in PSPACE [Horrocks *et al.*, 1999].

One theoretically derived technique that is widely used in practice is the *trace* technique. This is a method for minimizing the amount of space used by the algorithm to store the tableau expansion tree. The idea is to impose an ordering on the application of expansion rules so that local *propositional reasoning* (finding a clash-free expansion of conjunctions and disjunctions using the ⊓-rule and ⊔-rule) is completed before new nodes are created using the ∃-rule. A successor created by an application of the ∃-rule, and any possible applications of the ∀-rule, can then be treated as an independent subproblem that returns either *satisfiable* or *unsatisfiable*, and the space used to solve it can be re-used in solving the next subproblem. A node x returns *satisfiable* if there is a clash-free propositional solution for which any and all subproblems return *satisfiable*; otherwise it returns *unsatisfiable*. In algorithms where the trace technique can be used, the ∀-rule is often incorporated in the ∃-rule, giving a single rule as shown in Figure 9.2.

Apart from minimizing space usage, the trace technique is generally viewed as a sensible way of organizing the expansion and the flow of control within the algorithm. Ordering the expansion in this way may also be required by some blocking strategies [Buchheit *et al.*, 1993a], although in some cases it is possible to use a more efficient subset blocking technique that is independent of the ordering [Baader *et al.*, 1996].

The trace technique relies on the fact that node labels are not affected by the expansion of their successors. This is no longer true when the logic includes inverse roles, because universal value restrictions in the label of a successor of a node x can augment $\mathcal{L}(x)$. This could invalidate the existing propositional solution for $\mathcal{L}(x)$, or invalidate previously computed solutions to subproblems in other successor nodes. For example, if

$$\mathcal{L}(x) = \{\exists R.C, \exists S.(\forall S^-.(\forall R.\neg C))\},$$

then x is obviously unsatisfiable as expanding $\exists S.(\forall S^-.(\forall R.\neg C))$ will add $\forall R.\neg C$ to $\mathcal{L}(x)$, meaning that x must have an R-successor whose label contains both C and $\neg C$. The contradiction would not be discovered if the R-successor required by $\exists R.C \in \mathcal{L}(x)$ were generated first, found to be satisfiable and then deleted from the tree in order to save space.

The development of a PSPACE algorithm for the $\mathcal{SIN}$ logic has shown that a modified version of the trace technique can still be used with logics that include inverse roles [Horrocks *et al.*, 1999]. However, the modification requires that the propositional solution and all subproblems are re-computed whenever the label of a node is augmented by the expansion of a universal value restriction in the label of one of its successors.

9.4.2 Typical-case complexity

Although useful practical techniques can be derived from the study of theoretical algorithms, it should be borne in mind that minimizing worst-case complexity may require the use of techniques that clearly would not be sensible in typical cases. This is because the kinds of pathological problem that would lead to worst-case behavior do not seem to occur in realistic applications. In particular, the amount of space used by algorithms does not seem to be a practical problem, whereas the time taken for the computation certainly is. For example, in experiments with the FACT system using the DL'98 test suite, available memory (200Mb) was never exhausted in spite of the fact that some single computations required hundreds of seconds of CPU time [Horrocks and Patel-Schneider, 1998b]. In other experiments using the GALEN KB, computations were run for tens of thousands of seconds of CPU time without exhausting available memory.

In view of these considerations, techniques that save space by recomputing are unlikely to be of practical value. The modified trace technique used in the PSPACE $\mathcal{SIN}$ algorithm (see Subsection 9.4.1), for example, is probably not of practical value. However, the more sophisticated labeling and blocking strategy, which allows the establishment of a polynomial bound on the length of branches, could be used not only in an implementation of the $\mathcal{SIN}$ algorithm, but also in implementations of more expressive logics where other considerations mean that the PSPACE result no longer holds [Horrocks *et al.*, 1999].

In practice, the poor performance of tableau algorithms is due to non-determinism in the expansion rules (for example the ⊔-rule), and the resulting search of different possible expansions. This is often treated in a very cursory manner in theoretical presentations. For soundness and completeness it is enough to prove that the search will always find a solution if one exists, and that it will always terminate. For worst-case complexity, an upper bound on the size of the search space is all that is required. As this upper bound is invariably exponential with respect to the size of the problem, exploring the whole search space would inevitably lead to intractability for all but the smallest problems. When implementing an algorithm it is therefore vital to give much more careful consideration to non-deterministic expansion, in particular how to reduce the size of the search space and how to explore it in an efficient manner. Many of the optimizations discussed in subsequent sections will be aimed at doing this, for example by using *absorption* to localize non-determinism in the KB, *dependency directed backtracking* to prune the search tree, *heuristics* to guide the search, and *caching* to avoid repetitive search.

9.4.3 Reasoning with a knowledge base

One area in which the theory and practice diverge significantly is that of reasoning with respect to the axioms in a KB. This problem is rarely considered in detail: with less expressive logics the KB is usually restricted to being unfoldable, while with more expressive logics, all axioms can be treated as general axioms and dealt with via internalization. In either case it is sufficient to consider an algorithm that tests the satisfiability of a single concept, usually in negation normal form.

In practice, it is much more efficient to retain the structure of the KB for as long as possible, and to take advantage of it during subsumption/satisfiability testing. One way in which this can be done is to use *lazy unfolding* – only unfolding concepts as required by the progress of the subsumption or satisfiability testing algorithm [Baader *et al.*, 1992a]. With a tableau algorithm, this means that a defined concept A is only unfolded when it occurs in a node label. For example, if $\mathcal{T}$ contains the non-primitive definition axiom $A \equiv C$, and the $\sqcap$-rule is applied to a concept $(A \sqcap D) \in \mathcal{L}(x)$ so that A and D are added to $\mathcal{L}(x)$, then at this point A can be unfolded by replacing it with C.

Used in this way, lazy unfolding already has the advantage that it avoids unnecessary unfolding of irrelevant subconcepts, either because a contradiction is discovered without fully expanding the tree, or because a non-deterministic expansion choice leads to a complete and clash-free tree. However, a much greater increase in efficiency can be achieved if, instead of replacing concept names with their definitions, names are retained when their definitions are added. This is because the discovery of a clash between concept names can avoid expansion of their definitions [Baader *et al.*, 1992a].

In general, lazy unfolding can be described as additional tableau expansion rules, defined as follows:

$$
\begin{aligned}
&U_1\text{-rule} \quad \text{if} \ 1. \quad A \in \mathcal{L}(x) \text{ and } (A \equiv C) \in \mathcal{T} \\
&\qquad\qquad\qquad 2. \quad C \notin \mathcal{L}(x) \\
&\qquad\qquad \text{then} \quad \mathcal{L}(x) \longrightarrow \mathcal{L}(x) \cup \{C\} \\
&U_2\text{-rule} \quad \text{if} \ 1. \quad \neg A \in \mathcal{L}(x) \text{ and } (A \equiv C) \in \mathcal{T} \\
&\qquad\qquad\qquad 2. \quad \neg C \notin \mathcal{L}(x) \\
&\qquad\qquad \text{then} \quad \mathcal{L}(x) \longrightarrow \mathcal{L}(x) \cup \{\neg C\} \\
&U_3\text{-rule} \quad \text{if} \ 1. \quad A \in \mathcal{L}(x) \text{ and } (A \sqsubseteq C) \in \mathcal{T} \\
&\qquad\qquad\qquad 2. \quad C \notin \mathcal{L}(x) \\
&\qquad\qquad \text{then} \quad \mathcal{L}(x) \longrightarrow \mathcal{L}(x) \cup \{C\}.
\end{aligned}
$$

The U_1-rule and U_2-rule reflect the symmetry of the equality relation in the non-primitive definition $A \equiv C$, which is equivalent to $A \sqsubseteq C$ and $\neg A \sqsubseteq \neg C$. The U_3-rule on the other hand reflects the asymmetry of the subsumption relation in the primitive definition $A \sqsubseteq C$.

Treating all the axioms in the KB as general axioms, and dealing with them via internalization, is also highly inefficient. For example, if $\mathcal{T}$ contains an axiom $A \sqsubseteq C$, where A is a concept name not appearing on the left-hand side of any other axiom, then it is easy to deal with the axiom using the lazy unfolding technique, simply adding C to the label of any node in which A appears. Treating all axioms as general axioms would be equivalent to applying the following additional tableau expansion rules:

I_1-rule   if 1. $(C \equiv D) \in \mathcal{T}$
          2. $(D \sqcup \neg C) \notin \mathcal{L}(x)$
          then $\mathcal{L}(x) \longrightarrow \mathcal{L}(x) \cup \{(D \sqcup \neg C)\}$

I_2-rule   if 1. $(C \equiv D) \in \mathcal{T}$
          2. $(\neg D \sqcup C) \notin \mathcal{L}(x)$
          then $\mathcal{L}(x) \longrightarrow \mathcal{L}(x) \cup \{(\neg D \sqcup C)\}$

I_3-rule   if 1. $(C \sqsubseteq D) \in \mathcal{T}$
          2. $(D \sqcup \neg C) \notin \mathcal{L}(x)$
          then $\mathcal{L}(x) \longrightarrow \mathcal{L}(x) \cup \{(D \sqcup \neg C)\}.$

With $(\mathsf{A} \sqsubseteq C) \in \mathcal{T}$, this would result in the disjunction $(C \sqcup \neg \mathsf{A})$ being added to the label of every node, leading to non-deterministic expansion and search, the main cause of empirical intractability.

The solution to this problem is to divide the KB into two components, an unfoldable part $\mathcal{T}_u$ and a general part $\mathcal{T}_g$, such that $\mathcal{T}_g = \mathcal{T} \setminus \mathcal{T}_u$, and $\mathcal{T}_u$ contains unique, acyclic, definition axioms. This is easily achieved, e.g., by initializing $\mathcal{T}_u$ to $\emptyset$ (which is obviously unfoldable), then for each axiom X in $\mathcal{T}$, adding X to $\mathcal{T}_u$ if $\mathcal{T}_u \cup X$ is still unfoldable, and adding X to $\mathcal{T}_g$ otherwise.[3] It is then possible to use lazy unfolding to deal with $\mathcal{T}_u$, and internalization to deal with $\mathcal{T}_g$.

Given that the satisfiability-testing algorithm includes some sort of cycle checking, such as blocking, then it is even possible to be a little less conservative with respect to the definition of $\mathcal{T}_u$ by allowing it to contain cyclic primitive definition axioms, for example axioms of the form $\mathsf{A} \sqsubseteq \exists R.\mathsf{A}$. Lazy unfolding will ensure that $\mathsf{A}^{\mathcal{I}} \subseteq \exists R.\mathsf{A}^{\mathcal{I}}$ by adding $\exists R.\mathsf{A}$ to every node containing A, while blocking will take care of the non-termination problem that such an axiom would otherwise cause [Horrocks, 1997b]. Moreover, multiple primitive definitions for a single name can be added to $\mathcal{T}_u$, or equivalently merged into a single definition using the equivalence

$$(\mathsf{A} \sqsubseteq C_1), \ldots, (\mathsf{A} \sqsubseteq C_n) \quad \Longleftrightarrow \quad \mathsf{A} \sqsubseteq (C_1 \sqcap \cdots \sqcap C_n).$$

However, if $\mathcal{T}_u$ contains a non-primitive definition axiom $\mathsf{A} \equiv C$, then it cannot contain any other definitions for A, because this would be equivalent to allowing general axioms in $\mathcal{T}_u$. For example, given a general axiom $C \sqsubseteq D$, this could be added to $\mathcal{T}_u$ as $\mathsf{A} \sqsubseteq D$ and $\mathsf{A} \equiv C$, where A is a new name not appearing in $\mathcal{T}$. Moreover, certain kinds of non-primitive cycles cannot be allowed as they can be used to constrain possible models a way that would not be reflected by unfolding. For example, if $(\mathsf{A} \equiv \neg \mathsf{A}) \in \mathcal{T}$ for some concept

---

[3] Note that the result may depend on the order in which the axioms in $\mathcal{T}$ are processed.

name A, then the domain of all valid interpretations of $\mathcal{T}$ must be empty, and $\mathcal{T} \models C \sqsubseteq D$ for all concepts C and D [Horrocks and Tobies, 2000].

9.5 Optimization techniques

The KRIS system demonstrated that by taking a well-designed tableau algorithm, and applying some reasonable implementation and optimization techniques (such as lazy expansion), it is possible to obtain a tableau-based DL system that behaves reasonably well in typical cases, and compares favorably with systems based on structural algorithms [Baader *et al.*, 1992a]. However, this kind of system is still much too slow to be usable in many realistic applications. Fortunately, it is possible to achieve dramatic improvements in typical-case performance by using a wider range of optimization techniques.

As DL systems are often used to classify a KB, a hierarchy of optimization techniques is naturally suggested based on the stage of the classification process at which they can be applied.

1. Pre-processing optimizations that try to modify the KB so that classification and subsumption testing are easier.
2. Partial ordering optimizations that try to minimize the number of subsumption tests required in order to classify the KB.
3. Subsumption optimizations that try to avoid performing a potentially expensive satisfiability test, usually by substituting a cheaper test.
4. Satisfiability optimizations that try to improve the typical-case performance of the underlying satisfiability tester.

9.5.1 Pre-processing optimizations

The axioms that constitute a DL KB may have been generated by a human knowledge engineer, as is typically the case in ontological engineering applications, or be the result of some automated mapping from another formalism, as is typically the case in DB schema and query reasoning applications. In either case it is unlikely that a great deal of consideration was given to facilitating the subsequent reasoning procedures; the KB may, for example, contain considerable redundancy and may make unnecessary use of general axioms. As we have seen, general axioms are costly to reason with due to the high degree of non-determinism that they introduce.

It is, therefore, useful to preprocess the KB, applying a range of syntactic simplifications and manipulations. The first of these, *normalization*, tries to simplify the KB by identifying syntactic equivalences, contradictions and tautologies. The second, *absorption*, tries to eliminate general axioms by augmenting definition axioms.

9.5.1.1 Normalization

In realistic KBs, at least those manually constructed, large and complex concepts are seldom described monolithically, but are built up from a hierarchy of named concepts whose descriptions are less complex. The lazy unfolding technique described above can use this structure to provide more rapid detection of contradictions.

The effectiveness of lazy unfolding is greatly increased if a contradiction between two concepts can be detected whenever one is syntactically equivalent to the negation of the other; for example, we would like to discover a direct contradiction between $(C \sqcap D)$ and $(\neg D \sqcup \neg C)$. This can be achieved by transforming all concepts into a syntactic normal form, and by directly detecting contradictions caused by non-atomic concepts as well as those caused by concept names.

In Description Logics there is often redundancy in the set of concept-forming operators. In particular, logics with full negation often provide pairs of operators, either one of which can be eliminated in favor of the other by using negation. Conjunction and disjunction operators are an example of such a pair, and one can be eliminated in favor of the other using De Morgan's laws. In syntactic normal form, all concepts are transformed so that only one of each such pair appears in the KB (it does not matter which of the two is chosen, the important thing is uniformity). In $\mathcal{ALC}$, for example, all concepts could be transformed into (possibly negated) value restrictions, conjunctions and atomic concept names, with $(\neg D \sqcup \neg C)$ being transformed into $\neg(D \sqcap C)$. An important refinement is to treat conjunctions as sets (written $\sqcap\{C_1, \ldots, C_n\}$) so that reordering or repeating the conjuncts does not affect equivalence; for example, $(D \sqcap C)$ would be normalized as $\sqcap\{C, D\}$.[4] Normalization can also include a range of simplifications so that syntactically obvious contradictions and tautologies are detected; for example, $\exists R.\bot$ could be simplified to $\bot$.

Figure 9.3 describes normalization and simplification functions Norm and Simp for $\mathcal{ALC}$. These can be extended to deal with more expressive logics by adding appropriate normalizations (and possibly additional simplifications). For example, number restrictions can be dealt with by adding the normalizations $\mathsf{Norm}(\leqslant n\, R) = \neg \geqslant (n+1)R$ and $\mathsf{Norm}(\geqslant nR) = \geqslant nR$, and the simplification $\mathsf{Simp}(\geqslant 0R) = \top$.

---

[4] Sorting the elements in conjuctions, and eliminating duplicates, achieves the same result.

$$
\begin{aligned}
\mathsf{Norm}(A) &= A \text{ for atomic concept name } A \\
\mathsf{Norm}(\neg C) &= \mathsf{Simp}(\neg\,\mathsf{Norm}(C)) \\
\mathsf{Norm}(C_1 \sqcap \ldots \sqcap C_n) &= \mathsf{Simp}(\sqcap\{\mathsf{Norm}(C_1)\} \cup \cdots \cup \{\mathsf{Norm}(C_n)\}) \\
\mathsf{Norm}(C_1 \sqcup \ldots \sqcup C_n) &= \mathsf{Norm}(\neg(\neg C_1 \sqcap \cdots \sqcap \neg C_n)) \\
\mathsf{Norm}(\forall R.C) &= \mathsf{Simp}(\forall R.\,\mathsf{Norm}(C)) \\
\mathsf{Norm}(\exists R.C) &= \mathsf{Norm}(\neg\forall R.\neg C)
\end{aligned}
$$

$$
\mathsf{Simp}(A) = A \text{ for atomic concept name } A
$$

$$
\mathsf{Simp}(\neg C) = \begin{cases}
\bot & \text{if } C = \top \\
\top & \text{if } C = \bot \\
\mathsf{Simp}(D) & \text{if } C = \neg D \\
\neg C & \text{otherwise}
\end{cases}
$$

$$
\mathsf{Simp}(\sqcap \mathbf{S}) = \begin{cases}
\bot & \text{if } \bot \in \mathbf{S} \\
\bot & \text{if } \{C, \neg C\} \subseteq \mathbf{S} \\
\top & \text{if } \mathbf{S} = \emptyset \\
\mathsf{Simp}(\mathbf{S} \setminus \{\top\}) & \text{if } \top \in \mathbf{S} \\
\mathsf{Simp}(\sqcap \mathbf{P} \cup \mathbf{S} \setminus \{\sqcap\{\mathbf{P}\}\}) & \text{if } \sqcap\{\mathbf{P}\} \in \mathbf{S} \\
\sqcap \mathbf{S} & \text{otherwise}
\end{cases}
$$

$$
\mathsf{Simp}(\forall R.C) = \begin{cases}
\top & \text{if } C = \top \\
\forall R.C & \text{otherwise}
\end{cases}
$$

Fig. 9.3. Normalization and simplification functions for $\mathcal{ALC}$.

Normalized and simplified concepts may not be in negation normal form, but they can be dealt with by treating them exactly like their non-negated counterparts. For example, $\neg\sqcap\{C, D\}$ can be treated as $(\neg C \sqcup \neg D)$ and $\neg\forall R.C$ can be treated as $\exists R.\neg C$. In the remainder of this chapter we will use both forms interchangeably, choosing whichever is most convenient.

Additional simplifications would clearly be possible. For example, $\forall R.C \sqcap \forall R.D$ could be simplified to $\forall R.\,\mathsf{Norm}(C \sqcap D)$. Which simplifications it is sensible to perform is an implementation decision that may depend on a cost-benefit analysis with respect to some particular application. Empirically, simplification seems to be more effective with mechanically generated KBs and satisfiability problems, in particular those where the number of different roles is very small. With this kind of problem it is quite common for satisfiability tests to be greatly simplified, or even completely avoided, by simplifying part or all of the concept to either $\top$ or $\bot$. In the benchmark tests used for the Tableaux'98 comparison of modal logic theorem provers, for example, some classes of problems can be completely solved via this mechanism [Heuerding and Schwendimann, 1996; Balsiger and Heuerding, 1998].

If the subsumption-testing algorithm is to derive maximum benefit from normalization, it is important that it directly detects contradictions caused by non-atomic concepts as well as those caused by concept names; for example the occurrence of both $\sqcap\{C, D\}$ and $\neg\sqcap\{C, D\}$ in a node label should be detected as a contradiction without the need for further expansion. This can be achieved by replacing all equivalent (identically encoded) non-atomic concepts C in the KB with a new atomic concept name A, and adding the axiom $\mathsf{A} \equiv C$ to the KB. For example, all occurrences of $\sqcap\{C, D\}$ in a KB could be replaced with CD, and the axiom $\mathsf{CD} \equiv \sqcap\{C, D\}$ added to the KB.

It is necessary to distinguish these newly introduced *system* names from *user* names appearing in the original KB, as system names need not be classified (indeed, it would be very confusing for the user if they were). In practice, it is often more convenient to avoid this problem by using pointer or object identifiers to refer to concepts, with the same identifier always being associated with equivalent concepts. A contradiction is then detected whenever a pointer/identifier and its negation occur in a node label.

The advantages of the normalization and simplification procedure are:

- It is easy to implement and could be used with most logics and algorithms.
- Subsumption/satisfiability problems can often be simplified, and sometimes even completely avoided, by detecting syntactically obvious satisfiability and unsatisfiability.
- It complements lazy unfolding and improves early clash detection.
- The elimination of redundancies and the sharing of syntactically equivalent structures may lead to the KB being more compactly stored.

The disadvantages are:

- The overhead involved in the procedure, although this is relatively small.
- For very unstructured KBs there may be no benefit, and it might even slightly increase the size of the KB.

9.5.1.2 Absorption

As we have seen in Subsection 9.4.3, general axioms are costly to reason with due to the high degree of non-determinism that they introduce. With a tableau algorithm, a disjunction is added to the label of each node for each general axiom in the KB. This leads to an exponential increase in the search space as the number of nodes and axioms increases. For example, with 10 nodes and a KB containing 10 general axioms there are already 100 disjunctions, and they can be non-deterministically expanded in 2^{100} different ways. For a KB containing large numbers of general axioms (there are 1,214 in the GALEN medical terminology KB) this can degrade performance to the extent that subsumption testing is effectively non-terminating.

It therefore makes sense to eliminate general axioms from the KB whenever possible. Absorption is a technique that tries to do this by absorbing them into primitive definition axioms. The basic idea is that a general axiom of the form $C \sqsubseteq D$, where C may be a non-atomic concept, is manipulated

$$C_1 \sqcap C_2 \sqsubseteq D \iff C_1 \sqsubseteq D \sqcup \neg C_2$$
$$C \sqsubseteq D_1 \sqcap D_2 \iff C \sqsubseteq D_1 \text{ and } C \sqsubseteq D_2$$

Fig. 9.4. Axiom equivalences used in absorption.

(using the equivalences in Figure 9.4) so that it has the form of a primitive definition $A \sqsubseteq D'$, where A is an atomic concept name. This axiom can then be merged into an existing primitive definition $A \sqsubseteq C'$ to give $A \sqsubseteq C' \sqcap D'$. For example, an axiom stating that all three-sided geometric figures (i.e., triangles) also have three angles

geometric-figure $\sqcap$ ∃angles.three $\sqsubseteq$ ∃sides.three

could be transformed into an axiom stating that all geometric figures either have three sides or do not have three angles

geometric-figure $\sqsubseteq$ ∃sides.three $\sqcup$ ¬∃angles.three

and then absorbed into the primitive definition of geometric figure (geometric-figure $\sqsubseteq$ figure) to give

geometric-figure $\sqsubseteq$ figure $\sqcap$ (∃sides.three $\sqcup$ ¬∃angles.three).

Given a KB divided into an unfoldable part $\mathcal{T}_u$ and a general part $\mathcal{T}_g$, the following procedure can be used to try to absorb the axioms from $\mathcal{T}_g$ into primitive definitions in $\mathcal{T}_u$. First a set $\mathcal{T}'_g$ is initialized to be empty, and any axioms $(C \equiv D) \in \mathcal{T}_g$ are replaced with an equivalent pair of axioms $C \sqsubseteq D$ and $\neg C \sqsubseteq \neg D$. Then for each axiom $(C \sqsubseteq D) \in \mathcal{T}_g$:

1. Initialize a set $\mathbf{G} = \{\neg D, C\}$, representing the axiom in the form $\top \sqsubseteq \neg\sqcap\{\neg D, C\}$ (i.e., $\top \sqsubseteq D \sqcup \neg C$).
2. If for some $A \in \mathbf{G}$ there is a primitive definition axiom $(A \sqsubseteq C) \in \mathcal{T}_u$, then absorb the general axiom into the primitive definition axiom so that it becomes

$$A \sqsubseteq \sqcap\{C, \neg\sqcap(\mathbf{G} \setminus \{A\})\},$$

and exit.
3. If for some $A \in \mathbf{G}$ there is an axiom $(A \equiv D) \in \mathcal{T}_u$, then replace $A \in \mathbf{G}$ with D

$$\mathbf{G} \longrightarrow \{D\} \cup \mathbf{G} \setminus \{A\},$$

and return to step 2.
4. If for some $\neg A \in \mathbf{G}$ there is an axiom $(A \equiv D) \in \mathcal{T}_u$, then replace $\neg A \in \mathbf{G}$ with $\neg D$

$$\mathbf{G} \longrightarrow \{\neg D\} \cup \mathbf{G} \setminus \{\neg A\},$$

and return to step 2.

5. If there is some $C \in \mathbf{G}$ such that C is of the form $\sqcap\mathbf{S}$, then use associativity to simplify $\mathbf{G}$

$$\mathbf{G} \longrightarrow \mathbf{S} \cup \mathbf{G} \setminus \{\sqcap\mathbf{S}\},$$

and return to step 2.

6. If there is some $C \in \mathbf{G}$ such that C is of the form $\neg\sqcap\mathbf{S}$, then for every $D \in \mathbf{S}$ try to absorb (recursively)

$$\{\neg D\} \cup \mathbf{G} \setminus \{\neg\sqcap\mathbf{S}\},$$

and exit.

7. Otherwise, the axiom could not be absorbed, so add $\neg\sqcap\mathbf{G}$ to $\mathcal{T}'_g$

$$\mathcal{T}'_g \longrightarrow \mathcal{T}'_g \cup \neg\sqcap\mathbf{G},$$

and exit.

Note that this procedure allows parts of axioms to be absorbed. For example, given axioms $(\mathsf{A} \sqsubseteq D_1) \in \mathcal{T}_u$ and $(\mathsf{A} \sqcup \exists R.C \sqsubseteq D_2) \in \mathcal{T}_g$, then the general axiom would be partly absorbed into the definition axiom to give $(\mathsf{A} \sqsubseteq (D_1 \sqcap D_2)) \in \mathcal{T}_u$, leaving a smaller general axiom $(\neg\sqcap\{\neg D_2, \exists R.C\}) \in \mathcal{T}_g$.

When this procedure has been applied to all the axioms in $\mathcal{T}_g$, then $\mathcal{T}'_g$ represents those (parts of) axioms that could not be absorbed. The axioms in $\mathcal{T}'_g$ are already in the form $\top \sqsubseteq C$, so that $\sqcap\mathcal{T}'_g$ is the concept that must be added to every node in the tableau expansion. This can be done using a universal role, as described in Subsection 9.2.4, although in practice it may be simpler just to add the concept to the label of each newly created node.

The absorption process is clearly non-deterministic. In the first place, there may be more than one way to divide $\mathcal{T}$ into unfoldable and general parts. For example, if $\mathcal{T}$ contains multiple non-primitive definitions for some concept A, then one of them must be selected as a definition in $\mathcal{T}_u$ while the rest are treated as general axioms in $\mathcal{T}_g$. Moreover, the absorption procedure itself is non-deterministic as $\mathbf{G}$ may contain more than one primitive concept name into which the axiom could be absorbed. For example, in the case where $\{\mathsf{A}_1, \mathsf{A}_2\} = \mathbf{G}$, and there are two primitive definition axioms $\mathsf{A}_1 \sqsubseteq C$ and $\mathsf{A}_2 \sqsubseteq D$ in $\mathcal{T}_u$, then the axiom could be absorbed either into the definition of A_1 to give $\mathsf{A}_1 \sqsubseteq C \sqcap \neg\sqcap\{\mathsf{A}_2\}$ (equivalent to $\mathsf{A}_1 \sqsubseteq C \sqcap \neg\mathsf{A}_2$) or into the definition of A_2 to give $\mathsf{A}_2 \sqsubseteq C \sqcap \neg\sqcap\{\mathsf{A}_1\}$ (equivalent to $\mathsf{A}_2 \sqsubseteq C \sqcap \neg\mathsf{A}_1$).

It would obviously be sensible to choose the "best" absorption (the one that maximized empirical tractability), but it is not clear how to do this – in fact it is not even clear how to define "best" in this context [Horrocks and Tobies, 2000]. If $\mathcal{T}$ contains more than one definition axiom for a given concept name, then empirical evidence suggests that efficiency is improved by retaining as many non-primitive definition axioms in $\mathcal{T}_u$ as possible. Another intuitively obvious possibility is to preferentially absorb into the definition axiom of the most specific primitive concept, although this only helps in the case that $A_1 \sqsubseteq A_2$ or $A_2 \sqsubseteq A_1$. Other more sophisticated schemes might be possible, but have yet to be investigated.

The advantages of absorption are:

- It can lead to a dramatic improvement in performance. For example, without absorption, satisfiability of the GALEN KB (i.e., the satisfiability of $\top$) could not be proved by either FaCT or DLP, even after several weeks of CPU time. After absorption, the problem becomes so trivial that the CPU time required is hard to measure.
- It is logic and algorithm independent.

The disadvantage is the overhead required for the pre-processing, although this is generally small compared to classification times. However, the procedure described is almost certainly suboptimal, and trying to find an optimal absorption may be much more costly.

9.5.2 Optimizing classification

DL systems are often used to classify a KB, that is to compute a partial ordering or *hierarchy* of named concepts in the KB based on the subsumption relationship. As subsumption testing is always potentially costly, it is important to ensure that the classification process uses the smallest possible number of tests. Minimizing the number of subsumption tests required to classify a concept in the concept hierarchy can be treated as an abstract order-theoretic problem which is independent of the ordering relation. However, some additional optimization can be achieved by using the structure of concepts to reveal obvious subsumption relationships and to control the order in which concepts are added to the hierarchy (where this is possible).

The concept hierarchy is usually represented by a directed acyclic graph where nodes are labeled with sets of concept names (because multiple concept names may be logically equivalent), and edges correspond with subsumption relationships. The subsumption relation is both transitive and reflexive, so a classified concept A subsumes a classified concept B if either:

1. both A and B are in the label of some node x, or
2. A is in the label of some node x, there is an edge $\langle x, y \rangle$ in the graph, and the concept(s) in the label of node y subsume B.

It will be assumed that the hierarchy always contains a top node (a node whose label includes $\top$) and a bottom node (a node whose label includes $\bot$) such that the top node subsumes the bottom node. If the KB is unsatisfiable then the hierarchy will consist of a single node whose label includes both $\top$ and $\bot$.

Algorithms based on traversal of the concept hierarchy can be used to minimize the number of tests required in order to add a new concept [Baader *et al.*, 1992a]. The idea is to compute a concept's subsumers by searching down the hierarchy from the top node (the *top search* phase) and its subsumees by searching up the hierarchy from the bottom node (the *bottom search* phase).

When classifying a concept A, the top search takes advantage of the transitivity of the subsumption relation by propagating failed results down the hierarchy. It concludes, without performing a subsumption test, that if A is not subsumed by B, then it cannot be subsumed by any other concept that is subsumed by B:

$$\mathcal{T} \not\models \mathsf{A} \sqsubseteq \mathsf{B} \text{ and } \mathcal{T} \models \mathsf{B}' \sqsubseteq \mathsf{B} \quad \text{implies} \quad \mathcal{T} \not\models \mathsf{A} \sqsubseteq \mathsf{B}'.$$

To maximize the effect of this strategy, a modified breadth-first search is used [Ellis, 1992] which ensures that a test to discover if B subsumes A is never performed until it has been established that A is subsumed by all of the concepts known to subsume B.

The bottom search uses a corresponding technique, testing if A subsumes B only when A is already known to subsume all those concepts that are subsumed by B. Information from the top search is also used by confining the bottom search to those concepts which are subsumed by all of A's subsumers.

This abstract partial ordering technique can be enhanced by taking advantage of the structure of concepts and the axioms in the KB. If the KB contains an axiom $\mathsf{A} \sqsubseteq C$ or $\mathsf{A} \equiv C$, then C is said to be a *told subsumer* of A. If C is a conjunctive concept $(C_1 \sqcap \cdots \sqcap C_n)$, then from the structural subsumption relationship

$$D \sqsubseteq (C_1 \sqcap \cdots \sqcap C_n) \quad \text{implies} \quad D \sqsubseteq C_1 \text{ and } \ldots \text{ and } D \sqsubseteq C_n$$

it is possible to conclude that $C_1, \ldots, C_n$ are also told subsumers of A. Moreover, due to the transitivity of the subsumption relation, any told subsumers of $C_1, \ldots, C_n$ are also told subsumers of A. Before classifying A, all of its told subsumers which have already been classified, and all their subsumers, can be marked as subsumers of A; subsumption tests with respect to these concepts are therefore rendered unnecessary. This idea can be extended in the obvious way to take advantage of a structural subsumption relationship with respect to disjunctive concepts,

$$(C_1 \sqcup \cdots \sqcup C_n) \sqsubseteq D \quad \text{implies} \quad C_1 \sqsubseteq D \text{ and } \dots \text{ and } C_n \sqsubseteq D.$$

If the KB contains an axiom $\mathsf{A} \equiv C$ and C is a disjunctive concept $(C_1 \sqcup \cdots \sqcup C_n)$, then A is a told subsumer of $C_1, \dots, C_n$.

To maximize the effect of the told subsumer optimization, concepts should be classified in *definition order*. This means that a concept A is not classified until all of its told subsumers have been classified. When classifying an unfoldable KB, this ordering can be exploited by omitting the bottom search phase for primitive concept names and assuming that they only subsume (concepts equivalent to) $\bot$. This is possible because, with an unfoldable KB, a primitive concept can only subsume concepts for which it is a told subsumer. Therefore, as concepts are classified in definition order, a primitive concept will always be classified before any of the concepts that it subsumes. This additional optimization cannot be used with a general KB because, in the presence of general axioms, it can no longer be guaranteed that a primitive concept will only subsume concepts for which it is a told subsumer. For example, given a KB $\mathcal{T}$ such that

$$\mathcal{T} = \{\mathsf{A} \sqsubseteq \exists R.C, \; \exists R.C \sqsubseteq \mathsf{B}\},$$

then B is not a told subsumer of A, and A may be classified first. However, when B is classified the bottom search phase will discover that it subsumes A due to the axiom $\exists R.C \sqsubseteq \mathsf{B}$.

The advantages of the enhanced traversal classification method are:

- It can significantly reduce the number of subsumption tests required in order to classify a KB [Baader *et al.*, 1992a].
- It is logic and (subsumption) algorithm independent.

There appear to be few disadvantages to this method, and it is used (in some form) in most implemented DL systems.

9.5.3 Optimizing subsumption testing

The classification optimizations described in Subsection 9.5.2 help to reduce the number of subsumption tests that are performed when classifying a KB, and the combination of normalization, simplification and lazy unfolding facilitates the detection of "obvious" subsumption relationships by allowing unsatisfiability to be rapidly demonstrated. However, detecting "obvious" non-subsumption (satisfiability) is more difficult for tableau algorithms. This is unfortunate as concept hierarchies from realistic applications are typically

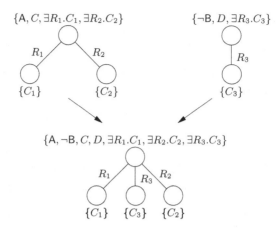

Fig. 9.5. Joining expansion trees for A and ¬B.

broad, shallow and tree-like. The top search phase of classifying a new concept A in such a hierarchy will therefore result in several subsumption tests being performed at each node, most of which are likely to fail. These failed tests could be very costly (if, for example, proving the satisfiability of A is a hard problem), and they could also be very repetitive.

This problem can be tackled by trying to use cached results from previous tableau tests to prove non-subsumption without performing a new satisfiability test. For example, given two concepts A and B defined by the axioms

$$A \equiv C \sqcap \exists R_1.C_1 \sqcap \exists R_2.C_2, \text{ and}$$
$$B \equiv \neg D \sqcup \forall R_3.\neg C_3,$$

then A is not subsumed by B if the concept $A \sqcap \neg B$ is satisfiable. If tableau expansion trees for A and ¬B have already been cached, then the satisfiability of the conjunction can be demonstrated by a tree consisting of the trees for A and ¬B joined at their root nodes, as shown in Figure 9.5 (note that $\neg B \equiv D \sqcap \exists R_3.C_3$).

Given two fully expanded and clash-free tableau expansion trees $\mathbf{T}_1$ and $\mathbf{T}_2$ representing models of (satisfiable) concepts A and ¬B respectively, the tree created by joining $\mathbf{T}_1$ and $\mathbf{T}_2$ at their root nodes is a fully expanded and clash-free tree representing a model of $A \sqcap \neg B$ provided that the union of the root node labels does not contain a clash and that no tableau expansion rules are applicable to the new tree. For most logics, this can be ascertained by examining the labels of the root nodes and the labels of the edges connecting them with their successors. With the $\mathcal{ALC}$ logic for example, if x_1 and x_2 are the two root nodes, then the new tree will be fully expanded and clash-free provided that:

1. the union of the root node labels does not contain an immediate contradiction, i.e., there is no C such that $\{C, \neg C\} \subseteq \mathcal{L}(x_1) \cup \mathcal{L}(x_2)$, and
2. there is no interaction between value restrictions in the label of one root node and edges connecting the other root node with its successors that might make the $\forall$-rule applicable to the joined tree, i.e., there is no R such that $\forall R.C \in \mathcal{L}(x_1)$ and $\mathbf{T}_2$ has an edge $\langle x_2, y \rangle$ with $\mathcal{L}(\langle x_2, y \rangle) = R$, or $\forall R.C \in \mathcal{L}(x_2)$ and $\mathbf{T}_1$ has an edge $\langle x_1, y \rangle$ with $\mathcal{L}(\langle x_1, y \rangle) = R$.

With more expressive logics it may be necessary to consider other interactions that could lead to the application of tableau expansion rules. With a logic that included number restrictions, for example, it would be necessary to check that these could not be violated by the root node successors in the joined tree.

It would be possible to join trees in a wider range of cases by examining the potential interactions in more detail. For example, a value restriction $\forall R.C \in \mathcal{L}(x_1)$ and an R labeled edge $\langle x_2, y \rangle$ would not make the $\forall$-rule applicable to the joined tree if $C \in \mathcal{L}(x_2)$. However, considering only root nodes and edges provides a relatively fast test and reduces the storage required by the cache. Both the time required by the test and the size of the cache can be reduced even further by only storing relevant components of the root node labels and edges from the fully expanded and clash-free tree that demonstrates the satisfiability of a concept. In the case of $\mathcal{ALC}$, the relevant components from a tree demonstrating the satisfiability of a concept A are the set of (possibly negated) atomic concept names in the root node label (denoted $\mathcal{L}_c(A)$), the set of role names in value restrictions in the root node label (denoted $\mathcal{L}_\forall(A)$), and the set of role names labeling edges connecting the root node with its successors (denoted $\mathcal{L}_\exists(A)$).[5] These components can be cached as a triple $(\mathcal{L}_c(A), \mathcal{L}_\forall(A), \mathcal{L}_\exists(A))$.

When testing if A is subsumed by B, the algorithm can now proceed as follows:

1. If any of $(\mathcal{L}_c(A), \mathcal{L}_\forall(A), \mathcal{L}_\exists(A))$, $(\mathcal{L}_c(\neg A), \mathcal{L}_\forall(\neg A), \mathcal{L}_\exists(\neg A))$, $(\mathcal{L}_c(B), \mathcal{L}_\forall(B),$ $\mathcal{L}_\exists(B))$ or $(\mathcal{L}_c(\neg B), \mathcal{L}_\forall(\neg B), \mathcal{L}_\exists(\neg B))$ are not in the cache, then perform the appropriate satisfiability tests and update the cache accordingly. In the case where a concept C is unsatisfiable, $\mathcal{L}_c(C) = \{\bot\}$ and $\mathcal{L}_c(\neg C) = \{\top\}$.
2. Conclude that A $\sqsubseteq$ B (A $\sqcap \neg$B is not satisfiable) if $\mathcal{L}_c(A) = \{\bot\}$ or $\mathcal{L}_c(B) = \{\top\}$.
3. Conclude that A $\not\sqsubseteq$ B (A $\sqcap \neg$B is satisfiable) if

---

[5] Consideration can be limited to atomic concept names because expanded conjunction and disjunction concepts are no longer relevant to the validity of the tree, and are only retained in order to facilitate early clash detection.

(a) $\mathcal{L}_c(\mathsf{A}) = \{\top\}$ and $\mathcal{L}_c(\mathsf{B}) \neq \{\top\}$, or

(b) $\mathcal{L}_c(\mathsf{A}) \neq \{\bot\}$ and $\mathcal{L}_c(\mathsf{B}) = \{\bot\}$, or

(c) $\mathcal{L}_\forall(\mathsf{A}) \sqcap \mathcal{L}_\exists(\mathsf{B}) = \emptyset$, $\mathcal{L}_\forall(\mathsf{B}) \sqcap \mathcal{L}_\exists(\mathsf{A}) = \emptyset$, $\bot \notin \mathcal{L}_c(\mathsf{A}) \cup \mathcal{L}_c(\mathsf{B})$, and there is no C such that $\{C, \neg C\} \subseteq \mathcal{L}_c(\mathsf{A}) \cup \mathcal{L}_c(\mathsf{B})$.

4. Otherwise perform a satisfiability test on $\mathsf{A} \sqcap \neg\mathsf{B}$, concluding that $\mathsf{A} \sqsubseteq \mathsf{B}$ if it is not satisfiable and that $\mathsf{A} \not\sqsubseteq \mathsf{B}$ if it is satisfiable.

When a concept A is added to the hierarchy, this procedure will result in satisfiability tests immediately being performed for both A and ¬A. During the subsequent top search phase, at each node x in the hierarchy such that some $C \in \mathcal{L}(x)$ subsumes A, it will be necessary to perform a subsumption test for each subsumee node y (unless some of them can be avoided by the classification optimizations discussed in Subsection 9.5.2). Typically only one of these subsumption tests will lead to a full satisfiability test being performed, the rest being shown to be obvious non-subsumptions using the cached partial trees. Moreover, the satisfiability test that is performed will often be an "obvious" subsumption, and unsatisfiability will rapidly be demonstrated.

The optimization is less useful during the bottom search phase as nodes in the concept hierarchy are typically connected to only one subsuming node. The exception to this is the bottom ($\bot$) node, which may be connected to a very large number of subsuming nodes. Again, most of the subsumption tests that would be required by these nodes can be avoided by demonstrating non-subsumption using cached partial trees.

The caching technique can be extended in order to avoid the construction of obviously satisfiable and unsatisfiable subtrees during tableau expansion. For example, if some leaf node x is about to be expanded, and $\mathcal{L}(x) = \{\mathsf{A}\}$, unfolding and expanding $\mathcal{L}(x)$ is clearly unnecessary if A is already known to be either satisfiable (i.e., $(\mathcal{L}_c(\mathsf{A}), \mathcal{L}_\forall(\mathsf{A}), \mathcal{L}_\exists(\mathsf{A}))$ is in the cache and $\mathcal{L}_c(\mathsf{A}) \neq \{\bot\}$) or unsatisfiable (i.e., $(\mathcal{L}_c(\mathsf{A}), \mathcal{L}_\forall(\mathsf{A}), \mathcal{L}_\exists(\mathsf{A}))$ is in the cache and $\mathcal{L}_c(\mathsf{A}) = \{\bot\}$).

This idea can be further extended by caching (when required) partial trees for all the syntactically distinct concepts discovered by the normalization and simplification process, and trying to join cached partial trees for all the concepts in a leaf node's label before starting the expansion process. For example, with the logic $\mathcal{ALC}$ and a node x such that

$$\mathcal{L}(x) = \{C_1, \ldots, C_n\},$$

x is unsatisfiable if for some $1 \leqslant i \leqslant n$, $\mathcal{L}_c(C_i) = \{\bot\}$, and x is satisfiable if for all $1 \leq i \leq n$ and $i < j \leq n$:

1. $\mathcal{L}_\forall(C_i) \sqcap \mathcal{L}_\exists(C_j) = \emptyset$,
2. $\mathcal{L}_\exists(C_i) \sqcap \mathcal{L}_\forall(C_j) = \emptyset$, and
3. there is no C such that $\{C, \neg C\} \subseteq \mathcal{L}_c(C_i) \cup \mathcal{L}_c(C_j)$.

As before, additional interactions may need to be considered with more expressive logics. Moreover, with logics that support inverse roles, the effect that the subtree might have on its predecessor must also be considered. For example, if x is an R-successor of some node y, and $R^- \in \mathcal{L}_\forall(C_i)$ for one of the $C_i \in \mathcal{L}(x)$, then the expanded $\mathcal{L}(x)$ represented by the cached partial trees would contain a value restriction of the form $\forall R^-.D$ that could augment $\mathcal{L}(y)$.

The advantages of caching partial tableau expansion trees are:

- When classifying a realistic KB, most satisfiability tests can be avoided. For example, the number of satisfiability tests performed by the FACT system when classifying the GALEN KB is reduced from 122,695 to 23,492, a factor of over 80%.
- Without caching, some of the most costly satisfiability tests are repeated (with minor variations) many times. The time saving due to caching is therefore even greater than the saving in satisfiability tests.

The disadvantages are:

- The overhead of performing satisfiability tests on individual concepts and their negations in order to generate the partial trees that are cached.
- The overhead of storing the partial trees. This is not too serious a problem as the number of trees cached is equal to the number of named concepts in the KB (or the number of syntactically distinct concepts if caching is used in subproblems).
- The overhead of determining if the cached partial trees can be merged, which is wasted if they cannot be.
- Its main use is when classifying a KB, or otherwise performing many similar satisfiability tests. It is of limited value when performing single tests.

9.5.4 Optimizing satisfiability testing

In spite of the various techniques outlined in the preceding sections, at some point the DL system will be forced to perform a "real" subsumption test, which for a tableau-based system means testing the satisfiability of a concept. For expressive logics, such tests can be very costly. However, a range of optimizations can be applied that dramatically improve performance in typical cases. Most of these are aimed at reducing the size of the search space explored by the algorithm as a result of applying non-deterministic tableau expansion rules.

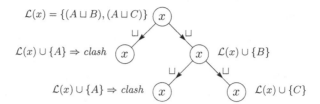

Fig. 9.6. Syntactic branching search.

9.5.4.1 Semantic branching search

Standard tableau algorithms use a search technique based on *syntactic branching*. When expanding the label of a node x, syntactic branching works by choosing an unexpanded disjunction $(C_1 \sqcup \cdots \sqcup C_n)$ in $\mathcal{L}(x)$ and searching the different models obtained by adding each of the disjuncts C_1, ..., C_n to $\mathcal{L}(x)$ [Giunchiglia and Sebastiani, 1996b]. As the alternative branches of the search tree are not disjoint, there is nothing to prevent the recurrence of an unsatisfiable disjunct in different branches. The resulting wasted expansion could be costly if discovering the unsatisfiability requires the solution of a complex subproblem. For example, tableau expansion of a node x, where $\{(A \sqcup B), (A \sqcup C)\} \subseteq \mathcal{L}(x)$ and A is an unsatisfiable concept, could lead to the search pattern shown in Figure 9.6, in which the unsatisfiability of $\mathcal{L}(x) \cup A$ must be demonstrated twice.

This problem can be dealt with by using a *semantic branching* technique adapted from the Davis–Putnam–Logemann–Loveland procedure (DPLL) commonly used to solve propositional satisfiability (SAT) problems [Davis and Putnam, 1960; Davis *et al.*, 1962; Freeman, 1996].[6] Instead of choosing an unexpanded disjunction in $\mathcal{L}(x)$, a single disjunct D is chosen from one of the unexpanded disjunctions in $\mathcal{L}(x)$. The two possible subtrees obtained by adding either D or $\neg D$ to $\mathcal{L}(x)$ are then searched. Because the two subtrees are strictly disjoint, there is no possibility of wasted search as in syntactic branching. Note that the order in which the two branches are explored is irrelevant from a theoretical viewpoint, but may offer further optimization possibilities (see Subsubsection 9.5.4.4).

The advantages of semantic branching search are:

• A great deal is known about the implementation and optimization of the DPLL algorithm. In particular, both *local simplification* (see Subsubsection 9.5.4.2) and *heuristic guided search* (see Subsubsection 9.5.4.4) can be used to try to minimize the size of the search tree (although it should be noted that both these techniques can also be adapted for use with syntactic branching search).

---

[6] An alternative solution is to enhance syntactic branching with "no-good" lists in order to avoid reselecting a known unsatisfiable disjunct [Donini and Massacci, 2000].

- It can be highly effective with some problems, particularly randomly generated problems [Horrocks and Patel-Schneider, 1999].

The disadvantages are:

- It is possible that performance could be degraded by adding the negated disjunct in the second branch of the search tree, for example if the disjunct is a very large or complex concept. However this does not seem to be a serious problem in practice, with semantic branching rarely exhibiting significantly worse performance than syntactic branching.
- Its effectiveness is problem dependent. It is most effective with randomly generated problems, particularly those that are over-constrained (likely to be unsatisfiable). It is also effective with some of the hand crafted problems from the Tableaux'98 benchmark suite. However, it appears to be of little benefit when classifying realistic KBs [Horrocks and Patel-Schneider, 1998a].

9.5.4.2 Local simplification

Local simplification is another technique used to reduce the size of the search space resulting from the application of non-deterministic expansion rules. Before any non-deterministic expansion of a node label $\mathcal{L}(x)$ is performed, disjunctions in $\mathcal{L}(x)$ are examined, and if possible simplified. The simplification most commonly used (although by no means the only one possible) is to deterministically expand disjunctions in $\mathcal{L}(x)$ that present only one expansion possibility and to detect a clash when a disjunction in $\mathcal{L}(x)$ has no expansion possibilities. This simplification has been called Boolean constraint propagation (BCP) [Freeman, 1995]. In effect, the inference rules

$$\frac{\neg C_1, \ldots, \neg C_n, C_1 \sqcup \cdots \sqcup C_n \sqcup D}{D} \quad \text{and} \quad \frac{C_1, \ldots, C_n, \neg C_1 \sqcup \cdots \sqcup \neg C_n \sqcup D}{D}$$

are being used to simplify the conjunctive concept represented by $\mathcal{L}(x)$.

For example, given a node x such that

$$\{(C \sqcup (D_1 \sqcap D_2)), (\neg D_1 \sqcup \neg D_2 \sqcup C), \neg C\} \subseteq \mathcal{L}(x),$$

BCP deterministically expands the disjunction $(C \sqcup (D_1 \sqcap D_2))$, adding $(D_1 \sqcap D_2)$ to $\mathcal{L}(x)$, because $\neg C \in \mathcal{L}(x)$. The deterministic expansion of $(D_1 \sqcap D_2)$ adds both D_1 and D_2 to $\mathcal{L}(x)$, allowing BCP to identify $(\neg D_1 \sqcup \neg D_2 \sqcup C)$ as a clash (without any branching having occurred), because $\{D_1, D_2, \neg C\} \subseteq \mathcal{L}(x)$.

BCP simplification is usually described as an integral part of SAT-based algorithms [Giunchiglia and Sebastiani, 1996a], but it can also be used with syntactic branching. However, it is more effective with semantic branching as the negated concepts introduced by failed branches can result in additional

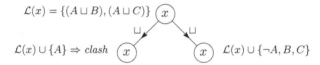

Fig. 9.7. Semantic branching search.

simplifications. Taking the above example of $\{(A \sqcup B), (A \sqcup C)\} \subseteq \mathcal{L}(x)$, adding $\neg A$ to $\mathcal{L}(x)$ allows BCP to deterministically expand both of the disjunctions using the simplifications $(A \sqcup B) \wedge \neg A \Rightarrow B$ and $(A \sqcup C) \wedge \neg A \Rightarrow C$. The reduced search space resulting from the combination of semantic branching and BCP is shown in Figure 9.7.

The advantages of local simplification are:

- It is applicable to a wide range of logics and algorithms.
- It can never increase the size of the search space.

The disadvantages are:

- It may be costly to perform without using complex data structures [Freeman, 1995].
- Its effectiveness is relatively limited and problem dependent. It is most effective with randomly generated problems, particularly those that are over-constrained [Horrocks and Patel-Schneider, 1998a].

9.5.4.3 Dependency directed backtracking

Inherent unsatisfiability concealed in subproblems can lead to large amounts of unproductive backtracking search, sometimes called thrashing. The problem is exacerbated when blocking is used to guarantee termination, because blocking may require that subproblems only be explored after all other forms of expansion have been performed. For example, expanding a node x (using semantic branching), where

$$\mathcal{L}(x) = \{(C_1 \sqcup D_1), \dots, (C_n \sqcup D_n), \exists R.(A \sqcap B), \forall R.\neg A\},$$

could lead to the fruitless exploration of 2^n possible R-successors of x before the inherent unsatisfiability is discovered (note that if $\mathcal{L}(x)$ simply included $\exists R.A$ instead of $\exists R.(A \sqcap B)$, then the inherent unsatisfiability would have been detected immediately due to the normalization of $\exists R.A$ as $\neg \forall R.\neg A$). The search tree resulting from the tableau expansion is illustrated in Figure 9.8.

This problem can be addressed by identifying the causes of clashes, and using this information to prune or restructure the search space – a technique known as *dependency directed backtracking*. The form most commonly used in practice, called *backjumping*, is adapted from a technique that has been

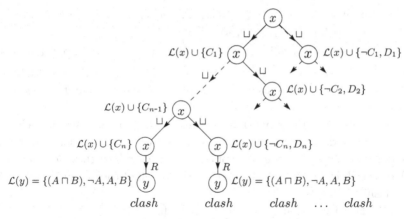

Fig. 9.8. Thrashing in backtracking search.

used in solving constraint satisfiability problems [Baker, 1995] (a similar technique was also used in the HARP theorem prover [Oppacher and Suen, 1988]). Backjumping works by labeling each concept in a node label and each role in an edge label with a dependency set indicating the branching points on which it depends. A concept $C \in \mathcal{L}(x)$ depends on a branching point if C was added to $\mathcal{L}(x)$ at the branching point or if C depends on another concept D (or role R), and D (or R) depends on the branching point. A concept $C \in \mathcal{L}(x)$ depends on a concept D (or role R) when C was added to $\mathcal{L}(x)$ by the application of a deterministic expansion rule that used D (or R); a role $R = \mathcal{L}(\langle x, y \rangle)$ depends on a concept D when $\langle x, y \rangle$ was labeled R by the application of a deterministic expansion rule that used D. For example, if $A \in \mathcal{L}(y)$ was derived from the expansion of $\forall R.A \in \mathcal{L}(x)$, then $A \in \mathcal{L}(y)$ depends on both $\forall R.A \in \mathcal{L}(x)$ and $R = \mathcal{L}(\langle x, y \rangle)$.

Labeling roles with dependency sets can be avoided in algorithms where a combined $\exists\forall$-rule is used, as the dependency sets for concepts in the label of the new node can be derived in a single step. On the other hand, more complex algorithms and optimization techniques may lead to more complex dependencies. For example, if $C_n \in \mathcal{L}(x)$ was derived from a BCP simplification of $\{(C_1 \sqcup \cdots \sqcup C_n), \neg C_1, \ldots, \neg C_{n-1}\} \subseteq \mathcal{L}(x)$, then it depends on the disjunction $(C_1 \sqcup \cdots \sqcup C_n)$ and all of $\neg C_1, \ldots, \neg C_{n-1}$.

When a clash is discovered, the dependency sets of the clashing concepts can be used to identify the most recent branching point where exploring the other branch might alleviate the cause of the clash. It is then possible to jump back over intervening branching points *without* exploring any alternative branches. Again, more complex algorithms and optimizations may lead to more complex dependencies. For example, if the clash results from a BCP simplification of $\{(C_1 \sqcup \cdots \sqcup C_n), \neg C_1, \ldots, \neg C_n\} \subseteq \mathcal{L}(x)$, then it depends on the disjunction $(C_1 \sqcup \cdots \sqcup C_n)$ and all of $\neg C_1, \ldots, \neg C_n$.

When testing the satisfiability of a concept C, the dependency set of $C \in \mathcal{L}(x)$ is initialized to $\emptyset$ (the empty set) and a branching depth counter b is initialized to 1. The search algorithm then proceeds as follows:

1. Perform deterministic expansion, setting the dependency set of each concept added to a node label and each role assigned to an edge label to the union of the dependency sets of the concepts and roles on which they depend.
   (a) If a clash is discovered, then return the union of the dependency sets of the clashing concepts.
   (b) If a clash-free expansion is discovered, then return $\{0\}$.
2. Branch on a concept $D \in \mathcal{L}(y)$, trying first $\mathcal{L}(y) \cup \{D\}$ and then $\mathcal{L}(y) \cup \{\neg D\}$.
   (a) Add D to $\mathcal{L}(y)$ with a dependency set $\{b\}$, and increment b.
   (b) Set $\mathbf{D}_1$ to the dependency set returned by a recursive call to the search algorithm, and decrement b.
   (c) If $b \notin \mathbf{D}_1$, then return $\mathbf{D}_1$ *without* exploring the second branch.
   (d) If $b \in \mathbf{D}_1$, then add $\neg D$ to $\mathcal{L}(y)$ with a dependency set $\mathbf{D}_1 \setminus \{b\}$ and return to step 1.

If the search returns $\{0\}$, then a successful expansion was discovered and the algorithm returns "satisfiable", otherwise all possible expansions led to a clash and "unsatisfiable" is returned.

Let us consider the earlier example and suppose that $\exists R.(A \sqcap B)$ has a dependency set $\mathbf{D}_i$, $\forall R.\neg A$ has a dependency set $\mathbf{D}_j$ and $b = k$ (meaning that there have already been $k - 1$ branching points in the search tree). Note that the largest values in $\mathbf{D}_i$ and $\mathbf{D}_j$ must be less than k, as neither concept can depend on a branching point that has not yet been reached.

At the kth branching point, C_1 is added to $\mathcal{L}(x)$ with a dependency set $\{k\}$ and b is incremented. The search continues in the same way until the $(k + n - 1)$th branching point, when C_n is added to $\mathcal{L}(x)$ with a dependency set $\{k + n - 1\}$. Next, $\exists R.(A \sqcap B)$ is deterministically expanded, generating an R-successor y with $R = \langle x, y \rangle$ labeled $\mathbf{D}_i$ and $(A \sqcap B) \in \mathcal{L}(y)$ labeled $\mathbf{D}_i$. Finally, $\forall R.\neg A$ is deterministically expanded, adding $\neg A$ to $\mathcal{L}(y)$ with a label $\mathbf{D}_i \cup \mathbf{D}_j$ (because it depends on both $\forall R.\neg A \in \mathcal{L}(x)$ and $R = \langle x, y \rangle$).

The expansion now continues with $\mathcal{L}(y)$, and $(A \sqcap B)$ is deterministically expanded, adding A and B to $\mathcal{L}(y)$, both labeled $\mathbf{D}_i$. This results in a clash as $\{A, \neg A\} \subseteq \mathcal{L}(y)$, and the set $\mathbf{D}_i \cup \mathbf{D}_i \cup \mathbf{D}_j = \mathbf{D}_i \cup \mathbf{D}_j$ (the union of the dependency sets from the two clashing concepts) is returned. The algorithm will then backtrack through each of the preceding n branching points without exploring the second branches, because in each case $b \notin \mathbf{D}_i \cup \mathbf{D}_j$ (remember

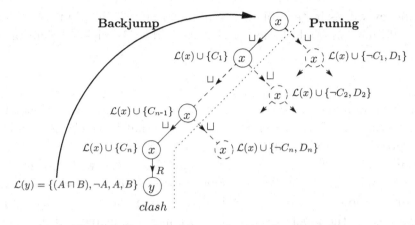

Fig. 9.9. Pruning the search using backjumping.

that the largest values in $\mathbf{D}_i$ and $\mathbf{D}_j$ are less than k), and will continue to backtrack until it reaches the branching point equal to the maximum value in $\mathbf{D}_i \cup \mathbf{D}_j$ (if $\mathbf{D}_i = \mathbf{D}_j = \emptyset$, then the algorithm will backtrack through all branching points and return "unsatisfiable"). Figure 9.9 illustrates the pruned search tree, with the number of R-successors explored being reduced by $2^n - 1$.

Backjumping can also be used with syntactic branching, but the procedure is slightly more complex as there may be more than two possible choices at a given branching point, and the dependency set of the disjunction being expanded must also be taken into account. When expanding a disjunction of size n with a dependency set $\mathbf{D}_d$, the first $n - 1$ disjuncts are treated like the first branch in the semantic branching algorithm, an immediate backtrack occurring if the recursive search discovers a clash that does not depend on b. If each of these branches returns a dependency set $\mathbf{D}_i$ such that $b \in \mathbf{D}_i$, then the nth disjunct is added with a dependency set $(\mathbf{D}_1 \cup \cdots \cup \mathbf{D}_{n-1} \cup \mathbf{D}_d) \setminus b$.

The advantages of backjumping are:

- It can lead to a dramatic reduction in the size of the search tree and thus a huge performance improvement. For example, when trying to classify the GALEN model using either FACT or DLP with backjumping disabled, single satisfiability tests were encountered that could not be solved even after several weeks of CPU time.
- The size of the search space can never be increased.

The disadvantage is the overhead of propagating and storing the dependency sets. The storage overhead can be alleviated to some extent by using a pointer-based implementation so that propagating a dependency set only requires the copying of a pointer. A simpler scheme using single maximal dependency values instead of sets would also be possible, but some dependency information would be lost and this could lead to less efficient pruning of the search tree.

9.5.4.4 Heuristic guided search

Heuristic techniques can be used to guide the search in a way that tries to minimize the size of the search tree. A method that is widely used in DPLL SAT algorithms is to branch on the disjunct that has the Maximum number of Occurrences in disjunctions of Minimum Size – the well-known MOMS heuristic [Freeman, 1995]. By choosing a disjunct that occurs frequently in small disjunctions, the MOMS heuristic tries to maximize the effect of BCP. For example, if the label of a node x contains the unexpanded disjunctions $C \sqcup D_1, \ldots, C \sqcup D_n$, then branching on C leads to their deterministic expansion in a single step: when C is added to $\mathcal{L}(x)$, no further expansion of the disjunctions is required (they are all fully expanded) and when $\neg C$ is added to $\mathcal{L}(x)$, BCP will expand all of the disjunctions, causing $D_1, \ldots, D_n$ to be added to $\mathcal{L}(x)$. Branching first on any of $D_1, \ldots, D_n$, on the other hand, would only cause a single disjunction to be expanded.

The MOMS value for a candidate concept C is computed simply by counting the number of times C or its negation occur in minimally sized disjunctions. There are several variants of this heuristic, including the heuristic from [Jeroslow and Wang, 1990]. The Jeroslow–Wang heuristic considers all occurrences of a disjunct, weighting them according to the size of the disjunction in which they occur. The heuristic then selects the disjunct with the highest overall weighting, again with the objective of maximizing the effect of BCP and reducing the size of the search tree.

When a disjunct C has been selected from the disjunctions in $\mathcal{L}(x)$, a BCP maximizing heuristic can also be used to determine the order in which the two possible branches, $\mathcal{L}(x) \cup \{C\}$ and $\mathcal{L}(x) \cup \{\neg C\}$, are explored. This is done by separating the two components of the heuristic weighting contributed by occurrences of C and $\neg C$, trying $\mathcal{L}(x) \cup \{C\}$ first if C made the *smallest* contribution, and trying $\mathcal{L}(x) \cup \{\neg C\}$ first otherwise. The intention is to prune the search tree by maximizing BCP in the first branch.

Unfortunately, MOMS-style heuristics can interact adversely with the backjumping optimization because they do not take dependency information into account. This was first discovered in the FaCT system, when it was noticed that using MOMS heuristic often led to much worse performance. The cause of this phenomenon turned out to be the fact that, without the heuristic, the data structures used in the implementation naturally led to "older" disjunctions (those dependent on earlier branching points) being expanded before "newer" ones, and this led to more effective pruning if a clash was discovered. Using the heuristic disturbed this ordering and reduced the effectiveness of backjumping [Horrocks, 1997b].

Moreover, MOMS-style heuristics are of little value themselves in DL systems because they rely for their effectiveness on finding the same disjuncts recurring in multiple unexpanded disjunctions: this is likely in hard propositional problems, where the disjuncts are propositional variables, and where the number of different variables is usually small compared to the number of disjunctive clauses (otherwise problems would, in general, be trivially satisfiable); it is unlikely in concept satisfiability problems, where the disjuncts are (possibly non-atomic) concepts, and where the number of different concepts is usually large compared to the number of disjunctive clauses. As a result, these heuristics will often discover that all disjuncts have similar or equal priorities, and the guidance they provide is not particularly useful.

An alternative strategy is to employ an *oldest-first* heuristic that tries to maximize the effectiveness of backjumping by using dependency sets to guide the expansion [Horrocks and Patel-Schneider, 1999]. When choosing a disjunct on which to branch, the heuristic first selects those disjunctions that depend on the least recent branching points (i.e., those with minimal maximum values in their dependency sets), and then selects a disjunct from one of these disjunctions. This can be combined with the use of a BCP maximizing heuristic, such as the Jeroslow–Wang heuristic, to select the disjunct from amongst the selected disjunctions.

Although the BCP and backjumping maximizing heuristics described above have been designed with semantic branching in mind they can also be used with syntactic branching. The oldest-first heuristic actually selects disjunctions rather than disjuncts, and is thus a natural candidate for a syntactic branching heuristic. BCP maximizing heuristics could also be adapted for use with syntactic branching, for example by first evaluating the weighting of each disjunct and then selecting the disjunction whose disjuncts have the highest average, median or maximum weightings.

The oldest-first heuristic can also be used to advantage when selecting the order in which existential role restrictions, and the labels of the R-successors which they generate, are expanded. One possible technique is to use the heuristic to select an unexpanded existential role restriction $\exists R.C$ from the label of a node x, apply the $\exists$-rule and the $\forall$-rule as necessary, and expand the label of the resulting R-successor. If the expansion results in a clash, then the algorithm will backtrack; if it does not, then continue selecting and expanding existential role restrictions from $\mathcal{L}(x)$ until it is fully expanded. A better technique is to first apply the $\exists$-rule and the $\forall$-rule exhaustively, creating a set of successor nodes. The order in which to expand these successors can then be based on the minimal maximum values in the dependency sets of all the concepts in their label, some of which may be due to universal role restrictions in $\mathcal{L}(x)$.

The advantages of using heuristics are:

- They can be used to complement other optimizations. The MOMS and Jeroslow–Wang heuristics, for example, are designed to increase the effectiveness of BCP while the oldest-first heuristic is designed to increase the effectiveness of backjumping.
- They can be selected and tuned to take advantage of the kinds of problem that are to be solved (if this is known). The BCP maximization heuristics, for example, are generally quite effective with large randomly generated and hand crafted problems, whereas the oldest-first heuristic seems to be more effective when classifying realistic KBs.

The disadvantages are:

- They can add a significant overhead as the heuristic function may be expensive to evaluate and may need to be re-evaluated at each branching point.
- They may not improve performance, and may significantly degrade it.
  - Heuristics can interact adversely with other optimizations, as was the case with the MOMS heuristic and backjumping in the FaCT system.
  - When they work badly, heuristics can increase the frequency with which pathological worst cases can be expected to occur. For example, with problems that are highly disjunctive but relatively under-constrained, using a BCP maximizing heuristic to select highly constraining disjuncts can force backtracking search to be performed when most random branching choices would lead rapidly to a clash-free expansion.
  - The cost of computing the heuristic function can outweigh the benefit (if any).
- Heuristics designed to work well with purely proposition reasoning, such as the BCP maximizing heuristics, may not be particularly effective with Description Logics, where much of the reasoning is modal (it involves roles and subproblems). There has been little work on finding good heuristics for modal reasoning problems.

9.5.4.5 Caching satisfiability status

During a satisfiability check there may be many successor nodes created. Some of these nodes can be very similar, particularly as the labels of the R-successors for a node x each contain the same concepts derived from the universal role restrictions in $\mathcal{L}(x)$. Considerable time can thus be spent re-computing the satisfiability of nodes that have the same label. As the satisfiability algorithm only needs to know whether a node is satisfiable or not, this time is wasted. Moreover, when classifying a KB, similar satisfiability tests may be performed many times, and may provide further opportunities for the re-use of satisfiability results for node labels if these are retained across multiple concept satisfiability tests.

If the expansion of existential value restrictions in the label of a node x is delayed until all other expansion possibilities have been exhausted (as in the trace technique), then as each existential role restriction $\exists R.C$ is expanded it is possible to generate the complete set of concepts that constitute the initial label of the R-successor; this will consist of C plus all the concepts derived from universal role restrictions in $\mathcal{L}(x)$.[7] If there exists another node with the same set of initial concepts, then the two nodes will have the same satisfiability status. Work need be done only on one of the two nodes, potentially saving a considerable amount of processing, as not only is the work at one of the nodes saved, but also the work at any of the successors of this node.

Care must be taken when using caching in conjunction with blocking as the satisfiability status of blocked nodes is not completely determined but is simply taken to be equal to that of the blocking node. Another problem with caching is that the dependency information required for backjumping cannot be effectively calculated for nodes that are found to be unsatisfiable as a result of a cache lookup. Although the set of concepts in the initial label of such a node is the same as that of the expanded node whose (un)satisfiability status has been cached, the dependency sets attached to the concepts that made up the two labels may not be the same. However, a weaker form of backjumping can still be performed by taking the dependency set of the unsatisfiable node to be the union of the dependency sets from the concepts in its label.

A general procedure for using caching when expanding a node x can be described as follows:

1. Exhaustively perform all local expansions, backtracking as required, until only existential value restrictions (if any) remain to be expanded.
2. If there are no unexpanded existential value restrictions in $\mathcal{L}(x)$, then return the satisfiability status *satisfiable* to the predecessor node.
3. Select (heuristically) an unexpanded existential role restriction from $\mathcal{L}(x)$, expanding it and any applicable universal role restrictions to create a new node y with an initial label $\mathcal{L}(y)$ (or create all such nodes and heuristically select the order in which they are to be examined).
4. If y is blocked, then its satisfiability status S is directly determined by the algorithm (normally *satisfiable*, but may depend on the kind of cycle that has

---

[7] This ordering is used in the trace technique to minimize space usage, and may be useful or even required for effective blocking.

been detected [Baader, 1991]).

    (a) If $S = satisfiable$, then return to step 2 without expanding $\mathcal{L}(y)$.

    (b) If $S = unsatisfiable$, then backtrack without expanding $\mathcal{L}(y)$. The dependency set will need to be determined by the blocking algorithm.

5. If a set equal to $\mathcal{L}(y)$ is found in the cache, then retrieve the associated satisfiability status S (this is called a cache "hit").

    (a) If $S = satisfiable$, then return to step 2 without expanding $\mathcal{L}(y)$.

    (b) If $S = unsatisfiable$, then backtrack without expanding $\mathcal{L}(y)$, taking the dependency set to be the union of the dependency sets attached to the concepts in $\mathcal{L}(y)$.

6. If a set equal to $\mathcal{L}(y)$ is not found in the cache, then set $L = \mathcal{L}(y)$ and expand $\mathcal{L}(y)$ in order to determine its satisfiability status S.

    (a) If $S = satisfiable$ and there is no descendant z of y that is blocked by an ancestor x' of y, then add L to the cache with satisfiability status S and return to step 2.

    (b) If $S = satisfiable$ and there is a descendant z of y that is blocked by an ancestor x' of y, then return to step 2 *without* updating the cache.

    (c) If $S = unsatisfiable$, then add L to the cache with satisfiability status S and backtrack, taking the dependency set to be the one returned by the expansion of $\mathcal{L}(y)$.

The problem of combining caching and blocking can be dealt with in a more sophisticated way by allowing the cached satisfiability status of a node to assume values such as *"unknown"*. These values can be updated as the expansion progresses and the satisfiability status of blocking nodes is determined. Such a strategy is implemented in the DLP system.

A further refinement is to use subset and superset instead of equality when retrieving satisfiability status from the cache: if $\mathcal{L}(x)$ is satisfiable, then clearly any $\mathcal{L}(y) \subseteq \mathcal{L}(x)$ is also satisfiable, and if $\mathcal{L}(x)$ is unsatisfiable, then clearly any $\mathcal{L}(y) \supseteq \mathcal{L}(x)$ is also unsatisfiable [Hoffmann and Koehler, 1999; Giunchiglia and Tacchella, 2000]. However, using subsets and supersets significantly increases the complexity of the cache, and it is not yet clear if the performance cost of this added complexity will be justified by the possible increase in cache hits.

The advantages of caching the satisfiability status are:

• It can be highly effective with some problems, particularly those with a repetitive structure. For example, the DLP system has been used to demonstrate that some of the problem sets from the Tableaux'98 benchmark suite are trivial when caching is used (all problems were solved in less than 0.1 s and there was little evidence of increasing difficulty with increasing problem size). Without caching, the same problems demonstrated a clearly exponential growth in solution time with increasing problem size, and the system was unable to solve the larger problems within the 100 s time limit imposed in the test [Horrocks and Patel-Schneider, 1999].

- It can be effective with both single satisfiability tests and across multiple tests (as in KB classification).
- It can be effective with both satisfiable and unsatisfiable problems, unlike many other optimization techniques that are primarily aimed at speeding up the detection of unsatisfiability.

The disadvantages are:

- Retaining node labels and their satisfiability status throughout a satisfiability test (or longer, if the results are to be used in later satisfiability tests) involves a storage overhead. As the maximum number of different possible node labels is exponential in the number of different concepts, this overhead could be prohibitive, and it may be necessary to implement a mechanism for clearing some or all of the cache. However, experiments with caching in the DLP system suggest that this is unlikely to be a problem in realistic applications [Horrocks and Patel-Schneider, 1999].
- The adverse interaction with dependency directed backtracking can degrade performance in some circumstances.
- Its effectiveness is problem dependent, and (as might be expected) is most evident with artificial problems having a repetitive structure. It is highly effective with some of the hand crafted problems from the Tableaux'98 benchmark suite, it is less effective with realistic classification problems, and it is almost completely ineffective with randomly generated problems [Horrocks and Patel-Schneider, 1999].
- The technique described depends on the logic having the property that the satisfiability of a node is completely determined by its initial label set. Extending the technique to logics that do not have this property, for example those which support inverse roles, may involve a considerable increase in both complexity and storage requirements.

9.6 Discussion

To be useful in realistic applications, DL systems need both expressive logics and fast reasoners. Procedures for deciding subsumption (or equivalently satisfiability) in such logics have discouragingly high worst-case complexities, normally exponential with respect to problem size. In spite of this, implemented DL systems have demonstrated that acceptable performance can be achieved with the kinds of problem that typically occur in realistic applications.

This performance has been achieved through the use of optimization techniques, a wide variety of which have been studied in this chapter. These techniques can operate at every level of a DL system; they can simplify the

KB, reduce the number of subsumption tests required to classify it, replace tableau subsumption tests with less costly tests, and reduce the size of the search space resulting from non-deterministic tableau expansion. Amongst the most effective of these optimizations are absorption and backjumping; both have the desirable properties that they impose a very small additional overhead, can dramatically improve typical case performance, and hardly ever degrade performance (to any significant extent). Other widely applicable optimizations include enhanced traversal, normalization, lazy unfolding, semantic branching and local simplification; their effects are less general and less dramatic, but they too impose low overheads and rarely degrade performance. Various forms of caching can also be highly effective, but they do impose a significant additional overhead in terms of memory usage, and can sometimes degrade performance. Finally, heuristic techniques, at least those currently available, are not particularly effective and can often degrade performance.

Several exciting new application areas are opening up for very expressive Description Logics, in particular reasoning about database schemata and queries, and providing reasoning support for the Semantic Web. These applications require logics even more expressive than those implemented in existing systems, in particular logics that include both inverse roles and number restrictions, as well as reasoning with general axioms. The challenge for DL implementors is to demonstrate that highly optimized reasoners can provide acceptable performance even for these logics. This may require the extension and refinement of existing techniques, or even the development of completely new ones.

One promising possibility is to use a more sophisticated form of dependency directed backtracking, called *dynamic backtracking* [Ginsberg, 1993], that preserves as much work as possible while backtracking to the source of a contradiction. Another useful approach, indicative of the increasing maturity of existing implementations, is to focus on problematical constructors and devise methods for dealing with them more efficiently. Good examples of this can be seen in the RACER system, where significant improvements in performance have been achieved by using more sophisticated techniques to deal with domain and range constraints on roles (see Chapter 2 for an explanation of these constructs) and qualified number restrictions [Haarslev and Möller, 2001c; 2001d; 2001a].

Finally, it should be re-emphasized that, given the immutability of theoretical complexity, no (complete) implementation can guarantee to provide good performance in all cases. The objective of optimized implementations is to provide acceptable performance in typical applications and, as the definition of "acceptable" and "typical" will always be application dependent, their effectiveness can only be assessed by empirical testing. Hopefully, the new generation of highly optimized DL systems will demonstrate their effectiveness by finding more widespread use in applications than did their predecessors.

Part III

Applications

10

Conceptual Modeling with Description Logics

Alex Borgida
Ronald J. Brachman

Abstract

The purpose of the chapter is to help someone familiar with DLs to understand the issues involved in developing an ontology for some universe of discourse, which is to become a conceptual model or knowledge base represented and reasoned about using Description Logics.

We briefly review the purposes and history of conceptual modeling, and then use the domain of a university library to illustrate an approach to conceptual modeling that combines general ideas of object-centered modeling with a look at special modeling/ontological problems, and DL-specific solutions to them.

Among the ontological issues considered are the nature of individuals, concept specialization, non-binary relationships, materialization, aspects of part–whole relationships, and epistemic aspects of individual knowledge.

10.1 Background

Information modeling is concerned with the construction of computer-based symbol structures that model some part of the real world. We refer to such symbol structures as information bases, generalizing the term from related terms in Computer Science, such as databases and knowledge bases. Moreover, we shall refer to the part of a real world being modeled by an information base as its *universe of discourse (UofD)*. The information base is checked for consistency, and sometimes queried and updated through special-purpose languages. As with all models, the advantage of information models is that they abstract away irrelevant details, and allow more efficient examination of both the current, as well as past and projected future states of the UofD.

An information model is built up using some language, and this language influences (more or less subtly) the kinds of details that are considered. For example, early information models (e.g., relational data models) were built on conventional programming notions such as records, and as a result focused on the implementation aspects of the information being captured, as opposed to the representational aspects. *Conceptual models* offer more expressive facilities for modeling applications *directly and naturally* [Hammer and McLeod, 1981], and for *structuring* information bases. These languages provide semantic terms for modeling an application, such as entity and relationship (or even activity, agent and goal), as well as means for organizing information.

Conceptual models play an important part in a variety of areas. The following is a brief summary of these areas, as reviewed in [Mylopoulos, 1998]:

- Artificial intelligence programs turned out to require the representation of a great deal of human knowledge in order to act "intelligently". As a result, they relied on conceptual models built up using knowledge representation languages, such as semantic networks – directed graphs labeled with natural language identifiers. DLs are the historical descendants of attempts to formalize semantic networks.
- The design of database systems was seen to have as an important initial phase the construction of a *"conceptual level schema"*, which determined the information needs of the users, and which was eventually converted to a physical implementation schema. Chen's Entity–Relationship model [Chen, 1976], and later semantic data models [Hull and King, 1987], were the result of efforts in this direction.
- More generally, the development of all software has an initial *requirements acquisition* stage, which nowadays is seen to consist of a *requirements model* that describes the relationship of the proposed system and its environment. The environment in this case is likely to be a conceptual model.
- Independently, the object-oriented software community has also proposed viewing software components (classes/objects) as models of real-world entities. This was evident in the features of Simula, the first object-oriented programming language, and became a cornerstone of most object-oriented techniques, including the current leader, UML [Rumbaugh *et al.*, 1998].

One interesting aspect of conceptual modeling in the database context has been the identification of a number of *abstraction mechanisms* that support the development of large models by abstracting details initially, and then introducing them in a stepwise and systematic manner. Among the important abstractions are the following:

- thinking of objects as wholes, not just a collection of their attributes/components ("aggregation");

- abstracting away the detailed differences between individuals, so that a class can represent the commonalities ("classification"[1]);
- abstracting the commonalities of several classes into a superclass ("generalization").

An important claim regarding the benefits of abstraction in conceptual modeling is that it results in a *structured* information model, which is easier to build and maintain. Interestingly, Description Logics further this goal by supporting the *automatic* classification of concepts with respect to others, thereby revealing generalizations that may not have been recognized by the modeler.

10.2 Elementary Description Logic modeling

Most conceptual models, including Description Logics, subscribe to an *object-centered* view of the world. Thus, their ontology includes notions like individual objects, which are associated with each other through (usually binary) relationships, and which are grouped into classes. In this chapter we use freely the notation and concrete syntax of Description Logics (see Appendix), and extend it with additional constructs that make it more suitable for modeling.

In the domain of a university library, we might encounter a particular person, GIANNI, or a particular book, BOOK23. Most of the information about the state of the world is captured by the interrelationships between individuals, such as GIANNI having borrowed BOOK23. Binary relationships are modeled directly in Description Logics using *roles* and *attributes*: either GIANNI is a filler of the lentTo role for BOOK23, or BOOK23 is the filler of the hasBorrowed role for GIANNI. Note that lentTo and hasBorrowed are converse relationships, and this should be captured in a model, since frequently one wants to access information about associations in either direction. In Description Logics, this is accomplished using the role constructor **inverse**:

hasBorrowed $\equiv$ (**inverse** lentTo).

Note that in order to avoid inadvertent errors during modeling due to confusion between a role and its converse, or between a role and the kind of values filling it, one heuristic is to use a natural language name that is asymmetric, and adopt the convention that the relationship $R(a, b)$ should be read as "a R b"; therefore in the above case lentTo(BOOK23,GIANNI) reads

---

[1] This term is used in a completely different way than in DL terminology, where it refers to the DL-KBMS service of finding the lowest subsumers of a concept or individual.

"BOOK23 lentTo GIANNI," while lentTo(GIANNI,BOOK23) reads "GIANNI lentTo BOOK23", which makes it clear that the first, but not the second, is the proper way to use the role lentTo in the model. On the other hand, loan would be a poor choice of a role identifier because one could equally well imagine loan as a role of books or of persons, so that neither loan(GIANNI,BOOK23) nor loan(BOOK23,GIANNI) "reads" properly.

In addition, it is always important to distinguish functional relationships, like lentTo (a book can be loaned to at most one borrower at any time) from non-functional ones, like hasBorrowed. This is done most cleanly if the particular Description Logic being used allows the declaration of functional relationships, sometimes called "attributes" or "features". Attributes themselves come in two flavors: total and partial. Thus lentTo is a partial attribute because a book can only be loaned to one person, but may not be on loan at some point of time; on the other hand, every book has to have an isbnNr. It is important to check which interpretation of attributes is offered by the particular Description Logic being used. In the rest of this chapter we assume that attributes are total, and the concept constructor **the** will be used as an abbreviation, so that (**the** p C) is equivalent to the conjunction of (**all** p C), (**at-most** 1 p) and (**at-least** 1 p).

Individuals are grouped into classes; for example, Book might be a natural class in our domain. Classes usually abstract out common properties of their instances, e.g., every book in the library has a call number. Classes are modeled by concepts in Description Logics, and usually the common properties are expressed as subsumption axioms about the concept. These conditions usually involve superconcepts, as well as the kinds of values that can fill roles, and limits on the number of (various kinds of) role fillers. By design, these are exactly the kinds of things that can be expressed using DL constructors:

```
/* Books are materials, whose callNr is an integer */
Book  ⊑  (and Material
            (the callNr Integer)
            ...).
```

As mentioned in earlier chapters, one of the fundamental properties of Description Logics is support for the distinction between primitive/atomic concepts – for which instances can only be declared explicitly – and defined concepts – which offer necessary and sufficient conditions for membership. So, for example, we can distinguish the notion of "borrower" as someone who *can* borrow a book (an approved customer of the library)

> /* Borrower is previously declared as a primitive concept.
>
>   Here it is indicated what restrictions on borrowing are in force for this concept */
> Borrower ⊑ (**all** hasBorrowed Book)

from the notion of "borrower" as someone who has actually borrowed a book from the library

> /* Borrower is defined as someone who has borrowed books */
> Borrower ≡ (**and** (**all** hasBorrowed Book)
>   (**at-least** 1 hasBorrowed)).

We now turn to a variety of more subtle issues that arise when modeling a domain. Almost all of these issues arise independently of the modeling language used; what we emphasize here is the range of possible solutions in the DL framework.

10.3 Individuals in the world

Some individuals are quite concrete, like a particular person, Gianni, or a particular copy of a book. Some are more abstract, like the subject matter covered by a book. The important property of most individuals is that they have an *identity*, which allows them to be distinguished from one another and to be *counted*.

Modeling of individuals is therefore made easier if they have unique identifiers. Unfortunately, this may not always be the case. For example, if one sees on a bookshelf two brand new copies of a book, which may not be distinguishable by any property known to us, one can still say that they are different copies of the book. In information management systems, and sometimes in the real world, this leads us to devise some kind of "extrinsic" identification scheme. For example, books on the library shelf are assigned a copy number. In this paper, as in object-oriented software systems, we will tend to assign arbitrary internal identifiers to objects, such as GIANNI or BOOK23.

The following examples concerning books show that what constitutes a relevant individual in a UofD depends very much on what we want to do with the information. In a domain concerning literature courses, one might consider something like Dickens' HARD-TIMES as the kind of individual appearing on an assigned reading list. For an Internet book-seller interface, it is necessary to consider a more concrete level of modeling – that of book editions, since these may have different prices. Finally, in a library, we need to keep track of actual physical book copies.

In the last two cases, one must then decide whether to model books (as opposed to editions or copies) as individuals, or as concepts that have the other kinds of individuals as instances. A general heuristic is that if we expect certain notions to be counted, then they must be modeled as individuals. Another heuristic is that notions that do not have an inception time are usually modeled as concepts.

Modeling of the particular kind of relationship that exists, for example, between a book and its editions is further examined in Subsection 10.7.2.

10.3.1 Values vs. objects

It is important to distinguish what we may call *individual objects*, such as GIANNI, from *values*, such as integers, strings, lists, tuples, etc. The former have an associated intrinsic and immutable identity, and need to be created in the knowledge base. The later are "eternal" mathematical abstractions, whose identity is determined by some procedure usually involving the structure of the individual. For example, the two strings "abc" and "abc" are the same individual value because they have the same sequence of characters; similarly for dates, such as 1925/12/20, which can be considered as 3-tuples.

Many Description Logics only support reasoning with objects, in which case composite values such as dates need to be modeled as objects with attributes for day, month and year. The danger here is that, for example, multiple date individuals can be created with the same attribute values, in which case they are treated as distinct for the purposes of counting and identity checking, resulting in reasoning anomalies. Implemented Description Logics such as CLASSIC support values from the underlying programming language (so-called "host values"), and relatively simple concept hierarchies over them. Others, such as $\mathcal{ALC}(\mathcal{D})$ [Baader and Hanschke, 1991a] and $\mathcal{SHOQ}(\mathcal{D})$ [Horrocks and Sattler, 2001] allow attributes to have values from so-called "concrete domains", which can contain entirely new kinds of values. These concrete domains are required to have their own, independent reasoners, which are then coupled with the DL reasoner.

Equally desirable would be mathematical types such as sets, bags, sequences, and tuples, as supported by modern programming languages and certain semantic data models.

Currently, only the highly expressive $\mathcal{DLR}$ languages support notions such as n-tuples and recursive fixed-point structures, from which one can build lists, trees, etc. Even here, one can only provide the description of concepts ("list of Persons"), as opposed to the specification of individuals ("the list [GIANNI,ANNA]").

10.3.2 Individuals vs. references to them

It is important to distinguish an individual from various references to it: Gianni vs. "the person whose first name is the 6-letter string "Gianni" vs. "the borrower with library card number 32245" vs. "the chairman of the Psychology Department". This distinction becomes crucial when we express relationships: there is a difference between relating two objects and relating their names, because we usually want objects to remain related, even if names are changed. Thus "GIANNI hasBorrowed BOOK25" is different from "card-holder number 32245 hasBorrowed BOOK25", because if Gianni gets a new card (after losing his old one, say), then the relationship between Gianni and the book is lost. So, in general, one should always deal with the individual objects, unless there is a bijection between a class of objects and a class of referents to them, and this bijection is universal (it always exists) and is unchanging.[2] Kent [1979] has eloquently argued the importance of these issues in record-based database systems, and shows that in the real world such bijections are much rarer than assumed. For example, Neumann [1992] reports that the same US social security number (the prototypical identifier for persons in the USA) has been issued to two people, who even have the same name and birth-date!

Conversely, in some cases one wants to state relationships between intensional references, rather than specific objects. For example, we might want to say that, in general, the director of the library is the head of the book selection committee (COMMITTEE3). If Gianni happens to be the current director of the NBU library, then asserting headOf(GIANNI,COMMITTEE3) is improper because, for example, if Gianni steps down as director, according to the above model he would still be committee chair. One needs the ability to use unnamed expressions as arguments of relationships, along the lines of the predicate logic expression headOf(directorOf(NBU-LIBRARY),COMMITTEE3).

In Description Logics, intensional referents can be expressed as roles that are applied to individuals. (The roles may often be complex chains, resulting

---

[2] Such bijections are exactly the "keys" used in the database context.

from the composition of atomic roles, as in "the zipCode of the address of the lentTo".) Assuming that we use the notation NBU-LIBRARY.director to refer to the filler of the director role for the NBU-LIBRARY individual, the above relationship is actually stated as "NBU-LIBRARY.director is identical to COMMITTEE3.head". The concept constructor **same-as**, indicating that two chains of roles have the same value, is used to express exactly such relationships, so the above situation might be modeled, naively, using the concept (**same-as** director head). The problem is that we need a single individual of which to assert this property, yet it is libraries that have directors while committees have heads. In such situations, in Description Logics one must find or create some chain of attributes relating the two individuals NBU-LIBRARY and COMMITTEE3. The natural relationship in this case is the attribute hasBookSelectionCommittee. Therefore the appropriate way of modeling this situation is

```
/* NBU-LIBRARY has book selection committee COMMITTEE3 */
hasBookSelectionCommittee(NBU-LIBRARY, COMMITTEE3)
```

```
/* NBU-LIBRARY.director equals
     NBU-LIBRARY.hasBookSelectionCommittee.head */
(same-as director (hasBookSelectionCommittee ∘ head))(NBU-LIBRARY).
```

10.4 Concepts

For the university library, some obvious classes of individuals include people, institutions, the material that can be loaned by the library, the staff, dates, library cards, and fines. These classes are normally modeled using atomic/primitive concepts in Description Logics.

It may be worth noting that in Description Logics the same individual may be an instance of multiple classes, without one being necessarily a subclass of another: some book might be an instance of both hardcover and science books. This is in contrast with many other object-oriented software systems, where one is forced to create a special subclass for this notion, in order to guarantee a unique "minimal" class for every individual. However, this is not a modeling principle – it is an implementation obstacle.

10.4.1 Essential vs. incidental properties of concepts

As explained in the earlier example involving the two possible meanings for the term "borrower", an important feature of Description Logics is the ability to distinguish primitive from defined concepts, where the latter have necessary and sufficient conditions for concept membership.

For example, BookOnLoan might naturally be defined as

```
/* A book is on loan if it is borrowed by someone */
BookOnLoan  ≡  (and Book (at-least 1 lentTo)).
```

Suppose that we also want to require that only hardcover books can be loaned out. There seem to be two options for modeling this:

```
/* Option 1 – being hardcover is part of the definition */
BookOnLoan  ≡  (and Book
                      (at-least 1 lentTo)
                      (fills binding 'hardcover))
```

```
/* Option 2 – being hardcover is an additional necessary condition */
BookOnLoan  ≡  (and Book (at-least 1 lentTo))
BookOnLoan  ⊑  (fills binding 'hardcover).
```

The first approach is not quite right because being hardcover is an *incidental* property of books on loan, albeit one universally shared by all such objects. Among other things, this means that if the system is to recognize some individual book as being on loan, it is enough to know that it has been lent to someone – one does not also need to know it is hardcover. Hence the second modeling option is the right one, since one can actually deduce that a book on loan is hardcover, if this was not known ahead of time.

The distinction between definitional and incidental properties is also important if we consider the task of classifying concepts into a taxonomy, since it has been argued that the taxonomy should not depend on contingent facts. This suggests that incidental properties, even universal inclusion assertions like the one for hardcover books in Option 2 above, should appear in the ABox, not the TBox defining the terminology.

Another subtle problem arises when there are multiple sufficient conditions for a concept. For example, suppose we associated a due date with books on loan (in the physical world, this might be recorded as a date stamped in the back of the book). Then encountering a book with a due date in the future would rightly classify it as a book on loan. If we model the due date as an attribute of books, which has a value only as long as the date is in the future, then we would represent this situation as

```
(and Book (at-least 1 dueDate))  ⊑  BookOnLoan
```

and, of course, requiring books on loan to have a due date would lead to

BookOnLoan ⊑ (**at-least** 1 dueDate).

We thus have multiple sufficient conditions for being a book on loan, although one of them appears to be the primary definition.

10.4.2 Reified concepts and meta-roles

In some cases it seems natural to associate information with an entire concept, rather than with each of its individual instances. One situation where this arises is in capturing aggregate information, such as the count of current individual instances of the concept, or the average value of their attributes. In the library example, attributes such as numberOfBooks and mostRequestedBooks would fall into this category.

In some object-oriented systems this can be modeled directly because classes are themselves objects, and as such are instances of meta-classes and have meta-properties. Currently, Description Logics do not have a facility to treat classes as objects. One must therefore create a separate "meta-individual" that is related to the concept by some naming convention, for example. In our example, we would create the individual BOOK-CLASS-OBJECT, and then attach the information regarding numberOfBooks, mostRequestedBooks, etc., as roles of this individual. In the CLASSIC system, given a named concept, this meta-individual can be retrieved using a special, new knowledge base operation.

10.4.3 Concepts dependent on relationships

The following interesting modeling problem arises in many situations: some concepts, such as Book, stand on their own. Others, such as Borrower, rely on the *implied existence of some relation/event* (e.g., lending), which has a second argument, and from which their meaning is derived. It is important to discern this second category of concepts, and explicitly introduce the corresponding binary relationship in the model. In the data modeling literature (e.g., [Albano *et al.*, 1993]) categories of this second type, such as Borrower, are called "roles", but to avoid confusion with DL roles, we will call them *"relationship roles"*. The modeling of these will be considered further in Subsection 10.7.1.

10.5 Subconcepts

For many of the above concepts, there are specialized subconcepts representing subsets of individuals that are also of interest. For example, the concept Material (referring to the holdings of libraries) could have specializations Book, Journal, Videotape, etc. In turn, Book may have subconcepts Monograph, EditedCollection, Proceedings, etc.[3] And Borrowers may be Institutions or Individuals, with the latter being divided into Faculty, Student, Staff.

There are a number of special aspects of the subclass relationship that should be modeled in order to properly capture the semantics of the UofD.

10.5.1 Disjointness of subconcepts

In many cases, subclasses are disjoint from each other. For example, Book and Journal are disjoint subclasses of Material. In Description Logics that support negation, this is modeled by adding the complement of one concept to the necessary properties of the other concept:

Book ⊑ **not** Journal

Often, entire collections of subclasses are disjoint.[4] For this purpose, some Description Logics provide the ability to describe disjointness by naming a *discriminator*, and a special declaration operation for primitive subclasses. For example, one might discriminate between various kinds of material on the basis of the medium as follows:

Print ⊑ (**disjointPrim** Material **in group** medium **with discriminant** paper)
Video ⊑ (**disjointPrim** Material **in group** medium **with discriminant** light)
Audio ⊑ (**disjointPrim** Material **in group** medium **with discriminant** sound)

At the same time, one might discriminate between different kinds of material on the basis of the format:

Book   ⊑ (**disjointPrim** Material **in group** format **with discriminant** book)
Journal ⊑ (**disjointPrim** Material **in group** format **with discriminant** journal)
      . . .

Two points are worth making here: (i) the advantage of a syntax based on discriminators is that it avoids the multiplicative effect of having to state

---

[3] For this section, we will think of the material to be loaned as physical individuals that can be carried out the door of the library, so to speak.
[4] This is especially the case at the top of the subclass hierarchy: Person, Material, etc.

disjointness for every pair of disjoint concepts; (ii) as in the above example, it is important to allow during modeling for multiple groups of disjoint subconcepts for the same concept.

10.5.2 Covering by subconcepts

In addition to disjointness, it is natural to consider whether some set of subclasses fully covers the superclass. For example, we might want to say that Circulating material must be either short-term or long-term.

For Description Logics that support concept disjunction, this is easy:

Circulating   ⊑   (**or** ShortTerm LongTerm).

Note that since ShortTerm, in turn, has Circulating as a superclass, the possibility arises of modeling Circulating as a definition:

Circulating   ≡   (**or** ShortTerm LongTerm).

However, this approach is not available for languages like CLASSIC, which avoid disjunction in order to gain tractable reasoning. We discuss in the next section an approach to the problem based on subconcept definitions and enumerated values.

10.5.3 Defined vs. primitive subconcepts

In the case of material that is either circulating or non-circulating, the name of the second class provides a hint: after introducing Material and Circulating as primitives, NonCirculating should be *defined*:

Circulating   ⊑   Material
NonCirculating ≡   (**and** Material (**not** Circulating)).

In this case, the Description Logic can deduce both the disjointness of Circulating and NonCirculating, and the fact that Material is the union of Circulating and NonCirculating, without having stated anything explicitly about either. This shows clearly the power of a reasoning system that is capable of supporting definitions.

By joining covering and disjointness one gets the partitioning of a class by some group of subclasses. In some Description Logics – those supporting the constructor **one-of** – it is possible to simulate the effect of declaring concepts as partitioned into subconcepts through the use of a special attribute. For example, we could add the attribute format to Books, with an enumerated set of possible values:

Book ⊑ (**the** format (**one-of** 'monograph 'journal 'editedCollection))

and then define the corresponding subclasses:

Monograph   ≡   (**and** Book (**fills** format 'monograph))
Journal   ≡   (**and** Book (**fills** format 'journal))
EditedCollection ≡   (**and** Book (**fills** format 'editedCollection)).

These concepts will be disjoint because format can have at most one value, and they cover the original class Book, because format must have (at least) one value from among the set enumerated.

10.5.4 Dynamics of (sub)concept membership

When changes in the model are allowed, there is a distinction between concepts that represent inherent properties of objects that do not change over time (called "rigid" in [Guarino and Welty, 2000]) such as Book, and concepts that represent more transient properties, such as MisplacedBook. Note that while it is possible for a transient property to be a subconcept of rigid one, the converse does not make sense.

Standard Description Logics have not developed modeling tools for issues involving the dynamics of the world, and hence usually cannot represent such distinctions. Description Logics extended with the notion of time, such as [Artale and Franconi, 1998], are of course well suited to express them.

10.5.5 The structure of the subconcept hierarchy

Recent work by Guarino and Welty (e.g., [Guarino and Welty, 2000]) has presented several interesting ontological dimensions along which a concept can be positioned.

The dimensions are related to many of the topics we discuss elsewhere in this chapter, including the existence or absence of criteria for identifying individuals (Section 10.3), the rigid vs. non-rigid nature of concept membership (Subsection 10.5.4), the nature of the part–whole relationship (Subsection 10.7.3), and aspects resembling relationship roles (Subsection 10.7.1).

The significance of these dimensions is that they can be used to both clarify the intended meaning of concepts in an ontology, and to better organize the taxonomy of primitive concepts. The conditions for proper taxonomies are based on observations such as *"a concept some of whose current instances may cease to be instances at some point in the future (e.g.,* Student*) cannot subsume a concept whose membership cannot change (e.g.,* Person*)."*

We refer the reader to the original paper for further details.

10.6 Modeling relationships

As mentioned earlier, binary relationships are modeled in Description Logics using roles and attributes. Just as with subclasses, there are a number of special constraints that are frequently expressed about relationships: cardinality constraints state the minimum and maximum number of objects that can be related via a role; domain constraints state the kinds of objects that can be related via a role; and inverse relationships between roles need to be recorded. For example, a book has exactly one title, which is a string, and exactly one call number, which is some value that depends on the cataloging technique used. On the other hand, there may be zero or more authors for a book:

> Book ⊑ (**and** (**the** title String)
> (**the** callNr MaterialIdentifier)
> (**all** author Person)).

As mentioned in Section 10.2, we can use the attribute lentTo to model when someone borrows a book:

> Book ⊑ (**all** lentTo Borrower).

Suppose we also want to record that the material in the library may be on loan, available or missing. This can be modeled by adding appropriate roles to the library:

> Library ⊑ (**and** (**all** hasOnLoan Material)
> (**all** hasAvailable Material)
> (**all** hasMissing Material)).

In such a case we would like to say that these roles are non-overlapping. This could be accomplished through the use of a concept constructor

non-overlapping, syntactically similar to **same-as**: (**non-overlapping** hasOn-Loan hasAvailable). However, if only one library is involved, it would be better to model the situation using an appropriate subclass of Material, such as MissingMaterial, because we already have tools for modeling disjointness of subclasses, and reasoning with them is not inherently hard as is the case of general constructors such as **same-as** and **non-overlapping**.

10.6.1 Reified relationships

It is sometimes useful to be able to give "properties of properties". For example, when some material is lent to a borrower, it is useful to record on what date the loan took place and when the material is due back. In the Entity–Relationship approach this would be modeled by the creation of a relationship class, called Loan, which would have attributes onLoan, lentTo, as well as lentOn and dueOn, describing the loan. This can be thought of as the *reification* of the relationship, and results in the following DL class specification:

```
Loan  ⊑  (and (the lentTo Borrower)
              (the onLoan Material)
              (the lentOn Date)
              (the dueOn Date)
              (the NrOfRenewals (max 3))).
```

Unless the DL supports n-ary relations, reified relationships become essential when modeling associations that involve more than two objects, as would be the case, for example, if we had several libraries (or branches), and we wanted to record from which library the loan was made.

Reified relationships have the disadvantage of requiring the modeler to distinguish somehow the subset of attributes determining the relationship $R(a, b, \ldots)$ from those qualifying it. In the above case, we may imagine that Loan represents a binary relationship Loan(Borrower,Material) between lentTo and onLoan (in which case lentOn is there just to qualify the relation); alternatively, we may interpret Loan as a ternary relationship Loan(Borrower,Material,Date) between lentTo, onLoan and lentOn. The former records loans (a borrower may have a book at most once) while the latter records the *history* of loans. The notion of "keys/unique identifiers" from databases, as adapted to Description Logics [Borgida and Weddell, 1997] can be used for this task, by marking the collection of attributes that describe the relationship as a key.

We remark that the $\mathcal{DLR}$ Description Logic can express n-ary relationships directly, so it does not require reification for this purpose.

10.6.2 Role hierarchies

In many applications, two roles on the same concept may be related by the constraint that every filler of the first role must be a filler of the second role. For example, in the library domain, the fillers of the role hasOnShort-TermLoan, recording a borrower's materials that need to be returned within a week, are also fillers of hasBorrowed, recording all the materials borrowed (this would be true by definition). Similarly, the editorInChief of a journal would be included in its editorialStaff.

One of the important features of frame knowledge representation schemes, and Description Logics in particular, is that they encourage the modeler to think of roles as first-class citizens. This includes support for the notion of a role taxonomy (subroles). This is all the more reasonable, since once we reify a relationship, we would be allowed to create subconcepts of it at will.

As a result, the above kinds of constraints on the containment of role fillers can be modeled through the use of role hierarchies – a notion supported by most Description Logics, at least for primitive roles:

hasOnShortTermLoan $\sqsubseteq$ hasBorrowed.

10.7 Modeling ontological aspects of relationships

The material in this section deals with some special kinds of relationships and approaches to modeling them. The cognoscenti will recognize these as issues related to the ontological aspects of a UofD (constructs relating to the essence of objects), as opposed to epistemological aspects (constructs relating to the structure of objects), which are captured by notions such as InstanceOf and IS-A. The kinds of relationships to be discussed below do however occur relatively frequently, and pose difficulties to the uninitiated.

10.7.1 Relationship roles

A subtle, but important, distinction can be drawn between objects that *may* participate in a relationship (the domain restrictions on the role) and the objects that actually do take part in one or more relationships. For example, the objects participating in a lending relationship can be said to be playing certain "roles": LentObject and Borrower. It was exactly this second meaning of borrower – as a relationship role – that was contrasted with the original meaning of "potential borrower" in our example of Section 10.2.

Description Logics allow one to define the relationship roles associated with a relationship. In the case when the relationship is modeled by a regular DL role, such as borrowedBy, we can define lent objects as ones that are being borrowed, and borrowers as objects that are the values of borrowedBy:

LentObject $\equiv$ (**at-least** 1 borrowedBy)
Borrower $\equiv$ (**at-least** 1 (**inverse** borrowedBy)).

In the case of the reified Loan relationship, the definition of these classes would be

LentObject $\equiv$ (**at-least** 1 (**inverse** onLoan))
Borrower $\equiv$ (**at-least** 1 (**inverse** lentTo)).

10.7.2 Materialization

There is a family of situations whose modeling is complicated by the fact that several concepts can be referred to by the same natural language term. For example, one might say "Shakespeare wrote 'Hamlet'," "The 'Hamlet' in London this season is a success," and "'Hamlet' was canceled tonight." But there is a difference between the abstract notion of the play 'Hamlet', various stagings of the play, and particular performances. Other familiar distinctions of this kind include the difference between an airline flight ("Air France flight 25 from Paris to London") and a particular "instance" of it – the one that will leave on May 24, 2002. Failure to model such differences can result in the same kind of problem that arises with any other form of ambiguity – inappropriate use in a context. So one can only buy tickets to play performances, but theatrical awards are given to stagings.

In each of these cases there is a relationship between a general notion (e.g., play staging) and 0-to-N more specific notions (e.g., performance of that play staging), which has been called *materialization*, and was investigated in [Pirotte *et al.*, 1994].

Let us first model some information that we would like to capture in the library domain:

```
/* Books have information about authors, etc. */
Book   ⊑  (and ...
                (all hasAuthors Person)
                (the hasTitle String))
/* Editions of books are related to the book (in a way yet to be specified)
   but have their own roles too */
BookEdition   ⊑  (and ...
                        (the publishedBy PublishingCompany)
                        (the isbnNr IsbnNumber)
                        (the format (one-of 'printed 'audio)))

/* Book copies are related to book editions, and in turn have their own roles */
BookCopy   ⊑  (and ...
                    (the callNr CallNumber)
                    (the atBranch LibraryBranch)).
```

There are several alternative ways of proceeding with the modeling of such a UofD.

Since objects in each of these classes are seen to naturally have attributes like hasTitle, it is tempting to think of BookCopy as being a subclass of BookEdition so that this attribute is *inherited*. However, this would mean that each individual instance of BookCopy is a separate BookEdition, which seems wrong.

If we are *not* committed to modeling separate individual instances of each of these concepts, it is possible to combine their description into a single concept that records all the relevant information. So, for example, we could define Books to have all the attributes of the three concepts above, and thus really refer to book copies. (But see below.)

Finally, according to the results in [Pirotte *et al.*, 1994], a more appropriate approach is to view each edition of a book as determining a *subclass* of BookCopy. Each of these subclasses can then be viewed as an instance of BookEdition, for which it provides so-called "meta-roles." Materialization is the combination of these ideas.

The materialization relationship can be modeled in Description Logics by a role materializationOf, connecting in our case book editions and books, and book copies and book editions. However, this sounds very unnatural when read out loud, so a better approach may be to create *subroles* of the general role materializationOf. This means that the above model would be completed by adding the following assertions

/* editionOf is a kind of materialization relationship */
editionOf ⊑ materializationOf

/* Book editions are materializations of books */
BookEdition ⊑ (**the** editionOf Book)
/* copyOf is a kind of materialization relationship */
copyOf ⊑ materializationOf

/* Book copies are materializations of book editions */
BookCopy ⊑ (**the** copyOf BookEdition).

Often, the properties of the more abstract concept are inherited by the materialization. For example, the book edition, and then the book copy, has the same title and author as the book. In Description Logics, this relationships can be expressed by identifying the appropriate attribute values on the general and the materialized object:

BookEdition ⊑ (**same-as** hasTitle (editionOf ∘ hasTitle)).

Several additional kinds of relationships between attributes of an object and its materialization are identified in [Pirotte *et al.*, 1994], but they are rather unclear and cannot be represented in Description Logics. Probably the most interesting is the case when an attribute of the more general concept has no correspondent on materialized individuals. For example, though a book edition may reasonably record the date when it was *first* and *last* printed, it seems very questionable to say that a book copy has a *last* printing date.

This looks like a case of meta-roles of the kind mentioned earlier. The main importance is that if one wants to have in the model attributes such as firstPrinting, then one cannot "melt" objects (book editions) into their various materializations (book copies), and is forced to model them separately.

10.7.3 Part–whole aggregation

The part–whole relationship distinguishes roles of a book such as its chapters, from others such as its publisher. There is a long history of discussions concerning this topic, with [Artale *et al.*, 1996b] being an excellent and comprehensive survey that considers, among other things, a variety of DL solutions to the problem. We present here some interesting observations.

Cognitive scientists have distinguished a variety of part–whole relationships, whose mixture has caused apparent paradoxes; according to one

hypothesis these can be distinguished by differentiating three kinds of wholes
– *complexes, collections* and *masses* – with parts called *components, members* and *quantities* respectively; furthermore parts can be *portions* (sharing
intrinsic properties with the whole) and *segments*. Most physical objects, like
book copies, are complexes of their parts (e.g., pages), but in the book domain we also find uses for collections in modeling books that are anthologies
of other literary pieces.

In addition, one can qualify the nature of two aspects of the relationship
between parts and wholes:

- Existence: A whole may depend on particular individual(s) for its continued existence and identity, as in the case when the part is irreplaceable (e.g., a book
  must have an author); or it may depend generically on a class of parts (e.g., a
  book copy must have a cover). Conversely, the part may depend on the whole for
  its existence (e.g., the chapter of a book). Finally, a part may belong exclusively
  to only one whole or it might be shared.
- Properties: Properties may be "inherited" from the whole to the part (e.g.,
  ownedBy) or from the part to the whole (e.g., isDefective).

At the very least, the above provides a checklist of issues to consider
whenever a part–whole relationship is encountered during modeling.

In the realm of Description Logics, Sattler [1995] offers an approach to
dealing with these topics, exploiting various role-forming operators such as
role hierarchies, role inverse, and transitive closure to capture the semantics
of aggregation.

Specifically, special roles are introduced for the different kinds of part–
whole relationships mentioned above: hasDComponent, hasDMember, has-
DSegment, hasDQuantity, hasDStuff, hasDIngredient, where "D" stands for
"direct". One then defines more complex relationships from these primitives:

hasComponent   ≡   (**transitive-closure**
                        (**or**$_{role}$ hasDComponent (hasDMember ∘ hasDComponent)))
hasPart   ≡   (**or**$_{role}$ hasComponent hasMember ...)

indicating that members of collections of components are also components,
and that hasPart is the union of the various subkinds of relationships.

Let us concentrate here on the component-of relationship, which is probably the one most frequently encountered in practical applications. We shall
consider the table of contents of a book as an exemplar of a component
attribute.

One idea is to declare attributes and roles that represent components (e.g., tableOfContents) as specializations of hasDComponent. This allows us to distinguish such component roles from other roles, like lentTo and publisher.

Obviously, the inverses of such roles provide access from a part to its containing whole:

isDComponentOf   ≡   (**inverse** hasDComponent)
hasTableOfContents ≡   (**inverse** contentsOf).

Turning to "existence" constraints, a book (but not a *copy* of a book!) depends on the existence of its specific table of contents, and conversely. Although we can specify that a book must have table of contents, as with earlier "dynamic" aspects (such as (im)mutable class membership) standard Description Logics are not currently equipped to express constraints stating that an attribute value cannot change.

To model the fact that each table of contents belongs exclusively to one book, we can use qualified number restrictions

TableOfContents ⊑ (**the** contentsOf Book).

Finally, the inheritance of properties (e.g., isDefective) across component-like attributes is modeled using constructs such as **same-as**, which relate attribute/role chains set-theoretically, in the same manner as shown with materialization:

Book ⊑ (**same-as** isDefective (hasTableOfContents ∘ isDefective)).

Note however that several of these representations require quite expressive language constructs, whose combination may result in a language for which subsumption is undecidable.

10.7.4 General constraints

In many modeling exercises one will encounter general constraints that characterize valid states of the world. For example, the dueDate of a book must be later than the lentOn date.

Except for a few cases involving identity of attribute paths, these constraints will not be expressible in standard Description Logics, due to their limited expressive power. Several widely distributed systems, such as CLAS-SIC and LOOM, offer "escape hatches" – concept constructors that allow one to describe sets of individuals using some very powerful language, such as a programming language (CLASSIC's test-concepts) or some variant of first-order logic (LOOM's assertions). These concept definitions are usually opaque as far as concept-level reasoning is concerned, because the system cannot guarantee correctness for such an expressive formalism. However, these concepts can have an impact as far as the ABox reasoning is concerned, since the latter resembles a logical model, and therefore we can do relatively simple "evaluation" as a way of recognizing individuals. Thus, in CLASSIC, the test-concept (**test** date-after (dueDate lentOn)) would invoke the date-after function on the dueDate and lentOn attributes of an individual object, and check that the first is temporally after the second, thus classifying individuals, or detecting errors in the ABox.

More general than these procedural extensions are DL systems that are *extensible* in the sense that a "knowledge language engineer" can add new concept constructors, and extend the implementation in a principled way. For example, if we wanted to deal with dates and durations (clearly a desirable feature for libraries), we would want to be able to compare dates, add durations to dates, etc. General approaches to extending Description Logics have been described, among others, in [Baader and Hanschke, 1991b; Borgida, 1999; Horrocks and Sattler, 2001].

10.7.5 Views and contexts

Although the initial goal is usually to provide a single model of the UofD, it turns out to be very important to preserve the various "views" of the information seen by different stake-holders and participants. For example, a book that is in the library (and by definition, this would mean that it has no value for the lentTo role) is of interest to the staff, for example to help find it; for this, it may have a role location, which might specify some shelf or sorting area; this attribute may be attached to the MaterialInLibrary concept.

On the other hand, a view of Material called MaterialOnLoan (which *requires* a lentTo role value), would be a natural place to keep information about dueDate and nrOfRenewals – attributes that would normally appear on the relationship itself. This view is of particular interest to the borrower, but also the staff in charge of sending overdue notices.

Incidentally, the above pattern of replacing a binary relationship having attributes by two views can be applied any time one of the participants in the relationship is restricted to appear in at most one tuple (e.g., every book can be loaned to at most one borrower).

10.8 A conceptual modeling methodology

The world of object-oriented software development has produced a vast literature on methodologies (e.g., [Shlaer and Mellor, 1988]) for identifying objects, classes, methods, etc., for a particular application. Instead of considering this voluminous material here, we will recapitulate some of the issues raised above by extending the outline of a simple DL knowledge engineering methodology first presented in [Brachman *et al.*, 1991]. The reader is referred to that article for more details, including a long worked-out example.

We present the main steps of modeling, with suggestions for refinements to be accomplished in later passes; this is in order to avoid the modeler becoming overwhelmed by details:

- Identify the individuals one can encounter in the UofD. Revisit this later considering issues such as materialization and values.
- Enumerate concepts that group these values.
- Distinguish independent concepts from relationship-roles.
- Develop a taxonomy of concepts. Revisit this later considering issues such as disjointness and covering for subconcepts.
- Identify any individuals (usually enumerated values) that are of interest in all states of the world in this UofD.
- Systematically search for part–whole relationships between objects, creating roles for them. Later, make them subroles of the categories of roles mentioned in Section 10.7.3.
- Identify other "properties" of objects, and then general relationships in which objects participate.
- Determine local constraints involving roles such as cardinality limits and value restrictions. Elaborate any concepts introduced as value restrictions.
- Determine more general constraints on relationships, such as those that can be modeled by subroles or **same-as**. (The latter often correspond to "inheritance" across some relationship other than IS-A, and have been mentioned in several places earlier.)
- Distinguish essential from incidental properties of concepts, as well as primitive from defined concepts.
- Consider properties of concepts such as rigidity, identifiers, etc., and use the techniques of [Guarino and Welty, 2000] to simplify and realign the taxonomy of primitive concepts.

10.9 The ABox: modeling specific states of the world

So far, we have concentrated on describing the conceptual model at the level of concepts. In some applications we may want to use our system to keep models of specific states of the world – somewhat like a database. As discussed in Chapter 2, this involves stating for each specific individual zero or more fillers for its attributes and roles, and asserting membership in zero or more concepts (primitive, but also possibly defined).

One of the challenging aspects of modeling the state of the world with Description Logics is remembering that unlike databases, DL systems *do not make the closed-world assumption*. Thus, in contrast with standard databases, if some relationship is not known to hold, it is not assumed to be false.

One consequence of this is that any question about the membership of an individual in a concept, or its relationship to another individual, has *three* possible answers: definitely yes, definitely no, or unknown. The positive side of this is that it allows the modeling of states with partial information: one can model that BOOK22 is an instance of Book, and hence has exactly one filler for isbnNr, yet not know what that value is. Chapter 12 shows how this feature has been exploited in developing a family of DL applications for configuring various devices.

Another consequence of the above stance is that in some cases individuals are not recognized as satisfying definitions when one might expect them to. For example, suppose we only know that hasAuthor relates BOOK22 to SHAKESPEARE, who in turn is known to be an instance of Englishman. This, by itself, is not enough to classify BOOK22 as an instance of concept (**all** hasAuthor Englishman); we must also know that there are no other possible fillers for BOOK22's hasAuthor role – i.e., that BOOK22 is an instance of (**at-most** 1 hasAuthor) – before we can *try* to answer definitively whether BOOK22 is an instance of (**all** hasAuthor Englishman). Even in this case, if the answer is not "yes", we may get "no" or "maybe".

A final consequence of not making the closed-world assumption is that there is a clear distinction between the state of the world (out there) and our (system's) *knowledge* of it. This is reflected by the terminology used above (e.g., "we must also *know* there are no other possible fillers"). As a result, in modeling a domain one may find it necessary to specify concepts that involve the state of our knowledge base, rather than the state of the world. For example, we might want to find out exactly which books in the KB are not known to have a ISBN number. The description (**and** Book (**at-most** 0 isbnNr)) will not do the job, because the second constraint would conflict with one of the the necessary conditions of Book, which is that it must have have exactly one isbnNr. What is happening here is that the **at-most** 1 constraint concerns the state of the world, while the **at-most** 0 condition involves the KB's knowledge of the world. To deal with this, we need some form of *epistemic* operator, so we can define the concept

UnknownIsbnBook $\equiv$ (**and** Book (**at-most** 0 (**known** isbnNr))).

The general problem of adding an epistemic operator to Description Logics is considered in [Donini *et al.*, 1998a], but this is not available in currently implemented Description Logics. A "hack" would be to introduce for such roles a subrole, whose identifier indicates its epistemic nature:

knownToHaveAuthor $\sqsubseteq$ hasAuthor

and then be sure to assert fillers only about the "known" variant. Unfortunately, there is no way to tell a Description Logic that such roles automatically have the "closed-world assumption".

10.10 Conclusions

There are a wide variety of sources that discuss the application of object-oriented approaches to modeling a domain. The same principles apply to conceptual modeling in general. For this reason, we have concentrated here on some of the more subtle ontological issues that arise during modeling, and the different ways in which these can be encoded in Description Logics. In some cases the issues examined were suggested by features of Description Logics themselves.

In the process, we covered most of the kinds of questions that would have to be addressed while modeling something like the library domain, and uncovered some of the strengths and also some of the weaknesses of Description Logics in representing this conceptual model. The latter include difficulty in representing (structured) values, constraints related to the dynamic aspects of the domain, certain forms of "inheritance" (e.g., for materialization), and meta-information. These were balanced by the multitude of features dealing with primitive and defined concepts, necessary and sufficient conditions for concept specification, and the treatment of roles as first-class citizens in subclasses and composition.

Probably the biggest problem in developing an appropriate conceptual model for a domain is that of testing it for correctness and completeness. The former is supported by the reasoning and explanation facilities provided by Description Logics. The latter, as usual, is much more difficult to achieve.

11

Software Engineering

Christopher A. Welty

Abstract

This chapter reviews the application of Description Logics to software engineering, following a steady evolution of DL-based systems used to support the program understanding process for programmers involved in software maintenance.

11.1 Introduction

One of the first large applications of Description Logics was in the area of software engineering. In software, programmers and maintainers of large systems are plagued with information overload. These systems are typically over a million lines of code, some approach fifty million. The size of the workforce dedicated to maintaining these enormous systems is often over a thousand. In addition, turnover is quite high, as is the training investment required to make someone a productive member of the team. This seems, on the surface, to be a problem crying out for a knowledge-based solution, but understanding precisely how Description Logics can play a role requires understanding the basic problems of software engineering "in the large".

11.2 Background

The three principal software maintenance tasks are pro-active (testing), re-active (debugging), and enhancement. Central to effective performance of these tasks is *understanding the software*. In the 1980s, cognitive studies of programmers involved in program understanding [Soloway *et al.*, 1987] revealed two things:

1. Programmers typically solve problems by realizing "plans" in their programs. This seems to tie the notion of program understanding to plan recognition [Soloway *et al.*, 1986].
2. *Delocalized plans* (plans which are not implemented in localized regions of code) are a serious impediment to plan recognition, for both humans and automated methods [Soloway and Letovsky, 1986].

While these observations were interesting, the studies from which they were derived were slightly flawed from the industrial perspective described above: the subjects of these studies were almost exclusively students working alone with small domain-independent programs (i.e., sorting, searching, etc.). It was not clear how these results applied to experienced programmers working in teams with huge domain-specific programs.

An ambitious effort launched by AT&T [Brachman *et al.*, 1990] attempted to address this problem by studying maintainers of a large software system, and measuring the time they spent performing different categories of tasks. What they found was a bit startling: up to 60% of the time was spent performing simple searches across the entire software system. A part of what was termed *discovery*, and as pointed out later in [Welty, 1997], the need for these searches was the result of the delocalization not only of plans in software, but of information in general; information a maintainer needs to understand a section of code is frequently not found in the vicinity of that section of code, but may be before or after in the file, in a different file, in a different directory, etc. For a large software system whose source code is spread out over a large number of files in a deep and complex directory structure, finding something as simple as, e.g., the definition of a datatype, with tools such as *find* (the Unix program that runs another program on all files recursively down a directory structure) and *grep* (the Unix program that searches files for strings) was both difficult and time-consuming.

Another more comprehensive study was performed by MCC around the same time [Curtis *et al.*, 1988], which concluded, among other things, that a prerequisite to understanding the software is understanding the domain in which the software operates and is a part – if you don't know what a "dial tone" is, you can't be expected to debug the code that generates a dial tone.

11.3 LASSIE

In an attempt to have a direct impact on the maintenance group, the researchers at AT&T developed the notion of a *Software Information System*

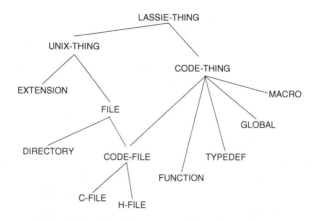

Fig. 11.1. The LASSIE code-level ontology.

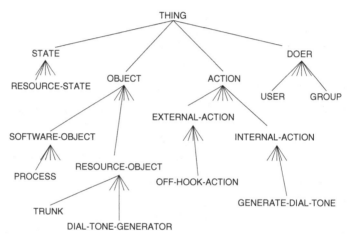

Fig. 11.2. The LASSIE telephony ontology.

(SIS) [Brachman *et al.*, 1990]. An SIS is basically an information system which treats the software system source code itself as data, and stores relationships that can provide the information maintainers frequently search for during discovery.

The first SIS, LASSIE [Devanbu *et al.*, 1991], was developed to assist the understanding of AT&T's Definity 75/85 software system. Influenced by their own study and that of MCC, it contained two components: a *domain model* and a *code model*.

The code model was implemented with a simple ontology of source code elements, shown in Figure 11.1, which was derived empirically from the basic kinds of searches maintainers performed. The knowledge base (the actual assertions about individual functions, files, datatypes, etc.) was populated automatically from the source code.

The domain model was reverse engineered from the code and contact with the domain experts, and contained knowledge about the *telephony* domain, i.e. the things the software system dealt with. These included entities such as telephones, microphones, cables, cable-trunks, etc. A sample of the ontology is shown in Figure 11.2.

One of the most interesting aspects of this work, and perhaps the most significant from the perspective of exploring Description Logics, is an analysis of the differences between these two models. The code model was founded on a very simple ontology, containing perhaps twenty concepts, and was populated with a large number of individuals, on the order of thousands (at least one for each file, datatype, function, and variable in the system). The domain model had a large and complex ontology, containing perhaps two hundred concepts, *but very few individuals.*

The reason for this difference was that the trivial searches that characterized software discovery were performed for two reasons:

1. Discovering specific information about the software, e.g., what is the datatype of the variable `dial-tone`?
2. Discovering specific information about the domain, e.g., what is a dial tone?

In case 1, the maintainer requires specific information about the software, and thus raw data that represents that information is required. For example, by far the most common question asked during discovery is, "Where is this variable used?" [Welty, 1997]. Normally, a maintainer would *grep* for the variable in the rest of the code to find the answers to this question, and as if this didn't take enough time and effort, the results would have to be pruned by hand to remove various kinds of "semantic noise" such as:

1. variables with longer names that include the desired variable name
2. names of functions that include the desired variable name
3. comments that include the variable name
4. other non-variable string matches.

In this particular case, the amount of semantic noise was quite high as a result of mandated naming conventions whose intent was to make the source code easier to understand (semantic noise, also known as *false positives*, is a general problem with string-based search methods, and will be discussed further in Chapter 14).

The SIS code model immediately solved these problems by identifying "variable" as a semantic category (as well as file, function, etc. See Figure 11.1). This meant, quite simply, that where a string search for places in which e.g., the variable `error-value` was used might yield such unwanted results as: `compute-error-value`, `display-error-value-result-code`, `error-value-lookup-table`, etc., limiting the search to variables would remove up to 80% of the noise.

In addition to trivially being able to restrict searches to specific categories, other information that could be extracted automatically was mined from the code. For variables, it is simple to automatically determine:

- the file it was defined in
- each function in which the variable was used.

In addition, for each function, information was extracted regarding the file it was defined in. From this, a simple inference could be made as follows:

$$\text{Variable} \equiv \forall \text{usedInFile.File} \sqcap \forall \text{usedInFunction.Function} \sqcap$$
$$\text{usedInFile} = \text{usedInFunction} \circ \text{definedInFile.}$$

In other words, if a function uses a variable then the variable is used in the file that function is defined in; this produces all the locations where the variable is used. In this manner, the LaSSIE system augmented the basic data in a number of ways through inference.

A similar and nearly as common maintenance task was, e.g., after modifying a function, searching for all the places that function is used to see if the changes affect other sections of the code. Information about what functions call others (i.e., the call graph) was also kept in the code model, and an expression similar to the one in the example above can be used to derive all the files in which a function is called.

The code model alone was able to simplify several of the common discovery tasks maintainers experienced during code modification, but as suggested in case 2 of the reasons for engaging in discovery listed above, there are other reasons for a maintainer to be searching through the code. For these cases, in which domain information is the desired result of a search, a robust description of the domain is required, and was provided by the domain model (see Figure 11.2).

For example, a maintainer may want to know what kinds of actions a user of the system can take by themselves. To answer this question from the code – the usual approach before LaSSIE – would be quite difficult. One method might be to *grep* through the code for the string "user" – hoping of course that the documentation is up to date or consistent with respect to user actions. Clearly the semantic noise would be quite high in such a case.

Another approach might be to start with a piece of code the maintainer is familiar with, and draw some clues from that for where to look next. The point here is that, whereas for code-model queries the goal is quite specific, domain-oriented queries are not, and imply a lot of time browsing, searching for new ideas, etc. The code is organized around specific functions, not around specific domain concepts, and of course multiple "views" of the code are not supported.

To address this type of need, the LaSSIE domain model expressed knowledge about the domain of telephony. It presented numerous key concepts that let maintainers view the knowledge in the code in a variety of different ways. The domain model was mostly terminological, since it was a description of the things that the software could do. An action concept, such as "generating a dial tone" was a description of the action, whereas an individual would be an actual action of generating a dial tone at some fixed time. These individuals did not normally exist in the domain model, except as examples. The concept would roughly be

$$\mathsf{GenerateDialToneAction} \;\equiv\; \mathsf{Action} \sqcap \forall \mathsf{initiatedBy.LatBox} \sqcap$$
$$\forall \mathsf{follows.OffHookAction} \sqcap$$
$$\forall \mathsf{recipient.LocalPhone} \sqcap \;\geqslant 1\; \mathsf{hasConnection}.$$

In other words, a "generate dial tone action" is an action that is initiated by a local telephone service following an "off hook action." The recipient of the product of the action (the dial tone) is a phone for which a connection has been allocated.

Other domain concepts described things that the software reacted to, such as

$$\mathsf{OffHookAction} \;\equiv\; \mathsf{Action} \sqcap \forall \mathsf{initiatedBy.User} \sqcap \;\leqslant 0\; \mathsf{follows} \sqcap$$
$$\forall \mathsf{recipient.LatBox} \sqcap \forall \mathsf{activates.AllocateConnectionAction}.$$

In other words, an "off hook action" is an action that is initiated by a user (more commonly the result of pressing a button these days than lifting the receiver off the hook). It follows no previous action, and the recipient of the product of the action is the local telephone service (on which the software is running). The action activates a search for a connection.

Returning to the randomly chosen example above, the maintainer looking for all actions that can be initiated by a user would simply enter a query such as

$$\mathsf{Action} \sqcap \forall \mathsf{initiatedBy.User}$$

and the system would find all the concepts subsumed by that expression. LaSSIE contained a facility for defining new domain concepts identified by maintainers during discovery, and adding them to the domain model by simply assigning them a name (e.g., USER-ACTION in this example).

While these two models independently solved existing problems, it soon became clear that integrating the two models was an important requirement.

Using the tool exposed the fact that most domain queries were followed by code queries. For example, after exploring the domain model to discover the significance of a "connect action", the maintainer will typically ask, "What are the functions that implement it?" In addition, classifying software components by their relevance in the domain was viewed to be a very significant bit of functionality, as this permitted components to be found and retrieved with this information – something that was not previously possible.

This integration between the two models made it possible to use subsumption to find different software objects. For example, all functions that implement connect actions would be

$$\text{Function} \sqcap \text{ConnectAction}.$$

Variables used in functions that implement user actions would be

$$\text{Variable} \sqcap \forall \text{usedInFunction.UserAction}.$$

The LASSIE system underwent steady development for several years at AT&T, and was shown to cut down on the time maintainers spent in discovery. In order to further improve the process, it was observed that:

- The connection between the domain and code models needed to be made by hand. This was time-consuming to create, and difficult to maintain since the domain model changed over time as new features were added to the software system. Maintainers began to lose faith in the domain model, as a result, and usage deteriorated.
- The code model, though extremely simple, was used far more frequently than the domain model, and became an important part of every maintainer's tool set. It did not, however eliminate the searches maintainers made, and therefore did not completely replace *find* and *grep*.

11.4 CODEBASE

Because the code model proved quite useful and easy to maintain, the demand for it began to increase. This introduced two problems for the LASSIE SIS:

- Like all DL-systems, it was based on main memory. The software contained many thousands of functions, variables, and files. More importantly, the complexity of the function call graph, variable usage graph, and location maps, exceeded one million. It was not possible to store this amount of information in main memory of any computer at that time.
- The natural language interface, while simple and easy to understand, did not *facilitate* using the system quickly. One still had to compose a proper query and type it in. If the result of one query were to be used in another, the maintainer had

to re-type the name(s) of the concepts or individuals involved. Increased usage demanded a better user interface.

The CODEBASE system [Selfridge and Heineman, 1994] offered solutions to both of these problems. Perhaps the most significant achievement was the development of a system for off-line storage of individuals. The relatively small code-model TBox was always kept in memory, but individuals were kept on a disk, in a technique similar to virtual memory. The difference was in the heuristics used for predicting what portions of the ABox to pre-load.

Whereas a virtual memory system normally uses heuristics based on temporal or spatial proximity, for a knowledge base like LaSSIE, this was not relevant. The location of an individual in physical memory was no indication of its relevance to other individuals near it in physical memory.

The heuristics for virtual memory are based on the empirical observation that when one location is accessed, it is probable that the next access will be to a nearby location in memory. The LaSSIE developers observed that, in a DL ABox, when an individual is accessed it is probable that the next access will be *to one of its role fillers*, or to objects along some role path from the accessed individual. Because a role may have many fillers, and because an individual may have many roles, there is no way to arrange the individuals in memory so that the normal virtual memory heuristics will be efficient.

CODEBASE also provided numerous graphical tools for viewing and browsing the information in the knowledge base. While this is less significant from the general perspective of Description Logics, it is important from the standpoint of developing knowledge-based systems. One must never forget that these systems interact with people, and can not be considered as viable systems unless the human is "in the loop".

11.5 CSIS and CBMS

Development of LaSSIE was eventually halted by the trivestiture of AT&T in 1995. Research into software information systems did not stop, however, and Description Logics have played an important role in this continued development.

Two issues were brought to light by the LaSSIE system:

• The deterioration of the domain model over time was another manifestation of the classic software documentation problem: the same information being stored in different ways. The code model stayed relevant because it was automatically generated from the only thing that *had* to be maintained: the software. It did not, therefore, need to be maintained separately to remain accurate. The documentation and the domain model were different representations of the knowledge that was, perhaps implicitly, in the code. These representations always lagged the "real" one, since they had to be maintained independently.

- The delocalization of information in software, which is the central obstacle to code understanding, required new ways of viewing the code. Looking at code on the screen, analogously to the heuristics for operating system virtual memories, is inherently two-dimensional. It does not allow relationships between code-level entities to be viewed, or localized.

The first step in determining how to address these problems was to perform further studies of programmers involved in discovery to gain more detailed insight into specifically what they were doing. One such study, in this case of programmers maintaining a moderate-sized object-oriented software system, found that the most common high level queries were:

1. Where is this variable modified?
2. What are the available slots and methods on this instance?
3. What is the datatype of this variable or function?
4. What are the superclasses of this class?
5. What does this function return?
6. Does this function have side-effects?
7. Is this datatype used?

Clearly, to provide answers to questions like these requires far more fine-grained information about the software than simply the locations of the definitions. Furthermore, this study confirmed that object-oriented languages actually increase understanding problems by delocalizing much more information than their imperative predecessors [Huitt and Wilde, 1992]. Inheritance, in particular, spreads method and slot (instance variable) declarations up the class hierarchy, making it harder to find answers to questions about class composition, among other things.

These issues spurred research into *Comprehensive Software Information Systems* [Welty, 1995], which soon became *Code-Based Management Systems*. The idea of CBMS was to define the most precise level of granularity of representation needed to have *complete knowledge of the software system in the knowledge base*. In other words, to have the knowledge-based representation be the artifact that is maintained.

From a DL perspective, such a comprehensive representation of software in a knowledge base required the ability to deal with large amounts of information efficiently. In addition, such a deep representation made it possible for a wide range of inferences that were well-suited for subsumption reasoning.

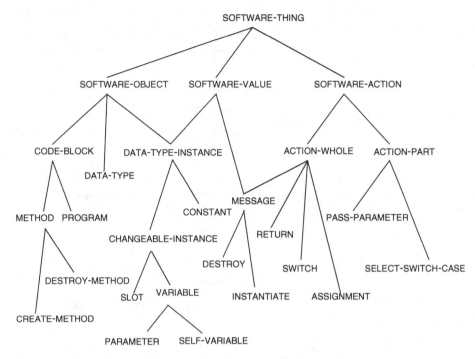

Fig. 11.3. A simplified code-level ontology.

A CBMS is based on a full-scale parse of the code to construct an *abstract syntax tree* (AST), which is basically the parse tree. The AST has all the information of the source code, such that the source code can be completely generated from the AST. The AST is augmented with semantic information that can be derived automatically from the syntax. In C++, for example, we know that the left side of an assignment operator is the variable to be changed, and the right side is the new value.

The ability to represent everything in the code requires a deeper ontology of code-level software elements than the original LaSSIE ontology, that includes statements, blocks, conditions, etc. In fact, every syntactic element of the programming language is in the ontology. A simplified ontology for an object-oriented language is shown in Figure 11.3.

In addition to these concepts representing the syntactic elements of the source language, roles were use to relate instances of these concepts to each other for control flow, data flow, call graphs, etc. For example, take the following C++ code fragment:

```
void group_deliver (
      MAIL_MESSAGE message,
      GROUP group)
```

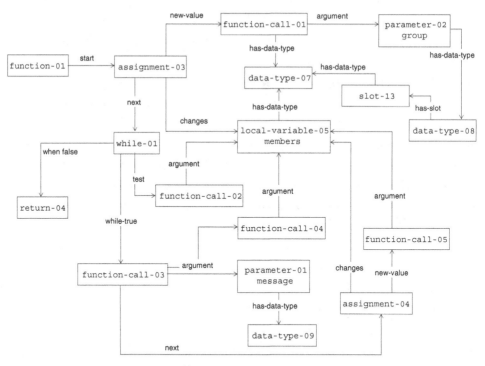

Fig. 11.4. A CBMS representation of the code fragment.

```
{ LIST members;
  members = get_members(group);
  while (! empty(members)) {
    ind_deliver(message,car(members));
    members = cdr(members);
  }
}
```

The CBMS representation of that fragment is shown in Figure 11.4. Note
that Figure 11.4 shows only the ABox corresponding to the small code fragment, and that role fillers are shown as binary relations.

With an interface that showed individuals in the code representation with
role fillers displayed as hypertext links (see [Welty, 1996a]), this ontology
alone localizes far more information than the standard text view of software
displayed in an editor window. Again, an editor window localizes only the
control flow information; a maintainer looking, e.g., at the code fragment
shown above, only sees the text. The lines are arranged in roughly control-
flow order.

Using a CBMS representation, a maintainer's view is focused on a particular object, such as the assignment statement on the first line of the function.

This view would be:

```
ASSIGNMENT-STATEMENT-23:
   implementation-of: {FUNCTION-03: group_deliver}
   next: {WHILE-STATEMENT-14}
   changes: {LOCAL-VARIABLE-16: members}
   new-value: {FUNCTION-INVOCATION-34: get-members(group)}
```

In this kind of view, anything in {...} is a hypertext link to a similar description of the individual named in the link, and localization takes on a new meaning: the number of hypertext links a desired piece of information is from the current context (individual being viewed). For example, information about control flow is accessible through a chain of **next** links, but in addition, information about data flow is accessible through the **new-value** link, about the function being implemented, about the variable being used, etc.

Another advantage of the CBMS approach is that reasoning can be employed to augment the data and automate the localization of even more information. In existing work in CLASSIC, three types of reasoning were employed:

Role inverses. Every role in the ontology has an inverse, and this provides a tremendous amount of simple bookkeeping information useful to maintainers. In the example above, the **changes** role is filled through parsing with **members**, and the inverse relationship, that the variable **members** is changedBy ASSIGNMENT-STATEMENT-23, is added as well. The power of this simple inference can not be overstated. Studies showed that this was the most useful kind of information the system provided, as it answered the most common question asked by maintainers.

Path tracing. Many useful pieces of information were a few clicks away, but would be more useful if brought within one click (i.e., one link). A simple set of forward chaining "filler" rules in CLASSIC are capable of handling this. For example, it is also useful to know within which functions a variable is changed. Without inference, the maintainer must click on the changedBy role for a variable to get to the statement that changes it (or statements), and then must click on the implementationOf role for the statement to get to the function. Instead, with "path-tracing rules", we can fill the changedInFunction role automatically with all the values from the path (changedBy implementationOf). Thus in our example we can conclude that **members** is changedInFunction group_deliver.

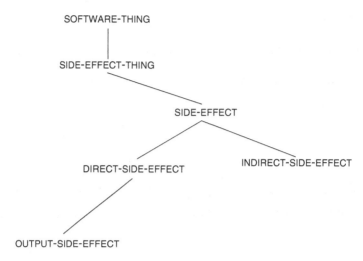

Fig. 11.5. The side-effect ontology.

Subsumption. With subsumption reasoning, membership in a number of useful classes can be inferred for individuals representing pieces of the code. For example, the concept GlobalAssignmentStatement is defined:

$$\text{GlobalAssignmentStatement} \equiv \text{AssignmentStatement} \sqcap \\ \forall \text{changes.GlobalVariable}$$

which allows all the assignment statements that modify global variables to be identified.

The most compelling result that came out of the CBMS work so far has been the automatic detection of side-effects, answering the sixth most commonly asked question. This detection was not originally believed to be possible. To simplify the discussion, we assume a pure object-oriented language without pointers or call-by-reference parameters. The latter can be handled in a similar way, the former is still believed to be undecidable.

There can be two kinds of *direct* side-effects in a method: a change to a global variable, and any sort of output. A third kind of side-effect is a call to a method that has a side-effect. In this case, the side-effect does not actually occur within the calling method, yet a side-effect will occur when the calling method itself is invoked, so it can be important to discover it. A change to a global variable occurs whenever that variable appears in an assignment statement as the variable to be changed.

The CBMS ontology contains a fairly simple extension which can automatically detect side-effects on global variables and calls to methods with side-effects. Output methods must be specifically identified as such in order that calls to them may be recognized. This is not really a problem, since output functions are generally part of a support library which would be provided to any developer. The extension begins with a new part of the code-level ontology, shown in Figure 11.5. This new ontology of primitive concepts fits under the **SoftwareThing** concept. Next, any individual of **GlobalAssignmentStatement** (defined above) is a side-effect – an **AssignmentSideEffect**.

In order to put individuals of **AssignmentSideEffect** into the side-effect ontology shown in Figure 11.5, a forward chaining rule is added:

$$\text{AssignmentSideEffect} \ \Rightarrow \ \text{DirectSideEffect}.$$

This rule is required because if the relationship it specifies were part of the defined concept, being a direct side-effect would become a sufficient condition for recognizing assignment side-effects, and they would never be found automatically. In other words, the rule says "once an assignment side-effect is recognized, it should be also be classified as a direct side-effect", whereas putting direct side-effect after assignment in the defined concept definition would say, "An assignment side-effect must already be known to be a direct side-effect to be recognized." The latter is not productive.

At this point we can classify all assignments that change global variables as assignment side-effects and direct side-effects. The next addition is a set of roles that will help identify the methods that contain these side-effects: **hasDirectSideEffect**, its inverse **directSideEffectOf**, and their role parents **hasSideEffect** and **SideEffectOf**. With these roles defined, a path-tracing rule is added for **DirectSideEffect** that says **directSideEffectOf = implementationOf**. In other words, the **directSideEffectOf** role should be filled with the value in the **implementationOf** role of the assignment. Through the role hierarchy, this also adds the **SideEffectOf** role, and through the inverse, the individual of **Method** that fills this role gets the **hasDirectSideEffect** and **hasSideEffect** roles pointing back to the assignment.

With these inverse roles filled in, we can create a new defined concept to recognize methods with side-effects:

$$\text{MethodWithSideEffects} \ \equiv \ \text{Method} \sqcap \geqslant 1\,\text{hasSideEffects}$$

and a more specific one for methods with direct side-effects:

$$\text{MethodWithDirectSideEffects} \ \equiv \ \text{Method} \sqcap \geqslant 1\,\text{hasDirectSideEffects}.$$

Note that the second concept will automatically be classified under the first. Now, as a result of the rules that added the **hasSideEffect** links, every method that has in its implementation a slot assignment side-effect will have at least one filler in its hasDirectSideEffects role, and will be classified as a method with direct side-effects.

The next case is detecting indirect side-effects, which first requires recognizing invocations of methods that have side-effects (in object-oriented terms, a method invocation is a message):

$$\text{MessageSideEffect} \equiv \text{Message} \sqcap \forall \text{callMethod.MethodWithSideEffects.}$$

Individuals of this new concept can be recognized since *all methods with side-effects have been found with the previous two defined concepts.* A simple forward chaining rule then links these message side-effects back into the side-effect ontology:

$$\text{MessageSideEffect} \Rightarrow \text{IndirectSideEffect.}$$

Next we define two more roles: hasIndirectSideEffect and its inverse indirectSideEffectOf, and make them children of hasSideEffect and SideEffectOf, respectively. Once these roles have been defined, and the message side-effects have been found, we can identify all the methods that have them in a similar manner to assignment side-effects. First, create a path-tracing rule for IndirectSideEffect: indirectSideEffectOf = implementationOf which will fill in roles. Now we identify all these methods with indirect side-effects with the concept

$$\text{MethodWithIndirectSideEffects} \equiv \text{Method} \sqcap \geqslant 1 \text{ hasIndirectSideEffects}$$

The final step is simply to link methods with side-effects into the side-effect ontology with one last forward chaining rule:

$$\text{MethodWithSideEffects} \Rightarrow \text{SideEffectThing}$$

The addition of this rule basically creates the side-effect ontology shown in Figure 11.5.

Not only do these definitions identify functions with side-effects, but they also lead a maintainer directly to the side-effect itself. The point here, from a software understanding perspective, is that subsumption makes it possible to *localize* information that otherwise would be difficult (or at least time-consuming) to discover.

The inferences for finding side-effects are clearly very deep, yet the developer or maintainer need not be aware of them. All these side-effect inferences come with no extra work by the developer or maintainer at all. In fact, answers to *all* of the top questions asked by maintainers during discovery can be localized to within one link, therefore one mouse click in the simple hypertext interface described.

12

Configuration

Deborah L. McGuinness

Abstract

Description Logics are used to solve a wide variety of problems, with configuration applications being some of the largest and longest-lived. There is concrete, commercial evidence that shows that DL-based configurators have been successfully fielded for over a decade. Additionally, it appears that configuration applications have a number of characteristics that make them well-suited to DL-based solutions. This chapter will introduce the problem of configuration, describe some requirements of configuration applications that make them candidates for DL-based solutions, show examples of these requirements in a configuration example, and introduce the largest and longest-lived family of DL-based configurators.

12.1 Introduction

In order to solve a configuration problem, a configurator (human or machine) must find a set of components that fit together to solve the problem specification. Typically, that means the answer will be a parts list that contains a set of components that work together and that the system comprising the components meets the specification. This task can be relatively simple, such as choosing stereo components in order to create a home stereo system. The problem can also be extremely complex, such as choosing the thousands of components that must work together in order to build complicated telecommunications equipment such as cross-connect devices or switches.

One important factor that makes configuration challenging is that making a choice for one component typically generates constraints on other components as well. For example, a customer who chooses a receiver that only supports up to four speakers may not conveniently support a surround sound system with a subwoofer (since this would require more than four speakers).

Configuration continues to have strong interest in the academic and commercial communities. It has been a prominent area in artificial intelligence at least since the R1/XCON [McDermott, 1982] work on configuring computer systems. Since then, many configuration systems have been built in domains including communication networks, trucks, cars, operating systems, buildings, furniture layout, and even wine properties to match a meal description. Today, there are active mailing lists, workshops and conferences (such as the configuration workshops at ECAI-2002 [ECAI, 2002] IJCAI 2001 [Soininen *et al.*, 2001], AAAI'99 [Faltings *et al.*, 1999], and the Fall Symposium Workshop on Configuration [Faltings and Freuder, 1996]), special issues of journals (such as *IEEE Intelligent Systems* [Faltings and Freuder, 1998] and *Artificial Intelligence for Engineering Design, Analysis and Manufacturing* [Darr *et al.*, 1998]), and research groups at a number of universities and companies. Approaches include constraints, expert systems, model-based reasoning, and case-based reasoning as well as Description Logics.

Configuration is an important and growing commercial concern. There are a number of companies dedicated to configuration such as Trilogy, Calico, etc. Other companies in broader markets such as the enterprise integration software companies, Baan and SAP, have a major emphasis in configuration. Companies that sell complicated products, such as computers, are providing their own configurators (e.g., the Dell personal computer online configurators). There are spinoff companies of general configuration companies that are aiming at particular domain areas, such as PCOrder (a spinoff of Trilogy focusing on personal computer configuration). There are also some domain-oriented companies that include configuration as a major component such as CarsDirect's configuration of United States consumer car orders.

Although the commercial configuration market may appear to be a recent event since it has been exploding recently, it does have at least a decade of history. Trilogy, for example, one of the earlier companies focusing primarily on configuration, was founded in 1989. Forrester Research reports that the configuration market was valued at 8 billion dollars in 1997 and it predicts that the market will grow to 327 billion in 2002. Configuration is also seen as important by companies not originally classifying themselves as "configuration companies". In a study of fifty eCommerce executives from top firms in the business-to-business and business-to-consumer space, Forrester Research found that search and configurators were considered the two tools most critical for customer support [Koetzle *et al.*, 2001].

The DL community has been addressing configuration needs for over a decade as well. Owsnicki-Klewe [1988] presented a view of configuration as a consistency maintenance task for Description Logics and AT&T independently began work in 1988 on its family of configurators for telecommunications equipment [Wright *et al.*, 1993; McGuinness *et al.*, 1995; McGuinness and Wright, 1998b; 1998a]. Similarly Ford Motor Company has had a DL-based configurator [Rychtyckyj, 1996] in the field for over 10 years. Others in the DL area have explored Description Logics for configuration as well, e.g., [Buchheit *et al.*, 1994c; Kessel *et al.*, 1995].

12.2 Configuration description and requirements

In this chapter, we will be considering large-scale configuration problems. If one only has a small number of constraints to satisfy and a small number of possible component choices, then any somewhat reasonable solution will work. If however the final product is complicated and there are thousands of choices and constraints, then there is more need for a well-suited solution. We will consider the generic configuration problem where there is a complex artifact being assembled from components. Potentially the components have subcomponents, and thus the artifact may be modular or hierarchical in nature. Also, each of the components typically has a number of properties, such as power restrictions, connections to other components, etc., and thus components may be tightly interconnected. If one looks at modern configuration descriptions [Fleischanderl *et al.*, 1998; Juengst and Heinrich, 1998], one can see only large, interconnected, tightly constrained, complex systems.

The input description for the configuration problems we will consider will be a specification of a complex, probably highly interconnected system. The input should be able to be entered incrementally by a user as well as being able to be uploaded from sales programs. The input specification may be:

- incomplete
- ambiguous
- incrementally evolving
- granular to different levels of specificity
- inconsistent
- entered in any arbitrary order
- interconnected
- nested with complex structure.

The output for the system, in its simplest form, will be some kind of parts list. The parts list may be organized hierarchically so that there is a parts list of high level components (such as bays in switching systems or speaker sets in home theater systems) as well as a detailed parts list of the individual components. In this chapter, we will only address configuration and not the related area of parts layout.

The output of the system should be:

- correct
- complete
- consistent (with respect to other parts, preferences, pre-existing components in the customer's environment)
- modifiable
- understandable / explainable
- capable of being queried
- interconnected and interoperable with related data.

The configurator needs to accept the problem input along with any previously entered domain information concerning valid configurations. It must then check the constraints it has (calculating the constraints that are implicit in the input data from the input and background information) in order to start building a parts list. It may find that a complete and correct parts list may not be built from the given input. In actuality, it is common for the problem specification to be either overconstrained (i.e., contain a contradiction such as "I want a pair of speakers that is of the highest quality available yet I do not want to pay more than fifty dollars for them") or underconstrained (i.e., "I want to buy a high quality stereo system"). In the first case, the configurator needs to identify the source of the conflicting information and determine (probably along with user input) which conflicting constraint(s) to relax. In the second case, the configurator needs either to solicit more specific information from the user, or to generate a list of possible configurations, or both. If the configurator makes arbitrary choices for the user (e.g., it chooses some receiver for the stereo system yet there were many possible choices), then it needs to make it possible for the user to change the arbitrary choices and also to find out which choices were arbitrary and which choices were mandated by constraints. Additionally it needs to let the user enter partial additional input that would further constrain the choices.

The configurator also needs to accept information from multiple data sources. There will be a number of databases with which a configurator may need to interact. Typically, there will be databases of parts and prices, other databases of parts and availability, and possibly many other databases with user information or just information about different product families.

It is likely that information (such as pricing and availability) will change frequently. Also, there will be information concerning what parts are compatible together and how the choice of one part constrains the choices of other parts. These might be considered the configuration rules. Although these rules might not change on a frequent basis, modifications are typically necessary. The rules may come from multiple sources as well. They may need to be imported from many different source languages and they may need to be input by people who have no training in computer science, let alone knowledge representation systems.

Finally, the system may be long-lived and thus require support and maintenance. It may be necessary to staff a help desk to help users of the system. The customer service representatives may know very little about any one individual product about which they are answering questions (because they are supporting a large number of products). The technical staff maintaining the individual configurator may not include people who originally built the system, and over time, it may not even include people who know much about the product (although they may be quite capable of researching the product if necessary). Also, the technical staff may need to generate new configurators for updated or similar products.

We might summarize the requirements from the input, output, and core configurator requirements starting from the requirements presented in one configurator family of applications [McGuinness and Wright, 1998b] and augmenting them slightly here. A solution methodology should have the following properties:

- object-oriented modeling
- rule representation, organization, and triggering
- active inference and knowledge completion
- explanation, product training, and help desk support
- ability to handle incrementally evolving specifications
- extensible schemas
- reasoning mechanisms that handle incomplete or ambiguous information
- inconsistency detection, error handling, and retraction
- modularity
- maintainability.

This list of needs represents those in many complicated reasoning tasks. Although we could argue that this general architecture and approach is more broadly applicable, we will limit our discussion to configuration applications. In the next set of subsections, we will describe each of these needs with respect to the task of configuring a stereo system (based on the configurator demo by AT&T [McGuinness *et al.*, 1995; 1998] and mention how the

DL-based solution met the need. When useful or necessary, we will mention how the need was addressed in the larger PROSE configurator family.

In the stereo configuration application, the goal was to require the user to enter a small number of constraints concerning the end system and generate a complete, correct, and consistent parts list. Although the system would accept a large set of constraints as input as well, the goal was to reduce the user's task and thus require minimal input. The system used the user input along with its extensive domain knowledge and parts information to determine if the user's input specification was consistent. It used the underlying theorem prover within the DL system to compute the deductive closure of the input and generated a more complete input description. User input was solicited on the system quality (high, medium, or low with associated price ranges) and the typical use (audio only, home theater only, or combination), and then the application deduced applicable consequences. This typically generated descriptions for 6–20 subcomponents which restrict properties such as price range, television diagonal, power rating, etc. A user might then inspect any of the individual components possibly adding further requirements to it which may, in turn, cause further constraints to appear on other components of the system. Also, a user may ask the system to "complete" the configuration task (even if the user specification was incomplete), completely specifying each component so that a parts list is generated and an order may be completed. An online demonstration of the web configurator application is available at Stanford (`http://www.ksl.stanford.edu/people/dlm/dls/stereo-demo/`) and a number of examples are available in the extended online version of the IJCAI paper [McGuinness *et al.*, 1995] available at: `http://www.research.att.com/sw/tools/classic/tm/ijcai-95-with-scenario.html`.

This application is convenient for illustrating our points since it is small and in a broadly understandable domain. It is potentially more interesting than some simple pedagogical examples since it was developed as an application that had representation and reasoning requirements that were isomorphic to the needs observed in the PROSE family [Wright *et al.*, 1993; McGuinness and Wright, 1998b] of configurators. The examples in this paper can be seen in more detail in [McGuinness *et al.*, 1995; 1998].

12.2.1 Object-oriented modeling

A system that is being configured may be viewed as a structured object composed of smaller objects. Even our simple example domain of stereo equipment presents a natural hierarchy of concept descriptions and instances that have a number of properties. We have a top level node like ElectricalThing and then have subclasses of that node such as HomeTheaterSystem and Stereo-OrVideoComponent. Further, subclasses of StereoOrVideoEquipment might include Receiver, Speaker, and Television. Any particular term may have properties associated with it. For example, a Television might have a property called diagonal (that must be filled with a positive integer), another called price (that must be filled with a monetary value), a repairHistory (that must be filled with one of the following values: {BAD, OK, GOOD}), a manufacturer (that must be filled with a company), and a height, width, and depth (all of which must be filled with a positive number). All of the properties might have cardinality requirements on them. For example, there must be at least one manufacturer (although possibly more than one manufacturer), there must be exactly one filler for the diagonal role, etc.

In the simple examples so far, we have seen a need for number (cardinality) restrictions, value restrictions (choosing the type of a filler for a role), roles, and class hierarchies. Further we should note in the description that the objects are compositional. The value restriction on the manufacturer role is naturally determined to be a company. Companies themselves might have further properties like headquarter locations, CEOs, etc. A user might subsequently want to choose speakers made by companies in the United States and televisions made by companies headquartered in Japan.

It is argued more extensively elsewhere [McGuinness and Wright, 1998a] and in this book in Chapter 10 that Description Logics are convenient modeling tools for such objects. We can show a simple example of this diagrammatically where a HomeTheaterSystem inherits a price role with a value restriction of MonetaryUnit. We might also have a particular HomeTheaterSystem named MY-HTS that is the system we will be building through the example. It will also have a price role with some unknown value at the moment. We might also have a subclass of HomeTheaterSystem called High-QualSystem. In our simple example, this might be defined simply as a home theater system that costs at least 6000 dollars. In a Description Logic system, once MY-HTS contains either a price that is over 6000, or contains a partial description such as "a minimum price of 8000 dollars" that restricts the price to be greater than 6000, then it can be recognized to be an instance of a HighQualSystem. This kind of automatic recognition and organization of terms based on their definitions is a convenience for organizing and maintaining partial descriptions and is arguably one reason that Description Logics are thought to be particularly useful for modeling and maintenance of applications that require object-oriented models.

12.2.2 Rule representation

A knowledge base that contains information about active deductions will contain some sort of rules. Typical large configuration systems will contain many rules. Also, these rules may change frequently. It is reported that 40% of the rules in R1 changed yearly. Thus, support for modeling, organizing, and later, maintaining the rules will be important in large configuration systems. A simple rule may take the form of "If something is an A, then it is a B". For example, if something is a HighQualSystem, then its television is a HighQualTelevision (which has a minimum price and diagonal value), its speakers are HighQualSpeakers (which have minimum price restrictions), etc. In fact, in our stereo demo, there are dozens of rules that fire once a system is determined to be a HighQualSystem. If the minimum price restriction were ever removed from the specification requirement, we would want the results of those rules retracted automatically (unless the same results could be deduced in other ways as well).

A DL-based system can support modeling of rules described above in a hierarchical fashion. Rules can be associated at what ever level of the hierarchy is appropriate. Thus, we might associate minimum price and diagonal for televisions at the level of a HighQualSystem and we might associate repair-history restrictions with another concept such as HighReliabilitySystem. If we just wanted to have this kind of simple rule encoding, we would not need to use a separate mechanism. If one has an encoding scheme that includes negation and disjunction (or some other way of encoding an "if–then" rule), as do most of the modern Description Logic languages, then one does not need to introduce a separate rule notion. For example, one might encode a simple if–then relationship such as (or (not HighReliabilitySystem) GoodRepairHistory). This states that either something is not a high reliability system or it has a good repair history, which is typically viewed as equivalent to "if something is a high reliability system, then it has a good repair history".

The Description Logic that this example was encoded in (CLASSIC [Borgida *et al.*, 1989; Brachman *et al.*, 1991; Patel-Schneider *et al.*, 1991; McGuinness and Patel-Schneider, 1998]) had a rather limited set of constructors and also had the simple rules introduced above and also more sophisticated rules such as those which compute role values based on context. In some configuration applications of this Description Logic, the more sophisticated rules in combination with other constructors have encoded expressive rule-based reasoning, and in fact many of the rules in those configuration system required CLASSIC's more sophisticated rule representation system. The examples we have seen in this chapter only use a simple form of if–then rules. For a more detailed discussion of how powerful these rules can be in practice, see [Borgida *et al.*, 1996].

Description logics are not required of course in order to capture rule representation and reasoning; this example simply shows that they can be a convenient technique for capturing rules and reasoning with them.

12.2.3 Active inference

Description logics deduce logical consequences of information and are thus said to provide active inference. In fact, one of the typical patterns of inference observed in many DL-based configuration systems includes:

- asserting new information about an existing term
- recognizing that the updated term is an instance of a class
- firing a rule on the term that is associated with the class
- propagating information from the updated term to related terms.

For example, let's consider MY-HTS again. Let it have a hasTelevision slot filled with a particular television TV-11. Once it is asserted that the user is willing to pay more than 8000 dollars for this system, it is recognized to be an instance of the HighQualSystem. The rules associated with that concept fire and now it becomes an instance of something that has a television diagonal minimum of 50 inches (or possibly a high definition television with a smaller diagonal) and a television price of a minimum of 1000 dollars. These restrictions are propagated onto TV-11.

This kind of deduction chain comprises over 50% of the inferences that are done in the stereo configurator example. In this manner, users only need to specify a small number of restrictions on their system and they can have a large number of deductions performed for them.

It should be noted that this particular example configurator was built on a Description Logic that did not contain default reasoning. Some Description Logics have been expanded to include default reasoning (i.e., if it is not known to be otherwise, use the default rule) [Padgham and Zhang, 1993; Baader and Hollunder, 1995a; Quantz and Royer, 1992]. For example, if a manufacturer has not been specified for a television, use Sony as the manufacturer. If the underlying formalism had had a default representation, this would have been used.

As the demonstration system was encoded, the stereo configurator used two sets of concepts on which to hang rules: a concept for all provably correct rules (such as power compatibility) and another concept for the default rules, called a "guidance" concept (for more subjective rules such as minimum prices). The deployed configurators on which this system was based actually used defaults as completion – at a particular point in the specification input process, if information is unknown, then "complete" it using the "default" or subjective rules [McGuinness and Wright, 1998b]. This provided one very simple method of implementing a kind of "default" as completion that can be viewed as one of the simplest forms of default reasoning.

12.2.4 Explanation

Customer help desk staff need to be able to help users understand potentially everything about a configuration specification and the final parts list. In fact, the PROSE family of configurators faced extinction had it not been able to respond with a full explanation capability. It was evident that consumers needed to be able to find out why some particular part was in their final system, why it had the particular value restrictions it did, what the possible alternatives were, and from what portion of the specification this information had been derived. In this simple example, a customer might want to find out why the television in the final system costs over 1000 dollars or why it has a particular minimum diagonal requirement. The explanation would be that a high quality system was requested and high quality systems include a suggested minimum diagonal size and a minimum price on their television components.

The demonstration system allows customers to point to particular components and ask questions about everything that has been deduced about them. It also anticipates the most common explanation questions that users ask and provides pulldown menus containing explanation question that were dynamically generated based on the item a user was pointing to and that a user could just click on to ask quickly. An extensive explanation foundation was designed for the underlying DL-based system in order to support that [McGuinness, 1996; McGuinness and Borgida, 1995]. The explanation system provides a proof-theoretic foundation for explaining any deduction in terms of proof rules and arguments. It also provides an automatic followup capability that generates the questions that would lead to this inference being deducible. The followup question generation was found to be needed since user studies showed that users wanted fairly simple explanations along with the capability to ask followup questions. Further studies found that users appreciated help in generating syntactically correct followup questions that made sense given the previous question that was asked. The followup questions were automatically generated from the model-theoretic form of the explanation.

The basic explanation structure was originally done for a normalize–compare DL-based system but has since been used as the foundation for a tableau-based Description Logic [Borgida *et al.*, 1999] and also a model-elimination theorem prover in an implementation of the ATP and JTP theorem proving systems at Stanford University.

Explanation in general is one of the strengths of Description Logics as opposed to some of the other configuration approaches. It may be much more difficult to explain a line of reasoning in a typical constraint-based approach than it is to filter and prune an inference-rule-based theorem prover such as a DL prover. Filtering object presentations and explanations in Description Logic has also been addressed in [McGuinness, 1996; Borgida and McGuinness, 1996; Baader *et al.*, 1999a]. Also, it has been argued elsewhere [McGuinness and Patel-Schneider, 1998; Brachman *et al.*, 1999] that explanation is a requirement for many kinds of applications, but is particularly important for configuration systems [McGuinness and Wright, 1998a].

Recent work has been done in constraint-based approaches that starts to address explanation in constraint-based configurators. While progress is being made, the more interesting constraint-based explanation systems [Freuder *et al.*, 2001] utilize extensive domain specific information and are not generic solutions to the problem of understanding explanations.

12.2.5 Evolving specifications

In many common configuration scenarios, a user begins with an incomplete set of specifications for an end product. Configuration applications built to support users should take input of the known specifications (in an order that is convenient for the user and not just an order convenient for the program), and then solicit remaining required input.

A configurator system should allow mixed initiative input, where the user may input the specifications the user is aware of at a particular time and the system should request input that it needs to meet a task. Description Logics can allow users to input descriptions of end products or individual components at any time. For example, in the home theater system, a user could specify information about the entire system – such as a requirement for the entire system to be high quality – and also could specify information about any of the particular components that was known at a particular time. The user might, for example, prefer to buy a particular model television or might want to set a diagonal size and a number of other constraints on the television, but might not know anything at the moment about the restrictions on the DVD player.

A user interface, such as the one depicted in the stereo example, allowed a user to choose components from dropdown menus. The dropdown menus were generated on the fly in order to take into account all of the information that the system currently had about a component. This was used as a query to the database of all components that met that specification. Thus, the user was kept from choosing many components that would be incompatible with the system that was configured to date.

The user could also browse the current configuration and delete any requirements that were stated. (The user was not allowed to delete requirements that were inferred, but was allowed to ask how a particular requirement was deduced, thereby discovering the source of that requirement.) Once a requirement was deleted, then new dropdown menus were generated to include components that met the current set of specifications instead of the previous set.

This architecture provides a great deal of flexibility for incrementally evolving (sometimes non-monotonically evolving) specifications. It worked well to provide users with menus of choices that were recalculated as needed, with updated component lists that met the current specifications that were stated or implied about any component.

For example, if a user specified a high quality stereo system and then decided to choose an amplifier for the system, the configurator would only present options for amplifiers that had been determined to be of high quality. Description Logics are not the only modeling scheme that supports evolving specifications, but this section attempts to point out that they can be used rather easily to support evolving configuration specifications.

12.2.6 Extensible schemas

Many configuration applications find that information about components is continually updated. It is not always the case that only the simple data about components is updated but sometimes properties of the components change or new properties are discovered after an application has been encoded. Thus, it becomes important to work with a schema or a description of a component that can be updated. For example, in our home theater application, when we began development, DVD players were not in the consumer market. It later became common for home theater systems to include DVD players, and thus our schema needed to be extended with the new class – DVDPlayer – as well as with roles that were appropriate for DVD players.

This need for updatable and configurable schemas is sometimes a requirement for design. For example, in AT&T evaluation of software, one criterion is extensible schemas. Our experience in the deployed PROSE and QUESTAR configurator family was that products were extended often in practice.

12.2.7 Reasoning for incomplete information

Many configuration specifications are almost by necessity incomplete when input initially. In large systems, it may be common for one person who may be an expert in one area to input specifications for that area while another person who is an expert in another area may update the specification later. For example, in a two-person household, one person may be much more literate in audio quality and thus may input the requirements for speakers, while the others may have more interest and knowledge in video displays and thus may input specifications for the television (along with its input and output requirements). It may be important to allow specification to be done across multiple sessions as well.

One would not want a configurator that could not make deductions until all of the input requirements had been presented. For example, in the stereo system, one would want a configurator that could infer the implications of the speaker restrictions on say minimum power requirements for the amplifier, even though the television specifications had not been input yet.

Description Logics have been demonstrated to be useful at determining logical consequences of information even when that information is incomplete. They can also be used to determine information that is still required. For example, they can determine that two speakers need to be input as parts in the parts list before the configuration can be considered complete. Thus, it is not enough to say that two high quality main speakers are required but the parts list actually needs to have the actual speakers chosen before the job is considered complete.

In the home theater application, there was a one-pane display dedicated to showing which final component choices still remained before a configuration could be considered completed. The display could be used to view the current parts already implied and/or chosen along with the other components yet to be chosen. The other components could be clicked on to obtain the current description of the component so that a user could view what had been derived to date about that component. The application allowed a user to save a partial specification of a configuration for further requirements to be input at another point. The application also allowed a user to "complete" the configuration at any point that would force the system to make consistent decisions for remaining underconstrained components. The user could also inspect individual component choices and click on them and see a pulldown menu list of alternative choices that the system could have made. The user could also click on the component and view a description of the constraints that the application had determined must hold for that component. The description of the component was what was used to query the knowledge base about components that would fit the characteristics. The description could also be passed along to another user (or another application) so that it could see what constraints had been deduced so far and then have that other user (or application) either add new constraints or make the ultimate product choice, thereby facilitating collaborative configuration.

12.2.8 Inconsistency detection

Configuration applications should minimize the chances for users to generate inconsistent specifications. The stereo configurator, for example, uses the information that can be deduced about any particular component in order to form a query to the database about possible components. This greatly limits the chances that a user may choose a component in their system that will cause an inconsistent specification to result. The deployed application did not take a greater step, however, before choosing to put a component on a pulldown list. It did not make the hypothetical choice of the component for the user and then check to see if the remaining components that were still unspecified could be completed with a component in the database. (Of course, this would be an exponential search with the remaining components yet to be specified.) Thus the deployed example could still allow a user to generate an inconsistent specification – the application just made it more difficult for this to happen. The back end reasoning system was required to determine when an incremental specification became inconsistent.

Sometimes users of other deployed configurators generate a large set of constraints and want to input them into other (connected) configuration applications. Thus one additional requirement on a user friendly configurator (that is expected to interact with other configuration applications) is for the reasoner to take input constraints and determine if they are inconsistent. The PROSE configurator family, for example, supported batch input of requirements with consistency checking.

Reasoners may choose different methods of handling inconsistencies. A requirement for a configuration system is that the underlying reasoner must be able to identify the inconsistency and notify the user. A helpful reasoner will also support users by allowing them to ask how the inconsistency was deduced. The reasoner could also give users the option to "roll back" the specification to the last consistent state. For example, the CLASSIC knowledge representation system required its information to be consistent, and thus once an inconsistency was detected, it disallowed the last statement that generated the inconsistency (maintaining a separate error state for debugging support) and then rolled back to the last consistent state. This was common for early DL-based systems. Today, however, Description Logics do not necessarily require consistent axioms to function. They may allow a set of inconsistent axioms to be input and then configurators can be built that utilize the Description Logic to identify if a description is satisfiable. This model of allowing inconsistent input with a user-identified checkpoint may be a model that supports collaboration and web-oriented development most naturally.

12.2.9 Modularity

In large systems, it is important to allow multiple people to work on specifications in what appears to be a simultaneous environment. In PROSE for example, care was taken to design a set of classes and roles that a number of developers could use. Multiple users were then allowed to work on specifications of different portions of the configuration information simultaneously, with previously defined upper level classes and roles for their use in specifying more specific classes. When the users were finished with their particular component descriptions, loads were done to see if the different portions interacted. This model of individual users being in charge of specific portions of the ontology while possibly one chief ontologist is in charge of the upper level ontology is not uncommon. Cycorp, for example, publishes its upper level ontology which is maintained by a core Cycorp group while many other people develop more specialized mid-level ontologies. VerticalNet also has a number of ontologies with many different authors of specific ontologies that use an upper level ontology that is maintained by a core ontology team. Description Logics can be used to support such modeling, with PROSE being an example of one such development.

Another notion of modularity support can be considered with environmental support features. Some systems such as ONTOBUILDER [Das *et al.*, 2001] at VerticalNet have been built to support multiple users working on the same portion of an ontology in a more integrated manner. VerticalNet's system allows users to be notified if someone is modifying a portion of the ontology that they are using. While ONTOBUILDER does not have a DL back end, its input language is quite similar to OIL [Fensel *et al.*, 2001] and thus it is not a hard task to imagine that an ONTOBUILDER-like system could be integrated with today's DL systems.

12.2.10 Maintainability

Once systems are used for a long time period or are used enough so that they require support from someone other than their original author, maintainability becomes an issue. We have used examples from the stereo configurator for all of the other sections, but in this section we will draw from our experience with the PROSE–QUESTAR family of configurators. The stereo configurator has been up on the web for some years, yet it has not had many maintenance requirements because it is a demonstration system that is not updated when new stereo information becomes available. However, deployed configurators typically have help desk support and require data (and sometimes schema) updates.

There are at least three components of maintenance that require some thought when planning a configurator:

- product data updates
- product specification updates
- help desk support.

The first is the simplest. Typically, product data requires updates over time. Simple things like prices and availability need updating and sometimes small updates are made with revisions. Typically, this kind of information is not hard to update – someone who does not know much about the encoding can typically find a way to do things such as updating price fields in many applications, whether they are DL-based or not. Description Logics support this requirement since they are aimed at working with incomplete information (e.g., Subsection 12.2.7), and thus updates from incomplete to more complete information are natural for DL-based systems to handle. Similarly, an object-oriented modeling scheme may make updates simpler, but this area alone would not be enough to drive a potential user to a DL-based approach.

The second issue of updates to product specification might be viewed by a database designer as a schema update. This kind of information is typically more challenging to update in applications since it requires product specification descriptions and not just simple, data changes. It could be simple, requiring say a change to the range of a field; for example, possibly an age range may move from 18–65 to 18–70. Similarly, a business that used to accept only US currency may now accept other currencies, such as euros, requiring updates to the price field value restriction. More complicated product specification updates may be done when new components become available (thus requiring someone to model the new components and their features). These types of specification updates are facilitated in Description Logics by the kinds of features that we noted in Subsections 12.2.6, 12.2.5, 12.2.1, and 12.2.9.

The third issue of help desk support has been noted as a strength of DL-based systems. One of the goals with the PROSE configurator systems was to allow the help desk personnel to appear to perform at a level above the amount of training they had on individual products. The enabling infrastructure toolset was to provide information to the help desk staff at the time they needed it in real time (instead of requiring them to have been previously trained on products so that they could answer questions from knowledge that they had learned instead of from knowledge that they could look up on demand).

The tools were to allow them to explain any of the deductions that the system made when customers called in asking why something was (or was not) in their configuration and also allowed them to answer questions about why configurations were (or were not) valid. This was most facilitated by the functionality described in Subsection 12.2.4 but also by others such as Subsection 12.2.8. Similarly, they could answer hypothetical questions such as "what would happen if I chose component X instead of component Y in my configuration?" The goal was to meet individual customer needs without requiring engineering support to answer such questions. Our claim is that it is a combination of the strengths of Description Logics as discussed in the previous sections that helps support maintainability of the applications and in fact, helps support maintainability by people who have not taken classes in Description Logics or knowledge representation.

12.3 The PROSE and QUESTAR family of configurators

The longest-lived and most prolific family of DL-based configurators has been the PROSE and QUESTAR product line [Wright *et al.*, 1993; McGuinness and Wright, 1998b]. AT&T began development on configuration problems in 1988 in response to business requests for help in the streamlining of the Engineer, Furnish, and Install process. The goal in the process is to solicit a specification request from the customer through the sales process, and then engineer a solution that can be "furnished" and of course manufactured and delivered to the customer in a timely and cost effective manner. The initial goals of the project were to decrease the time from specification to installation and to minimize the impact of contradictions in the specifications and mistakes in the engineering. The initial configurator was built for a fiber optic transmission system (the FT Series G) although the initial deployment was for a digital cross-connect system (the DACS IV-2000).

The initial configurator was successful enough that a family of configurators was built around it. The history of the project proceeded from a research involvement to one of development. AT&T's research division collaborated with developers in order to build the initial system. Researchers helped generate and critique the initial conceptual models and programming effort. Developers generated the initial system but with interactive assistance from research. As the product evolved, project needs emerged for developer independence and an environment was produced that allowed domain knowledgeable people to input configuration rules in a language that was comfortable to them. Developers had the lead responsibility; in the initial deployment they had the assistance of research but in the second through seventeenth system they required little assistance from research for either generation or maintenance of individual configurators. As the development environment evolved, the developers saw much less of the DL back end – essentially the DL back end verified input and deduced conclusions and was otherwise hidden behind the interface of the system.

There are a few points worth noting about this family of applications. First, the configurator family has shown longevity with some configurators deployed a decade after work began. Second, the majority of the generation and maintenance of the configurators was done by people who knew very little about Description Logics (thus showing empirical evidence that applications do not require PhDs in Description Logics to build and maintain them). An evolution interface was developed by domain literate developers aimed at users who knew the products but did not know Description Logics or sometimes computer science at all. This interface allowed users both to maintain configurators and also to generate new configurators in the same product family. Third, there is a consensus that the DL-based approach both facilitates conceptual modeling (e.g., [McGuinness and Wright, 1998b]), and also makes maintenance much easier. Ford Motor Company has also stated similar findings with its long-lived DL-based configurator applications.

12.4 Summary

We have introduced the problem of configuration, describing briefly the nature of the problem and why many communities consider it important. We have described properties inherent in the problem that make it an area for which one might consider DL-based approaches. We have provided examples of all of properties in the setting of a stereo configurator, mentioning how a DL-based approach was used to solve the problem. We made parallel connections to the much larger configurators used for telecommunications equipment that also included the same issues and had DL-based solutions.

We have also introduced the largest family of DL-based configurators – the PROSE–QUESTAR family of systems (noting also that at least one other commercial configurator at Ford Motor Company also has a similar lifespan and a similar Description Logic-based approach). We observe that the PROSE–QUESTAR configurator family has been in continuous use for over a decade and has configured billions of dollars of equipment. We finally note that the commercial configuration examples with long histories state that the DL approach has alleviated the problems of conceptual modeling and configurator maintenance. Additionally, we speculate that this general architecture that meets the list of configuration needs might also be used in problem areas with similar needs.

Acknowledgements

While of course all errors in the chapter are the responsibility of the author, the chapter has been enhanced by contributions from a number of people. Much of the discussion has been in the setting of either PROSE–QUESTAR or CLASSIC work that has been done in conjunction with Jon Wright, Lori Alperin Resnick, Peter Patel-Schneider, Ron Brachman, Alex Borgida, Charles Isbell, Elia Weixelbaum, Gregg Vesonder, Harry Moore, Pat Saleh, Charlie Foster, Chris Welty, Matt Parker, and a number of other important contributors. Also, Nestor Rychtyckyj provided many valuable comments on a previous version of this chapter.

13

Medical Informatics

Alan Rector

Abstract

Description Logics and related formalisms are being applied in at least five applications in medical informatics – terminology, intelligent user interfaces, decision support and semantic indexing, language technology, and systems integration. Important issues include size, complexity, connectivity, and the wide range of granularity required – medical terminologies require on the order of 250,000 concepts, some involving a dozen or more conjuncts with deep nesting; the nature of anatomy and physiology is that everything connects to everything else; and notions to be represented range from psychology to molecular biology. Technical issues for expressivity have focused on problems of part–whole relations and the need to provide "frame-like" functionality – i.e., the ability to determine efficiently what can sensibly be said about any particular concept and means of handling at least limited cases of defaults with exceptions. There are also significant problems with "semantic normalization" and "clinical pragmatics" because understanding medical notions often depends on implicit knowledge and some notions defy easy logical formulation. The two best-known efforts – *Open*GALEN and SNOMED-RT – both use idiosyncratic Description Logics with generally limited expressivity but specialized extensions to cope with issues around part–whole and other transitive relations. There is also a conflict between the needs for re-use and the requirement for easy understandability by domain expert authors. *Open*GALEN has coped with this conflict by introducing a layered architecture with a high level "Intermediate Representation" which insulates authors from the details of the Description Logic, which is treated as an "assembly language" rather than the primary medium for expressing the ontology.

13.1 Background and history

13.1.1 Knowledge representation in medical applications

Description Logics and related frame-based and conceptual graph formalisms are being applied in at least five applications in medical informatics:

- Terminology development and, more broadly, the representation of information in health records.
- Intelligent user interfaces.
- Decision support and semantic indexing.
- Semantics-oriented natural language processing.
- Semantic integration of information systems.

The seminal early work in the use of Description Logics in medical applications focused on the dilemma between expressiveness and tractability. Doyle and Patil [1991] attempted to apply NIKL to medical vocabulary and came to the firm conclusion that the NIKL TBox language was too restrictive to be useful for this purpose. More explicitly they despaired of users accepting the restrictions of minimally expressive TBox languages and predicted that users would find "work-arounds" which defeated the logical rigor which was their raison d'être. A first attempt at a more appropriate representation was made by Jang and Patil [1989].

However, as providing a standard controlled medical vocabulary came to be seen as one of the central issues of medical informatics, some researchers saw "compositional systems" as the only plausible route forward. The perceived urgency of the task motivated "pragmatic" approaches. Masarie *et al.* [1991] used a large frame-based AI environment to produce an "interlingua" linking three of the then current terminologies in one of the exploratory projects to what became the Unified Medical Language System [Evans, 1987].

Although the US National Library of Medicine chose to use lexical methods to cross map existing terminologies rather than to develop Masarie's approach to a logical interlingua, the project gave rise indirectly to the CANON group who became strong advocates of formal representations in medical terminologies [Cimino, 1994; Evans *et al.*, 1994]. A special issue of the *American Journal of Medical Informatics* (volume 1, issue 3) summarised the material from its seminal workshop.

The CANON group brought together several other strands of then current work:

- The Medical Entities Dictionary developed by Cimino *et al.* [1989] as a large semantic network.

- The related GALEN [Rector *et al.*, 1993; Rector and Nowlan, 1994] and PEN&PAD [Nowlan *et al.*, 1991a; 1991b; Nowlan and Rector, 1991] programs from Europe.
- A series of projects on the use of Sowa's conceptual graphs for representing medical vocabularies, the best known of which is the one by Campbell *et al.* [1994] but the series includes also work by Bell *et al.* [1994].

In addition, the group interacted with more linguistic work by Friedman *et al.* [1994] and Sager *et al.* [1994] which, along with Tuttle [1994], served as a contrast and a reality check.

There have been two large scale outcomes of this work:

- The SNOMED-Reference Terminology (SNOMED-RT) and SNOMED-Clinical Terms (SNOMED-CT) projects under the College of American Pathologists,[1] which seek to produce a terminology all of whose concepts are represented in a subset of KRSS and formally classified, and which were released at the end of 2000 [Spackman *et al.*, 1997]. A further cooperation with the UK Clinical Terms project is to produce an international version to be released in 2002.[2]
- *Open*GALEN, which seeks to produce a reference ontology in a specialized Description Logic for use in developing and managing other terminologies and indexing knowledge required for decision support, user interfaces and other knowledge management tasks.[3]

In addition there have been a number of projects on language processing in medicine which have included significant work on formal knowledge representation, particularly the work by Hahn using LOOM [Hahn *et al.*, 1999a; 1999c], which has produced a range of large scale results in both language engineering and ontologies proper, and by Zweigenbaum using a specially restricted frame representation in a similar way [Zweigenbaum *et al.*, 1995]. Another important task is the indexing and retrieval of medical literature, which has been addressed by McGuinness [1999].

Applications of ontologies within medicine, not based on Description Logics, include the work by Musen [1998] on re-usable problem solving methods and ontology driven knowledge acquisition in the PROTÉGÉ project which, at least so far, has specifically not used a Description Logic or other formal basis for its ontology, but rather based its ontologies around the OKBC and DAML standards. As these standards are converging with Description Logics in OIL and DAML+OIL [Fensel *et al.*, 2001;

---

[1] http://www.snomed.org/
[2] http://www.coding.nhsia.nhs.uk/
[3] http://www.opengalen.org

Horrocks and Patel-Schneider, 2001], convergence with PROTÉGÉ is under active discussion.

Stefannelli and Schreiber likewise have produced a body of work based around adaptations of the KADS architecture using ontologies as the basis for intelligent systems and agent architectures [Schreiber *et al.*, 1993; Vanheijst *et al.*, 1995; Falasconi *et al.*, 1997].

Another major effort on knowledge representation in medicine is the Digital Anatomist project [Rosse *et al.*, 1998; Agoncillo *et al.*, 1999; Mejino and Rosse, 1999], which currently does not use a Description Logic but which represents a benchmark for a comprehensive, carefully curated and validated knowledge base based on carefully analyzed ontological commitments and distinctions manifest in a meticulously defined hierarchy of high level concepts such as "organ", "tissue", etc. It poses a challenge to any system aspiring to a comprehensive representation of medical knowledge.

13.1.2 The medical environment

Behind most of these applications is the aspiration to re-use clinical data – either to integrate systems, to link patient records to decision support and knowledge management, or to re-use information collected in the course of patient care for management, remuneration, quality assurance or research.

There has been a widespread move to greater integration and to "Electronic Patient Records" (EPRs), also known variously as "Computer based Patient Records" (CPRs) or (CBPRs). The goal behind these moves is threefold:

- To improve patient care through providing better information on current patients, warnings, and decision support to healthcare professionals – e.g., to be able to identify patients' known problems and treatments, warn of potential drug interactions and contraindications, or suggest management based on established guidelines.
- To capture improved information for planning and management within healthcare institutions by re-using information collected at the point of care for all secondary functions – e.g., to re-use diagnosis and treatment information collected during patient care for statistical reporting, quality assurance, and remuneration.
- To integrate the disparate information systems typical of most healthcare institutions.

Major reports justifying electronic patient records have been issued, amongst others, the Institute of Medicine [Dick and Steen, 1991], the Computer based Patient Record Institute (CPRI), and the UK National Health

Service [NHS National Health Service Executive, 1998]. This pressure is increasing with moves to greater clinical accountability and concern with clinical errors [Kohn *et al.*, 2000]. That every patient should have an electronic medical record is now government policy in a number of western countries, including the UK and US.

Despite the widespread use of management, billing, and laboratory systems in medicine, the vast majority of the information required for such medical records currently exists only as unstructured narrative text. Capturing more of this information in structured form is a central task of medical informatics. The absence of a standard "controlled vocabulary" or "coding system" is seen as a major barrier to this task [Sittig, 1994] while its presence is a key to its success [Rossi Mori and Consorti, 1999]. Hence several countries have mandated, or will soon mandate, standard terminologies for use in medical records.

However, most existing terminologies or "coding systems" are monohierarchical classifications developed either for public health reporting (the International Classification of Diseases – ICD) or bibliographic retrieval (the Medical Subject Headings – MeSH). They are much too coarse grained for recording care of individual patients. Attempts to extend them to make them finer grained have run into combinatorial explosions with some systems now running to over 250,000 "terms" which are beyond manual maintenance. Their structure is largely implicit, and writing software to use them is therefore problematic. An alternative faceted system, SNOMED-International, has existed for some time, but has no strong semantics defining the relationships amongst the facets and has always been considered difficult to use outside its origin in Pathology – both because of its unfamiliar structure and an organization which reflects its origins in pathology and often does not cater for the needs of other medical specialities.

The US National Library of Medicine has mounted a major program to tame this chaos in its Unified Medical Language System (UMLS) which cross maps, insofar as possible, all of the general and special purpose vocabularies [Lindberg *et al.*, 1993]. It has developed into a massive (15 Gb) cross reference and cataloging system.[4] However, although cross referenced, the Unified Medical Language System is fundamentally limited by the nature of the underlying systems which it cross maps. It itself provides only a minimal amount of additional semantic information – less than 200 categories in a loose semantic network.

---

[4] http://umlsks.nlm.nih.gov/

Hence the hope by various researchers that DL-based ontologies can provide a better solution for at least some of the problems of terminology, decision support, language processing and integration.

13.2 Example applications

13.2.1 Description Logics in terminology development and "coding"

13.2.1.1 SNOMED-RT*: tightly coupled development and pre-coordination*

SNOMED-RT is a cooperative enterprise between the College of American Pathologists and Kaiser Permanente, a large health maintenance organization. It has re-represented in a subset of KRSS the information in the SNOMED-International. In a first approximation, the SNOMED facets for anatomy, morphology, function, etc. have been turned into roles, hasTopography, hasMorphology, etc. [Campbell *et al.*, 1998]. The initial mechanical translation has then been re-modeled in place by domain experts using a set of tools with a highly developed change management mechanism [Campbell, 1998]. The development methodology has placed a high emphasis on achieving repeatability of domain experts' results, and made extensive use of lexical tools to suggest additional relationships which are implied by the rubrics but may not be explicitly present in the faceted representation; for example the term "retinal vasculitis" was correctly related to "eye" but not to "vasculitis" (inflammation of the blood vessels) in early versions of SNOMED-International [Campbell *et al.*, 1996]

The first released version consists of a pre-enumerated set of 180,000 or more disease and procedure codes, each defined in an ontology represented in KRSS and classified accordingly into an acyclic directed graph. The intention appears to be a standard pre-coordinated (i.e., pre-defined) set of concepts and associated terms to be presented and used in a form analogous to that of traditional hierarchical coding schemes.

Recently a collaboration has been formed between SNOMED-RT and the UK Clinical Terms (Read Codes) project to produce a combined product which is aimed at being a standard English controlled vocabulary for medicine. Details have not yet been announced, but it is assumed that the form will be closely related to that of SNOMED-RT.

The ontology used is relatively shallow, including under ten roles in its pre-release version, and avoiding embedded expressions wherever possible. However, the standard semantics of KRSS has been enhanced by the inclusion of right-identities to cater for part–whole relations (see Subsection 13.3.2).

SNOMED-RT itself includes no tools or transformations for data entry or for other applications involving dynamic post-coordination. However, a range of tools based on SNOMED-RT, including the authoring suite, is available from the company that supplies the development tools (Apelon[5]), which are descended in part from K-REP, a DL-style KR system used in many of the early experiments which led up to the project [Mays *et al.*, 1991a; 1996].

13.2.1.2 GALEN : *loosely coupled development and post-coordination*

GALEN is the result of a series of European Commission funded projects and its ontologies and specifications as well as some of the tools are available in open source form from `http://www.opengalen.org/`.

The GALEN tools are designed for loosely coupled development, and the ontology is aimed primarily at post-coordinated applications, such as intelligent user interfaces, and tools to empower users to adapt core terminologies to their specific needs. It is based around the idea of a dynamic "terminology server" rather than an enumerated table of pre-coordinated terms [Nowlan *et al.*, 1994; Rector *et al.*, 1995a], although there is a limited set of common concepts pre-defined.

An important feature of GALEN is the clean separation of functions within the server architecture:

- logical representation in the Description Logic;
- language generation and text recognition;
- mapping to and from existing coding systems;
- indexing of non-terminological information;
- additional calculations such as unit and coordinate transformations.

GALEN's ontology was created de novo but with close reference to the standard classifications, particularly the International Classification of Diseases. It uses the GRAIL Description Logic [Rector *et al.*, 1997] whose core includes the subset of operations of the KRSS used by SNOMED-RT, including transitive roles, with the addition of inverse roles and role subsumption. (See Subsubsection 13.3.2.2 for a further discussion of transitive roles and related issues.) In addition GRAIL provides a construct "sanctioning", analogous to slot definitions in frame systems or function signatures in object-oriented systems, which supports answering queries of the form "what can be said about this?" GRAIL is implemented using a graph comparison algorithm which, although known to be incomplete, has still proved to be extremely useful in practice.

---

[5] `http://www.apelon.com/`

GALEN's most distinctive feature is the use in authoring tools for domain experts of a much simplified "intermediate representation" which is then translated into the Description Logic, which is relegated to the status of an "assembly language" (see Subsection 13.5.1 below).

The GALEN project has also devoted much effort to mapping to existing coding systems – a more complex task than is at first apparent because of the idiosyncratic construction of the target schemes. Each code in such schemes is mapped to the disjunction of one or more GALEN concepts. A GALEN concept is taken as being mapped to the most specific code mapped to a subsuming concept, and conversely, a code is mapped to all those GALEN concepts subsumed by its mapping except those subsumed by a more specific mapping. This mechanism deals with almost all of the complex sets of exclusions and inclusions in the International Classification of Diseases – e.g., "Hypertension excluding hypertension in pregnancy" is coped with automatically simply by mapping to the general concept "Hypertension", because there is a mapping to a specific concept "Hypertension in pregnancy" which will cause it, and its descendants, to be excluded automatically. In the very few cases where conflicts occur they are resolved by separate exception-handling tables.

A similar mechanism provides a surrogate for inheritance with exceptions as a means of indexing information ranging from triggers for decision support rules to data entry forms and user interface specifications. Any information may be labeled and attached to the ontology, and the server provides operations to retrieve the set of all the values "inherited". The GALEN server makes no attempt to reduce the set to a single value; if required this is a matter for the client application.

13.2.2 Description Logics and language processing

13.2.2.1 Language analysis and information extraction

Most medical information originates and is stored as natural language text. Medical texts present classic "sublanguages" with peculiarities of vocabulary and syntax. Many utterances are telegraphic or highly elliptical, and cannot be easily parsed without semantic knowledge. These features seem natural to combine with lexicalized grammars in which most or all syntactic information is stored with the lexical item rather than in a separate grammar, e.g., Tree-Adjoining Grammars (TAG) [Joshi, 1994], Lexical-Functional Grammar, and Combinatory Categorical Grammar (CCG) [Steedman, 1996].[6]

---

[6] However, it should be noted that the classic medical natural language work, the Linguistic String Project [Sager *et al.*, 1987; 1994], while it makes extensive use of semantics, makes no use of ontologies or related mechanisms.

Hahn's work on medSYNDICATE [Hahn *et al.*, 1999a], provides a detailed example using a specially constructed ontology in LOOM. The medSYNDICATE architecture features close coupling of the ontology ("Domain knowledge base") with the parser and extensive use of learning techniques to deepen and extend both the ontology and the grammar. It uses the integrity conditions, and conceptual constraints, and cardinality restrictions in the ontology to reduce ambiguity and select plausible interpretations. It makes use of knowledge within the ontology to complete ellipses within the original text – e.g., to know that the connection between a gland and its product is "secretes". It also makes extensive use of partonomic information using a unique approach discussed in Subsection 13.3.2.3 below.

Rassinoux and Baud have used the GALEN ontology to augment a strongly semantic approach likewise to constrain ambiguous or incomplete parsings [Baud *et al.*, 1993; Rassinoux, 1998]. Zweigenbaum has used a restricted application specific ontology to similar purpose [Zweigenbaum *et al.*, 1995].

Ceusters, by contrast, attempted to use natural language processing to understand the text attached to codes (the "rubrics") to build and make mappings to the GALEN ontology. Ceusters' work was based on a range of pre-existing tools and experienced significant difficulty because of serious differences in the information-processing-oriented ontology developed by GALEN and the language-oriented ontologies which underlay his tools. For example, the distinctions between location and part–whole relations and the distinctions amongst different part–whole relations have no direct linguistic counterpart. An adaptation of the GALEN Intermediate representation was used to bridge this gap, but with only partial success [Ceusters and Spyns, 1997; Ceusters, 1998; Ceusters *et al.*, 1999].

13.2.2.2 Language generation, user interfaces, and quality assurance

Any ontology intended for use by domain experts presents a problem of quality assurance, or curation, by those experts. Any post-coordinated use of an ontology also presents a serious problem for the user interface – standard DL expressions are not acceptable for most uses by most domain experts. Even if they are simplified to an "intermediate representation" or transformed to conceptual graphs, the complexity is too great for most domain experts to take in quickly.

One way to make such expressions accessible to users is to generate language expressions from them. Not only are the language expressions more readable, they are usually much more compact. GALEN has found language generation to be essential in virtually all applications involving post-coordination including most approaches to independent quality assurance of the ontology.

One of the major applications of GALEN technology has been by the French government to produce unambiguous definitions for their new national classification of surgical procedures. Curiously, in this application, the usual language generation goals of concise idiomatic expression do not apply. The value of the technique is its pedantic, but completely unambiguous, presentation of the underlying formal definitions. Once the definitions are agreed and quality assured, idiomatic "preferred terms" can be composed manually where required [Baud *et al.*, 1997; Rodrigues *et al.*, 1997].

13.2.3 Decision support, indexing, and re-usable ontologies for problem solving

Many decision support methodologies, notably Musen's PROTÉGÉ and AEÓN [Tu *et al.*, 1995; Musen *et al.*, 1996; Musen, 1998; Grosso *et al.*, 1999] and Stefanelli's GAMES [Schreiber *et al.*, 1993; Vanheijst *et al.*, 1995; Falasconi *et al.*, 1997], are based around the existence of a domain ontology, but in general the ontologies are constructed specifically for one application and have proved less re-usable than the problem-solving methods they support. Both use ontologies primarily as frame systems.

A more specific use of the classification reasoning in Description Logics is provided by GALEN's work on drug ontologies carried out in collaboration with the PRODIGY project on computerized guidelines for prescribing in UK general practice [Johnson *et al.*, 2000]. Traditional classifications for diseases and drugs have only a single axis of generalization which conflates several different criteria. For example, standard drug classifications conflate indication (e.g., for "treatment of asthma"), molecular effects (e.g., "stimulates alpha adrenergic receptors"), physiological effects (e.g., "dilates the airways") and chemical structure. As result, even simple generalizations such as "steroids reduce inflammation" are difficult to operationalize using the classification because various steroids may be classified in many different ways – under anti-asthmatic drugs, topical skin preparations, anti-rheumatic drugs, etc.

Separating the conflated axes and then using them as the basis of formal descriptions which can be classified by a Description Logic offers a potential solution. After early prototype demonstrations [Solomon and Heathfield, 1994], GALEN is now being used to construct an ontology of drugs and related conditions to be used as part of the PRODIGY project, a system of protocols for prescribing for patients with chronic diseases which is being developed by the UK Department of Health [Solomon *et al.*, 1999; Wroe *et al.*, 2000].

Experience to date suggests that the ontology provides efficiently precise indexing at the varying levels of granularity required and can provide a framework for the necessary default reasoning via the mechanisms described in Subsection 13.2.1.1 for coding. Further evaluation awaits the next phase of the project.

13.2.4 Intelligent data entry

Data capture is the largest single barrier to greater information use in healthcare. GALEN developed from the PEN&PAD project [Nowlan *et al.*, 1991a; 1991b] which aimed to improve user interfaces for healthcare professionals and which placed particular emphasis on data entry by attempting to construct forms which would capture most, if not all, of the information currently recorded as narrative text.

The ontology provides two services in PEN&PAD – both related to the question "What can be sensibly said in this situation?":

• Indicating how a given concept could be refined by modifiers.
• Indexing the form associated with each starting concept – often a disease or a symptom. Each such form may contain numerous subforms allowing further refinement of a concept or inclusion of further less common signs and symptoms.

The total number of forms required to provide a clinical interface is very large – certainly hundreds of thousands and possibly more. The goal of the system is to assemble forms dynamically from the indexed "recipes" in such a way that it would fail soft – i.e., that forms for important frequently encountered situations could be highly tailored at a very fine granularity whereas rarely encountered areas could be served by a form related only to the broad class of condition. In its commercial version, Clinergy™, a knowledge base of under 10,000 concepts and a similar number of auxiliary facts and forms specifications covered essentially all data entry for British general practice – a task requiring several hundreds of thousands of forms.[7]

Related systems were developed by Poon and Fagan [1994] and Lussier *et al.* [1992]. using conceptual graph representations of SNOMED-International.

13.2.5 Integration

A major ostensible goal for common terminologies in medicine is system integration [Evans *et al.*, 1994; Rector *et al.*, 1995b; Spackman *et al.*, 1997].

---

[7] See http://www.galen-organisation.com/furthertut.html for further information.

While specialized terminology systems are being used in a few places as part of an enterprise wide effort at integration [Rocha *et al.*, 1993; 1994; Cimino *et al.*, 1998], ontologies based on Description Logics have yet to be demonstrated convincingly in this context. Much of the reason for this is the sheer scale and coverage required for such mediation tasks.

13.3 Technical issues in medical ontologies

13.3.1 Issues of scaling

13.3.1.1 Size

The fundamental issue in any medical ontology intended to capture clinical terminology is scale. The smallest useful medical terminologies contain on the order of 10,000 concepts; "comprehensive" terminologies require on the order of 250,000 or more concepts. The *Open*GALEN model of basic anatomy alone contains over 5000 concepts, the model of surgical procedures some 15,000. SNOMED-RT currently has some 180,000 concepts, and the combined Clinical Terms (Read Codes) SNOMED-CT expects to have substantially more. The Unified Medical Language System has issued nearly a million "Unique Concept Identifiers" with over a million lexical variants.

13.3.1.2 Connectivity

Medical ontologies are notoriously highly connected. Most medical concepts depend on anatomy, and every anatomical structure is ultimately connected to every other, at least trivially, by virtue of being part of the body. The causal and functional interrelationships are of similar density. SNOMED-RT reduces connectivity by omitting inverses. GRAIL supports role inverses and transitive roles, but GALEN's ontology explicitly avoids expressions of the form "A which is part of B which has part C", for which the classifier is known to be incomplete. It is not known whether complete and decidable reasoning for a Description Logic including role transitivity and inverses is practical for a large scale comprehensive medical ontology: some form of heuristic constraint on the depth or computational resources used for individual inferences may prove necessary.

13.3.1.3 Range of granularity or organization

Common medical notions span the range from the molecular to the physiological to the behavioural. To form a truly re-usable framework for medical knowledge representation, the ontology needs to encompass concepts such as "substances which cause mood change and tremor by binding to specific receptor sites". If the promise of "genomics" is to be realized, this may soon need to be extended to include concepts which add "... by stimulating the expression of a genetic sequence homologous to some specified allele in some reference source".

13.3.1.4 Complexity of concepts to be represented

The areas of medicine most resistant to traditional manual terminologies and therefore most ripe for formal representation tend to include very complicated concepts. For example, a not untypical surgical procedure rubric to be represented might be "Removal of the gall bladder using an endoscope inserted via an abdominal incision" or "Fixation of fracture of the femur by means of insertion of pins". More complex rubrics may go on for several lines in their natural language formulation. The full expansion in a Description Logic may include several dozen conjuncts nested five or six levels deep. This complexity is not an academic artifact; these are the categories used to determine payment, quality of outcome, and prognosis.

13.3.1.5 How much to represent – detail of the ontology

SNOMED-RT has a relatively simple ontology with less than ten roles. The GALEN ontology is relatively complex, with some fifty roles, including seven different partonomic roles, and sharp distinctions between two-dimensional and three-dimensional objects. The Digital Anatomist appears to be a representation of similar complexity to GALEN's anatomical representation. At the extreme, Gangemi *et al.* [1996] have produced a high level ontology which claims strong philosophical grounding but is yet more elaborate. How much of this complexity is required for which purposes is still not established.

13.3.2 Issues of expressivity: part–whole relations

13.3.2.1 Transitivity and anatomy

A large fraction of all medical terminology is based on anatomy and dependent on part–whole relations. "Fracture of foot" must be classified as "trauma to lower extremity", "repair of the aortic valve" must be classified as an "operation on heart", etc.

Conflation of part–whole and IS-A relations is ubiquitous in informal clinical classifications and thesauri [Rector, 1998]. In general this works because for the key locative attributes it is, in general, true that a disease of the part is a disease of the whole and a procedure on a part is a procedure on the whole. This is closely related to CYC's TRANSFERS-THRO notion and to some frame systems' notion of inheritance of certain slots via relations other than IS-A.

13.3.2.2 GALEN's specialisedBy axioms and SNOMED-RT's right identity axioms

All medical ontologies must face this problem in one way or another. GALEN allows axioms equivalent to $R \circ S \sqsubseteq R$ (R specialisedBy S in GRAIL notation). SNOMED-RT allows the declaration that S is a right identity for R, which appears to be equivalent [Spackman, 2000].

Hence if R is hasLocation and S is isPartOf, then

$$\exists \mathsf{hasLocation}.(\exists \mathsf{isPartOf}.\mathsf{Heart}) \sqsubseteq \exists \mathsf{hasLocation}.\mathsf{Heart}$$

where hasLocation is the relation used to link lesions and diseases to anatomy. Given axioms such as that

$$\mathsf{AorticValve} \sqsubseteq \exists \mathsf{isPartOf}.\mathsf{Heart},$$

the required inferences that lesions of the aortic valve are lesions of the heart follows, i.e., it can be inferred that

$$\exists \mathsf{hasLocation}.\mathsf{AorticValve} \sqsubseteq \exists \mathsf{hasLocation}.\mathsf{Heart}.$$

There are, in practice, a variety of other situations in which this construct seems essential, for example to say that the "risk of a syndrome involving a disease" is subsumed by a "risk of the disease itself".

GALEN also makes extensive use of the implication of such axioms for the inverse roles, i.e., $S^- \circ R^- \sqsubseteq R^-$. For example, let S be isSubProcessOf and R be isActedOnBy, then S^- and R^- are hasSubprocess and actsOn respectively. The implication of such an axiom for the inverse roles then allows us to express the rule that surgical procedures can be said to act on all those structures acted on by their subprocedures, e.g.:

$$\exists \mathsf{hasSubprocess}.(\exists \mathsf{actsOn}.\mathsf{FemoralArtery}) \sqsubseteq \exists \mathsf{actsOn}.\mathsf{FemoralArtery}.$$

This is a practical example. The femoral artery is the usual route by which the heart is catheterized. Without such inferred subsumptions, cardiac catheterization would not be found as a target for the procedure – e.g., by a decision support system seeking to identify possible causes of damage to the femoral artery. Numerous parts of the classification of surgical procedures depend on such inferences.

The GRAIL language allows chains of such axioms, which can imply complex paths. Such axioms also interact strongly with the role hierarchy. Re-representing these paths as regular expressions of roles taking into account the role hierarchy is a current topic of research.

13.3.2.3 The "triples" approach

Hahn *et al.* [1999c; 1999b] have developed an alternative representation for partonomic relations based on what they have termed "SEP-triples", which captures much partonomic reasoning within a framework compatible with the standard $\mathcal{ALC}$ Description Logic. In the SEP-triple formulation, each anatomical part X is represented by a parent concept X_s, and two subsumed concepts X_e and X_p. X_e represents the entity as a whole, and X_p the concept of its parts. For all parts Y of X, X_p subsumes Y_s, and since Y_s subsumes both Y_e and Y_p, both the entire part Y_e and all of its parts Y_p are subsumed by the parts of X.

$$Y_p \sqsubseteq Y_s \sqsubseteq X_p \sqsubseteq X_s$$
$$X_p \sqsubseteq \exists \mathsf{anatomicalPartOf}.X_e.$$

This captures the transitive relation, i.e., that any part of Y is a part of X.

For invariant anatomical relations, a separate existentially qualified role called $\mathsf{hasAnatomicalPart}$ links X_e to Y_e.

$$X_e \sqsubseteq \exists \mathsf{hasAnatomicalPart}.Y_e.$$

This scheme allows Hahn to capture the notion that something is always part of the whole if it is present, but that it may not necessarily be present (e.g., that it may have been removed or be congenitally absent) – this is achieved by omitting the third axiom.

This allows inferences such as that a disease of a part must be a disease of the whole structure (s) node, but not of the whole taken as in its entirety (e) node. By careful selection of which of the three members of an SEP-triple is used in an assertion, it appears to be possible to be selective about which properties are "inherited". For example: "diseases of parts are diseases of the whole", but "surfaces of parts are not surfaces of the whole". Hence in Hahn's schema, "surface of" should always refer to an entity (e) node representing the entire object, whereas diseases should refer to the structure (s) node representing the complex of the entire object and all of its parts.

Detailed comparison of the expressiveness of SEP-triples with SNOMED-RT's right identities and GALEN's `specialisedBy` axioms is not yet known. However, the scheme presents a number of advantages and is relatively easy to implement with existing classifier technology.

13.3.2.4 Construct not implemented in any major medical ontology

Padgham and Lambrix [1994] point out a number of other potential patterns for relationships between parts and wholes of which at least one is potentially important for anatomical reasoning but not implemented in any current Description Logic. This formalizes the pattern that from "the hand is part of the arm" we may infer that "the skin of the hand is a part of the skin of the arm". One way to capture the essence of this notion formally would be to allow axioms of the form $R \circ S \sqsubseteq S \circ R$ so that we have

$$\text{isLayerOf} \circ \text{isPartOf} \sqsubseteq \text{isPartOf} \circ \text{isLayerOf},$$

from which may be inferred, for example,

$$\exists\text{isLayerOf}.(\exists\text{isPartOf}.\text{Arm}) \sqsubseteq \exists\text{isPartOf}.(\exists\text{isLayerOf}.\text{Arm}).$$

The GALEN ontology makes the necessary distinctions between different partonomic relations but the GRAIL language does not implement this inference.

13.3.3 Other issues of expressivity

Both GALEN and SNOMED-RT use Description Logics with a very limited range of core constructors – usually only existential quantification and conjunction. Both even exclude conjunctions of primitives. Neither uses universal quantification in its constructors, although GRAIL's "sanctioning" mechanism provides constraints which serve some of the same functions [Rector *et al.*, 1997]. (Hahn uses LOOM, but exploits only a limited subset of the concept language.) On the other hand, both include constructs for transitive relations as described above. Two other issues deserve mention.

13.3.3.1 Negation

Neither GALEN nor SNOMED-RT uses negation, at least in the subset of the DL used in the ontology itself. This reflects real questions about the appropriate interpretation of negative statements in clinical records. In the context of medical records, there needs to be a clear differentiation at all levels between "false" and "not done" or "unknown". GALEN simulates some of the effects in the ontology by the use of "modalities" such as "presence/absence" and "done/not-done" [Rector and Rogers, 2002; Rector *et al.*, 2002].

13.3.3.2 General inclusion axioms

GALEN makes extensive use of a subset of general inclusion axioms – i.e., axioms which state that one defined concept is classified under another concept. In GALEN the subsuming term is restricted to be a conjunction of existentially qualified constructed concepts. GALEN uses such expressions for two purposes:

- To indicate which structures, states and processes are normal, abnormal but harmless, or pathological, i.e., to be treated as "diseases". In many cases it is the presence of specific modifiers which implies that a structure or process is "pathological".
- To bridge levels of granularity and add implied meaning, e.g., to indicate that "ulcer of stomach" really occurs in the "lining of the stomach" or to cope with normalization as discussed in Subsection 13.4.2.2.

Many Description Logics have explicitly disallowed general inclusion axioms because of the difficulty of devising suitable algorithms and worries about intractability. However, motivated by GALEN, Horrocks has shown effective optimizations for Description Logics including general inclusion axioms. Furthermore, he has shown that all such axioms in GALEN are of a particular form which can be transformed so as to be "absorbed" within term definitions, and therefore reasoned with relatively efficiently [Horrocks and Rector, 1996; Horrocks *et al.*, 1996; Horrocks, 1997b; 1998b].

13.3.4 Frame-like behavior

The use of Description Logics in both decision support and data entry systems stemmed from the use of frame systems to manage default inheritance and identify the slots relevant to a particular object. Neither is easy to implement directly in Description Logics. Both are particularly important in medical applications. Because of their size and variability, exhaustive manual enumeration of cases is neither practical initially nor maintainable.

13.3.4.1 Defaults and indexing

A major function of an ontology in a decision support system is to index information. However, the natural representation for a domain expert of this indexing is usually in terms of generalizations with exceptions. For example drug indications, interactions and side effects are all almost invariably expressed as general principles plus exceptions (chemical structure, biochemical and physiological actions can usually be treated as being indefeasible). To require all statements to be indefeasible in the domain users' environment drastically limits its usability and usefulness.

GALEN's approach is to attach "extrinsic" statements to the ontology and provide operations in the server which deliver all potential most specific candidates as described in Subsection 13.2.1.2. Experience has shown that if the ontology is well constructed, the incidence of conflict is small and almost always represents a real requirement for additional information. Often this information is application specific – how seriously a drug's side effects should be viewed in a given situation, for example, or which of several minor variant codes matches the World Health Organization's detailed coding criteria – and not appropriate to a re-usable ontology.

It has been suggested that similar behavior could be achieved by "compiling" all defaults at the user level to explicit exclusions in the underlying Description Logic. A practical demonstration of this approach on a large scale in the medical field has yet to be seen.

13.3.4.2 Available "slots": "what is it reasonable to say?"

GALEN's original approach was to represent "all and only what it is medically sensible to say". PEN&PAD (as well as non-medical uses of GRAIL such as the BioInformatics project TAMBIS [Baker *et al.*, 1998]) depends on assembling data entry forms and queries dynamically. The total number of potential forms is vastly greater than could be enumerated individually. Both applications depend on being able to determine which roles are "sensibly" applicable to a particular concept. GRAIL's sanctioning mechanism provides this information directly, but there is no direct way to form such a query within a standard DL framework. How best to address this issue remains a topic for research.

A key part of the GALEN experience in this regard is that only part of this "sanctioning" information is re-usable. In the original PEN&PAD application, changes to the user interface were made by changing the underlying ontology. In GALEN, and in the commercial version of PEN&PAD, Clinergy™, changing the re-usable ontology to fit an application specific requirement was unacceptable, so an additional layer of "perspectives" was interposed between the ontology itself and applications. This layered architecture now seems essential to many applications of ontologies which aspire to be re-usable.

13.4 Ontological issues in medical ontologies

13.4.1 Normative statements and abnormalities

Congenital and other deformities present a major difficulty to clinical knowledge representations, because they require that statements which would otherwise be absolute be made somehow contingent and that an extremely wide variety of statements be permitted in exceptional circumstances. They also require drawing distinctions that seem odd. Even in a thalidomide patient with an absent left arm, we still need to be able to make statements about the left arm. Hence physical and potential presence must somehow be distinguished.

Likewise, in determining what it is "sensible" to say, congenital anomalies make a nonsense of the usual constraints. For example, most patients have their heart on their left side, three lobes to their right lung, and two lobes to their left. Most patients have a "right middle lobe" but no "left middle lobe" of the lung. However, a small percentage of patients reverse the pattern. The anomaly is not always complete, so many combinations of abnormalities are possible. Doctors tend to be highly intolerant of being presented with options such as "left middle lobe" in normal circumstances. Unfortunately, they are equally intolerant of the inability to express the notion of a "left middle lobe" in that small number ($\ll 1\%$) of cases where it is needed. Taken individually, such anomalies are rare. Taken collectively, they are surprisingly common, i.e., a significant percentage of all patients are atypical in one respect or another.

13.4.2 Clinical pragmatics

13.4.2.1 Conventional idioms

As in any language, many terms or phrases have conventional meanings different from their literal interpretation. Such differences are not always immediately obvious. A typical example is "endocrine surgery" which it might seem natural to define as "surgery on an endocrine organ". However, procedures on both the male and female reproductive organs are normally excluded, even though no doctor would dispute that they are endocrine organs. Similarly, "heart valve" might naively be defined as a "structure in the heart with valvular function", but this includes numerous embryonic and sometimes congenitally deformed structures as well as the four "major valves" which serve the four "great vessels" entering and leaving the heart. Much of the effort of formulating a satisfactory medical ontology goes into reconciling such conventional usages with their apparent meaning.

13.4.2.2 Normalization and implied information

Many medical notions, particularly of actions and procedures, carry strong implications about their purpose. O'Neil's classic example illustrates this problem [O'Neil *et al.*, 1995; Brown *et al.*, 1998]. A common procedure to treat hip fractures is "insertion of pins in the femur". The only reason to insert pins in the femur is to "fixate" a fracture, and the operation is expected to be classified under both "insertion of pins" and "procedures to fixate fractures of long bones". Should the ontology contain axioms to extend the procedure definition automatically by adding "... to fixate fracture of femur"? If so, should the procedure be "fixation of fracture of femur by means of insertion of pins in the femur" or "insertion of pins in order to fixate fracture of femur"? Ordinarily such "qua-induced" duals are distinct – e.g., the "infection caused by a virus" is very different from the "virus caused by an infection". In these cases, two or more logically distinct possible representations are clinically equivalent. Most systems cope with this situation by imposing external "guidelines" on domain expert authors to normalize such expressions to one form or the other, but the problem is far from solved.

13.4.3 Semantic normalization and level of intent

Consider the problem of what constitutes a "surgical procedure". It is easy to agree that all surgical procedures are constituted by an "act" on some "thing" which either is, or is located in, an anatomical structure. It is less easy to agree on what constitutes an "act" when there is a hierarchy of motivations: for example, "inserting pins to fixate a fracture of a long bone" or "destruction of a polyp by cautery" or "removal of a polyp (by excision)". Furthermore, important classifications hang on notions of motivation such as "palliative surgery" versus "corrective surgery". In addition, some systems wish to be able to record operations just as "correction of X" without describing the exact "act", while others wish to record "insertion of pins in fractured bone" without recording that the purpose is fixation. To address this problem within GALEN, Rossi Mori *et al.* [1997] proposed a classification into four levels:

L4 clinical goal (palliation, cure);
L3 physiological goal: (correction, destruction, ...);
L2 primary surgical method (excision, insertion, lysis, ...);
L1 low level surgical act (cutting, cautery, ...).

It is tempting to believe that a list of concepts in each category could be agreed, so that resolution could be done automatically. However, at least within the GALEN project, intuitions and requirements clashed sufficiently to make this difficult. For example, "cautery" can sometimes be a low level act or sometimes a primary method. This ambiguity is dealt with in the formal ontology by having separate concepts for "simple cautery" and "removal by cauterization", and by care in formulating the intermediate representation (see Subsection 13.5.1). However, achieving consistent usage amongst a range of authors with different applications requires vigilance and careful quality assurance.

13.5 Architectures: terminology servers, views, and change management

13.5.1 Intermediate representations and views: GALEN's layered architecture

There is an inevitable conflict between the need for an ontology to be re-usable and the requirement that it be easily understood by the domain experts who must author and maintain it. SNOMED-RT addresses this problem by keeping the ontology relatively simple. GALEN addresses this problem by placing an "intermediate representation" and views ("perspectives") between the re-usable ontology and user-oriented applications [Rector *et al.*, 1999; 2001]. The intermediate representation and perspective layers in the architecture hide complexities irrelevant to the current application from domain experts and other users. It also allows for variations amongst domain experts in the vocabulary, structure, and – critically for an international project – language. In this layered architecture, the DL ontology is effectively reduced to a role analogous to that of an assembly language program. Using an intermediate representation both allows loose coupling amongst authors and simplifies the authoring task.

Within the GALEN project, use of an intermediate representation reduced training time for new authors from months to days. It also drastically reduced the time required centrally to harmonize the work of different authors so that the resulting classification would pass an agreed quality assurance. Prior to the introduction of the intermediate representation, central harmonization had consumed over fifty percent of the effort; following introduction of the intermediate representation this dropped to less than ten percent. This is a major saving given that the knowledge engineers required for central harmonization take a year or more to train fully. The experience of developing the drug ontology in PRODIGY (see Subsection 13.2.3) has been roughly comparable. In addition, in the drug ontology, the use of the intermediate representation has allowed the quality assurance experts to participate directly in correcting the authored ontology – something which would be entirely impractical in its expanded formulation in the Description Logic.

13.5.2 Learning vs. building

Given the scale of medical ontologies, it would obviously be attractive to use learning techniques for at least some of their construction. Hahn *et al.* [1999a] are focusing on using language plus the structure of the Unified Medical Language System as a major source for inducing their ontology. Campbell *et al.* [1998] have outlined a strategy which makes use of lexical "suggestions" to guide manual modeling as part of the SNOMED-RT methodology. GALEN has experimented with various linguistic techniques but so far with limited success [Ceusters *et al.*, 1999].

13.5.3 Version and change management

Any medical ontology for general use must be a living developing structure. There are both clinical and technical issues to be dealt with. Campbell *et al.* [1996] have developed a tightly coupled methodology for change management in conjunction with SNOMED-RT, while Oliver *et al.* [1999] and Cimino [1996] have discussed the issues of changes in medical vocabulary.

13.6 Discussion: key lessons from medical ontologies

Medicine is big and complicated. It has a long tradition of controlled vocabularies and coding systems. Developing re-usable medical ontologies presents at least three major classes of issue to the DL community:

- Developing implementations which scale.
- Developing architectures which reconcile the needs of users for simplicity with the formal constraints required for tractability and the ontological richness required for re-use.
- Developing formalisms expressive enough to cope with constructs of particular concern to medicine, particularly part–whole relations but also other spatio-temporal constructs such as adjacency.

Perhaps most critically, medicine poses the challenge of presenting DL notations in forms which users can use to meet real problems – whether in representation of medical records, indexing of information for decision support, or supporting user interfaces and natural language processing.

14

OWL: a Description-Logic-Based Ontology Language for the Semantic Web

Ian Horrocks
Peter F. Patel-Schneider
Deborah L. McGuinness
Christopher A. Welty

Abstract

It has long been realized that the web could benefit from having its content understandable and available in a machine processable form. The Semantic Web aims to achieve this via annotations that use terms defined in ontologies to give well defined meaning to web accessible information and services. OWL, the ontology language recommended by the W3C for this purpose, was heavily influenced by Description Logic research. In this chapter we review briefly some early efforts that combine Description Logics and the web, including predecessors of OWL such as OIL and DAML+OIL. We then go on to describe OWL in some detail, including the various influences on its design, its relationship with RDFS, its syntax and semantics, and a range of tools and applications.[1]

14.1 Background and history

The World Wide Web, while wildly successful in growth, may be viewed as being limited by its reliance on languages such as HTML that are focused on *presentation* (i.e., text formatting) rather than *content*. Languages such as XML do add some support for capturing the meaning of web content (instead of simply how to render it in a browser), but more is needed in order to support intelligent applications that can better exploit the ever increasing range of information and services accessible via the web. Such

---

[1] This chapter provides an update to the chapter in the first edition of this book entitled "Digital Libraries and Web-Based Information Systems" by Ian Horrocks, Deborah L. McGuinness, and Christopher A. Welty. That chapter was written prior to the completion of OWL, and focused on earlier Description-Logic-based ontology languages for the Semantic Web. Some of the material in the current chapter has previously appeared in other forms in conference and journal publications, in particular in [Horrocks *et al.*, 2003].

applications are urgently needed in order to avoid overwhelming users with the sheer volume of information becoming available.

The Semantic Web has been envisaged as an evolution of the existing web from a linked document repository into an application platform where "information is given well-defined meaning, better enabling computers and people to work in cooperation" [Berners-Lee *et al.*, 2001]. This is to be achieved by augmenting the existing layout information with semantic annotations that add descriptive terms to web content, with the meaning of such terms being defined in *ontologies*.

In order for the meaning of semantic annotations to be accessible to applications (as well as humans), the ontology language being used should have a precisely defined semantics and should be amenable to automated processing. Description Logics appear to be ideally suited to this role: they have a formal, logic-based semantics, and are often equipped with decision procedures that have been designed with the objective of being implemented in automated reasoning systems. This view of the potential place of Description Logics in the Semantic Web led to the development of a number of languages that brought Description Logic concepts to the Semantic Web, culminating in the development of the Web Ontology Language OWL. OWL is the World Wide Web Consortium (W3C) recommended ontology language for the Semantic Web, and exploits many of the strengths of Description Logics, including well defined semantics and practical reasoning techniques.

In this chapter we first review briefly the history of Description Logic efforts related to the Semantic Web, in particular OIL and DAML+OIL. We then go on to describe OWL in some detail, and to show how it brings Description Logic concepts fully into the Semantic Web.

14.1.1 Early uses of Description Logics in the Semantic Web

Before the development of Description Logic-related languages designed for the Semantic Web, there were several systems that used Description Logics in the context of the web. We will describe some salient features of two systems, UNTANGLE and FINDUR, that illustrate early Description Logic usage on the web.

The relationship between hypertext and semantic networks has long been realized, but one of the earliest Description Logic systems to realize this relationship was the UNTANGLE system [Welty and Jenkins, 2000], a Description Logic system for representing bibliographic (card-catalog) information. The UNTANGLE project began as a bit of exploratory research in using Description Logics for digital libraries [Welty, 1994], but out of sheer temporal coincidence with the rise of the web, a web interface was added and the first web-based Description Logic system was born.

The original UNTANGLE web interface was developed in 1994 [Welty, 1996a], and combined LISP-CLASSIC and the COMMONLISP Hypermedia Server (CL-HTTP) [Mallery, 1994] to implement a hypertext view of the ABox and TBox semantic networks, and used nested bullet lists to view the concept taxonomy, with in-page cross references for concepts having multiple parents. The interface was interesting in some respects as a tool to visualize Description Logic and semantic network information, though this aspect was never fully developed.

As the World Wide Web (WWW) became the primary means of dissemination of Computer Science research, the goals of the UNTANGLE project shifted in 1995 to cataloging and classifying pages on the web [Welty, 1996b], which was viewed as a massive and unstructured digital library [Welty, 1998].

Another early project using Description Logics for the web was the FINDUR system at AT&T [McGuinness, 1998; McGuinness *et al.*, 1997]. The basic notion of FINDUR was *query expansion*,[2] that is, taking synonyms or hyponyms (more specific terms) and including them in the input terms, thereby expanding the query.

The FINDUR system represented a simple background knowledge base containing mostly thesaurus information built in a Description Logic (CLASSIC) using the most basic notions of Wordnet (synsets and hyper/hyponyms) [Miller, 1995]. Concepts corresponding to sets of synonyms (synsets) were arranged in a taxonomy. These synsets also contained an informal list of related terms. Site-specific search engines (built on Verity – a commercial search engine) were hooked up to the knowledge base. Any search term would first be checked in the knowledge base, and if it was contained in any synset, a new query would be constructed consisting of the disjunction of all the synonymous terms, as well as all the more specific terms (hyponyms).

The background knowledge was represented in CLASSIC, but the Description Logic was not itself part of the on-line system. Instead, the information used by the search engine was statically generated on a regular basis and used to populate the search engine. The true power of using a Description Logic as the substrate for the knowledge base was realized mainly in the maintenance task. The Description Logic allowed the maintainer of the knowledge base to maintain some amount of consistency, such as discovering cycles in the

---

[2] Work on a subsequent Description-Logic-based approach to query expansion addressed some formal issues in evaluating the soundness and completeness of alternative approaches [Rousset, 1999b]. Other work on Description Logic (or Description Logic-inspired) approaches to retrieval also exists, e.g., [Meghini *et al.*, 1997; Calvanese *et al.*, 1999c].

taxonomy and disjoint synsets. These simple constraints proved effective tools for maintaining the knowledge since the knowledge itself was very simple.

Additional use of the Description Logic approach in FindUR was realized in applications that exposed more structured searches, exploiting subclass hierarchies and property relationships, such as the medical applications of FindUR in the P-CHIP Primary Care Search Application [McGuinness, 1999]. This type of structured search, exploiting background ontologies and relationships between terms, can also be seen in later work, e.g., in the SHOE project [Heflin *et al.*, 2003].

14.2 Steps towards integration with the Semantic Web: OIL and DAML+OIL

The first major effort to build a language that combined Description Logics and the Semantic Web was OIL (the Ontology Inference Layer) [Horrocks *et al.*, 2000a], a part of the On-To-Knowledge research project funded by the European Union. The OIL language was explicitly designed as "a web-based representation and inference language for ontologies [combining] the widely used modeling primitives from frame-based languages with the formal semantics and reasoning services provided by description logics" (`http://www.ontoknowledge.org/oil/oilhome.shtml`).

Description Logics provide the semantics for OIL, so much so that the semantics of OIL is specified via a mapping to the Description Logic $\mathcal{SHIQ}$ [Fensel *et al.*, 2001; Horrocks *et al.*, 1999]. OIL has a syntax based on the Resource Description Framework (RDF), as well as an XML syntax, that provided the connection to the Semantic Web of the time.[3] OIL allows the grouping of Description Logic constructs in a way similar to frame systems, providing a more intuitive feel to the language as opposed to the logically inspired syntax usually used for Description Logics. These three influences – Description Logics, frames, and the Semantic Web – are present not only in OIL, but also in all of its successors.[4]

14.2.1 $\mathcal{SHIQ}$ and $\mathcal{SHOIN}$

In this subsection we will briefly introduce the syntax and semantics of the Description Logics on which OIL, DAML+OIL and OWL are based, i.e.,

---

[3] At the time that OIL was developed, RDF– the base language of the Semantic Web – was without a fully specified semantic foundation.

[4] The correspondence between Description Logics and frame systems is also discussed in Subsection 4.1.2.

Construct Name	Syntax	Semantics	
atomic concept	A	$A^{\mathcal{I}} \subseteq \Delta^{\mathcal{I}}$	
atomic role	R	$R^{\mathcal{I}} \subseteq \Delta^{\mathcal{I}} \times \Delta^{\mathcal{I}}$	
transitive role	$R \in \mathbf{R}_+$	$R^{\mathcal{I}} = (R^{\mathcal{I}})^+$	
conjunction	$C \sqcap D$	$C^{\mathcal{I}} \cap D^{\mathcal{I}}$	
disjunction	$C \sqcup D$	$C^{\mathcal{I}} \cup D^{\mathcal{I}}$	$\mathcal{S}$
negation	$\neg C$	$\Delta^{\mathcal{I}} \setminus C^{\mathcal{I}}$	
exists restriction	$\exists R.C$	$\{x \mid \exists y.(x,y) \in R^{\mathcal{I}} \text{ and } y \in C^{\mathcal{I}}\}$	
value restriction	$\forall R.C$	$\{x \mid \forall y.(x,y) \in R^{\mathcal{I}} \text{ implies } y \in C^{\mathcal{I}}\}$	
role hierarchy	$R \sqsubseteq S$	$R^{\mathcal{I}} \subseteq S^{\mathcal{I}}$	$\mathcal{H}$
nominal	$\{o\}$	$\{o^{\mathcal{I}}\}$	$\mathcal{O}$
inverse role	R^-	$\{(x,y) \mid (y,x) \in R^{\mathcal{I}}\}$	$\mathcal{I}$
number restrictions	$\geqslant n\,P$	$\{x \mid \sharp\{y.(x,y) \in P^{\mathcal{I}}\} \geqslant n\}$	$\mathcal{N}$
	$\leqslant n\,P$	$\{x \mid \sharp\{y.(x,y) \in P^{\mathcal{I}}\} \leqslant n\}$	
qualifying number restrictions	$\geqslant n\,P.C$	$\{x \mid \sharp\{y.(x,y) \in P^{\mathcal{I}} \text{ and } y \in C^{\mathcal{I}}\} \geqslant n\}$	$\mathcal{Q}$
	$\leqslant n\,P.C$	$\{x \mid \sharp\{y.(x,y) \in P^{\mathcal{I}} \text{ and } y \in C^{\mathcal{I}}\} \leqslant n\}$	

Fig. 14.1. Syntax and semantics of the $\mathcal{S}$ family of Description Logics

$\mathcal{SHIQ}$ and $\mathcal{SHOIN}$. These logics are based on an extension of the well-known DL $\mathcal{ALC}$ [Schmidt-Schauß and Smolka, 1991] to include transitively closed primitive roles [Sattler, 1996]; this logic has been called $\mathcal{S}$ due to its relationship with the propositional (multi-) modal logic $\mathbf{S4_m}$ [Schild, 1991].[5] This logic is then extended to include features such as role inclusion axioms ($\mathcal{H}$), nominals ($\mathcal{O}$), inverse roles ($\mathcal{I}$) and (possibly qualified) number restrictions ($\mathcal{Q}$ if qualified, $\mathcal{N}$ otherwise).

The syntax and semantics of these features are summarised in Figure 14.1, where A is a concept name, C and D are concepts, R and S are roles, $\mathbf{R}_+$ is the set of transitive roles, o is an individual name, P is a simple role (i.e., one that is not transitive and has no transitive subrole), and n is a nonnegative integer. Further details can be found in Chapter 2, and in [Horrocks et al., 1999] and [Horrocks and Sattler, 2005].

These logics can also be extended with a simple form of concrete domains known as datatypes; this is denoted by appending ($\mathbf{D}$) to the name of the logic, e.g., $\mathcal{SHOIN}(\mathbf{D})$. Concrete domains are discussed in detail in Chapter 6, and the datatype variant is described in [Horrocks and Sattler, 2001].

---

[5] This logic has previously been called $\mathcal{ALC}_{R^+}$, but this becomes too cumbersome when adding letters to represent additional features.

14.2.2 OIL

The OIL language is designed to combine frame-like modeling primitives with the increased (in some respects) expressive power, formal rigor and automated reasoning services of an expressive Description Logic [Fensel *et al.*, 2000]. OIL also comes "web enabled" by having both XML- and RDFS-based serializations (as well as a formally specified "human readable" form, which we will use here). In frame languages, classes (concepts) are described by *frames*, whose main components are a list of superclasses and a list of *slot–filler* pairs. A slot corresponds to a role in a Description Logic, and a slot–filler pair corresponds to either a value restriction (a concept of the form $\forall R.C$) or an existential quantification (a concept of the form $\exists R.C$) – one of the criticisms leveled at frame languages is that they are often unclear as to exactly which of these is intended by a slot–filler pair.

OIL extends this basic frame syntax so that it can capture the full power of an expressive Description Logic.

In order to allow users to choose the expressive power appropriate to their application, and to allow for future extensions, a layered family of OIL languages was described. The base layer, called "Core OIL" [Bechhofer *et al.*, 2000], is a cut-down version of the language that closely corresponds with RDFS (i.e., it includes only class and slot inclusion axioms, and slot range and domain constraints). The standard language is called "Standard OIL", and when extended with ABox axioms (i.e., the ability to assert that individuals and tuples are, respectively, instances of classes and slots), it is called "Instance OIL". Finally, "Heavy OIL" was the name given to a further layer that was to include still unspecified language extensions.

Figure 14.2 illustrates an OIL ontology (using the human readable serialization) corresponding to an example terminology from Chapter 2. A full specification of OIL, including DTDs for the XML and RDFS serializations, can be found in [Horrocks *et al.*, 2000a].

Standard OIL can be seen as a syntactic variant of the Description Logic $\mathcal{SHIQ}$ [Horrocks *et al.*, 1999] extended with simple concrete datatypes [Baader and Hanschke, 1991a; Horrocks and Sattler, 2001], otherwise known as $\mathcal{SHIQ(D)}$. Rather than providing the usual model-theoretic semantics, OIL defines a translation that maps an OIL ontology into an equivalent $\mathcal{SHIQ(D)}$ terminology. From this mapping, OIL derives both a clear semantics and a means to exploit the reasoning services of Description Logic systems such as FaCT [Horrocks, 1998b], RACER [Haarslev and Möller, 2001e] and Pellet [Pellet, 2003] that implement (most of) $\mathcal{SHIQ(D)}$.

```
name "Family"
documentation "Example ontology describing family relationships"
definitions
  slot-def hasChild
    inverse isChildOf

  class-def defined Woman
    subclass-of Person Female

  class-def defined Man
    subclass-of Person not Woman

  class-def defined Mother
    subclass-of Woman
    slot-constraint hasChild
      has-value Person

  class-def defined Father
    subclass-of Man
    slot-constraint hasChild
      has-value Person

  class-def defined Parent
    subclass-of or Father Mother

  class-def defined Grandmother
    subclass-of Mother
    slot-constraint hasChild
      has-value Parent

  class-def defined MotherWithManyChildren
    subclass-of Mother
    slot-constraint hasChild
      min-cardinality 3

  class-def defined MotherWithoutDaughter
    subclass-of Mother
    slot-constraint hasChild
      value-type not Woman
```

Fig. 14.2. OIL "family" ontology.

14.2.3 The DAML project and DAML+OIL

At about the same time as OIL was being developed, the DARPA Agent Markup Language (DAML) program was started in the United States. DAML was initiated in order to provide the foundation for the next generation of the web which, it was anticipated, would increasingly utilize agents and programs rather than relying so heavily on human interpretation of web information [Hendler and McGuinness, 2000].

One of the early widely distributed contributions of the DAML program was DAML-ONT– a proposal for an ontology language for the web [Hendler and McGuinness, 2000; McGuinness *et al.*, 2002]. This language began with the requirement to build on the best practice in web languages of the time, and in particular to extend W3C's Resource Description Framework, with the aim of adding expressive power suited to agent and service interoperation.

It became obvious that the goals of DAML-ONT and OIL were so similar that these objectives could best be served by combining the two efforts. The resulting language, DAML+OIL, has a formal (model-theoretic) semantics that provides machine and human understandability [van Harmelen *et al.*, 2001], an axiomatization [Fikes and McGuinness, 2001], and a reconciliation of the language constructors from the two precursor languages.

DAML+OIL is similar to OIL in many respects, but is more tightly integrated with RDFS, which provides the only specification of the language and its only serialization. While the dependence on RDFS has some advantages in terms of the re-use of existing RDFS infrastructure and the portability of DAML+OIL ontologies, using RDFS to completely define the syntax of DAML+OIL is quite difficult as, unlike XML, RDFS is not designed for the precise specification of syntactic structure. For example, there is no way in RDFS to state that a restriction (slot constraint) should consist of exactly one property (slot) and one class, and as a result the following axiom is perfectly legal in DAML+OIL, in spite of the fact that the restriction specifies two properties and two classes:

```
<daml:Class rdf:ID="Person">
  <rdfs:subClassOf>
    <daml:Restriction>
        <daml:onProperty rdf:resource="#hasFather"/>
        <daml:onProperty rdf:resource="#hasMother"/>
        <daml:toClass rdf:resource="#Man"/>
        <daml:toClass rdf:resource="#Woman"/>
    </daml:Restriction>
```

```
        </rdfs:subClassOf>
      </daml:Class>
```

The solution to this problem adopted by DAML+OIL is to define the semantics of the language in such a way that it gives a meaning to any (parts of) ontologies that conform to the RDFS specification, including "strange" constructs such as the one shown above. This is made easier by the fact that, unlike OIL, the semantics of DAML+OIL is directly defined, although a translation into a suitable DL would also have been possible: the above DAML+OIL axiom is, for example, equivalent to the following DL axioms:

$$\text{Person} \sqsubseteq \exists\text{hasFather.Man}$$
$$\text{Person} \sqsubseteq \exists\text{hasFather.Woman}$$
$$\text{Person} \sqsubseteq \exists\text{hasMother.Man}$$
$$\text{Person} \sqsubseteq \exists\text{hasMother.Woman}$$
$$\exists\text{hasFather.Man} \equiv \exists\text{hasFather.Woman}$$
$$\exists\text{hasFather.Woman} \equiv \exists\text{hasMother.Man}$$
$$\exists\text{hasMother.Man} \equiv \exists\text{hasMother.Woman}.$$

This may seem strange, but has the advantage of giving a consistent and unambiguous semantics to DAML+OIL restrictions consisting of multiple properties and/or classes. The DAML+OIL specification strongly recommends, however, that the use of such restrictions (and other "strange" constructs) be avoided.

Another effect of DAML+OIL's tight integration with RDFS is that the frame structure of OIL's syntax is much less evident: a DAML+OIL ontology is more Description Logic-like in that it consists largely of a relatively unstructured collection of subsumption and equality axioms. This can make it more difficult to use DAML+OIL with frame-based tools such as PROTÉGÉ [Grosso *et al.*, 1999] or OILED [Bechhofer *et al.*, 2001b], because the axioms may be susceptible to many different frame-like groupings [Bechhofer *et al.*, 2001a].

From the point of view of language constructs, the differences between OIL and DAML+OIL are relatively trivial. Although there is some difference in "keyword" vocabulary, there is usually a one-to-one mapping of constructors, and in the cases where the constructors are not completely equivalent, simple translations are possible.

The initial release of DAML+OIL did not include any specification of datatypes. The language was, however, subsequently extended with arbitrary datatypes from the XML Schema type system, which can be used in restrictions (slot constraints) and range constraints. As in $\mathcal{SHOQ(D)}$ [Horrocks and Sattler, 2001], a clean separation is maintained between instances of "object" classes (defined using the ontology language) and instances of datatypes (defined using the XML Schema type system). In particular, it is assumed that the domain of interpretation of object classes is disjoint from the domain of interpretation of datatypes, so that an instance of an object class (e.g., the individual Italy) can never have the same interpretation as a value of a datatype (e.g., the integer 5), and that the set of object properties (which relate individuals to individuals) is disjoint from the set of datatype properties (which relate individuals to datatype values).

14.3 Full integration into the Semantic Web: OWL

With its tighter integration with RDF and RDFS, DAML+OIL was the first Description Logic-inspired language to be completely integrated into the fabric of the Semantic Web (as it was then defined). There was, however, no formal semantic integration of DAML+OIL with RDF and RDFS, as RDF and RDFS did not have a formal semantics at the time when DAML+OIL was being developed. DAML+OIL also lacked any formal status, having been the product of a group of researchers operating under the auspices of the so-called "Joint EU/US ad hoc Agent Markup Language Committee". This group published DAML+OIL as a W3C Note on December 18, 2001 (see http://www.w3.org/Submission/2001/12/).

To fix these problems, the W3C chartered two working groups in 2001. The RDF Core Working Group was to be responsible for updating the RDF recommendation and providing a formal semantics for RDF and thus for the Semantic Web. The Web Ontology Working Group was to be responsible for designing an ontology language for the web, compatible with the new version of RDF. The Web Ontology Working Group developed the Web Ontology Language OWL [Bechhofer *et al.*, 2004], which became a W3C recommendation on 10 February 2004 (see http://www.w3.org/2004/OWL/). In parallel, the RDF Core Working Group developed a formal semantics for RDF and RDFS [Hayes, 2004].

The OWL recommendation defines a family of three languages in order to address concerns ranging from level of expressiveness to degree of compatibility with RDF. Two of these so-called "species" of OWL, OWL Full and OWL DL, provide the same set of Description Logic constructors, but differ in the way the constructors can be used: in OWL Full they can be used in arbitrary RDF graphs, whereas in OWL DL their use is restricted so that OWL DL ontologies correspond directly to Description Logic knowledge bases. The third species of OWL, OWL Lite, is very similar to OWL DL, but provides a reduced set of constructors.

14.3.1 Influences on the Design of OWL

The design of OWL was subject to a variety of influences. These included influences from established formalisms and knowledge representation paradigms, influences from existing ontology languages, and influences from existing Semantic Web languages.

Some of the most important influences on the design of OWL came, via its predecessor DAML+OIL, from Description Logics, from the frames paradigm, and from RDF. In particular, the formal specification of the language was influenced by Description Logics, the surface structure of the language (as seen in the abstract syntax) was influenced by the frames paradigm, and the RDF/XML exchange syntax was influenced by a requirement for upwards compatibility with RDF.

Description Logics, and insights from Description Logic research, had a strong influence on the design of OWL, particularly on the formalization of the semantics, the choice of language constructors, and the integration of datatypes and data values (see, e.g., Chapters 2–6). In fact OWL DL and OWL Lite (two of the three species of OWL) can be viewed as expressive Description Logics, with an ontology being equivalent to a Description Logic knowledge base. More precisely, OWL DL and OWL Lite are equivalent to $\mathcal{SHIF}(\mathbf{D})$ and $\mathcal{SHOIN}(\mathbf{D})$ respectively (see Subsections 14.3.3 and 14.3.5 for more details).

This design was motivated by practical considerations. The designers of OWL wanted to have some idea as to how difficult it would be for tools and applications to support the language. It was therefore important to understand its formal properties, e.g., with respect to the decidability and complexity of key inference problems. These properties followed directly from the correspondences with Description Logics (see Chapter 3). These correspondences would allow tools and applications to exploit known reasoning algorithms and even (highly optimized) implementations (see, e.g., Chapters 7–9).

In the Semantic Web context, where users with a wide range of expertise might be expected to create or modify ontologies, readability and general ease of use are important considerations for an ontology language. In the design of OIL [Fensel *et al.*, 2001], these requirements were addressed by providing a surface syntax based on the frames paradigm. Frames group together information about each class, making ontologies easier to read and understand, particularly for users not familiar with (Description) Logics. The frames paradigm has been used in a number of well-known knowledge representation and ontology environment systems including the PROTÉGÉ ontology design tool [Grosso *et al.*, 1999], the Ontolingua ontology environment tool [Farquhar *et al.*, 1996], the OKBC knowledge model [Chaudhri *et al.*, 1998b], and the Chimaera Ontology Evolution Environment [McGuinness *et al.*, 2000b]. The design of OIL was influenced by XOL [Karp *et al.*, 1999] – a proposal for an XML syntax for OKBC Lite (a cut-down version of the OKBC knowledge model).

In frame-based languages, each class is described by a frame. The frame includes the name of the class, identifies the more general class (or classes) that it specializes, and lists a set of "slots". A slot may consist of a property–value pair, or a constraint on the values that can act as slot "fillers" (in this context, value means either an individual or a data value). This structure was used in the OIL language, with some enrichment of the syntax for specifying classes and slot constraints so as to enable the full power of a Description Logic-style language to be captured. In addition, property frames were used to describe properties, e.g., specifying more general properties, range and domain constraints, transitivity and inverse property relationships.

A class frame is semantically equivalent to a Description Logic axiom asserting that the class being described by the frame is a subclass of each of the classes that it specializes and of each of the property restrictions corresponding to the slots. As well as a richer slot syntax, OIL also offered the possibility of asserting that the class being described by the frame was exactly equivalent to the relevant intersection class (i.e., that they were mutually subsuming). A property frame is equivalent to a set of axioms asserting the relevant subproperty relationships, range and domain constraints etc. OIL was designed so that OIL frames could easily be mapped to equivalent axioms in the $\mathcal{SHOQ}(\mathcal{D})$ Description Logic [Decker *et al.*, 2000].

The formal specification and semantics of OWL are given by an abstract syntax [Patel-Schneider *et al.*, 2004] that has been heavily influenced by frames in general and by the design of OIL in particular. In the abstract syntax, axioms are compound constructions that are very like an OIL-style frame. For classes, they consist of the name of the class being described, a *modality* of "partial" or "complete" (indicating that the axiom is asserting a subclass or equivalence relationship respectively), and a sequence of property restrictions and names of more general classes. Similarly, a property axiom specifies the name of the property and its various features.

The frame style of the abstract syntax, which borrows heavily in spirit from the human readable syntax for OIL, makes it *much* easier to read (compared to the RDF/XML syntax), and also easier (for non-logicians) to understand and to use. Moreover, abstract syntax axioms have a direct correspondence with Description Logic axioms, and they can also be mapped to a set of RDF triples (as we will see in the following subsection).

The third major influence on the design of OWL was the requirement to maintain the maximum upwards compatibility with existing web languages, and in particular with RDF [Manola and Miller, 2004]. On the face of it this requirement made good sense as RDF (and in particular RDF Schema) already included several of the basic features of a class- and property-based ontology language, e.g., it allows subclass and subproperty relationships to be asserted. Moreover, the development of RDF preceded that of OWL, and it seemed reasonable to try to appeal to any user community already established by RDF.

It may seem easy to meet this requirement simply by giving OWL an RDF-based syntax, but, in order to provide maximum upwards compatibility, it was also thought necessary to ensure that the semantics of OWL ontologies was consistent with the semantics of RDF. This proved to be difficult, however, given the greatly increased expressive power provided by OWL. This will be discussed in more detail in Subsection 14.3.2.

14.3.2 Layering (on RDFS) and three "species" of OWL

On the face of it, maintaining maximum upwards compatibility with RDF made good sense, but this requirement led to a number of problems in the design of OWL.

In the first place, RDF/XML is extremely verbose. Compare, for example, information about a class as it would be given in a Description Logic syntax

$$\texttt{Student} \equiv \texttt{Person} \sqcap \geqslant 1\,\texttt{enrolledIn}$$

(a `Student` is a `Person` who is `enrolledIn` at least 1 thing), or the OWL abstract syntax

```
Class(Student partial Person
            restriction(enrolledIn minCardinality(1)))
```

with how it would most naturally be written using the OWL RDF/XML syntax[6]

```
<owl:Class rdf:ID="Student">
    <owl:intersectionOf rdf:parsetype="Collection">
        <owl:Class rdfs:about="Person" />
        <owl:Restriction>
            <owl:onProperty rdf:resource="enrolledIn" />
            <owl:minCardinality rdfs:datatype="&xsd;Integer">
                1
            </owl:minCardinality>
        </owl:Restriction>
    </owl:intersectionOf>
</owl:Class>
```

This verbosity of OWL's RDF/XML syntax may not, in itself, be a serious problem given the capabilities and bandwidths of modern computers and communication systems, and that this syntax is mainly intended for exchanging data between OWL applications. The RDF/XML syntax does, however, lead to some more serious problems. RDF is itself a graph-based formalism, with graphs-expressed as sets of subject–predicate–object triples, where each triple represents a labeled edge (the predicate) connecting two vertices (the subject and object). This means that many OWL constructs, such as property restrictions, have to be encoded as several triples. There is no requirement that these triples occur together, so parsing becomes difficult as it may be necessary to scan the entire input in order to locate all of the components of a given construction. Moreover, circular and other unusual structures with ill defined meanings cannot be ruled out.

Even more problematical is the relationship between the semantics of an OWL ontology and the semantics of the RDF triples used to encode it. This was not as much of an issue when OIL and DAML+OIL were designed, as at that time the meaning of RDF was not precisely specified. OIL in particular did not bother to relate the RDF meaning of its RDF/XML syntax to the OIL meaning of this syntax – the RDF/XML syntax for some OIL constructs does more or less line up with the RDF meaning of these constructs, but this is by no means the case for all such constructs.

DAML+OIL did a better job of abiding by the RDF meaning of its syntax. The DAML+OIL model theory [van Harmelen *et al.*, 2001] included a semantic condition for triples that was close to the RDF meaning (as defined at that time) for triples. Moreover, DAML+OIL used the built-

---

[6] Full details on the OWL RDF/XML syntax can be found in the OWL reference document [Bechhofer *et al.*, 2004].

in RDF and RDFS vocabulary to a greater extent than did OIL, and used it in a way generally compatible with the RDF or RDFS meaning. For example DAML+OIL uses `rdfs:subClassOf` to relate classes to superclasses.

By the time OWL was being designed, RDF was being given a formal meaning via the RDF model theory [Hayes, 2004]. It proved to be difficult to design an RDF syntax for OWL such that the Description Logic semantics assigned by OWL to its various constructs was compatible with the semantics of the RDF triples used to encode them. Moreover, there was an incompatibility between the requirement to be fully backwards compatible with OWL (i.e., to allow arbitrary RDF graphs to be interpreted as OWL ontologies), and the requirement for OWL to be equivalent to an expressive Description Logic. (See [Horrocks *et al.*, 2003] for a detailed discussion of these issues.)

These problems were eventually "resolved" by defining two "species" of OWL: OWL Full and OWL DL. Only a subset of RDF graphs correspond to OWL DL ontologies. In particular, the graph cannot include cyclical and other problematical constructions (including "malformed" OWL syntax), and the sets of class, property, and individual names must be disjoint. For RDF graphs that satisfy these syntactic restrictions, a fairly standard Description Logic-style model theory is used to define the semantics of the resulting OWL constructs. In contrast, OWL Full uses an RDF-style model theory to give a semantic account of the use of OWL constructors in arbitrary RDF graphs. (See Subsections 14.3.4 and 14.3.5 for more details.)

As well as arguments about the importance of compatibility with RDF, there were also tensions within the working group regarding the expressive power that was appropriate for OWL, with some members arguing that OWL DL was too complex to be understood by new users or implemented by application developers. Weight was lent to these arguments by the fact that, at the time, no tableaux decision procedure was known for $\mathcal{SHOIN}(\mathbf{D})$ (the Description Logic language underlying OWL DL), and no implemented system supported it. In response to these concerns, a third OWL species was defined, namely OWL Lite.

OWL Lite is a syntactic subset of OWL DL that prohibits and/or restricts the use of certain constructors and axioms with the aim of making the language easier to understand and/or implement. It has subsequently been shown, however, that by combining other constructors and axioms, most of the expressive power of OWL DL can be regained, and that OWL Lite is expressively equivalent to $\mathcal{SHIF}(\mathbf{D})$ [Horrocks and Patel-Schneider, 2003].

Given that OWL Full does not correspond either syntactically or semantically to a Description Logic, in the remainder of this chapter we will focus our attention on OWL DL and OWL Lite.

14.3.3 OWL DL abstract syntax and semantics

OWL DL has some differences from standard Description Logics. These differences provide a bridge between the formal Description Logic world and the Semantic Web world.

- OWL uses URI references as names, and constructs these URI references in the same manner as that used by RDF. It is thus common in OWL to use qualified names as shorthand for URI references, using, for example, the qualified name owl:Thing for the URI reference `http://www.w3.org/2002/07/owl#Thing`.
- OWL gathers information into ontologies, which are generally stored as Web documents written in RDF/XML. Ontologies can import other ontologies, adding the information from the imported ontology to the current ontology.
- OWL allows RDF annotation properties to be used to attach information to classes, properties, and ontologies, such as `owl:DeprecatedClass`. These annotations are RDF triples, and are therefore required to carry a full semantic weight in RDF. In OWL DL, however, such annotations carry a separate, limited meaning.
- OWL uses the facilities of RDF datatypes and XML Schema datatypes to provide datatypes and data values (a very restricted form of concrete domains; see Subsection 6.2.1).
- OWL DL and OWL Lite have a frame-like abstract syntax, whereas RDF/XML is the official exchange syntax for all three species of OWL.

As mentioned above, OWL DL is very closely related to $\mathcal{SHOIN}(\mathbf{D})$, which extends $\mathcal{SHOIQ}$ [Horrocks and Sattler, 2005] with datatypes like those in $\mathcal{SHOQ}(\mathcal{D})$ [Horrocks and Sattler, 2001], but allows only unqualified number restrictions (see Subsection 2.4.2). OWL DL can form descriptions of classes, datatypes, individuals and data values using the constructs shown in Figure 14.3. In this table the first column gives the OWL abstract syntax for the construction, while the second column gives the equivalent Description Logic syntax. The letters A, D, R, U, o, and v represent, respectively, names for classes (concepts), data ranges, object properties (abstract roles), datatype properties (concrete roles), individuals (nominals), and data values; C, possibly subscripted, represents an arbitrary class description. In OWL, data values are RDF literals (i.e., instances of datatypes such as string or integer), and all other names are URI references. As mentioned above, owl:Thing and owl:Nothing are

Abstract Syntax	DL Syntax
Descriptions (C)	
A	A
`owl:Thing`	$\top$
`owl:Nothing`	$\bot$
`intersectionOf`$(C_1 \ldots C_n)$	$C_1 \sqcap \cdots \sqcap C_n$
`unionOf`$(C_1 \ldots C_n)$	$C_1 \sqcup \cdots \sqcup C_n$
`complementOf`(C)	$\neg C$
`oneOf`$(o_1 \ldots o_n)$	$\{o_1\} \sqcup \cdots \sqcup \{o_n\}$
`restriction`$(R$ `someValuesFrom`$(C))$	$\exists R.C$
`restriction`$(R$ `allValuesFrom`$(C))$	$\forall R.C$
`restriction`$(R$ `hasValue`$(o))$	$R : o$
`restriction`$(R$ `minCardinality`$(n))$	$\geqslant n\,R$
`restriction`$(R$ `maxCardinality`$(n))$	$\leqslant n\,R$
`restriction`$(U$ `someValuesFrom`$(D))$	$\exists U.D$
`restriction`$(U$ `allValuesFrom`$(D))$	$\forall U.D$
`restriction`$(U$ `hasValue`$(v))$	$U : v$
`restriction`$(U$ `minCardinality`$(n))$	$\geqslant n\,U$
`restriction`$(U$ `maxCardinality`$(n))$	$\leqslant n\,U$
Data Ranges (D)	
D	D
`oneOf`$(v_1 \ldots v_n)$	$\{v_1\} \sqcup \ldots \sqcup \{v_n\}$
Object Properties (R)	
R	R
`inv`(R)	R^-
Datatype Properties (U)	
U	U
Individuals (o)	
o	o
Data Values (v)	
v	v

Fig. 14.3. OWL DL descriptions, data ranges, properties, individuals, and data values

shorthand for the URI references `http://www.w3.org/2002/07/owl#Thing` and `http://www.w3.org/2002/07/owl#Nothing` respectively.

The treatment of concrete values in OWL is somewhat different from the usual treatment of concrete values in Description Logics [Baader and Hanschke, 1991a; Lutz, 2002], and is instead based on the more restricted concrete datatypes introduced in [Horrocks and Sattler, 2001]. OWL uses datatypes from XML Schema datatypes as its concrete types, so `xsd:integer` is a concrete type in OWL, namely the type of integers. OWL uses the RDF syntax for these concrete values, so `"2"^^xsd:integer` is the way to write the integer 2. OWL also allows plain RDF literals, which are a combination of a string and an optional language tag. These plain literals belong to the datatype `rdfs:Literal`. OWL also allows sets of data values to be used in concept expressions, as in `oneOf("1"^^xsd:integer "2"^^xsd:integer "3"^^xsd:integer)`.

OWL uses these description-forming constructs in axioms that provide information about classes, properties, and individuals, as shown in Figure 14.4. Again, the frame-like abstract syntax is given in the first column, and the standard Description Logic syntax is given in the second column. The notation is the same as in Figure 14.3.

Either partial or complete information can be stated about a class, as in

```
Class(ex:Country partial owl:Thing)
Class(ex:Person partial owl:Thing)
Class(ex:Student partial ex:Person)
Class(ex:Canadian complete ex:Person
                hasValue(ex:nationality ex:Canada))
```

which makes `ex:Country` and `ex:Person` classes, `ex:Student` a subclass of `ex:Person`, and `ex:Canadian` precisely those people who have `ex:nationality ex:Canada`.[7]

In OWL DL properties are divided into object properties, such as `ex:nationality`, which relate individuals to other individuals, datatype properties, such as `ex:age`, which relate individuals to data values, and annotation properties, which can be used to add uninterpreted information (such as versioning information) to individuals, classes, and properties. Constraints, such as domains and ranges, can be given for object properties and datatype properties, but not for annotation properties.

```
DatatypeProperty(ex:age domain(ex:Person)
                        range(xsd:integer))
ObjectProperty(ex:nationality domain(ex:Person)
                        range(ex:Country))
```

---

[7] For a more extensive example of how to use OWL, see the OWL guide [Smith *et al.*, 2004].

Abstract Syntax	DL Syntax
Class(A partial $C_1 \ldots C_n$)	$A \sqsubseteq C_1 \sqcap \cdots \sqcap C_n$
Class(A complete $C_1 \ldots C_n$)	$A \equiv C_1 \sqcap \cdots \sqcap C_n$
EnumeratedClass(A $o_1 \ldots o_n$)	$A \equiv \{o_1\} \sqcup \cdots \sqcup \{o_n\}$
SubClassOf(C_1 C_2)	$C_1 \sqsubseteq C_2$
EquivalentClasses($C_1 \ldots C_n$)	$C_1 \equiv \cdots \equiv C_n$
DisjointClasses($C_1 \ldots C_n$)	$C_i \sqcap C_j \sqsubseteq \bot, i \neq j$
Datatype(D)	
ObjectProperty(R super(R_1)$\ldots$super(R_n)	$R \sqsubseteq R_i$
$\quad$ domain(C_1)$\ldots$domain(C_m)	$\geqslant 1\,R \sqsubseteq C_i$
$\quad$ range(C_1)$\ldots$range(C_ℓ)	$\top \sqsubseteq \forall R.C_i$
$\quad$ [inverseOf(R_0)]	$R \equiv R_0^-$
$\quad$ [Symmetric]	$R \equiv R^-$
$\quad$ [Functional]	$\top \sqsubseteq \leqslant 1\,R$
$\quad$ [InverseFunctional]	$\top \sqsubseteq \leqslant 1\,R^-$
$\quad$ [Transitive])	$Tr(R)$
SubPropertyOf(R_1 R_2)	$R_1 \sqsubseteq R_2$
EquivalentProperties($R_1 \ldots R_n$)	$R_1 \equiv \cdots \equiv R_n$
DatatypeProperty(U super(U_1)$\ldots$super(U_n)	$U \sqsubseteq U_i$
$\quad$ domain(C_1)$\ldots$domain(C_m)	$\geqslant 1\,U \sqsubseteq C_i$
$\quad$ range(D_1)$\ldots$range(D_ℓ)	$\top \sqsubseteq \forall U.D_i$
$\quad$ [Functional])	$\top \sqsubseteq \leqslant 1\,U$
SubPropertyOf(U_1 U_2)	$U_1 \sqsubseteq U_2$
EquivalentProperties($U_1 \ldots U_n$)	$U_1 \equiv \cdots \equiv U_n$
AnnotationProperty(S)	
OntologyProperty(S)	
Individual(o type(C_1)$\ldots$type(C_n)	$o \in C_i$
$\quad$ value(R_1 o_1)$\ldots$value(R_n o_n)	$\langle o, o_i \rangle \in R_i$
$\quad$ value(U_1 v_1)$\ldots$value(U_n v_n))	$\langle o, v_i \rangle \in U_i$
SameIndividual($o_1 \ldots o_n$)	$\{o_1\} \equiv \cdots \equiv \{o_n\}$
DifferentIndividuals($o_1 \ldots o_n$)	$\{o_i\} \sqsubseteq \neg\{o_j\}, i \neq j$

Fig. 14.4. OWL DL axioms and facts

Object properties can also be specified to be transitive, symmetric, functional, and inverse functional. In order to retain decidability, OWL DL restricts how these specifications can be combined for a particular object property: properties that are specified as being transitive, and their super-properties and their inverses, cannot have their cardinality restricted, either via the functional part of property axioms or in cardinality restrictions (see [Horrocks *et al.*, 1999]).

Annotation properties are a way of associating uninterpreted information with classes, properties, and individuals. The syntax for annotations is not given in Figure 14.4 (as they do not contribute to the corresponding Description Logic syntax), but some examples of their use are given below. Many axioms (`Class`, `EnumeratedClass`, `Datatype`, `ObjectProperty`, `DatatypeProperty`, `AnnotationProperty`, `OntologyProperty`, and `Individual` axioms) can have an annotation that provides uninterpreted information about that class, property, or individual. To prevent annotations influencing the semantics of OWL DL, little can be said about annotation properties: they cannot participate in restrictions, nor can they be given domains, ranges, or any other aspect of other kinds of properties. These limitations result in only trivial inferences being possible in relation to annotation properties in OWL DL.

One use of annotation properties is to provide comment information for classes and properties, as in

```
Class(ex:Country partial
      annotation(rdfs:comment "Countries of the world")
      owl:Thing)
```

This is, perhaps, the most useful purpose for annotations in OWL DL.

Information about individuals can also be provided in OWL, for either named individuals or anonymous individuals, as in:

```
Individual(ex:Canada type(ex:Country))
Individual(ex:England type(ex:Country))
Individual(ex:Peter type(ex:Canadian)
                 value(ex:age "48"^^xsd:integer))
Individual(value(ex:nationality ex:England)
           value(ex:age "44"^^xsd:integer))
```

In OWL, axioms and facts are grouped into ontologies, with the result that an OWL DL ontology is equivalent to a Description Logic knowledge base, i.e., a TBox plus an ABox (see Chapter 2). This is not completely standard, as ontologies are more typically thought of as describing only the structure of a domain (in terms of classes and properties), and not as describing a particular situation (in terms of instances of classes and properties); in this more common usage, an ontology is therefore equivalent

to a Description Logic TBox, and not to the combination of a TBox and an
ABox.

Ontologies can be given annotations, just like classes, properties, and individuals. Ontologies can also have ontology properties as annotations. Most
ontology properties act just like annotation properties (i.e., they provide
uninterpreted information), but one special property, `owl:imports`, can be
used to "import" other ontologies. Importing an ontology effectively treats
the content of a web page as part of the current ontology, as in:

```
Ontology(Simple
    Annotation(rdfs:comment "A simple ontology for nationality")
    Annotation(owl:imports http://www.foo.ex/simpler.owl)
    ...
)
```

The meaning of the above imports statement is that the set of axioms in
the `Simple` ontology is taken to include the set of axioms in the `simpler.owl`
ontology.

14.3.4 Semantics for OWL DL

A formal semantics, very similar to the semantics provided for Description
Logics (see Subsection 2.2.1), is provided for this style of using OWL. Full
details on this model theory can be found in the OWL Semantics and Abstract Syntax [Patel-Schneider *et al.*, 2004].

Because OWL includes datatypes, the semantics for OWL is very similar
to that of Description Logics that also incorporate datatypes, in particular
$\mathcal{SHOQ(D)}$. However, the particular datatypes used in OWL are taken from
RDF and XML Schema Datatypes [Biron and Malhotra, 2001]. Data values
such as `"44"^^xsd:integer` thus mean what they would mean as XML
Schema data values.

The semantics for OWL DL does include some aspects that may be viewed
as unusual from a Description Logic perspective. Annotations are given a
simple separate meaning, not shown here, that can be used to associate information with classes, properties, and individuals in a manner compatible
with the RDF semantics. Ontologies also live within the semantics and can
be given annotation information. Finally, `owl:imports` is given a meaning
that involves finding the referenced ontology (if possible) and adding its
meaning to the meaning of the current ontology. In other respects, however,
the meaning of an OWL ontology should be exactly equivalent to the meaning of the Description Logic knowledge base derived via the correspondences
given in Figures 14.3 and 14.4.

What makes OWL DL (and OWL Lite) a Semantic Web language, therefore, is not its semantics, which is quite standard for a Description Logic, but instead the use of URI references for names, the use of XML Schema datatypes for data values, and the ability to connect to documents in the World Wide Web.

14.3.5 OWL Lite and OWL Full

As we have seen, OWL DL is related to $\mathcal{SHOIN}(\mathbf{D})$, a very expressive Description Logic. This Description Logic is somewhat difficult to present to naive users, as it is possible to build complex Boolean descriptions using, for example, union and complement. $\mathcal{SHOIN}(\mathbf{D})$ is also difficult to reason with, as key inference problems have NExpTime complexity, and the potential for complex descriptions makes it somewhat difficult to build tools such as editors.

For these reasons, a subset of OWL DL has been identified that should be easier on all the above metrics; this subset is called OWL Lite. OWL Lite prohibits unions and complements, restricts intersections to the implicit intersections in the frame-like class axioms, limits all embedded descriptions to class names, does not allow individuals to occur in descriptions or class axioms, and limits cardinalities to 0 or 1.

These restrictions make OWL Lite expressively equivalent to $\mathcal{SHIF}(\mathbf{D})$. As in $\mathcal{SHIF}(\mathbf{D})$, key inferences in OWL Lite can be computed in worst-case exponential time (ExpTime), and there are already several optimized reasoners for logics equivalent to OWL Lite (see Subsection 14.3.7). This improvement in tractability comes with relatively little loss in expressive power – although OWL Lite syntax is more restricted than that of OWL DL, it is still possible to express complex descriptions by introducing new class names, and exploiting the duality between allValuesFrom and someValuesFrom restrictions [Horrocks and Patel-Schneider, 2003]. For example, the OWL Lite axioms

```
Class(C complete A B)
ObjectProperty(p)
Class(C complete restriction(p allValuesFrom(Nothing)))
Class(D complete restriction(p someValuesFrom(Thing)))
```

result in the class D being equivalent to the union of the negations of A and B, i.e., $D \equiv \neg A \sqcup \neg B$. Using these techniques, all OWL DL descriptions can be captured in OWL Lite except those containing either individual names or cardinalities greater than 1.

OWL DL and OWL Lite are extensions of a restricted use of RDF and RDFS, because, unlike RDF and RDFS, they do not allow classes to be used as individuals, and the language constructors cannot be applied to the language itself. For users who want these capabilities, a version of OWL that is upward compatible with RDF and RDFS has been provided; this version is called OWL Full. In OWL Full, all RDF and RDFS combinations are allowed. For example, in OWL Full, it is possible to impose a cardinality constraint on `rdfs:subClassOf`, if so desired.

OWL Full contains OWL DL, but goes well outside the standard Description Logic framework. The penalty to be paid here is two-fold. First, reasoning in OWL Full is undecidable. Showing the undecidability is trivial, because restrictions required in order to maintain the decidability of OWL DL do not apply to OWL Full [Horrocks *et al.*, 1999], but also as a result of the ability to apply OWL's expressive power to RDF syntax, as exemplified above [Motik, 2005]. Second, the abstract syntax for OWL DL is inadequate for OWL Full (the abstract syntax would not, for example, allow for the representation of cyclical RDF graphs or for graphs that contain only parts of OWL DL syntactic constructs), and the official OWL exchange syntax, RDF/XML, must be used.

OWL Full has been given a model-theoretic semantics that is a vocabulary extension of the RDF model theory [Patel-Schneider *et al.*, 2004; Hayes, 2004]. A correspondence between this semantics and the semantics of OWL DL has also been established: it has been shown that the model theory for OWL DL has very similar consequences to this RDF-style model theory for those OWL ontologies that can be written in the OWL DL abstract syntax [Patel-Schneider *et al.*, 2004].

More formally, given two OWL DL ontologies $\mathcal{O}_1$ and $\mathcal{O}_2$, written in the abstract syntax, if $\mathcal{O}_1$ entails $\mathcal{O}_2$ according to the OWL DL model theory then the mapping of $\mathcal{O}_1$ into RDF triples will entail the mapping of $\mathcal{O}_2$ into RDF triples according to the OWL Full model theory.

The converse, however, is not true. Although the correspondence is usually exact, it has been shown that there are at least some pathological cases where the correspondence breaks down. For example, in OWL Full `owl:Thing` contains individuals corresponding to the RDFS and OWL vocabularies (such as `rdf:Property`, `rdfs:subClassOf`, and `owl:hasValue`). (There are no such individuals in the model theory for OWL DL.) Limiting the extent of `owl:Thing`, for example as in

    SubClassOf(owl:Thing oneOf(ex:foo))

forces equalities in this vocabulary, which have truly unusual effects in the OWL Full model theory. For example, because there would be only one individual, and OWL syntax tokens are individuals in OWL Full, an `allValuesFrom` restriction would imply a `someValuesFrom` restriction.

In order to avoid any possible confusion as to the meaning of OWL DL, the OWL Full model theory has been given "non-normative" status (i.e., it is only informative) for OWL ontologies that can be written in the abstract syntax – for such ontologies, the definitive semantics is given by the OWL DL model theory.

14.3.6 OWL datatypes

As well as dealing with "abstract" classes such as `Person` and `Animal`, many practical applications need to represent and reason about datatypes and values such as integers and strings. The integration of datatypes in the OWL language is again heavily influenced by Description Logic research, which has demonstrated that care is required in order to avoid complexity blow-ups or even undecidability being caused by datatypes [Lutz, 2002]. In the $\mathcal{SHOQ}(\mathcal{D})$ Description Logic it was shown that this could be achieved by strictly separating the interpretation of datatypes and values from that of classes and individuals: $\mathcal{SHOQ}(\mathcal{D})$ interpretations include an additional interpretation domain for data values $\Delta_{\mathbf{D}}^{\mathcal{I}}$ which is disjoint from the domain of individuals $\Delta^{\mathcal{I}}$. Datatypes, such as integer, are interpreted as a subset of $\Delta_{\mathbf{D}}^{\mathcal{I}}$, and values such as the integer "35" are interpreted as elements of $\Delta_{\mathbf{D}}^{\mathcal{I}}$. The separation is further strengthened by dividing properties into two disjoint sets of abstract and datatype properties. Abstract properties such as `brother` are interpreted as binary relations on $\Delta^{\mathcal{I}}$ (i.e., subsets of $\Delta^{\mathcal{I}} \times \Delta^{\mathcal{I}}$), while datatype properties such as `age` are interpreted as binary relations between $\Delta^{\mathcal{I}}$ and $\Delta_{\mathbf{D}}^{\mathcal{I}}$ (i.e., subsets of $\Delta^{\mathcal{I}} \times \Delta_{\mathbf{D}}^{\mathcal{I}}$).

This design has the advantage that reasoning with datatypes and values can be almost entirely separated from reasoning with classes and individuals – a class-based reasoner simply needs access to a datatype "oracle" that can answer simple questions with respect to datatypes and values (e.g., "is -5 a nonNegative Integer?"). Moreover, the language remains decidable if datatype and value reasoning is decidable, i.e., if the oracle can guarantee to answer all questions of the relevant kind for supported datatypes. This can easily be achieved for a range of common datatypes such as integers, decimals, and strings [Lutz, 2002].

As well as these practical considerations, it can also be argued that the separation of classes and datatypes makes sense from a philosophical standpoint as datatypes are already structured by built-in predicates such as greater-than and less-than. From this point of view, it does not make sense to use ontology axioms to add further structure to datatypes or to form "hybrid" classes such as the class of red integers.

14.3.7 Reasoners, tools, and applications

As discussed in Subsection 14.3.1, an important motivation for the design of OWL DL and OWL Lite was the ability for applications to exploit known reasoning algorithms and existing (highly optimized) reasoner implementations. This meant that, even before the OWL specification was finalized, prototype tools and applications could make use of Description Logic reasoning systems such as FaCT [Horrocks, 1998a], Pellet [Pellet, 2003] and RACER [Haarslev and Möller, 2001e]. The use of these systems was also facilitated by the fact that they provide a standard application interface designed by the Description Logic Implementation Group (DIG) [Bechhofer *et al.*, 1999].

At the time when OWL achieved recommendation status (the final stage in the W3C standardization process), the above systems were only able to support OWL Lite reasoning. This was because, at that time, no suitable algorithm was known for $\mathcal{SHOIN}$, and all of the implementations were based on the $\mathcal{SHIQ}$ algorithms described in [Horrocks *et al.*, 1999] and [Horrocks *et al.*, 2000c]. In order to process OWL DL ontologies, reasoning systems typically applied some "work-around" with respect to nominals, e.g., by treating them as primitive classes. This work-around is sound but incomplete for subsumption. I.e., given ontologies $\mathcal{O}$ and $\mathcal{O}'$, where $\mathcal{O}'$ has been derived from $\mathcal{O}$ by replacing each occurrence of a nominal o with a primitive class C_o, a class C is subsumed by a class D with respect to $\mathcal{O}$ if C is subsumed by a D with respect to $\mathcal{O}'$, but if C is *not* subsumed by a D with respect to $\mathcal{O}'$, then we cannot be sure that C is *not* subsumed by a D with respect to $\mathcal{O}$. Clearly, the work-around is unsound for satisfiability, i.e., there may be concepts that are satisfiable with respect to $\mathcal{O}'$, but unsatisfiable with respect to $\mathcal{O}$.

This situation was clearly very unsatisfactory given the motivation for OWL's Description Logic-based design, and it was always anticipated that existing tableaux decision procedures for $\mathcal{SHIQ}$ and $\mathcal{SHOQ}$ would soon be extended to $\mathcal{SHOIQ}$. Although this took a little longer than anticipated, a tableaux decision procedure for $\mathcal{SHOIQ}$ was eventually developed [Horrocks and Sattler, 2005], and both the Pellet system and the FaCT++ system [Tsarkov and Horrocks, 2005] (the successor of the FaCT system) now use this algorithm to fully support OWL DL. It is expected that other reasoners, including Racer, will soon follow suit.

It is interesting to note that OWL is now supported by commercial Description Logic systems. These include the Cerebra system from Cerebra Inc. (formerly Network Inference), and RacerPro, a commercial version of the RACER system. There are also several OWL reasoners that are not based on tableaux decision procedures. These include KAON2, a system that uses a reduction of $\mathcal{SHIQ}(\mathcal{D})$ to disjunctive datalog [Hustadt *et al.*, 2004], and Hoolet, a system that uses the Vampire First Order Theorem prover via a translation of $\mathcal{SHOIN}(\mathbf{D})$ into FOL [Tsarkov *et al.*, 2004].

The growing importance of ontologies, and the emergence of the OWL standard, has also given impetus to the development of ontology engineering tools, including tools for editing, validating, visualizing, merging, and debugging OWL ontologies. Several Application Programming Interfaces (APIs) for OWL are also available.

Of the available OWL Editing tools, probably the best-known and most widely used is PROTÉGÉ [Gennari *et al.*, 2003]. PROTÉGÉ is a frame-based editor that supports OWL via an OWL Plugin. The Plugin uses a range of techniques (some of which were first developed in the OilEd editor [Bechhofer *et al.*, 2001b]) to extend the language that can be dealt with, e.g., by explicitly specifying quantification with slots and allowing for multiple necessary and sufficient conditions in class definitions. In addition to the frame editor, there are additional PROTÉGÉ plugins supporting, e.g., ontology visualization, ontology documentation, and "wizards" that can automate some basic steps in the ontology development process. PROTÉGÉ can connect to any Description Logic reasoner with a DIG compliant interface, and uses the reasoner to check class consistency, to compute the class hierarchy, and to compute the most specific class(es) that each individual is an instance of.

Several other OWL editing tools are also available. These include OilEd [Bechhofer *et al.*, 2001b] (from Manchester University), SWOOP [Kalyanpur *et al.*, 2005a] (from the Pellet team) and Construct (from Cerebra). The design of OilEd is based on that of PROTÉGÉ, but it provides more complete support for OWL DL. Like PROTÉGÉ, OilEd can use any DIG compliant reasoner to reason over the ontology. SWOOP is browser-based, and is much more tightly linked to OWL's syntactic structure; it provides both abstract syntax and RDF/XML syntax editing modes, and fully supports OWL DL. SWOOP uses the Pellet system for reasoning support, and also has an integrated debugger [Kalyanpur *et al.*, 2005b]. Construct is a graphical tool that uses a UML-like notation; it uses the Cerebra reasoner to provide reasoning support.

OWL editing tools are also expanding into the software engineering realm, as tools such as Sandpiper Software's Medius Visual Ontology Modeler supports ontology development using UML modeling tools with output in OWL (see `http://www.sandsoft.com/`). This enables broader communities to model, edit, and integrate with OWL ontologies.

Although OWL was initially developed as an ontology language for the Semantic Web, OWL has also been widely adopted as a de facto standard for ontology-based applications. These include "traditional" applications in e-Science and -Medicine, as well as applications in industry and government. The advantages of using OWL in such applications include the relative stability and interoperability conferred by a W3C standard, and the availability of an expanding range of reasoners and tools.

Examples of OWL ontology applications include:

- Ontologies developed by members of the Open Biomedical Ontologies Consortium (see `http://obo.sourceforge.net/`), which recommends OWL as the exchange language for all Life Science ontologies. These include the widely used Gene Ontology (GO) and Microarray Gene Expression Data (MGED) ontology.
- The US National Cancer Institute (NCI) "thesaurus", an ontology containing the working vocabulary used in NCI data system (see `http://ncicb.nci.nih.gov/NCICB/core/EVS/`).
- United Nations Food and Agriculture Organization (FAO) is using OWL to develop a range of ontologies covering areas such as agriculture and fisheries (see `http://www.fao.org/agris/aos/Applications/intro.htm`).
- The Semantic Web for Earth and Environmental Terminology (SWEET) ontologies developed at the US National Aeronautics and Space Administration (NASA) Jet Propulsion Laboratory (see `http://sweet.jpl.nasa.gov/ontology/`). These include ontologies describing space, the biosphere, and the sun. SWEET is now being expanded by a number of earth and space science efforts, and has been augmented in the GEON project (see `http://www.geongrid.org/`) to cover the solid earth, and by the Virtual Solar Terrestrial Observatory Project (see `http://vsto.hao.ucar.edu/`) to include much more information on the atmosphere.
- An ontology used at General Motors in a project to help quality improvement activities for assembly line processes in different production sites [Morgan *et al.*, 2005].

14.4 Summary

The Semantic Web is envisaged as an evolution of the existing Web where terms defined in ontologies will be used to give well defined and machine-processable meaning to Web accessible information and services. OWL, a Description Logic-based ontology language, has been designed for this purpose.

Because of the ambitious design goals for OWL, because of the multiple influences on OWL, and also because of the structural requirements constraining OWL, the development of OWL has not been without problems. Through hard work and compromise, these problems have largely been overcome, resulting in an ontology language that is truly part of the Semantic Web.

It was not possible to simultaneously satisfy all of the constraints on OWL, so two styles of using OWL have been developed, each appropriate under different circumstances.

One style of OWL usage is motivated by the need to unambiguously represent information in an expressive language, but one that can still be reasoned with predictably. When this is a primary goal, OWL DL will be the target language, and it has been used in a number of existing applications. When using OWL DL, some compatibility with RDF is lost, mostly having to do with using classes and properties as individuals. On the other hand, users of OWL DL benefit from decidable inference, and the availability of an increasingly wide range of tools and infrastructure, including efficient reasoning systems and sophisticated ontology development environments. OWL DL also has a frame-like alternative syntax that can be used to make working with OWL easier.

Even though OWL DL is, essentially, a Description Logic, it also includes features that place it firmly in the Semantic Web. OWL DL uses the datatyping mechanisms from RDF and many of the built-in XML Schema datatypes. OWL DL uses RDF URI references as names, including the names from RDF, RDFS, and XML Schema datatypes that are relevant. Entailment in OWL DL is compatible with entailment in RDF and RDFS.

For users who still need unambiguous representation and predictable reasoning, but for whom simplicity is more important than expressive power, the OWL Lite subset of OWL DL may be a good choice. This sublanguage rules out some of the things that can be said in OWL DL, but still retains considerable expressive power. Moreover, OWL Lite is supported by a wider range of reasoning tools, and as key reasoning tasks are of lower worst-case complexity, these reasoners might be expected to be more efficient, in general, than OWL DL reasoners.

The other style of OWL usage is one where compatibility with RDF is the overarching concern. In this case, OWL Full would be an appropriate choice. OWL Full extends RDF and RDFS to a full ontology language, with a well-specified entailment relationship that extends entailment in RDF and RDFS, while avoiding any paradoxes that might arise. However, entailment in OWL Full is undecidable, which is a significant issue in most circumstances, and no effective tools for reasoning are available for OWL Full, nor are they expected to appear. Also, the user-friendly alternative syntax is not adequate for OWL Full, so RDF/XML must be used.

In practice, relatively few OWL Full applications have emerged to date, and where OWL Full ontologies are found, they often turn out to be outside the OWL DL subset only as the result of minor syntactic errors. Fragments of OWL are, however, sometimes used as ad hoc extensions to RDFS. A common example is the use of OWL functional properties, and explicit equivalences and (in)equalities, in what would otherwise be an RDFS ontology.

There remain, of course, significant issues that are deliberately not handled by OWL, but which are definitely relevant to many Semantic Web use cases:

- OWL avoids anything related to non-monotonicity (such as default reasoning and localized closed-world assumptions);
- OWL's limited expressiveness excludes operations such as property-chaining, or, more generally, axioms with variables, such as rules (although there are already proposals for extensions in this direction [Horrocks *et al.*, 2005; Eiter *et al.*, 2004; Motik *et al.*, 2004; Rosati, 2005], some of which are based on earlier work on integrating Description Logics and logic programming rules as described in Chapter 2);
- like the Description Logics on which it is based, OWL does not support N-ary relations (although Description Logics supporting N-ary relations are known [Calvanese *et al.*, 1999c]);
- OWL does not allow for the use of data values as database style keys [Lutz *et al.*, 2004], or for functionality or path constraints [Calvanese *et al.*, 1999c; Khizder *et al.*, 2001];
- OWL's import mechanism is limited, and does not support fine-grained operations (such as the importation of parts of ontologies);
- OWL integrates datatypes in a very clean way, but there is no notion of operations on these datatypes (such as integer arithmetic or string operations).

Extending the current Semantic Web with some or all of these features not only will require a standardization effort, but sets a significant research challenge to the community.

15

Natural Language Processing

Enrico Franconi

Abstract

In most natural language processing applications, Description Logics have been used to encode in a knowledge base some syntactic, semantic, and pragmatic elements needed to drive the semantic interpretation and the natural language generation processes. More recently, Description Logics have been used to fully characterize the semantic issues involved in the interpretation phase. In this chapter the various proposals that have appeared in the literature about the use of Description Logics for natural language processing will be analyzed.

15.1 Introduction

Since the early days of the KL-ONE system, one of the main applications of Description Logics has been for *semantic interpretation* in natural language processing [Brachman *et al.*, 1979]. Semantic interpretation is the derivation process from the syntactic analysis of an utterance to its *logical form* – intended here as the representation of its literal deep and context-dependent meaning. Typically, Description Logics have been used to encode in a knowledge base both syntactic and semantic elements needed to drive the semantic interpretation process. One part of the knowledge base constitutes the *lexical semantics* knowledge, relating words and their syntactic properties to concept structures, while the other part describes the *contextual* and *domain* knowledge, giving a deep meaning to concepts. By developing this idea further, a considerable part of the research effort has been devoted to the development of linguistically motivated ontologies, i.e., large knowledge bases where both concepts closely related to lexemes and domain concepts coexist. Logical forms and various kinds of internal semantics representations based on Description Logics may also provide the basis for further computational processing such as representing common meanings in machine translation applications, generating coherent text starting from its semantic content, answering database queries, and dialog management.

After a big success in the 1980s and the beginning of the 1990s (see, e.g., the collection of papers in [Sowa, 1991]), the interest of the applied computational linguistic community in Description Logics began to drop, as did its interest in well-founded theories on syntax or semantics. At the time of writing this chapter, there is no major applied project in natural language processing making use of Description Logics. This is due to the positive achievements in real applications of the systems based on shallow analysis and statistical approaches to semantics, initiated by the applications in the message understanding area.

In this chapter the basic uses of Description Logics for natural language processing will be analyzed, together with a little bit of history, and the role of Description Logics in the current state of the art in computational linguistics will be pointed out. Obviously, space constraints will lead to several omissions and over-simplifications.

15.2 Semantic interpretation

In order to understand the role of Description Logics in semantic interpretation, let us first introduce a general setting for the process of deriving a logical form of an utterance.

A basic property of a logical form as a semantic representation of a natural language constituent – such as a noun phrase (NP) or a verb phrase (VP) – is *compositionality*, i.e., the semantic representation of a constituent is a function of the semantic interpretation of its subconstituents. Thus, a close correspondence between syntactic structure and logical form is allowed. In this way, a parser working according to some grammar rules can incrementally build up the semantic interpretation of an utterance using the corresponding lexical semantic rules of logical composition – specifying how the logical terms associated to the subconstituents are to be combined in order to give the formula for the constituent. Thus, each lexeme has an associated (possibly complex) logical term, which forms its contribution to the meaning of the utterance it is part of.

In the context of such a formalism, an effective semantic lexical discrimination process could be carried out during parsing, by cutting out the exponential factor due to the explicit treatment all the possible derivations. Semantically implausible interpretations can be discarded, by checking –

whenever the parser tries to build a constituent – the inconsistency of the logical form compositionally obtained at that stage. This leaves out many syntactically plausible but semantically implausible interpretations. Such a discrimination step is highly effective in restricted domain applications, where knowledge of the world considerably reduces the number of possible models. Clearly, the more the contextual and domain knowledge is taken into consideration when evaluating a logical form, the more effective is the discrimination process. Thus, consistency checking of logical forms plays the role of a generalized selectional restrictions mechanism.

But what is the relationship between a syntactic constituent and its range of possible lexical semantic contributions? The conceptual content of a lexeme should convey both the lexical relations – such as, for example, synonymy, hyponymy, incompatibility – and the subcategorization information about the expected arguments (aka complements) of the lexical entry. For example the verb *paint* may be conceptualized as an event having an *agent* thematic role corresponding to the *subject* syntactic argument, with a specified selectional restriction being the concept *animate*. It is important to distinguish the syntactic information – such as the lexical relations and the subcategorization frame constraining the complements to have specific syntactic structures – from the semantic information – such as the thematic roles and their selectional restrictions. A semantic lexical entry will specify the appropriate mappings between the syntactic structure of the lexeme and the conceptual information.

The situation is, of course, a bit more complex, since, for example, there is no direct obvious conceptual content to lexemes belonging to particular syntactic categories like adjectives or adverbs. Moreover there is a distinction between complements (which are considered as internal arguments) and *adjuncts* (which are considered as modifiers). It is outside the scope of this chapter to analyze the correspondence between syntax and semantics and its compositional nature (see, e.g., [Jackendoff, 1990; Pustejovsky, 1988]).

For example, the sentence "A painter paints a fresco" involves the concepts Painter, Fresco, and Paint, where the concept Paint has two thematic roles associated to it, an agent and a goal, with the concepts Animate and Inanimate as respective selectional restrictions. Moreover, the conceptualizations should include the facts that a Painter is a subconcept of Animate, a Fresco is a subconcept of Inanimate, and the concepts Animate and Inanimate are disjoint. This information is enough, for example, to validate the above sentence, while it would discard as semantically implausible the sentence "A fresco paints a painter". This conceptualization and its relationship with the lexical knowledge can be encoded in a DL knowledge base.

Many studies have been done about building a good DL knowledge base for natural language processing (also called *ontology*) [Bateman, 1990; Hovy and Knight, 1993; Knight and Luk, 1994; Bateman *et al.*, 1995]– see also Chapter 14. A good linguistically motivated ontology ought to be partitioned into a language-dependent but domain-independent part (the *upper model*) and a language-independent but domain-dependent part (the *domain model*) – but this result is theoretically very hard to achieve [Bateman, 1990; Lang, 1991]. A good linguistically motivated ontology should be used both for semantic interpretation and for natural language generation (see Section 15.4). The conceptualization in the ontology should be at a level of granularity which may depend on the application: if selectional restrictions are too specific, disambiguation is achieved, but probably many correct sentences will be rejected (e.g., the sentences involving some form of metaphor, type shifting, or metonymy); if selectional restrictions are too general, the opposite problem may appear. In principle, a good linguistically motivated ontology should be abstract, large-scale, re-usable. However, these goals are very hard to achieve since they conflict with the practical need to implement effective and discriminating ontologies in specialized domains.

The ideas just sketched form the theoretical background of any application of Description Logics for semantic interpretation, since the early works where KL-ONE was involved [Bobrow and Webber, 1980; Sondheimer *et al.*, 1984; Brachman and Schmolze, 1985; Jacobs, 1991]. Every realized system relies on the so-called *multilevel semantics architecture* [Lavelli *et al.*, 1992], where a sequence of processing phases is distinguished:

- Lexical discrimination: whenever the parser tries to build a constituent, the *consistency* of the semantic part of such a constituent is checked. In parallel, a first logical form is built up – where references and quantifier scoping are still ambiguous – expressing the meaning of the sentence in the most specialized way with respect to the semantic lexicon and the background knowledge. Heuristics are applied to the minimal form in order to obtain a preferential ordering of the semantically consistent but still lexically ambiguous interpretations.
- Anaphora and quantifier scoping resolution: the semantically plausible referents for linguistic expressions such as definite NPs, pronouns and deictic references are identified, and the scope of quantifiers is resolved by making explicit the different unambiguous interpretations. Syntax-based heuristics are used to cut down the various derivations to a unique unambiguous one.
- Contextual interpretation: decides how to react in a given dialogic situation, considering the type of request, the context, and the model of the user interest.

It makes use of knowledge about the speech acts, the dialog and the user model.

It has to be emphasized that all the approaches aim at deriving a unique unambiguous logical form. For this purpose, the logical form is treated as a mere compositionally obtained data structure on which to operate ad hoc algorithms for solving ambiguities, with the support of the information represented in the knowledge base. There is no attempt to give a logic-based semantics to the "logical form" during the disambiguation phases. The role of Description Logics is thus limited to serving a lexically motivated knowledge base, which is used for building the logical form. Some approaches purport to represent the logical form itself as DL assertions, but in fact they use it just as a support for somehow computing the real logical form. Section 15.3 will discuss the few DL-based well-founded approaches, where the whole semantic interpretation process has been given a logical foundation.

A number of recent important projects involving Description Logics for semantic interpretation are listed below.

- The JANUS system [Weischedel, 1989], where the consistency check of the selectional restrictions was implemented as a double up-and-down subsumption check.
- The XTRA system [Allgayer et al., 1989], proposing a clear distinction between the domain independent linguistically motivated part of the knowledge base (called Functional-Semantic Structure, FSS), and the domain-dependent part (called Conceptual Knowledge Base, CKB) modeling the knowledge of an underlying expert system.
- The PRACMA project [Fehrer et al., 1994], in which an expressive Description Logic has been studied to support special inferences such as probabilistic reasoning, non-monotonic reasoning, and abductive reasoning.
- The LILOG project [Herzog and Rollinger, 1991], funded by IBM, a very ambitious research project for studying the logical foundations of the semantics of natural language, with an emphasis on computational aspects. The project belongs to the category of projects where the whole semantic interpretation process has been given a logical foundation – by means of a sorted first-order logic. However, the role of Description Logics is again just as a knowledge server during the various interpretation and disambiguation phases.
- The ALFRESCO system, a multi-modal dialog prototype for the exploration of fourteenth century Italian painters and frescoes [Stock et al., 1991; 1993], and the natural language interface for the *concierge* of the system MAIA, a mobile robot with intelligent capabilities in the domain of office activities [Samek-Lodovici and Strapparava, 1990; Lavelli et al., 1992; Franconi, 1994]. These systems are characterized by the presence of natural language dialogs, so that logical form becomes central to conveying the meaning for the evolving *behavior* of the system.

- The VERBMOBIL project [Wahlster, 2000], a large speech-to-speech translation project, with translations into German, English, and Japanese. In VERBMOBIL, the role of Description Logics is limited to the off-line pre-computation of a taxonomy of concepts with thematic roles and selectional restrictions, which are then used by ad hoc rules during the runtime disambiguation phase.
- The Ford Direct Labor Management System (DLMS) [Rychtyckyj, 1996; 1999] is one of the few industrial level examples of a DL-based application involving natural language. DLMS utilizes a DL knowledge base in a fairly standard way to build the semantic interpretation of *process sheets* – natural language documents containing specific information about work instructions – and to generate from them structured descriptions of the parts and the tools required for allocating labor at the car plant floor.

15.3 Reasoning with the logical form

Traditionally, the logical form has been considered in computational linguistics as only representing the literal – i.e., context-independent – meaning of an utterance, as clearly distinguished from the representation of the surface syntactic constituent structure, and from a deeper semantic representation, which is a function of discourse context and world knowledge. Thus, the logical form plays in these cases an intermediate role between syntax and the deep semantics, and it is therefore not intended to fully contain the meaning in context of the utterance. Moreover, quite often a further distinction is introduced between *quasi* logical forms – i.e., literal under-specified semantic representations – and proper logical forms – i.e., literal unambiguous derivations.

The reasons for separating the literal under-specified, the literal unambiguous, and the deep meaning representations are mainly pragmatic rather than theoretical. Pure linguists would say that any sentence has just one unambiguous meaning, and that any ambiguity is introduced by under-constraining the interpretation process – e.g., by not adequately considering the context knowledge. In such a case, they would speak of different possible ending paths in the derivation (i.e., interpretation) process, each one of them being again unambiguous. Clearly, this approach is infeasible from a computational point of view: first, because the number of derivations might combinatorially increase; and secondly because the interdependencies among the derivations are lost.

On the other hand, computational linguists consider ambiguities as part of the meaning of utterances, with the ultimate goal of being able to reason with such under-specified expressions, in order to increase compactness in the representation and efficiency in the processing. Allen [1993] argues that one of the crucial issues facing future natural language systems is the development of knowledge representation formalisms that can effectively handle ambiguity.

We can identify two main approaches. The classical *computational* approaches – like the ones described above – rely on the modularity of the semantic analysis process – the multilevel semantics architecture – starting from the under-specified representation and ending up with an unambiguous and context-dependent representation. The *semantics-oriented* approaches usually propose a very expressive logical language – possibly with an expressivity greater than first-order logic – with the goal of giving a clear semantics to many natural language phenomena, and in particular to ambiguities and under-specification. Ambiguities can be roughly classified as follows: lexical ambiguities introduced by, e.g., prepositions, nouns, and verbs; structural ambiguities such as PP-attachment ambiguities – involving prepositional phrases; referential ambiguities such as quantification scoping and anaphora.

A disadvantage of the first approach is that there are no solid formal grounds for the proper use of the logical form, and in particular for the treatment of ambiguity, so that operations on the logical form are often based on heuristics and ad hoc procedures. This can be justified by the fact that reasoning on logical forms including – among other things – domain knowledge, incomplete and ambiguous terms, unsolved references, and under-specified quantifications, is considered a hard computational task. Computational linguists have devised structural processing techniques based on syntax, selectional restrictions, case grammars, and structured information such as frames and type hierarchies – carefully trying to avoid or to drastically reduce the inclusion in the computational machinery of logical inference mechanisms for treating ambiguities. Of course, these techniques often need ad hoc mechanisms when such ambiguities come into play. The computational approach is an example of *"knowledge representation as engineering"*.

On the other hand, a number of recent works in applying Description Logics to natural language processing ([Quantz, 1995; Franconi, 1996; Ludwig *et al.*, 2000]) are getting closer to a semantics-oriented approach, but they follow a minimalist conceptualization, and they emphasize the computational aspects. Instead of trying to solve sophisticated semantic problems of natural language, they try to logically reconstruct some *basic* issues in a general way, which is *compositional, homogeneous, principled,* and interesting from an applicative point of view. The main idea of these approaches is to take logical forms seriously: they represent not only the literal meaning of the fragment but also lexical ambiguities, represent unresolved referents via variables and equality, interpret plural entities and (generalized) quantifiers, and are linked to a rich theory of the domain. To that end, an expressive logical language should have a proper reasoning mechanism, and nonetheless be compositional.

In this section an abstract overview will be given by means of examples, in such a way that, we believe, common ideas will be captured.

Let us first try to understand how a logical form can be characterized in terms of proper logical constructs. It is observed that, assuming the widely accepted Davidsonian view on eventualities, natural language phrases – such as an NP or a VP – explicitly introduce discourse referents stating the existence of individuals or events of the domain model. Introduced referents are represented as existentially quantified variables. The possibility of having variables and constants allows for the representation of referential ambiguities. This is the basis of most works on logical formalizations of the logical form.

For example, the NP *A fresco of Giotto* might be given the logical form

$$\exists b.\ \mathsf{Fresco}(b) \wedge \mathsf{of}(b, \mathsf{GIOTTO})$$

while the NP *A fresco painted by Giotto* might be given the logical form

$$\exists b, e.\ \mathsf{Fresco}(b) \wedge \mathsf{Paint}(e) \wedge \mathsf{agent}(e, \mathsf{GIOTTO}) \wedge \mathsf{goal}(e, b). \qquad (15.1)$$

As we have pointed out above, consistency checking of a (partial) logical form corresponding to a constituent may help in the semantic discrimination process. Thus, in a restricted application domain, we would like to discard a sentence like *A fresco paints Giotto*, since its logical form

$$\exists b, e.\ \mathsf{Fresco}(b) \wedge \mathsf{Paint}(e) \wedge \mathsf{agent}(e, b) \wedge \mathsf{goal}(e, \mathsf{GIOTTO})$$

would be inconsistent with respect to a general domain theory of frescoes and animate things that we could attach to the lexicon:

$$\forall x, y.\ \mathsf{Paint}(x) \rightarrow (\mathsf{agent}(x, y) \rightarrow \mathsf{Animate}(y))$$
$$\forall x.\ \mathsf{Animate}(x) \rightarrow \neg \mathsf{Inanimate}(x)$$
$$\forall x.\ \mathsf{Fresco}(x) \rightarrow \mathsf{Inanimate}(x).$$

Such an axiomatic theory plays the role of *meaning postulates* for the predicates appearing in the logical form; they can be also considered as a set of *predicate level axioms*. Using a DL-based formalism, this will be written as the following theory:

$$\text{Paint} \sqsubseteq \forall \text{agent.Animate}$$
$$\text{Animate} \sqsubseteq \neg \text{Inanimate}$$
$$\text{Fresco} \sqsubseteq \text{Inanimate}.$$

This is the place where Description Logics play a formal role as general domain theories representing the basic ontological properties of common-sense domain knowledge.

Let us consider the *deep* meaning of *A fresco of Giotto*. The NP is ambiguous (at least) with respect to the two readings *A fresco painted by Giotto* and *A fresco owned by Giotto*. We could reformulate the ambiguous logical form, by enumerating the unambiguous derivations, i.e., by disjoining the logical forms of the two readings. However, it is infeasible to explicitly enumerate all the (exponentially large) number of readings; moreover, this would not add any information to the logical form. Note however that traditional computational approaches purport to always find a unique unambiguous representation for the final logical form, based on syntactically and contextually motivated heuristics; in this case, the enumeration will be the basis for an ad hoc preferential ordering. If the logical form is written instead as

$$\exists b. \text{ Fresco}(b) \land (\text{paintedBy} \sqcup \text{ownedBy})(b, \text{GIOTTO}) \qquad (15.2)$$

then each of the two readings clearly entails this *ambiguous* (or, better, under-specified) representation. Of course, the use of an explicit disjunction to encode the ambiguity requires a particular treatment of the natural language negation, which cannot be represented as a classical negation in the logical form. In fact, derivations from the ambiguous content are independent traces and, for example, De Morgan's law would not hold anymore. The treatment of natural language negation has never been considered in DL-based approaches. So, we assume the logical form to be always positive; of course, this is not necessary for the DL-based domain theory.

In this way, the lexicon – which can be considered as an associated theory – may contain a meaning postulate for the relation of:

$$\forall x, y. \text{ of}(x, y) \leftrightarrow \text{paintedBy}(x, y) \lor \text{ownedBy}(x, y)$$

which can be rewritten using Description Logics as

$$\text{of} \equiv \text{paintedBy} \sqcup \text{ownedBy}.$$

Moreover, if one writes *reification* axioms (see [Franconi and Rabito, 1994]) of the kind

$$\forall x, y. \; \mathsf{paintedBy}(y, x) \leftrightarrow \exists z. \; \mathsf{Paint}(z) \wedge \mathsf{agent}(z, x) \wedge \mathsf{goal}(z, y)$$

then the logical form (15.1) with the explicit event also entails the ambiguous representation (15.2). In Description Logics, this would be written as

$$\mathsf{paintedBy} \equiv \mathsf{goal}^- |_{\mathsf{Paint}} \circ \mathsf{agent}.$$

The ambiguity of *A fresco of Giotto* can be *monotonically* refined later on in the dialog by uttering, e.g., either *Giotto painted the fresco in Siena* or *Giotto sold his fresco*. The refinement process is monotonic, since it is not necessary to revise the knowledge asserted by means of the logical form (15.2).

Lexical ambiguities of nouns can also be represented, as in the example *The pilot was out* – where pilot can be a small flame used to start a furnace, or a person who flies airplanes. The sentence *He was on the toilet* monotonically refines the previous one, because the pronoun *he* may refer only to a person, thus excluding the reading with flame. Of course, in order to make possible such a reasoning by cases, axioms at the predicate level having negation and, more generally, partitioning capabilities have to be added to the theory – specifying and reducing the possible models:

$$\mathsf{Pilot} \equiv \mathsf{Flame} \sqcup \mathsf{Aviator}$$
$$\mathsf{Flame} \sqsubseteq \mathsf{Process}$$
$$\mathsf{Aviator} \sqsubseteq \mathsf{Human}$$
$$\mathsf{Human} \sqsubseteq \mathsf{Animate}$$
$$\mathsf{Animate} \sqcap \mathsf{Process} \sqsubseteq \bot.$$

Verb ambiguity is also captured in the same manner. For example, it is possible to rule out the sentence *The door opens the door*, given the two senses of *open* as "cause to open" – transitive, with an animate agent – and "become open" – intransitive. According to these two senses, both the constituents "*The door opens*" and "*opens the door*" are consistent, but the whole sentence is inconsistent.

Talking briefly about structural ambiguities, a general theory of common-sense knowledge will allow only for one interpretation of *Giotto paints the fresco with a brush* where the PP attaches to the painting event – "*paints with a brush*" – ruling out the interpretation "*the fresco representing a brush*". An early detection of the semantic inconsistency solving the PP-attachment problem is very important in practical applications, since the non-deterministic choice among the different interpretations is usually left to the parser. Thus, the parser does not need to compute a combinatorial number of derivations. Clearly, any metaphoric aspect of language is excluded in these approaches.

Following a semantics-oriented approach as sketched in this section, Quantz [1993; 1995] proposes a preferential DL-based approach to disambiguation in natural language processing. He gives a particular emphasis to the problem of anaphora resolution, showing that an adequate disambiguation strategy has to be based on factors which take globally into account heterogeneous information (e.g., from syntax, semantics, domain knowledge) and yield *preferences* with varying degrees of relevance. For this purpose, Quantz introduced and developed a sound and complete proof theory for a *preferential Description Logic*, including a non-monotonic extension with weighted defaults. In his approach, a DL theory comprises syntactic, semantic, domain, and pragmatic knowledge, which globally contributes to the preferential disambiguation process, following the proposal by [Hobbs *et al.*, 1993].

Franconi [1996] proposes a formalism based on expressive Description Logics complemented with the ability to express logical forms as *conjunctive queries* [Calvanese *et al.*, 1998a], i.e., formulae in the conjunctive existential fragment of first-order logic. The formalism allows for both underspecified semantic representations and encapsulation of contextual and domain knowledge in the form of meaning postulates. In particular, lexical ambiguities, structural ambiguities, and quantification scoping ambiguities [Franconi, 1993] are considered, and an account of the structure of events and processes in terms of tense and aspect is given [Franconi *et al.*, 1993; 1994]. It is shown how to apply this logic for lexical discrimination based on semantic knowledge.

Ludwig *et al.* [2000] present a modified version of Discourse Representation Theory (DRT) and show that its Discourse Representation Structures (DRSs) may be expressed as assertional statements in a Description Logic. This allows lexical discrimination during the parsing process based on the domain model. In order to capture situations where the available information is insufficient to characterize the meaning of an utterance, a partial logic (called *first-order ionic logic*) is introduced to represent and reason with the logical form. The approach combines in an elegant way linguistic and contextual semantics – both represented in the DL domain model.

15.4 Knowledge-based natural language generation

In the previous sections an architecture for semantic interpretation was introduced, where Description Logics were used to build a knowledge base with lexical and conceptual information. The knowledge base encodes the necessary data for building the logical form from the analysis of some natural language text. In this section we mention another task which makes use of the same body of knowledge expressed in a DL-based ontology, but with the dual goal of generating a coherent (multi-sentential) natural language text, starting from an abstract non-linguistic specification of its meaning. Examples are in the context of dialogs (see, e.g., [Stock *et al.*, 1991; 1993]), of natural language instructions (see, e.g., [Moore and Paris, 1993; Di Eugenio, 1994; 1998; Paris and Vander Linden, 1996a; 1996b]), of language translation (see, e.g., [Dorr, 1992; Dorr and Voss, 1993; 1995; Knight *et al.*, 1995; Quantz and Schmitz, 1994; Wahlster, 2000]), or of multimedia presentations (see, e.g., [Wahlster *et al.*, 1993; André and Rist, 1995; André *et al.*, 1996]).

The lexical and conceptual knowledge base classifier is the main driving component for the algorithms used to solve the problem of *lexical choice*, i.e., the task of choosing an appropriate target language term in generating text from an underlying logical form [Dorr *et al.*, 1994; Stede, 1999]. The lexicalization problem is a non-trivial one, since it is possible to have alternative lexical choices covering various (overlapping) parts of the content representation – a translation *divergence* – or it may be necessary to change the conveyed information content in order to find a viable lexical choice – a translation *mismatch*. The problem is usually solved by using ad hoc algorithms which make use of the classifier for determining which lexical units can potentially be used to express parts of the logical form representing the content.

The choice and the realization of the most appropriate verbalization should be made in the context of the previous utterances (in the case of a dialog), of the surrounding environment (in the case of multimedia presentation), and of the overall goal of the ongoing communicative act. For these tasks, it is not enough to have an underlying representation of the content of the text to be generated, but a *pragmatic* aspect has to be considered as well. The pragmatic knowledge about the *rhetorical* interrelationships which occur among the various parts of the broader linguistic and extra-linguistic context of the communication is needed to generate a coherent presentation in agreement with its communicative goals. In other words, on the one hand there is the content to be presented, on the other hand there is the style of its presentation which should use the most appropriate linguistic expressions to convey the message.

In order to generate a text satisfying the communicative goals and the coherence requirements, a planning algorithm is used to generate an overall structured text (or discourse) strategy, giving the general shape of the text.

Using the lexical and conceptual information in the knowledge base, the planner – by taking into account the grammar of the target language – converts the text plans into a specialized unambiguous representation of the semantic and syntactic information necessary to select the appropriate target language terms [Moore and Paris, 1993; Paris and Vander Linden, 1996b].

16

Description Logics for Databases

Alex Borgida
Maurizio Lenzerini
Riccardo Rosati

Abstract

In contrast to the relatively complex information that can be expressed in DL ABoxes (which we might call knowledge or information), databases and other sources such as files, semistructured data, and the World Wide Web provide rather simpler *data*, which must however be managed effectively. This chapter surveys the major classes of application of Description Logics and their reasoning facilities to the issues of data management, including: (i) expressing the conceptual domain model/ontology of the data source, (ii) integrating multiple data sources, and (iii) expressing and evaluating queries. In each case we utilize the standard properties of Description Logics, such as the ability to express ontologies at a level closer to that of human conceptualization (e.g., representing conceptual schemas), determining consistency of descriptions (e.g., determining if a query or the integration of some schemas is consistent), and automatically classifying descriptions that are definitions (e.g., queries are really definitions, so we can classify them and determine subsumption between them).

16.1 Introduction

According to [ElMasri and Navathe, 1994], a database is a coherent collection of related data, which have some "inherent meaning". Databases are similar to knowledge bases because they are usually used to maintain *models* of some universe of discourse (UofD). Of course, the purpose of such computer models is to support end-users in finding out things about the world, and therefore it is important to maintain an up-to-date and error-free model. The main difference between databases and knowledge bases is that while the former concentrate on manipulating *large and persistent* models of relatively simple data, the latter provide more support for *inference* – finding answers about the model which had not been explicitly told to it – and involve fewer but more complex data.

Following the functional view of knowledge bases advocated by Levesque, we expect a number of operations that can be applied to the KB, such as **define**, **tell**, and **ask**. Each of these operations involves one or more languages, such as the schema/constraint language, the update language, the query language and the answer language. In an earlier paper surveying the application of Description Logics to data management [Borgida, 1995], it has been argued that Description Logics offer advantages for each of these languages, as well as the internal processing of queries.

We begin by providing a review of the important notions involving databases, their development and use, in preparation for examining the application of Description Logics in these tasks.

First, one needs to describe the UofD about which the database will be knowledgeable. This is a form of requirements specification, which is normally undertaken using some high-level language, because the requirements will have to be understandable both to end-users and implementors, so they can agree on the goals. In databases, the best known such language is the Entity–Relationship (ER) data model,[1] but many other so-called *semantic modeling languages* have been proposed [Hull and King, 1987]. The ER data model will be described in considerable detail and precision in Section 16.2; for now, suffice it to say that it views the world as populated by entities, which are related to each other by *n*-ary relationships, and are described by attributes having atomic values. Note that a semantic model may be concerned with the UofD as well as the data to be stored in the computer, and consists of mostly time-invariant generic information (e.g., "every department has exactly one manager") as opposed to specific facts (e.g., "Edna manages the shipping department"). The semantic model introduces the terms to be used in talking about the domain, and captures their meaning by their interrelationships and constraints on them.

From this generic description of the UofD, the database designer develops a *logical schema*, describing the structure of data stored in the database, including the data types, interconnections, and constraints that must hold. Different data models are used for this purpose, but the *relational data model* has become the logical model of choice. While in the semantic modeling phase the emphasis was on a natural and direct mapping to the UofD, in this case the driving force is the existence of large software systems called

---

[1] The term "data model" refers to a language or set of concepts for describing a class of databases.

Database Management Systems (DBMSs), which support the management of the data in the model. For example, the relational data model views data as being stored in the form of tables/relations, with rows/tuples containing primitive data types (e.g., integers, strings). In this case, the schema contains, among other things, the name of each table, with its columns and their datatype. For example, table Supplies may have columns for the material, the supplier, the recipient, as well as the shipment date and the amount of material supplied. Relational DBMSs require that each table be given a subset of attributes (called a "key") which uniquely identifies each tuple. DBMSs may offer additional ways to capture integrity constraints – assertions distinguishing valid from invalid states of the data.

More recently, *Object-Oriented DBMSs* have been developed. These support the management of persistent objects with intrinsic identity, which can be related to (collections of) other objects, not just atomic values. Such OO-DBMSs can be used, among other things, for providing persistence for object-oriented languages. Object-oriented languages and databases also support the notion of "method" or procedure attached to a class, as well as implementation encapsulation, but these aspects will not be considered in this chapter.

The database is used of course to store facts about the (current) state of the world. Databases make the so-called "closed-world assumption", which states that a fact is false unless it has been explicitly stated as true. This assumption works well, with the restriction that the database represents only a very limited form of partial information. In particular, databases do not allow the representation of disjunctive information, and support only a very limited form of existential quantification: if there is no information about an attribute, it is given the *null* value.

In order to provide access to the data stored in databases, DBMSs support a variety of *query languages* – languages for specifying declaratively what data is to be retrieved. For relational databases, SQL is the practical query language of choice. However, from the theoretical point of view, first-order logic formulae with free variables are a much more elegant form, based on the observation that tables can be viewed as predicates. For example,

$$\exists m, d1, d2.\, \mathsf{supplies}('\mathtt{intel}', r, m, d1) \wedge \mathsf{supplies}('\mathtt{intel}', r, m, d2) \wedge (d2 \neq d1)$$

would be asking for recipients (values of the free variable r) who had received from $'\mathtt{intel}'$ shipments of the same material (m) on different dates ($d1, d2$).

Query languages of varying expressive power can be obtained by restricting or extending the above "standard". For example, the so-called "conjunctive" or "select–join–project" queries only allow formulae with existential quantifiers and conjunction, while Datalog is a query language that permits the use of intermediate tables derived using Horn rules, and thereby supports recursion [Ullman, 1988]. For example, if we want to describe when one company depends on another through a chain of suppliers, we could state the rules[2]

$$\mathsf{dependsOn}(x, y) \quad \leftarrow \quad \mathsf{supplies}(x, y, m, d).$$
$$\mathsf{dependsOn}(x, y) \quad \leftarrow \quad \mathsf{supplies}(x, z, m, d, a) \wedge \mathsf{dependsOn}(z, y, m_2, d_2, a_2).$$

In many DBMSs, the result of a query is another structure of the kind found in the schema (e.g., relational queries return tables as answers). In some situations, either because a query is asked frequently or because we want to restrict the access of some users to a subset of the database, a query can be named, in which case it is called a *view*. If a view is *materialized*, then its value is stored rather than re-computed on demand, and it is kept correct after every update to the basic database.

The DBMS performs a number of hidden functions, insulating users from the considerable details of the *physical* level. For example, the DBMS places the incoming data physically onto storage media, and provides data structures and other information that permits efficient access to certain data at some later point of time. In particular, given a query, the DBMS attempts to optimize the time in which it is answered by looking at access structures available and statistical information, and using the ability to reformulate queries into other, equivalent ones.

Over time, additional, more complex kinds of databases and DBMSs have appeared. For example, *distributed databases* keep information at a variety of sites connected by networks (e.g., so that data might be closer to where it is used most frequently). Note however that the user is unaware of this detail, and perceives a single database. Heterogeneous and federated databases are collections of independent databases which choose to share information but are maintained autonomously. Users may even be interested in obtaining information from all kinds of sources, including non-databases such as files, etc. In such situations, a significant problem is relating the logical schemas at the various sites in order to provide a schema that can be presented to the user. The rest of the chapter is devoted to showing a variety of roles that Description Logics (and reasoning with them) can play in database management. In particular, in Section 16.2 we take a detailed look at their use in semantic/conceptual modeling. We then examine the possible uses of Description Logics in querying and query processing in Section 16.3, while

---

[2] Variables appearing only on the right hand side of "→" are assumed to be existentially quantified.

in Section 16.4 we will consider the utility of Description Logics in providing integrated access to multiple information sources. We summarize the material in Section 16.5.

16.2 Data models and Description Logics

Recall that a "data model" is essentially a language or set of concepts for describing a class of certain kinds of databases. This section attempts to answer some questions about the relationship between data models and Description Logics:

What are some examples of such relationships? First, we will consider in detail the translation of Entity-Relationship models into knowledge bases expressed in the $\mathcal{DLR}$ Description Logic. In Subsection 16.2.5, we will consider more cursorily several other data models, such as OODB and semistructured data.

How are relationships established? The answer is by (i) formalizing the data model (ER in this case), (ii) choosing an appropriate Description Logic ($\mathcal{DLR}$ in this case), (iii) defining a translation function from the former to the latter, and (iv) proving that this translation is "information-preserving" (not done here, but detailed in [Calvanese *et al.*, 1999e]).

What benefits can be derived from having established relationships? Most significant is the use of automated DL reasoning services to support the development and maintenance of correct models (Subsection 16.2.4). In addition, since Description Logics are often more expressive, it is possible to suggest extensions to database data models that allow further information about the structure of the data to be captured (Subsection 16.2.3).

16.2.1 The Entity–Relationship model

In order to talk about the relationship between the Entity–Relationship (ER) model and Description Logics, it is necessary first to introduce the reader to the ER data model (see also Subsection 4.3.1 and Chapter 10). ER is the most widespread semantic data model, and it has become a standard, extensively used in the design phase of commercial applications. The ER model was introduced in [Chen, 1976], with minor variants and extensions proposed over the years (e.g., [Teorey, 1989; Batini *et al.*, 1992; Thalheim, 1992; 1993]).

The basic elements of the ER model are entities, relationships, and attributes. An *entity set* (or simply *entity*) denotes a set of objects, called its *instances*, that have common properties. Elementary properties are modeled through *attributes*, whose values belong to one of several pre-defined domains, such as Integer, String, or Boolean. Properties that are due to relations to other entities are modeled through the participation of the entity in relationships. A *relationship set* (or simply *relation*) denotes a set of tuples (also called its instances), each of which represents an association among a different combination of instances of the entities that participate in the relationship. Since each entity can participate in a relationship more than once (e.g., a company can be the recipient or sender in a "supply" relationship), the notion of *ER-role* is introduced to represent such a participation, and a distinguishing identifier within the relationship is assigned to it. The *arity* of a relationship is the number of its ER-roles. We assume that, for each relationship of arity n, the identifiers $1, \ldots, n$ are assigned to the roles of the relationship.

An entity B is said to be a specialization or IS-A of another entity A, if all the instances of B are also instances of A. Relationships can be similarly related by IS-A. This induces an inheritance of the attributes of an entity to its subentities, and of the roles of a relationship to its subroles. The ER schema produced as a result of ER modeling is usually represented in a graphical notation, which is particularly useful for an easy visualization of the data dependencies. In the commonly accepted notation, entities are represented as boxes, whereas relationships are represented as diamonds. An attribute is shown as a circle attached to the entity for which it is defined. ER-roles are graphically depicted by connecting the relationship to the participating entities, and labeling the edges with the corresponding role identifier. An IS-A relation between two entities is denoted by an arrow from the more specific to the more general entity (analogously for IS-A relations between two relationships). *Cardinality constraints* can be attached to an ER-role in order to restrict the number of times each instance of an entity is allowed to participate via that ER-role in instances of the relationship.

Such constraints can be used to specify both existence dependencies and functionality of relations [Cosmadakis and Kanellakis, 1986]. They are often used only in a restricted form, where the minimum cardinality is either 0 or 1 and the maximum cardinality is either 1 or ∞. Cardinality constraints in the form considered here have already been introduced in [Abrial, 1974], and subsequently studied in [Grant and Minker, 1984; Lenzerini and Nobili, 1990; Ferg, 1991; Ye *et al.*, 1994; Thalheim, 1992; Calvanese and Lenzerini, 1994b].

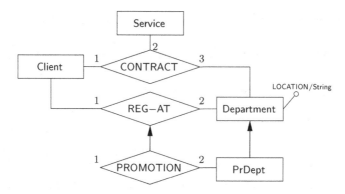

Fig. 16.1. Example of an ER schema.

An example of an ER schema is reported in Figure 16.1. Such a schema models information, handled by an enterprise, about contracts between customers and departments for services, and about registration of customers at departments. Some customers may be registered at "promotion departments".

For the purpose of relating the ER model to Description Logics it is better to have a more formal description, which also abstracts out the most important common characteristics present in the different variants.

An *ER schema S* is constructed starting from pairwise disjoint sets of entity symbols, relationship symbols, ER-role symbols, attribute symbols, and domain symbols. Each domain symbol D has an associated predefined basic domain $D^{\mathcal{B}_D}$, and we assume the basic domains to be pairwise disjoint. For each entity symbol, a set of attribute symbols is defined, and to each such attribute a unique domain symbol is associated. A relationship symbol of arity n has n associated ER-role symbols, each with an associated entity symbol, and defines a relationship between these entities. We assume that each ER-role symbol belongs to a unique relationship, thus determining also a unique entity. The cardinality constraints are represented by two functions $cmin_S$, from ER-role symbols to nonnegative integers, and $cmax_S$, from ER-role symbols to positive integers union the special symbol ∞. IS-A relations between entities and between relationships are modeled by means of a binary relation $\preceq_S$. We do not need to make any special assumption on the form of $\preceq_S$, such as acyclicity or injectivity.

The semantics of an ER schema can be given by specifying which database states are consistent with the information structure represented by the schema. Formally, a database state $\mathcal{B}$ corresponding to an ER schema S is constituted by a nonempty *finite* set $\Delta^{\mathcal{B}}$, assumed to be disjoint from all basic domains, and a function $\cdot^{\mathcal{B}}$ that maps

- every domain symbol D to the corresponding basic domain $D^{\mathcal{B}_\mathcal{D}}$,
- every entity E to a subset $E^\mathcal{B}$ of $\Delta^\mathcal{B}$,
- every attribute A to a set $A^\mathcal{B} \subseteq \Delta^\mathcal{B} \times \bigcup_{D \in \mathcal{D}_S} D^{\mathcal{B}_\mathcal{D}}$, and
- every relationship R to a set $R^\mathcal{B}$ of labeled tuples over $\Delta^\mathcal{B}$.

A *labeled tuple* over a domain $\Delta^\mathcal{B}$ is a function from a set of ER-roles to $\Delta^\mathcal{B}$. The labeled tuple T that maps ER-role U_i to o_i, for $i \in \{1, \ldots, n\}$, is denoted $\langle U_1 : o_1, \ldots, U_n : o_n \rangle$. We also write $T[U_i]$ to denote o_i, and call it the U_i-*component of* T. The elements of $E^\mathcal{B}$, $A^\mathcal{B}$, and $R^\mathcal{B}$ are called *instances* of E, A, and R respectively.

A database state is considered acceptable if it satisfies all integrity constraints that are part of the schema. This is captured by the notion of legal database state. A database state $\mathcal{B}$ is *legal for* an ER schema $\mathcal{S}$, if it satisfies the following conditions:

- For each pair of entities E_1, E_2 with $E_1 \preceq_S E_2$, we have $E_1^\mathcal{B} \subseteq E_2^\mathcal{B}$.
- For each pair of relationships R_1, R_2 with $R_1 \preceq_S R_2$, we have $R_1^\mathcal{B} \subseteq R_2^\mathcal{B}$.
- For each entity E, if E has an attribute A with domain D, then for each instance $e \in E^\mathcal{B}$ there is exactly one element $a \in A^\mathcal{B}$ with e as first component, and the second component of a is an element of $D^{\mathcal{B}_\mathcal{D}}$.
- For each relationship R of arity n between entities $E_1, \ldots, E_n$, to which R is connected by means of ER-roles $U_1, \ldots, U_n$ respectively, all instances of R are of the form $\langle U_1 : e_1, \ldots, U_n : e_n \rangle$, where $e_i \in E_i^\mathcal{B}$, $i \in \{1, \ldots, n\}$.
- For each ER-role U of relationship R associated with entity E, and for each instance e of E, we have

$$cmin_S(U) \le |\{r \in R^\mathcal{B} \mid r[U] = e\}| \le cmax_S(U).$$

16.2.2 Transforming Entity–Relationship schemas into $\mathcal{DLR}$ knowledge bases

In order to represent ER schemas in terms of DL knowledge bases, we make use of the Description Logic $\mathcal{DLR}$, which has been formally introduced in Chapter 5. We recall here the syntax of $\mathcal{DLR}$, which is a natural generalization of Description Logics to n-ary relations: in particular, atomic relations, of given arity between 2 and n_{max}, belong to the basic elements of $\mathcal{DLR}$, and, besides concept expressions, arbitrary relation expressions can be formed, according to the following syntax:

$$\begin{aligned} \mathbf{R} &::= \top_n \mid \mathbf{P} \mid (\$i/n : C) \mid \neg\mathbf{R} \mid \mathbf{R}_1 \sqcap \mathbf{R}_2 \\ C &::= \top_1 \mid A \mid \neg C \mid C_1 \sqcap C_2 \mid \exists[\$i]\mathbf{R} \mid \leqslant k\,[\$i]\mathbf{R} \end{aligned}$$

where $\mathbf{P}$ and $\mathbf{R}$ denote respectively atomic and arbitrary relations, i denotes components of relations, i.e., integers between 1 and n_{max}, n denotes the arity of a relation, i.e., an integer between 2 and n_{max}, and k denotes a nonnegative integer. In what follows, we abbreviate $(\$i/n\colon C)$ by $(\$i\colon C)$ when n is clear from the context. Moreover, we use the following abbreviations:

$$
\begin{array}{rcl}
\forall[\$i]\mathbf{R} & \text{for} & \neg\exists[\$i]\neg\mathbf{R} \\
\geqslant (k+1)\,[\$i]\mathbf{R} & \text{for} & \neg(\leqslant k\,[\$i]\mathbf{R}) \\
= k\,[\$i]\mathbf{R} & \text{for} & (\leqslant (k+1)\,[\$i]\mathbf{R}) \sqcap (\geqslant k\,[\$i]\mathbf{R}).
\end{array}
$$

In $\mathcal{DLR}$, n-ary relations are interpreted as sets of tuples of arity n, and the $\mathcal{DLR}$ constructs generalize those of traditional Description Logics. In particular, besides the Boolean constructs on concepts and relations, the construct $(\$i/n\colon C)$ denotes all tuples of arity n in which the ith component is an instance of concept C, and thus represents a unary selection. The construct $\exists[\$i]\mathbf{R}$ denotes all objects that participate as the ith component in a tuple of relation $\mathbf{R}$, and thus represents a unary projection. Finally $\leqslant k\,[\$i]\mathbf{R}$ is a generalization of number restrictions to n-ary relations. We refer to Chapter 5, Section 5.7, for the formal semantics of the $\mathcal{DLR}$ constructs.

We now show that the semantics of the ER model can be captured in $\mathcal{DLR}$ by defining a translation ϕ from ER schemas to $\mathcal{DLR}$ knowledge bases, and then establishing a correspondence between legal database states and models of the derived knowledge base. In the following, for each relationship R of arity n in $\mathcal{S}$, we denote by μ_R a mapping from the set of ER-roles associated with R to the integers $1, \ldots, n$.

The knowledge base $\phi(\mathcal{S})$ derived from an ER schema $\mathcal{S}$ is defined as follows:

- The set of atomic concepts of $\phi(\mathcal{S})$ consists of the set of entity and domain symbols in $\mathcal{S}$.[3]
- The set of atomic relations of $\phi(\mathcal{S})$ is obtained from the set of relationship and attribute symbols in $\mathcal{S}$. More specifically:
  - each symbol R in $\mathcal{S}$, denoting a relation of arity n, is mapped into a symbol $\mathbf{P}_R$ in $\phi(\mathcal{S})$, denoting a relation of arity n.
  - each attribute symbol A in $\mathcal{S}$ is mapped into a symbol $\mathbf{P}_A$ in $\phi(\mathcal{S})$, denoting a relation of arity 2. Thus, each instance of the relation $\mathbf{P}_A$ is a tuple such that its first component corresponds to an entity, while the second component denotes an element of the concept corresponding to the attribute domain.
- The set of inclusion axioms of $\phi(\mathcal{S})$ consists of the following elements:

---

[3] For the sake of simplicity, we model domains of ER schemas as concepts in $\mathcal{DLR}$.

– for each pair of entities E_1, E_2 such that $E_1 \preceq_S E_2$, the inclusion axiom

$$E_1 \sqsubseteq E_2$$

– for each pair of relationships R_1, R_2 such that $R_1 \preceq_S R_2$, the inclusion axiom

$$\mathbf{P}_{R_1} \sqsubseteq \mathbf{P}_{R_2}$$

– for each attribute A with domain D of an entity E, the inclusion axiom

$$E \sqsubseteq (\forall[\$1](\mathbf{P}_A \sqcap (\$2\colon D))) \sqcap = 1\,[\$1]\mathbf{P}_A$$

– for each relationship R of arity n with ER-roles $U_1, \ldots, U_n$ in which each U_i is associated with the entity E_i, the inclusion axiom

$$\mathbf{P}_R \sqsubseteq (\$\mu_R(U_1)\colon E_1) \sqcap \cdots \sqcap (\$\mu_R(U_n)\colon E_n)$$

– for each ER-role U of relationship R associated with entity E, with cardinality constraints $m = cmin_S(U)$ and $n = cmax_S(U)$,
 * if $m \neq 0$, the inclusion axiom

$$E \sqsubseteq \geqslant m\,[\$\mu_R(U)]\mathbf{P}_R$$

 * if $n \neq \infty$, the inclusion axiom

$$E \sqsubseteq \leqslant n\,[\$\mu_R(U)]\mathbf{P}_R.$$

Based on the results presented in [Calvanese *et al.*, 1999e], the correctness of the translation presented above can be formally proved. More specifically; let S be an ER schema. Then, there is a one-to-one correspondence between legal database states of S and models of the $\mathcal{DLR}$ knowledge base $\phi(S)$. For example, an entity E can be populated in a legal database state for S if and only if $\phi(S)$ admits a model in which E has a nonempty extension. This allows us to exploit reasoning techniques developed for the logic $\mathcal{DLR}$ in order to reason on ER schemas.

For example, by applying the translation presented above to the ER schema in Figure 16.1, presented earlier, we obtain the following $\mathcal{DLR}$ knowledge base:

$$
\begin{aligned}
\text{CONTRACT} &\sqsubseteq (\$1\colon \text{Client}) \sqcap (\$2\colon \text{Service}) \sqcap (\$3\colon \text{Department}) \\
\text{REG–AT} &\sqsubseteq (\$1\colon \text{Client}) \sqcap (\$2\colon \text{Department}) \\
\text{PROMOTION} &\sqsubseteq \text{REG–AT} \sqcap (\$2\colon \text{PrDept}) \\
\text{Department} &\sqsubseteq \forall[\$1](\text{LOCATION} \sqcap (\$2\colon \text{String})) \sqcap = 1\,[\$1]\text{LOCATION} \\
\text{PrDept} &\sqsubseteq \text{Department.}
\end{aligned}
$$

16.2.3 Additions to the Entity–Relationship model

The ER model does not provide several features which would prove useful
in order to represent complex dependencies between data. On the other
hand, the richness of constructs that is typical of Description Logics, and
the correspondence between the two formalisms established in the previous
subsection, makes it possible to add such constructs to the basic model and
take them fully into account when reasoning on a schema. We provide several
examples of useful additions to the basic ER Model that arise as a natural
consequence of the correspondence with the Description Logic $\mathcal{DLR}$. We
also consider a feature of the original ER Model that appears to force $\mathcal{DLR}$
itself to be extended.

- *Arbitrary Boolean constructs on entities.* The only direct relationship between
  entities that can be expressed in the basic ER model is the IS-A relation. A
  common extension is by so-called *generalization hierarchies* (see e.g., [Batini *et al.*,
  1992]), which allow one to express that the extension of an entity should be the
  disjoint union of the extensions of other entities. Such construct can easily be
  translated by making use of union and negation of $\mathcal{DLR}$.
- *Refinement of properties along an IS-A hierarchy.* Another important extension
  that should be considered is the ability to specify more complex forms of refinement of properties of entities along IS-A hierarchies, than the mere addition of
  attributes. This is already an essential feature of the more recent object-oriented
  models. In particular, cardinality constraints could be refined by restricting the
  range of values, and the participation in relationships can be restricted. One may
  require for specific instances of an entity that the objects they are related to via
  a certain relationship belong to a more specific entity than the one directly associated to the ER-role. Such forms of constraints can be naturally expressed in
  $\mathcal{DLR}$ by making use of universal quantification over relations.
- *Definitions of classes by means of complex properties.* In the ER model (and more
  generally in semantic data models) one can specify only necessary conditions that
  the instances of entities (or more generally classes) must satisfy. This means that
  in a database that conforms to the schema one cannot deduce that a certain object
  is an instance of an entity unless this fact is explicitly stated. When modeling
  a complex domain, however, in order to capture more precisely the intended
  semantics, one would like to be able to define classes of objects through necessary
  and sufficient conditions, or even to state just sufficient conditions for an object
  to be an instance of a class. The former correspond in fact to *views*, which are
  important parts of database schemas. By using the different types of axioms of
  $\mathcal{DLR}$, necessary and sufficient (and even just sufficient) conditions can be easily
  imposed and become part of the schema.
- *Key constraints.* Because of their utility in physical database design, even the
  original ER model allowed the specification of key attributes/roles. Extending

Description Logics with key constraints (roles which uniquely identify objects) has been the subject of several investigations [Borgida and Weddell, 1997]. In particular, Calvanese *et al.* [2000b] have shown that reasoning about $\mathcal{DLR}$ augmented by key constraints can be performed without increasing the worst-case computational complexity.

- *Temporal constraints.* Recent efforts in the conceptual modeling community have been devoted to properly capturing time-varying information, and several proposals of temporally enhanced Entity–Relationship (ER) exist. [Artale and Franconi, 1999; 2001; Artale *et al.*, 2001] provide a DL-based logical formalization of the various properties that characterize and extend different temporal ER models which are found in literature. In particular, [Artale *et al.*, 2001] define the Description Logic $\mathcal{DLR}_{\mathcal{US}}$, an extension of $\mathcal{DLR}$ with temporal constructs, and study decidability and complexity of reasoning in such a logic.

16.2.4 Reasoning about Entity–Relationship schemas

Providing a formalization of the ER schema in terms of the logic $\mathcal{DLR}$ allows several forms of reasoning on the ER schema to be supported. Typical reasoning tasks at the conceptual level supporting the designer of an ER schema $\mathcal{S}$ (see [Calvanese *et al.*, 1998e]) include:

- *Entity satisfiability*, i.e., whether for every concept C, $\mathcal{S}$ admits a model in which it has a nonempty extension. If C must always have an empty extension then there is an inconsistency in its specification, or at the very least the concept is inappropriately named since it is a synonym for "EmptyEntity".
- *Relation satisfiability*, i.e., whether $\mathcal{S}$ admits a model in which a certain relation has a nonempty extension. (Similar to the above.)
- *Consistency of the ER schema*, i.e., whether $\mathcal{S}$ admits a finite model. Without this, there is no database that satisfies the schema, which indicates that the totality of the definitions is inconsistent or requires an infinite model, which is a clear sign of incorrectness. Ideally, the reasoning system could provide *explanations* [McGuinness and Borgida, 1995; Borgida *et al.*, 2000] for the source of inconsistencies, which could focus the search for modifications.
- *Redundancy of the ER schema.* Various forms of redundancy in the ER schema can be detected: e.g., if A, B are entities and both $A \sqsubseteq B$ and $B \sqsubseteq A$ hold, we can conclude that one of the entities is redundant.
- *Stronger constraints on relationship roles.* The concept and relationship specifications may combine to yield stronger cardinality or domain constraints than those explicitly specified by the designer. (The simplest example is when we permit (multiple) inheritance.)
- *Entity subsumption*, i.e., whether the extension of one concept B is a subset of the extension of another concept A in every model of $\mathcal{S}$. This property suggests that the designer check for the possible omission of an explicit IS-A relationship

between B and A. Alternatively, if conceptually all B's are not supposed to be A's, then something is wrong in the rest of the schema, since it is forcing an undesired conclusion.

- *Relation subsumption*, i.e., whether the extension of one relation is a subset of the extension of another relation in every model of S. (Similar to the above.)

Ideas such as the ones above have been been pursued, for example, within the DWQ European Project [Bouzeghoub *et al.*, 1999], where the DL system FACT [Horrocks, 1998b] has been successfully used as reasoning tool supporting the analysis and the integration of diverse database conceptual schemas [Franconi and Ng, 2000].

16.2.5 Description Logics and other data models

Several other investigations have been carried out on the relationships between Description Logics and database models:

- [Bergamaschi and Nebel, 1994; Artale *et al.*, 1996a; Calvanese *et al.*, 1999e] provide formal models of object-oriented DBMSs using Description Logics.
- [Borgida *et al.*, 1989; Beck *et al.*, 1989; Bergamaschi and Sartori, 1992] introduce semantic data models based directly on Description Logics, which are different from ER and previous database semantic data models.
- More generally, class-based knowledge representation schemes, such as semantic networks, conceptual structures and frames [Lehmann, 1992; Sowa, 1991] have been considered as database models, or as ways to enrich the deductive capabilities of data models. These are related to Description Logics as suggested in Chapter 4.

A recent important development in the field of data management has been the need to represent data whose structure is less rigid and strict than that held in conventional databases. Such *semistructured data* are important in many application areas, such as web information systems, biological databases, and digital libraries. Semistructured data is neither raw text, nor strictly typed as in conventional database systems [Abiteboul, 1997]. In many recent formalisms, semistructured data is modeled by graphs with labeled edges, where the label keeps information on both the values and the schema of the data. Many authors have noticed that this model coincides with the ontology of Description Logics, where roles correspond to edges. In [Calvanese *et al.*, 1998c] it is shown that expressive Description Logics can not only capture semistructured data schemas, but can also add the ability to express several new kinds of constraints. The same kind of investigation has been carried out in [Calvanese *et al.*, 1999d] for the case of the XML language, which is currently a very popular formalism for semistructured data on the web (see Chapter 4, Subsection 4.3.3 for more details).

16.3 Description Logics and database querying

We have seen that descriptions can be used to present the schema of a database. For example, to emulate object-oriented databases, classes are equated with primitive concepts, while type restrictions on attributes are presented as necessary conditions that apply to these primitive classes in the form of role restrictions. In addition, certain integrity constraints can be expressed as rules of the form "if C then D", or axioms $C \sqsubseteq D$. On the other hand, since a concept description provides *necessary and sufficient* conditions for objects to satisfy it, it is natural to treat it as a query. So, in systems like CLASSIC [Borgida *et al.*, 1989] and CANDIDE [Beck *et al.*, 1989], we have a unification of two traditionally distinct languages: the data definition and data manipulation languages.

16.3.1 Description Logics as query languages

Once the query is viewed as a concept description, we can perform the standard operations on it. For example, the query description can be compared to the inconsistent description. If they are equivalent, this is almost surely a mistake on the part of the user – who would want to ask a query that never returns an object? The most likely reason for this is that the person asking the query is unfamiliar with the application domain. Since the query can be quite complex, and the schema quite large, a really helpful system would then assist the user in understanding the problem by isolating the specific parts of the query and of the schema that are responsible for the contradiction. Such a tool can be built on top of explanation facilities available for certain Description Logics [McGuinness and Borgida, 1995; Borgida *et al.*, 2000].

More generally, in situations where the query returns no individuals in the current database, it has been argued that the query is "not interesting", and should be generalized until a non-empty answer set is returned. As suggested by Anwar *et al.* [1992], this relaxation can be performed using the semilattice of descriptions provided by the subsumption relationship, which can guide the systematic weakening of terms in the query.

The query can be classified with respect to the concepts in the schema. This can be used to help users pose queries in an unfamiliar domain, as follows: if the answer set contains unwanted values, the immediate subsumers and subsumees of the query reveal other *potentially relevant* concepts (and, through subsumption assertions in the schema, roles as well) which the user may want to use for restricting the query. The result is a process of *query specification by iterative refinement* introduced by Tou *et al.* [1982].

Queries can also be classified with respect to each other into a subsumption hierarchy. In an environment where several people are asking exploratory questions about the data over a long period of time (e.g., data mining by humans), it is very useful to have the questions organized so that the results of *previous* related queries can be reviewed [Brachman *et al.*, 1992]. This prevents duplication of effort and, again, helps the user to pose queries that are more precise.

Unfortunately, in exchange for a more expressive description of the schema, Description Logics pay the price of a weaker query language than usual: queries can only return subsets of existing objects, rather than creating new objects (as in standard SQL databases); furthermore, the selection conditions are rather limited. In fact, it has been shown [Borgida, 1996] that even the most expressive Description Logics discussed in the literature until recently, could only express a variant of the "3-variable" subset of formulae of first-order logic – i.e., formulae that only use 3 variables, although allowing numeric quantifiers, like "exists at least n".

Given the expressive limitations of DL concepts alone as queries, it is reasonable to consider extending standard queries (in Datalog) with Description Logics. Two different approaches have been pursued: In one, inspired by the work of Aït-Kaci and Nasr [1986] on LOGIN, and exemplified by the $\mathcal{AL}$-LOG language [Donini *et al.*, 1998b], descriptions are used essentially as *type constraints* on variables appearing in Horn clauses. In this case, a crucial condition is that concept and role names form a disjoint set from the relations used in expressing rules. The second approach, exemplified by the CARIN language [Levy and Rousset, 1996; 1998], treats concepts and roles as ordinary unary and binary predicates that can also appear in query atoms. This is significant because it allows for the first time conjunctive queries to be expressed over DL databases/Aboxes.

A second important distinction is between recursive and non-recursive Datalog queries. For the non-recursive case (which covers a large portion of practically useful queries), it seems possible to combine some expressive decidable Description Logics with Datalog, while keeping query answering and even reasoning on queries decidable (see Section 16.4). For the recursive case, undecidability arises sooner, but some studies have identified suitable restrictions on the DL language and/or on the form of Datalog rules, for preserving decidability of query answering.

Consider first $\mathcal{AL}$-LOG. In the rule

$$\mathsf{happy}(x) \leftarrow \mathsf{marriedTo}(x,y) \wedge \mathsf{employedBy}(y,z)$$
$$\& \; \mathsf{Person}(x) \wedge \mathsf{Person}(y) \wedge \mathsf{StartUp}(z)$$

the tests after the ampersand & are for concept membership, while those before it are for n-ary relations, as in relational databases. The processing of such queries is complicated by the fact that the DL "type database" may contain disjunction or be otherwise incomplete. Instead of the standard answers, one gets a "conditional result", with a side condition c describing necessary DL constraints on the variables in the query. For example, for the above query one might get as answer

$$\mathsf{happy}(\mathsf{ANNA}) \;\; \mathrm{if} \;\; \mathsf{Person}(\mathsf{ANNA})$$

in a database containing

$$\mathsf{marriedTo}(\mathsf{ANNA}, \mathsf{JOE}), \mathsf{employedBy}(\mathsf{JOE}, \mathsf{IBM}), \mathsf{Person}(\mathsf{JOE}), \mathsf{StartUp}(\mathsf{IBM}).$$

Donini *et al.* [1998b] establish that answering queries in recursive $\mathcal{AL}$-LOG is decidable in the case when the Description Logic used is $\mathcal{ALC}$. The framework of $\mathcal{AL}$-LOG is further extended in [Rosati, 1999] to the case of *disjunctive* Datalog, i.e., Datalog with negation as failure in rule bodies and disjunction in the head of rules.

The CARIN approach is more general, but this increase in expressive power comes at a price: for general Datalog rules, the query answering problem is now undecidable as soon as one allows $\forall R.C$ or $\leqslant n\,R$ as concept constructors. (These appear in most Description Logics.) However, if Datalog rules are restricted to avoid recursion, then query answering is decidable even for the $\mathcal{ALCNR}$ Description Logic. Numerous other results circumscribing the cases when query processing is decidable may be found in [Levy and Rousset, 1998].

16.3.2 *Query optimization*

In the case when queries can be classified (as when they are descriptions or when the query implication problem is decidable), classification of queries has been proposed as a technique for *query processing and optimization*. In [Beck *et al.*, 1989], queries are classified with respect to schema concepts; if the query concept Q is classified below concept C, then only instances of C need to be checked whether they satisfy the full query. Of course, in this classification process one uses the axioms describing the schema of the database.

If the answers to previous queries are cached, then the query concepts can be left in the classification hierarchy, together with the other concepts in the schema. The result is a simple form of the query optimization technique known as "query answering using cached views": find the most specific views V that subsume the query Q; check only the individual instances of V (which, recall, are locally available) to see if they satisfy the query. Potentially, this could provide considerable savings, especially when gathering information from multiple sites, for example.

Buchheit *et al.* [1994b] elaborate on this by using a more powerful query language. In particular, in order to achieve the expressiveness of full first-order logic, expressing a query is viewed as a two-phase process: as much of the query as possible is written in the "query Description Logic" (yielding the so-called "structural part"), and the remainder of the query is written as a constraint in a first-order logic notation (yielding the so-called "dirty part"). For example, the following query asks for students whose advisor is the same as their committee chair and at least 5 years older than the student:

QueryClass QueryStudent **isa** Student **with**
    derived
        $I1$: advisor: Prof
        $I2$: committee.(chair: Thing)
    where $I1=I2$ **constraint** forall s/QueryStudent $(s.\text{age} + 5 < s.\text{advisor.age})$.

In this case, assuming that cached views have only structural conditions, the query is classified using only its own structural conditions. Thereafter, only the instances of the view are tested using both the structural and dirty parts of the query.

Finally, Bergamaschi *et al.* [1997] have investigated the use of Description Logics in optimizing query evaluation in object-oriented DBMSs by eliminating redundant terms. This is accomplished by first expanding the query as much as possible using the information in the schema; for example, subsumption is used to test when the antecedent of a rule can be applied to the query (subsumes it) so that its consequent can be added to it. By repeatedly applying this process, an expanded query is obtained. Then, all the query subterms that subsume the rest of the query (and are therefore redundant) are eliminated one by one. The result is a semantically equivalent description/query which may be more concise than the original one; hence it may have fewer tests to evaluate. Furthermore, the new expanded query may be classified further down the pre-existing class/view hierarchy, providing more efficient query evaluation, using the query classification technique described earlier. These are forms of so-called "semantic query optimization".

An issue related to efficient processing of large numbers of individuals is the situation where the user needs to query the conceptual model for DL instances, while the data are presented in a relational database, say. In other words, we need to obtain the proper ABox instances of the DL query (which involves concepts and roles) from the database. The main problem is that processing hundreds of thousands of individuals is not feasible with DL technology because in each case we try to perform complex inferences. However, most of the data in the database is very straightforward, and the corresponding individuals do not generate new inferences. The solution proposed in [Borgida and Brachman, 1993] is to associate with the *primitive* concepts (resp. roles) of the DL knowledge base unary (resp. binary) view tables defined over the DBMS. One can then automatically translate complex descriptions into complex SQL queries over these views. The important effect is that one gets the full benefit of DBMS optimization for the SQL query, and if only a few values satisfy the query, then only a few DL individuals need to be created. For example, for a primitive DL class **Student**, we might take the values appearing in the **enrollee** column of relational table **Enrollment_R**, and use this subset of the **Person_R** table to generate appropriate individuals in a special view **Student_R**, which has only one column. (The generation of unique identifiers for these individuals is in itself a research issue.) Similarly, for example, one would generate a two-column view **visitor_R** corresponding to the role **visitor**. Complex descriptions over **Student** and **visitor** are then translated algorithmically into SQL queries over the corresponding views. Additional optimizations turn out to be necessary to deal properly with multiple queries and functional roles [Borgida and Brachman, 1993].

16.4 Data integration

Integrating different data sources is one of the fundamental problems faced in the last decades by the database community [Batini *et al.*, 1986]. Generally speaking, the goal of a data integration system is to provide a uniform interface to various data sources [Levy, 2000], so as to enable users to focus on specifying what they want. As a result, the data integration system frees the users from tasks such as finding the relevant data sources, interacting with each source in isolation, and selecting, cleaning, and combining data from multiple sources.

The design of a data integration system is a very complex task, which comprises several different aspects. Our goal in this section is to discuss the use of Description Logics in two important aspects, namely:

- The specification of the content of the various data sources.
- The process of computing the answer to queries posed to the data integration system, based on the specification of the sources.

16.4.1 Specifying the content of data sources

The typical architecture of a data integration system allows one to explicitly model data and information needs – i.e., a specification of the data that the system provides to the user – at various levels:

- The *conceptual level* contains a conceptual representation of the sources and of the reconciled integrated data, together with an explicit declarative account of the relationships among their components.
- The *logical level* contains a representation of the sources in terms of a logical data model.

The conceptual level As we have seen before, the conceptual level contains a formal description of the concepts, the relationships between concepts, and the information requirements that the integration application has to deal with. The key feature of this level is that such a description is independent of any system consideration, and is oriented towards the goal of expressing the semantics of the application. In particular, we distinguish among the following elements:

- The *Enterprise Conceptual Schema* is a representation of the global concepts and relationships that are of interest to the application. It corresponds roughly to the notion of global conceptual schema in the traditional approaches to schema integration and to the notion of *world view*, as introduced in [Levy *et al.*, 1995; Kirk *et al.*, 1995].
- For an information source S, the *Source Conceptual Schema* of S is a conceptual representation of the data residing in S.
- The term *Domain Conceptual Schema* is used to denote the union of both the Enterprise Conceptual Schema and the various Source Conceptual Schemas, plus possible inter-schema relationships [Catarci and Lenzerini, 1993].

We have seen in Section 16.2 that Description Logics are very well suited for data modeling at the conceptual level, so it comes as no surprise that Description Logics have also been used in data integration projects to represent Source and Enterprise Conceptual Schemas [Catarci and Lenzerini, 1993; Arens *et al.*, 1993; 1996; Levy *et al.*, 1995; Goasdoue *et al.*, 2000]. In this section, following [Calvanese *et al.*, 1998e], we will continue to use the $\mathcal{DLR}$ DL for specifying these conceptual schemas.

As stated above, the Domain Conceptual Schema contains *inter-schema relationships*. In particular, since the sources are of interest in the system, integration does not simply mean producing the Enterprise Conceptual Schema, but rather being able to establish the correct interdependencies both between the Source Conceptual Schemas and the Enterprise Conceptual Schema, and between the various Source Conceptual Schemas.

To specify inter-schema relationships, we make use of the special kinds of assertions available in DL reasoning. In particular, following [Catarci and Lenzerini, 1993], one can use assertions of the following forms:

$$L_i \sqsubseteq_{ext} L_j$$
$$L_i \sqsubseteq_{int} L_j$$

where L_i and L_j are expressions of different schemas. In particular, L_i and L_j are either two relation expressions of the same arity, or two concept expressions. Intuitively, the first assertion states that L_i is extensionally included in L_j, which means that every object that satisfies the expression L_i in source i also satisfies the expression L_j in source j. For example, if the designer knows that the set of students stored in source 1 is a subset of those stored in source 2, then this knowledge is captured by the inter-schema assertion

$$\text{Student}_1 \sqsubseteq_{ext} \text{Student}_2.$$

The second assertion states that the concept denoted by the expression L_i in source i is a subconcept of the one denoted by the expression L_j in source j, which means that every object in source i satisfying L_i also satisfies L_j in source j, provided that it does appear in source j. For example, if the designer knows that the concept of student in source 1 is a subconcept of person in source 2, then s/he can use the inter-schema assertion

$$\text{Student}_1 \sqsubseteq_{int} \text{Person}_2.$$

It is worth noting that the possibility of reasoning about $\mathcal{DLR}$ schemas allows sophisticated forms of reasoning on inter-schema assertions, e.g., for inferring those extensional relationships between concepts that are implied by the knowledge on the intensional interdependencies. More details about these forms of reasoning can be found in [Catarci and Lenzerini, 1993; Calvanese *et al.*, 1998e].

The logical level The logical level provides a description of the logical content of each source, called the *Source Schema*. Typically, a Source Schema is provided in terms of a set of relations using the relational logical model of data. So-called *wrappers* can be used to hide how the source actually stores its data, the data model it adopts, etc., and present the source as a set of relations.

The link between the logical representation of a source and the Domain Conceptual Schema can be specified in two different ways.

- According to the so-called *global-as-view approach*, a query over the source relations is associated to each concept in the Domain Conceptual Schema. Every such concept is thus seen as a view over the sources.
- In the alternative *local-as-view approach*, one associates with each source relation a query that describes its content in terms of the Domain Conceptual Schema. In other words, the logical content of a source relation is described in terms of a view over the Domain Conceptual Schema.

In [Levy, 2000], it is argued that the local-as-view approach has several advantages, and we will follow this approach in the rest of the chapter.

To describe the content of the sources through views, one needs a notion of query such as the union of conjunctive queries over the Domain Conceptual Schema. Specifically, a source relation is described in terms of a *query* of the form

$$q(\vec{\mathbf{x}}) \;\leftarrow\; conj_1(\vec{\mathbf{x}}, \vec{\mathbf{y}}_1) \vee \cdots \vee conj_m(\vec{\mathbf{x}}, \vec{\mathbf{y}}_m)$$

where:

- The *head* $q(\vec{\mathbf{x}})$ defines the schema of the relation in terms of a name, and the number of columns.
- The *body* describes the content of the relation in terms of the Domain Conceptual Schema.

In [Calvanese *et al.*, 2001c], $conj_i(\vec{\mathbf{x}}, \vec{\mathbf{y}}_i)$ is a conjunction of *atoms*, and $\vec{\mathbf{x}}, \vec{\mathbf{y}}_i$ are all the variables appearing in the conjunct (we use $\vec{\mathbf{x}}$ to denote a tuple of variables $x_1, \ldots, x_n$, for some n). Each atom is of the form $E(t)$, $R(\vec{\mathbf{t}})$, or $A(t, t')$, where $\vec{\mathbf{t}}$, t, and t' are variables in $\vec{\mathbf{x}}, \vec{\mathbf{y}}_i$ or constants, and E, R, and A are respectively entities, relationships, and attributes appearing in the Domain Conceptual Schema.

The semantics of queries is as follows. Given a database that satisfies the Domain Conceptual Schema, a query q of arity n is interpreted as the set of n-tuples $(d_1, \ldots, d_n)$, with each d_i an object of the database, such that, when substituting each d_i for x_i, the formula

$$\exists \vec{\mathbf{y}}_1.conj_1(\vec{\mathbf{x}}, \vec{\mathbf{y}}_1) \vee \cdots \vee \exists \vec{\mathbf{y}}_m.conj_m(\vec{\mathbf{x}}, \vec{\mathbf{y}}_m)$$

evaluates to true.

Analogously to the case of the conceptual level, it is interesting to perform several reasoning tasks on the DL representation of the sources, for example for inferring redundancies and/or inconsistencies among data stored in different sources. Since queries that include atoms from the Conceptual Schema are more expressive, new algorithms are required to answer the following problems:

- *Query containment.* Given two queries q_1 and q_2 (of the same arity n), check whether q_1 is *contained in* q_2, i.e., check whether the set of tuples denoted by q_1 is contained in the set of tuples denoted by q_2 in every database satisfying the Conceptual Schema. Papers that contain results relating to this question include [Levy and Rousset, 1998; Calvanese *et al.*, 1998a; Goasdoue and Rousset, 2000].
- *Query consistency.* Check whether a query q over the Conceptual Schema is *consistent*, i.e., check whether there exists a database satisfying the Conceptual Schema in which the set of tuples denoted by q is not empty.
- *Query disjointness.* Check whether two queries q_1 and q_2 (of the same arity) over the Conceptual Schema are *disjoint*, i.e., check whether the intersection of the set of tuples denoted by q_1 and the set of tuples denoted by q_2 is empty, in every database satisfying the Conceptual Schema.

16.4.2 Query answering

The ultimate goal of a data integration system is to allow the user to pose queries over the global view, and to answer the queries by accessing the sources in a transparent way. The mechanism for answering queries differs depending on the approach adopted for specifying the sources. The possibility of reasoning about queries can provide useful support in both the global-as-view and the local-as-view approaches. As in the previous subsection, here we focus on the local-as-view approach, that is the one in which query answering is most complex.

In the local-as-view approach, relations at the sources are modeled as views over the virtual database represented by the Domain Conceptual Schema. Since the database is virtual, in order to answer a query Q formulated over the Domain Conceptual Schema, we can only use the source views. In other words, query processing cannot simply be done by looking at a set of relations, as in traditional databases, but requires reasoning on both the form of the query, and the content of the source views. This motivates the idea that query answering in data integration becomes the problem of *view-based query processing*. There are two approaches to view-based query processing, called *query rewriting* and *query answering*, respectively.

In the former approach, we are given a query Q and a set of view definitions, and the goal is to reformulate the query into an equivalent expression that refers only to the views available, and provides the answer to Q.

In the latter approach, besides Q and the view definitions, we also take into account the extensions of the views, and the goal is to compute the set of tuples that are implied by these extensions, i.e., the set of tuples t such that t satisfies Q in all the databases that are consistent with the views.

Notice the difference between the two approaches. In query rewriting, query processing is divided in two steps, where the first re-expresses the query in terms of a given query language over the alphabet of the view names, and the second step evaluates the rewriting over the view extensions. In query answering, we do not pose any limit on query processing, and the only goal is to exploit all possible information, including view extensions, to compute the answer to the query.

View-based query processing has been extensively investigated by the database community [Levy, 2000]. Only recently has the problem been studied for the case where the Domain Conceptual Schema is expressed in Description Logics. For example, [Baader *et al.*, 2000] addresses the problem of rewriting queries that are concepts in terms of concepts in the conceptual schema. Query rewriting for more general queries (e.g., ones involving conjunctions of atoms) has been studied in [Beeri *et al.*, 1997; Levy and Rousset, 1998; Goasdoue *et al.*, 2000; Calvanese *et al.*, 2001c], in some cases taking into consideration complex constraints expressed in Description Logic as part of the Conceptual Schema. One issue that must be addressed here is that the original query Q may not be rewritable as an expression over the views because of limitations of the language for combining views. In this case, one must find heuristic best-effort approximations. Another issue is finding a minimum-cost rewriting (e.g., by eliminating unnecessary lookups in some of the views).

Finally, we mention that Goasdoue *et al.* [2000] describe an implemented information integration system, which uses a combination of global-as-view and limited local-as-view approaches applied to the $\mathcal{ALN}$ DL and non-recursive Horn rules.

Among the pioneering attempts at solving the query answering problem is the Information Manifold system [Levy *et al.*, 1996; 1995], which has detailed algorithms for query rewriting. In the context of heterogeneous databases, Mena *et al.* [2000] propose that each source has its own conceptual schema/ontology expressed in a Description Logic, and these are interrelated by adding "hyponym" (subsumption) relationships between concepts in each. (This is reminiscent of the approach in [Catarci and Lenzerini, 1993].) One of the interesting features of this system is that it takes seriously the approximations resulting from the fact that some queries may not be expressible in terms of the combined ontologies. Among others, they study the notions of "precision" and "accuracy" of recall to quantify this approximation. A solution to the query answering approach is presented in [Calvanese *et al.*, 2000a], which, among other things, illustrates the relationship between view-based query answering and ABox reasoning in Description Logics.

16.5 Conclusions

We have reviewed a number of ways in which Description Logics can be useful in the development and utilization of databases.

Probably the most successful applications are in areas where the conceptual model of the UofD is required. This includes the initial development stage, as well as access to heterogeneous data sources.

Concerning the initial conceptual modeling: First, Description Logics are powerful enough to capture the domain semantics represented by various entity–relationship data models, as well as other data models introduced in the database literature. In fact, with most Description Logics, one can represent additional constraints. Second, because Description Logics have a clear semantics, the meaning of the DL model is unambiguous and precise. Third, not only can information be represented, but it can also be reasoned with: one can look for inconsistent class/entity definitions (ones that cannot have any individual instances) and more generally, one can check for the consistency of the entire model. Both of these are signs to the developer that there are modeling errors. Arguably, it is this third aspect, concerning reasoning with the model, that is the greatest advantage of DL models.

DL descriptions can be viewed as necessary and sufficient conditions, and hence as queries (or views!) for a database. Description Logics are somewhat less successful in this regard (at least in their pure form), because they have limited expressive power compared to the standard calculi known from relational databases, and because they cannot generate new objects – only select subsets of existing objects.

However, if one accepts a Description Logic as a data model, then DL queries can be classified with respect to schema concepts and previous queries, supporting query by refinement and data exploration. The subsumption relationship can also be used for semantic query optimization.

Combining Description Logics with Datalog rules, or at least supporting conjunctive queries from concepts, is a promising way to obtain a more expressive query language. The evaluation of the resulting queries appears to be decidable with a wide range of Description Logics if the rules are not recursive. The addition of recursion appears to lead to undecidability relatively quickly. However, full recursion is not an necessity for practical applications, such as information integration, so further research in the possible combinations of Description Logics and Datalog restrictions is warranted.

The ability to represent the semantics of a UofD is also the reason why Description Logics are useful in situations where information is to be integrated from various sources, such as heterogeneous or federated databases. It is widely agreed that the integration needs to be achieved at the conceptual level. The Description Logic can be used to define the ontology of each site, and then these ontologies are inter-related; alternatively, a global ontology is specified, and then the sites are described as views over it.

Appendix

Description Logic Terminology

Franz Baader

Abstract

The purpose of this appendix is to introduce (in a compact manner) the syntax and semantics of the most prominent DLs occurring in this handbook. More information and explanations as well as some less familiar Description Logics can be found in the respective chapters. For DL constructors whose semantics cannot be described in a compact manner, we will only introduce the syntax and refer the reader to the respective chapter for the semantics. Following Chapter 2 on basic Description Logics, we will first introduce the basic Description Logic $\mathcal{AL}$, and then describe several of its extensions. Thereby, we will also fix the notation employed in this handbook. Finally, we will comment on the naming schemes for Description Logics that are employed in the literature and in this handbook.

A.1 Notational conventions

Before starting with the definitions, let us introduce some notational conventions. The letters A, B will often be used for atomic concepts, and C, D for concept descriptions. For roles, we often use the letters R, S, and for functional roles (features, attributes) the letters f, g. Nonnegative integers (in number restrictions) are often denoted by n, m, and individuals by a, b. In all cases, we may also use subscripts. This convention is followed when defining syntax and semantics and in abstract examples. In concrete examples, the following conventions are used: concept names start with an uppercase letter followed by lowercase letters (e.g., Human, Male), role names (also functional ones) start with a lowercase letter (e.g., hasChild, marriedTo), and individual names are all uppercase (e.g., CHARLES, MARY).

A.2 Syntax and semantics of common Description Logics

In this section, we introduce the standard concept and role constructors as well as knowledge bases. For more information see Chapter 2.

A.2.1 Concept and role descriptions

Elementary descriptions are *atomic concepts* and *atomic roles* (also called *concept names* and *role names*). Complex descriptions can be built from them inductively with *concept constructors* and *role constructors*. Concept descriptions in $\mathcal{AL}$ are formed according to the following syntax rule:

$$
\begin{aligned}
C, D \longrightarrow \quad &A \mid && \text{(atomic concept)} \\
&\top \mid && \text{(universal concept, top concept)} \\
&\bot \mid && \text{(bottom concept)} \\
&\neg A \mid && \text{(atomic negation)} \\
&C \sqcap D \mid && \text{(intersection)} \\
&\forall R.C \mid && \text{(value restriction)} \\
&\exists R.\top && \text{(limited existential quantification).}
\end{aligned}
$$

Following our convention, A denotes an atomic concept and C, D denote concept descriptions. The role R is atomic since $\mathcal{AL}$ does not provide role constructors.

An *interpretation* $\mathcal{I}$ consists of a non-empty set $\Delta^{\mathcal{I}}$ (the domain of the interpretation) and an interpretation function, which assigns to every atomic concept A a set $A^{\mathcal{I}} \subseteq \Delta^{\mathcal{I}}$ and to every atomic role R a binary relation $R^{\mathcal{I}} \subseteq \Delta^{\mathcal{I}} \times \Delta^{\mathcal{I}}$. The interpretation function is extended to concept descriptions by the following inductive definitions:

$$
\begin{aligned}
\top^{\mathcal{I}} &= \Delta^{\mathcal{I}} \\
\bot^{\mathcal{I}} &= \emptyset \\
\neg A^{\mathcal{I}} &= \Delta^{\mathcal{I}} \setminus A^{\mathcal{I}} \\
(C \sqcap D)^{\mathcal{I}} &= C^{\mathcal{I}} \cap D^{\mathcal{I}} \\
(\forall R.C)^{\mathcal{I}} &= \{a \in \Delta^{\mathcal{I}} \mid \forall b.\ (a, b) \in R^{\mathcal{I}} \rightarrow b \in C^{\mathcal{I}}\} \\
(\exists R.\top)^{\mathcal{I}} &= \{a \in \Delta^{\mathcal{I}} \mid \exists b.\ (a, b) \in R^{\mathcal{I}}\}.
\end{aligned}
$$

There are several possibilities for extending $\mathcal{AL}$ in order to obtain a more expressive Description Logic. The three most prominent are adding additional concept constructors, adding role constructors, and formulating restrictions on role interpretations. Below, we start with the third possibility, since we need to refer to restrictions on roles when defining certain concept constructors. For these extensions, we also introduce a naming scheme.

Basically, each extension is assigned a letter or symbol. For concept constructors, the letters/symbols are written after the starting $\mathcal{AL}$, for role constructors, we write the letters/symbols as superscripts, and for restrictions on the interpretation of roles as subscripts. As an example, the Description Logic $\mathcal{ALCQ}_{R^c}^{-1}$ extends $\mathcal{AL}$ with the concept constructors negation ($\mathcal{C}$) and qualified number restrictions ($\mathcal{Q}$), the role constructor inverse ($^{-1}$), and the restriction that some roles are transitive ($_{R^c}$).

Restrictions on role interpretations

These restrictions force the interpretations of roles to satisfy certain properties, such as functionality and transitivity. We consider these two prominent examples in more detail. Others would be symmetry or connections between different roles.[1]

1. *Functional roles.* Here one considers a subset N_F of the set of role names N_R; its elements are called *features*. An interpretation must map features f to functional binary relations $f^{\mathcal{I}} \subseteq \Delta^{\mathcal{I}} \times \Delta^{\mathcal{I}}$, i.e., relations satisfying $\forall a, b, c. f^{\mathcal{I}}(a, b) \wedge f^{\mathcal{I}}(a, c) \rightarrow b = c$. Sometimes functional relations are viewed as partial functions, and thus one writes $f^{\mathcal{I}}(a) = b$ rather than $f^{\mathcal{I}}(a, b)$. $\mathcal{AL}$ extended with features is denoted by $\mathcal{AL}_f$.
2. *Transitive roles.* Here one considers a subset N_{R+} of N_R. Role names $R \in N_{R+}$ are called *transitive roles*. An interpretation must map transitive roles $R \in N_{R+}$ to transitive binary relations $R^{\mathcal{I}} \subseteq \Delta^{\mathcal{I}} \times \Delta^{\mathcal{I}}$. $\mathcal{AL}$ extended with transitive roles is denoted by $\mathcal{AL}_{R+}$.

Concept constructors

Concept constructors take concept and/or role descriptions and transform them into more complex concept descriptions. Table A.1 shows the syntax and semantics of common concept constructors. In order to have them all in one place, we also repeat the ones from $\mathcal{AL}$, minus atomic negation and limited existential quantification since they are special cases of negation and existential quantification.

Some explanatory remarks are in order. The symbols u_1, u_2 in the agreement constructor stand for chains of functional roles, i.e., $u_1 = f_1 \ldots f_m$ and $u_2 = g_1 \ldots g_n$ where $n, m \geq 0$ and the f_i, g_j are features. The semantics of such a chain is given by the composition of the partial functions interpreting its components, i.e., $u_1^{\mathcal{I}}(a) = f_m^{\mathcal{I}}(\ldots f_1^{\mathcal{I}}(a) \ldots)$. Nominals (or individuals) in concept expressions are interpreted as singleton sets, consisting of one element of the domain. We assume that names for individuals come from a

---

[1] One could also count role hierarchies as imposing such restrictions. Here we will, however, treat role hierarchies in the context of knowledge bases.

Table A.1. *Some Description Logic concept constructors.*

Name	Syntax	Semantics	Symbol
Top	$\top$ $\Delta^{\mathcal{I}}$		$\mathcal{AL}$
Bottom	$\bot$ $\emptyset$		$\mathcal{AL}$
Intersection	$C \sqcap D$ $C^{\mathcal{I}} \cap D^{\mathcal{I}}$		$\mathcal{AL}$
Union	$R \sqcup S$ $C^{\mathcal{I}} \cup D^{\mathcal{I}}$		$\mathcal{U}$
Negation	$\neg C$ $\Delta^{\mathcal{I}} \setminus C^{\mathcal{I}}$		$\mathcal{C}$
Value restriction	$\forall R.C$	$\{a \in \Delta^{\mathcal{I}} \mid \forall b.\ (a,b) \in R^{\mathcal{I}} \rightarrow b \in C^{\mathcal{I}}\}$	$\mathcal{AL}$
Existential quant.	$\exists R.C$	$\{a \in \Delta^{\mathcal{I}} \mid \exists b.\ (a,b) \in R^{\mathcal{I}} \wedge b \in C^{\mathcal{I}}\}$	$\mathcal{E}$
Unqualified number restriction	$\geqslant n\,R$ $\leqslant n\,R$ $= n\,R$	$\{a \in \Delta^{\mathcal{I}} \mid \mid\{b \in \Delta^{\mathcal{I}} \mid (a,b) \in R^{\mathcal{I}}\}\mid \geq n\}$ $\{a \in \Delta^{\mathcal{I}} \mid \mid\{b \in \Delta^{\mathcal{I}} \mid (a,b) \in R^{\mathcal{I}}\}\mid \leq n\}$ $\{a \in \Delta^{\mathcal{I}} \mid \mid\{b \in \Delta^{\mathcal{I}} \mid (a,b) \in R^{\mathcal{I}}\}\mid = n\}$	$\mathcal{N}$
Qualified number restriction	$\geqslant n\,R.C$ $\leqslant n\,R.C$ $= n\,R.C$	$\{a \in \Delta^{\mathcal{I}} \mid \mid\{b \in \Delta^{\mathcal{I}} \mid (a,b) \in R^{\mathcal{I}} \wedge b \in C^{\mathcal{I}}\}\mid \geq n\}$ $\{a \in \Delta^{\mathcal{I}} \mid \mid\{b \in \Delta^{\mathcal{I}} \mid (a,b) \in R^{\mathcal{I}} \wedge b \in C^{\mathcal{I}}\}\mid \leq n\}$ $\{a \in \Delta^{\mathcal{I}} \mid \mid\{b \in \Delta^{\mathcal{I}} \mid (a,b) \in R^{\mathcal{I}} \wedge b \in C^{\mathcal{I}}\}\mid = n\}$	$\mathcal{Q}$
Role-value-map	$R \subseteq S$ $R = S$	$\{a \in \Delta^{\mathcal{I}} \mid \forall b.(a,b) \in R^{\mathcal{I}} \rightarrow (a,b) \in S^{\mathcal{I}}\}$ $\{a \in \Delta^{\mathcal{I}} \mid \forall b.(a,b) \in R^{\mathcal{I}} \leftrightarrow (a,b) \in S^{\mathcal{I}}\}$	
Agreement and disagreement	$u_1 \doteq u_2$ $u_1 \not\doteq u_2$	$\{a \in \Delta^{\mathcal{I}} \mid \exists b \in \Delta^{\mathcal{I}}.\ u_1^{\mathcal{I}}(a) = b = u_2^{\mathcal{I}}(a)\}$ $\{a \in \Delta^{\mathcal{I}} \mid \exists b_1, b_2 \in \Delta^{\mathcal{I}}.\ u_1^{\mathcal{I}}(a) = b_1 \neq b_2 = u_2^{\mathcal{I}}(a)\}$	$\mathcal{F}$
Nominal	I	$I^{\mathcal{I}} \subseteq \Delta^{\mathcal{I}}$ with $\mid I^{\mathcal{I}} \mid = 1$	$\mathcal{O}$

name space disjoint from the set of concept and role names. Since role-value-maps cause undecidability and thus are no longer used in DL systems, there is no special symbol for them in the last column of Table A.1.

Many DL systems employ a LISP-like concrete syntax. Table A.2 introduces this syntax and gives a translation into the abstract syntax introduced in Table A.1.

Role constructors

Role constructors take role and/or concept descriptions and transform them into more complex role descriptions. Table A.3 shows the syntax and semantics of common role constructors.

The symbol $\circ$ denotes the usual composition of binary relations, i.e.,

$$R^{\mathcal{I}} \circ S^{\mathcal{I}} = \{(a,c) \mid \exists b.\ (a,b) \in R^{\mathcal{I}} \wedge (b,c) \in S^{\mathcal{I}}\}.$$

Table A.2. *Concrete syntax of concept constructors.*

Name	Concrete syntax	Abstract syntax
Top	`TOP`	$\top$
Bottom	`BOTTOM`	$\bot$
Intersection	`(and C`$_1$` ... C`$_n$`)`	$C_1 \sqcap \cdots \sqcap C_n$
Union	`(or C`$_1$` ... C`$_n$`)`	$C_1 \sqcup \cdots \sqcup C_n$
Negation	`(not C)`	$\neg C$
Value restriction	`(all R C)`	$\forall R.C$
Limited existential quantification	`(some R)`	$\exists R.\top$
Existential quantification	`(some R C)`	$\exists R.C$
At-least number restriction	`(at-least n R)`	$\geqslant n\,R$
At-most number restriction	`(at-most n R)`	$\leqslant n\,R$
Exact number restriction	`(exactly n R)`	$= n\,R$
Qualified at-least restriction	`(at-least n R C)`	$\geqslant n\,R.C$
Qualified at-most restriction	`(at-most n R C)`	$\leqslant n\,R.C$
Qualified exact restriction	`(exactly n R C)`	$= n\,R.C$
Same-as, agreement	`(same-as u`$_1$` u`$_2$`)`	$u_1 \doteq u_2$
Role-value-map	`(subset R`$_1$` R`$_2$`)`	$R_1 \subseteq R_2$
Role fillers	`(fillers R I`$_1$` ... I`$_n$`)`	$\exists R.I_1 \sqcap \cdots \sqcap \exists R.I_n$
One-of	`(one-of I`$_1$` ... I`$_n$`)`	$I_1 \sqcup \cdots \sqcup I_n$

Table A.3. *Some Description Logic role constructors.*

Name	Syntax	Semantics	Symbol
Universal role	U	$\Delta^{\mathcal{I}} \times \Delta^{\mathcal{I}}$	U
Intersection	$R \sqcap S$	$R^{\mathcal{I}} \cap S^{\mathcal{I}}$	$\sqcap$
Union	$R \sqcup S$	$R^{\mathcal{I}} \cup S^{\mathcal{I}}$	$\sqcup$
Complement	$\neg R$	$\Delta^{\mathcal{I}} \times \Delta^{\mathcal{I}} \setminus R^{\mathcal{I}}$	$\neg$
Inverse	R^-	$\{(b,a) \in \Delta^{\mathcal{I}} \times \Delta^{\mathcal{I}} \mid (a,b) \in R^{\mathcal{I}}\}$	-1
Composition	$R \circ S$	$R^{\mathcal{I}} \circ S^{\mathcal{I}}$	$\circ$
Transitive closure	R^+	$\bigcup_{n \geq 1}(R^{\mathcal{I}})^n$	$+$
Reflexive–transitive closure	R^*	$\bigcup_{n \geq 0}(R^{\mathcal{I}})^n$	$*$
Role restriction	$R|_C$	$R^{\mathcal{I}} \cap (\Delta^{\mathcal{I}} \times C^{\mathcal{I}})$	r
Identity	$id(C)$	$\{(d,d) \mid d \in C^{\mathcal{I}}\}$	id

Table A.4. *Concrete syntax of role constructors.*

Name	Concrete syntax	Abstract syntax
Universal role	`top`	U
Intersection	`(and R`$_1$ $\cdots$ `R`$_n$`)`	$R_1 \sqcap \cdots \sqcap R_n$
Union	`(or R`$_1$ $\cdots$ `R`$_n$`)`	$R_1 \sqcup \cdots \sqcup R_n$
Complement	`(not R)`	$\neg R$
Inverse	`(inverse R)`	R^-
Composition	`(compose R`$_1$ $\cdots$ `R`$_n$`)`	$R_1 \circ \cdots \circ R_n$
Transitive closure	`(transitive-closure R)`	R^+
Reflexive–transitive closure	`(reflexive-transitive-closure R)`	R^*
Role restriction	`(restrict R C)`	$R|_C$
Identity	`(identity C)`	$id(C)$

Iterated composition is denoted in the form $(R^{\mathcal{I}})^n$. To be more precise,

$$(R^{\mathcal{I}})^0 = \{(d,d) \mid d \in \Delta^{\mathcal{I}}\} \quad \text{and} \quad (R^{\mathcal{I}})^{n+1} = (R^{\mathcal{I}})^n \circ R^{\mathcal{I}}.$$

Transitive and reflexive–transitive closure are the only constructors among the ones introduced so far that cannot be expressed in first-order predicate logic.

The LISP-like concrete syntax for role constructors can be found in Table A.4.

A.2.2 Knowledge bases

A DL knowledge base usually consists of a set of terminological axioms (often called a TBox) and a set of assertional axioms or assertions (often called an ABox). The syntax and semantics of these axioms can be found in Table A.5. An interpretation $\mathcal{I}$ is called a *model* of an axiom if it satisfies the statement in the last column of the table.

An equality whose left-hand side is an atomic concept (role) is called a concept (role) *definition*. A finite set of definitions is called a *terminology* or *TBox* if the definitions are unambiguous, i.e., no atomic concept occurs more than once as left-hand side. Axioms of the form $C \sqsubseteq D$ for a complex description C are often called *general inclusion axioms*. A set of axioms of the form $R \sqsubseteq S$ where both R and S are atomic is called a *role hierarchy*. Such a hierarchy obviously imposes restrictions on the interpretation of roles. Thus, the fact that the knowledge base may contain a role hierarchy

Table A.5. *Terminological and assertional axioms.*

Name	Syntax	Semantics
Concept inclusion	$C \sqsubseteq D$	$C^{\mathcal{I}} \subseteq D^{\mathcal{I}}$
Role inclusion	$R \sqsubseteq S$	$R^{\mathcal{I}} \subseteq S^{\mathcal{I}}$
Concept equality	$C \equiv D$	$C^{\mathcal{I}} = D^{\mathcal{I}}$
Role equality	$R \equiv S$	$R^{\mathcal{I}} = S^{\mathcal{I}}$
Concept assertion	$C(a)$	$a^{\mathcal{I}} \in C^{\mathcal{I}}$
Role assertion	$R(a, b)$	$(a^{\mathcal{I}}, b^{\mathcal{I}}) \in R^{\mathcal{I}}$

Table A.6. *Concrete syntax of axioms.*

Name	Concrete syntax	Abstract syntax
Concept definition	`(define-concept A C)`	$A \equiv C$
Primitive concept introduction	`(define-primitive-concept A C)`	$A \sqsubseteq C$
General inclusion axiom	`(implies C D)`	$C \sqsubseteq D$
Role definition	`(define-role R S)`	$R \equiv S$
Primitive role introduction	`(define-primitive-role R S)`	$R \sqsubseteq S$
Concept assertion	`(instance a C)`	$C(a)$
Role assertion	`(related a b R)`	$R(a, b)$

is sometimes indicated by appending a subscript $\mathcal{H}$ to the name of the Description Logic (see "Restrictions on role interpretations" above).

The concrete LISP-like syntax in Table A.6 distinguishes between terminological axioms with atomic concepts as left-hand sides and the more general ones. Following the convention mentioned at the beginning of this appendix, A denotes an atomic concept, and R denotes an atomic role.

A.3 Additional constructors

Here we mention some of the additional constructors that occur somewhere in the handbook. For most of them, the semantics cannot be described in a compact manner, and thus we refer to the respective chapter for details.

A.3.1 Concept and role constructors

Many additional constructors are introduced in Chapter 6. In Description Logics with *concrete domains* one can use concrete predicates to constrain fillers of feature chains, similarly to the use of the equality predicate in feature agreements. For example, if hasAge is a feature and $\geq_{18}$ the unary concrete predicate consisting of all nonnegative integers greater than or equal to 18, then $\exists$hasAge.$\geq_{18}$ describes the individuals whose age is greater than or equal to 18. In general, an *existential predicate restriction* is of the form

$$\exists(u_1, \ldots, u_n).P,$$

where P is an n-ary predicate of the underlying concrete domain and $u_1, \ldots, u_n$ are feature chains. One can also use concrete domain predicates to define new roles. For example, $\exists$(hasAge)(hasAge).$>$ consists of all pairs of individuals having an age such that the first individual is older than the second one. The general form of such a *complex role* is

$$\exists(u_1, \ldots, u_n)(v_1, \ldots, v_m).P,$$

where P is an $(n + m)$-ary predicate of the underlying concrete domain and $u_1, \ldots, u_n$, and $v_1, \ldots, v_m$ are feature chains.

In *modal extensions* of Description Logics, one can apply modal operators to concepts and/or roles, i.e., if $\Box$ is such a modal operator, C is a concept, and R is a role, then

$$\Box C \quad \text{and} \quad \Box R$$

are a concept and a role, respectively. Similarly, one can also use diamond operators $\Diamond$ to obtain new concepts and roles. A special such modal operator is the *epistemic operator* **K**, which can be used to talk about things that are known to the knowledge base.

Chapter 5 introduces several additional constructors. Least and greatest fixpoint semantics for cyclic terminologies (see Chapter 2) can be generalized by introducing *fixpoint constructors* directly into the description language. Let X be a concept name and C a concept description containing the name X. Then

$$\mu X.C \quad \text{and} \quad \nu X.C$$

are new concept descriptions respectively obtained by applying the least and the greatest fixpoint constructor to C. To ensure that the least and the greatest fixpoint exist, one must restrict C to be syntactically monotonic, i.e., every occurrence of X in C must be in the scope of an even number of complement operators. For example, given an interpretation $\mathsf{Man}^{\mathcal{I}}$ of Man and $\mathsf{hasChild}^{\mathcal{I}}$ of hasChild, the concept $\nu\mathsf{Momo}.(\mathsf{Man} \sqcap \forall\mathsf{hasChild}.\mathsf{Momo})$ looks for the greatest interpretation $\mathsf{Momo}^{\mathcal{I}}$ of Momo such that $\mathsf{Momo}^{\mathcal{I}} = (\mathsf{Man} \sqcap \forall\mathsf{hasChild}.\mathsf{Momo})^{\mathcal{I}}$. It is easy to see that this is the set of all men having only male offspring (see Chapter 2 for the corresponding example with a cyclic TBox).

Chapter 5 also considers the Description Logic $\mathcal{DLR}$, in which the restriction to at most binary predicates is no longer enforced. If $\mathbf{R}$ is an n-ary predicate, $i \in \{1, \ldots, n\}$, and k is a nonnegative integer, then

$$\exists[\$i]\mathbf{R}$$

denotes the concept collecting those individuals that occur as the ith component in some tuple of $\mathbf{R}$, and

$$\leqslant k\,[\$i]\mathbf{R}$$

denotes the concept collecting those individuals d for which the predicate $\mathbf{R}$ contains at most k tuples whose ith component is d. Conversely, if C is a concept, n a nonnegative integer, and $i \in \{1, \ldots, n\}$, then

$$(\$i/n : C)$$

denotes the n-ary predicate consisting of the tuples whose ith component belongs to C. The Description Logic $\mathcal{DLR}$ also allows Boolean operators on both concepts and predicates.[2]

A.3.2 Axioms

In addition to the semantics for terminological axioms introduced above, Chapter 2 also considers fixpoint semantics for cyclic TBoxes.

Chapter 6 introduces several ways of extending the terminological and the assertional component of a DL system. In Description Logics with *concrete domains* one can use concrete predicates also in the ABox in assertions of the form

$$P(x_1, \ldots, x_n),$$

where P is an n-ary predicate of the underlying concrete domain and $x_1, \ldots, x_n$ are names for concrete individuals.

In some *modal extensions* of Description Logics, one can apply modal and Boolean operators also to terminological and assertional axioms: if φ, ψ are axioms, then so are

$$\varphi \wedge \psi, \quad \neg\varphi, \quad \Box\varphi.$$

---

[2] Note, however, that negation on predicates has a non-standard semantics (see Chapter 5 for details).

In *probabilistic extensions* of Description Logics, one can use probabilistic terminological axioms of the form

$$P(C|D) = p,$$

which state that the conditional probability for an object known to be in D to belong to C is p.

The integration of Reiter's default logic into Description Logics yields *terminological defaults* of the form

$$\frac{C(x) : D(x)}{E(x)},$$

where C, D, E are concept descriptions (viewed as first-order formulae with one free variable x). Intuitively, such a default rule can be applied to an ABox individual a, i.e., $E(a)$ is added to the current set of beliefs, if its prerequisite $C(a)$ is already believed for this individual and its justification $D(a)$ is consistent with the set of beliefs.

Rules of the form

$$C \Rightarrow E$$

(as introduced in Chapter 2) can be seen as a special case of terminological defaults where the justification is empty. Their intuitive meaning is: "if an individual is known to be an instance of C, then add the information that it is also an instance of E."

A.4 A note on the naming scheme for Description Logics

In Section A.2 we have introduced a naming scheme for Description Logics, which extends the naming scheme for the $\mathcal{AL}$-family introduced in Chapter 2 by writing letters/symbols for role constructors as superscripts, and for restrictions on the interpretation of roles as subscripts. The reason was that this yields a consistent naming scheme, which distinguishes typographically between the three different possibilities for extending the expressive power of $\mathcal{AL}$.

In the literature, and also in this handbook, other naming schemes are employed as well. One reason for this, in addition to the fact that such schemes have evolved over time, is that it is very hard to pronounce a name like $\mathcal{ALCQ}_{R^+}^{-1}$. We will here point out the most prominent such naming schemes.

The historically first scheme is the one for the $\mathcal{AL}$-family introduced in Chapter 2, and extended in this appendix. However, in the literature the typographical distinction between role constructors, concept constructors, and restrictions on the interpretation of roles is usually not made. For example, many papers use $\mathcal{I}$ to denote inverse of roles, $\mathcal{R}$ to denote intersection of roles, and $\mathcal{H}$ to denote role hierarchies. Thus, $\mathcal{ALCRI}$ denotes the extension of $\mathcal{ALC}$ by intersection and inverse of roles, and $\mathcal{ALCH}$ denotes the extension of $\mathcal{ALC}$ by role hierarchies. In some cases, the letter $\mathcal{F}$, which we have employed to express the presence of feature agreements and disagreements, is used with a different meaning. Its presence states that number restrictions of the form $\leqslant 1\,R$ can be used to express functionality of roles.[3] The subscript "trans" (or "reg") is often employed to express the presence of union, composition, and transitive closure of roles (sometimes also including the identity role). The Greek letter μ in front of a language name, as in $\mu\mathcal{ALC}$, usually indicates the extension of this Description Logic by fixpoint operators.

All members of the $\mathcal{AL}$-family include $\mathcal{AL}$ as a sublanguage. In some cases one does not want all the constructors of $\mathcal{AL}$ to be present in the language. The Description Logic $\mathcal{FL}^-$ is obtained from $\mathcal{AL}$ by disallowing atomic negation, and $\mathcal{FL}_0$ is obtained from $\mathcal{FL}^-$ by, additionally, disallowing limited existential quantification. If these languages are extended by other constructors, one can indicate this in a way analogous to extensions of $\mathcal{AL}$. For example, $\mathcal{FL}^-\mathcal{U}$ denotes the extension of $\mathcal{FL}^-$ by union of concepts.

All the Description Logics mentioned so far contain the concept constructors intersection and value restriction as a common core. Description Logics that allow intersection of concepts and existential quantification (but not value restriction) are collected in the $\mathcal{EL}$-family. The only constructors available in $\mathcal{EL}$ are intersection of concepts and existential quantification. Extensions of $\mathcal{EL}$ are again obtained by adding appropriate letters/ symbols.

In order to avoid very long names for expressive Description Logics, the abbreviation $\mathcal{S}$ has been introduced for $\mathcal{ALC}_{R^+}$, i.e., the Description Logic that extends $\mathcal{ALC}$ by transitive roles. Prominent members of the $\mathcal{S}$-family are $\mathcal{SIN}$ (which extends $\mathcal{ALC}_{R^+}$ with number restrictions and inverse roles), $\mathcal{SHIF}$ (which extends $\mathcal{ALC}_{R^+}$ with role hierarchies, inverse roles, and number restrictions of the form $\leqslant 1\,R$), and $\mathcal{SHIQ}$ (which extends $\mathcal{ALC}_{R^+}$ with role hierarchies, inverse roles, and qualified number restrictions). Actually, the Description Logics $\mathcal{SIN}$, $\mathcal{SHIF}$, and $\mathcal{SHIQ}$ are somewhat less expressive than indicated by their name since the use of roles in number restrictions

---

[3] Unlike the restriction of R to be functional, which we express with a subscript f, this allows *local* functionality statements, i.e., R is functional at a certain place, but may be non-functional at other places.

is restricted: roles that have a transitive subrole must not occur in number restrictions.

The Description Logic $\mathcal{DLR}$ mentioned in the previous section also gives rise to a family of Description Logics, with members like $\mathcal{DLR}_{reg}$, which extends $\mathcal{DLR}$ with union, composition, and transitive closure of binary relations obtained as projections of n-ary predicates onto two of their components.

Bibliography

[Abiteboul, 1997] Serge Abiteboul. Querying semi-structured data. In *Proc. of the 6th Int. Conf. on Database Theory (ICDT'97)*, pages 1–18, 1997.

[Abiteboul and Kanellakis, 1989] Serge Abiteboul and Paris Kanellakis. Object identity as a query language primitive. In *Proc. of the ACM SIGMOD Int. Conf. on Management of Data*, pages 159–173, 1989.

[Abiteboul et al., 1995] Serge Abiteboul, Richard Hull, and Victor Vianu. *Foundations of Databases*. Addison Wesley Publ. Co., Reading, Massachussetts, 1995.

[Abiteboul et al., 1997] Serge Abiteboul, Dallan Quass, Jason McHugh, Jennifer Widom, and Janet L. Wiener. The Lorel query language for semistructured data. *Int. J. on Digital Libraries*, 1(1):68–88, 1997.

[Abiteboul et al., 2000] Serge Abiteboul, Peter Buneman, and Dan Suciu. *Data on the Web: from Relations to Semistructured Data and XML*. Morgan Kaufmann, Los Altos, 2000.

[Abrahams et al., 1996] Merryll K. Abrahams, Deborah L. McGuinness, Rich Thomason, Lori Alperin Resnick, Peter F. Patel-Schneider, Violetta Cavalli-Sforza, and Cristina Conati. NeoClassic tutorial: Version 1.0. Technical report, Artificial Intelligence Principles Research Department, AT&T Labs Research and University of Pittsburgh, 1996. Available as http://www.bell-labs.com/project/classic/papers/ NeoTut/NeoTut.html.

[Abrett and Burstein, 1987] Glen Abrett and Mark H. Burstein. The KREME knowledge editing environment. *Int. J. of Man-Machine Studies*, 27(2):103–126, 1987.

[Abrial, 1974] J. R. Abrial. Data semantics. In J. W. Klimbie and K. L. Koffeman, editors, *Data Base Management*, pages 1–59. North-Holland Publ. Co., Amsterdam, 1974.

[Achilles et al., 1991] E. Achilles, B. Hollunder, A. Laux, and J. P. Mohren. $\mathcal{KRIS}$: Knowledge Representation and Inference System – User guide. Technical Report D91-14, Deutsches Forschungszentrum für Künstliche Intelligenz (DFKI), 1991.

[Agoncillo et al., 1999] A. V. Agoncillo, J. L. Mejin Jr, and C. Rosse. Influence of the digital anatomist foundational model on traditional representations of anatomical concepts. *J. of the American Medical Informatics Association*, pages 2–6, 1999. Annual Symposium Issue.

[Aït-Kaci and Nasr, 1986] H. Aït-Kaci and R. Nasr. LOGIN: A logic programming language with built-in inheritance. *J. of Logic Programming*, 3:185–215, 1986.

[Albano *et al.*, 1991] Antonio Albano, Giorgio Ghelli, and Renzo Orsini. A relationship mechanism for strongly typed Object-Oriented database programming languages. In *Proc. of the 17th Int. Conf. on Very Large Data Bases (VLDB'91)*, pages 565–575, Barcelona (Spain), 1991.

[Albano *et al.*, 1993] Antonio Albano, Roberto Bergamini, Giorgio Ghelli, and Renzo Orsini. An object data model with roles. In *Proc. of the 19th Int. Conf. on Very Large Data Bases (VLDB'93)*, pages 39–51, 1993.

[Allen, 1983] James F. Allen. Maintaining knowledge about temporal intervals. *Communications of the ACM*, 26(11):832–843, 1983.

[Allen, 1991] James F. Allen. The RHET system. *SIGART Bull.*, 2(3):1–7, 1991.

[Allen, 1993] James F. Allen. Natural language, knowledge representation, and logical form. In M. Bates and R. Weischedel, editors, *Challenges in Natural Language Processing*. Cambridge University Press, 1993.

[Allgayer, 1990] Jürgen Allgayer. SB-ONE+: Dealing with sets efficiently. In *Proc. of the 9th Eur. Conf. on Artificial Intelligence (ECAI'90)*, pages 13–18, 1990.

[Allgayer *et al.*, 1989] J. Allgayer, R. Jansen-Winkeln, C. Reddig, and N. Reithinger. Bidirectional use of knowledge in the multi-modal NL access system XTRA. In *Proc. of the 10th Int. Joint Conf. on Artificial Intelligence (IJCAI'87)*, 1989.

[Amarger *et al.*, 1991] S. Amarger, D. Dubois, and H. Prade. Constraint propagation with imprecise conditional probabilities. In *Proc. of the 7th Annual Conf. on Uncertainty in Artificial Intelligence (UAI'91)*, pages 26–34. Morgan Kaufmann, Los Altos, 1991.

[André and Rist, 1995] Elisabeth André and Thomas Rist. Generating coherent presentations employing textual and visual material. *Artificial Intelligence Rev.*, 9(2/3):147–165, 1995.

[André *et al.*, 1996] E. André, J. Müller, and T. Rist. WIP/PPP: Automatic generation of personalized multimedia presentations. In *Proc. of the 4th ACM Int. Multimedia Conference (Multimedia'96)*, pages 407–408, 1996.

[Andréka *et al.*, 1996] Hajnal Andréka, Johan van Benthem, and Istvaán Németi. Modal languages and bounded fragments of predicate logic. Technical Report ML-96-03, ILLC, University of Amsterdam, 1996.

[Anwar *et al.*, 1992] T. W. Anwar, H. Beck, and S. Navathe. Knowledge mining by imprecise querying: A classification-based approach. In *Proc. of the 8th IEEE Int. Conf. on Data Engineering (ICDE'92)*, pages 622–630, 1992.

[Areces, 2000] Carlos Areces. *Logic Engineering. The Case of Description and Hybrid Logics*. PhD thesis, ILLC, University of Amsterdam, 2000. ILLC Dissertation Series 2000-5.

[Areces and de Rijke, 1998] Carlos Areces and Marteen de Rijke. Expressiveness revisited. In *Proc. of the 1998 Description Logic Workshop (DL'98)*. CEUR Electronic Workshop Proceedings, http://ceur-ws.org/Vol-11/, 1998.

[Areces *et al.*, 2000] Carlos Areces, Patrick Blackburn, and Maarten Marx. The computational complexity of hybrid temporal logics. *J. of the Interest Group in Pure and Applied Logic*, 8(5), 2000.

[Arens *et al.*, 1993] Y. Arens, C. Y. Chee, C. Hsu, and C. A. Knoblock. Retrieving and integrating data from multiple information sources. *J. of Intelligent and Cooperative Information Systems*, 2(2):127–158, 1993.

[Arens *et al.*, 1996] Y. Arens, C. A. Knoblock, and W. Shen. Query reformulation for dynamic information integration. *J. of Intelligent Information Systems*, 6:99–130, 1996.

[Artale and Franconi, 1994] Alessandro Artale and Enrico Franconi. A computational account for a Description Logic of time and action. In J. Doyle, E. Sandewall, and P. Torasso, editors, *Proc. of the 4th Int. Conf. on the Principles of Knowledge Representation and Reasoning (KR'94)*, pages 3–14, Bonn (Germany), 1994. Morgan Kaufmann, Los Altos.

[Artale and Franconi, 1998] Alessandro Artale and Enrico Franconi. A temporal Description Logic for reasoning about actions and plans. *J. of Artificial Intelligence Research*, 9:463–506, 1998.

[Artale and Franconi, 1999] Alessandro Artale and Enrico Franconi. Temporal ER modeling with Description Logics. In *Proc. of the 18th Int. Conf. on Conceptual Modeling (ER'99)*, volume 1728 of Lecture Notes in Computer Science, pages 81–95. Springer, 1999.

[Artale and Franconi, 2000] Alessandro Artale and Enrico Franconi. A survey of temporal extensions of Description Logics. *Ann. of Mathematics and Artificial Intelligence*, 1–4:171–210, 2000.

[Artale and Franconi, 2001] Alessandro Artale and Enrico Franconi. Temporal Description Logics. In D. Gabbay, M. Fisher, and L. Vila, editors, *Handbook of Time and Temporal Reasoning in Artificial Intelligence*. The MIT Press, 2001.

[Artale *et al.*, 1996a] Alessandro Artale, Francesca Cesarini, and Giovanni Soda. Describing database objects in a concept language environment. *IEEE Trans. on Knowledge and Data Engineering*, 8(2):345–351, 1996.

[Artale *et al.*, 1996b] Alessandro Artale, Enrico Franconi, Nicola Guarino, and Luca Pazzi. Part-whole relations in object-centered systems: An overview. *Data and Knowledge Engineering*, 20:347–383, 1996.

[Artale *et al.*, 2001] Alessandro Artale, Enrico Franconi, Milenko Mosurovic, Frank Wolter, and Michael Zakharyaschev. The $\mathcal{DLR}$(US) temporal Description Logic. In *Proc. of the 2001 Description Logic Workshop (DL 2001)*. CEUR Electronic Workshop Proceedings, http://ceur-ws.org/Vol-49/, 2001.

[Baader, 1990a] Franz Baader. Terminological cycles in KL-ONE-based knowledge representation languages. In *Proc. of the 8th Nat. Conf. on Artificial Intelligence (AAAI'90)*, pages 621–626, Boston (MA, USA), 1990.

[Baader, 1990b] Franz Baader. Terminological cycles in KL-ONE-based knowledge representation languages. Technical Report RR-90-01, Deutsches Forschungszentrum für Künstliche Intelligenz (DFKI), Kaiserslautern (Germany), 1990. An abridged version appeared in *Proc. of the 8th Nat. Conf. on Artificial Intelligence (AAAI'90)*, pp. 621–626.

[Baader, 1991] Franz Baader. Augmenting concept languages by transitive closure of roles: An alternative to terminological cycles. In *Proc. of the 12th Int. Joint Conf. on Artificial Intelligence (IJCAI'91)*, 1991.

[Baader, 1996a] Franz Baader. A formal definition for the expressive power of terminological knowledge representation languages. *J. of Logic and Computation*, 6:33–54, 1996.

[Baader, 1996b] Franz Baader. Using automata theory for characterizing the semantics of terminological cycles. *Ann. of Mathematics and Artificial Intelligence*, 18:175–219, 1996.

[Baader, 1998] Franz Baader. Personal communication, 1998.

[Baader and Hanschke, 1991a] Franz Baader and Philipp Hanschke. A schema for integrating concrete domains into concept languages. In *Proc. of the 12th Int. Joint Conf. on Artificial Intelligence (IJCAI'91)*, pages 452–457, 1991.

[Baader and Hanschke, 1991b] Franz Baader and Philipp Hanschke. A scheme for integrating concrete domains into concept languages. Technical Report RR-91-10, Deutsches Forschungszentrum für Künstliche Intelligenz (DFKI), 1991.

[Baader and Hanschke, 1992] Franz Baader and Philipp Hanschke. Extensions of concept languages for a mechanical engineering application. In *Proc. of the 16th German Workshop on Artificial Intelligence (GWAI'92)*, volume 671 of Lecture Notes in Computer Science, pages 132–143. Springer, 1992.

[Baader and Hollunder, 1991a] Franz Baader and Bernhard Hollunder. $\mathcal{KRIS}$: $\mathcal{K}$nowledge $\mathcal{R}$epresentation and $\mathcal{I}$nference $\mathcal{S}$ystem. *SIGART Bull.*, 2(3):8–14, 1991.

[Baader and Hollunder, 1991b] Franz Baader and Bernhard Hollunder. A terminological knowledge representation system with complete inference algorithm. In *Proc. of the Workshop on Processing Declarative Knowledge (PDK'91)*, volume 567 of Lecture Notes in Artificial Intelligence, pages 67–86. Springer, 1991.

[Baader and Hollunder, 1992] Franz Baader and Bernhard Hollunder. Embedding defaults into terminological knowledge representation formalisms. In *Proc. of the 3rd Int. Conf. on the Principles of Knowledge Representation and Reasoning (KR'92)*, pages 306–317. Morgan Kaufmann, Los Altos, 1992.

[Baader and Hollunder, 1993] Franz Baader and Bernhard Hollunder. How to prefer more specific defaults in terminological default logic. In *Proc. of the 13th Int. Joint Conf. on Artificial Intelligence (IJCAI'93)*, pages 669–674. Morgan Kaufmann, Los Altos, 1993.

[Baader and Hollunder, 1995a] Franz Baader and Bernhard Hollunder. Embedding defaults into terminological knowledge representation formalisms. *J. of Automated Reasoning*, 14:149–180, 1995.

[Baader and Hollunder, 1995b] Franz Baader and Bernhard Hollunder. Priorities on defaults with prerequisites and their application in treating specificity in terminological default logic. *J. of Automated Reasoning*, 14:41–68, 1995.

[Baader and Küsters, 1998] Franz Baader and Ralf Küsters. Computing the least common subsumer and the most specific concept in the presence of cyclic $\mathcal{ALN}$-concept descriptions. In *Proc. of the 22nd German Annual Conf. on Artificial Intelligence (KI'98)*, volume 1504 of Lecture Notes in Computer Science, pages 129–140. Springer, 1998.

[Baader and Küsters, 1999] Franz Baader and Ralf Küsters. Matching in
· Description Logics with existential restrictions. In *Proc. of the 1999 Description Logic Workshop (DL'99)*. CEUR Electronic Workshop Proceedings, http://ceur-ws.org/ Vol-22/, 1999.

[Baader and Küsters, 2000] Franz Baader and Ralf Küsters. Matching in Description Logics with existential restrictions. In *Proc. of the 7th Int. Conf. on Principles of Knowledge Representation and Reasoning (KR 2000)*, pages 261–272, 2000.

[Baader and Küsters, 2001] Franz Baader and Ralf Küsters. Unification in a Description Logic with transitive closure of roles. In Robert Nieuwenhuis and Andrei Voronkov, editors, *Proc. of the 8th Int. Conf. on Logic for*

Programming, Artificial Intelligence and Reasoning (LPAR 2001), volume 2250 of Lecture Notes in Computer Science, pages 217–232. Springer, 2001.

[Baader and Laux, 1995] Franz Baader and Armin Laux. Terminological logics with modal operators. In *Proc. of the 14th Int. Joint Conf. on Artificial Intelligence (IJCAI'95)*, pages 808–814, 1995. Morgan Kaufmann, Los Altos.

[Baader and Molitor, 1999] Franz Baader and Ralf Molitor. Rewriting in Description Logics using terminologies. In *Proc. of the 1999 Description Logic Workshop (DL'99)*. CEUR Electronic Workshop Proceedings, http://ceur-ws.org/ Vol-22/, 1999.

[Baader and Narendran, 1998] Franz Baader and Paliath Narendran. Unification of concept terms in Description Logics. In H. Prade, editor, *Proc. of the 13th Eur. Conf. on Artificial Intelligence (ECAI'98)*, pages 331–335. John Wiley & Sons, 1998.

[Baader and Narendran, 2001] Franz Baader and Paliath Narendran. Unification of concept terms in Description Logics. *J. of Symbolic Computation*, 31(3):277–305, 2001.

[Baader and Ohlbach, 1993] Franz Baader and Hans-Jürgen Ohlbach. A multi-dimensional terminological knowledge representation language. In *Proc. of the 13th Int. Joint Conf. on Artificial Intelligence (IJCAI'93)*, pages 690–695, 1993.

[Baader and Ohlbach, 1995] Franz Baader and Hans-Jürgen Ohlbach. A multi-dimensional terminological knowledge representation language. *J. of Applied Non-classical Logics*, 5:153–197, 1995.

[Baader and Sattler, 1996a] Franz Baader and Ulrike Sattler. Description logics with symbolic number restrictions. In *Proc. of the 12th Eur. Conf. on Artificial Intelligence (ECAI'96)*, pages 283–287. John Wiley & Sons, 1996.

[Baader and Sattler, 1996b] Franz Baader and Ulrike Sattler. Number restrictions on complex roles in Description Logics: A preliminary report. In *Proc. of the 5th Int. Conf. on the Principles of Knowledge Representation and Reasoning (KR'96)*, pages 328–338, 1996.

[Baader and Sattler, 1999] Franz Baader and Ulrike Sattler. Expressive number restrictions in Description Logics. *J. of Logic and Computation*, 9(3):319–350, 1999.

[Baader and Schlechta, 1993] Franz Baader and Karl Schlechta. A semantics for open normal defaults via a modified preferential approach. In *Proceedings of the European Conference on Symbolic and Quantitative Approaches to Reasoning und Uncertainty, (ECSQARU'93)*, volume 747 of Lecture Notes in Computer Science, pages 9–16. Springer, 1993.

[Baader et al., 1991] Franz Baader, Hans-Jürgen Bürkert, Jochen Heinsohn, Bernhard Hollunder, Jürgen Müller, Bernhard Nebel, Werner Nutt, and Hans-Jürgen Profitlich. Terminological knowledge representation: A proposal for a terminological logic. Technical Report TM-90-04, Deutsches Forschungszentrum für Künstliche Intelligenz (DFKI), Kaiserslautern (Germany), 1991.

[Baader et al., 1992a] Franz Baader, Enrico Franconi, Bernhard Hollunder, Bernhard Nebel, and Hans-Jürgen Profitlich. An empirical analysis of optimization techniques for terminological representation systems, or: Making KRIS get a move on. In *Proc. of the 3rd Int. Conf. on the Principles of Knowledge Representation and Reasoning (KR'92)*, pages 270–281, 1992.

[Baader *et al.*, 1992b] Franz Baader, Bernhard Hollunder, Bernhard Nebel, Hans-Jürgen Profitlich, and Enrico Franconi. An empirical analysis of optimization techniques for terminological representation systems. In *Proc. of the 3rd Int. Conf. on the Principles of Knowledge Representation and Reasoning (KR'92)*, pages 270–281. Morgan Kaufmann, Los Altos, 1992.

[Baader *et al.*, 1993] Franz Baader, Hans-Jürgen Bürckert, Bernhard Nebel, Werner Nutt, and Gert Smolka. On the expressivity of feature logics with negation, functional uncertainty, and sort equations. *J. of Logic, Language and Information*, 2:1–18, 1993.

[Baader *et al.*, 1994] Franz Baader, Enrico Franconi, Bernhard Hollunder, Bernhard Nebel, and Hans-Jürgen Profitlich. An empirical analysis of optimization techniques for terminological representation systems or: Making KRIS get a move on. *Applied Artificial Intelligence. Special Issue on Knowledge Base Management*, 4:109–132, 1994.

[Baader *et al.*, 1996] Franz Baader, Martin Buchheit, and Bernhard Hollunder. Cardinality restrictions on concepts. *Artificial Intelligence*, 88(1–2):195–213, 1996.

[Baader *et al.*, 1998a] Franz Baader, Ralf Küsters, and Ralf Molitor. Structural subsumption considered from an automata theoretic point of view. In *Proc. of the 1998 Description Logic Workshop (DL'98)*. CEUR Electronic Workshop Proceedings, http://ceur-ws.org/Vol-11/, 1998.

[Baader *et al.*, 1998b] Franz Baader, Ralf Molitor, and Stephan Tobies. On the relation between Description Logics and conceptual graphs. LTCS-Report 98-11, LuFG Theoretical Computer Science, RWTH Aachen, Germany, 1998.

[Baader *et al.*, 1999a] Franz Baader, Ralf Küsters, Alex Borgida, and Deborah L. McGuinness. Matching in Description Logics. *J. of Logic and Computation*, 9(3):411–447, 1999.

[Baader *et al.*, 1999b] Franz Baader, Ralf Küsters, and Ralf Molitor. Computing least common subsumers in Description Logics with existential restrictions. In *Proc. of the 16th Int. Joint Conf. on Artificial Intelligence (IJCAI'99)*, pages 96–101, 1999.

[Baader *et al.*, 1999c] Franz Baader, Ralf Molitor, and Stephan Tobies. Decidable and tractable fragments of conceptual graphs. In William Tepfenhart and Walling Cyre, editors, *Proc. of the 7th Int. Conf. on Conceptual Structures (ICCS'99)*, volume 1640 of Lecture Notes in Artificial Intelligence, pages 480–493. Springer, 1999.

[Baader *et al.*, 2000] Franz Baader, Ralf Küsters, and Ralf Molitor. Rewriting concepts using terminologies. In *Proc. of the 7th Int. Conf. on Principles of Knowledge Representation and Reasoning (KR 2000)*, pages 297–308, 2000.

[Baader *et al.*, 2001] Franz Baader, Sebastian Brandt, and Ralf Küsters. Matching under side conditions in Description Logics. In *Proc. of the 17th Int. Joint Conf. on Artificial Intelligence (IJCAI 2001)*, pages 213–218, 2001.

[Baker, 1995] A. B. Baker. *Intelligent Backtracking on Constraint Satisfaction Problems: Experimental and Theoretical Results*. PhD thesis, University of Oregon, 1995.

[Baker *et al.*, 1998] P. Baker, A. Brass, S. Bechhofer, C. Goble, N. Paton, and R. Stevens. TAMBIS: Transparent access to multiple bioinformatics information sources. In *Proc. of the 6th Int. Conf. on Intelligent Systems for Molecular Biology (ISMB'98)*, pages 25–34, 1998.

[Balcazar, 1996] José L. Balcazar. The complexity of searching implicit graphs. *Artificial Intelligence*, 86:171–188, 1996.

[Balsiger and Heuerding, 1998] P. Balsiger and A. Heuerding. Comparison of theorem provers for modal logics—introduction and summary. In H. de Swart, editor, *Proc. of the 2nd Int. Conf. on Analytic Tableaux and Related Methods (TABLEAUX'98)*, volume 1397 of Lecture Notes in Artificial Intelligence, pages 25–26. Springer, 1998.

[Balsiger *et al.*, 1996] P. Balsiger, G. Jäger, S. Schwendimann, and M. Seyfried. A logics workbench. *AI Communications – The Eur. J. on Artificial Intelligence*, 9(2):53–58, 1996.

[Bancilhon and Khoshafian, 1989] François Bancilhon and Setrag Khoshafian. A calculus for complex objects. *J. of Computer and System Sciences*, 38(2):326–340, 1989.

[Bateman, 1990] John A. Bateman. Upper modeling: Organizing knowledge for natural language processing. In *Proc. of the 5th Int. Workshop on Natural Language Generation*, pages 54–61, Dawson, PA, 1990.

[Bateman *et al.*, 1995] John A. Bateman, Bernardo Magnini, and Giovanni Fabris. The generalized upper model knowledge base: Organization and use. In *Proc. of the 2nd Int. Conf. on Building and Sharing of Very Large-Scale Knowledge Bases*, Twente (The Netherlands), April 1995.

[Batini *et al.*, 1986] Carlo Batini, Maurizio Lenzerini, and Shamkant B. Navathe. A comparative analysis of methodologies for database schema integration. *ACM Computing Surveys*, 18(4):323–364, 1986.

[Batini *et al.*, 1992] Carlo Batini, Stefano Ceri, and Shamkant B. Navathe. *Conceptual Database Design, an Entity-Relationship Approach*. Benjamin and Cummings Publ. Co., Menlo Park, California, 1992.

[Baud *et al.*, 1993] R. Baud, C. Lovis, L. Alpay, A.-M. Rassinoux, J.-R. Scherrer, A. Nowlan, and A. Rector. Modelling for natural language understanding. In *Proc. of the 17th Annual Symposium on Computer Applications in Medical Care (SCAMC'93)*, pages 289–293, 1993.

[Baud *et al.*, 1997] R. H. Baud, J.-M. Rodrigues, J. C. Wagner, A.-M. Rassinoux, C. Lovis, P. Rush, B. Trombert-Paviot, and J.-R. Scherrer. Validation of concept representation using natural language generation. *J. of the American Medical Informatics Association*, 1997. Fall Symposium Supplement.

[Bechhofer *et al.*, 1999] Sean Bechhofer, Ian Horrocks, Peter F. Patel-Schneider, and Sergio Tessaris. A proposal for a Description Logic interface. In *Proc. of the 1999 Description Logic Workshop (DL'99)*, pages 33–36. CEUR Electronic Workshop Proceedings, http://ceur-ws.org/Vol-22/, 1999.

[Bechhofer *et al.*, 2000] Sean Bechhofer, Jeen Broekstra, Stefan Decker, Michael Erdmann, Dieter Fensel, Carole Goble, Frank van Harmelen, Ian Horrocks, Michel Klein, Deborah L. McGuinness, Enrico Motta, Peter F. Patel-Schneider, Steffen Staab, and Rudi Studer. An informal description of OIL-Core and Standard OIL: a layered proposal for DAML-O. Technical Report KSL-00-19, Stanford University KSL, November 2000. Available at http://www.ontoknowledge.org/oil/ downl/dialects.pdf.

[Bechhofer *et al.*, 2001a] Sean Bechhofer, Carole Goble, and Ian Horrocks. DAML+OIL is not enough. In *Proc. of the 2001 Int. Semantic Web Working Symposium (SWWS 2001)*, pages 151–159, 2001. Available at http://www.semanticweb.org/SWWS/program/full/SWWSProceedings.pdf.

[Bechhofer *et al.*, 2001b] Sean Bechhofer, Ian Horrocks, Carole Goble, and Robert Stevens. OilEd: A Reason-able ontology editor for the semantic web. In *Proc. of the Joint German/Austrian Conf. on Artificial Intelligence (KI 2001)*, number 2174 in Lecture Notes in Artificial Intelligence, pages 396–408. Springer, 2001. Appeared also in *Proc. of the 2001 Description Logic Workshop (DL 2001)*.

[Bechhofer *et al.*, 2004] Sean Bechhofer, Frank van Harmelen, Jim Hendler, Ian Horrocks, Deborah L. McGuinness, Peter F. Patel-Schneider, and Lynn Andrea Stein. OWL Web Ontology Language reference. W3C Recommendation, February 2004. Available at http://www.w3.org/TR/owl-ref/.

[Beck *et al.*, 1989] Howard W. Beck, Sunit K. Gala, and Shamkant B. Navathe. Classification as a query processing technique in the CANDIDE semantic data model. In *Proc. of the 5th IEEE Int. Conf. on Data Engineering (ICDE'89)*, pages 572–581, 1989.

[Beeri *et al.*, 1997] Catriel Beeri, Alon Y. Levy, and Marie-Christine Rousset. Rewriting queries using views in Description Logics. In *Proc. of the 16th ACM SIGACT SIGMOD SIGART Symp. on Principles of Database Systems (PODS'97)*, pages 99–108, 1997.

[Bell *et al.*, 1994] D. S. Bell, E. Pattison-Gordon, and R. A. Greenes. Experiments in concept modeling for radiographic image reports. *J. of the American Medical Informatics Association*, 1(3), 1994.

[Ben-Ari *et al.*, 1982] Mordechai Ben-Ari, Joseph Y. Halpern, and Amir Pnueli. Deterministic propositional dynamic logic: Finite models, complexity, and completeness. *J. of Computer and System Sciences*, 25:402–417, 1982.

[Bennett, 1997] Brandon Bennett. Modal logics for qualitative spatial reasoning. *J. of the Interest Group in Pure and Applied Logic*, 4(1), 1997.

[Bergamaschi and Nebel, 1994] Sonia Bergamaschi and Bernhard Nebel. Acquisition and validation of complex object database schemata supporting multiple inheritance. *Applied Intelligence*, 4(2):185–203, 1994.

[Bergamaschi and Sartori, 1992] Sonia Bergamaschi and Claudio Sartori. On taxonomic reasoning in conceptual design. *ACM Trans. on Database Systems*, 17(3):385–422, 1992.

[Bergamaschi *et al.*, 1997] Sonia Bergamaschi, Domenico Beneventano, Claudio Sartori, and Maurizio Vincini. ODB-QOPTIMIZER: A tool for semantic query optimization in oodb. In *Proc. of the 13th IEEE Int. Conf. on Data Engineering (ICDE'97)*, 1997.

[Berger, 1966] R. Berger. The undecidability of the dominoe problem. *Mem. Amer. Math. Soc.*, 66:1–72, 1966.

[Berners-Lee *et al.*, 2001] Tim Berners-Lee, James Hendler, and Ora Lassila. The Semantic Web. *Scientific American*, 284(5):34–43, May 2001.

[Bernholtz *et al.*, 1994] Orna Bernholtz, Moshe Y. Vardi, and Pierre Wolper. An automata-theoretic approach to branching-time model checking. In *Proc. of the 6th Int. Conf. on Computer Aided Verification (CAV'94)*, volume 818 of Lecture Notes in Computer Science, pages 142–155. Springer, 1994.

[Bettini, 1997] Claudio Bettini. Time-dependent concepts: Representation and reasoning using temporal Description Logics. *Data and Knowledge Engineering*, 22:1–38, 1997.

[Biron and Malhotra, 2001] Paul V. Biron and Ashok Malhotra. XML Schema Part 2: Datatypes. W3C Recommendation, May 2001. Available at http://www.w3.org/TR/xmlschema-2/.

[Blackburn, 1993] Patrick Blackburn. Nominal tense logic. *Notre Dame J. of Formal Logic*, 34(1):56–83, 1993.

[Blackburn and Seligman, 1995] Patrick Blackburn and Jerry Seligman. Hybrid languages. *J. of Logic, Language and Information*, 4:251–272, 1995.

[Blackburn and Spaan, 1993] Patrick Blackburn and Edith Spaan. A modal perspective on computational complexity of attribute value grammars. *J. of Logic, Language and Information*, 2:129–169, 1993.

[Blackburn et al., 2001] Patrick Blackburn, Maarten de Rijke, and Yde Venema. *Modal Logic*, volume 53 of Cambridge Tracts in Theoretical Computer Science. Cambridge University Press, 2001.

[Bobrow and Webber, 1980] R. Bobrow and B. Webber. Knowledge representation for syntactic/semantic processing. In *Proc. of the 1st Nat. Conf. on Artificial Intelligence (AAAI'80)*, 1980.

[Borgida, 1992a] Alexander Borgida. Description logics are not just for the flightless-birds: a new look at the utility and foundations of Description Logics. Technical Report DCS-TR-295, New Brunswick Department of Computer Science, Rutgers University, 1992.

[Borgida, 1992b] Alexander Borgida. From type systems to knowledge representation: natural semantics specifications for Description Logics. *J. of Intelligent and Cooperative Information Systems*, 1(1):93–126, 1992.

[Borgida, 1995] Alexander Borgida. Description logics in data management. *IEEE Trans. on Knowledge and Data Engineering*, 7(5):671–682, 1995.

[Borgida, 1996] Alexander Borgida. On the relative expressiveness of Description Logics and predicate logics. *Artificial Intelligence*, 82(1–2):353–367, 1996.

[Borgida, 1999] Alexander Borgida. Extensible knowledge representation: the case of description reasoners. *J. of Artificial Intelligence Research*, 10:399–434, 1999.

[Borgida and Brachman, 1993] Alexander Borgida and Ronald J. Brachman. Loading data into description reasoners. In *Proc. of the ACM SIGMOD Int. Conf. on Management of Data*, pages 217–226, 1993.

[Borgida and Etherington, 1989] Alexander Borgida and David W. Etherington. Hierarchical knowledge bases and efficient disjunctive reasoning. In Ron J. Brachman, Hector J. Levesque, and Ray Reiter, editors, *Proc. of the 1st Int. Conf. on the Principles of Knowledge Representation and Reasoning (KR'89)*, pages 33–43, 1989.

[Borgida and Küsters, 2000] Alexander Borgida and Ralf Küsters. What's not in a name: Some properties of a purely structural approach to integrating large DL knowledge bases. In *Proc. of the 2000 Description Logic Workshop (DL 2000)*, pages 65–78. CEUR Electronic Workshop Proceedings, http://ceur-ws.org/Vol-33/, 2000.

[Borgida and McGuinness, 1996] Alexander Borgida and Deborah L. McGuinness. Asking queries about frames. In *Proc. of the 5th Int. Conf. on the Principles of Knowledge Representation and Reasoning (KR'96)*, pages 340–349, 1996.

[Borgida and Patel-Schneider, 1994] Alexander Borgida and Peter F. Patel-Schneider. A semantics and complete algorithm for subsumption in the CLASSIC Description Logic. *J. of Artificial Intelligence Research*, 1:277–308, 1994.

[Borgida and Weddell, 1997] Alexander Borgida and Grant E. Weddell. Adding uniqueness constraints to Description Logics (preliminary report). In *Proc. of the 5th Int. Conf. on Deductive and Object-Oriented Databases (DOOD'97)*, pages 85–102, 1997.

[Borgida *et al.*, 1989] Alexander Borgida, Ronald J. Brachman, Deborah L. McGuinness, and Lori Alperin Resnick. CLASSIC: a structural data model for objects. In *Proc. of the ACM SIGMOD Int. Conf. on Management of Data*, pages 59–67, 1989.

[Borgida *et al.*, 1996] Alex Borgida, Charles Isbell, and Deborah L. McGuinness. Reasoning with black boxes: handling test concepts in CLASSIC. In *Proc. of the 1996 Description Logic Workshop (DL'96)*, number WS-96-05 in AAAI Technical Report. AAAI Press/The MIT Press, 1996.

[Borgida *et al.*, 1999] Alex Borgida, Enrico Franconi, Ian Horrocks, Deborah L. McGuinness, and Peter F. Patel-Schneider. Explaining $\mathcal{ALC}$ subsumption. In *Proc. of the 1999 Description Logic Workshop (DL'99)*. CEUR Electronic Workshop Proceedings, http://ceur-ws.org/Vol-22/, 1999.

[Borgida *et al.*, 2000] Alex Borgida, Enrico Franconi, and Ian Horrocks. Explaining $\mathcal{ALC}$ subsumption. In *Proc. of the 14th Eur. Conf. on Artificial Intelligence (ECAI 2000)*, 2000.

[Bouzeghoub *et al.*, 1999] Mokrane Bouzeghoub, Francoise Fabret, Helena Galhardas, Maja Matulovic-Broqué, Joao Pereira, and Eric Simon. Data warehouse refreshment. In Matthias Jarke, Maurizio Lenzerini, Yannis Vassiliou, and Panos Vassiliadis, editors, *Fundamentals of Data Warehouses*, pages 47–86. Springer, 1999.

[Brachman, 1977a] Ronald J. Brachman. *A Structural Paradigm for Representing Knowledge*. PhD thesis, Harvard University, Cambridge, MA, 1977. Revised version published as BBN Report No. 3605, Bolt Beranek and Newman, Inc., Cambridge, MA, July, 1978.

[Brachman, 1977b] Ronald J. Brachman. What's in a concept: structural foundations for semantic networks. *Int. Journal of Man-Machine Studies*, 9(2):127–152, 1977.

[Brachman, 1978] Ronald J. Brachman. Structured inheritance networks. In W. A. Woods and R. J. Brachman, editors, *Research in Natural Language Understanding*, Quarterly Progress Report No. 1, BBN Report No. 3742, pages 36–78. Bolt, Beranek and Newman Inc., Cambridge, MA, 1978.

[Brachman, 1979] Ronald J. Brachman. On the epistemological status of semantic networks. In Nicholas V. Findler, editor, *Associative Networks*, pages 3–50. Academic Press, 1979. Republished in [Brachman and Levesque, 1985].

[Brachman, 1983] Ronald J. Brachman. What IS-A is and isn't. *IEEE Computer*, 16(10):30–36, 1983.

[Brachman, 1985] Ronald J. Brachman. "I lied about the trees": or, defaults and definitions in knowledge representation. *AI Magazine*, 6(3):80–93, 1985.

[Brachman, 1992] Ronald J. Brachman. "Reducing" CLASSIC to practice: Knowledge representation meets reality. In *Proc. of the 3rd Int. Conf. on the Principles of Knowledge Representation and Reasoning (KR'92)*, pages 247–258. Morgan Kaufmann, Los Altos, 1992.

[Brachman, 1994] Ronald J. Brachman. Viewing databases through a knowledge representation lens. In K. Fuchi and T. Yokoi, editors, *Proc. of Knowledge Building and Knowledge Sharing Conference (KB&KS'93)*, pages 121–124, Tokyo, 1994. Ohmsha, Ltd.

[Brachman and Levesque, 1984] Ronald J. Brachman and Hector J. Levesque. The tractability of subsumption in frame-based description languages. In *Proc. of the 4th Nat. Conf. on Artificial Intelligence (AAAI'84)*, pages 34–37, 1984.

[Brachman and Levesque, 1985] Ronald J. Brachman and Hector J. Levesque, editors. *Readings in Knowledge Representation*. Morgan Kaufmann, Los Altos, 1985.

[Brachman and Schmolze, 1985] Ronald J. Brachman and James G. Schmolze. An overview of the KL-ONE knowledge representation system. *Cognitive Science*, 9(2):171–216, 1985.

[Brachman *et al.*, 1979] R. Brachman, R. Bobrow, P. Cohen, J. Klovstad, B. Webber, and W. Woods. Research in natural language understanding, annual report. Technical Report 4274, Bolt Beranek and Newman, Cambridge, MA (USA), 1979.

[Brachman *et al.*, 1983a] Ronald J. Brachman, Richard E. Fikes, and Hector J. Levesque. KRYPTON: A functional approach to knowledge representation. *IEEE Computer*, October:67–73, 1983.

[Brachman *et al.*, 1983b] Ronald J. Brachman, Richard E. Fikes, and Hector J. Levesque. KRYPTON: integrating terminology and assertion. In *Proc. of the 3rd Nat. Conf. on Artificial Intelligence (AAAI'83)*, pages 31–35, 1983.

[Brachman *et al.*, 1985] Ronald J. Brachman, Victoria Pigman Gilbert, and Hector J. Levesque. An essential hybrid reasoning system: Knowledge and symbol level accounts in KRYPTON. In *Proc. of the 9th Int. Joint Conf. on Artificial Intelligence (IJCAI'85)*, pages 532–539, 1985.

[Brachman *et al.*, 1990] Ronald J. Brachman, Premkumar Devanbu, Peter G. Selfridge, David Belanger, and Yun Chen. Toward a software information system. *AT&T Technical J.*, 69(2):22–41, 1990.

[Brachman *et al.*, 1991] Ronald J. Brachman, Deborah L. McGuinness, Peter F. Patel-Schneider, Lori Alperin Resnick, and Alexander Borgida. Living with CLASSIC: When and how to use a KL-ONE-like language. In John F. Sowa, editor, *Principles of Semantic Networks*, pages 401–456. Morgan Kaufmann, Los Altos, 1991.

[Brachman *et al.*, 1992] Ronald J. Brachman, Peter G. Selfridge, Loren G. Terveen, B. Altman, Alexander Borgida, F. Halper, Thomas Kirk, A. Lazar, Deborah L. McGuinness, and Lori Alperin Resnick. Knowledge representation support for data archeology. In Y. Yesha, editor, *Proc. of the Int. Conf. on Information and Knowledge Management (CIKM'92)*, pages 457–464, 1992.

[Brachman *et al.*, 1993] Ronald J. Brachman, Peter G. Selfridge, Loren G. Terveen, B. Altman, F. Halper, Thomas Kirk, A. Lazar, Deborah L. McGuinness, and Lori Alperin Resnick. Integrated support for data archeology. *Int. J. of Cooperative Information Systems*, 2(2):159–185, 1993.

[Brachman *et al.*, 1999] Ronald J. Brachman, Alexander Borgida, Deborah L. McGuinness, and Peter Patel-Schneider. Reducing CLASSIC to practice: Knowledge representation theory meets reality. *Artificial Intelligence*, 114(1–2):203–237, 1999.

[Brandt *et al.*, 2001] Sebastian Brandt, Ralf Küsters, and Anni-Yasmin Turhan. Approximation in Description Logics. LTCS-Report 01-06, LuFG Theoretical Computer Science, RWTH Aachen, Germany, 2001. Available at http://www-lti.informatik.rwth-aachen.de/Forschung/Reports.html.

[Bray *et al.*, 1998] Tim Bray, Jean Paoli, and C. M. Sperberg-McQueen. Extensible Markup Language (XML) 1.0—W3C recommendation. Technical report, World Wide Web Consortium, 1998. Available at http://www.w3.org/TR/1998/REC-xml-19980210.

[Bresciani *et al.*, 1995] P. Bresciani, E. Franconi, and S. Tessaris. Implementing and testing expressive Description Logics: Preliminary report. In *Proc. of the 1995 Description Logic Workshop (DL'95)*, pages 131–139, 1995.

[Brill, 1994] David Brill. *Loom Reference Manual, Version 2.0*. Marina del Rey, 1994.

[Brown *et al.*, 1998] P. Brown, M. O'Neil, and C. Price. Semantic definition of disorders in version 3 of the read codes. *Methods of Information in Medicine*, 37:415–419, 1998.

[Buchheit *et al.*, 1993a] Martin Buchheit, Francesco M. Donini, and Andrea Schaerf. Decidable reasoning in terminological knowledge representation systems. *J. of Artificial Intelligence Research*, 1:109–138, 1993.

[Buchheit *et al.*, 1993b] Martin Buchheit, Francesco M. Donini, and Andrea Schaerf. Decidable reasoning in terminological knowledge representation systems. Technical Report RR-93-10, Deutsches Forschungszentrum für Künstliche Intelligenz (DFKI), Saarbrücken (Germany), 1993. An abridged version appeared in *Proc. of the 13th Int. Joint Conf. on Artificial Intelligence (IJCAI'93)*.

[Buchheit *et al.*, 1993c] Martin Buchheit, Francesco M. Donini, and Andrea Schaerf. Decidable reasoning in terminological knowledge representation systems. In *Proc. of the 13th Int. Joint Conf. on Artificial Intelligence (IJCAI'93)*, pages 704–709. Morgan Kaufmann, Los Altos, 1993.

[Buchheit *et al.*, 1994a] Martin Buchheit, Francesco M. Donini, Werner Nutt, and Andrea Schaerf. Terminological systems revisited: terminology = schema + views. In *Proc. of the 12th Nat. Conf. on Artificial Intelligence (AAAI'94)*, pages 199–204, Seattle (USA), 1994.

[Buchheit *et al.*, 1994b] Martin Buchheit, Manfred A. Jeusfeld, Werner Nutt, and Martin Staudt. Subsumption between queries to object-oriented databases. *Information Systems*, 19(1):33–54, 1994. Special issue on Extending Database Technology, EDBT'94.

[Buchheit *et al.*, 1994c] Martin Buchheit, Rudiger Klein, and Werner Nutt. Configuration as model construction: the constructive problem solving approach. In *Proc. of the 4th Int. Conf. on Artificial Intelligence in Design*, Lausanne (Switzerland), August 1994.

[Buchheit *et al.*, 1998] Martin Buchheit, Francesco M. Donini, Werner Nutt, and Andrea Schaerf. A refined architecture for terminological systems: terminology = schema + views. *Artificial Intelligence*, 99(2):209–260, 1998.

[Bull, 1970] R. Bull. An approach to tense logic. *Theoria*, 12:171–182, 1970.

[Buneman *et al.*, 1997] Peter Buneman, Susan Davidson, Mary F. Fernandez, and Dan Suciu. Adding structure to unstructured data. In *Proc. of the 6th Int. Conf. on Database Theory (ICDT'97)*, pages 336–350, 1997.

[Cadoli *et al.*, 2000] Marco Cadoli, Marco Schaerf, Andrea Giovanardi, and Massimo Giovanardi. An algorithm to evaluate quantified boolean formulae and its experimental evaluation. In Ian Gent, Hans van Maaren, and Toby Walsh, editors, *SAT2000 – Highlights of Satisfiability Research in the Year 2000*, pages 485–521. IOS Press, 2000.

[Calvanese, 1990] Diego Calvanese. Integrazione tra linguaggi logici e linguaggi per la descrizione di concetti. Master's thesis, Università di Roma "La Sapienza", 1990.

[Calvanese, 1996a] Diego Calvanese. Finite model reasoning in Description Logics. In Luigia C. Aiello, John Doyle, and Stuart C. Shapiro, editors, *Proc. of the*

5th Int. Conf. on the Principles of Knowledge Representation and Reasoning (KR'96), pages 292–303. Morgan Kaufmann, Los Altos, 1996.

[Calvanese, 1996b] Diego Calvanese. Reasoning with inclusion axioms in Description Logics: Algorithms and complexity. In *Proc. of the 12th Eur. Conf. on Artificial Intelligence (ECAI'96)*, pages 303–307. John Wiley & Sons, 1996.

[Calvanese, 1996c] Diego Calvanese. *Unrestricted and Finite Model Reasoning in Class-Based Representation Formalisms*. PhD thesis, Dipartimento di Informatica e Sistemistica, Università di Roma "La Sapienza", 1996. Available at http://www.dis.uniroma1.it/pub/calvanes/thesis.ps.gz.

[Calvanese and Lenzerini, 1994a] Diego Calvanese and Maurizio Lenzerini. Making object-oriented schemas more expressive. In *Proc. of the 13th ACM SIGACT SIGMOD SIGART Symp. on Principles of Database Systems (PODS'94)*, pages 243–254, Minneapolis (Minnesota, USA), 1994. ACM Press and Addison Wesley.

[Calvanese and Lenzerini, 1994b] Diego Calvanese and Maurizio Lenzerini. On the interaction between ISA and cardinality constraints. In *Proc. of the 10th IEEE Int. Conf. on Data Engineering (ICDE'94)*, pages 204–213, Houston (Texas, USA), 1994. IEEE Computer Society Press.

[Calvanese et al., 1994] Diego Calvanese, Maurizio Lenzerini, and Daniele Nardi. A unified framework for class based representation formalisms. In J. Doyle, E. Sandewall, and P. Torasso, editors, *Proc. of the 4th Int. Conf. on the Principles of Knowledge Representation and Reasoning (KR'94)*, pages 109–120, Bonn (Germany), 1994. Morgan Kaufmann, Los Altos.

[Calvanese et al., 1995] Diego Calvanese, Giuseppe De Giacomo, and Maurizio Lenzerini. Structured objects: Modeling and reasoning. In *Proc. of the 4th Int. Conf. on Deductive and Object-Oriented Databases (DOOD'95)*, volume 1013 of Lecture Notes in Computer Science, pages 229–246. Springer, 1995.

[Calvanese et al., 1997] Diego Calvanese, Giuseppe De Giacomo, and Maurizio Lenzerini. Conjunctive query containment in Description Logics with n-ary relations. In *Proc. of the 1997 Description Logic Workshop (DL'97)*, pages 5–9, 1997.

[Calvanese et al., 1998a] Diego Calvanese, Giuseppe De Giacomo, and Maurizio Lenzerini. On the decidability of query containment under constraints. In *Proc. of the 17th ACM SIGACT SIGMOD SIGART Symp. on Principles of Database Systems (PODS'98)*, pages 149–158, 1998.

[Calvanese et al., 1998b] Diego Calvanese, Giuseppe De Giacomo, and Maurizio Lenzerini. Semi-structured data with constraints and incomplete information. In *Proc. of the 1998 Description Logic Workshop (DL'98)*, pages 11–20. CEUR Electronic Workshop Proceedings, http://ceur-ws.org/Vol-11/, 1998.

[Calvanese et al., 1998c] Diego Calvanese, Giuseppe De Giacomo, and Maurizio Lenzerini. What can knowledge representation do for semi-structured data? In *Proc. of the 15th Nat. Conf. on Artificial Intelligence (AAAI'98)*, pages 205–210, 1998.

[Calvanese et al., 1998d] Diego Calvanese, Giuseppe De Giacomo, Maurizio Lenzerini, Daniele Nardi, and Riccardo Rosati. Description logic framework for information integration. In *Proc. of the 6th Int. Conf. on Principles of Knowledge Representation and Reasoning (KR'98)*, pages 2–13, 1998.

550   *Bibliography*

[Calvanese *et al.*, 1998e] Diego Calvanese, Giuseppe De Giacomo, Maurizio Lenzerini, Daniele Nardi, and Riccardo Rosati. Information integration: Conceptual modeling and reasoning support. In *Proc. of the 6th Int. Conf. on Cooperative Information Systems (CoopIS'98)*, pages 280–291, 1998.

[Calvanese *et al.*, 1998f] Diego Calvanese, Giuseppe De Giacomo, Maurizio Lenzerini, Daniele Nardi, and Riccardo Rosati. Source integration in data warehousing. In *Proc. of the 9th Int. Workshop on Database and Expert Systems Applications (DEXA'98)*, pages 192–197. IEEE Computer Society Press, 1998.

[Calvanese *et al.*, 1998g] Diego Calvanese, Maurizio Lenzerini, and Daniele Nardi. Description logics for conceptual data modeling. In Jan Chomicki and Günter Saake, editors, *Logics for Databases and Information Systems*, pages 229–264. Kluwer Academic Publishers, 1998.

[Calvanese *et al.*, 1999a] Diego Calvanese, Giuseppe De Giacomo, and Maurizio Lenzerini. Answering queries using views in Description Logics. In *Proc. of the 1999 Description Logic Workshop (DL'99)*, pages 9–13. CEUR Electronic Workshop Proceedings, `http://ceur-ws.org/Vol-22/`, 1999.

[Calvanese *et al.*, 1999b] Diego Calvanese, Giuseppe De Giacomo, and Maurizio Lenzerini. Modeling and querying semi-structured data. *Network and Information Systems*, 2(2), 1999.

[Calvanese *et al.*, 1999c] Diego Calvanese, Giuseppe De Giacomo, and Maurizio Lenzerini. Reasoning in expressive Description Logics with fixpoints based on automata on infinite trees. In *Proc. of the 16th Int. Joint Conf. on Artificial Intelligence (IJCAI'99)*, pages 84–89, 1999.

[Calvanese *et al.*, 1999d] Diego Calvanese, Giuseppe De Giacomo, and Maurizio Lenzerini. Representing and reasoning on XML documents: a Description Logic approach. *J. of Logic and Computation*, 9(3):295–318, 1999.

[Calvanese *et al.*, 1999e] Diego Calvanese, Maurizio Lenzerini, and Daniele Nardi. Unifying class-based representation formalisms. *J. of Artificial Intelligence Research*, 11:199–240, 1999.

[Calvanese *et al.*, 2000a] Diego Calvanese, Giuseppe De Giacomo, and Maurizio Lenzerini. Answering queries using views over Description Logics knowledge bases. In *Proc. of the 17th Nat. Conf. on Artificial Intelligence (AAAI 2000)*, pages 386–391, 2000.

[Calvanese *et al.*, 2000b] Diego Calvanese, Giuseppe De Giacomo, and Maurizio Lenzerini. Keys for free in Description Logics. In *Proc. of the 2000 Description Logic Workshop (DL 2000)*, pages 79–88. CEUR Electronic Workshop Proceedings, `http://ceur-ws.org/Vol-33/`, 2000.

[Calvanese *et al.*, 2001a] Diego Calvanese, Giuseppe De Giacomo, and Maurizio Lenzerini. Identification constraints and functional dependencies in Description Logics. In *Proc. of the 17th Int. Joint Conf. on Artificial Intelligence (IJCAI 2001)*, pages 155–160, 2001.

[Calvanese *et al.*, 2001b] Diego Calvanese, Giuseppe De Giacomo, Maurizio Lenzerini, and Daniele Nardi. Reasoning in expressive Description Logics. In Alan Robinson and Andrei Voronkov, editors, *Handbook of Automated Reasoning*, pages 1581–1634. Elsevier Science Publishers (North-Holland), Amsterdam, 2001.

[Calvanese *et al.*, 2001c] Diego Calvanese, Giuseppe De Giacomo, Maurizio Lenzerini, Daniele Nardi, and Riccardo Rosati. Data integration in data warehousing. *Int. J. of Cooperative Information Systems*, 10(3):237–271, 2001.

[Campbell, 1998] K. Campbell. Scalable methodologies for distributed development of logic-based convergent medical terminology. *Methods of Information in Medicine*, 37:426–439, 1998.

[Campbell *et al.*, 1994] K. E. Campbell, A. K. Das, and M. A. Musen. A logical foundation for representation of clinical data. *J. of the American Medical Informatics Association*, 1(3):218–232, 1994.

[Campbell *et al.*, 1996] K. Campbell, S. Cohn, C. Chute, G. Rennels, and E. Shortliffe. Gálapagos: Computer-based support for evolution of a convergent medical terminology. In *Proc. of AMIA Fall Symposium*, pages 269–273, 1996.

[Campbell *et al.*, 1998] K. E. Campbell, M. S. Tuttle, and K. A. Spackman. A "lexically-suggested logical closure" metric for medical terminology maturity. *J. of the American Medical Informatics Association*, pages 785–789, 1998. Fall Symposium Special Issue.

[Catarci and Lenzerini, 1993] Tiziana Catarci and Maurizio Lenzerini. Representing and using interschema knowledge in cooperative information systems. *J. of Intelligent and Cooperative Information Systems*, 2(4):375–398, 1993.

[Cattell and Barry, 1997] Roderick G. G. Cattell and Douglas K. Barry, editors. *The Object Database Standard: ODMG 2.0*. Morgan Kaufmann, Los Altos, 1997.

[Ceusters, 1998] W. Ceusters. The distinction between linguistic and conceptual semantics in medical terminology and its implications for NLP-based knowledge acquisition. *Methods of Information in Medicine*, 37:327–333, 1998.

[Ceusters and Spyns, 1997] W. Ceusters and P. Spyns. From natural language to formal language: when MultiTALE meets GALEN. In *Proc. of Medical Informatics Europe (MIE'97)*, pages 396–400, 1997.

[Ceusters *et al.*, 1999] W. Ceusters, J. Rogers, F. Consorti, and A. Rossi Mori. Syntactic-semantic tagging as a mediator between linguistic representations and formal models: an exercise in linking SNOMED to GALEN. A.I.M., 15(1):5–23, 1999.

[Chagrov and Zakharyaschev, 1997] Alexander Chagrov and Michael Zakharyaschev. *Modal Logic*, volume 35 of Oxford Logic Guides. Clarendon Press, 1997.

[Chandra and Merlin, 1977] Ashok K. Chandra and Philip M. Merlin. Optimal implementation of conjunctive queries in relational data bases. In *Proc. of the 9th ACM Symp. on Theory of Computing (STOC'77)*, pages 77–90, 1977.

[Chaudhri *et al.*, 1997] Vinay K. Chaudhri, Adam Farquhar, Richard Fikes, Peter D. Karp, and James Rice. The Generic Frame Protocol 2.0. Technical report, Artificial Intelligence Center, SRI International, Menlo Park, CA (USA), July 1997.

[Chaudhri *et al.*, 1998a] Vinay K. Chaudhri, Adam Farquhar, Richard Fikes, and Peter D. Karp. Open Knowledge Base Connectivity 2.0. Technical Report KSL-09-06, Stanford University KSL, 1998.

[Chaudhri *et al.*, 1998b] Vinay K. Chaudhri, Adam Farquhar, Richard Fikes, Peter D. Karp, and James Rice. OKBC: A programmatic foundation for knowledge base interoperability. In *Proc. of the 15th Nat. Conf. on Artificial Intelligence (AAAI'98)*, pages 600–607, 1998.

[Chein and Mugnier, 1992] Michel Chein and Marie-Laure Mugnier. Conceptual graphs: Fundamental notions. *Revue d'Intelligence Artificielle*, 6(4):365–406, 1992.

[Chen, 1976] P. P. Chen. The Entity–Relationship model: toward a unified view of data. *ACM Trans. on Database Systems*, 1(1):9–36, March 1976.

[Christaller *et al.*, 1992] Thomas Christaller, Franco di Primio, Uwe Schnepf, and Angi Voß. *The AI-Workbench BABYLON – an Open and Portable Development Environment for Expert Systems*. Academic Press, 1992.

[Cimino, 1994] J. Cimino. Controlled medical vocabulary construction: Methods from the CANON group. *J. of the American Medical Informatics Association*, 1(3), 1994.

[Cimino, 1996] J. Cimino. Formal descriptions and adaptive mechanisms for changes in controlled medical vocabularies. *Methods of Information in Medicine*, 35:202–210, 1996.

[Cimino *et al.*, 1989] J. Cimino, G. Hripcsak, S. Johnson, and P. Clayton. Designing an introspective controlled medical vocabulary. In *Proc. of the 13th Annual Symposium on Computer Applications in Medical Care (SCAMC'89)*, pages 202–210, 1989.

[Cimino *et al.*, 1998] J. Cimino, S. Huff, C. T. M. Broverman, and S. Nelson. Development of a standard terminology to support medication messages. *J. of the American Medical Informatics Association*, 1998. Fall Symposium Special Issue.

[Cohen and Hirsh, 1994a] William W. Cohen and Haym Hirsh. Learnability of Description Logics with equality constraints. *Machine Learning*, 17(2/3):169–200, 1994.

[Cohen and Hirsh, 1994b] William W. Cohen and Haym Hirsh. Learning the CLASSIC Description Logics: Theoretical and experimental results. In J. Doyle, E. Sandewall, and P. Torasso, editors, *Proc. of the 4th Int. Conf. on the Principles of Knowledge Representation and Reasoning (KR'94)*, pages 121–133, 1994.

[Cohen *et al.*, 1992] William W. Cohen, Alex Borgida, and Haym Hirsh. Computing least common subsumers in Description Logics. In William Swartout, editor, *Proc. of the 10th Nat. Conf. on Artificial Intelligence (AAAI'92)*, pages 754–760. AAAI Press/The MIT Press, 1992.

[Collins, 1975] G. E. Collins. Quantifier elimination for real closed fields by cylindric algebraic decomposition. In H. Brakhage, editor, *Proc. of the 2nd GI Conference on Automata Theory and Formal Languages*, volume 33 of Lecture Notes in Computer Science, pages 134–183, 1975. Springer.

[Collins and Quillian, 1970] A. M. Collins and M. R. Quillian. Facilitating retrieval from semantic memory: The effect of repeating part of an inference. *Acta Psychologica*, 33:304–314, 1970.

[Cosmadakis and Kanellakis, 1986] Stavros S. Cosmadakis and Paris C. Kanellakis. Functional and inclusion dependencies – a graph theoretical approach. In P. C. Kanellakis and F. P. Preparata, editors, *Advances in Computing Research, Vol. 3*, pages 163–184. JAI Press, 1986.

[Cosmadakis *et al.*, 1990] S. S. Cosmadakis, P. C. Kanellakis, and M. Vardi. Polynomial-time implication problems for unary inclusion dependencies. *J. of the ACM*, 37(1):15–46, January 1990.

[Coupey and Faron, 1998] Pascal Coupey and Catherine Faron. Towards correspondences between conceptual graphs and Description Logics. In

Marie-Laure Mugnier and Michel Chein, editors, *Proc. of the 6th Int. Conf. on Conceptual Structures (ICCS'98)*, volume 1453 of Lecture Notes in Artificial Intelligence. Springer, 1998.

[Curtis *et al.*, 1988] B. Curtis, N. Iscoe, and H. Krasner. A field study of the software design process for large systems. *Communications of the ACM*, 31(11):1268–1287, November 1988.

[Danecki, 1984] Ryszard Danecki. Nondeterministic Propositional Dynamic Logic with intersection is decidable. In *Proc. of the 5th Symp. on Computation Theory*, volume 208 of Lecture Notes in Computer Science, pages 34–53. Springer, 1984.

[Darr *et al.*, 1998] Tim Darr, Mark Fox, and Deborah McGuinness (editors). Special issue on configuration. *Artificial Intelligence for Engineering Design, Analysis, and Manufacturing*, 1998.

[Das *et al.*, 2001] Aseem Das, Wei Wu, and Deborah L. McGuinness. An industrial strength distributed ontology environment. In *Proc. of the 2001 Int. Semantic Web Working Symposium (SWWS 2001)*, 2001. Available at `http://www.semanticweb.org/SWWS/program/full/SWWSProceedings.pdf`.

[Davis, 1973] Martin Davis. Hilbert's tenth problem is unsolvable. *American Mathematical Monthly*, 80:233–269, 1973.

[Davis and Putnam, 1960] Martin Davis and Hilary Putnam. A computing procedure for quantification theory. *J. of the ACM*, 7(3):201–215, 1960.

[Davis *et al.*, 1962] M. Davis, G. Logemann, and D. Loveland. A machine program for theorem proving. *Communications of the ACM*, 5:394–397, 1962.

[de Bakker, 1980] Jaco de Bakker. *Mathematical Theory of Program Correctness*. Prentice-Hall, Englewood Cliffs, New Jersey, 1980.

[De Giacomo, 1995] Giuseppe De Giacomo. *Decidability of Class-Based Knowledge Representation Formalisms*. PhD thesis, Dipartimento di Informatica e Sistemistica, Università di Roma "La Sapienza", 1995.

[De Giacomo, 1996] Giuseppe De Giacomo. Eliminating "converse" from Converse PDL. *J. of Logic, Language and Information*, 5:193–208, 1996.

[De Giacomo and Lenzerini, 1994a] Giuseppe De Giacomo and Maurizio Lenzerini. Boosting the correspondence between Description Logics and propositional dynamic logics. In *Proc. of the 12th Nat. Conf. on Artificial Intelligence (AAAI'94)*, pages 205–212. AAAI Press/The MIT Press, 1994.

[De Giacomo and Lenzerini, 1994b] Giuseppe De Giacomo and Maurizio Lenzerini. Concept language with number restrictions and fixpoints, and its relationship with μ-calculus. In *Proc. of the 11th Eur. Conf. on Artificial Intelligence (ECAI'94)*, pages 411–415, 1994.

[De Giacomo and Lenzerini, 1994c] Giuseppe De Giacomo and Maurizio Lenzerini. Description logics with inverse roles, functional restrictions, and n-ary relations. In *Proc. of the 4th Eur. Workshop on Logics in Artificial Intelligence (JELIA'94)*, volume 838 of Lecture Notes in Artificial Intelligence, pages 332–346. Springer, 1994.

[De Giacomo and Lenzerini, 1994d] Giuseppe De Giacomo and Maurizio Lenzerini. On the correspondence between Description Logics and logics of programs (position paper). In *Proc. of the Description Logics Workshop*, pages 1–4, 1994.

[De Giacomo and Lenzerini, 1995] Giuseppe De Giacomo and Maurizio Lenzerini. What's in an aggregate: Foundations for Description Logics with tuples and sets. In *Proc. of the 14th Int. Joint Conf. on Artificial Intelligence (IJCAI'95)*, pages 801–807, 1995.

[De Giacomo and Lenzerini, 1996] Giuseppe De Giacomo and Maurizio Lenzerini. TBox and ABox reasoning in expressive Description Logics. In Luigia C. Aiello, John Doyle, and Stuart C. Shapiro, editors, *Proc. of the 5th Int. Conf. on the Principles of Knowledge Representation and Reasoning (KR'96)*, pages 316–327. Morgan Kaufmann, Los Altos, 1996.

[De Giacomo and Lenzerini, 1997] Giuseppe De Giacomo and Maurizio Lenzerini. A uniform framework for concept definitions in Description Logics. *J. of Artificial Intelligence Research*, 6:87–110, 1997.

[De Giacomo and Massacci, 1996] Giuseppe De Giacomo and Fabio Massacci. Tableaux and algorithms for propositional dynamic logic with converse. In Michael A. McRobbie and John K. Slaney, editors, *Proc. of the 13th Int. Conf. on Automated Deduction (CADE'96)*, volume 1104 of Lecture Notes in Artificial Intelligence, pages 613–628. Springer, 1996.

[De Giacomo et al., 1999] Giuseppe De Giacomo, Luca Iocchi, Daniele Nardi, and Riccardo Rosati. A theory and implementation of cognitive mobile robots. *J. of Logic and Computation*, 9(5):759–785, 1999.

[De Rosa et al., 1998] Mattia De Rosa, Tiziana Catarci, Luca Iocchi, Daniele Nardi, and Giuseppe Santucci. Materializing the Web. In *Proc. of the 6th Int. Conf. on Cooperative Information Systems (CoopIS'98)*, pages 24–31, 1998.

[Decker et al., 2000] Stefan Decker, Dieter Fensel, Frank van Harmelen, Ian Horrocks, Sergey Melnik, Michel Klein, and Jeen Broekstra. Knowledge representation on the web. In *Proc. of the 2000 Description Logic Workshop (DL 2000)*, pages 89–97. CEUR Electronic Workshop Proceedings, http://ceur-ws.org/Vol-33/, 2000.

[Dershowitz and Jouannaud, 1990] N. Dershowitz and J. Jouannaud. Rewrite systems. In J. van Leeuven, editor, *Handbook of Theoretical Computer Science*, volume B, chapter 6, pages 243–320. Elsevier Science Publishers (North-Holland), Amsterdam, 1990.

[Devanbu et al., 1991] Premkumar Devanbu, Ronald J. Brachman, Peter J. Selfridge, and Bruce W. Ballard. LASSIE: A knowledge-based software information system. *Communications of the ACM*, 34(5):36–49, 1991.

[Di Battista and Lenzerini, 1993] Giuseppe Di Battista and Maurizio Lenzerini. Deductive entity–relationship modeling. *IEEE Trans. on Knowledge and Data Engineering*, 5(3):439–450, 1993.

[Di Eugenio, 1994] Barbara Di Eugenio. Action representation for interpreting purpose clauses in natural language instructions. In *Proc. of the 4th Int. Conf. on the Principles of Knowledge Representation and Reasoning (KR'94)*, pages 158–169, 1994.

[Di Eugenio, 1998] Barbara Di Eugenio. An action representation formalism to interpret natural language instructions. *Computational Intelligence*, 14(1):89–133, 1998.

[Dick and Steen, 1991] R. S. Dick and E. B. Steen, editors. *The Computer-Based Patient Record: An Essential Technology for Health Care*. National Academy Press, 1991.

[Dionne et al., 1992] Robert Dionne, Eric Mays, and Frank J. Oles. A non-well-founded approach to terminological cycles. In *Proc. of the 10th Nat. Conf. on Artificial Intelligence (AAAI'92)*, pages 761–766. AAAI Press/The MIT Press, 1992.

[Donini and Massacci, 2000] Francesco M. Donini and Fabio Massacci. EXPTIME tableaux for *ALC*. *Artificial Intelligence*, 124(1):87–138, 2000.

[Donini *et al.*, 1990] Francesco M. Donini, Maurizio Lenzerini, and Daniele Nardi. Using terminological reasoning in hybrid systems. *AI Communications—The Eur. J. on Artificial Intelligence*, 3(3):128–138, 1990.

[Donini *et al.*, 1991a] Francesco M. Donini, Maurizio Lenzerini, Daniele Nardi, and Werner Nutt. The complexity of concept languages. In James Allen, Richard Fikes, and Erik Sandewall, editors, *Proc. of the 2nd Int. Conf. on the Principles of Knowledge Representation and Reasoning (KR'91)*, pages 151–162. Morgan Kaufmann, Los Altos, 1991.

[Donini *et al.*, 1991b] Francesco M. Donini, Maurizio Lenzerini, Daniele Nardi, and Werner Nutt. Tractable concept languages. In *Proc. of the 12th Int. Joint Conf. on Artificial Intelligence (IJCAI'91)*, pages 458–463, Sydney (Australia), 1991.

[Donini *et al.*, 1992a] Francesco M. Donini, Bernhard Hollunder, Maurizio Lenzerini, Alberto Marchetti Spaccamela, Daniele Nardi, and Werner Nutt. The complexity of existential quantification in concept languages. *Artificial Intelligence*, 2–3:309–327, 1992.

[Donini *et al.*, 1992b] Francesco M. Donini, Maurizio Lenzerini, Daniele Nardi, Werner Nutt, and Andrea Schaerf. Adding epistemic operators to concept languages. In *Proc. of the 3rd Int. Conf. on the Principles of Knowledge Representation and Reasoning (KR'92)*, pages 342–353. Morgan Kaufmann, Los Altos, 1992.

[Donini *et al.*, 1994a] Francesco M. Donini, Maurizio Lenzerini, Daniele Nardi, Werner Nutt, and Andrea Schaerf. Queries, rules and definitions as epistemic sentences in concept languages. In *Proc. of the ECAI Workshop on Knowledge Representation and Reasoning*, volume 810 of Lecture Notes in Artificial Intelligence, pages 113–132. Springer, 1994.

[Donini *et al.*, 1994b] Francesco M. Donini, Maurizio Lenzerini, Daniele Nardi, and Andrea Schaerf. Deduction in concept languages: From subsumption to instance checking. *J. of Logic and Computation*, 4(4):423–452, 1994.

[Donini *et al.*, 1995] Francesco M. Donini, Daniele Nardi, and Riccardo Rosati. Non-first-order features in concept languages. In M. Gori and G. Soda, editors, *Proc. of the 4th Conf. of the Ital. Assoc. for Artificial Intelligence (AI*IA'95)*, volume 992 of Lecture Notes in Artificial Intelligence, pages 91–102. Springer, 1995.

[Donini *et al.*, 1996a] Francesco M. Donini, Giuseppe De Giacomo, and Fabio Massacci. EXPTIME tableaux for *ALC*. In *Proc. of the 1996 Description Logic Workshop (DL'96)*, number WS-96-05 in AAAI Technical Report, pages 107–110. AAAI Press/The MIT Press, 1996.

[Donini *et al.*, 1996b] Francesco M. Donini, Maurizio Lenzerini, Daniele Nardi, and Andrea Schaerf. Reasoning in Description Logics. In Gerhard Brewka, editor, *Principles of Knowledge Representation*, Studies in Logic, Language and Information, pages 193–238. CSLI Publications, 1996.

[Donini *et al.*, 1997a] Francesco M. Donini, Maurizio Lenzerini, Daniele Nardi, and Werner Nutt. The complexity of concept languages. *Information and Computation*, 134:1–58, 1997.

[Donini *et al.*, 1997b] Francesco M. Donini, Daniele Nardi, and Riccardo Rosati. Autoepistemic Description Logics. In *Proc. of the 15th Int. Joint Conf. on Artificial Intelligence (IJCAI'97)*, pages 136–141, 1997.

[Donini *et al.*, 1997c] Francesco M. Donini, Daniele Nardi, and Riccardo Rosati. Ground nonmonotonic modal logics. *J. of Logic and Computation*, 7(4):523–548, August 1997.

[Donini *et al.*, 1998a] Francesco M. Donini, Maurizio Lenzerini, Daniele Nardi, Werner Nutt, and Andrea Schaerf. An epistemic operator for Description Logics. *Artificial Intelligence*, 100(1–2):225–274, 1998.

[Donini *et al.*, 1998b] Francesco M. Donini, Maurizio Lenzerini, Daniele Nardi, and Andrea Schaerf. $\mathcal{AL}$-log: Integrating Datalog and Description Logics. *J. of Intelligent Information Systems*, 10(3):227–252, 1998.

[Donini *et al.*, 1999] Francesco M. Donini, Maurizio Lenzerini, Daniele Nardi, and Werner Nutt. Tractability and intractability in Description Logics. Available at `ftp://ftp.dis.uniroma1.it/pub/ai/papers/dlnn99d.ps.gz`, 1999.

[Donini *et al.*, 2002] Francesco M. Donini, Daniele Nardi, and Riccardo Rosati. Description Logics of minimal knowledge and negation as failure. *TOCL*, 3(2):177–225, 2002.

[Dorr, 1992] Bonnie J. Dorr. The use of lexical semantics in interlingual machine translation. *J. of Machine Translation*, 7:135–193, 1992.

[Dorr and Voss, 1993] Bonnie J. Dorr and Clare R. Voss. Machine Translation of spatial expressions: Defining the relation between an interlingua and a knowledge representation system. In *Proc. of the 11th Nat. Conf. on Artificial Intelligence (AAAI'93)*, 1993.

[Dorr and Voss, 1995] Bonnie J. Dorr and Clare R. Voss. Toward a lexicalized grammar for interlinguas. *J. of Machine Translation*, 10(1):139–180, 1995.

[Dorr *et al.*, 1994] B. Dorr, C. Voss, E. Peterson, and M. Kiker. Concept-based lexical selection. In *Working notes of the AAAI Fall Symposium on "Knowledge Representation for Natural Language Processing in Implemented Systems"*, 1994.

[Doyle and Patil, 1991] Jon Doyle and Ramesh S. Patil. Two theses of knowledge representation: Language restrictions, taxonomic classification, and the utility of representation services. *Artificial Intelligence*, 48:261–297, 1991.

[ECAI, 2002] *Proc. of the 15th Eur. Conf. on Artifical Intelligence* (ECAI-2002).

[Edelmann and Owsnicki, 1986] J. Edelmann and B. Owsnicki. Data models in knowledge representation systems: A case study. In C. R. Rollinger and W. Horn, editors, *GWAI-86 and 2. Österreichische Artificial-Intelligence-Tagung*, volume 124 of *Informatik-Fachberichte*, pages 69–74. Springer, 1986.

[Eiter *et al.*, 2004] Thomas Eiter, Thomas Lukasiewicz, Roman Schindlauer, and Hans Tompits. Combining answer set programming with description logics for the semantic web. In *Proc. of the 9th Int. Conf. on Principles of Knowledge Representation and Reasoning (KR 2004)*, pages 141–151. Morgan Kaufmann, Los Altos, 2004.

[Ellis, 1992] Gerard Ellis. Compiled hierarchical retrieval. In T. Nagle, J. Nagle, L. Gerholz, and P. Eklund, editors, *Conceptual Structures: Current Research and Practice*, pages 285–310. Ellis Horwood, 1992.

[ElMasri and Navathe, 1994] Ramez A. ElMasri and Shamkant B. Navathe. *Fundamentals of Database Systems*. Benjamin and Cummings Publ. Co., Menlo Park, California, 2nd edition, 1994.

[Emerson, 1996] E. Allen Emerson. Automated temporal reasoning about reactive systems. In Faron Moller and Graham Birtwistle, editors, *Logics for*

Concurrency: Structure versus Automata, volume 1043 of Lecture Notes in Computer Science, pages 41–101. Springer, 1996.

[Emerson and Jutla, 1991] E. Allen Emerson and Charanjit S. Jutla. Tree automata, mu-calculus and determinacy. In *Proc. of the 32nd Annual Symp. on the Foundations of Computer Science (FOCS'91)*, pages 368–377, 1991.

[Etherington, 1987] David W. Etherington. *Reasoning with Incomplete Information*. Morgan Kaufmann, Los Altos, 1987.

[Euzenat, 2001] Jérôme Euzenat. Preserving modularity in XML encoding of Description Logics. In *Proc. of the 2001 Description Logic Workshop (DL 2001)*, pages 20–29. CEUR Electronic Workshop Proceedings, http://ceur-ws.org/Vol-49/, 2001.

[Evans, 1987] D. Evans. Final report on the MedSORT-II project: Developing and managing medical thesauri. Technical report, Carnegie Mellon University, 1987.

[Evans et al., 1994] D. A. Evans, J. Cimino, W. R. Hersh, S. M. Huff, D. S. Bell, and The CANON Group. Position statement: Towards a medical concept representation language. *J. of the American Medical Informatics Association*, 1(3):207–217, 1994.

[Fagin et al., 1995] Ronald Fagin, Joseph Y. Halpern, Yoram Moses, and Moshe Y. Vardi. *Reasoning about Knowledge*. The MIT Press, 1995.

[Falasconi et al., 1997] S. Falasconi, G. Lanzola, and M. Stefanelli. An ontology-based multi-agent architecture for distributed health-care information systems. *Methods of Information in Medicine*, 36:20–29, 1997.

[Faltings and Freuder, 1996] Boi Faltings and Eugene Freuder, editors. *Working Notes of the AAAI Fall Symposium on Configuration*, November 1996. Technical Report FS-96-03.

[Faltings and Freuder, 1998] Boi Faltings and Eugene Freuder. Configuration: Getting it right. *IEEE Intelligent Systems*, 13(4), 1998.

[Faltings et al., 1999] Boi Faltings, Eugene Freuder, Gerhard Friedrich, and Alexander Felfernig, editors. *Proc. of AAAI Worshop on Configuration*, July 1999. Technical Report WS-99-05.

[Farquhar et al., 1996] Adam Farquhar, Richard Fikes, and James Rice. The Ontolingua server: A tool for collaborative ontology construction. In *Proc. of the 10th Knowledge Acquisition for Knowledge-Based Systems Workshop*, November 1996. Also available as Stanford University Knowledge Systems Lab Tech Report: KSL-TR-96-26.

[Fattorosi-Barnaba and De Caro, 1985] M. Fattorosi-Barnaba and F. De Caro. Graded modalities I. *Studia Logica*, 44:197–221, 1985.

[Fehrer et al., 1994] D. Fehrer, U. Hustadt, M. Jaeger, A. Nonnengart, H.-J. Ohlbach, R. Schmidt, C. Weidenbach, and E. Weydert. Description logics for natural language processing. In *Proc. of the 1994 Description Logic Workshop (DL'94)*, 1994. Deutsches Forschungszentrum für Künstliche Intelligenz (DFKI) Technical Report D-94-10.

[Fensel et al., 2000] Dieter Fensel, Ian Horrocks, Frank van Harmelen, Stefan Decker, Michael Erdmann, and Michel Klein. OIL in a nutshell. In R. Dieng, editor, *Proc. of the 12th European Workshop on Knowledge Acquisition, Modeling, and Management (EKAW 2000)*, number 1937 in Lecture Notes in Artificial Intelligence, pages 1–16. Springer, 2000.

[Fensel et al., 2001] Dieter Fensel, Frank van Harmelen, Ian Horrocks, Deborah L. McGuinness, and Peter F. Patel-Schneider. OIL: An ontology infrastructure for the semantic web. *IEEE Intelligent Systems*, 16(2):38–45, 2001.

[Ferg, 1991] S. Ferg. Cardinality concepts in entity-relationship modeling. In *Proc. of the 10th Int. Conf. on the Entity–Relationship Approach (ER'91)*, pages 1–30, 1991.

[Fikes, 1982] Richard E. Fikes. Klonetalk. In Schmolze and Brachman [1982]. Published as BBN Research Report 4842, Bolt Beranek and Newman Inc., June 1982.

[Fikes and Kehler, 1985] Richard Fikes and Tom Kehler. The role of frame-based representation in reasoning. *Communications of the ACM*, 28(9):904–920, 1985.

[Fikes and McGuinness, 2001] Richard E. Fikes and Deborah L. McGuinness. An axiomatic semantics for RDF, RDF Schema, and DAML+OIL. Technical Report KSL-01-01, Stanford University KSL, 2001. Available at `http://www.ksl.stanford.edu/people/dlm/daml-semantics/abstract-axiomatic-semantics.html`.

[Fine, 1972] K. Fine. In so many possible worlds. *Notre Dame J. of Formal Logic*, 13(4):516–520, 1972.

[Finger and Gabbay, 1992] Michael Finger and Dov Gabbay. Adding a temporal dimension to a logic system. *J. of Logic, Language and Information*, 2:203–233, 1992.

[Fischer, 1992] Michael J. Fischer. The integration of temporal operators into a terminological representation system. KIT-Report 92, Fachbereich Informatik, Technische Universität Berlin, Berlin (Germany), 1992.

[Fischer and Ladner, 1979] Michael J. Fischer and Richard E. Ladner. Propositional dynamic logic of regular programs. *J. of Computer and System Sciences*, 18:194–211, 1979.

[Fitting, 1993] Melvin Fitting. Basic modal logic. In *Handbook of Logic in Artificial Intelligence and Logic Programming*, volume 1, pages 365–448. Oxford Science Publications, 1993.

[Fleischanderl et al., 1998] Gerhard Fleischanderl, Gerhard E. Friedrich, Alis Haselboeck, Herwig Schreiner, and Markus Stumptner. Configuring large systems using generative constraint satisfaction. *IEEE Intelligent Systems*, pages 59–68, 1998.

[Flex, 1999] Lpa-flex. `http://www.lpa.co.uk/`, 1999.

[Franconi, 1993] Enrico Franconi. A treatment of plurals and plural quantifications based on a theory of collections. *Minds and Machines*, 3(4):453–474, 1993.

[Franconi, 1994] Enrico Franconi. Description logics for natural language processing. In *Working Notes of the AAAI Fall Symposium on "Knowledge Representation for Natural Language Processing in Implemented Systems"*, pages 37–44, 1994.

[Franconi, 1996] Enrico Franconi. Logical form and knowledge representation: Towards a reconciliation. In *Working Notes of the AAAI Fall Symposium on "Knowledge Representation Systems based on Natural Language"*, pages 20–24, 1996.

[Franconi and Ng, 2000] Enrico Franconi and Gary Ng. The i.com tool for intelligent conceptual modeling. In *Proc. of the 7th Int. Workshop on Knowledge Representation meets Databases (KRDB 2000)*, pages 45–53. CEUR Electronic Workshop Proceedings, `http://ceur-ws.org/Vol-29/`, 2000.

[Franconi and Rabito, 1994] Enrico Franconi and Vania Rabito. A relation-based Description Logic. In *Proc. of the 1994 Description Logic Workshop (DL'94)*, pages 62–66. Deutsches Forschungszentrum für Künstliche Intelligenz (DFKI), 1994. Deutsches Forschungszentrum für Künstliche Intelligenz (DFKI) Technical Report D-94-10.

[Franconi *et al.*, 1993] Enrico Franconi, Alessandra Giorgi, and Fabio Pianesi. Tense and aspect: a mereological approach. In *Proc. of the 13th Int. Joint Conf. on Artificial Intelligence (IJCAI'93)*, pages 1222–1228, 1993.

[Franconi *et al.*, 1994] Enrico Franconi, Alessandra Giorgi, and Fabio Pianesi. A mereological characterization of temporal and aspectual phenomena. In Carlos Martin-Vide, editor, *Current Issues in Mathematical Linguistics*, North-Holland Linguistic Series, pages 269–278. Elsevier Science Publishers (North-Holland), Amsterdam, 1994.

[Frazier and Pitt, 1994] Michael Frazier and Leonard Pitt. Classic learning. In *Proc. of the 7th Annual ACM Conference on Computational Learning Theory*, pages 23–34, New Brunswick, New Jersey, 1994. ACM Press and Addison Wesley.

[Freeman, 1995] J. W. Freeman. *Improvements to Propositional Satisfiability Search Algorithms*. PhD thesis, Department of Computer and Information Science, University of Pennsylvania, 1995.

[Freeman, 1996] J. W. Freeman. Hard random 3-SAT problems and the Davis–Putnam procedure. *Artificial Intelligence*, 81:183–198, 1996.

[Freuder *et al.*, 2001] Eugene C. Freuder, Chavalit Likitvivatanavong, and Richard J. Wallace. Explanation and implication for configuration problems. In *Proc. of the 17th Int. Joint Conf. on Artificial Intelligence (IJCAI 2001) Workshop on Configuration*, 2001.

[Friedman *et al.*, 1994] C. Friedman, J. J. Cimino, and S. B. Johnson. A schema for representing medical language applied to clinical radiology. *J. of the American Medical Informatics Association*, 1(3):233–248, 1994.

[Gabbay, 1972] Dov M. Gabbay. Craig's interpolation theorem for modal logics. In *Proceedings of the Logic Conference*, volume 255 of Lecture Notes in Mathematics, pages 111–127. Springer, 1972.

[Gabbay *et al.*, 1994] Dov M. Gabbay, Ian Hodkinson, and Mark Reynolds. *Temporal Logic: Mathematical Foundations and Computational Aspects*, volume 28 of Oxford Logic Guides. Oxford University Press, 1994.

[Gabbay *et al.*, 2003] Dov Gabbay, Agnes Kurusz, Frank Wolter, and Michael Zakharyaschev. *Many-Dimensional Modal Logics: Theory and Applications*. Elsevier, 2003.

[Gangemi *et al.*, 1996] A. Gangemi, G. Steve, and F. Giacomelli. ONIONS: An ontological methodology for taxonomic integration. In *Proc. of ECAI'96 Workshop on Ontological Engineering*, 1996.

[Garey and Johnson, 1979] M. R. Garey and D. S. Johnson. *Computers and Intractability – a guide to NP-completeness*. W. H. Freeman and Company, San Francisco (CA, USA), 1979.

[Gargov and Goranko, 1993] George Gargov and Valentin Goranko. Modal logic with names. *J. of Philosophical Logic*, 22:607–636, 1993.

[Gargov and Passy, 1988] George Gargov and Solomon Passy. Determinism and looping in combinatory PDL. *Theoretical Computer Science*, 61:259–277, 1988.

[Gehrke *et al.*, 1991] Manfred Gehrke, Gerrit Burkert, Peter Forster, and Enrico Franconi. Natural language processing and Description Logics. In Christof Peltason, Kai von Luck, and Carsten Kindermann, editors, *Proc. of the*

Terminological Logic Users Workshop, pages 162–164. Department of Computer Science, Technische Universität Berlin (Germany), 1991.

[Gen, 1995] Gensym Corporation, 125 Cambridge Park Drive, Cambridge (MA), USA. *G2 Reference Manual for G2 version 4.0.*, 1995.

[Genesereth and Fikes, 1992] Michael R. Genesereth and Richard E. Fikes. Knowledge Interchange Format, version 3.0 reference manual. Technical Report Logic-92-1, Stanford University, 1992.

[Gennari *et al.*, 2003] John H. Gennari, Mark A. Musen, William E. Grosso, Monica Crubézy, Henrik Eriksson, Natalya F. Noy, and Samson W. Tu. The evolution of Protégé. *International Journal of Human Computer Studies*, 58(1):89–123, 2003.

[Gent and Walsh, 1999] I. P. Gent and T. Walsh. Beyond NP: the QSAT phase transition. In *Proc. of the 16th Nat. Conf. on Artificial Intelligence (AAAI'99)*. AAAI Press/The MIT Press, 1999.

[Gil and Melz, 1996] Yolanda Gil and Eric Melz. Explicit representations of problem-solving strategies to support knowledge acquisition. In *Proc. of the 13th Nat. Conf. on Artificial Intelligence (AAAI'96)*, pages 469–476, 1996.

[Ginsberg, 1987] Matthew L. Ginsberg, editor. *Readings in Nonmonotonic Reasoning*. Morgan Kaufmann, Los Altos, 1987.

[Ginsberg, 1993] Matthew L. Ginsberg. Dynamic backtracking. *J. of Artificial Intelligence Research*, 1:25–46, 1993.

[Giunchiglia and Sebastiani, 1996a] Fausto Giunchiglia and Roberto Sebastiani. Building decision procedures for modal logics from propositional decision procedures – the case study of modal K. In Michael A. McRobbie and John K. Slaney, editors, *Proc. of the 13th Int. Conf. on Automated Deduction (CADE'96)*, volume 1104 of Lecture Notes in Artificial Intelligence, pages 583–597. Springer, 1996.

[Giunchiglia and Sebastiani, 1996b] Fausto Giunchiglia and Roberto Sebastiani. A SAT-based decision procedure for $\mathcal{ALC}$. In *Proc. of the 5th Int. Conf. on the Principles of Knowledge Representation and Reasoning (KR'96)*, pages 304–314, 1996.

[Giunchiglia and Tacchella, 2000] Enrico Giunchiglia and Armando Tacchella. A subset-matching size-bounded cache for satisfiability in modal logics. In *Proc. of the 4th Int. Conf. on Analytic Tableaux and Related Methods (TABLEAUX 2000)*, number 1847 in Lecture Notes in Artificial Intelligence, pages 237–251. Springer, 2000.

[Giunchiglia *et al.*, 1999] Enrico Giunchiglia, Fausto Giunchiglia, and Armando Tacchella. *SAT, KSATC, DLP and TA: A comparative analysis. In *Proc. of the 1999 Description Logic Workshop (DL'99)*, pages 110–114. CEUR Electronic Workshop Proceedings, http://ceur-ws.org/Vol-22/, 1999.

[Giunchiglia *et al.*, 2001] Enrico Giunchiglia, Massimo Narizzano, and Armando Tacchella. QuBE: A system for deciding boolean formulas satisfiability. In *Proc. of the Int. Joint Conf. on Automated Reasoning (IJCAR 2001)*, number 2083 in Lecture Notes in Artificial Intelligence, pages 364–369. Springer, 2001.

[Giunchiglia *et al.*, 2002] Enrico Giunchiglia, Armando Tacchella, and Fausto Giunchiglia. SAT-based decision procedures for classical modal logics. *J. of Automated Reasoning*, 28(2):143–171, 2001.

[Goasdoue and Rousset, 2000] Francois Goasdoue and Marie-Christine Rousset. Rewriting conjunctive queries using views in Description Logics with existential restrictions. In *Proc. of the 2000 Description Logic Workshop*

(DL 2000), pages 113–122. CEUR Electronic Workshop Proceedings, `http://ceur-ws.org/Vol-33/`, 2000.

[Goasdoue *et al.*, 2000] Francois Goasdoue, Veronique Lattes, and Marie-Christine Rousset. The use of CARIN language and algorithms for information integration: The Picsel system. *Int. J. of Cooperative Information Systems*, 9(4):383–401, 2000.

[Gonçalvès and Grädel, 2000] E. Gonçalvès and E. Grädel. Decidability issues for action guarded logics. In *Proc. of the 2000 Description Logic Workshop (DL 2000)*, pages 123–132. CEUR Electronic Workshop Proceedings, `http://ceur-ws.org/Vol-33/`, 2000.

[Gräber *et al.*, 1995] A. Gräber, H. Bürckert, and A. Laux. Terminological reasoning with knowledge and belief. In A. Laux and H. Wansing, editors, *Knowledge and Belief in Philosophy and Artificial Intelligence*, pages 29–61. Akademie Verlag, 1995.

[Grädel, 1998] Erich Grädel. Guarded fragments of first-order logic: a perspective for new Description Logics? In *Proc. of the 1998 Description Logic Workshop (DL'98)*. CEUR Electronic Workshop Proceedings, `http://ceur-ws.org/Vol-11/`, 1998.

[Grädel, 1999] Erich Grädel. On the restraining power of guards. *J. of Symbolic Logic*, 64:1719–1742, 1999.

[Grädel and Walukiewicz, 1999] Erich Grädel and Igor Walukiewicz. Guarded fixed point logic. In *Proc. of the 14th IEEE Symp. on Logic in Computer Science (LICS'99)*, pages 45–54. IEEE Computer Society Press, 1999.

[Grädel *et al.*, 1997a] Erich Grädel, Phokion G. Kolaitis, and Moshe Y. Vardi. On the decision problem for two-variable first-order logic. *Bulletin of Symbolic Logic*, 3(1):53–69, 1997.

[Grädel *et al.*, 1997b] Erich Grädel, Martin Otto, and Eric Rosen. Two-variable logic with counting is decidable. In *Proc. of the 12th IEEE Symp. on Logic in Computer Science (LICS'97)*, pages 306–317. IEEE Computer Society Press, 1997.

[Grant and Minker, 1984] John Grant and Jack Minker. Numerical dependencies. In H. Gallaire, J. Minker, and J.-M. Nicolas, editors, *Advances in Database Theory II*. Plenum Publ. Co., New York, 1984.

[Grosso *et al.*, 1999] W. E. Grosso, H. Eriksson, R. W. Fergerson, J. H. Gennari, S. W. Tu, and M. A. Musen. Knowledge modelling at the millennium (The design and evolution of Protégé-2000). In *Proc. of Knowledge Acquisition Workshop (KAW'99)*, 1999.

[Guarino and Welty, 2000] Nicola Guarino and Christopher A. Welty. Ontological analysis of taxonomic relationships. In *Proc. of the 19th Int. Conf. on Conceptual Modeling (ER 2000)*, pages 210–224, 2000.

[Günsel and Wittmann, 2001] Christian Günsel and Marco Wittmann. Towards an implementation of the temporal Description Logic $\mathcal{TL_{ALC}}$. In *Proc. of the 2001 Description Logic Workshop (DL 2001)*, pages 162–169. CEUR Electronic Workshop Proceedings, `http://ceur-ws.org/Vol-49/`, 2001.

[Haarslev and Möller, 1999] Volker Haarslev and Ralf Möller. RACE system description. In *Proc. of the 1999 Description Logic Workshop (DL'99)*, pages 130–132. CEUR Electronic Workshop Proceedings, `http://ceur-ws.org/Vol-22/`, 1999.

[Haarslev and Möller, 2000] Volker Haarslev and Ralf Möller. Expressive ABox reasoning with number restrictions, role hierarchies, and transitively closed roles. In *Proc. of the 7th Int. Conf. on Principles of Knowledge Representation and Reasoning (KR 2000)*, pages 273–284, 2000.

[Haarslev and Möller, 2001a] Volker Haarslev and Ralf Möller. Combining tableaux and algebraic methods for reasoning with qualified number restrictions. In *Proc. of the 2001 Description Logic Workshop (DL 2001)*, pages 152–161. CEUR Electronic Workshop Proceedings, http://ceur-ws.org/Vol-49/, 2001.

[Haarslev and Möller, 2001b] Volker Haarslev and Ralf Möller. Description of the RACER system and its applications. In *Proc. of the 2001 Description Logic Workshop (DL 2001)*, pages 132–141. CEUR Electronic Workshop Proceedings, http://ceur-ws.org/Vol-49/, 2001.

[Haarslev and Möller, 2001c] Volker Haarslev and Ralf Möller. High performance reasoning with very large knowledge bases: A practical case study. In *Proc. of the 17th Int. Joint Conf. on Artificial Intelligence (IJCAI 2001)*, pages 161–168, 2001.

[Haarslev and Möller, 2001d] Volker Haarslev and Ralf Möller. Optimizing reasoning in Description Logics with qualified number restrictions. In *Proc. of the 2001 Description Logic Workshop (DL 2001)*, pages 142–151. CEUR Electronic Workshop Proceedings, http://ceur-ws.org/Vol-49/, 2001.

[Haarslev and Möller, 2001e] Volker Haarslev and Ralf Möller. RACER system description. In *Proc. of the Int. Joint Conf. on Automated Reasoning (IJCAR 2001)*, volume 2083 of Lecture Notes in Artificial Intelligence, pages 701–705. Springer, 2001.

[Haarslev et al., 1998] Volker Haarslev, Carsten Lutz, and Ralf Möller. Foundations of spatioterminological reasoning with Description Logics. In *Proc. of the 6th Int. Conf. on Principles of Knowledge Representation and Reasoning (KR'98)*, pages 112–123, 1998.

[Haarslev et al., 1999] Volker Haarslev, Carsten Lutz, and Ralf Möller. A Description Logic with concrete domains and role-forming predicates. *J. of Logic and Computation*, 9(3):351–384, 1999.

[Haarslev et al., 2001] Volker Haarslev, Ralf Möller, and Michael Wessel. The Description Logic $\mathcal{ALCNH}_{R+}$ extended with concrete domains: A practically motivated approach. In *Proc. of the Int. Joint Conf. on Automated Reasoning (IJCAR 2001)*, pages 29–44, 2001.

[Hagen et al., 1999] Paul Hagen, David Weisman, Harley Manning, and Randy Souza. Guided search for eCommerce. In *The Forrester Report*. Cambridge, MA, January 1999.

[Hahn et al., 1999a] U. Hahn, M. Romacker, and S. Schulz. How knowledge drives understanding – matching medical ontologies with the needs of medical language processing. *AI Magazine*, 15(1):25–52, 1999.

[Hahn et al., 1999b] Udo Hahn, Stefan Schulz, and Martin Romacker. Part-whole reasoning: a case study in medical ontology engineering. *IEEE Intelligent Systems*, 14(5):59–67, 1999.

[Hahn et al., 1999c] Udo Hahn, Stefan Schulz, and Martin Romacker. Partonomic reasoning as taxonomic reasoning in medicine. In *Proc. of the 16th Nat. Conf. on Artificial Intelligence (AAAI'99)*, pages 271–276, 1999.

[Halpern and Moses, 1992] Joseph Y. Halpern and Yoram Moses. A guide to completeness and complexity for modal logics of knowledge and belief. *Artificial Intelligence*, 54:319–379, 1992.

[Halpern and Shoham, 1991] Joseph Y. Halpern and Yoav Shoham. A propositional modal logic of time intervals. *J. of the ACM*, 38:935–962, 1991.

[Hammer and McLeod, 1981] Michael Hammer and Dennis McLeod. Database description with SDM: A semantic database model. *ACM Trans. on Database Systems*, 6(3):351–386, 1981.

[Hanschke, 1992] Philipp Hanschke. Specifying role interaction in concept languages. In *Proc. of the 3rd Int. Conf. on the Principles of Knowledge Representation and Reasoning (KR'92)*, pages 318–329. Morgan Kaufmann, Los Altos, 1992.

[Harel, 1984] David Harel. Dynamic logic. In D. M. Gabbay and F. Guenthner, editors, *Handbook of Philosophical Logic*, volume II, pages 497–604. D. Reidel Publishing Company, 1984.

[Harel, 1985] David Harel. Recurring dominoes: Making the highly undecidable highly understandable. *Ann. of Discrete Mathematics*, 24:51–72, 1985.

[Harel, 1986] David Harel. Effective transformations of infinite trees, with applications to high undecidability, dominoes, and fairness. *J. of the ACM*, 33(1):224–248, 1986.

[Harel *et al.*, 2000] David Harel, Dexter Kozen, and Jerzy Tiuryn. *Dynamic Logic*. The MIT Press, 2000.

[Hayes, 1977] Patrick J. Hayes. In defense of logic. In *Proc. of the 5th Int. Joint Conf. on Artificial Intelligence (IJCAI'77)*, pages 559–565, 1977. A longer version appeared in *The Psychology of Computer Vision* (1975). Republished in [Brachman and Levesque, 1985].

[Hayes, 1979] Patrick J. Hayes. The logic of frames. In D. Metzing, editor, *Frame Conceptions and Text Understanding*, pages 46–61. Walter de Gruyter and Co., 1979. Republished in [Brachman and Levesque, 1985].

[Hayes, 2004] Patrick Hayes. RDF semantics. W3C Recommendation, February 2004. Available at http://www.w3.org/TR/rdf-mt/.

[Heflin and Hendler, 2001] Jeff Heflin and James Hendler. A portrait of the semantic web in action. *IEEE Intelligent Systems*, 16(2):54–59, 2001.

[Heflin *et al.*, 2003] Jeff Heflin, James Hendler, and Sean Luke. SHOE: A blueprint for the Semantic Web. In D. Fensel, J. Hendler, H. Lieberman, and W. Wahlster, editors, *Spinning the Semantic Web*. MIT Press, Cambridge, MA, 2003.

[Heinsohn, 1994] Jochen Heinsohn. Probabilistic Description Logics. In Ramon Lopez de Mantaras and David Poole, editors, *Proc. of the 10th Conf. on Uncertainty in Artificial Intelligence*, pages 311–318, Seattle, Washington, 1994. Morgan Kaufmann, Los Altos.

[Heinsohn *et al.*, 1992] Jochen Heinsohn, Daniel Kudenko, Bernhard Nebel, and Hans-Jürgen Profitlich. An empirical analysis of terminological representation systems. In *Proc. of the 10th Nat. Conf. on Artificial Intelligence (AAAI'92)*, pages 767–773. AAAI Press/The MIT Press, 1992.

[Heinsohn *et al.*, 1994] Jochen Heinsohn, Daniel Kudenko, Bernhard Nebel, and Hans-Jürgen Profitlich. An empirical analysis of terminological representation systems. *Artificial Intelligence*, 68:367–397, 1994.

[Hemaspaandra, 1999] Edith Hemaspaandra. The complexity of poor man's logic. In J. Gerbrandy, M. Marx, M. de Rijke, and Y. Venema, editors, *Essays Dedicated to Johan van Benthem on the Occasion of His 50th Birthday*. Amsterdam University Press, 1999.

[Hendler and McGuinness, 2000] James Hendler and Deborah L. McGuinness. The DARPA agent markup language. *IEEE Intelligent Systems*, 15(6):67–73, 2000.

[Herzog and Rollinger, 1991] O. Herzog and C. R. Rollinger, editors. *Text Understanding in LILOG.* Springer, 1991.

[Heuerding and Schwendimann, 1996] A. Heuerding and S. Schwendimann. A benchmark method for the propositional modal logics K, KT, and S4. Technical report IAM-96-015, University of Bern, Switzerland, 1996.

[Hobbs *et al.*, 1993] J. R. Hobbs, M. Stickel, D. Appelt, and P. Martin. Interpretation as abduction. *Artificial Intelligence*, 63:69–142, 1993.

[Hoffmann and Koehler, 1999] Jörg Hoffmann and Jana Koehler. A new method to index and query sets. In *Proc. of the 16th Int. Joint Conf. on Artificial Intelligence (IJCAI'99)*, pages 462–467, 1999.

[Hollunder, 1990] Bernhard Hollunder. Hybrid inferences in KL-ONE-based knowledge representation systems. In *Proc. of the German. Workshop on Artificial Intelligence*, pages 38–47. Springer, 1990.

[Hollunder, 1994a] Bernhard Hollunder. *Algorithmic Foundations of Terminological Knowledge Representation Systems.* PhD thesis, University of Saarbrücken, Department of Computer Science, 1994.

[Hollunder, 1994b] Bernhard Hollunder. An alternative proof method for possibilistic logic and its application to terminological logics. In Ramon Lopez de Mantaras and David Poole, editors, *Proc. of the 10th Conf. on Uncertainty in Artificial Intelligence*, pages 327–335, Seattle, Washington, 1994. Morgan Kaufmann, Los Altos.

[Hollunder, 1996] Bernhard Hollunder. Consistency checking reduced to satisfiability of concepts in terminological systems. *Ann. of Mathematics and Artificial Intelligence*, 18(2–4):133–157, 1996.

[Hollunder and Baader, 1991a] Bernhard Hollunder and Franz Baader. Qualifying number restrictions in concept languages. Technical Report RR-91-03, Deutsches Forschungszentrum für Künstliche Intelligenz (DFKI), Kaiserslautern (Germany), 1991. An abridged version appeared in *Proc. of the 2nd Int. Conf. on the Principles of Knowledge Representation and Reasoning (KR'91).*

[Hollunder and Baader, 1991b] Bernhard Hollunder and Franz Baader. Qualifying number restrictions in concept languages. In *Proc. of the 2nd Int. Conf. on the Principles of Knowledge Representation and Reasoning (KR'91)*, pages 335–346, 1991.

[Hollunder and Nutt, 1990] Bernhard Hollunder and Werner Nutt. Subsumption algorithms for concept languages. Technical Report RR-90-04, Deutsches Forschungszentrum für Künstliche Intelligenz (DFKI), Kaiserslautern (Germany), 1990.

[Hollunder *et al.*, 1990] Bernhard Hollunder, Werner Nutt, and Manfred Schmidt-Schauß. Subsumption algorithms for concept description languages. In *Proc. of the 9th Eur. Conf. on Artificial Intelligence (ECAI'90)*, pages 348–353, London (United Kingdom), 1990. Pitman.

[Hollunder *et al.*, 1991] Berhnard Hollunder, Armin Laux, Hans-Jürgen Profitlich, and T. Trenz. $\mathcal{KRIS}$-manual. Technical report, Deutsches Forschungszentrum für Künstliche Intelligenz (DFKI), 1991.

[Hoppe *et al.*, 1993] Thomas Hoppe, Carsten Kindermann, Joachim Quantz, Albrecht Schmiedel, and Martin Fischer. BACK V5: tutorial and manual.

KIT-Report 100, Fachbereich Informatik, Technische Universität Berlin, Berlin (Germany), 1993.

[Horrocks, 1997a] Ian Horrocks. Optimisation techniques for expressive Description Logics. Technical Report UMCS-97-2-1, University of Manchester, Department of Computer Science, 1997.

[Horrocks, 1997b] Ian Horrocks. *Optimising Tableaux Decision Procedures for Description Logics.* PhD thesis, University of Manchester, 1997.

[Horrocks, 1998a] Ian Horrocks. The FaCT system. In Harrie de Swart, editor, *Proc. of the 2nd Int. Conf. on Analytic Tableaux and Related Methods (TABLEAUX'98)*, volume 1397 of Lecture Notes in Artificial Intelligence, pages 307–312. Springer, 1998.

[Horrocks, 1998b] Ian Horrocks. Using an expressive Description Logic: FaCT or fiction? In *Proc. of the 6th Int. Conf. on Principles of Knowledge Representation and Reasoning (KR'98)*, pages 636–647, 1998.

[Horrocks, 1999] Ian Horrocks. FaCT and iFaCT. In *Proc. of the 1999 Description Logic Workshop (DL'99)*, pages 133–135. CEUR Electronic Workshop Proceedings, http://ceur-ws.org/Vol-22/, 1999.

[Horrocks and Patel-Schneider, 1998a] Ian Horrocks and Peter F. Patel-Schneider. Comparing subsumption optimizations. In *Proc. of the 1998 Description Logic Workshop (DL'98)*, pages 90–94. CEUR Electronic Workshop Proceedings, http://ceur-ws.org/Vol-11/, 1998.

[Horrocks and Patel-Schneider, 1998b] Ian Horrocks and Peter F. Patel-Schneider. DL systems comparison. In *Proc. of the 1998 Description Logic Workshop (DL'98)*, pages 55–57. CEUR Electronic Workshop Proceedings, http://ceur-ws.org/Vol-11/, 1998.

[Horrocks and Patel-Schneider, 1998c] Ian Horrocks and Peter F. Patel-Schneider. FaCT and DLP: Automated reasoning with analytic tableaux and related methods. In *Proc. of the 2nd Int. Conf. on Analytic Tableaux and Related Methods (TABLEAUX'98)*, pages 27–30, 1998.

[Horrocks and Patel-Schneider, 1998d] Ian Horrocks and Peter F. Patel-Schneider. Optimising propositional modal satisfiability for Description Logic subsumption. In *Proc. of the 4th Int. Conf. on Artificial Intelligence and Symbolic Computation (AISC'98)*, 1998.

[Horrocks and Patel-Schneider, 1999] Ian Horrocks and Peter F. Patel-Schneider. Optimizing Description Logic subsumption. *J. of Logic and Computation*, 9(3):267–293, 1999.

[Horrocks and Patel-Schneider, 2001] Ian Horrocks and Peter F. Patel-Schneider. The generation of DAML+OIL. In *Proc. of the 2001 Description Logic Workshop (DL 2001)*, pages 30–35. CEUR Electronic Workshop Proceedings, http://ceur-ws.org/Vol-49/, 2001.

[Horrocks and Patel-Schneider, 2003] Ian Horrocks and Peter F. Patel-Schneider. Reducing OWL entailment to description logic satisfiability. In *Proc. of the 2003 International Semantic Web Conference (ISWC 2003)*, volume 2870 of *Lecture Notes in Computer Science*, pages 17–29. Springer, 2003.

[Horrocks and Rector, 1996] Ian Horrocks and Alan Rector. Using a Description Logic with concept inclusions. In *Proc. of the 1996 Description Logic Workshop (DL'96)*, number WS-96-05 in AAAI Technical Report, pages 132–135. AAAI Press/The MIT Press, 1996.

[Horrocks and Sattler, 1999] Ian Horrocks and Ulrike Sattler. A Description Logic with transitive and inverse roles and role hierarchies. *J. of Logic and*

Computation, 9(3):385–410, 1999.

[Horrocks and Sattler, 2001] Ian Horrocks and Ulrike Sattler. Ontology reasoning in the $\mathcal{SHOQ}$(D) Description Logic. In *Proc. of the 17th Int. Joint Conf. on Artificial Intelligence (IJCAI 2001)*, pages 199–204, 2001.

[Horrocks and Sattler, 2005] Ian Horrocks and Ulrike Sattler. A tableaux decision procedure for $\mathcal{SHOIQ}$. In *Proc. of the 19th Int. Joint Conf. on Artificial Intelligence (IJCAI 2005)*, pages 448–453, 2005.

[Horrocks and Tessaris, 2000] Ian Horrocks and Sergio Tessaris. A conjunctive query language for Description Logic ABoxes. In *Proc. of the 17th Nat. Conf. on Artificial Intelligence (AAAI 2000)*, pages 399–404, 2000.

[Horrocks and Tobies, 2000] Ian Horrocks and Stephan Tobies. Reasoning with axioms: Theory and practice. In *Proc. of the 7th Int. Conf. on Principles of Knowledge Representation and Reasoning (KR 2000)*, pages 285–296, 2000.

[Horrocks et al., 1996] Ian Horrocks, Alan Rector, and Carole Goble. A description logic based schema for the classification of medical data. In *Proc. of the 3rd Int. Workshop on Knowledge Representation meets Databases (KRDB'96)*, pages 24–28. CEUR Electronic Workshop Proceedings, http://ceur-ws.org/Vol-4/, 1996.

[Horrocks et al., 1999] Ian Horrocks, Ulrike Sattler, and Stephan Tobies. Practical reasoning for expressive Description Logics. In Harald Ganzinger, David McAllester, and Andrei Voronkov, editors, *Proc. of the 6th Int. Conf. on Logic for Programming and Automated Reasoning (LPAR'99)*, number 1705 in Lecture Notes in Artificial Intelligence, pages 161–180. Springer, 1999.

[Horrocks et al., 2000a] I. Horrocks, D. Fensel, J. Broekstra, S. Decker, M. Erdmann, C. Goble, F. van Harmelen, M. Klein, S. Staab, R. Studer, and E. Motta. OIL: The Ontology Inference Layer. Technical Report IR-479, Vrije Universiteit Amsterdam, Faculty of Sciences, September 2000.

[Horrocks et al., 2000b] Ian Horrocks, Ulrike Sattler, and Stephan Tobies. Practical reasoning for very expressive Description Logics. *J. of the Interest Group in Pure and Applied Logic*, 8(3):239–264, 2000.

[Horrocks et al., 2000c] Ian Horrocks, Ulrike Sattler, and Stephan Tobies. Reasoning with individuals for the Description Logic $\mathcal{SHIQ}$. In David McAllester, editor, *Proc. of the 17th Int. Conf. on Automated Deduction (CADE 2000)*, volume 1831 of Lecture Notes in Computer Science, pages 482–496. Springer, 2000.

[Horrocks et al., 2003] Ian Horrocks, Peter F. Patel-Schneider, and Frank van Harmelen. From $\mathcal{SHIQ}$ and RDF to OWL: The making of a web ontology language. *J. of Web Semantics*, 1(1):7–26, 2003.

[Horrocks et al., 2005] Ian Horrocks, Peter F. Patel-Schneider, Sean Bechhofer, and Dmitry Tsarkov. OWL Rules: A proposal and prototype implementation. *J. of Web Semantics*, 3(1):23–40, 2005.

[Horty et al., 1987] J. F. Horty, R. H. Thomason, and D. S. Touretzky. A skeptical theory of inheritance in nonmonotonic semantic networks. In *Proc. of the 6th Nat. Conf. on Artificial Intelligence (AAAI'87)*, pages 358–363, 1987.

[Hovy and Knight, 1993] E. H. Hovy and K. Knight. Motivation for shared ontologies: An example from the Pangloss collaboration. In *Proc. of the IJCAI'93 Workshop on Knowledge Sharing and Information Interchange*, 1993.

[Huitt and Wilde, 1992] R. Huitt and N. Wilde. Maintenance support for object-oriented programs. *IEEE Trans. on Software Engineering*, 18(12), 1992.

[Hull, 1988] Richard Hull. A survey of theoretical research on typed complex
    database objects. In J. Paredaens, editor, *Databases*, pages 193–256.
    Academic Press, 1988.
[Hull and King, 1987] R. B. Hull and R. King. Semantic database modelling:
    Survey, applications and research issues. *ACM Computing Surveys*,
    19(3):201–260, September 1987.
[Hustadt and Schmidt, 1997] Ulrich Hustadt and Renate A. Schmidt. On
    evaluating decision procedures for modal logic. In *Proc. of the 15th Int. Joint
    Conf. on Artificial Intelligence (IJCAI'97)*, pages 202–207, 1997.
[Hustadt and Schmidt, 2000] Ulrich Hustadt and Renate A. Schmidt. Issues of
    decidability for Description Logics in the framework of resolution. In
    R. Caferra and G. Salzer, editors, *Automated Deduction in Classical and
    Non-Classical Logics*, volume 1761 of Lecture Notes in Artificial Intelligence,
    pages 191–205. Springer, 2000.
[Hustadt et al., 2004] Ullrich Hustadt, Boris Motik, and Ulrike Sattler. Reducing
    $\mathcal{SHIQ}$-description logic to disjunctive datalog programs. In *Proc. of the 9th
    Int. Conf. on Principles of Knowledge Representation and Reasoning
    (KR 2004)*, pages 152–162, 2004.
[Israel and Brachman, 1984] David J. Israel and Ronald J. Brachman. Some
    remarks on the semantics of representation languages. In M. L. Brodie,
    J. Mylopoulos, and J. W. Schmidt, editors, *On Conceptual Modeling:
    Perspectives from Artificial Intelligence Databases and Programming
    Languages*. Springer, 1984.
[Jackendoff, 1990] Ray Jackendoff. *Semantic Structures*. Current Studies in
    Linguistics Series. The MIT Press, 1990.
[Jacobs, 1991] Paul S. Jacobs. Integrating language and meaning in structured
    inheritance networks. In [Sowa, 1991], pages 527–542.
[Jacobson et al., 1998] Ivar Jacobson, Grady Booch, and James Rumbaugh. *The
    Unified Modeling Language User Guide*. Addison Wesley Publ. Co., Reading,
    Massachussetts, 1998.
[Jaeger, 1994] Manfred Jaeger. Probabilistic reasoning in terminological logics. In
    Pietro Torasso, Jon Doyle, and Erik Sandewall, editors, *Proc. of the 4th Int.
    Conf. on the Principles of Knowledge Representation and Reasoning
    (KR'94)*, pages 305–316, 1994.
[Jang and Patil, 1989] Y. Jang and R. Patil. KOLA: a knowledge organisation
    language. In *Proc. of the 13th Annual Symposium on Computer Applications
    in Medical Care (SCAMC'89)*, pages 71–75, 1989.
[Jeroslow and Wang, 1990] R. Jeroslow and J. Wang. Solving propositional
    satisfiability problems. *Ann. of Mathematics and Artificial Intelligence*,
    1:167–187, 1990.
[Johnson, 1990] D. S. Johnson. A catalog of complexity classes. In *Handbook of
    Theoretical Computer Science*, volume A, chapter 2. Elsevier Science
    Publishers (North-Holland), Amsterdam, 1990.
[Johnson et al., 2000] P. D. Johnson, S. Tu, N. Booth, B. Sugden, and I. Purves.
    Using scenarios in chronic disease management guidelines for primary care. In
    Proc. of the American Medical Informatics Society Annual Fall Symposium,
    pages 389–393, 2000.
[Joshi, 1994] Aravind K. Joshi. Introduction to special issue on tree-adjoining
    grammars. *Computational Intelligence*, 10(4):vii–xv, 1994.
[Juengst and Heinrich, 1998] Werner E. Juengst and Michael Heinrich. Using
    resource balancing to configure modular systems. *IEEE Intelligent Systems*,

pages 50–58, 1998.

[Kaczmarek *et al.*, 1986] Thomas S. Kaczmarek, Raymond Bates, and Gabriel Robins. Recent developments in NIKL. In *Proc. of the 5th Nat. Conf. on Artificial Intelligence (AAAI'86)*, pages 978–985, 1986.

[Kalmes, 1988] J. Kalmes. SB-Graph user manual. Technical Report SFB 314, Memo Nr. 30, Universität des Saarlandes, Fachbereich Informatik, Saarbrücken (Germany), 1988.

[Kalmes, 1990] J. Kalmes. SB-Graph. Technical Report SFB 314, Memo Nr. 44, Universität des Saarlandes, Fachbereich Informatik, Saarbrücken (Germany), 1990. In German.

[Kalyanpur *et al.*, 2005a] Aditya Kalyanpur, Bijan Parsia, and James Hendler. A tool for working with web ontologies. *Int. J. on Semantic Web and Information Systems*, 1(1):36–49, 2005.

[Kalyanpur *et al.*, 2005b] Aditya Kalyanpur, Bijan Parsia, Evren Sirin, and James Hendler. Debugging unsatisfiable classes in OWL ontologies. *J. of Web Semantics – Special Issue on the Semantic Web Track of WWW 2005*, 3(4), 2005.

[Karp, 1992] Peter D. Karp. The design space of knowledge representation systems. Technical Report SRI AI Technical Note 520, SRI International, Menlo Park (CA, USA), 1992.

[Karp *et al.*, 1999] P. D. Karp, V. K. Chaudhri, and J. Thomere. XOL: An XML-based ontology exchange language.

[Kent, 1979] William Kent. Limitations of record-base information models. *ACM Trans. on Database Systems*, 4(1):107–131, 1979.

[Kerdiles and Salvat, 1997] Gwen Kerdiles and Eric Salvat. A sound and complete CG proof procedure combining projections with analytic tableaux. In D. Lukose, H. Delugach, M. Keeler, L. Searle, and J. Sowa, editors, *Proc. of the 5th Int. Conf. on Conceptual Structures (ICCS'97)*, volume 1257 of Lecture Notes in Computer Science, pages 371–385. Springer, 1997.

[Kessel *et al.*, 1995] T. Kessel, F. Rousselot, M. Schlick, and O. Stern. Use of DL within the framework of DBMS. In *Proc. of the 2nd Int. Workshop on Knowledge Representation meets Databases (KRDB'95)*. CEUR Electronic Workshop Proceedings, http://ceur-ws.org/Vol-2/, 1995.

[Khizder *et al.*, 2001] Vitaliy L. Khizder, David Toman, and Grant E. Weddell. On decidability and complexity of description logics with uniqueness constraints. In *Proc. of the 8th Int. Conf. on Database Theory (ICDT 2001)*, 2001.

[Kim, 1990] Won Kim. *Introduction to Object-Oriented Databases*. The MIT Press, 1990.

[Kim and Lochovsky, 1989] Won Kim and Frederick H. Lochovsky, editors. *Object-Oriented Concepts, Databases, and Applications*. ACM Press and Addison Wesley, New York (USA), 1989.

[Kindermann, 1992] Carsten Kindermann. Retraction of object descriptions in BACK. KIT-Report 105, Fachbereich Informatik, Technische Universität Berlin, Berlin (Germany), 1992.

[Kindermann and Randi, 1990] C. Kindermann and P. Randi. Object recognition and retrieval in the BACK system. KIT-Report 86, Fachbereich Informatik, Technische Universität Berlin, Berlin (Germany), 1990.

[Kirk *et al.*, 1995] Thomas Kirk, Alon Y. Levy, Yehoshua Sagiv, and Divesh Srivastava. The Information Manifold. In *Proceedings of the AAAI 1995 Spring Symp. on Information Gathering from Heterogeneous, Distributed*

Enviroments, pages 85–91, 1995.

[Knight and Luk, 1994] K. Knight and S. Luk. Building a large knowledge base for machine translation. In *Proc. of the 12th Nat. Conf. on Artificial Intelligence (AAAI'94)*, 1994.

[Knight *et al.*, 1995] K. Knight, I. Chander, M. Haines, V. Hatzivassiloglou, E. Hovy, M. Iida, S. K. Luk, R. Whitney, and K. Yamada. Filling knowledge gaps in a broad-coverage machine translation system. In *Proc. of the 14th Int. Joint Conf. on Artificial Intelligence (IJCAI'95)*, pages 1390–1396, 1995.

[Kobsa, 1991a] Alfred Kobsa. First experiences with the SB-ONE knowledge representation workbench in natural-language applications. *SIGART Bull.*, 2(3):70–76, 1991.

[Kobsa, 1991b] Alfred Kobsa. Utilizing knowledge: The components of the SB-ONE knowledge representation workbench. In [Sowa, 1991], pages 457–486.

[Koetzle *et al.*, 2001] Laura Koetzle, Paul Hagen, Hillary Drohan, and Moira Dorsey. Smarter sales of complex goods. In *The Forrester Report*. Cambridge, MA, September 2001.

[Kohn *et al.*, 2000] L. T. Kohn, J. M. Corrigan, and M. S. Donaldson, editors. *To Err is Human: Building a Safer Health System*. National Academy Press, 2000.

[Koller *et al.*, 1997] Daphne Koller, Alon Levy, and Avi Pfeffer. P-CLASSIC: A tractable probabilistic Description Logic. In *Proc. of the 14th Nat. Conf. on Artificial Intelligence (AAAI'97)*, pages 390–397. AAAI Press/The MIT Press, 1997.

[Kozen, 1983] Dexter Kozen. Results on the propositional μ-calculus. *Theoretical Computer Science*, 27:333–354, 1983.

[Kozen and Tiuryn, 1990] Dexter Kozen and Jerzy Tiuryn. Logics of programs. In Jan van Leeuwen, editor, *Handbook of Theoretical Computer Science – Formal Models and Semantics*, pages 789–840. Elsevier Science Publishers (North-Holland), Amsterdam, 1990.

[Kripke, 1980] S. Kripke. *Naming and Necessity*. Harvard University Press, 1980.

[Kuper and Vardi, 1993] Gabriel M. Kuper and Moshe Y. Vardi. On the complexity of queries in the logical data model. *Theoretical Computer Science*, 116:33–58, 1993.

[Kurtonina and de Rijke, 1997] Natasha Kurtonina and Maarten de Rijke. Classifying Description Logics. In *Proc. of the 1997 Description Logic Workshop (DL'97)*, pages 49–53, 1997.

[Küsters, 1998] Ralf Küsters. Characterizing the semantics of terminological cycles in $\mathcal{ALN}$ using finite automata. In *Proc. of the 6th Int. Conf. on Principles of Knowledge Representation and Reasoning (KR'98)*, pages 499–510, 1998.

[Küsters, 2001] Ralf Küsters. *Non-standard Inferences in Description Logics*, volume 2100 of Lecture Notes in Artificial Intelligence. Springer, 2001.

[Küsters and Borgida, 2001] Ralf Küsters and Alexander Borgida. What's in an attribute? Consequences for the least common subsumer. *J. of Artificial Intelligence Research*, 14:167–203, 2001.

[Küsters and Molitor, 2001a] Ralf Küsters and Ralf Molitor. Approximating most specific concepts in Description Logics with existential restrictions. In Franz Baader, Gerd Brewka, and Thomas Eiter, editors, *Proc. of the Joint German/Austrian Conf. on Artificial Intelligence (KI 2001)*, volume 2174 of Lecture Notes in Artificial Intelligence, pages 33–47. Springer, 2001.

[Küsters and Molitor, 2001b] Ralf Küsters and Ralf Molitor. Computing least common subsumers in $\mathcal{ALEN}$. In *Proc. of the 17th Int. Joint Conf. on Artificial Intelligence (IJCAI 2001)*, pages 219–224, 2001.

[Ladner, 1977] Richard E. Ladner. The computational complexity of provability in systems of modal propositional logic. *SIAM J. on Computing*, 6(3):467–480, 1977.

[Lambrix *et al.*, 1998] P. Lambrix, N. Shahmehri, and N. Wahlöf. A default extension to Description Logics for use in an intelligent search engine. In *Proc. of the 31st Hawaii Int. Conf. on System Sciences, Volume V – Modeling Technologies and Intelligent Systems Track*, pages 28–35, 1998.

[Lang, 1991] Ewald Lang. The LILOG ontology from a linguistic point of view. In [Herzog and Rollinger 1991], pages 464–481.

[Laux, 1994] Armin Laux. Beliefs in multi-agent worlds: A terminological approach. In *Proc. of the 11th Eur. Conf. on Artificial Intelligence (ECAI'94)*, pages 299–303, Amsterdam, The Netherlands, 1994.

[Lavelli *et al.*, 1992] Alberto Lavelli, Bernardo Magnini, and Carlo Strapparava. An approach to multilevel semantics for applied systems. In *Proc. of the 3rd ACL Conference on Applied Natural Language Processing (ANLP'92)*, pages 17–24, 1992.

[Lecluse and Richard, 1989] Christophe Lecluse and Philippe Richard. Modeling complex structures in object-oriented databases. In *Proc. of the 8th ACM SIGACT SIGMOD SIGART Symp. on Principles of Database Systems (PODS'89)*, pages 362–369, 1989.

[Lehmann, 1992] Fritz Lehmann, editor. *Semantic Networks in Artificial Intelligence*. Pergamon Press, Oxford (United Kingdom), 1992.

[Lenzerini and Nobili, 1990] Maurizio Lenzerini and Paolo Nobili. On the satisfiability of dependency constraints in entity-relationship schemata. *Information Systems*, 15(4):453–461, 1990.

[Lenzerini and Schaerf, 1991] Maurizio Lenzerini and Andrea Schaerf. Concept languages as query languages. In *Proc. of the 9th Nat. Conf. on Artificial Intelligence (AAAI'91)*, pages 471–476, 1991.

[Lenzerini *et al.*, 1991] Maurizio Lenzerini, Daniele Nardi, and Maria Simi, editors. *Inheritance Hierarchies in Knowledge Representation and Programming Languages*. John Wiley & Sons, 1991.

[Levesque, 1984] Hector J. Levesque. Foundations of a functional approach to knowledge representation. *Artificial Intelligence*, 23:155–212, 1984.

[Levesque and Brachman, 1987] Hector J. Levesque and Ron J. Brachman. Expressiveness and tractability in knowledge representation and reasoning. *Computational Intelligence*, 3:78–93, 1987.

[Levy, 2000] Alon Y. Levy. Logic-based techniques in data integration. In Jack Minker, editor, *Logic Based Artificial Intelligence*. Kluwer Academic Publishers, 2000.

[Levy and Rousset, 1996] Alon Y. Levy and Marie-Christine Rousset. CARIN: a representation language combining Horn rules and Description Logics. In *Proc. of the 12th Eur. Conf. on Artificial Intelligence (ECAI'96)*, pages 323–327, 1996.

[Levy and Rousset, 1997] Alon Y. Levy and Marie-Christine Rousset. CARIN: a representation language combining Horn rules and Description Logics. Technical report, AT&T, 1997.

[Levy and Rousset, 1998] Alon Y. Levy and Marie-Christine Rousset. Combining

Horn rules and Description Logics in CARIN. *Artificial Intelligence*, 104(1–2):165–209, 1998.

[Levy et al., 1995] Alon Y. Levy, Divesh Srivastava, and Thomas Kirk. Data model and query evaluation in global information systems. *J. of Intelligent Information Systems*, 5:121–143, 1995.

[Levy et al., 1996] Alon Y. Levy, Anand Rajaraman, and Joann J. Ordille. Query answering algorithms for information agents. In *Proc. of the 13th Nat. Conf. on Artificial Intelligence (AAAI'96)*, pages 40–47, 1996.

[Libkin, 2000] Leonid Libkin. Logics with counting and local properties. *ACM Trans. on Computational Logic*, 1(1), 2000.

[Lifschitz, 1991] Vladimir Lifschitz. Nonmonotonic databases and epistemic queries. In *Proc. of the 12th Int. Joint Conf. on Artificial Intelligence (IJCAI'91)*, pages 381–386, 1991.

[Lifschitz, 1994] Vladimir Lifschitz. Minimal belief and negation as failure. *Artificial Intelligence*, 70:53–72, 1994.

[Lindberg et al., 1993] D. Lindberg, B. Humphreys, and A. McCray. The unified medical language system. In J. van Bemmel, editor, *Yearbook of Medical Informatics*, pages 41–53. International Medical Informatics Association, 1993.

[Lipkis, 1982] Thomas A. Lipkis. A KL-ONE classifier. In [Schmolze and Brachman 1982], pages 128–145. Published as BBN Research Report 4842, Bolt Beranek and Newman Inc., June 1982.

[Ludwig et al., 2000] Bernd Ludwig, Günther Görz, and Heinrich Niemann. Combining expression and content in domains for dialog managers. *J. of Logic and Computation*, 1(2):241–258, 2000.

[Lussier et al., 1992] Y. A. Lussier, M. Maksud, B. Desruisseaux, P.-P. Yale, and R. St-Arneault. PureMD: a computerized patient record software for direct data entry by physicians using keyboard-free pen-based portable computer. In *Proc. of the 16th Annual Symposium on Computer Applications in Medical Care (SCAMC'92)*, pages 261–263, 1992.

[Lutz, 1999a] Carsten Lutz. Complexity of terminological reasoning revisited. In *Proc. of the 6th Int. Conf. on Logic for Programming and Automated Reasoning (LPAR'99)*, volume 1705 of Lecture Notes in Artificial Intelligence, pages 181–200. Springer, 1999.

[Lutz, 1999b] Carsten Lutz. Reasoning with concrete domains. In Thomas Dean, editor, *Proc. of the 16th Int. Joint Conf. on Artificial Intelligence (IJCAI'99)*, pages 90–95, Stockholm, Sweden, 1999. Morgan Kaufmann, Los Altos.

[Lutz, 2001a] Carsten Lutz. Interval-based temporal reasoning with general TBoxes. In *Proc. of the 17th Int. Joint Conf. on Artificial Intelligence (IJCAI 2001)*, pages 89–94, 2001.

[Lutz, 2001b] Carsten Lutz. NEXPTIME-complete Description Logics with concrete domains. In *Proc. of the Int. Joint Conf. on Automated Reasoning (IJCAR 2001)*, volume 2083 of Lecture Notes in Artificial Intelligence, pages 45–60. Springer, 2001.

[Lutz, 2002] Carsten Lutz. *The Complexity of Reasoning with Concrete Domains*. PhD thesis, Teaching and Research Area for Theoretical Computer Science, RWTH Aachen, 2002.

[Lutz and Sattler, 2000a] Carsten Lutz and Ulrike Sattler. The complexity of reasoning with boolean modal logic. In *Proc. of Advances in Modal Logic 2000 (AiML 2000)*, 2000.

[Lutz and Sattler, 2000b] Carsten Lutz and Ulrike Sattler. Mary likes all cats. In *Proc. of the 2000 Description Logic Workshop (DL 2000)*, pages 213–226. CEUR Electronic Workshop Proceedings, `http://ceur-ws.org/Vol-33/`, 2000.

[Lutz and Sattler, 2001] Carsten Lutz and Ulrike Sattler. The complexity of reasoning with boolean modal logics. In F. Wolter, H. Wansing, M. de Rijke, and M. Zakharyaschev, editors, *Advances in Modal Logics*, volume 3. CSLI Publications, 2001.

[Lutz et al., 1999] Carsten Lutz, Ulrike Sattler, and Stephan Tobies. A suggestion for an *n*-ary Description Logic. In *Proc. of the 1999 Description Logic Workshop (DL'99)*, pages 81–85. CEUR Electronic Workshop Proceedings, `http://ceur-ws.org/Vol-22/`, 1999.

[Lutz et al., 2001a] Carsten Lutz, Ulrike Sattler, and Frank Wolter. Description logics and the two-variable fragment. In *Proc. of the 2001 Description Logic Workshop (DL 2001)*, pages 66–75. CEUR Electronic Workshop Proceedings, `http://ceur-ws.org/Vol-49/`, 2001.

[Lutz et al., 2001b] Carsten Lutz, Holger Sturm, Frank Wolter, and Michael Zakharyaschev. Tableaux for temporal Description Logic with constant domain. In *Proc. of the Int. Joint Conf. on Automated Reasoning (IJCAR 2001)*, volume 2083 of Lecture Notes in Artificial Intelligence, pages 121–136. Springer, 2001.

[Lutz et al., 2002] Carsten Lutz, Holger Sturm, Frank Wolter, and Michael Zakharyaschev. A tableau decision algorithm for modalized $\mathcal{ALC}$ with constant domains. *Studia Logica*, 72:199–232, 2002.

[Lutz et al., 2004] Carsten Lutz, Carlos Areces, Ian Horrocks, and Ulrike Sattler. Keys, nominals, and concrete domains. 23:667–726, 2004.

[MacGregor, 1988] Robert MacGregor. A deductive pattern matcher. In *Proc. of the 7th Nat. Conf. on Artificial Intelligence (AAAI'88)*, pages 403–408, 1988.

[MacGregor, 1991a] Robert MacGregor. The evolving technology of classification-based knowledge representation systems. In John F. Sowa, editor, *Principles of Semantic Networks*, pages 385–400. Morgan Kaufmann, Los Altos, 1991.

[MacGregor, 1991b] Robert MacGregor. Inside the LOOM description classifier. *SIGART Bull.*, 2(3):88–92, 1991.

[MacGregor, 1994] Robert MacGregor. A description classifier for the predicate calculus. In *Proc. of the 12th Nat. Conf. on Artificial Intelligence (AAAI'94)*, pages 213–220, 1994.

[MacGregor and Bates, 1987] Robert MacGregor and R. Bates. The Loom knowledge representation language. Technical Report ISI/RS-87-188, University of Southern California, Information Science Institute, Marina del Rey (CA, USA), 1987.

[MacGregor and Brill, 1992] Robert MacGregor and David Brill. Recognition algorithms for the LOOM classifier. In *Proc. of the 10th Nat. Conf. on Artificial Intelligence (AAAI'92)*, pages 774–779. AAAI Press/The MIT Press, 1992.

[MacGregor and Burstein, 1991] Robert MacGregor and Mark H. Burstein. Using a description classifier to enhance knowledge representation. *IEEE Expert*, pages 41–46, July 1991.

[Mallery, 1994] John Mallery. A Common LISP hypermedia server. In *Proc. of the 1st Int. Conf. on The World-Wide Web*. CERN, 1994. Available at `http:`

//www.ai.mit.edu/projects/iiip/doc/cl-http/server-abstract.html.

[Mameide and Montero, 1993] Margarida Mameide and Luis Montero. Decidability of a terminological language with role negation and conjunction. In *Proc. of the Compulog Net area meeting on Knowledge Representation and Reasoning*, Lisbon, Portugal, 1993. Departamento de Informatica, Universidade Nova de Lisboa.

[Manola and Miller, 2004] Frank Manola and Eric Miller. RDF primer. W3C Recommendation, 10 February 2004.

[Mark, 1982] W. Mark. Realization. In [Schmolze and Brachman 1982]. Published as BBN Research Report 4842, Bolt Beranek and Newman Inc., June 1982.

[Masarie *et al.*, 1991] F. Masarie, R. Miller, O. Bouhaddou, N. Giuse, and H. Warner. An interlingua for electronic interchange of medical information: Using frames to map between clinical vocabularies. *Computers in Biomedical Research*, 24(4):379–400, 1991.

[Massacci, 1999] Fabio Massacci. TANCS non classical system comparison. In *Proc. of the 3rd Int. Conf. on Analytic Tableaux and Related Methods (TABLEAUX'99)*, volume 1617 of Lecture Notes in Artificial Intelligence. Springer, 1999.

[Massacci, 2001] Fabio Massacci. Decision procedures for expressive Description Logics with intersection, composition, converse of roles and role identity. In *Proc. of the 17th Int. Joint Conf. on Artificial Intelligence (IJCAI 2001)*, pages 193–198, 2001.

[Matiyasevich, 1971] Y. Matiyasevich. Diophantine representation of recursively enumerable predicates. *Isv. Ak. Nauk SSSR, Ser. Mat.*, 35:3–30, 1971.

[Mays *et al.*, 1988] E. Mays, C. Apté, J. Griesmer, and J. Kastner. Experience with K-Rep: An object-centered knowledge representation language. In *Proc. of the 4th IEEE Conference on Artificial Intelligence Application (CAIA'88)*, pages 62–67, Orlando, FL, 1988.

[Mays *et al.*, 1991a] Eric Mays, Robert Dionne, and Robert Weida. K-Rep system overview. *SIGART Bull.*, 2(3):93–97, 1991.

[Mays *et al.*, 1991b] Eric Mays, Sitaram Lanka, Robert Dionne, and Robert Weida. A persistent store for large shared knowledge bases. *IEEE Trans. on Knowledge and Data Engineering*, 3(1):33–41, 1991.

[Mays *et al.*, 1996] E. Mays, R. Weida, R. Dionne, M. Laker, B. White, C. Liang, and F. J. Oles. Scalable and expressive medical terminologies. In *Proc. of the American Medical Informatics Society Annual Fall Symposium*, pages 259–263, 1996.

[McAllester, 1982] David A. McAllester. Reasoning utility package user's manual. Technical Report AI Memo 551, Massachusetts Institute of Technology, Artificial Intelligence Laboratory, 1982.

[McAllester *et al.*, 1996] David A. McAllester, Robert Givan, Carl Witty, and Dexter Kozen. Tarskian set constraints. In *Proc. of the 11th IEEE Symp. on Logic in Computer Science (LICS'96)*, pages 138–147, 1996.

[McDermott, 1982] John McDermott. R1: A rule-based configurer of computer systems. In *Artificial Intelligence*, volume 19, 1982.

[McGuinness, 1996] Deborah L. McGuinness. *Explaining Reasoning in Description Logics*. PhD thesis, Department of Computer Science, Rutgers University, October 1996. Also available as Rutgers Technical Report Number LCSR-TR-277.

[McGuinness, 1998] Deborah L. McGuinness. Ontological issues for knowledge-enhanced search. In *Proceedings of Formal Ontology in Information Systems*, 1998. Also published in *Frontiers in Artificial Intelligence and Applications*, IOS-Press, 1998.

[McGuinness, 1999] Deborah L. McGuinness. Ontology-enhanced search for primary care medical literature. In *Proc. of the Int. Medical Informatics Association Working Group 6 – Conference on Natural Language Processing and Medical Concept Representation (IMIA'99)*, 1999. Available at `http://www.ksl.stanford.edu/people/dlm/papers/imia99-abstract.html`.

[McGuinness and Borgida, 1995] Deborah L. McGuinness and Alex Borgida. Explaining subsumption in Description Logics. In *Proc. of the 14th Int. Joint Conf. on Artificial Intelligence (IJCAI'95)*, pages 816–821, 1995.

[McGuinness and Patel-Schneider, 1998] Deborah L. McGuinness and Peter F. Patel-Schneider. Usability issues in knowledge representation systems. In *Proc. of the 15th Nat. Conf. on Artificial Intelligence (AAAI'98)*, pages 608–614, 1998.

[McGuinness and Wright, 1998a] Deborah McGuinness and Jon R. Wright. Conceptual modelling for configuration: A Description Logic-based approach. *Artificial Intelligence for Engineering Design, Analysis, and Manufacturing. Special Issue on Configuration*, 12:333–344, 1998.

[McGuinness and Wright, 1998b] Deborah L. McGuinness and Jon R. Wright. An industrial strength Description Logic-based configuration platform. *IEEE Intelligent Systems*, pages 69–77, 1998.

[McGuinness *et al.*, 1994] Deborah L. McGuinness, Merryll K. Abrahams, Lori Alperin Resnick, Peter F. Patel-Schneider, Rich Thomason, Violetta Cavalli-Sforza, and Cristina Conati. CLASSIC knowledge representation system tutorial. Technical report, Artificial Intelligence Principles Research Department, AT&T Labs Research and University of Pittsburgh, 1994. Available as `http://www.bell-labs.com/project/classic/papers/ClassTut/ClassTut.html`.

[McGuinness *et al.*, 1995] Deborah L. McGuinness, Lori Alperin Resnick, and Charles Isbell. Description Logic in practice: a CLASSIC application. In *Proc. of the 14th Int. Joint Conf. on Artificial Intelligence (IJCAI'95)*, pages 2045–2046, 1995.

[McGuinness *et al.*, 1997] Deborah L. McGuinness, Harley Manning, and Tom Beattie. Knowledge augmented intranet search. In *Proc. of the 6th World Wide Web Conference CDROM version*, 1997.

[McGuinness *et al.*, 1998] Deborah McGuinness, Peter F. Patel-Schneider, Lori Alperin Resnick, Charles Isbell, Matt Parker, and Chris Welty. A Description Logic based configurator for the web. *SIGART Bull.*, 9(2):20–22, 1998.

[McGuinness *et al.*, 2000a] Deborah L. McGuinness, Richard Fikes, James Rice, and Steve Wilder. The Chimaera ontology environment. In *Proc. of the 17th Nat. Conf. on Artificial Intelligence (AAAI 2000)*, pages 1123–1124, 2000.

[McGuinness *et al.*, 2000b] Deborah L. McGuinness, Richard Fikes, James Rice, and Steve Wilder. An environment for merging and testing large ontologies. In *Proc. of the 7th Int. Conf. on Principles of Knowledge Representation and Reasoning (KR 2000)*, pages 483–493, 2000.

[McGuinness *et al.*, 2002] Deborah L. McGuinness, Richard Fikes, Lynn A. Stein, and James Hendler. DAML-ONT: an ontology language for the semantic web. In Dieter Fensel, Hendler, Henry Lieberman, and Wolfgang Wahlster, editors, *The Semantic Web: Why, What, and How*. The MIT Press, 2002.

[Meghini *et al.*, 1997] Carlo Meghini, Fabrizio Sebastiani, and Umberto Straccia. Modelling the retrieval of structured documents containing texts and images. In Costantino Thanos, editor, *Proc. of the 1st European Conf. on Research and Advanced Technology for Digital Libraries (ECDL'97)*, volume 1324 of Lecture Notes in Computer Science. Springer, 1997.

[Mejino and Rosse, 1999] J. L. V. Mejino and C. Rosse. Conceptualization of anatomical spatial entities in the digital anatomist foundation model. *J. of the American Medical Informatics Association*, pages 112–116, 1999. Annual Symposium Special Issue.

[Mena *et al.*, 2000] E. Mena, A. Illarramendi, V. Kashyap, and A. Sheth. OBSERVER: An approach for query processing in global information systems based on interoperation across pre-existing ontologies. *Distributed and Parallel Databases*, 8(2):223–271, 2000.

[Mendelzon *et al.*, 1997] Alberto Mendelzon, George A. Mihaila, and Tova Milo. Querying the World Wide Web. *Int. J. on Digital Libraries*, 1(1):54–67, 1997.

[Meyer and van der Hoek, 1995] J. J. Meyer and W. van der Hoek. *Epistemic Logic for AI and Computer Science*. Cambridge University Press, 1995.

[Michaeli *et al.*, 1997] David Michaeli, Werner Nutt, and Yehoshua Sagiv. Classification rules for semistructured data. In *Proc. of the 1997 Description Logic Workshop (DL'97)*, pages 59–64, 1997.

[Miller, 1995] George A. Miller. WordNet: A lexical database for English. *Communications of the ACM*, 38(11):39–41, 1995.

[Milne, 1928] A. A. Milne. *The House at Pooh Corner*. Dutton, 1928.

[Minsky, 1981] Marvin Minsky. A framework for representing knowledge. In J. Haugeland, editor, *Mind Design*. The MIT Press, 1981. A longer version appeared in *The Psychology of Computer Vision* (1975). Republished in [Brachman and Levesque, 1985].

[Molitor and Tresp, 2000] Ralf Molitor and Christopher B. Tresp. Extending Description Logics to vague knowledge in medicine. In P. Szczepaniak, P. J. G. Lisboa, and J. Kacprzyk, editors, *Fuzzy Systems in Medicine*, volume 41 of *Studies in Fuzziness and Soft Computing*, pages 617–635. Springer, 2000.

[Moore, 1985] Robert C. Moore. Semantical considerations on nonmonotonic logic. *Acta Informatica*, 25:75–94, 1985.

[Moore and Paris, 1993] Johanna D. Moore and Cécile Paris. Planning text for advisory dialogues: Capturing intentional and rhetorical information. *Computational Linguistics*, 19(4):651–694, 1993.

[Morgan *et al.*, 2005] Alexander P. Morgan, John A. Cafeo, Kurt Godden, Ronald M. Lesperance, Andrea M. Simon, Deborah L. McGuinness, and James L. Benedict. The General Motors Variation-Reduction Adviser. *AI Magazine*, 26(2), 2005.

[Mortimer, 1975] Michael Mortimer. On languages with two variables. *Zeitschrift für Mathematische Logik und Grundlagen der Mathematik*, 21:135–140, 1975.

[Mosurovic and Zakharyaschev, 1999] M. Mosurovic and M. Zakharyaschev. On the complexity of Description Logics with modal operators. In P. Kolaitos and G. Koletos, editors, *Proceedings of the 2nd Panhellenic Logic Symposion*, pages 166–171, Delphi, Greece, 1999.

[Motik, 2005] Boris Motik. On the properties of metamodeling in OWL. In *Proc.*

of the 2005 International Semantic Web Conference (ISWC 2005), volume 3729 of *Lecture Notes in Computer Science*, pages 548–562. Springer, 2005.

[Motik *et al.*, 2004] Boris Motik, Ulrike Sattler, and Rudi Studer. Query answering for OWL-DL with rules. In *Proc. of the 2004 International Semantic Web Conference (ISWC 2004)*, pages 549–563, 2004.

[Motschnig-Pitrik and Mylopoulous, 1992] Renate Motschnig-Pitrik and John Mylopoulous. Classes and instances. *J. of Intelligent and Cooperative Information Systems*, 1(1), 1992.

[Mugnier and Chein, 1992] Marie-Laure Mugnier and Michel Chein. Polynomial algorithms for projection and matching. In Heather D. Pfeiffer and Timothy E. Nagle, editors, *Proc. of the 7th Annual Workshop on Conceptual Structures: Theory and Implementation*, volume 754 of Lecture Notes in Artificial Intelligence, pages 239–251. Springer, 1992.

[Muller and Schupp, 1987] D. E. Muller and P. E. Schupp. Alternating automata on infinite trees. *Theoretical Computer Science*, 54:267–276, 1987.

[Musen, 1998] M. Musen. Modern architectures for intelligent systems: Reusable ontologies and problem-solving methods. *J. of the American Medical Informatics Association*, pages 46–54, 1998. Annual Symposium Special Issue.

[Musen *et al.*, 1996] M. Musen, S. Tu, A. Das, and Y. Shahar. EON: a component-based architecture for automation of protocol-directed therapy. *J. of the American Medical Informatics Association*, 3:367–383, 1996.

[Mylonas and Renear, 1999] Elli Mylonas and Allen Renear. The text encoding initiative at 10. *Computers and the Humanities*, 33(1–2):1–10, 1999.

[Mylopoulos, 1998] John Mylopoulos. Information modeling in the time of the revolution. *Information Systems*, 23(3–4):127–155, 1998.

[Nado and Fikes, 1987] Robert Nado and Richard Fikes. Semantically sound inheritance for a formally defined frame language with defaults. In *Proc. of the 6th Nat. Conf. on Artificial Intelligence (AAAI'87)*, pages 443–448, 1987.

[Nardi and Rosati, 1995] Daniele Nardi and Riccardo Rosati. A preference semantics for ground nonmonotonic modal logics. In *Proc. of the 7th Portuguese Conf. on Artificial Intelligence (EPIA'95)*, volume 990 of Lecture Notes in Artificial Intelligence. Springer, 1995.

[Nebel, 1988] Bernhard Nebel. Computational complexity of terminological reasoning in BACK. *Artificial Intelligence*, 34(3):371–383, 1988.

[Nebel, 1990a] Bernhard Nebel. *Reasoning and Revision in Hybrid Representation Systems*, volume 422 of Lecture Notes in Artificial Intelligence. Springer, 1990.

[Nebel, 1990b] Bernhard Nebel. Terminological reasoning is inherently intractable. *Artificial Intelligence*, 43:235–249, 1990.

[Nebel, 1991] Bernhard Nebel. Terminological cycles: semantics and computational properties. In John F. Sowa, editor, *Principles of Semantic Networks*, pages 331–361. Morgan Kaufmann, Los Altos, 1991.

[Nebel and Smolka, 1991] Bernhard Nebel and Gert Smolka. Attributive description formalism and the rest of the world. In O. Herzog and C.-R. Rollinger, editors, *Textunderstanding in LILOG: Integrating Computational Linguistics and Artificial Intelligence*. Springer, Berlin (Germany), 1991.

[Nebel and von Luck, 1987] Bernhard Nebel and Kai von Luck. Issues of integration and balancing in hybrid knowledge representation systems. In K. Morik, editor, *Proc. of the 11th German Workshop on Artificial Intelligence (GWAI'87)*, pages 114–123. Springer, 1987.

[Nebel and von Luck, 1988] Bernhard Nebel and Kai von Luck. Hybrid reasoning in BACK. In *Proc. of the 3rd Int. Symp. on Methodologies for Intelligent Systems (ISMIS'88)*, pages 260–269. North-Holland Publ. Co., Amsterdam, 1988.

[Neumann, 1992] Peter G. Neumann. What's in a name? *Communications of the ACM*, 35(1):186, 1992.

[Neuwirth, 1993] A. Neuwirth. Inferences for temporal object descriptions in a terminological representation system. KIT-Report 107, Fachbereich Informatik, Technische Universität Berlin, Berlin (Germany), 1993.

[Newell, 1982] Allen Newell. The knowledge level. *Artificial Intelligence*, 18(1):87–127, 1982.

[NHS National Health Service Executive, 1998] NHS National Health Service Executive. Information for health: An information strategy for the modern NHS 1998–2005, 1998.

[Nowlan and Rector, 1991] W. Nowlan and A. Rector. Medical knowledge representation and predictive data entry. In *Proc. of Artificial Intelligence in Medicine Europe (AIME'91)*, pages 105–116, 1991.

[Nowlan et al., 1991a] W. Nowlan, S. Kay, A. Rector, B. Horan, and A. Wilson. PEN&PAD: A multi-lingual patient care workstation based on a unified representation of the medical record and medical terminology. In *Proc. of Medical Informatics Europe (MIE'91)*, pages 1043–1048, 1991.

[Nowlan et al., 1991b] W. Nowlan, A. Rector, S. Kay, B. Horan, and A. Wilson. A patient care workstation based on a user centred design and a formal theory of medical terminology: PEN&PAD and the SMK formalism. In *Proc. of the 15th Annual Symposium on Computer Applications in Medical Care (SCAMC'91)*, pages 855–857, 1991.

[Nowlan et al., 1994] W. Nowlan, A. Rector, T. Rush, and W. Solomon. From terminology to terminology services. In *Proc. of the 18th Annual Symposium on Computer Applications in Medical Care (SCAMC'94)*, pages 150–154, 1994.

[Noy and McGuinness, 2000] Natalya Fridman Noy and Deborah L. McGuinness. Ontology development 101: A guide to creating your first ontology. Technical Report KSL-01-05, Stanford University KSL, 2000. Available also as Stanford Medical Informatics Technical Report no. SMI-2001-0880. Available at http://www.ksl.stanford.edu/people/dlm/papers/ontology-tutorial-noy-mcg uinness-abstract.html.

[Ohlbach and Koehler, 1999] Hans Jürgen Ohlbach and Jana Koehler. Modal logics, Description Logics and arithmetic reasoning. *Artificial Intelligence*, 109(1–2):1–31, 1999.

[Oliver et al., 1999] D. E. Oliver, Y. Shahar, E. H. Shortliffe, and M. A. Musen. Representing change in controlled medical vocabularies. *J. of the American Medical Informatics Association*, 15(1):53–76, 1999.

[O'Neil et al., 1995] M. O'Neil, C. Payne, and J. Read. Read codes version 3: A user led terminology. *Methods of Information in Medicine*, 34:187–192, 1995.

[Oppacher and Suen, 1988] F. Oppacher and E. Suen. HARP: A tableau-based theorem prover. *J. of Automated Reasoning*, 4:69–100, 1988.

[Owsnicki-Klewe, 1988] B. Owsnicki-Klewe. Configuration as a consistency maintenance task. In *Proc. of the 12th German Workshop on Artificial Intelligence (GWAI'88)*, pages 77–87. Springer, 1988.

[Pacholski et al., 1997] Leszek Pacholski, Wieslaw Szwast, and Lidia Tendera.

Complexity of two-variable logic with counting. In *Proc. of the 12th IEEE Symp. on Logic in Computer Science (LICS'97)*, pages 318–327. IEEE Computer Society Press, 1997.

[Pacholski *et al.*, 2000] Leszek Pacholski, Wieslaw Szwast, and Lidia Tendera. Complexity results for first-order two-variable logic with counting. *SIAM J. on Computing*, 29(4):1083–1117, 2000.

[Padgham and Lambrix, 1994] Lin Padgham and Patrick Lambrix. A framework for part-of hierarchies in terminological logics. In *Proc. of the 4th Int. Conf. on the Principles of Knowledge Representation and Reasoning (KR'94)*, pages 485–496, 1994.

[Padgham and Nebel, 1993] Lin Padgham and Bernhard Nebel. Combining classification and non-monotonic inheritance reasoning: A first step. In J. Komorowski and Z. W. Raś, editors, *Proc. of the 7th Int. Symp. on Methodologies for Intelligent Systems (ISMIS'93)*, 1993.

[Padgham and Zhang, 1993] Lin Padgham and Tingting Zhang. A terminological logic with defaults: A definition and an application. In *Proc. of the 13th Int. Joint Conf. on Artificial Intelligence (IJCAI'93)*, pages 662–668, 1993.

[Paley *et al.*, 1997] Suzanne M. Paley, John D. Lawrence, and Peter D. Karp. A generic knowledge-base browser and editor. In *Proc. of the 14th Nat. Conf. on Artificial Intelligence (AAAI'97)*, pages 1045–1051, 1997.

[Papadimitriou, 1994] Christos H. Papadimitriou. *Computational Complexity*. Addison Wesley Publ. Co., Reading, Massachussetts, 1994.

[Paramasivam and Plaisted, 1998] M. Paramasivam and David A. Plaisted. Automated deduction techniques for classification in Description Logic systems. *J. of Automated Reasoning*, 20(3):337–364, 1998.

[Parikh, 1981] Rohit Parikh. Propositional dynamic logic of programs: A survey. In *Proc. of the 1st Workshop on Logics of Programs*, volume 125 of *Lecture Notes in Computer Science*, pages 102–144. Springer, 1981.

[Paris and Vander Linden, 1996a] C. Paris and K. Vander Linden. Building knowledge bases for the generation of software documentation. In *Proc. of the 16th Int. Conf. on Computational Linguistics (COLING'96)*, pages 734–739, 1996.

[Paris and Vander Linden, 1996b] C. Paris and K. Vander Linden. DRAFTER: An interactive support tool for writing multilingual instructions. *IEEE Computer*, pages 49–56, July 1996.

[Park, 1970] David Park. Fixpoint induction and proofs of program properties. *Machine Intelligence*, 5:59–78, 1970.

[Park, 1976] David Park. Finiteness is mu-ineffable. *Theoretical Computer Science*, 3:173–181, 1976.

[Passy and Tinchev, 1985] Solomon Passy and Tinko Tinchev. PDL with data constraints. *Information Processing Lett.*, 20:35–41, 1985.

[Passy and Tinchev, 1991] Solomon Passy and Tinko Tinchev. An essay in combinatory dynamic logic. *Information and Computation*, 93:263–332, 1991.

[Patel-Schneider, 1984] Peter F. Patel-Schneider. Small can be beautiful in knowledge representation. In *Proc. of the IEEE Workshop on Knowledge-Based Systems*, 1984. An extended version appeared as Fairchild Tech. Rep. 660 and FLAIR Tech. Rep. 37, October 1984.

[Patel-Schneider, 1986] Peter F. Patel-Schneider. A four-valued semantics for frame-based description languages. In *Proc. of the 5th Nat. Conf. on Artificial Intelligence (AAAI'86)*, pages 344–348, 1986.

[Patel-Schneider, 1987a] Peter F. Patel-Schneider. *Decidable, Logic-Based Knowledge Representation.* PhD thesis, Department of Computer Science, University of Toronto, Ontario, Canada, 1987. Available as Technical report 201/87.

[Patel-Schneider, 1987b] Peter F. Patel-Schneider. A hybrid, decidable, logic-based knowledge representation system. *Computational Intelligence,* 3(2):64–77, 1987.

[Patel-Schneider, 1989a] Peter F. Patel-Schneider. A four-valued semantics for terminological logic. *Artificial Intelligence,* 38(1):319–351, 1989.

[Patel-Schneider, 1989b] Peter F. Patel-Schneider. Undecidability of subsumption in NIKL. *Artificial Intelligence,* 39:263–272, 1989.

[Patel-Schneider, 1998] P. F. Patel-Schneider. DLP system description. In *Proc. of the 1998 Description Logic Workshop (DL'98),* pages 87–89. CEUR Electronic Workshop Proceedings, http://ceur-ws.org/Vol-11/, 1998.

[Patel-Schneider, 1999] Peter F. Patel-Schneider. DLP. In *Proc. of the 1999 Description Logic Workshop (DL'99),* pages 9–13. CEUR Electronic Workshop Proceedings, http://ceur-ws.org/Vol-22/, 1999.

[Patel-Schneider and Swartout, 1993] Peter F. Patel-Schneider and Bill Swartout. Description-logic knowledge representation system specification from the KRSS group of the ARPA knowledge sharing effort. Technical report, AI Principles Research Department, AT&T Bell Laboratories, 1993. Available at http://dl.kr.org/.

[Patel-Schneider *et al.,* 1990] P. F. Patel-Schneider, B. Owsnicki-Klewe, A. Kobsa, N. Guarino, R. MacGregor, W. S. Mark, D. L. McGuinness, B. Nebel, A. Schmiedel, and J. Yen. Report on the workshop on term subsumption languages in knowledge representation. *AI Magazine,* 11(2):16–22, 1990.

[Patel-Schneider *et al.,* 1991] Peter F. Patel-Schneider, Deborah L. McGuiness, Ronald J. Brachman, Lori Alperin Resnick, and Alexander Borgida. The CLASSIC knowledge representation system: guiding principles and implementation rationale. *SIGART Bull.,* 2(3):108–113, 1991.

[Patel-Schneider *et al.,* 2004] Peter Patel-Schneider, Patrick Hayes, and Ian Horrocks. OWL Web Ontology Language semantics and abstract syntax. W3C Recommendation, February 2004. Available at http://www.w3.org/TR/owl-semantics/.

[Pellet, 2003] Pellet OWL reasoner. Technical report, Maryland Information and Network Dynamics Lab, 2003. Available at http://www.mindswap.org/2003/pellet/index.shtml.

[Peltason, 1991] Christof Peltason. The BACK system—an overview. *SIGART Bull.,* 2(3):114–119, 1991.

[Pirotte *et al.,* 1994] Alain Pirotte, Esteban Zimányi, David Massart, and Tatiana Yakusheva. Materialization: a powerful and ubiquitous abstraction pattern. In *Proc. of the 20th Int. Conf. on Very Large Data Bases (VLDB'94),* pages 630–641, 1994.

[Poon and Fagan, 1994] A. D. Poon and L. M. Fagan. PEN-Ivory: The design and evaluation of a pen-based system for structured data entry. In *Proc. of the 18th Annual Symposium on Computer Applications in Medical Care (SCAMC'94),* pages 447–552, 1994.

[Pratt, 1979] Vaughan R. Pratt. Models of program logic. In *Proc. of the 20th Annual Symp. on the Foundations of Computer Science (FOCS'79),* pages 115–122, 1979.

[Pratt, 1980] Vaughan R. Pratt. A near-optimal method for reasoning about action. *J. of Computer and System Sciences*, 20:231–255, 1980.

[Pratt, 1981] Vaughan R. Pratt. A decidable μ-calculus (preliminary report). In *Proc. of the 22nd Annual Symp. on the Foundations of Computer Science (FOCS'81)*, pages 421–428. IEEE Computer Society Press, 1981.

[Prior, 1967] Arthur Prior. *Past, Present, and Future*. Oxford University Press, 1967.

[Pustejovsky, 1988] J. Pustejovsky. Constraints on the acquisition of semantic knowledge. *Int. J. of Intelligent Systems*, 3:247–268, 1988.

[Quantz, 1993] Joachim Quantz. Interpretation as exception minimization. In *Proc. of the 13th Int. Joint Conf. on Artificial Intelligence (IJCAI'93)*, pages 1310–1315, 1993.

[Quantz, 1995] Joachim Quantz. *Preferential Disambiguation in Natural Language Processing*. PhD thesis, Technische Universität Berlin (Germany), 1995.

[Quantz and Kindermann, 1990] Joachim Quantz and Carsten Kindermann. Implementation of the BACK system version 4. KIT-Report 78, Fachbereich Informatik, Technische Universität Berlin, Berlin (Germany), 1990.

[Quantz and Royer, 1992] Joachim Quantz and Veronique Royer. A preference semantics for defaults in terminological logics. In *Proc. of the 3rd Int. Conf. on the Principles of Knowledge Representation and Reasoning (KR'92)*, pages 294–305. Morgan Kaufmann, Los Altos, 1992.

[Quantz and Schmitz, 1994] J. Quantz and B. Schmitz. Knowledge-based disambiguation for machine translation. *Minds and Machines*, 4:39–57, 1994.

[Quantz et al., 1995] J. Quantz, G. Dunker, F. Bergmann, and I. Kellner. The FLEX system. KIT-Report 124, Fachbereich Informatik, Technische Universität Berlin, Berlin (Germany), 1995.

[Quillian, 1967] M. Ross Quillian. Word concepts: A theory and simulation of some basic capabilities. *Behavioral Science*, 12:410–430, 1967. Republished in [Brachman and Levesque, 1985].

[Quillian, 1968] M. Ross Quillian. Semantic memory. In M. Minsky, editor, *Semantic Information Processing*, pages 216–270. The MIT Press, 1968.

[Randell et al., 1992] David A. Randell, Zhan Cui, and Anthony G. Cohn. A spatial logic based on regions and connection. In *Proc. of the 3rd Int. Conf. on the Principles of Knowledge Representation and Reasoning (KR'92)*, pages 165–176. Morgan Kaufmann, Los Altos, 1992.

[Rassinoux, 1998] A.-M. Rassinoux. Modeling just the important and relevant concepts in medical language understanding. *Methods of Information in Medicine*, 37:361–372, 1998.

[Rector, 1998] A. Rector. Thesauri and formal classifications: Terminologies for people and machines. *Methods of Information in Medicine*, 37(4–5):501–509, 1998.

[Rector and Nowlan, 1994] A. L. Rector and W. Nowlan. A reusable application independent model of medical terminology: GALEN's GRAIL. In *Proc. of the 4th Int. Conf. on the Principles of Knowledge Representation and Reasoning (KR'94)*, 1994.

[Rector and Rogers, 2002] A. Rector and J. Rogers. Ontological issues in using a Description Logic to represent medical concepts: experience from GALEN. *Methods of Information in Medicine*, 2002. To appear.

[Rector et al., 1993] A. L. Rector, W. A. Nowlan, and A. Glowinski. Goals for concept representation in the GALEN project. In *Proc. of the 17th Annual*

Symposium on Computer Applications in Medical Care (SCAMC'93), pages 414–418, Washington DC, USA, 1993.

[Rector *et al.*, 1995a] A. Rector, W. Solomon, W. Nowlan, and T. Rush. A terminology server for medical language and medical information systems. *Methods of Information in Medicine*, 34:147–157, 1995.

[Rector *et al.*, 1995b] A. Rector, P. Zanstra, W. Solomon, and The GALEN Consortium. GALEN: terminology services for clinical information systems. In M. Laires, M. Ladeira, and J. Christensen, editors, *Health in the New Communications Age*, pages 90–100. IOS Press, 1995.

[Rector *et al.*, 1997] A. Rector, S. Bechhofer, C. A. Goble, I. Horrocks, W. A. Nowlan, and W. D. Solomon. The GRAIL concept modelling language for medical terminology. *Artificial Intelligence in Medicine*, 9:139–171, 1997.

[Rector *et al.*, 1999] A. L. Rector, P. E. Zanstra, W. D. Solomon, J. E. Rogers, R. Baud, W. Ceusters, W. Claassen, J. Kirby, J.-M. Rodrigues, A. R. Mori, E. Haring, and J. Wagner. Reconciling users' needs and formal requirements: Issues in developing a re-usable ontology for medicine. *IEEE Transactions on Information Technology in BioMedicine*, 2(4):229–242, 1999.

[Rector *et al.*, 2001] A. Rector, C. Wroe, J. Rogers, and A. Roberts. Untangling taxonomies and relationships: Personal and practical problems in loosely coupled development of large ontologies. In Y. Gil, M. Musen, and J. Shavlik, editors, *Proc. of the 1st Int. Conf. on Knowledge Capture (K-CAP 2001)*. ACM Press and Addison-Wesley, 2001.

[Rector *et al.*, 2002] A. L. Rector, J. E. Rogers, and W. D. Solomon. Ontological issues in using a Description Logic to represent medical concepts: Part II: The GALEN high level schemata. *Methods of Information in Medicine*, 2002. To appear.

[Reiter, 1980] Raymond Reiter. A logic for default reasoning. *Artificial Intelligence*, 13:81–132, 1980.

[Reiter, 1990] Raymond Reiter. On asking what a database knows. In John W. Lloyd, editor, *Computational Logics, Symposium Proceedings*, pages 96–113. Springer, 1990.

[Reiter and Criscuolo, 1981] R. Reiter and G. Criscuolo. On interacting defaults. In *Proc. of the 7th Int. Joint Conf. on Artificial Intelligence (IJCAI'81)*, pages 270–276, 1981.

[Resnick *et al.*, 1995] Lori Alperin Resnick, Alexander Borgida, Ronald J. Brachman, Deborah L. McGuinness, Peter F. Patel-Schneider, and Kevin C. Zalondek. CLASSIC: description and reference manual for the Common Lisp implementation, version 2.3. Technical report, AT&T Bell Labs, Murray Hill, NY, 1995.

[Rich, 1991] Charles Rich, editor. Special issue on implemented knowledge representation and reasoning systems. *SIGART Bulletin*, 2(3), 1991.

[Rintanen, 1999] Jussi T. Rintanen. Improvements to the evaluation of quantified boolean formulae. In *Proc. of the 16th Int. Joint Conf. on Artificial Intelligence (IJCAI'99)*, pages 1192–1197, 1999.

[Robins, 1986] Gabriel Robins. The NIKL manual. Technical report, University of Southern California, Los Angeles, Information Sciences Institutes, The Knowledge Representation Project, 1986.

[Robinson, 1971] R. Robinson. Undecidability and nonperiodicity of tilings on the plane. *Inventiones Math.*, 12:177–209, 1971.

[Rocha *et al.*, 1993] R. Rocha, B. Rocha, and S. Huff. Automated translation between medical vocabularies using a frame-based interlingua. In *Proc. of the*

17th Annual Symposium on Computer Applications in Medical Care (SCAMC'93), pages 690–694, 1993.

[Rocha *et al.*, 1994] R. A. Rocha, S. M. Huff, P. J. Haug, and H. R. Warner. Designing a controlled medical vocabulary server: the VOSER project. *Computers and Biomedical Research*, 27:472–507, 1994.

[Rodrigues *et al.*, 1997] J. M. Rodrigues, B. Trombert-Paviot, R. Baud, J. Wagner, P. Rusch, and F. Meusnier. GALEN-In-Use: an EU project applied to the development of a new national coding system for surgical procedures: NCAM. In *Proc. of Medical Informatics Europe (MIE'97)*, pages 897–901, 1997.

[Rosati, 1998] Riccardo Rosati. Autoepistemic Description Logics. *AI Communications – The Eur. J. on Artificial Intelligence*, 11(3–4):219–221, 1998.

[Rosati, 1999] Riccardo Rosati. Towards expressive KR systems integrating Datalog and Description Logics: Preliminary report. In *Proc. of the 1999 Description Logic Workshop (DL'99)*, pages 160–164. CEUR Electronic Workshop Proceedings, http://ceur-ws.org/Vol-22/, 1999.

[Rosati, 2005] Riccardo Rosati. On the decidability and complexity of integrating ontologies and rules. *J. of Web Semantics*, 3(1):61–73, 2005.

[Rosse *et al.*, 1998] C. Rosse, I. G. Shapiro, and J. F. Brinkley. The digital anatomist foundational model: Principles for defining and structuring its concept domain. *J. of the American Medical Informatics Association*, 1998. Fall Symposium Special Issue.

[Rossi Mori and Consorti, 1999] A. Rossi Mori and F. Consorti. Structuring clinical information in electronic healthcare records. In *Proc. of Medical Informatics Europe (MIE'99)*, 1999. Tutorial.

[Rossi Mori *et al.*, 1997] A. Rossi Mori, A. Gangemi, G. Steve, F. Consorti, and E. Galeazzi. An ontological analysis of surgical deeds. In *Proc. of Artificial Intelligence in Medicine Europe (AIME'97)*, pages 361–372, 1997.

[Rousset, 1999a] Marie-Christine Rousset. Backward reasoning in ABoxes for query answering. In *Proc. of the 1999 Description Logic Workshop (DL'99)*, pages 18–22. CEUR Electronic Workshop Proceedings, http://ceur-ws.org/Vol-22/, 1999.

[Rousset, 1999b] Marie-Christine Rousset. Query expansion in Description Logics and CARIN. In *Working Notes of the AAAI Fall Symposium on "Question Answering Systems"*, 1999.

[Rumbaugh *et al.*, 1998] James Rumbaugh, Ivar Jacobson, and Grady Booch. *The Unified Modeling Language Reference Manual*. Addison Wesley Publ. Co., Reading, Massachussetts, 1998.

[Rychtyckyj, 1996] Nestor Rychtyckyj. DLMS: An evaluation of KL-ONE in the automobile industry. In *Proc. of the 5th Int. Conf. on the Principles of Knowledge Representation and Reasoning (KR'96)*, pages 588–596, 1996.

[Rychtyckyj, 1999] Nestor Rychtyckyj. DLMS: Ten years of AI for vehicle assembly process planning. In *Proc. of the 11th Annual Conf. on Innovative Appplications of Artificial Intelligence (IAAI'99)*, pages 821–828, 1999.

[Sager *et al.*, 1987] N. Sager, C. Friedman, and M. Lyman. *Medical Language Processing – Computer Management of Narrative Data*. Addison Wesley Publ. Co., Reading, Massachussetts, 1987.

[Sager *et al.*, 1994] N. Sager, M. S. Lyman, C. Bucknall, N. T. Nhan, and L. J. Tick. Natural language processing and the representation of clinical data. *J.*

of the American Medical Informatics Association, 1(1):142–160, 1994.

[Samek-Lodovici and Strapparava, 1990] Vieri Samek-Lodovici and Carlo Strapparava. Identifying noun phrase references: the topic module of the AlFresco system. In *Proc. of the 9th Eur. Conf. on Artificial Intelligence (ECAI'90)*, pages 573–578, 1990.

[Sattler, 1995] Ulrike Sattler. A concept language for an engineering application with part-whole relations. In *Proc. of the 1995 Description Logic Workshop (DL'95)*, pages 119–123, 1995.

[Sattler, 1996] Ulrike Sattler. A concept language extended with different kinds of transitive roles. In Günter Görz and Steffen Hölldobler, editors, *Proc. of the 20th German Annual Conf. on Artificial Intelligence (KI'96)*, number 1137 in Lecture Notes in Artificial Intelligence, pages 333–345. Springer, 1996.

[Sattler and Vardi, 2001] Ulrike Sattler and Moshe Y. Vardi. The hybrid μ-calculus. In *Proc. of the Int. Joint Conf. on Automated Reasoning (IJCAR 2001)*, pages 76–91, 2001.

[Savitch, 1970] W. J. Savitch. Relationship between nondeterministic and deterministic tape complexities. *J. of Computer and System Sciences*, 4:177–192, 1970.

[Schaerf, 1993] Andrea Schaerf. On the complexity of the instance checking problem in concept languages with existential quantification. *J. of Intelligent Information Systems*, 2:265–278, 1993.

[Schaerf, 1994a] Andrea Schaerf. *Query Answering in Concept-Based Knowledge Representation Systems: Algorithms, Complexity, and Semantic Issues.* PhD thesis, Dipartimento di Informatica e Sistemistica, Università di Roma "La Sapienza", 1994.

[Schaerf, 1994b] Andrea Schaerf. Reasoning with individuals in concept languages. *Data and Knowledge Engineering*, 13(2):141–176, 1994.

[Schank, 1975] Roger C. Schank. *Conceptual Information Processing.* North-Holland Publ. Co., Amsterdam, 1975.

[Schild, 1989] Klaus Schild. Towards a theory of frames and rules. Technical report, Fachbereich Informatik, Technische Universität Berlin, Berlin (Germany), 1989.

[Schild, 1991] Klaus Schild. A correspondence theory for terminological logics: Preliminary report. In *Proc. of the 12th Int. Joint Conf. on Artificial Intelligence (IJCAI'91)*, pages 466–471, 1991.

[Schild, 1993] Klaus Schild. Combining terminological logics with tense logic. In *Proc. of the 6th Portuguese Conf. on Artificial Intelligence (EPIA'93)*, volume 727 of Lecture Notes in Computer Science, pages 105–120. Springer, 1993.

[Schild, 1994] Klaus Schild. Terminological cycles and the propositional μ-calculus. In J. Doyle, E. Sandewall, and P. Torasso, editors, *Proc. of the 4th Int. Conf. on the Principles of Knowledge Representation and Reasoning (KR'94)*, pages 509–520, Bonn (Germany), 1994. Morgan Kaufmann, Los Altos.

[Schmidt, 1991] R. Schmidt. Algebraic terminological representation. Technical report, Max Planck Institute for Computer Science, MPI-Report MPI-I-91-216, 1991.

[Schmidt-Schauß, 1989] Manfred Schmidt-Schauß. Subsumption in KL-ONE is undecidable. In Ron J. Brachman, Hector J. Levesque, and Ray Reiter, editors, *Proc. of the 1st Int. Conf. on the Principles of Knowledge Representation and Reasoning (KR'89)*, pages 421–431. Morgan Kaufmann,

Los Altos, 1989.

[Schmidt-Schauß and Smolka, 1991] Manfred Schmidt-Schauß and Gert Smolka. Attributive concept descriptions with complements. *Artificial Intelligence*, 48(1):1–26, 1991.

[Schmiedel, 1988] Albrecht Schmiedel. A temporal constraint handler for the BACK system. KIT-Report 70, Fachbereich Informatik, Technische Universität Berlin, Berlin (Germany), 1988.

[Schmiedel, 1990] Albrecht Schmiedel. A temporal terminological logic. In *Proc. of the 8th Nat. Conf. on Artificial Intelligence (AAAI'90)*, pages 640–645, 1990.

[Schmiedel, 1993] Albrecht Schmiedel. Persistent maintenance of object descriptions using BACK. KIT-Report 112, Fachbereich Informatik, Technische Universität Berlin, Berlin (Germany), 1993.

[Schmolze, 1985] James G. Schmolze. The language and semantics of NIKL. Technical report, BBN Laboratories, Cambridge, MA, 1985.

[Schmolze, 1989] James G. Schmolze. Terminological knowledge representation systems supporting n-ary terms. In *Proc. of the 1st Int. Conf. on the Principles of Knowledge Representation and Reasoning (KR'89)*, pages 432–443, 1989.

[Schmolze and Brachman, 1982] James G. Schmolze and Ronald J. Brachman, editors. *Proc. of the 1981 KL-ONE Workshop*, 1982. Published as BBN Research Report 4842, Bolt Beranek and Newman Inc., June 1982.

[Schmolze and Israel, 1983] James G. Schmolze and David J. Israel. KL-ONE: Semantics and classification. Technical report, Research in Knowledge Representation for Natural Language Understanding – Annual Report 1983, BBN Report No. 5421, BBN Laboratories, Cambridge, MA, 1983.

[Schmolze and Lipkis, 1983] James G. Schmolze and Thomas A. Lipkis. Classification in the KL-ONE knowledge representation system. In *Proc. of the 8th Int. Joint Conf. on Artificial Intelligence (IJCAI'83)*, pages 330–332, 1983.

[Schmolze and Mark, 1991] James G. Schmolze and William S. Mark. The NIKL experience. *Computational Intelligence*, 7(1):48–69, 1991.

[Schreiber *et al.*, 1993] A. Schreiber, G. van Heijst, G. Lanzola, and M. Stefanelli. Knowledge organisation in medical KBS construction. In *Proc. of Medical Informatics Europe (MIE'93)*, pages 394–405, 1993.

[Selfridge and Heineman, 1994] Peter Selfridge and George Heineman. Graphical support for code-level software understanding. In Douglas Smith, editor, *Proc. of the 9th Conf. on Knowledge-Based Software Engineering (KBSE'94)*. IEEE Computer Society Press, 1994.

[Selman and Levesque, 1993] Bart Selman and Hector J. Levesque. The complexity of path-based defeasible inheritance. *Artificial Intelligence*, 62(2):303–339, 1993.

[Shlaer and Mellor, 1988] Sally Shlaer and Stephen J. Mellor. *Object Oriented Systems Analysis: Modeling the World in Data*. Yourdon Press, 1988.

[Shoham, 1987] Yoav Shoham. A semantical approach to nonmonotonic logics. In *Proc. of the 2nd IEEE Symp. on Logic in Computer Science (LICS'87)*, pages 275–279, 1987.

[Simmons, 1973] Robert F. Simmons. Semantic networks: Their computation and use for understanding English sentences. In Roger C. Schank and Kenneth M. Colby, editors, *Computer Models of Thought and Language*, pages 63–113. W. H. Freeman, San Francisco, CA, 1973.

[Sittig, 1994] D. F. Sittig. Grand challenges in medical informatics. *J. of the American Medical Informatics Association*, 1:412–413, 1994.

[Smith et al., 2004] Michael K. Smith, Chris Welty, and Deborah L. McGuinness. OWL Web Ontology Language guide. W3C Recommendation, February 2004. Available at http://www.w3.org/TR/owl-guide/.

[Smolka, 1988] Gert Smolka. A feature logic with subsorts. Technical Report 33, IWBS, IBM Deutschland, P.O. Box 80 08 80 D-7000 Stuttgart 80, Germany, 1988.

[Soininen et al., 2001] Timo Soininen, Michel Aldanondo, Gerhard Friedrich, Eugene Freuder, Deborah McGuinness, and Markus Stumptner, editors. *Proc. of the 17th Int. Joint Conf. on Artificial Intelligence (IJCAI 2001) Workshop on Configuration*, 2001.

[Solomon and Heathfield, 1994] W. Solomon and H. Heathfield. Conceptual modelling used to represent drug interactions. In *Proc. of Medical Informatics Europe (MIE'94)*, pages 186–190, 1994.

[Solomon et al., 1999] D. S. Solomon, C. Wroe, J. E. Rogers, and A. Rector. A reference terminology for drugs. *J. of the American Medical Informatics Association*, 1999. Conference Special Issue.

[Soloway and Letovsky, 1986] Elliot Soloway and Stan Letovsky. Delocalized plans and program comprehension. *IEEE Software*, 3(3), 1986.

[Soloway et al., 1986] Elliot Soloway, Stan Letovsky, Juan Pinto, and Diane Littman. Mental models and software maintenance. In *Proceedings of the Conference on Empirical Studies of Programmers*, pages 80–98. Ablex Publishers, 1986.

[Soloway et al., 1987] E. Soloway, S. Sheppard, and G. Olson, editors. *Proceedings of the Second Workshop on Empirical Studies of Programmers*. Ablex Publishers, December 1987.

[Sondheimer et al., 1984] N. Sondheimer, R. Weischedel, and R. Bobrow. Semantic interpretation using KL-ONE. In *Proc. of the 14th Int. Conf. on Computational Linguistics (COLING'94)*, 1984.

[Sowa, 1984] John F. Sowa. *Conceptual Structures: Information Processing in Mind and Machine*. Addison Wesley Publ. Co., Reading, Massachussetts, 1984.

[Sowa, 1991] John F. Sowa, editor. *Principles of Semantic Networks: Explorations in the Representation of Knowledge*. Morgan Kaufmann, Los Altos, 1991.

[Spackman, 2000] K. A. Spackman. Managing clinical terminology hierarchies using algorithmic calculation of subsumption: experience with SNOMED-RT. *J. of the American Medical Informatics Association*, 2000. Fall Symposium Special Issue.

[Spackman et al., 1997] K. A. Spackman, K. E. Campbell, and R. A. Côté. SNOMED-RT: A reference terminology for health care. *J. of the American Medical Informatics Association*, pages 640–644, 1997. Fall Symposium Special Issue.

[Speel et al., 1995] P.-H. Speel, F. van Raalte, P. E. van der Vet, and N. J. I. Mars. Runtime and memory usage performance of Description Logics. In G. Ellis, R. A. Levinson, A. Fall, and V. Dahl, editors, *Knowledge Retrieval, Use and Storage for Efficiency: Proc. of the 1st Int. KRUSE Symposium*, pages 13–27, 1995.

[Staab and Maedche, 2000] S. Staab and A. Maedche. Ontology engineering beyond the modeling of concepts and relations. In *Proc. of the ECAI'00 workshop on Applications of Ontologies and Problem-solving Methods*, 2000.

[Stede, 1999] Manfred Stede. *Lexical Semantics and Knowledge Representation in Multilingual Text Generation*. Kluwer Academic Publishers, 1999.

[Steedman, 1996] M. Steedman. *Syntactic Structure and Interpretation*. Number 30 in Linguistic Inquiry Monographs. The MIT Press, 1996.

[Steele, 1990] G. Steele. *Common Lisp, The Language*. Digital Press, second edition, 1990.

[Stickel, 1982] Mark E. Stickel. A nonclausal connection-graph resolution theorem-proving program. In *Proc. of the 2nd Nat. Conf. on Artificial Intelligence (AAAI'82)*, pages 229–233, 1982.

[Stirling, 1996] Colin Stirling. Modal and temporal logics for processes. In Faron Moller and Graham Birtwistle, editors, *Logics for Concurrency: Structure versus Automata*, volume 1043 of Lecture Notes in Computer Science, pages 149–237. Springer, 1996.

[Stock et al., 1991] O. Stock, G. Carenini, F. Cecconi, E. Franconi, A. Lavelli, B. Magnini, F. Pianesi, M. Ponzi, V. Samek-Lodovici, and C. Strapparava. Natural language and exploration of an information space: the AlFresco interactive system. In *Proc. of the 12th Int. Joint Conf. on Artificial Intelligence (IJCAI'91)*, pages 972–978, 1991.

[Stock et al., 1993] O. Stock, G. Carenini, F. Cecconi, E. Franconi, A. Lavelli, B. Magnini, F. Pianesi, M. Ponzi, V. Samek-Lodovici, and C. Strapparava. AlFresco: Enjoying the combination of natural language processing and hypermedia for information exploration. In Mark T. Maybury, editor, *Intelligent Multimedia Interfaces*, chapter 9, pages 197–224. The MIT Press, 1993.

[Straccia, 1993] Umberto Straccia. Default inheritance reasoning in hybrid KL-ONE-style logics. In *Proc. of the 13th Int. Joint Conf. on Artificial Intelligence (IJCAI'93)*, pages 676–681. Morgan Kaufmann, Los Altos, 1993.

[Straccia, 1998] Umberto Straccia. A fuzzy Description Logic. In *Proc. of the 15th Nat. Conf. on Artificial Intelligence (AAAI'98)*, pages 594–599. AAAI Press/The MIT Press, 1998.

[Straccia, 2001] Umberto Straccia. Reasoning within fuzzy Description Logics. *J. of Artificial Intelligence Research*, 14:137–166, 2001.

[Streett, 1982] Robert S. Streett. Propositional Dynamic Logic of looping and converse is elementarily decidable. *Information and Control*, 54:121–141, 1982.

[Streett and Emerson, 1989] Robert S. Streett and E. Allen Emerson. An automata theoretic decision procedure for the propositional μ-calculus. *Information and Computation*, 81:249–264, 1989.

[Sturm and Wolter, 2002] Holger Sturm and Frank Wolter. A tableau calculus for temporal Description Logic: the expanding domain case. *J. of Logic and Computation*, 12:809–838, 2002.

[Swartout and Gil, 1996] William R. Swartout and Yolanda Gil. EXPECT: A user-centered environment for the development and adaptation of knowledge-based planning aids. In Austin Tate, editor, *Advanced Planning Technology: Technological Achievements of the ARPA/Rome Laboratory Planning Initiative*, Menlo Park (CA, USA), 1996. AAAI Press/The MIT Press.

[Tarski, 1951] Alfred Tarski. *A Decision Method for Elementary Algebra and Geometry*. University of California Press, Berkeley, 1951.

[Tarski, 1955] Alfred Tarski. A lattice-theoretical fixpoint theorem and its applications. *Pacific Journal of Mathematics*, 5:285–309, 1955.

[Teorey, 1989] Toby J. Teorey. *Database Modeling and Design: The Entity-Relationship Approach*. Morgan Kaufmann, Los Altos, 1989.

[Tessaris, 2001] Sergio Tessaris. *Questions and Answers: Reasoning and Querying in Description Logic*. PhD thesis, University of Manchester, Department of Computer Science, April 2001.

[Thalheim, 1992] Bernhard Thalheim. Fundamentals of cardinality constraints. In G. Pernoul and A. M. Tjoa, editors, *Proc. of the 11th Int. Conf. on the Entity–Relationship Approach (ER'92)*, pages 7–23. Springer, 1992.

[Thalheim, 1993] Bernhard Thalheim. *Fundamentals of the Entity Relationship Model*. Springer, 1993.

[The Gene Ontology Consortium, 2000] The Gene Ontology Consortium. Gene ontology: Tool for the unification of biology. *Nature Genetics*, 25(1):25–29, 2000.

[Tobies, 1999a] Stephan Tobies. A NEXPTIME-complete Description Logic strictly contained in C^2. In J. Flum and M. Rodríguez-Artalejo, editors, *Proc. of the Annual Conf. of the Eur. Assoc. for Computer Science Logic (CSL'99)*, volume 1683 of *Lecture Notes in Computer Science*, pages 292–306. Springer, 1999.

[Tobies, 1999b] Stephan Tobies. On the complexity of counting in Description Logics. In *Proc. of the 1999 Description Logic Workshop (DL'99)*, pages 105–109. CEUR Electronic Workshop Proceedings, http://ceur-ws.org/Vol-22/, 1999.

[Tobies, 1999c] Stephan Tobies. A PSPACE algorithm for graded modal logic. In H. Ganzinger, editor, *Proc. of the 16th Int. Conf. on Automated Deduction (CADE'99)*, volume 1632 of Lecture Notes in Artificial Intelligence, pages 52–66. Springer, 1999.

[Tobies, 2000] Stephan Tobies. The complexity of reasoning with cardinality restrictions and nominals in expressive Description Logics. *J. of Artificial Intelligence Research*, 12:199–217, 2000.

[Tobies, 2001a] Stephan Tobies. *Complexity Results and Practical Algorithms for Logics in Knowledge Representation*. PhD thesis, LuFG Theoretical Computer Science, RWTH-Aachen, Germany, 2001.

[Tobies, 2001b] Stephan Tobies. PSPACE reasoning for graded modal logics. *J. of Logic and Computation*, 11(1):85–106, 2001.

[Tou et al., 1982] F. Tou, M. Williams, R. Fikes, A. Henderson, and T. Malone. RABBIT: An intelligent database assistant. In *Proc. of the 2nd Nat. Conf. on Artificial Intelligence (AAAI'82)*, pages 314–318, 1982.

[Touretzky et al., 1987] David S. Touretzky, John F. Horty, and Richmond H. Thomason. A clash of intuitions: the current state of nonmonotonic multiple inheritance systems. In *Proc. of the 10th Int. Joint Conf. on Artificial Intelligence (IJCAI'87)*, pages 476–482, 1987.

[Touretzky et al., 1991] David S. Touretzky, Richmond Thomason, and Jeff Horty. A skeptic's menagerie: conflictors, preemptors, reinstaters, and zombies in nonmonotonic inheritance. In *Proc. of the 12th Int. Joint Conf. on Artificial Intelligence (IJCAI'91)*, pages 478–483, 1991.

[Tresp and Molitor, 1998] Christopher B. Tresp and Ralf Molitor. A Description Logic for vague knowledge. In *Proc. of the 13th Eur. Conf. on Artificial Intelligence (ECAI'98)*, pages 361–365, 1998.

[Tsarkov and Horrocks, 2005] Dmitry Tsarkov and Ian Horrocks. Ordering heuristics for description logic reasoning. In *Proc. of the 19th Int. Joint Conf. on Artificial Intelligence (IJCAI 2005)*, pages 609–614, 2005.

[Tsarkov et al., 2004] Dmitry Tsarkov, Alexandre Riazanov, Sean Bechhofer, and Ian Horrocks. Using Vampire to reason with OWL. In Sheila A. McIlraith, Dimitris Plexousakis, and Frank van Harmelen, editors, *Proc. of the 2004 International Semantic Web Conference (ISWC 2004)*, number 3298 in Lecture Notes in Computer Science, pages 471–485. Springer, 2004.

[Tu et al., 1995] S. Tu, H. Eriksson, J. Gennari, Y. Shahar, and M. Musen. Ontology-based configuration of problem-solving methods and generation of knowledge-acquisition tools: Application of Protégé-II to protocol-based decision-support. *AI Magazine*, 7:257–289, 1995.

[Tuttle, 1994] M. S. Tuttle. The position of the CANON group: A reality check. *J. of the American Medical Informatics Association*, 1(3):298–299, 1994.

[Ullman, 1988] Jeffrey D. Ullman. *Principles of Database and Knowledge Base Systems*, volume 1. Computer Science Press, Potomac, Maryland, 1988.

[Valiant, 1984] L. G. Valiant. A theory of the learnable. *Communications of the ACM*, 27(11):1134–1142, 1984.

[van Benthem, 1983] Johan van Benthem. *Modal Logic and Classical Logic*. Bibliopolis, Napoli, 1983.

[van Benthem, 1984] Johan van Benthem. Correspondence theory. In D. M. Gabbay and F. Guenthner, editors, *Handbook of Philosophical Logic*, volume II, pages 167–247. D. Reidel Publishing Company, 1984.

[van Benthem, 1996] Johan van Benthem. Temporal logic. In D. Gabbay, C. Hogger, and J. Robinson, editors, *Handbook of Logic in Artificial Intelligence and Logic Programming, Volume 4*, pages 241–350. Oxford Scientific Publishers, 1996.

[Van der Hoek, 1992] Wiebe Van der Hoek. On the semantics of graded modalities. *J. of Applied Non-classical Logics*, 2(1):81–123, 1992.

[Van der Hoek and de Rijke, 1995] Wiebe Van der Hoek and Maarten de Rijke. Counting objects. *J. of Logic and Computation*, 5(3):325–345, 1995.

[van Emde Boas, 1997] Peter van Emde Boas. The convenience of tilings. In A. Sorbi, editor, *Complexity, Logic, and Recursion Theory*, volume 187 of Lecture Notes in Pure and Applied Mathematics, pages 331–363. Marcel Dekker Inc., 1997.

[van Harmelen et al., 2001] Frank van Harmelen, Peter F. Patel-Schneider, and Ian Horrocks. A model-theoretic semantics for DAML+OIL, March 2001. Available at http://www.daml.org/2001/03/model-theoretic-semantics.html.

[Vanheijst et al., 1995] G. Vanheijst, S. Falasconi, A. Abuhanna, G. Schreiber, and M. Stefanelli. A case-study in ontology library construction. *AI Magazine*, 7(3):227–255, 1995.

[Vardi, 1982] Moshe Y. Vardi. The complexity of relational query languages. In *Proc. of the 14th ACM SIGACT Symp. on Theory of Computing (STOC'82)*, pages 137–146, 1982.

[Vardi, 1985] Moshe Y. Vardi. The taming of converse: Reasoning about two-way computations. In R. Parikh, editor, *Proc. of the 4th Workshop on Logics of Programs*, volume 193 of Lecture Notes in Computer Science, pages 413–424. Springer, 1985.

[Vardi, 1996] Moshe Y. Vardi. An automata-theoretic approach to linear temporal logic. In Faron Moller and Graham Birtwistle, editors, *Logics for Concurrency: Structure versus Automata*, volume 1043 of Lecture Notes in Computer Science, pages 238–266. Springer, 1996.

[Vardi, 1997] Moshe Y. Vardi. Why is modal logic so robustly decidable. In *DIMACS Series in Discrete Mathematics and Theoretical Computer Science*, volume 31, pages 149–184. American Mathematical Society, 1997.

[Vardi, 1998] Moshe Y. Vardi. Reasoning about the past with two-way automata. In *Proc. of the 25th Int. Coll. on Automata, Languages and Programming (ICALP'98)*, volume 1443 of Lecture Notes in Computer Science, pages 628–641. Springer, 1998.

[Vardi and Wolper, 1986] Moshe Y. Vardi and Pierre Wolper. Automata-theoretic techniques for modal logics of programs. *J. of Computer and System Sciences*, 32:183–221, 1986. A preliminary version appeared in *Proc. of the 16th ACM SIGACT Symp. on Theory of Computing (STOC'84)*.

[Veith, 1997] Helmut Veith. Languages represented by boolean formulas. *Information Processing Lett.*, 63:251–256, 1997.

[Vilain, 1985] Marc Vilain. The restricted language architecture of a hybrid representation system. In *Proc. of the 9th Int. Joint Conf. on Artificial Intelligence (IJCAI'85)*, pages 547–551. Morgan Kaufmann, Los Altos, 1985.

[Wahlöf, 1996] N. Wahlöf. A default extension to Description Logics and its applications. Master's thesis, Linköping University, Thesis 591, Department of Computer and Information Science, 1996.

[Wahlster, 2000] Wolfgang Wahlster, editor. *Verbmobil: Foundations of Speech-to-Speech Translation*. Springer, 2000.

[Wahlster *et al.*, 1993] Wolfgang Wahlster, Elisabeth André, Wolfgang Finkler, Hans-Jürgen Profitlich, and Thomas Rist. Plan-based integration of natural language and graphics generation. *Artificial Intelligence*, 63(1–2):387–428, 1993.

[Weida, 1996] Robert A. Weida. Closed terminologies in Description Logics. In *Proc. of the 13th Nat. Conf. on Artificial Intelligence (AAAI'96)*, pages 592–599, 1996.

[Weida and Litman, 1992] Robert Weida and Diane Litman. Terminological reasoning with constraint networks and an application to plan recognition. In *Proc. of the 3rd Int. Conf. on the Principles of Knowledge Representation and Reasoning (KR'92)*, pages 282–293. Morgan Kaufmann, Los Altos, 1992.

[Weischedel, 1989] R. M. Weischedel. A hybrid approach to representation in the Janus natural language processor. In *Proc. of the 27th Annual Meeting of the Association for Computational Linguistics (ACL'89)*, pages 193–202, 1989.

[Welty, 1994] Christopher Welty. A knowledge-based email distribution system. In *Proc. of the 1994 Florida AI Research Symposium*. AAAI Press/The MIT Press, May 1994.

[Welty, 1995] Christopher Welty. *An Integrated Representation for Software Development and Discovery*. PhD thesis, Rensselaer Polytechnic Institute, 1995.

[Welty, 1996a] Christopher Welty. An HTML interface for Classic. In *Proc. of the 1996 Description Logic Workshop (DL'96)*, number WS-96-05 in AAAI Technical Report. AAAI Press/The MIT Press, 1996.

[Welty, 1996b] Christopher Welty. Intelligent assistance for navigating the web. In *Proc. of the 1996 Florida AI Research Symposium*. AAAI Press/The MIT Press, May 1996.

[Welty, 1997] Christopher Welty. Augmenting abstract syntax trees for program understanding. In *Proc. of the 1997 Automated Software Engineering Conf.* IEEE Computer Society Press, 1997.

[Welty, 1998] Christopher Welty. The ontological nature of subject taxonomies. In *Proc. of the Int. Conf. on Formal Ontology in Information Systems (FOIS'98)*, Frontiers in Artificial Intelligence. IOS Press, 1998.

[Welty and Guarino, 2001] Christopher Welty and Nicola Guarino. Support for ontological analysis of taxonomic relationships. *Data and Knowledge Engineering*, 39(1):51–74, 2001.

[Welty and Jenkins, 2000] Christopher Welty and Jessica Jenkins. Untangle: a new ontology for card catalog systems. In *Proc. of the 17th Nat. Conf. on Artificial Intelligence (AAAI 2000)*, pages 1137–1138. AAAI Press/The MIT Press, 2000.

[Wermelinger, 1995] Michel Wermelinger. Conceptual graphs and first-order logic. In Gerard Ellis, Robert Levinson, William Rich, and John F. Sowa, editors, *Proc. of the 3rd Int. Conf. on Conceptual Structures (ICCS'95)*, volume 954 of Lecture Notes in Artificial Intelligence, pages 323–337. Springer, 1995.

[Wielinga et al., 2001] B. J. Wielinga, A. T. Schreiber, J. Wielemaker, and J. A. C. Sandberg. From thesaurus to ontology. In *Proc. of the 1st Int. Conf. on Knowledge Capture (K-CAP 2001)*. ACM Press and Addison Wesley, 2001.

[Wolter, 2000] Frank Wolter. The product of converse PDL and polymodal K. *J. of Logic and Computation*, 10(2):223–251, 2000.

[Wolter and Zakharyaschev, 1998] Frank Wolter and Michael Zakharyaschev. Satisfiability problem in Description Logics with modal operators. In *Proc. of the 6th Int. Conf. on Principles of Knowledge Representation and Reasoning (KR'98)*, pages 512–523, 1998.

[Wolter and Zakharyaschev, 1999a] Frank Wolter and Michael Zakharyaschev. Dynamic Description Logic. In K. Segerberg, M. de Rijke, H. Wansing, and M. Zakharyaschev, editors, *Advances in Modal Logic, Volume 2*. CSLI Publications, 1999.

[Wolter and Zakharyaschev, 1999b] Frank Wolter and Michael Zakharyaschev. Modal Description Logics: modalizing roles. *Fundamenta Informaticae*, 39(4):411–438, 1999.

[Wolter and Zakharyaschev, 1999c] Frank Wolter and Michael Zakharyaschev. Multi-dimensional Description Logics. In *Proc. of the 16th Int. Joint Conf. on Artificial Intelligence (IJCAI'99)*, pages 104–109, 1999.

[Wolter and Zakharyaschev, 1999d] Frank Wolter and Michael Zakharyaschev. Temporalizing Description Logic. In D. Gabbay and M. de Rijke, editors, *Frontiers of Combining Systems*, pages 379–402. Studies Press/Wiley, 1999.

[Wolter and Zakharyaschev, 1999e] Frank Wolter and Michael Zakharyaschev. Temporalizing Description Logics. In M. de Rijke and D. Gabbay, editors, *Proc. of the 2th Int. Workshop on Frontiers of Combining Systems (FroCoS'98)*, Amsterdam, 1999. Wiley.

[Wood, 1995] Derick Wood. Standard Generalized Markup Language: Mathematical and philosophical issues. In Jan van Leeuwen, editor, *Computer Science Today, Recent Trends and Developments*, volume 1000 of Lecture Notes in Computer Science, pages 344–365. Springer, 1995.

[Woods, 1975] William A. Woods. What's in a link: Foundations for semantic networks. In D. G. Bobrow and A. M. Collins, editors, *Representation and Understanding: Studies in Cognitive Science*, pages 35–82. Academic Press,

1975. Republished in [Brachman and Levesque, 1985].

[Woods, 1991] William A. Woods. Understanding subsumption and taxomony: A framework for progress. In J. F. Sowa, editor, *Principles of Semantic Networks*, pages 45–94. Morgan Kaufmann, Los Altos, 1991.

[Woods and Schmolze, 1992] William A. Woods and James G. Schmolze. The KL-ONE family. In F. W. Lehmann, editor, *Semantic Networks in Artificial Intelligence*, pages 133–178. Pergamon Press, 1992. Published as a special issue of *Computers & Mathematics with Applications*, Volume 23, Number 2–9.

[Wright *et al.*, 1993] Jon R. Wright, Elia S. Weixelbaum, Gregg T. Vesonder, Karen E. Brown, Stephen R. Palmer, Jay I. Berman, and Harry H. Moore. A knowledge-based configurator that supports sales, engineering, and manufacturing at AT&T network systems. *AI Magazine*, 14(3):69–80, 1993.

[Wroe *et al.*, 2000] C. Wroe, W. Solomon, A. Rector, and J. Rogers. Inheritance of drug information. *J. of the American Medical Informatics Association*, 2000. Annual Symposium Special Issue.

[Ye *et al.*, 1994] Xian Ye, Christine Parent, and Stefano Spaccapietra. Cardinality consistency of derived objects in DOOD systems. In P. Loucopoulos, editor, *Proc. of the 13th Int. Conf. on the Entity-Relationship Approach (ER'94)*, volume 881 of Lecture Notes in Computer Science, pages 278–295, 1994. Springer.

[Yelland, 2000] Philip Y. Yelland. An alternative combination of Bayesian networks and Description Logics. In *Proc. of the 7th Int. Conf. on Principles of Knowledge Representation and Reasoning (KR 2000)*, pages 225–234, 2000.

[Yen, 1991] John Yen. Generalizing term subsumption languages to fuzzy logic. In Ray Reiter and John Myopoulos, editors, *Proc. of the 12th Int. Joint Conf. on Artificial Intelligence (IJCAI'91)*, pages 472–477, 1991.

[Yen *et al.*, 1991a] J. Yen, H.-L. Juang, and R. MacGregor. Using polymorphism to improve expert system maintainability. *IEEE Expert*, 6(2):48–55, 1991.

[Yen *et al.*, 1991b] John Yen, Robert Neches, and Robert MacGregor. CLASP: Integrating term subsumption systems and production systems. *IEEE Trans. on Knowledge and Data Engineering*, 3(1):25–31, 1991.

[Zakharyaschev, 2000] Michael Zakharyaschev. Personal communication, 2000.

[Zweigenbaum *et al.*, 1995] P. Zweigenbaum, B. Bachimont, J. Bouaud, and J. Charlet. Issues in the structuring and acquisition of an ontology for medical language understanding. *Methods of Information in Medicine*, 34(1/2):15–24, 1995.

Index

Printed in the United States
by Baker & Taylor Publisher Services

Printed in the United States
by Baker & Taylor Publisher Services